A Textual Commentary on the Greek New Testament

A Companion to the Sixth Edition of the
United Bible Societies' Greek New Testament

by

H. A. G. Houghton

DEUTSCHE BIBELGESELLSCHAFT

The German Bible Society is a not for profit religious foundation.
Its mission, in collaboration with other members of the United Bible Societies,
is to promote biblical research and worldwide Bible translation work in
order to make the Bible available to everybody
in their own language.

ISBN 978-3-438-05331-2

A Textual Commentary on the Greek New Testament
H. A. G. Houghton
© 2025 Deutsche Bibelgesellschaft, Stuttgart

Satz: C.H.Beck, Nördlingen
Druck: C.H.Beck, Nördlingen

Product safety information:
Deutsche Bibelgesellschaft, Balinger Str. 31 A,
70567 Stuttgart, product-safety@dbg.de

Printed in Germany
All rights reserved

06.2025

Table of Contents

Preface VII
Abbreviations IX
Apparatus Symbols XI
Principal Greek Manuscripts XIII

Introduction 1*

The Gospel according to Matthew 1
The Gospel according to Mark 71
The Gospel according to Luke 119
The Gospel according to John 195

The Acts of the Apostles 279

The Catholic Epistles 331
   The Letter of James 333
   The First Letter of Peter 341
   The Second Letter of Peter 349
   The First Letter of John 357
   The Second Letter of John 367
   The Third Letter of John 369
   The Letter of Jude 371

The Pauline Epistles 379
   The Letter to the Romans 382
   The First Letter to the Corinthians 410
   The Second Letter to the Corinthians 438
   The Letter to the Galatians 451
   The Letter to the Ephesians 465
   The Letter to the Philippians 478
   The Letter to the Colossians 483
   The First Letter to the Thessalonians 495
   The Second Letter to the Thessalonians 503
   The Letter to the Hebrews 507

The First Letter to Timothy	523
The Second Letter to Timothy	528
The Letter to Titus	531
The Letter to Philemon	533
The Revelation to John	537
Glossary	563
Bibliography	569

Preface

This is a commentary on all the textual variations presented in the sixth edition of the United Bible Societies' *Greek New Testament* (UBS6). It covers every unit listed in the apparatus at the foot of the page, as well as readings in the text indicated by square brackets. Its aim is to describe the differing readings at each point, consider the evidence in support of each and explain why the form in the editorial text has been chosen. In many cases an indication is given of the reason the variation unit was selected for inclusion in the apparatus, be that its significance for translation, its theological implications, or the light it sheds on the textual transmission of the New Testament. Like the edition itself, this commentary is intended for an audience of translators, students and non-specialists. It is hoped that the English rendering of variants will also make it accessible to those with limited facility in New Testament Greek who encounter textual variation in footnotes in contemporary translations.

This volume is a successor to both the *Textual Commentary on the Greek New Testament* by Bruce M. Metzger (1971, 1994) and its adapted version for translators, the *Textual Guide to the Greek New Testament* by Roger L. Omanson (2006). Although it was written independently of these, in order to present a new guide based on current scholarship, the final text was compared with both in order to ensure full coverage in places where they overlap. Indications are also given of other publications which may be useful to those wishing to study a particular variant in more detail or to explore a differing interpretation of the data. However, it is beyond the scope of this commentary to offer a comprehensive guide to scholarship at each place of variation. An overview of the textual tradition of the New Testament and the principles of textual criticism is provided in the Introduction, along with information on the background to UBS6 and the creation of this commentary. Technical terms are also explained in a Glossary towards the end of the volume.

I thank the German Bible Society for the invitation to write this book, and my colleagues on the Editorial Board of the United Bible Societies'

Greek New Testament for entrusting me with this task and providing feedback on drafts. I am particularly grateful for Klaus Wachtel's detailed engagement with the sections on the Acts of the Apostles and the Catholic Epistles. In addition, Tommy Wasserman generously shared his publications and offered comments on the entries for Mark, John, Acts, the Catholic Epistles and most of the Pauline Epistles, leading to numerous improvements in these books. Amy Myshrall gave helpful feedback on Galatians and Ephesians, and Elijah Hixson kindly provided me with copies of two other commentaries. Florian Voss (German Bible Society) was instrumental in enabling the production of the edition and this commentary to proceed in tandem and inform each other: it has been a pleasure to work with him, and his care and attention have significantly improved this volume.

The hybrid nature of the text of UBS6, described further in the Introduction, means that this book is neither a record of the committee's discussions nor an endorsement of every reading adopted as the editorial text. The persistence of scholarly disagreement as to the form which is most likely to be the earliest at each place of variation should make for humility when providing an account of the development of the text. In offering a personal understanding of the current state of the evidence, I have tried to allow for the fact that the consideration of additional material and the application of new analytical techniques will lead to further changes and differences in successive editions of the Greek New Testament. In order to extend the utility of this volume, I therefore invite its users to bring to my attention any inaccuracies or updates which may be listed on a companion website (www.hughhoughton.uk/tcgnt). My hope is that, as with the edition itself, such collaboration may further improve the understanding of the nature of the New Testament text, its transmission through the centuries and its significance in each generation.

Birmingham
St Hugh's Day, 2024

Abbreviations

Abbreviations used only in the bibliography are indicated there in a separate list. Abbreviations of biblical books follow the SBL Handbook of Style.

BDAG	*A Greek-English Lexicon of the New Testament* (Bauer, Danker, Arndt & Gingrich 2001)
CBGM	Coherence-Based Genealogical Method
ECM	Editio Critica Maior: *ECM Mark* (Strutwolf, Gäbel, Hüffmeier, Lakmann, Paulson & Wachtel 2021); *ECM Acts* (Strutwolf, Gäbel, Hüffmeier, Mink & Wachtel 2017); *ECM Catholic Epistles* (Aland, Aland, Mink, Strutwolf & Wachtel 2013); *ECM Revelation* (Karrer, Müller, Sigismund, Strutwolf, Hüffmeier, Paulson et al. 2024); *ECM Parallel Pericopes* (Strutwolf & Wachtel, 2011)
GA	Gregory-Aland (the standard system of numbers for Greek New Testament manuscripts)
IGNTP	International Greek New Testament Project
INTF	Institut für Neutestamentliche Textforschung
KJV	King James Version
LXX	Septuagint
NA29	Nestle-Aland *Novum Testamentum Graece*, 29th edition (2026)
NASB	New American Standard Bible
NIV	New International Version
NRSVue	New Revised Standard Version (updated edition)
SBLGNT	*The Greek New Testament: SBL Edition* (Holmes 2010)
THGNT	*The Greek New Testament Produced at Tyndale House Cambridge* (Jongkind & Williams 2017)
TS	*Teststelle(n)* (test passage[s])
TuT	Text und Textwert: *TuT Matthew* (Aland et al. 1999); *TuT Mark* (Aland et al. 1998); *TuT Luke* (Aland et al. 1999); *TuT John* (Aland & Wachtel 2005); *TuT Acts* (Aland et al. 1993);

	TuT Cath. (Aland et al. 1987); *TuT Romans, 1 Cor., 2 Cor., Galatians, Ephesians, Philippians, Colossians, Thessalonians, TuT Hebrews, Pastorals* (Aland et al. 1991); *TuT Rev.* (Lembke et al. 2017).
UBS1–6	*The United Bible Societies Greek New Testament*: first edition (1966); second edition (1968); third edition (1975); fourth edition (1994); fifth edition (2013); sixth edition (2025).

Apparatus Symbols

*	First hand reading
c	Corrector
1, 2, 3	Layers of correction, in sequence. ^{1} and ^{2} may also indicate the first and second occurrence of the same text within a single verse.
[ ]	Square brackets indicate witnesses which offer partial support for the reading
lem	The lemma reading of a commentary
mg	Marginal reading
ms	One manuscript
mss	Manuscripts
pt	Part of the tradition
supp	Supplement, a later addition to a manuscript
txt	The reading in the body of the manuscript
vid	*Ut videtur*, what seems to be the reading
v.r.	Variant reading in the same manuscript
𝔓	Papyrus
f^1	Family 1
f^{13}	Family 13
Byz	Byzantine text
Byz^A	Byzantine text in Andreas of Caesarea tradition (in Revelation)
Byz^K	Byzantine text in Koine tradition (in Revelation)
TR	*Textus Receptus*
Lect.	Lectionaries
lat ($^{vl, vg}$)	Latin translations (Old Latin, Vulgate)
sy ($^{c, s, f, p, ph, h}$)	Syriac translations (Curetonian, Sinaitic, Sinai New Find, Peshitta, Philoxenian, Harklean)
co ($^{sa, bo, mae, fa, ly, ac, pbo, cv, cw}$)	Coptic translations (Sahidic, Bohairic, Middle Egyptian, Fayyumic, Lycopolitan, Achmimic, Proto-Bohairic, Dialect V, Middle Egyptian Fayyumic)
cpa	Christian Palestinian Aramaic translation

eth	Ethiopic translation
got	Gothic translation

Principal Greek Manuscripts

A full list of manuscripts is provided in the Introduction to UBS6; those cited most frequently in the present volume or mentioned in the overviews are listed here for ease of reference.

The following abbreviations are used for the contents: e–Gospels, a–Acts, c–Catholic Epistles, p–Pauline Epistles, r–Revelation. *Dates are based on the online* Kurzgefasste Liste *(see Introduction).*

Siglum	Name	Contents	Current Location	Century
𝔓⁴	Papyrus 4	e: Luke	Paris	III
𝔓⁷	Papyrus 7	e: Luke	Kyiv	III/IV?
𝔓⁹	Papyrus 9	c: 1 John	Cambridge, MA	III/IV
𝔓¹¹	Papyrus 11	p: 1 Cor.	St Petersburg; Sinai	VI
𝔓¹³	Papyrus 13	p: Heb.	London; Cairo	III/IV
𝔓²⁰	Papyrus 20	c: James	Princeton, NJ	III
𝔓²³	Papyrus 23	c: James	Urbana, IL	early III
𝔓³³	Papyrus 33	a	Vienna	VI
𝔓⁴⁵	Papyrus 45	ea	Dublin; Vienna	III
𝔓⁴⁶	Papyrus 46	p	Dublin; Ann Arbor, MI	early III
𝔓⁴⁷	Papyrus 47	r	Dublin	late III
𝔓⁵¹	Papyrus 51	p: Gal.	Oxford	early V
𝔓⁵²	Papyrus 52	e: John	Manchester	mid II or III
𝔓⁶⁰	Papyrus 60	e: John	New York, NY	VII
𝔓⁶¹	Papyrus 61	p	New York, NY	early VIII
𝔓⁶⁴	Papyrus 64	e: Matt.	Oxford; Montserrat (Spain)	early III
𝔓⁶⁶	Papyrus 66	e: John	Cologny; Dublin; Cologne	early III or IV
𝔓⁶⁹	Papyrus 69	e: Luke	Oxford	III
𝔓⁷²	Papyrus 73	c: 12Peter Jude	Cologny; Vatican City	III/IV
𝔓⁷⁴	Papyrus 74	ac	Cologny	VII
𝔓⁷⁵	Papyrus 75	e: Luke, John	Vatican City	early III or IV
𝔓⁷⁷	Papyrus 77	e: Matt.	Oxford	II/III

A Textual Commentary

Siglum	Name	Contents	Current Location	Century
𝔓⁸⁴	Papyrus 84	e: Mark	Leuven	VI
𝔓⁸⁸	Papyrus 88	e: Mark	Milan	IV
𝔓⁹⁸	Papyrus 98	r	Cairo	II?
𝔓¹⁰⁰	Papyrus 100	c: James	Oxford	III/IV
𝔓¹¹¹	Papyrus 111	e: Luke	Oxford	III
𝔓¹¹⁵	Papyrus 115	r	Oxford	III/IV
𝔓¹²⁷	Papyrus 127	a	Oxford	V
01 (ℵ)	Codex Sinaiticus	epacr	London (New Testament)	IV
02 (A)	Codex Alexandrinus	eacpr	London	V
03 (B)	Codex Vaticanus	eacp	Vatican City	IV
04 (C)	Codex Ephraemi Rescriptus	eacpr	Paris	V
05 (D)	Codex Bezae	ea	Cambridge	V
06 (D)	Codex Claromontanus	p	Paris	VI
07 (E)	Codex Basiliensis	e	Basle	VIII
08 (E)	Codex Laudianus/Laudian Acts	a	Oxford	VI
09 (F)	Codex Boreelianus	e	Utrecht	IX
011 (G)	Codex Seidelianus	e	London; Cambridge	IX
012 (G)	Codex Boernerianus	p	Dresden	IX
015 (H)	Codex Coislinianus	p	Athos; Kyiv; Moscow; Paris; St Petersburg; Turin	VI
016 (I)	Codex Freerianus	p	Washington, DC	V
017 (K)	Codex Cyprius	e	Paris	IX or X
018 (K)	Codex Mosquensis	cp	Moscow	IX
019 (L)	Codex Regius	e	Paris	VIII or IX
020 (L)	Codex Angelicus	acp	Rome	IX
022 (N)	Codex Purpureus Petropolitanus	e	Athens; Lerma; London; New York, NY; Patmos; Vatican City; St Petersburg; Thessaloniki; Vienna	VI
025 (P)	Codex Porphyrianus	acpr	St Petersburg	IX
032 (W)	Codex Washingtonianus/Freer Gospels	e	Washington, DC	IV/V or VIII
035 (Z)	Codex Dublinensis	e: Matt.	Dublin	VI

Principal Greek Manuscripts

Siglum	Name	Contents	Current Location	Century
037 (Δ)	Codex Sangallensis	e	St Gall	IX
038 (Θ)	Codex Coridethianus/Koridethi Codex	e	Tbilisi	IX
040 (Ξ)	Codex Zacynthius	e: Luke	Cambridge	VI or VIII
042 (Σ)	Codex Rossanensis	e: Matt., Mark	Rossano	VI
044 (Ψ)	Codex Athous Lavrensis	eacp	Athos	IX/X
0141		e: John	Paris	X
0150		p	Patmos	IX
0207		r	Florence	IV
0233		e	Münster	VIII
0250	Codex Climaci Rescriptus	e	Washington, DC	VIII
0274		e: Mark	Cairo	V
0278		p	Sinai	IX
0281		e: Matt.	Sinai	VII/VIII
0285		cp	Sinai	VI
5		eacp	Paris	XIII
6		eacp	Paris	XIII
33		eacp	Paris	IX
35		eacpr	Paris	XIV
81		acp	Alexandria; London	XI (1044)
181		acpr	Vatican City	X
254		acpr	Athens	XIV
256		acpr	Paris	XI/XII
263		eacp	Paris	XIII
307		ac	Paris	X
365		eacp	Florence	XII
436		acp	Vatican City	XI/XII
565		e	St Petersburg	IX
579		e	Paris	XII or XIII
597		e	Venice	XI or XIII
614		acp	Milan	XIII
623		acp	Vatican City	XI (1037)
642		acp	London	XIV

A Textual Commentary

Siglum	Name	Contents	Current Location	Century
700		e	London	XI
892		e	London	IX
1006		er	Athos	XI
1071		e	Athos	XII
1175		acp	Patmos	X
1241		eacp	Sinai	XII or XIII
1243		eacp	Sinai	XI
1409		eacp	Athos	XIV
1424		eacpr	Drama	IX/X
1448		eacp	Athos	XII
1506		ep	Athos	XIV (1320)
1611		acpr	Athens	XII
1637		eacpr	Athos	XIV (1328)
1642		eacp	Athos	XIII (1278)
1735		acp	Athos	X
1739	Von der Goltz Codex	acp	Athos	X
1852		acpr	Uppsala	XIII
1854		acpr	Athos	XI
1881		cp	Sinai	XIV
1962		p	Vienna	XI/XII
2019		r	Naples	XIII
2050		r	El Escorial	XII (1107)
2053		r	Messina	XIII
2080		acpr	Patmos	XIV
2329		r	Meteora	X
2344		acpr	Paris	XI
2464		acp	Patmos	IX
2492		eacp	Sinai	XIV
2846		r	Paris	XII

Introduction

The Diversity of the Textual Tradition of the New Testament

Readers should not be surprised or dismayed that the text of the Greek New Testament exists in a variety of forms. Such a situation is only to be expected with a collection of books which has been transmitted across many centuries in thousands of handwritten documents, each of them unique and reflecting the circumstances in which they were produced and used. As with every writing from antiquity, these works circulated through the production of copies made by scribes with varying degrees of competence. Copying errors, material damage obscuring the text, editorial interventions seeking to correct apparent inconsistencies or to offer improvements to language or sense—all these may have contributed to the diversification of the textual tradition on each occasion that a copy was produced.

Evidence for thoroughgoing alteration of the New Testament text is very limited, however, and seems largely to be restricted to the first couple of centuries when the nature and form of the corpus were still under development (e.g. the assembly of letter collections, the production of an early harmony of the gospels, editorial activity such as that associated with Marcion). The translation of biblical books into other languages in this period also contributed to their textual diversity, in that this process inaugurated new traditions which could represent several potential wordings in the source language and which then went on to develop in their own ways. The scarcity of documents surviving from these centuries makes it difficult to establish the extent of textual variation commonly present in the earliest copies and the degree to which these writings may have circulated in 'free' forms alongside a more controlled tradition. Nevertheless, if the manuscripts which have been preserved are representative of the situation in antiquity, there are no grounds for serious doubt as to the consistency of the New Testament tradition.

In addition, the first generations of biblical scholars were aware of the challenges posed by manuscript transmission and took this into account in their interpretation of the text. Many early Christian writings provide information about differences between copies known to their authors. While the grounds on which they may have preferred one reading to another are not always the same as those adopted by modern editors, ancient interpreters often maintained the value of multiple readings for understanding the sacred text. In any case, copies of the Bible produced for use within Christian communities were treated as scripture regardless of the exact form of text they contained, just as contemporary readers accept differences between modern translations into a single language. Diversity was a characteristic of the New Testament from its beginning, given that it contains four separate accounts of the life of Jesus and letters written to specific communities and individuals which, even though they address particular situations, were still deemed by the early Church to be of broader value for subsequent readers. The oldest surviving documents offer little indication of strict control of textual production or uniformity in scribal practice: along with the various early translations of the New Testament, this shows that the spreading of the message was considered to be of greater importance than its specific wording.

The Need for an Edition

Just as the New Testament writings pass down the earliest traditions of Christianity, so their own textual history constitutes the record of their transmission across the centuries. A scholarly edition therefore fulfils two functions. It offers a specific form of text, usually that which is considered to be the earliest attainable wording, along with an indication of the development of the tradition as shown by differences within the surviving evidence. The earliest text can be described as 'original' insofar as it is considered to provide the origin for the variant readings, even though its relationship to the documents first produced by the authors or to the collections which stand at the head of the tradition may remain unclear.[1] A single text is desirable for the purposes of translation, interpretation and study, despite varying levels of editorial confidence in the reconstruction. The history of the tradition is illustrated by the criti-

---

[1] There are discussions of the term 'original text' in Epp 1999 and by Holmes in Ehrman & Holmes 2013: 637–688. The textual form which underlies all surviving evidence is often referred to as the 'initial text'.

cal apparatus in which variant readings and their attestation are listed. These alternative forms not only indicate options which were not adopted by the editors but also serve as a reminder that the editorial text is a composite form, a reconstruction based on and reflecting the diverse textual tradition of the New Testament. In a hand edition, such as the sixth edition of the United Bible Societies' *Greek New Testament* (UBS6), this apparatus is relatively slim and serves to highlight places of particular importance to users. The current Nestle-Aland *Novum Testamentum Graece* (NA29) is also a hand edition but with a fuller critical apparatus for more technical study.[2] Some of the more comprehensive editions represent the pinnacle of previous generations of scholarship, such as those edited by Tregelles, Tischendorf and Westcott & Hort in the latter half of the nineteenth century and by von Soden in the early twentieth century. In the present day, the understanding of the textual tradition of the Greek New Testament is being transformed by the ongoing *Editio Critica Maior* (ECM). This substantial edition, which will run to several volumes, aims to present the textual history of the first millennium. Following the examination of all available surviving documents, it cites between one hundred and two hundred manuscripts in each book, as well as ancient translations and quotations in early Christian writers. Such a project is only possible through the use of modern digital technology.[3]

As new material is taken into consideration and fresh techniques are applied, the understanding of the text and transmission of the New Testament continues to develop. A scholarly edition provides both a set of the historical data for the text and an interpretation of that evidence based on current knowledge and specific editorial principles (discussed in their own section below). It offers users a working text, enabling them to approach the original writings while reminding them that the tradition is one of diversity and requires further study and interpretation to be more fully appreciated. In addition, it demonstrates the continuity of the transmission and, accordingly, the confidence users may have both in the editorial text and the tradition of the work itself. In

---

[2] In addition to the introduction to the edition itself, Trobisch 2013 offers a guide for users.

[3] The ECM is introduced in Houghton et al. 2020, as well as in numerous recent overviews. The edition is accompanied by a range of online resources, some of which are described below.

this way, such an edition points beyond the wording of the text to the message of these writings and the way in which it has been received, understood and transmitted across the centuries.

Evidence for the Text of the New Testament[4]

There is a vast amount of material which transmits the books of the Greek New Testament. Sources may be divided into primary evidence (or 'direct tradition'), consisting of Greek manuscripts, and secondary evidence (or 'indirect tradition') from early translations and quotations in Christian writers.

Direct Tradition

The oldest surviving New Testament documents are written on papyrus, a writing material made from plant stems which was in regular use until around the eighth century. Most of these have only been rediscovered since the end of the nineteenth century, preserved in the dry climate of the Egyptian desert. Almost all are fragmentary, ranging from scraps of single pages to more substantial books lacking portions at the beginning or end. The dating of papyri is approximate and is usually assigned on the basis of palaeography (comparison of handwriting styles): techniques from the physical sciences have yet to provide more specific results.[5] Some New Testament papyrus manuscripts may have been copied as early as the second century but a range of at least fifty years (and probably much more) should be applied to palaeographical estimates. The date assigned to copies of literary texts is often subject to revision as more comparative material is published from excavations. Although many ancient papyrus documents were written as scrolls, most Christian books take the form of a codex, consisting of folded pages written on both sides and bound in the middle.

---

[4] An effort has been made to explain technical terms which appear in this account, but users may also wish to refer to the Glossary towards the end of this book.

[5] The calibration curve involved in Carbon-14 dating means that this often cannot be any more specific than palaeographic approaches. Recent developments in Raman spectroscopy or micro X-ray fluorescence analysis of ink offer a promising, non-invasive way of dating material, but this has not so far been widely applied. See further Nongbri 2018: 72–82 and Goler et al. 2019.

Parchment, a prepared form of animal skin, was used as a writing material from around the third to the sixteenth century. This is much more durable than plant-based material and also permitted the construction of larger documents. The oldest parchment codices are written in majuscule script (sometimes called 'uncial', consisting only of capital letters), as seen in New Testament papyri: these witnesses are also usually dated through palaeography. Greek minuscule script was developed during the eighth century and this type of writing soon became the standard for parchment manuscripts. Variations in letter forms, ornamentation and decoration sometimes enable palaeographers and art historians to identify where a manuscript was produced. In addition, information provided by the copyist in a colophon written after the end of a work can include their name, the location and the date of completion. Paper began to be adopted for copies of Christian books from the eleventh century onwards, eventually supplanting parchment around the fifteenth century even though the latter continued to be used for some early printed books. The adoption of the printing press for mass production of books in the sixteenth century led to a decline in the creation of manuscripts, although this never completely died out. Some later handwritten books of the Greek New Testament were actually copied from printed texts.

The writings of the New Testament may initially have circulated as individual books, but at an early date they were gathered into collections of related works. The most common groupings found in the manuscript tradition are the four canonical gospels, the Acts of the Apostles with the Catholic Epistles (James, Peter, John and Jude), and the Pauline Epistles (including Hebrews). Although the four major codices of the Greek Bible which survive from the fourth and fifth centuries appear to have contained all New Testament writings alongside the Septuagint (the Greek translation of the Hebrew Scriptures and other books), these are unusual. Most Greek New Testament manuscripts are gospel books (*Evangelia*), copies of the Acts and Epistles (*Praxapostoloi*), or the book of Revelation, which often circulated separately accompanied by a commentary. Manuscripts which contain a complete, uninterrupted text are known as continuous-text manuscripts. In contrast, collections of passages from the Greek Bible which were appointed to be read during Christian worship are called lectionaries. These consist of separate extracts arranged in the sequence of the Church calendar for ease of use. While there is evidence for the development of this type of collection as early as the fifth century, most surviving lectionaries are from a much later period. The New Testament is also transmitted in manuscripts which contain a commentary. Some of these are collections of extracts from multiple early Christian authors (known as *catenae*), while others are the work of a single writer. Not all of them provide a complete biblical text. A small proportion of biblical documents are bilingual, with the text is presented in two languages (for example, Greek and Coptic, or Greek and Latin) in order to facilitate comparison and study.

Indirect Tradition

Writings by early Christian authors often include quotations from the Bible or, in a few cases, reworkings of the biblical text. Among the latter is the genre of the gospel harmony, combining the four canonical texts into a single narrative. As ancient writers would have relied on manuscripts which no longer survive, their quotations (sometimes known as 'citations' or 'patristic testimony') may preserve important evidence for the scriptural text. In addition, as the place and time in which these works were composed can usually be established, their textual form may be associated with a particular location or period in a way which is not possible for most early manuscripts. On the other hand, many of these quotations may not have been made with direct reference to biblical manuscripts. They may also have been abbreviated or adapted in some way. In addition, these writings have their own textual tradition because they have been transmitted through the same processes as the New Testament itself. This may have resulted in alterations to their wording. Careful research is therefore required to establish the value of these references for the textual history of the Bible. Similar to quotations are epigraphic references to the biblical text, which take the form of inscriptions (for example on houses or gravestones) or illustrations (such as mosaics or paintings). Verses from the New Testament were sometimes scratched onto pieces of pottery ('ostraca') or other everyday items, which may have been used as talismans. Short extracts from the Bible are also found written on folded pieces of papyrus or parchment which were carried as amulets. There are even writing exercises or glossaries which appear to be based on biblical texts. Although this sort of evidence usually has little significance for the biblical text and is rarely cited in editions, it indicates some of the uses of Scripture in the early Church.

As noted above, the New Testament was translated into a variety of languages from early on in its history. The first of these were translations into Latin, Syriac and Coptic. These began around the end of the second century and were in wide circulation and general use by the fourth century, when they were joined by other languages such as Gothic, Ethiopic and Christian Palestinian Aramaic. Later versions include those in Armenian, Old Church Slavonic and Georgian. The first translations were made from early Greek copies of New Testament books. Nevertheless, as in the case of biblical quotations, their evidence must be carefully evaluated. The oldest translations often appear to be the loosest, with considerable variety in the rendering of the Greek such as paraphrase and omission. While some subsequent revisions may have been carried out through comparison with another Greek text, bringing the translation into closer correspondence with it, other variations may be linguistic or editorial improvements within a language tradition which have no bearing on the Greek. Examination of translation technique and other characteristics of these versions is therefore necessary to apply them to the tradition of the Greek New Testament, as well as the analysis of their own transmission history. Sometimes, the early history of these versions has to be reconstructed through quotations in Christian writers within that language tradition, adding a further layer of complexity to this indirect evidence.

Categories of Witnesses to the Greek New Testament

A register of Greek New Testament manuscripts, known as the *Kurzgefasste Liste* (or just the *Liste*), is maintained by the Institute for New Testament Textual Research (Institut fur neutestamentliche Textforschung, INTF) in Münster and is also accessible online in the New Testament Virtual Manuscript Room (NTVMR).[6] The witnesses are divided into four classes, providing a series of identifiers known as

---

[6] The second edition of the *Liste* is Aland 1994, and a third is in preparation; the web address is https://ntvmr.uni-muenster.de/liste. The numbers given in this section were taken from the online *Liste* in July 2024.

Gregory-Aland (GA) numbers. Built on earlier systems, the numbers indicate the point at which the manuscripts were added to the *Liste*, with the higher numbers correlating to more recent discoveries.

Papyri

Papyri are indicated with an initial P, usually in gothic lettering (𝔓), followed by superscript numerals. At present, the numbers go up to $\mathfrak{P}^{142}$, although some of these fragments are from the same manuscript (such as $\mathfrak{P}^{64}$ and $\mathfrak{P}^{67}$). Most papyrus documents are small fragments, containing just a few verses, but there are some substantial witnesses which are usually dated to the third century: $\mathfrak{P}^{45}$ contains parts of all four gospels and Acts; $\mathfrak{P}^{46}$ is the oldest collection of the Pauline Epistles; $\mathfrak{P}^{66}$ is an almost complete copy of the Gospel according to John; $\mathfrak{P}^{75}$ offers an excellent text of Luke and John. A full list of New Testament papyri is presented in the introduction to UBS6.

Majuscules

Manuscripts written in majuscule script on parchment are identified with an initial 0. In earlier editions, some of these were indicated by an alphabetical siglum, and several also have Latin names reflecting a place or person with which they are associated. These include four copies of the whole Greek Bible: Codex Vaticanus (03, B) is probably the earliest of these, copied slightly earlier than Codex Sinaiticus (01, ℵ) in the second half of the fourth century; Codex Alexandrinus (02, A) was produced in the fifth century, as was Codex Ephraemi Rescriptus (04, C). The last of these is a palimpsest, a manuscript from which the biblical text was erased in order to reuse the parchment for another writing. Three early majuscule witnesses have Greek and Latin on facing pages or alternating columns: the fifth-century Codex Bezae (05, D) of the Gospels and Acts, the sixth-century Codex Claromontanus (06, D) of the Pauline Epistles, and the Laudian Acts (08, E). Codex Augiensis (010, F) and Codex Boernerianus (012, G) are ninth-century Greek-Latin bilinguals of the Pauline Epistles, the latter with an interlinear format matching the gospels in Codex Sangallensis (037, Δ).[7] There are over forty Greek-Coptic

---

[7] A recent study has suggested that the Greek text of Codex Augiensis is a direct copy of that in Codex Boernerianus and therefore has no independent value (Fisher 2024).

bilinguals, including six papyri, while 0278 is the most substantial of six surviving Greek-Arabic manuscripts from the ninth century. Among the important majuscule gospel books are the eighth-century Codex Regius (019, L) and Codex Washingtonianus (032, W, Freer Gospels) which may have been copied in the sixth century. Some of the latest manuscripts included in the category of majuscules are tenth-century commentaries in which the biblical text is written in capital letters. A high proportion of the other majuscule manuscripts are fragments. At the time of writing, the highest number in this category is 0326. The introduction to UBS6 provides further details of the majuscule witnesses which have been used to establish the text of the ECM.

Minuscules

The majority of manuscripts of the Greek New Testament are written in minuscule script and identified simply by a number. One of the oldest, GA 33, sometimes called 'The Queen of the Minuscules', is a copy of the Gospels, Acts and Epistles made in the ninth century. GA 1582 (of the Gospels) and GA 1739 (of the Pauline Epistles) were both copied in the tenth century by a scribe named Ephrem from much earlier documents. The former is a member of a family of manuscripts which all descend from the same exemplar, known as Family 1 (because it also includes GA 1). Another well-known family in the Gospels is Family 13, several of whose members were produced by a priest called Leo in South Italy in the eleventh century. The text of these families is usually indicated by the sigla f^1 and f^{13} respectively. The fourteenth-century GA 35 is a good representative of the Byzantine text for the whole New Testament, which is attested in the majority of minuscule manuscripts ('Byz' or '𝔐').[8] The highest number in this category is currently 3026; the UBS6 introduction lists only the minuscules which are cited in the apparatus of the edition.

Lectionaries

A very large number of lectionaries are also included in the *Kurzgefasste Liste*. These are indicated by an initial letter l, written either as 'L'

---

[8] Technically, 'Byz' indicates a reconstruction of the Byzantine text, while '𝔐' denotes the reading of the majority of manuscripts. See further the discussion of editorial approaches below.

or (in italics) '*l*'. Some are copied in majuscule script but the majority are written in minuscules. This group consists of a variety of collections, some containing only the readings for Saturdays and Sundays, while others are focussed on the readings for saints' days. Most lectionaries correspond to the Constantinopolitan liturgical calendar of the Byzantine Church, although different types are attested, such as the early Jerusalem lectionary whose sequence is preserved in a number of translations. The numbers currently go up to L2577, but only a representative selection of lectionaries is cited in editions of the Greek New Testament. In UBS6, the lectionaries are grouped under the single siglum 'Lect', with 'Lect[pt]' used when the tradition is divided.

Early Translations

Six ancient translations of the New Testament are cited in UBS6. The three earliest are Latin, Syriac and Coptic. The Latin evidence consists of the Old Latin (or *Vetus Latina*, lat[vl]), translated around the end of the second century, and the Vulgate (lat[vg]), a revision made two hundred years later. The former is reconstructed from the few surviving manuscripts and quotations in Latin Christian authors: these are not listed independently because most stem from a single point of contact with Greek. In contrast, the two Old Syriac gospel manuscripts are cited whenever they are present: the Curetonian Syriac (sy[c]) and the Sinaitic Syriac (sy[s]). The later standard Syriac translation is the Peshitta (sy[p]), a revision from the early fifth century. Two further Syriac versions were revised against a Greek text, the Philoxenian Syriac of 507/8 (sy[ph]) and the Harklean Syriac of 615/6 (sy[h]), a literal rendering which often has significant variant readings marked in its margin (sy[hmg]). The Christian Palestinian Aramaic (cpa) is often classed with the Syriac witnesses. The principal early Coptic version is the third-century Sahidic (co[sa]), while the later standard is the Bohairic (co[bo]). Several translations into other Coptic dialects are preserved in part, including Middle Egyptian (co[mae]), Fayyumic (co[fa]), Lycopolitan (co[ly]), Achmimic (co[ach]) and proto-Bohairic (co[pbo]). The Ethiopic version (eth) and the Gothic version (got) are also cited occasionally. The rationale for including these versions is that they were all translated directly from the Greek and therefore may preserve readings which are no longer extant in Greek tradition. Nevertheless, differing linguistic structures and other aspects of translation technique mean that they cannot always be connected with particular Greek variants and in some places may represent independent secondary developments (such as glosses).

Biblical Quotations

Textual evidence from biblical quotations in a range of early Christian authors is also cited. A full list of these sources is given in the introduction to UBS6. Most are identified by name (e.g. Origen, Chrysostom), but occasionally a place name is added for disambiguation (e.g. Gregory-Nyssa for Gregory of Nyssa). In some cases, Greek writers are only available in translation (e.g. Irenaeus^{lat} for the Latin version of Irenaeus) or through quotation in another writer (e.g. Marcion$^{acc.\ to\ Epiphanius}$ for quotations of Marcion in Epiphanius). Only authors writing in Greek are included, with the exception of Tertullian who is believed to have translated his biblical quotations directly from a Greek source. Other early Latin writers are included by implication under the Old Latin siglum (lat^{vl}). Tatian's gospel harmony, known as the Diatessaron, is only known to be transmitted in quotations in other Christian writers, especially in Syriac and Armenian tradition.

Principles of Textual Criticism

Criteria for selecting between multiple readings transmitted in a textual tradition were first articulated in antiquity and have been developed across the centuries. They hold good for all writings preserved in manuscripts, not just the New Testament, and may be deployed in different ways by editors depending on the nature of the tradition and the aim and scope of the edition. The two main types are normally described as external criteria, based on the sources which transmit the work, and internal criteria, comprising matters of consistency, style and scribal practice. More recently, considerations of genealogical and stemmatic coherence have been introduced through the adoption of digital editing methods.[9]

---

[9] For a fuller discussion of these criteria, see Wasserman in Ehrman & Holmes 2013: 579–612.

External Criteria

External evidence involves the historical attestation of each textual form. The oldest surviving witnesses are usually considered to be of the greatest value for establishing the earliest text of a work, on the grounds that fewer instances of copying separate them from the original writing: as a result, their text is less likely to have undergone major alteration. In practice, however, the situation is often much more complex. Only a small proportion of manuscripts of the New Testament survive from the first few centuries, while apparent biblical quotations in the earliest Christian writers are often very loose and may have been adjusted as part of their own transmission. As noted above, the oldest manuscripts can only be assigned an approximate date and most of them are fragmentary. What is more, despite their age, there are already numerous differences between them, some resulting from copying errors and others from editorial adjustments. Although there may be an overall consistency to their text, it is unclear to what extent extant documents are representative of the texts in circulation in the earliest generations of Christianity or, indeed, of the writings which left the hands of those responsible for creating them. Even if there existed an autograph, a document written personally by an author—which is not the case for most writings from the first millennium, including those of the New Testament—it would still be difficult to determine whether the variant readings in circulation derived from another draft or revision produced by the same person or the intervention of a later editor.[10]

Given the gap between the composition of the writings of the New Testament and the oldest surviving witnesses, the age of a manuscript is not always a clear guide to the age of the text it transmits. Some of the earliest documents may contain a text deriving from a large number of intervening copies or extensive editorial revision, while later manuscripts may have been copied from an exemplar which was much older or whose text had been subject to fewer alterations.[11] The same is true of the quality of production. Carefully-copied manuscripts produced in

---

[10] The variant readings in the Acts of the Apostles are sometimes explained as stemming from two different authorial versions (e.g. Strange 1992a), although the nature of the additional material indicates that it is more likely to be the work of a later reviser (e.g. Epp 1966).

[11] Examples of the latter include the minuscules GA 1582 and 1739 mentioned above.

a controlled editorial setting may be based on ancient and valuable exemplars but it is also possible that they have been subject to thoroughgoing adjustment of the text or language. Likewise, documents which are more hasty in execution or contain a greater overall proportion of errors and anomalies may nonetheless preserve a layer of important readings.

A different approach to external criteria is to prefer the reading found in the majority of manuscripts because it is the most widely attested form. Even this, however, is subject to the haphazard nature of the preservation of manuscripts across the centuries and may also involve discrimination between categories of witness: taking into account the thousands of Greek lectionaries or biblical quotations in Christian writers (and the manuscripts in which they are transmitted) could result in differing readings with a numerical majority. The use of external evidence in this way is usually connected with an alternative understanding of textual authority, looking to ecclesiastical tradition or the outcome of the entire process of transmission as the principal indication of the value of the text rather than its putative origin (see further the section below on editorial approaches).

Despite agreement between earlier and later manuscripts on much of the wording of the Greek New Testament, at most points of variation there is no consistent division of witnesses. In cases where many or all of the oldest documents differ from the majority of minuscules, it is very likely that the latter represent a later editorial intervention or derive from a scribal change in one or more key witnesses. However, the possibility may remain that the majority reading was present in ancient documents which have not survived and could even be the earliest form. Readings which are shared by the majority of minuscules and a subset of early documents might be the original form or they might be an early alteration of the text preserved in another group of witnesses: at any rate, they show that the majority reading has ancient roots. Whether or not minority early readings—including those attested by just a single manuscript—transmit the original text or an ancient alternative not taken up in later tradition is up to editors to establish. This challenge is compounded by the problem that, although some patterns may be identified in the external attestation of readings, the oldest manuscripts often fluctuate between the groups supporting different texts.

While external evidence provides useful information about the age of a reading, it usually needs to be supplemented by other considerations such as the internal criteria described in the following section. These assist with determining the general reliability of the earliest witnesses, which may accordingly be given greater weight where the development of the text is less clear. Two well-known sayings are applied to the evaluation of external evidence: "witnesses are to be weighed rather than counted" and "knowledge of documents should precede final judgement upon readings".[12] The latter involves identifying not just the habits of the copyist responsible for producing the manuscript, but also the characteristics of the text it represents and any editorial interventions which may be reflected therein.

Internal Criteria

Internal criteria offer considerations based on the context in which a reading is found. Some of these are classified under the heading of 'intrinsic probability', identifying what an author was most likely to have written. This addresses questions such as whether a reading is consistent with the surrounding text as well as with the style and vocabulary of the rest of the work and any other writings attributed to the same author. There is an expectation that a reading will conform to the norms of grammar and language use of the time. The sources used in the composition of a text (for example, quotations from the Septuagint, or the reliance of Matthew and Luke on Mark) may be relevant here as well. While it is possible that a writer may have produced more than one edition of the same work, as was noted in the previous section, identifying the nature or probable reason for textual changes enables modern editors to set aside secondary alterations introduced as part of the transmission process.

Changes introduced by a copyist or editor are grouped under the heading of 'transcriptional probability'. Could a copyist have mistaken a rare word for a more common one or substituted one with a similar shape? Were the words confused phonetically, especially due to later changes in pronunciation? Two phenomena in the history of the Greek

---

[12] Westcott & Hort 1896: 31; for the formulation of the former (which derives from the legal maxim *ponderantur testes, non numerantur*), Metzger 1994: 12*.

language account for multiple variants: vowel isochrony and itacism. The former is the loss of the difference in the length of a vowel, which for example led to confusion between *omicron* and *omega* (ο and ω); the latter refers to the identical pronunciation in later Greek of certain vowels including ι, ει, οι, η and υ, resulting in substitutions such as ὑμᾶς ('you') for ἡμᾶς ('us'). Other similar developments included the overlap of consonantal υ and β (betacism) or the vowels ε and αι. Was an abbreviation misread or wrongly expanded? Might the change be due to duplicating text or omitting identical sequences? The repetition of one or more letters is called dittography, while the term for overlooking double letters or repeated groups is haplography. Was an omission caused by skipping between words with similar beginnings (homoeoarcton, also spelt homoeoarchon) or similar endings (homoeoteleuton)? Given that word divisions were not always clearly defined in the oldest Greek manuscripts, and such jumps between identical sequences of characters could happen at any point within a word or longer portion of text, it is simpler to refer to this type of variation as eyeskip (for which the equivalent Greek term is parablepsis).

On numerous occasions, a word or an idea in context may have motivated a subconscious alteration or even a deliberate change. The majority of variants in the New Testament comprise such instances of assimilation (also described as harmonisation), when one or more words have been changed due to the influence of another similar text or construction. This could be on the level of morphology, affecting the number or case of a noun or the person, number or tense of a verb, so as to match the pattern of a preceding sentence or clause. It might be lexical, leading to a change in the choice of word. In certain cases the scope is even broader, resulting in the introduction of details or phrases from other parts of the same work or even parallel passages from other writings: overlaps between the gospels, and the similar formulaic phrases or lists in the Pauline epistles, are among the reasons that that this sort of variation is particularly common. Sometimes, two variant readings circulating separately in the tradition are brought together into a conflation or 'doublet' (double reading), incorporating both into the text rather than choosing between them. This is also common in early translations, where differing renderings of a single Greek term may be conflated and give a false impression of the source text.

Editorial Approaches

Although the evaluation of the different criteria and the resultant textual decisions often vary from editor to editor, several broader types of editorial approach may be identified.[13] Editions which are based on a single manuscript adopt the approach known as 'copy text'. This was often the case for the first printed edition (the *editio princeps*) of ancient works, when editors seeking simply to make a text more widely available in the new medium would mark up a copy to be typeset by the printer. In other cases, it may represent an editor's preference for a particular manuscript (such as the oldest surviving witness). Among the drawbacks of this approach is the lack of any indication of how representative the chosen manuscript is of the overall textual tradition of the work. As no comparisons are made with other witnesses, any peculiarities or errors of this document are reproduced as authoritative (although an editor may intervene to standardise spelling or grammar). While each New Testament manuscript may have been regarded as representative of the scriptural text by the community which produced and used it, the copy-text approach ignores the evidence of the rest of the textual tradition. A related practice is the production of a 'diplomatic edition'. This reproduces the text of an individual document, with all its peculiarities, but does not treat it as representative of the broader work. Rather, this is a stepping stone towards further study of this particular witness or an edition of the work as a whole. The full electronic transcriptions created for the ECM constitute independent editions of the witnesses selected for each biblical book, making their full text available in the digital medium.

The nature of the text to be established is often a key to the editorial approach. While most editors seek to recover the earliest text, others may prefer a later form of text which has particular authority. For instance, given the development of the textual tradition over time, some may regard more recent witnesses as the culmination of this process. This is present in the concept of an 'ecclesiastical text', where a particular form may have official sanction. The authoritative forms of the New Testament used by the Greek Orthodox Church are known as the

---

[13] In addition to the works cited below, see also Epp 2015 (esp. pp. 33–37) and Aland & Aland 1989: 280–281.

Patriarchal Text (PT) and, for the lectionary, the *Apostoliki Diakonia* (AD).[14] These provide continuity with church practice through its use of later manuscripts before the move to printed texts. A similar approach is seen in the privileging of the Byzantine text, not least because it is the most common form attested by surviving manuscripts. This is sometimes equated with the Majority Text, created simply by calculating the numerical support for each reading and preferring that which has the most support. Although in most instances the choice is clearcut, in others the balance is less clear and the addition of new manuscripts or inclusion of other types of evidence may result in different readings.[15] Establishing a Byzantine or Majority text therefore still requires editorial decisions about which types of evidence are to be taken into consideration and what stage of development is represented by the edition.[16] In some cases, preference for a Byzantine form of text may be due to the use of this form by a translation which is taken as authoritative (such as the King James version in English), yet this has no bearing on the history of the Greek tradition.

Most modern editions adopt an 'eclectic' approach, constructing a text by choosing readings from among those transmitted by the surviving witnesses. Proponents of 'thoroughgoing eclecticism' argue that this choice should be made on internal grounds alone, without reference to the age or character of the manuscripts in which they are found.[17] Despite the haphazard nature of manuscript preservation, however, deciding to discount information from external evidence seems to be unduly restrictive. Accordingly, the majority of editors of the New Testament follow the principles of 'reasoned eclecticism' (also known as 'rational eclecticism'), in which a balance is struck between internal and external criteria. Each variation unit is assessed on its own merits, as described in the following section, with the resulting editorial text representing an attempt to

---

[14] The standard edition of the *Patriarchal Text* is Antoniades 1912 (a revision of his 1904 edition).

[15] This is shown in some of the variants presented in *Text und Textwert*, which only deals with continuous-text witnesses: if lectionaries are taken into account, a different majority reading might emerge.

[16] The edition of the Byzantine text used as a standard is currently Robinson & Pierpont 2018 (RP2018).

[17] This approach has not been widely practised: the two keenest advocates were G. D. Kilpatrick and J. K. Elliott (see further Elliott 2010).

reconstruct a particular stage in the tradition. Normally, such editors seek to recover the earliest attainable text from the evidence preserved in the available sources: it has already been noted above that this may or may not be identifiable with an 'original' form. Both the UBS and Nestle-Aland hand editions are founded on reasoned eclecticism, as will be seen in the individual entries of this Textual Commentary. The same is true of the ECM, which also takes into account genealogical coherence (see below). Given the volume of evidence for the text of the Greek New Testament as well as its scriptural status, modern editors tend to avoid the conjecture of readings which are not transmitted in any known witness. The age and abundance of surviving material makes it likely that one of the attested readings explains the others. On the other hand, this has not always been the case and there are still occasional instances where a conjecture is deemed to be necessary.[18] In some cases, suggestions proposed by earlier scholars have subsequently been found in witnesses of which they were not aware.

Evaluating Variation Units

The art of textual criticism is the balancing of possible explanations in order to determine which reading accounts best for the other forms which are found at that point in the tradition. This usually involves taking account of the external evidence regarding their attestation (the age and quality of the manuscripts or other witnesses) and internal considerations, such as contextual factors, which may have motivated a change. The key aspects of both of these have been described above. Although some scholars have sought to formulate a series of rules for text-critical decisions, most of these cannot be applied without careful examination of the circumstances in each variation unit. At the same time, the criterion of plausibility remains a key factor in making text-critical decisions. While multiple potential explanations could be put forward in favour of almost any variant reading, sometimes involving great ingenuity, the broader context means that usually only a few candidates are plausible options for the earliest form. For instance, in cases of assimilation to the immediate surroundings, copyists are more likely

---

[18] Thousands of conjectures have been collected in the *Amsterdam Database of New Testament Conjectural Emendation.* The editorial text of UBS6 contains a conjecture at Acts 13:33, along with a reading based solely on versional evidence at 2 Pet. 3:10.

to reproduce a word or form which they have already encountered than anticipate one which is a few verses further on in the text, unless the latter is a particularly well-known passage. Similarly, eyeskip usually involves a sequence of several letters or similar characters rather than homoeoarcton or homoeoteleuton to a single letter, especially in manuscripts written without word breaks (*scriptio continua*). A change or error, no matter how egregious, only needs to have happened once to be reflected in a large number of manuscripts.

One useful general consideration is to identify the 'harder' reading, expressed in Latin as *lectio difficilior potior* ('the more difficult reading is preferable'). A form which does not match the context or a reader's expectations is more likely to have given rise to one or more variants with a smoother or more fitting reading. Not only do readers expect a text to make sense, but they also bring a series of assumptions about its content which are then shaped and modified in the reading and copying of a work, both in general ways and in more specific details. The privileging of unusual forms is also connected with the predominance of assimilation in the textual tradition of the New Testament: the overarching tendency is to bring texts into correspondence with each other rather than differentiate them. Those who are familiar with more than one account of the same event will often align or confuse their wording. The same is true of alterations inspired by the immediate context, where the use of particular vocabulary or constructions sets up a pattern which leads to the substitution of a matching form. On a broader level, words or formulations which do not conform to common usage—especially if changes in the language over time have rendered them unusual or obsolete—are prime candidates for replacement: this might be termed assimilation to a linguistic standard. Interventions which introduce differences are largely restricted to stylistic considerations rather than those of content. Of course, there are occasions when a 'more difficult' reading may be a scribal error which violates grammatical norms or results in nonsense: clearly, this is unlikely to be the earliest form although it may still explain subsequent corrections. The internal consideration of the tendency towards a smoother reading in later texts is often corroborated by the external evidence of the age of the manuscripts, in which less common or more difficult forms are mostly attested in, or even restricted to, older witnesses.

Related to this consideration is the traditional claim that 'the shorter reading is preferable' (*lectio brevior potior*). This principle should not be applied mechanically because many shorter readings are the result of scribal oversight, whether this is the omission of a few letters or an entire sentence (see the discussion of eyeskip above). Paradoxically, however, while this phenomenon means that individual witnesses are almost all deficient in some way, the textual tradition as a whole gets longer over time. This is partly due, once again, to assimilation: the process of making texts more similar to each other nearly always involves extending them in order to supply words or details which a reader remembers from one passage and expects to be in corresponding text. In addition, the introduction of a smoother reading often results in an increase of words, either through supplying material to make explicit what was originally implied in context, or by the addition of glosses or explanations for the purpose of clarification. Readers are less likely to delete such material, especially from a scriptural writing, even if it accords with what they already know and expect. Rather, they might correct the text or enhance it with further information or explanations, perhaps in the form of marginal annotations which became incorporated into the text of a later copy.[19] The growth of the New Testament text in this way would have been promoted by its manuscript transmission: users and copyists who were aware of the general propensity towards omission would be more likely to ensure that additional material was included whose absence might represent a copying error.[20] One particular context in which the shortest reading is often preferred is when two different longer versions are found, suggesting that both are independent expansions. On the other hand, it is possible that one of the longer forms is original and was subsequently abbreviated, perhaps by accident, before being expanded in a different way. In such cases, comparison with the external attestation of each reading is advisable to determine the most likely scenario.

---

[19] For examples, see Schmid 2008 and 2011.

[20] The 'Western' readings of Acts, described below, provide a good example of this, both in individual passages and the book as a whole. Its editorial changes take the form of revision or expansion rather than deletion, and the appearance of some of these additions across a range of manuscripts (including, on occasion, the majority of minuscules) illustrates the way in which the tradition may grow in a haphazard way over time.

Genealogical Coherence

One of the problems facing editors of the New Testament is the phenomenon of mixture (sometimes called 'contamination') from multiple sources within the text of a single manuscript. This makes it very hard, if not impossible, to construct a stemma, or family tree, of how manuscripts relate to each other. In other textual traditions, this is often done based on 'shared errors' which demonstrate the dependence of certain witnesses on others and thereby indicate that their text is likely to be secondary.[21] The adoption of digital editing processes, however, has led to new methods of examining relationships within the textual tradition. Chief among these is the Coherence-Based Genealogical Method (CBGM), used in the production of the ECM.[22] A fundamental difference between this method and traditional stemmatics is the distinction between the manuscript and the text it carries. In the framework of the CBGM, the text is the witness, not the manuscript with its codicological and palaeographical properties. While traditional stemmatics focuses on common errors, the CBGM addresses the issue of textual contamination by considering different types of coherence. The first measure is the percentage agreement of the text of any two witnesses included in the edition (their 'pre-genealogical coherence'). By creating a 'local stemma' of how readings relate to each other in each variation unit, it is then possible to compare the relationship of witnesses wherever they differ, expressing it in terms of the proportions of 'prior' (earlier) and 'posterior' (later) readings. Each local stemma is constructed by the editors using traditional philological principles to establish how the readings are related in each unit, largely based on internal criteria. The ability of the computer to process the relationships of witnesses based on each place of variation provides editors with an indication of the closest potential ancestors for each witness and, beyond that, the textual shape of the tradition as a whole. The measure of 'genealogical coherence' is the extent to which each variant reading is attested in witnesses which are related overall ('coherent attestation') or whether it emerged

---

[21] This practice is known as Lachmannian stemmatics, through its association with Karl Lachmann (1793–1851).

[22] For a full account of the CBGM, illustrated with numerous examples, see Wasserman & Gurry 2017; other useful literature includes Mink 2004, 2009 and 2011 and Wachtel 2012, 2019 and 2020.

on multiple, unrelated occasions ('incoherent attestation'). Beyond this is the concept of 'stemmatic coherence', which expresses the extent to which the text of each witness can be explained by the smallest possible combination of its potential ancestors in an optimal substemma. Combining all substemmata creates a 'global stemma'.

This genealogical approach is used alongside the traditional criteria by the editors of the ECM when constructing the editorial text (described as the *Ausgangstext* or 'Initial Text').[23] It thus constitutes a novel means of enhancing reasoned eclecticism by adding information which can only be provided by computer processing. Like the understanding of the textual quality of individual documents, the CBGM data is built up in an iterative way, beginning with straightforward variation units and then using the genealogical relationships built up from these to consider more complex cases. It is worth underlining that the CBGM does not itself determine the earliest reading: rather, it provides analyses of the consistency of the textual tradition which may assist editors in identifying the earliest reading, especially in cases where other criteria are evenly balanced. In addition, the CBGM sheds new light on the development of the biblical text by indicating the extent to which particular readings are likely to be related or may have arisen independently.

Further Digital Approaches

Modern technology offers additional ways of analysing and visualising relationships within a textual tradition. Data from a critical apparatus in electronic form can be examined with a variety of computer programs. One example is the application of phylogenetic tools developed for the processing of DNA to generate indications of manuscript relationships or groups, based on the most economical way of accounting for the differences between them. Another is cladistics software, which calculates the most likely paths of textual development and locates witnesses on these.[24] In these, unlike the CBGM, the analysis of the vari-

---

[23] Genealogical criteria are regularly cited in the textual commentaries provided for the ECM, which is why they are considered in detail here. The CBGM data for the published volumes of the ECM is available to view at https://ntg.uni-muenster.de/.

[24] Carlson 2015 is a good example of the use of cladistics to illuminate the textual history of Galatians.

ants is entirely automated with no editorial input. Nevertheless, the comparison of results reached through these different processes can highlight fresh areas for research. In some cases, it is even possible to identify the key points of variation which characterise different forms of the text. New tools such as these do not replace or invalidate philological analysis: rather, they supplement traditional approaches with alternative information which may be useful in explaining the origin and transmission of variant readings.

Who Changed the Text and How?

When trying to reconstruct the development of a text, it is often important to distinguish between deliberate and accidental changes and consider how they were introduced. Previous scholarship has frequently uncritically ascribed all changes to scribes, as if copyists were at liberty to pick and choose readings from a variety of manuscripts during the process of producing a new book. Sometimes it is claimed that scribes freely adjusted the text to match their preferences and possibly even their theological presuppositions.[25] In practice, there is little evidence for such an inefficient and independent approach to copying in antiquity. Although professional scribes may have had some licence when composing letters for illiterate customers, such latitude in the copying of literary texts is extremely unlikely. The price for manuscript production was set in the form of stichometric lists which indicated the number of lines in each work. While the image of scholars surrounded by multiple books may be familiar from Renaissance paintings and the desks (or virtual desktops) of modern academics, almost all ancient depictions of copyists show them working from a single document on a book stand, with the work in progress on their lap. All accidental changes, including subconscious alterations, are the creation of scribes, but it is misleading to hold them solely accountable for the form of text in the final copy.[26] Instead, it is clear from ancient accounts of literary

---

[25] Examples of this are seen throughout the explanations in Metzger 1994, reflected in much subsequent literature including Ehrman 2011.

[26] On these topics, see further Schmid 2008 and Jongkind 2008. For more on the range of people involved in the production of New Testament texts and manuscripts, see Moss 2024.

scholarship that there were multiple stages in the production and use of texts in antiquity. These were not always the responsibility of the same person, whether in a commercial bookshop or a monastic scriptorium.

Book Production in the Ancient World

The first step in copying a new manuscript was the selection of an exemplar (source document) from which the copy would be made. In most cases, this would have been provided by the person commissioning the manuscript, whether a private individual or a scriptorium overseer. There are many possible reasons for producing a new copy: an existing book may have deteriorated; a newly established congregation or freshly appointed minister may have required their own set of books; a visitor may have brought a work which was desired by local readers. The production of books was expensive, and although booksellers in antiquity may have kept a stock of the more commonly-required works, it seems that most manuscripts would have been produced to order.

The next stage was the establishment of the text to be copied from the exemplar (known in antiquity as *diorthosis*) by someone with scholarly training. Their contribution might involve adjusting spellings, correcting obvious errors, providing indications of formatting and any other alterations associated with the purpose of the new copy (e.g. the insertion of titles, or pictures, or lectionary indications). If multiple copies were to be produced from a single exemplar, more thorough preparation might be expected in keeping with the concept of a new edition. In such a situation, extended comparison with one or more other copies of the same work is conceivable. For less formal productions, the preparation process may have been more *ad hoc*: the exemplar may already have contained multiple corrections and other evidence of use such as liturgical markings, annotations by earlier readers, alternative readings entered in the margin, and so on. In such cases, the decision as to how to handle this material may have been delegated to the copyist.

It is unclear whether making copies from dictation or by sight was more common in antiquity. Even in the latter case, studies have suggested that copyists would usually vocalise the text as they were copying it, in units of a few syllables at a time. This explains how variations reflecting sound change are seen alongside visual misreadings of letters or whole words in the same copy, as well as errors of memory.[27] In some manuscripts, it is possible to see where scribes refilled their pen with ink: this, and other distractions such as switching to new lines, columns or pages in the exemplar, provided further opportunities for error. Corrections were sometimes made by the first hand in the course of writing (*in scribendo*), erasing or overwriting letters. The copyist or another member of the production team may have performed a full check of the copy against the exemplar before the manuscript left the scriptorium: this is sometimes indicated in the colophon at the end of the work. Only on rare occasions would a manuscript have been compared with another copy of the same work: the most common scenario for this is when a later reader noted discrepancies in the margin or tried to adjust some or all of the text. Other users might annotate the manuscript in different ways, according to the purposes for which it was being used. When manuscripts became damaged, replacement pages ('supplements') were sometimes copied from another source in order to extend the life of the document.

Scribes and Editors

One key point from the preceding account of book production is that the preparation of the text was usually a separate stage and the responsibility of an editor. While this function may sometimes have been fulfilled by the person who physically wrote the copy, this would have been the exception rather than the rule and the two roles should not be confused. Mistakes due to inattention (including some types of assimilation) or for mechanical reasons (such as eyeskip or dittography) happened during the copying process, but the scope for deliberately altering the text at this point was minimal. Not only would it have made the task slower and more prone to error, but gratuitous or unauthorised changes would render the copy a less accurate version of its exemplar, against the wishes of the person who commissioned it. The surviving evidence indicates that copyists usually sought to copy accurately, even reproducing mistakes or other readings in the text of their exemplar

---

[27] See Jongkind 2008: 47–49 and 2022; the latter notes the prevalence of substitutions due to 'word image', the replacement of a term by one of similar appearance (Jongkind 2022: 149–152).

which may have made no sense to them. What is more, in the absence of this source document, one can rarely be confident about the origin of any variant readings in the copy. Not only are these readings not a deliberate 'choice' by the scribe, but they may not even have been introduced by the person who prepared the exemplar for copying: instead, they might reflect the interventions of an editor several generations earlier which had been faithfully reproduced in subsequent iterations. An alteration only needs to be made once for it to appear in hundreds of manuscripts. Claims that the same change, sometimes of considerable complexity, was independently introduced by hundreds of scribes are highly implausible.

The most frequent textual variations created as part of the process of book production are therefore accidental changes or subconscious alterations. These were not introduced for ideological reasons, even though the differences between readings can be interpreted as theologically significant. The omission of a particular phrase or a small word such as 'not', the alteration of a verb tense or a personal pronoun, the interchange between the terms 'Christ', 'Lord' and 'God' (all written as two- or three-letter abbreviations known as *nomina sacra*) can each have substantial impact on the meaning of a text, yet all of these examples involve common copying errors described above in the section on internal criteria, such as eyeskip, haplography, vowel isochrony, itacism and confusion between similar forms. When a variant can be explained in terms of a mechanical error or an accommodation to the context, such an explanation is normally preferable to treating it as a deliberate alteration, because this reflects the nature of the copying process underlying each manuscript.

In contrast, changes made by an editor were deliberate, and usually represent a thoroughgoing revision of the text. Typical editorial alterations include grammatical improvements, consistent stylistic adjustments, harmonisation between passages (e.g. in the form of quotations from other writings), substantial reworking and the introduction of additional material, whether explanatory, exegetical, or complementary. Some of these may have been motivated by theological concerns. Ehrman's concept of the 'orthodox corruption of Scripture' observes that textual changes which can be interpreted as doctrinally significant usually bring passages into accordance with mainstream Christian teaching.[28] Such elimination of readings which might support heretical positions, along with the addition of clarifications to remove ambiguity, can be seen as further justification for the principle that the 'hardest' or 'most difficult' reading is most likely to be the earliest. At the same time, it should be recognised that possible theologically-motivated alterations constitute a very small proportion of the textual variation in the New Testament. In most cases, doctrinal significance is likely to be secondary because other, more mundane, reasons are behind the introduction of a variant. Just because a theological implication can be identified does not mean that this is the most plausible explanation for a variant reading. Throughout Christian history, difficult or uncongenial passages of Scripture have largely been addressed through interpretation rather than the alteration of the biblical text.[29]

Manuscript Grouping and Selection

Both the large amount of evidence preserved for the Greek New Testament and the loss of many documents, particularly from the earliest period, pose a problem for modern editors. The majority of variants appear to have arisen during the first two or three centuries, the time from which the fewest witnesses survive. This means that, even though there are some substantial early New Testament manuscripts, it is not always straightforward to determine which of the variant readings represents the earliest text. The extensive use of the Scriptures within the early Church resulted in Christian readers and copyists being familiar with multiple forms of text, providing plenty of scope for assimilation between them. Anyone with experience of using more than one translation in the same modern language will know how easy it is inadvertently to blend the two. As noted earlier in the discussion of genealogical coherence, the degree of textual mixture means that it is not possible to construct a stemma of all the witnesses to the New Testament to assist with making textual decisions. The only occasion on which this can be

---

[28] Ehrman 2011.

[29] The literature on this is substantial. While allegations of tampering with the text of Scripture were sometimes made in the early Church (especially with regard to the activity of Marcion), even then such disputes were resolved by appeals to the breadth and diversity of the manuscript tradition.

done is in the case of a family of manuscripts which all descend from a common ancestor: the best known of these are Family 1 and Family 13 in the gospels. Where such an ancestor cannot be reconstructed, manuscripts with a similar text (and often other shared features, such as decoration or origin) may be more loosely described as a group.

Text Types and Categories

One way of simplifying the complexity of the vast number of New Testament witnesses has been to try to define broader types of text on the basis of certain shared readings. This began in the early eighteenth century, with groupings being identified by geographical names reflecting the supposed origin of each type. Readings shared with Latin witnesses were thus described as a 'Western' text; those matching the biblical text of Christian writers in the scholarly centre on the north coast of Egypt were called 'Alexandrian', sometimes divided into 'primary Alexandrian' and 'secondary Alexandrian'; another famous ancient library was associated with a 'Caesarean' text; the text typical of later ecclesiastical tradition, the church of the empire centred on Constantinople, was termed the 'Byzantine' (also 'Syrian', 'Koine' or 'Ecclesiastical') text. Given the antiquity at which these strands developed, based on the diversity of their attestation in early Christian writers, agreements between witnesses considered to be typical of the different branches were treated as particularly important for reconstructing the earliest text by previous generations of New Testament editors.[30] More recent scholarship has cast doubt on this approach to such an extent that it has now largely been abandoned. Formal attempts to define these groupings quantitatively on the basis of a selection of variants are difficult to maintain when the full text of each manuscript is compared: the gaps which previously differentiated representatives of different types become blurred when a large number of manuscripts is taken into consideration. What is more, witnesses traditionally allocated to the same type have been shown to differ more from each other than from the majority of manuscripts. As a result, the use of these groupings to assist with text-critical decisions is unsustainable. Nevertheless, it remains

---

[30] See further the lists of representative manuscripts of these types provided in Metzger 1994: 15*–16*.

useful to identify sets of readings which appear to constitute a specific editorial intervention (for example, the 'Western' readings in Acts, or 'Byzantine' expansions), even though these may be unevenly distributed across surviving witnesses.[31]

Another way of grouping manuscripts is set out in the introduction by Aland & Aland, which assigns them to one of five categories indicated by Roman numerals (I–V).[32] This maps onto the geographical text-types to a certain extent, with Category I including witnesses traditionally associated with the 'Alexandrian' text, Category IV the 'Western' readings, and Category V Byzantine forms. Category II comprises mixed forms (including an 'Egyptian text'), while Category III features distinctive groups such as the families of minuscule witnesses. This classification was intended as an interim approach based on *Text und Textwert* (see below), prior to the creation of the ECM: like the geographical text types, it has been overtaken by the provision of full-text transcriptions and collations. The categories were never adopted as part of the *Kurzgefasste Liste*, and should no longer be used in editions or publications.

The Byzantine and Majority Texts

The only broad textual grouping which continues to be widely recognised is the Byzantine tradition. This is attested by the majority of Greek minuscule manuscripts, as well as most of the later majuscules. The *Text und Textwert* (TuT) analysis of almost one thousand places of variation in the Greek New Testament has demonstrated that these witnesses have an overall agreement with each other of at least 90% (and sometimes far higher), providing a standard against which the rest of the tradition can be defined.[33] Given that there are occasions on which the Byzantine tradition can be split between two or more readings (indicated as Byz^{pt} in UBS6), it is not always the case that this is identical to the 'Majority Text', even though in practice the two often share the

---

[31] For more on the history and applicability of text-types, see Parker 2008: 171–174 and Epp in Ehrman & Holmes 2013: 519–577; earlier hesitations regarding the 'Western' type are seen in Aland & Aland 1989: 54–55.

[32] See Aland & Aland 1989: 96–138 (especially 106–107), 159–163 and 332–337; Ehrman 1989 offers a summary and criticism of this approach.

[33] For more on *Text und Textwert*, see Aland & Aland 1989: 317–332.

same majority reading.³⁴ It is also worth noting that the printed edition known as the *Textus Receptus* (*TR*), often taken as representative of this tradition, contains some unusual poorly attested readings which reflect the manuscripts on which it was based: over 1,800 differences have been noted between this and the Byzantine text.³⁵

Selection Principles

The practice in most current editions of the Greek New Testament is to select manuscripts on the basis of their age and divergence from the majority of witnesses. This provides a range of variants which circulated in antiquity and is thus likely to include the earliest reading. For the ECM, with the goal of presenting the first thousand years of the textual tradition, all papyri are included, along with a set of majuscules and minuscules determined by their percentage disagreement from the majority reading. The same principle is generally followed in the hand editions, including UBS6, although here the selection of majuscules and minuscules is refined on the basis of the CBGM and limited to those which are closest to the ECM's editorial text (*Ausgangstext*). The only witnesses which are represented by groups are the Byzantine tradition (*Byz*), a selection of Greek lectionaries (*Lect*), and the two families of gospel manuscripts (f^1 and f^{13}). The other Greek manuscripts are presented as independent witnesses, allowing users to draw their own conclusions about relationships between them and the likely origin and sequence of variant readings.

The United Bible Societies' *Greek New Testament*

The Bible Societies' edition of the Greek New Testament was conceived by Eugene Nida in the 1950s for use by translators and expositors.³⁶ The aim was to provide an editorial text, reconstructed according to the la-

---

³⁴ Compare the discussion in the section above on 'Editorial Approaches'. The Majority Text is often indicated in a critical apparatus as MT or 𝔐.

³⁵ Wallace 1989. The term *Textus Receptus* was first used in an edition from the Elzevir publishing house in Leiden in 1633 and is based on Erasmus' edition of 1516: the Oxford 1873 edition is often taken as a standard in modern scholarship. When the *TR* differs from Byzantine tradition, this is indicated in the apparatus of UBS6.

³⁶ For an account of its early history, see Crisp 2021 and Aland & Aland 1989: 31–36.

test scholarly principles, which represented the earliest form attainable on the basis of the surviving evidence. A full apparatus would be given for variants of particular importance for translation, exegesis, or the history of the text. In addition to resources in the volume of the edition, such as lists of manuscripts, parallel passages, and maps, various companion volumes were envisaged including a textual commentary setting out the reasoning of the editors at each place of variation. As the edition was sponsored by several national Bible Societies, an editorial committee was assembled which came to comprise scholars from a variety of Christian traditions. The involvement of Kurt Aland of the INTF provided the committee with the data from the established Nestle-Aland *Novum Testamentum Graece* hand edition (NA). The first edition of the *Greek New Testament* was published in 1966 (UBS1). From 1975 (UBS3, with NA26 appearing in 1979), these two editions have shared the same editorial text while presenting different forms of apparatus: NA treats more points of variation in a condensed way for those focussing on textual history, while UBS offers a selection of readings with a full apparatus for a more general audience.

The sixth edition (UBS6) stands in the tradition of its predecessors, but is a thorough revision in all aspects. In books for which the ECM has been published (Mark, Acts, the Catholic Epistles, Revelation), the reconstructed 'Initial Text' of that edition has been adopted and printed as the main text in UBS6.[37] In other books, the editorial text remains unchanged. The sequence of the writings has been rearranged to accord with that seen in the oldest complete Greek biblical manuscripts: the Catholic Epistles follow Acts, while Hebrews comes between 2 Thessalonians and 1 Timothy (dividing the congregational from the personal epistles). This matches the nineteenth-century editions by Tregelles, Tischendorf and Westcott & Hort, as well as the Robinson & Pierpont edition of the Majority Text: earlier UBS editions followed the Latin order popularised by Erasmus and the *Textus Receptus*. The selection of variation units was completely reviewed, giving consideration to the nature and attestation of the alternative readings as well as their treatment in Bible translations and commentaries. Over a hundred units

---

[37] Where the ECM presents two readings as equally possible (the 'split guiding line' or 'diamond readings'), UBS6 retains the reading in the editorial text of UBS5.

were added and many others removed in order to maintain the edition's focus on the most important variants for translation and exegesis, as well as those of pedagogical interest for textual transmission.[38] The definitions of the confidence ratings provided for the editorial text were revised as follows:

{A} The Committee is confident in this reconstruction of the text.
{B} The Committee is fairly confident in this reconstruction of the text.
{C} The Committee is doubtful about this reconstruction of the text.
{D} The Committee is extremely doubtful about this reconstruction of the text.
◆ A decision on the reconstruction of the text was left open.

These ratings were revisited at each variation unit; in addition, the committee considered square brackets in the editorial text (equivalent to a {C} or {D} rating, but not always with an accompanying apparatus unit) and removed some of these on the basis of the external evidence.[39] Changes were made to the witnesses cited in the apparatus, including the introduction of newly discovered papyri, alignment with the ECM, and a reduction in minuscules which often matched the majority reading. The treatment of versional evidence was made more consistent and the selection of early Christian writers reduced.

In this way, UBS6 offers a general-purpose edition of the Greek New Testament for those seeking a consensus view of the earliest text which can be reconstructed based on the entire range of surviving evidence as well as information on the attestation of around one thousand places of textual variation which are considered the most important for translation and interpretation. The simplification and improvement of this hand edition has been made possible by the appearance of the much fuller ECM, as well as further cutting-edge academic research and the range of digital resources now available. Those wishing to explore any witness or reading in greater detail may consult the ECM, or the re-

---

[38] The total number of variation units in UBS6 is 1,008; of these 135 did not appear in UBS5.

[39] The distribution of the ratings in UBS6 is as follows: A–269, B–441, C–233, D–18, ◆–47 (plus 224 sets of brackets not accompanied by an apparatus unit). Changes in the selection of variants as well as the definitions mean that direct comparison between editions does not treat like with like (cf. Clarke 2002: 113–114). Decisions about which variation units to include or exclude and changes to ratings were all made by a consensus of the members of the editorial committee.

Introduction

sources in progress for the volumes in preparation, as well as viewing digitised manuscript images (often with transcriptions) on the NTVMR.[40] Although work will continue on the ECM for years to come, the revision and updating of the UBS edition enables its users to benefit from the most recent scholarly findings and the latest understanding of the history of the textual tradition.

The Textual Commentary

In keeping with the original proposal of the Bible Societies, a textual commentary on the edition was produced by one of the committee members, Bruce M. Metzger. First published in 1971 as a companion to UBS3, this commentary purports to present the discussions of the editorial committee, with occasional notes from members who disagreed with the choice of reading in the reconstructed text. The survey comprises both the 1,440 variation units of this edition and around 600 additional entries, many from Acts.[41] The second edition appeared in 1994, reflecting changes to the selection of variation units in UBS4. A simplified version for the use of Bible translators was produced by Roger L. Omanson in 2006, but the commentary was not updated for UBS5.

The present volume is an entirely new composition although it matches the title and general structure of Metzger's commentary. It covers all of the 1,008 variation units selected for UBS6 along with a further 224 entries corresponding to instances of square brackets in the editorial text which are not provided with an apparatus. Accordingly, it offers a more detailed explanation of all text-critical indications in this edition. An overview is provided at the beginning of each book or collection of writings, in which the key witnesses and variation units are identified and information is given about the source of the editorial text and other resources. All references, indicated by author and date, are to a single bibliography at the end of the volume. Despite being written independently of Metzger and Omanson, it was cross-checked against their explanations to ensure that all relevant material was covered.

---

[40] See especially https://ntvmr.uni-muenster.de/ecm. Material for John is available at www.iohannes.org and for the Pauline Epistles at www.epistulae.org. Digital images of New Testament manuscripts are also available at https://manuscripts.csntm.org/.

[41] Metzger 1994: vii–viii.

The first line of each entry in the commentary consists of the biblical reference, the editorial text in the variation unit (sometimes expanded slightly to help with disambiguation), and the corresponding words from the New Revised Standard Version updated edition (NRSVue). Where this English version is based on a different text, a literal translation is sometimes provided instead ('lit.'). The last item in this row is the confidence rating of the committee, as described in the previous section: this is lacking for the instances of square brackets which are not accompanied by an apparatus entry. The entries usually begin by setting out the different readings in the apparatus. An English translation of each is provided, in order to make the discussion as accessible as possible for those with limited Greek. Only the first five or so witnesses are listed, for reasons of economy, but slightly more may be given when there is no apparatus entry in UBS6: users wishing to see the fuller list in other cases can simply refer to the edition. Because the first sigla in the apparatus are usually the earliest witnesses (consisting of the papyri and oldest majuscules), even this reduced selection provides a general indication of the attestation in Greek. The majority reading is always identified, except in cases where the Byzantine tradition is divided. Information is also given of variation units included in *Text und Textwert*, to which users can refer for the readings of all accessible Greek continuous-text manuscripts at this point: the printed or online ECM apparatus, where available, presents a comprehensive selection of witnesses.[42]

Arguments are given for and against the main variant readings as the earliest form of text, usually in the form of suggestions as to how secondary readings might have arisen. It is important to be clear that, unlike in Metzger's commentary, these observations do not represent the discussions or common opinion of the committee. The decision—also implemented in UBS5, NA28 and NA29—to adopt the editorial text of published volumes of the ECM and to retain the text of the previous edition unchanged in the other books means that the UBS6 committee did not discuss the choice of reading. This may serve to make the present textual commentary of broader value than its precursors: rather

---

[42] The occasional references to witnesses not cited in UBS6 have been taken from these sources or NA28. The ECM *Parallel Pericopes* volume is also cited when present.

than defend the committee's text, it seeks to present a rationale for each decision while indicating which of the alternative readings are worthy of serious consideration. The author has tried to make the best case for the reading printed in the editorial text, while representing differing possibilities and points of view. There are several occasions, however, on which the assessment of the evidence suggests that a different reading is more compelling than that chosen by the editors of UBS4, even though the latter persists in the editorial text: the UBS6 committee felt that there was little value in trying to anticipate the thoroughgoing evaluation of each book still to be published in the ECM. Even in books where the text is taken from the ECM there remains scope to prefer a different initial reading, as shown by the reports in the ECM textual commentaries of disagreements between the volume editors.

Particular attention is paid to the editorial text of two other recent hand-editions, the *SBL Greek New Testament* (SBLGNT; Holmes 2010) and *The Greek New Testament: Tyndale House Edition* (THGNT; Jongkind and Williams 2017), especially in variation units with a low confidence rating. Reference is also made to the ECM textual commentaries, where available, as well as other text-critical commentaries on substantial portions of text.[43] Indications are given in footnotes of more detailed discussions of particular units or the sources for information which has not been independently verified.[44] These include the commentaries of Metzger and Omanson as well as a variety of other academic publications from recent decades, in the hope that these may assist readers looking for further information.[45] These references are far from exhaustive and it has not been practicable to include information from the vast range of biblical commentaries currently avail-

---

[43] Most of the entries in the ECM textual commentaries are also available online at https://ntvmr.uni-muenster.de/forum/-/message_boards/category/1136042; for online access to the CBGM data, see the section on 'genealogical coherence' above. A textual commentary for the THGNT is in preparation but had not appeared at the time of writing; readers may also compare the six hundred text-critical notes in the NET Bible at www.netbible.org. Commentaries on individual books are mentioned in the Overview which begins each section of the present volume.

[44] Observations about usage which are not so indicated have been developed on the basis of the Accordance biblical software.

[45] The following introductory works provide useful overviews and orientations to the field of New Testament textual scholarship: Aland & Aland 1989; Parker 1997 and 2008; Ehrman & Holmes 2013; Hixson & Gurry 2019; Crawford and Wasserman 2025.

able, many of which are also worth consulting with regard to specific verses. In order to improve the usefulness of the present volume, it is intended to offer corrections and other updates on a dedicated website (http://hughhoughton.uk/tcgnt). Users are encouraged to refer to this and invited to contact the author with suggestions of bibliography or other items for inclusion there and in any subsequent editions.

The Gospel according to Matthew

Overview

Matthew is attested in seventeen fragmentary papyri from the second to the fourth century: the most substantial are Papyri 64/67 (two parts of the same document, identified as $\mathfrak{P}^{64}$) and Papyrus 45 ($\mathfrak{P}^{45}$), which contain portions of three and four chapters respectively. The principal sources for its text are the major majuscule codices of the fourth and fifth centuries: Codex Sinaiticus (01), Codex Alexandrinus (02), Codex Vaticanus (03), Codex Ephraemi Rescriptus (04) and Codex Bezae (05). Of these, Codex Alexandrinus is usually the oldest witness to the majority text, which is sometimes also reflected in the Greek-Latin bilingual Codex Bezae. The agreement of the other early witnesses is often paralleled in Codex Regius (019, from the eighth or ninth century), and the group of minuscule manuscripts known as Family 1 (f^1) which reflect a scholarly edition created in the tenth century. Other important minuscule witnesses are GA 33, 597, 892 and 1241. The text typical of the later Byzantine tradition is seen in most other majuscules, including Codex Washingtonianus (032, also called the Freer Gospels, whose date is uncertain), three ninth-century codices, 037 (a Latin-Greek bilingual), the Koridethi Codex (038) and 044. Family 13 (f^{13}) also usually agrees with the majority. Some of the early majuscules, especially 01 and 04, have multiple layers of corrections, which are indicated in sequence by superscript numerals.

All four gospels are present in the three principal early biblical translations: Latin, consisting of the Old Latin (lat^{vl}) and Jerome's fourth-century revision known as the Vulgate (lat^{vg}); the two main Old Syriac manuscripts (sy^s and sy^c), as well as the later Peshitta (sy^p) and Harklean version (sy^h); the Coptic versions, including the Sahidic (co^{sa}) and subsequent standard Bohairic (co^{bo}).[1] Among early Christian writers, the commentary on Matthew by the third-century writer Origen was par-

---

[1] Two further Old Syriac manuscripts have been discovered in recent years: sy^f, a palimpsest in St. Catherine's Monastery, Mount Sinai, with fragments of all four gospels, and a fragment of Matt. 11–12 in a double palimpsest in the Vatican Library.

ticularly influential (see Matt. 8:28 below), but it has not been preserved in its entirety. Second-century witnesses include Irenaeus and the Latin author Tertullian, as well as Tatian's *Diatessaron* (a Greek harmony of the four gospels which is only known through secondary sources).

Although Matthew usually comes first in collections of the four gospels, it was not the first to be written. It is generally accepted that Matthew was dependent on Mark; some also believe that it was a source for Luke. This means that comparisons with those two gospels may shed light on the development of the text. Nevertheless, Matthew was the principal gospel in antiquity, making it the main source for quotations and also meaning that the other accounts were assimilated to it. Despite ancient claims that Matthew was originally written in Hebrew, it is clearly a Greek composition as shown by its verbal dependence on Mark and its use of the Septuagint for quotations from the Jewish Scriptures. The identification of 'Semitic' constructions in its language or textual variants (apart from those in biblical quotations) is debatable.

There are three additional verses in the Byzantine tradition of Matthew not attested in the earliest manuscripts (Matt. 17:21, 18:11 and 23:14; see below). There is also one verse traditionally identified as a 'Western non-interpolation' (Matt. 27:49; see further the Overview for Luke), in which material from John appears to have been added at an early point. Three other verses are absent from a few ancient witnesses (Matt. 12:47, 16:2b–3 and 21:44). Other well-known variants include the inclusion of 'without cause' at Matt. 5:22, the forms of the doxology in the Lord's Prayer (Matt. 6:13), variations involving the teaching on adultery (Matt. 19:9), the sequence of the two sons in Matt. 21:29–31 and the question as to whether the Son knows the day and hour (Matt. 24:36). Names are a particularly common place of variation in this gospel, including the Gadarenes (Matt. 8:28), the apostle Thaddeus (Matt. 10:3) and Jesus Barabbas (Matt. 21:16–17).

The *Editio Critica Maior* of Matthew is in preparation and expected to appear in the next few years. Work towards this may be seen online in the form of transcriptions in the New Testament Virtual Manuscript Room (NTVMR) as well as the *Text und Textwert* (*TuT*) collations.[2]

---

[2] See further https://ntvmr.uni-muenster.de/. For more on *Text und Textwert* and the other material mentioned in this overview, see the Introduction above.

The text of Matthew in UBS6 remains identical to that of the two previous editions apart from the removal of some square brackets.

1:7-8   Ἀσάφ, Ἀσάφ (Asaph, and Asaph) {B}

The majority of Greek manuscripts read Ἀσά, Ἀσά ('Asa, and Asa'; 019 032 037 etc.), which is the name of the son of Abijah (or Abijam) at 1 Kings 15:8. Nevertheless, there is very strong early support for Ἀσάφ, Ἀσάφ ('Asaph, and Asaph'; 𝔓¹ᵛⁱᵈ 01 03 04 etc.). There are numerous instances of the name Asaph in the Septuagint (e.g. 2 Kings 18:18, 1 Chron. 16:5, Neh. 7:44, Psalms 73-83 [72-82 LXX]). Given the frequency of the latter name, it could be that it was erroneously substituted for Asa at an early point, or that it is simply a spelling variant for Asa. However, taking into account the attestation of Asaph (also seen in the Latin, Coptic and Ethiopic translations), it seems more likely that this was the earliest text which was then corrected by an editor who compared Matthew's account with that of the Septuagint. It is possible that the evangelist may have taken the genealogy from an independent list rather than drawing directly on biblical narrative, which could account for this error.[3] In any case, the principle of consistency in referring to a single person throughout the Bible means that many translations will use the name Asa here, regardless of which reading is considered original. See also the following variation unit.

1:10   Ἀμώς, Ἀμώς (Amos, and Amos) {B}

As in the previous unit, while early witnesses read Ἀμώς, Ἀμώς ('Amos, and Amos'; 01 03 04 etc.), most Byzantine manuscripts have Ἀμών, Ἀμών ('Amon, and Amon'; 019 032 f^{13} etc.). Again, the latter is the correct name for the son of Manasseh (or Manasses) at 2 Kings 21:18, while the name Amos is likely to have been more familiar as the father of Isaiah (2 Kings 19:2 etc.) and one of the Minor Prophets in his own right. While Ἀμώς could have been an early error for Ἀμών, the external evidence (which differs slightly from the pattern of attestation in Matt. 1:7-8) suggests that Ἀμών is a later correction. Even so, based in the principle of consistency mentioned in the previous unit, translations may prefer to use Amon to indicate this king.

---

[3] Metzger 1994: 1.

1:16 τὸν ἄνδρα Μαρίας, ἐξ ἧς ἐγεννήθη Ἰησοῦς ὁ λεγόμενος Χριστός (lit. the husband of Mary, of whom Jesus was born, who is called the Messiah) {A}

The editorial text is found in the oldest surviving manuscripts (𝔓¹ 01 03 04 etc.) as well as Byzantine tradition, and so is confidently adopted as the earliest form of text. Nevertheless, there are variant readings which are of theological interest in that they alter the description of Joseph and Mary in order to emphasise the virgin birth, even though the change in phrasing in the editorial text from the rest of the genealogy already indicates that Jesus' birth was different from those preceding. One group of witnesses reads ᾧ μνηστευθεῖσα παρθένος Μαριὰμ ἐγέννησεν Ἰησοῦν τὸν λεγόμενον Χριστόν ('to whom having been betrothed a virgin, Mary, bore Jesus who is called Christ'; 038 f^{13} lat^(vl·pt)). This is clearly an editorial change to indicate that Joseph was not Mary's husband at the time when Jesus was born, as well as underline Mary's virginity. A similar text is supported by the Curetonian Syriac, ᾧ μνηστευθεῖσα ἦν Μαριὰμ παρθένος, ἣ ἔτεκεν Ἰησοῦν Χριστόν ('to whom Mary, a virgin, was betrothed, who gave birth to Jesus Christ'), which is paralleled in the third-century Greek writer Hippolytus; the other Old Syriac manuscript, the Sinaitic, is close to this but, surprisingly, has Joseph as the subject of the verb ('Joseph ... begot Jesus'). This appears to be a unique reading produced by an unthinking adherence to the pattern of the rest of the genealogy in which each name is repeated twice, the second time at the beginning of the 'begot' clause. The full range of readings in continuous-text Greek manuscripts is given in *TuT Matthew* (TS2), while a variety of potential witnesses to the more unusual readings have been considered in greater detail elsewhere.[4]

1:18 γένεσις (birth) {C}

The majority of Greek witnesses read γέννησις ('birth'; 019 f^{13} etc.), while the oldest manuscripts have γένεσις (also 'birth'; 𝔓¹ 01 03 04 etc.). The difference between the two terms is that the latter has the sense of 'creation' (as in the book of Genesis) and 'genealogy' (for which it is used at Matt. 1:1), whereas the former refers to the physical process of

---

[4] e.g. Metzger 1972; Nolland 1996; Min 2005: 301–304.

giving birth. As such, γέννησις is the more appropriate word here and was used by early Christian writers to refer to the Nativity: it is attested in both Irenaeus and Origen. It is possible that this was original, with the evangelist making a deliberate change in terminology between Matt. 1:1 and 1:18. However, the attestation favours γένεσις, which is the harder reading in terms of sense although it is a simple substitution given its use in Matt. 1:1.[5] The similarity of the two words suggests that they might have been confused on multiple occasions. In certain languages, translators may have to choose between words with different nuances, whereas in others (such as English) it may be possible to render both in the same way. Both SBLGNT and THGNT have γένεσις.

1:25   υἱόν (a son) {A}

Most manuscripts read τὸν υἱὸν αὐτῆς τὸν πρωτότοκον ('her firstborn son'; 04 05* 032 etc.; see *TuT Matthew* TS4), but a group of important witnesses simply have υἱόν ('a son'; 01 03 035 *f*¹ etc.). The possibility that the additional phrase was omitted by eyeskip from the end of υἱόν to the end of πρωτότοκον is negligible, given the addition of τόν ('the') at the beginning and the fact that υἱόν is often written as a *nomen sacrum* (ΥΝ). Instead it seems that the shorter form, with its early attestation, has been expanded to the text found in the parallel passage at Luke 2:7.

2:18   κλαυθμός (wailing) {B}

The editorial text, κλαυθμός ('wailing'; 01 03 035 0250 etc.) differs from the form of the original quotation in the Septuagint (Jer. 31:15 [38:15 LXX]), which reads θρῆνος καὶ κλαυθμός ('mourning and wailing'; 04 05 019 032 etc.). It is possible that one of these words was omitted by a copyist in error, although the normal pattern for eyeskip would be to omit the second rather than the first term. The likely direction of editorial change is to conform a quotation to its source, which suggests that the longer reading is a correction. However, the relatively slim attestation of κλαυθμός leaves room for doubt as to whether it is original. If θρῆνος ('mourning') is read here, it would be the only occurrence of

---

[5] Ehrman 2011: 88–89 suggests that γέννησις was a deliberate substitution, but Wasserman 2012: 340 points to similar unmotivated variation elsewhere.

this noun in the New Testament. The full range of readings in continuous-text Greek manuscripts is given in *TuT Matthew* (TS5).

3:2 [καί] (and)

At the beginning of this verse, the textual tradition is split between witnesses which include καί ('and'; 01 03 04 032 f^1 f^{13} and numerous minuscules) and those which lack it (05 017 019 022^{vid} 036 037 etc.). In the absence of καί, the participle λέγων simply functions as a marker of direct speech. In the longer reading, which has the better external support and is preferred in SBLGNT and THGNT, the two participles are co-ordinated (κηρύσσων ... καὶ λέγων, 'proclaiming ... and saying').

3:16 [αὐτῷ] (to him) {C}

After the verb ἠνεῴχθησαν ('were opened'), most Greek manuscripts include the pronoun αὐτῷ ('to him' or 'for him'; 01^1 04 05^{supp} 019 etc.), indicating that only Jesus saw the opening of the heavens and the dove, or that they were for his benefit. The absence of the pronoun from two important manuscripts (01* 03) and some early versions may cast doubt on whether it was originally present, in which case the opening of the heavens could be interpreted as a more general event. However, the restriction to Jesus matches the source at Mark 1:10, and the pronoun could easily have been omitted from these few witnesses in error or through assimilation to the parallel at Luke 3:22, where both the heavens and the dove appear to be visible to all. Given the variations in the same manuscripts in the next two units, accidental omission seems less likely; THGNT includes the pronoun, whereas SBLGNT lacks it. The full range of readings in continuous-text Greek manuscripts is given in *TuT Matthew* (TS7).

3:16 [τὸ] πνεῦμα [τοῦ] θεοῦ (God's Spirit)

The two manuscripts which lack αὐτῷ in the previous unit also read πνεῦμα θεοῦ ('[a] spirit of God'; 01 03) here, rather than τὸ πνεῦμα τοῦ θεοῦ ('the Spirit of God'; 04 05^{supp} 019 etc.). The only other time this phrase appears in the gospels is at Matt. 12:28, which supports the shorter reading; the earlier references to the Holy Spirit in Matthew also lack a definite article (Matt. 1:18, 1:20, 3:11), but it is present in later ones (Matt. 4:1, 10:20, 12:32, 28:19). It is therefore possible that the form without the definite articles here is original, which was later expanded to the more standard construction which makes it clear that it is 'the Spirit' rather than 'a Spirit' (compare the parallels at Mark 1:10 and Luke 3:22). However, the attestation of the shorter reading is so slight, even though it is early, that it is very difficult to be confident about the earliest form. Again, the full range of readings in continuous-text Greek manuscripts is given in *TuT Matthew* (TS8).

3:16 [καὶ] ἐρχόμενον (and alighting)

For the fourth time in this verse, a small word is lacking from the first hand of Codex Sinaiticus and Codex Vaticanus (01* 03). All other manuscripts have καί ('and'), co-ordinating the two participles ('descending … and alighting'; 01² 04 05 etc.), whereas the shorter reading conveys a single idea ('descending like a dove alighting on him'). The single action is supported by the parallels at Mark 1:10 and Luke 3:22, whereas the twofold 'descending and remaining' matches John 1:33. This pattern of variation may suggest that there has been deliberate editorial intervention in the text reflected in these two witnesses, creating a shorter text which offers a better fit to certain parallels. On the other hand, because the longer text matches other parallels, this could be the result of later expansion. The limited support for the shorter text, especially in the light of the other units in this verse, means that it cannot be confidently adopted as the earliest form.

4:24 [καὶ] δαιμονιζομένους (and people possessed by demons)

A few important witnesses lack καί ('and'), reading just δαιμονιζομένους ('people possessed by demons'; 03 04* [037] f^{13}). Given the presence of καί before the other three elements of this list, it is likely that its omission here is due to eyeskip of KAI before ΔAI or deletion due to a misunderstanding of the preceding chiasmus.

5:4–5 μακάριοι … παρακληθήσονται. μακάριοι … τὴν γῆν.
(Blessed … for they will be comforted. Blessed … the earth)
{B}

A few witnesses have Matt. 5:4 and 5:5 in the opposite sequence, reading μακάριοι … τὴν γῆν. μακάριοι … παρακληθήσονται ('Blessed are the meek, for they will inherit the earth. Blessed are those who mourn, for they will be comforted'; 05 33 lat^{vl-pt, vg} sy^c co^{bo-ms} Origen Chrysostom^{pt}; see further *TuT Matthew* TS11). This is attractive, in that not only does it contrast 'the heavens' of Matt. 5:3 with 'the earth' in the following verse, but it also brings together two categories of people (οἱ πτωχοί ... οἱ πραεῖς, 'the poor ... the meek') followed by two activities (οἱ πενθοῦντες ... οἱ πεινῶντες, 'those who mourn ... those who hunger'). For this reason, it is likely that this is a subsequent editorial improvement, although it is not impossible that the majority reading adopted in the text may stem from an early error leading to a change of sequence: the parallel in Luke does not include either of these elements.

5:11 ψευδόμενοι (falsely) {B}

The word ψευδόμενοι (lit. 'lying') is lacking only from Codex Bezae, Old Latin manuscripts and the Sinaitic Syriac, as well as two ancient writers. While it may seem like a later gloss, this makes little sense in context. Rather, the location of this word results in an ambiguity ('lying for my sake'), which has been eliminated by an earlier editor or translators (note also the rearrangement in these witnesses of the previous two units). The absence of the word from the parallel at Luke 6:22 might favour the shorter reading, but it could also have led to assimilation here. The attestation in the present verse strongly indicates that ψευδόμενοι is original, and the brackets in UBS5 have been removed.[6]

5:22 τῷ ἀδελφῷ αὐτοῦ (with a brother or sister) {B}

After this phrase, the majority of witnesses include the qualification εἰκῇ ('without cause'; 01² 05 019 032 etc.). It is missing from a few witnesses, some of which are early and weighty (𝔓^{64} 01* 03 lat^{vl-pt, vg} Tertullian Origen and around 25 minuscules; see *TuT Matthew* TS13). As it is a mitigation of the commandment never to be angry, the longer reading has the appearance of a later insertion. Nevertheless, there is a qualification in the comparable prohibition at Matt. 5:32 (allowing a justification for divorce), which provides a parallel for an original limitation here. There is no mitigation to the commands on either side, which

---

[6] Holmes 1986 offers a discussion of this verse in its broader context, reaching the same conclusion.

means that εἰκῇ could have been omitted through assimilation, or possibly overlooked (it occurs at the end of a line in Codex Sinaiticus). With several studies in favour of the originality of the longer reading and the limited attestation of the shorter form, there is room for uncertainty.[7]

5:39 σιαγόνα [σου] ([your] cheek)

The word σου ('your') is superfluous here, and it is missing from numerous manuscripts (including 01 032 f^1 33 892 and 1241). It is possible that this is an omission due to several variants here in word order, or the accidental omission of a small word before another beginning with the same letter, or deliberate deletion in order to enhance the parallelism with the next clause. It seems less likely that σου was a later addition: although this might serve to explain some of the variations in word order, which is why earlier editors enclosed it in brackets, it is more probable that the short reading stems from the deletion of σου from its unexpected position between δεξιάν ('right') and σιαγόνα ('cheek') within part of Byzantine tradition, because in this context δεξιάν could be misinterpreted as 'right hand'. There is minimal difference in translation, as many languages will require a possessive here.

5:44 ἐχθροὺς ὑμῶν (your enemies) {A}

The majority of Greek witnesses include two extra phrases after the command to love your enemies, εὐλογεῖτε τοὺς καταρωμένους ὑμᾶς, καλῶς ποιεῖτε τοῖς μισοῦσιν ὑμᾶς ('bless those who curse you, do good to those who hate you'; 05 019 032 037 etc.). The shorter reading has early and varied support (01 03 f^1 lat[vl-pt] sy[c, s] co[sa, bo-pt] Irenaeus[lat vid] Origen), which suggests that the longer reading is a harmonisation to the parallel at Luke 6:27–28, although the clauses appear in the opposite sequence there. There is no obvious reason which would prompt the omission of both these lines: around sixty minuscules only have one of the extra phrases, as seen in the other variations here attested predominantly in early versions and Christian writers. This is presumably due

---

[7] Wernberg Møller 1956, Black 1988b and Victor 2009: 63–64 all prefer the longer text as original.

to eyeskip between the two instances of ὑμᾶς (see *TuT Matthew* TS14). The following variant confirms that the longer reading was a later accommodation.

5:44   διωκόντων ὑμᾶς (who persecute you) {A}

Around forty minuscules have ἐπηρεαζόντων ὑμᾶς ('who abuse you'; 1241 etc.: see *TuT Matthew* TS15), the reading found at the parallel in Luke 6:28. The majority of manuscripts read ἐπηρεαζόντων ὑμᾶς καὶ διωκόντων ὑμᾶς ('who abuse you and pursue you'; 05 019 032 037 etc.), while some Latin witnesses have both terms in the reverse order ('who pursue you and abuse you'; lat^(vl-pt, vg)). These seem to be straightforward conflations of the terms distinctive of Matthew and Luke: διωκόντων ὑμᾶς ('persecute you'; 01 03 f^1 etc.) is attested by exactly the same witnesses as the shorter reading in the previous unit, and indicates that the expansion there is due to assimilation to the parallel.

5:47   ἐθνικοί (gentiles) {B}

Most Greek manuscripts read τελῶναι ('tax collectors'; 019 032 037 038 etc.), matching the end of the previous verse. There is good evidence for a different term, ἐθνικοί ('gentiles'; 01 03 05 035 etc.), which suggests that the evangelist intended to vary the comparison: the combination of the two terms at Matt. 18:17 shows that they were considered as a pair. The likelihood that the variation was introduced by a later editor seems slim. The full range of readings in continuous-text Greek manuscripts is given in *TuT Matthew* (TS16).

6:1   προσέχετε [δέ] (beware)

The majority of witnesses lack a connective in this verse (03 05 015 032 037 etc.), whereas some important manuscripts have the contrastive δέ ('but'; 01 019 035 038 f^1 etc.). The same fluidity regarding δέ is seen in the other instances of this command in Matthew (Matt. 7:15, 10:17, 16:11) suggesting that it may have been added or dropped through assimilation. If δέ is present, its effect on interpretation would be to connect this verse more closely to the previous one; its absence would indicate the start of a new section, which is often also matched in the paragraph layout of these witnesses. The external evidence is slightly stronger for the shorter reading, but as the particle could also have been omitted through oversight (following three other two-letter combinations with *epsilon*), it is hard to be sure which is earlier.

6:4   σοι (you) {B}

Most of the oldest surviving witnesses end the verse with σοι ('you'; 01 03 05 035 etc., lat^(vl·pt, vg) sy^c co Origen). The majority of Greek manuscripts follow this with the phrase ἐν τῷ φανερῷ ('in the open'; 019 032 037 etc.; see *TuT Matthew* TS17), contrasting this with the secrecy of the previous two actions. There is no obvious reason for the accidental omission of this phrase: rather, it appears to have supplied by an editor who felt that the end of the verse was incomplete following the double appearance of 'in secret'. The antithesis between κρυπτός ('secret') and φανερός ('open') which may have inspired this at Mark 4:22 (cf. Luke 8:17) is not found in the parallel at Matt. 10:26, and the word φανερός only appears securely in this gospel at Matt. 12:16. The same variation is found at Matt. 6:6 and 6:18 (see below): there is an ethical implication to the reward being openly visible. The best case that can be made for the originality of the longer reading is that an early reader felt that God's activity was not always perceptible and therefore deleted the phrase.

6:6   ἀποδώσει σοι (will reward you) {B}

As at Matt. 6:4, the two instances of ἐν τῷ κρυπτῷ ('in secret') in this verse are followed in the majority of manuscripts by a contrast at the end with ἐν τῷ φανερῷ ('in the open'; 019 032 037 etc.; see *TuT Matthew* TS18). The attestation is almost the same as at Matt. 6:4, although f^{13} here agrees with the majority. Again, there is no obvious reason why the phrase would be overlooked: it seems to be an editorial addition presumably introduced at the same time as the one in Matt. 6:4 (see also Matt. 6:18 below).

6:12   ἀφήκαμεν (we have forgiven) {B}

The aorist tense, ἀφήκαμεν (lit. 'we forgave'; 01* 03 035 f^1 lat^(vg) sy^(p,h)), is the harder reading, given the focus of the rest of the prayer on the present. Nevertheless, a temporal distinction between human and divine forgiveness is also seen in Matt. 6:14–15, where the former clearly precedes the latter. It has been suggested that the aorist is a literal translation of an Aramaic perfect used with present force (compare the 'prophetic perfect' at Mark 11:24 below).[8] A smoother present tense appears in the majority of Greek manuscripts, either as ἀφίομεν ('we forgive'; 05 019 032 037 038 565) or ἀφίεμεν (also 'we forgive'; 01² f^{13} and most minuscules). The latter is the regular, more common form, also seen in the majority of manuscripts at Luke 11:4, but the former is adopted as the editorial text in that parallel which has no Greek evidence for the aorist. It is therefore possible that both present-tense forms here are due to assimilation to Luke: the present tense there may be that evangelist's adjustment of his source, a more idiomatic translation of an Aramaic form, or potential early evidence for ἀφίομεν in Matthew. The external evidence and the discontinuity in tense leads to the adoption of ἀφήκαμεν here as well as in the SBLGNT and THGNT. If the suggestion regarding an underlying Aramaic text is accepted, translators would be justified in using a present tense here; otherwise, a perfect tense would be idiomatic and also mark the difference between Matthew and Luke (cf. 'we have forgiven' NRSVue).

6:13 πονηροῦ (evil one) {A}

There is strong support for the ending of the Matthean Lord's Prayer with πονηροῦ ('the evil one'; 01 03 05 035 0170 f^1 lat[vl-pt, vg] co[bo-pt, mae] etc.): the Lukan version also lacks a doxology (Luke 11:4), and early commentaries on the Lord's Prayer by Tertullian, Origen, and Cyprian close here too. The standard addition, ὅτι σοῦ ἐστιν ἡ βασιλεία καὶ ἡ δύναμις καὶ ἡ δόξα εἰς τοὺς αἰῶνας. ἀμήν ('because yours is the kingdom and the power and the glory for ever, Amen'; 019 032 037 038 etc.), seen in the majority of Greek manuscripts, appears to be a liturgical addition perhaps modelled on 1 Chr. 29:11. A number of minor variations are attested, demonstrating the fluidity of the doxology: other early Coptic translations and the Didache lack ἡ βασιλεία καί ('the kingdom and'), the Old Latin Codex Bobiensis has neither ἡ βασιλεία nor καὶ ἡ δόξα (just reading 'yours is the power'), while some Greek minuscules expand it with a Trinitarian formula ('the glory of the Father and of the Son and of the Holy Spirit'; 157 and others not mentioned in

---

[8] Metzger 1994: 13. Victor 2009: 68, however, sees it as a later accommodation to the aorist imperatives of the other petitions.

UBS6). The full range of readings in continuous-text Greek manuscripts, numbering around thirty in total, is given in *TuT Matthew* (TS19). Most translations have a footnote indicating that there is precedent for the liturgical form in biblical manuscripts despite it not forming part of the earliest text.[9]

6:15 ἀνθρώποις (others) {C}

The majority of Greek manuscripts include τὰ παραπτώματα αὐτῶν ('their trespasses'; 03 019 032 etc.; see *TuT Matthew* TS20) after ἀνθρώποις ('humans'). This is seen following the verb ἀφῆτε ('forgive') in the previous verse and the following clause, but the direct object is lacking from the immediately preceding instance at the end of Matt. 6:14 (ἀφήσει καὶ ὑμῖν, 'will forgive you'). It is not clear whether the witnesses with the shorter reading (01 05 f^1 etc.) preserve an original chiasmus or reflect one created by an editorial deletion of the direct object: there is no obvious reason for accidental omission. Given that copyists were more likely to assimilate the beginning of this conditional clause to the previous one, regardless of the fact that the direct object appears in the following clause, the shorter reading has been preferred in the editorial text and the SBLGNT. Another factor in favour of the shorter reading is that this instance of τὰ παραπτώματα αὐτῶν ('their trespasses') is absent from Mark 11:25, an additional verse seen in the majority of Greek manuscripts which supplies this Matthean parallel. Nevertheless, the THGNT adopts the longer reading here based on the external evidence. In some languages, the verb 'to forgive' may require a direct as well as an indirect object, in which case the former must be supplied regardless of which reading is adopted.

6:18 σοι (you) {A}

The structure of this verse, with the double instance of ἐν τῷ κρυφαίῳ ('in secret'; the majority of manuscripts read ἐν τῷ κρυπτῷ, also 'in secret') matches that of Matt. 6:4 and 6:6. As in those verses, some manuscripts have a contrasting ἐν τῷ φανερῷ ('in the open'; 037 0233 157 etc.) at the end of the verse. Although this is attested by a large number

---

[9] Parker 1997: 54–60 offers a more extended discussion of this 'Matthean doxology' and the different witnesses.

of minuscules, it is not as widespread as in the earlier verses, which leads to the conclusion that it is a later assimilation to the previous longer readings. Again, there is nothing in context which would prompt its omission.

6:25 [ἢ τί πίητε] (or what you will drink) {C}

The majority of Greek manuscripts read καὶ τί πίητε ('and what you will drink'; 019 037 038 etc.), while a few important witnesses have ἢ τί πίητε ('or what you will drink'; 03 032 f^{13} etc.). Other early texts lack the phrase completely (01 f^1 892 lat[vl-pt, vg] sy[c] etc.): this could be through eyeskip (from HTE to HTE), or represent the earliest attainable text which was later expanded through assimilation to Matt. 6:31 (compare the shorter form in the parallel at Luke 12:22). The variety between καί ('and') and ἤ ('or') suggests that the longer readings are secondary. Conversely, the slim attestation of the shortest form and the early external support for ἢ τί πίητε makes it difficult to decide which reading is the earliest: the THGNT has the longer reading, while the SBLGNT lacks this phrase.

6:33 τὴν βασιλείαν [τοῦ θεοῦ] καὶ τὴν δικαιοσύνην αὐτοῦ (the kingdom of God and his righteousness) {C}

The longest form of this reading, including the words in brackets, is present in the majority of witnesses (019 032 037 etc.) and adopted in the THGNT. Various other forms are only attested by a few sources: Codex Sinaiticus and some early translations read τὴν βασιλείαν καὶ τὴν δικαιοσύνην αὐτοῦ ('the kingdom and his righteousness'; 01 lat[vl-pt, vg] co[sa, bo] Eusebius); in Codex Vaticanus alone, this is found in the sequence τὴν δικαιοσύνην καὶ τὴν βασιλείαν αὐτοῦ ('righteousness and his kingdom'; 03), perhaps because an editor wished to emphasise that righteousness was the key to entering the kingdom; some minuscules not cited in UBS6 and early writers have τὴν βασιλείαν τοῦ θεοῦ ('the kingdom of God'; Chrysostom[pt]) or τὴν βασιλείαν τῶν οὐρανῶν ('the kingdom of the heavens'; Justin Chrysostom[pt]). The full range of readings in continuous-text Greek manuscripts is given in *TuT Matthew* (TS21).[10]

---

[10] See Hendriks 2005 for early translations and quotations in Christian writers (although these are unreliable witnesses for shorter readings due to their tendency to abbreviate and paraphrase).

The absence of the second element is easily explained as eyeskip. The principal issue is whether τὴν βασιλείαν originally appeared with a qualifier or was later expanded by the addition of τοῦ θεοῦ or τῶν οὐρανῶν. The latter is the more common Matthean term, but there are a few instances of 'the kingdom of God' (e.g. Matt. 12:28, 19:24, 21:31, 21:43). If τοῦ θεοῦ is not read here, then the final αὐτοῦ must refer back to 'your heavenly Father' in the previous verse: this does not sit so well after 'the kingdom of the heavens', as αὐτοῦ usually refers to the immediately preceding noun. It is also worth noting that examples of βασιλεία ('kingdom') without qualification in Matthew are only slightly more common than βασιλεία τοῦ θεοῦ (e.g. Matt. 4:23, 8:12, 9:35, 13:19, 13:38 etc.), while the parallel at Luke 12:31 seems to have a qualifier (although one is lacking from 𝔓[75]). Obviously, if τοῦ θεοῦ were initially present, there would have been no reason to substitute it with τῶν οὐρανῶν (except through assimilation to other instances in Matthew). Conversely, if τῶν οὐρανῶν were the original form, the incongruity with the singular in τὴν δικαιοσύνην αὐτοῦ ('his righteousness') would explain both of the other readings, either deleting the qualifier or replacing it with the singular θεοῦ. However, the fact that this is not attested in any surviving manuscript militates against adopting it as the editorial text. Of the alternatives, the reading in Codex Sinaiticus is preferable (as chosen in the SBLGNT), with the addition of τοῦ θεοῦ as a clarification of αὐτοῦ, and the addition of τῶν οὐρανῶν an accommodation to Matthean usage.

7:14 τί (for) {B}

The editorial text is supported by the majority of Greek manuscripts, including some early witnesses (01¹ 04 019 etc.). In this case, τί is not an interrogative, but an exclamation ('how narrow!'), corresponding to Semitic usage.[11] Most variant readings conform the particle to the previous clause with ὅτι ('because'): the first hand of Codex Vaticanus has ὅτι δέ (lit. 'but because'), corrected to τί δέ ('but how'), while the first hand of Codex Sinaiticus, some minuscules and the *Textus Receptus* read just ὅτι ('because'; 01* 157 700ᶜ etc.). A few witnesses instead read καί ('and'; 205 Chrysostom).

---

[11] Metzger 1994: 16 cites the Hebrew text of Ps. 139:17 as an example.

7:24 ὁμοιωθήσεται (will be like) {B}

There is strong evidence in favour of the passive ὁμοιωθήσεται ('will be compared to'; 01 03 035 038 etc.), which is also found two verses later and at Matt. 25:1. The Byzantine tradition reads ὁμοιώσω αὐτόν ('I shall compare him'; 04 019 032 etc.), an active verb which only otherwise appears in this gospel at Matt. 11:16, but is the standard form in Mark and Luke. The majority reading is therefore likely to be assimilation to this, even though the parallel at Luke 6:47 has ὑποδείξω ('I will show'). Nonetheless, there remains a slight possibility that ὁμοιώσω αὐτόν was replaced at an early point by ὁμοιωθήσεται in anticipation of its appearance at Matt. 7:26.

8:13 ὁ παῖς [αὐτοῦ] (the servant)

Most manuscripts read ὁ παῖς αὐτοῦ ('his servant'; 04 017 019 022 etc.), but several important witnesses have only ὁ παῖς ('the servant'; 01 03 0281 f^1 33 lat co[mae, bo]). It is possible that the pronoun was added through assimilation to Matt. 8:8, yet it is also possible that it was omitted by oversight or even deliberately removed to avoid the ambiguity that it might apply to Jesus. While the external evidence favours the shorter reading, adopted in the SBLGNT and THGNT, it is difficult to decide on the editorial text. In some languages, a pronoun would be the natural translation of either reading. This verse is included in *ECM Parallel Pericopes*.

8:18 ὄχλον (lit. crowd) {C}

The editorial text, which is the shortest reading, is only found in Codex Vaticanus and some Sahidic manuscripts (ὄχλον, 'crowd'; 03 co[sa-mss]). Other poorly attested variants are ὄχλον πολύν ('a large crowd'; 032 [1424] lat[vl-pt] etc.), ὄχλους ('crowds'; 01* f^1 co[bo]), πολλούς ('many people'; 1071) and ὄχλους πολλούς ('many crowds'; lat[vl-pt, vg] eth[pp]). The majority of manuscripts read πολλοὺς ὄχλους ('many crowds'; 01² 04 019 etc.). In this gospel as a whole, the plural ὄχλοι occurs more frequently than the singular, with ὄχλοι πολλοί on several occasions (Matt. 4:25, 8:1, 13:2, 15:30 etc.) and multiple instances of the singular ὄχλος πολύς (Matt. 14:14, 20:29, 26:47), indicating that all of these variants are in keeping with the evangelist's style. However, there are no parallels for the sequence πολλοὺς ὄχλους, which could suggest that this is a later adjustment. Although SBLGNT and THGNT adopt the majority reading, the choice of ὄχλον is based on the opinion that alterations were more likely to increase the size of the crowd in order to explain Jesus' decision to cross over, given the lack of clarity provided by external and internal considerations.

8:21 τῶν μαθητῶν [αὐτοῦ] (of his disciples) {C}

The majority of Greek manuscripts read τῶν μαθητῶν αὐτοῦ ('of his disciples'; 04 019 032 etc.), in keeping with the tendency throughout Matthew to qualify the noun 'disciple' with a genitive. A few important witnesses, however, just read τῶν μαθητῶν ('of the disciples'; 01 03 33 lat[vl-pt] co[sa]). Given that the tendency would be to add the pronoun, the shorter reading seems preferable, and is adopted by the SBLGNT and THGNT. Nevertheless, this could be the result of a deliberate intervention in order to reduce the number of pronouns in this phrase. The observation that the previous interlocutor is described as a scribe rather than a disciple appears to have led to the replacement of the whole phrase with ἕτερός τις εἶπεν ('another person said'; Chrysostom). It is unlikely that an editor seeking to dissociate the scribe from the disciples would simply have removed αὐτοῦ but left the word μαθητῶν; the same variation is seen at Matt. 19:10 (see below). In some languages, a pronoun will be required whether or not it is present in Greek, and translators will need to pay attention to punctuation in order to avoid the implication that the scribe was a disciple.

8:25 σῶσον (save) {B}

The verb σῴζειν ('to save') usually requires a definite object, yet there is good early evidence in favour of the imperative by itself, σῶσον ('save!'; 01 03 04 f^1 etc.). There is no obvious reason why an object would have been removed if it were originally present, as in the majority reading σῶσον ἡμᾶς ('save us'; 019 032 037 etc.). The shorter reading makes tolerable sense in itself (compare the English 'help!'), but in certain languages it may be necessary to include an object even if the editorial text is followed.

8:28 Γαδαρηνῶν (of the Gadarenes) {C}

The majority of manuscripts have Γεργεσηνῶν ('of the Gergasenes'; 01² 019 032 *f*¹ *f*¹³ etc.), but there is significant early evidence for Γαδαρηνῶν ('of the Gadarenes'; 03 04 [037] 038 sy$^{s, p, h}$, as well as Γαζαρηνῶν ['of the Gazarenes'] in 01*). The readings Gadara and Gerasa were known to Origen, but he rejected them as being too far from the lake (*Commentary on John* 5.41). Instead, he preferred Gergesa on the basis of local tradition which he encountered during his visit and his interpretation of the etymology of the name. Other ancient sources, in the form of Josephus (*Life* 9.42) and coins of the time, suggest that the area of Gadara may have included the shore of the lake, and the external attestation supports its adoption here. In this verse, the reading Γερασηνῶν ('of the Gerasenes'; lat sy^{hmg} co$^{sa, mae}$) is poorly attested and likely to be a harmonisation to the other Synoptic Gospels (Mark 5:1, Luke 8:26, 8:37). It is surprising to observe that, despite reading 'Gergasenes' here, Byzantine tradition supports 'Gadarenes' in Mark and Luke. Earlier manuscripts are also inconsistent across the three gospels, leading to the choice—with hesitation—of 'Gerasenes' for the editorial text of Mark and Luke (see the corresponding entries below).[12] The predominance of 'Gergasenes' in the textual tradition of this verse appears to reflect the influence of Origen's attempt to establish the topography:[13] the adoption of 'Gadarenes' in the editorial text (and SBLGNT and THGNT) implies that Matthew also corrected the text of Mark with a reading which he thought was more plausible.

9:8 ἐφοβήθησαν (they were filled with awe) {A}

There is good early evidence for the reading ἐφοβήθησαν (lit. 'they were afraid'; 01 03 05 032 *f*¹ etc.), whereas Byzantine tradition has ἐθαύμασαν ('they were amazed'; 04 019 037 etc.). The latter is a standard response to Jesus' miracles in Matthew (e.g. Matt. 8:10, 8:27, 9:33 and 15:31: the last also has the combination 'they were amazed, and glorified'), suggesting that it may have been introduced here through

---

[12] A table of the three gospels is given in Metzger 1994: 18.

[13] The first half of Origen's *Commentary on Matthew* is no longer extant, but it is reasonable to assume that it provided the same geographical information preserved in his *Commentary on John*. See also Baarda 1969.

assimilation. It is also possible that this was a deliberate replacement: elsewhere in Matthew φοβοῦμαι usually has the sense of 'be afraid', but there is no obvious reason for fear as a response to the healing of the paralysed man. This makes ἐφοβήθησαν the more difficult reading, although its force in translation has sometimes been softened to 'awe' or 'alarm'.[14] One Old Latin manuscript has a doublet which combines the two alternatives, also seen in Ethiopic, while a few witnesses (033 Irenaeus) omit this verb altogether, possibly because ἐφοβήθησαν was seen as problematic in context or simply through eyeskip. The full range of readings in continuous-text Greek manuscripts (*TuT Matthew* TS2) shows that one minuscule even reads ἐπίστευσαν ('they believed'; 738*). The use of 'fear' in the parallel at Luke 5:26 can also be taken to support the originality of ἐφοβήθησαν here.

9:13 ἁμαρτωλούς (sinners) {A}

The majority of Greek manuscripts include εἰς μετάνοιαν ('to repentance'; 04 019 038 etc.), as is seen in the parallel at Luke 5:32. If it had originally been present here, there is no obvious reason for its absence from a range of early translations and important witnesses (01 03 05 etc.). Translations based on the Byzantine tradition feature the longer reading at this point.

9:14 νηστεύομεν [πολλά] (fast often) {C}

Almost all witnesses read νηστεύομεν πολλά ('we fast often'; 01² 04 05 019 etc.; see *TuT Matthew* TS28). However, a few early manuscripts just read νηστεύομεν ('we fast'; 01* 03 co^{sa-ms}), while the first corrector of Codex Sinaiticus introduced text from the parallel at Luke 5:33, reading νηστεύομεν πυκνά ('we fast frequently'; 01¹). The shortest reading matches the source at Mark 2:18; while it is possible that this was also the earliest reading in Matthew, to which a qualifier was later added under the influence of the Lukan parallel, it is more likely that its absence is due to assimilation to Mark, the following phrase, or an oversight. If the parallel in Luke had prompted an expansion, more instances of the unusual word πυκνά would be expected.

---

[14] Metzger 1994: 20.

9:27 [αὐτῷ] (him)

The pronoun αὐτῷ ('him') is missing from a few important manuscripts (03 05 892). This could be an oversight or a deliberate deletion: the preceding dative serves as the object of ἠκολούθησαν ('followed'), so the pronoun is redundant. However, given the frequency of the phrase ἠκολούθησαν αὐτῷ ('they followed him') in Matthew, it is possible that the pronoun was added in error at an early stage. While the external evidence favours the longer reading, translation is unaffected. This verse is included in *ECM Parallel Pericopes*.

10:3 Θαδδαῖος (Thaddaeus) {C}

The majority of manuscripts read Λεββαῖος ὁ ἐπικληθεὶς Θαδδαῖος ('Lebbaeus who was called Thaddeus'; 04² 019 032 037 etc., with the names reversed in some members of Family 13). The first hand of Codex Ephraemi Rescriptus seems to have written Λεββαῖος ὁ καὶ Θαδδαῖος ('Lebbaeus who was also Thaddaeus'; 04*), Each name is attested by itself in early witnesses: a few manuscripts have Θαδδαῖος ('Thaddaeus'; 01 03 f^{13pt} 892 lat$^{vl\text{-}pt,\ vg}$ co), while only Codex Bezae and some indirect tradition have Λεββαῖος ('Lebbaeus'; 05 lat$^{vl\text{-}pt}$ Origen^{lat}). It is striking that the latter witnesses also have Lebbaeus at Mark 3:18, where all other witnesses read Thaddaeus.[15] The parallel at Luke 6:15 has neither name, but instead includes 'Judas son of James' after Simon the Zealot in Luke 6:16: this explains the appearance of this name in the Sinaitic Syriac, and probably also the variant 'Judas the Zealot' seen here in Old Latin witnesses and a Christian Palestinian Aramaic manuscript. The movement towards harmonising names in early translations is striking. The external evidence could be taken to support Thaddaeus as the earliest form, which was then expanded to 'Lebbaeus who was called Thaddaeus' in the majority text, under the influence of the alternative seen in Codex Bezae. This explains the current editorial text, also adopted in the SBLGNT and THGNT. However, if Thaddeus was the principal form, one would expect it to come first in the longer reading;

---

[15] This variation unit is not discussed in Mark, as there is no variation there in the majority of manuscripts. Omanson 2006: 14 notes the suggestion that Judas son of James was the original name, which was substituted by Thaddaeus in the early church in order not to have more than one disciple with the name Judas. However, it would be surprising to have no trace of this in Mark and only minimal attestation in Matthew.

similarly, as the Bezan tradition did not influence the majority text in Mark, it is not obvious why it would have had this effect in Matthew. It is therefore possible that Matthew himself introduced Lebbaeus into the list of disciples, either by itself (leading to the alternative reading in some manuscripts of Mark and the majority reading as a later editorial expansion) or with the explanation 'who was called Thaddaeus' to explain his deviation from his Markan source. In this case, the early witnesses would represent assimilation back to Mark at a very early point in the tradition rather than an initial shorter reading. The full range of readings in continuous-text Greek manuscripts is given in *TuT Matthew* (TS29).

10:4 Καναναῖος (the Cananaean) {B}

The textual tradition is split between Καναναῖος ('the Zealot'; 03 04 05 019 etc.) and the majority reading Κανανίτης ('the Cananite'; 01 032 037 etc.). The same variation is attested at Mark 3:18 (see below), where the external evidence leads to the adoption of Καναναῖος. This is the more unusual term, which derives from the Aramaic word for 'zealot'; the regular word for someone from Cana is Κανανίτης, hence the majority reading. Translators can choose whichever reading seems more appropriate in context.

10:8 νεκροὺς ἐγείρετε, λεπροὺς καθαρίζετε, δαιμόνια ἐκβάλλετε (raise the dead; cleanse those with a skin disease; cast out demons) {B}

The phrase νεκροὺς ἐγείρετε ('raise the dead') has good attestation in the earliest surviving manuscripts (the editorial text is supported by 01 03 04* 022 etc.), indicating that it is likely to be authorial. The majority of manuscripts lack these words, however, reading just λεπροὺς καθαρίζετε, δαιμόνια ἐκβάλλετε ('cleanse those with a skin disease, cast out demons'; 04³ 019 038 etc.). Although it is unusual to find a shorter reading in Byzantine tradition, the theological implications of the disciples raising the dead could have prompted an editor to remove this command; equally, its absence could easily be due to eyeskip between the imperative verbs. Still, the appearance of the phrase in differing positions in other variant readings may be an argument against its originality: it is possible that it was added through assimilation to Luke 7:22, but this reflects a different context and makes no reference to demons. A more likely scenario is that the variety of sequences indicate multiple occasions on which the phrase was added back into the majority reading, as in λεπροὺς καθαρίζετε, δαιμόνια ἐκβάλλετε, νεκροὺς ἐγείρετε ('cleanse those with a skin disease, cast out demons, raise the dead'; 024 032 037, perhaps reordered in ascending sequence) or λεπροὺς καθαρίζετε, νεκροὺς ἐγείρετε, δαιμόνια ἐκβάλλετε ('cleanse those with a skin disease, raise the dead, cast out demons'; *TR*). Codex Bezae has a version in which the present imperatives are replaced with aorist imperatives: νεκροὺς ἐγείρατε, λεπροὺς καθαρίσατε καὶ δαιμόνια ἐκβάλετε ('raise the dead, cleanse those with a skin disease and cast out demons'; 05). This appears to be an editorial intervention, reflecting the one-off nature of each of these activities rather than the ongoing state implied by the present tense: in many languages, this will also be the natural translation.

10:32 ἐν [τοῖς] οὐρανοῖς (in heaven)

The majority of manuscripts lack the definite article before οὐρανοῖς ('heavens'; 𝔓¹⁹ᵛⁱᵈ 01 05 019 032 etc.), but it is present in some important witnesses (03 04 017 *f*¹³ 565 etc.). The practice of whether or not to include the definite article after the preposition ἐν ('in') is inconsistent throughout this gospel, and nearly always accompanied by variation in the manuscripts (see also the following verse). The decision largely depends on the external attestation, which here is split. Both SBLGNT and THGNT follow the shorter reading both here and in the next unit.

10:33 ἐν [τοῖς] οὐρανοῖς (in heaven)

The variation is identical to that in the previous unit, yet it is surprising that some manuscripts change reading despite the otherwise identical phrasing: in this verse 04, 017 and 565 lack the article, whereas 1424 includes it. Although only a few manuscripts include the article (03 *f*¹³ 892 1424), the importance of Codex Vaticanus has been considered sufficient to justify its presence in brackets. In either case, translation is unaffected.

11:2 διὰ τῶν μαθητῶν (by his disciples) {B}

There is strong external evidence for διὰ τῶν μαθητῶν (lit. 'through his disciples'; 01 03 04* 05 etc.), but this is the only instance in the New Testament of πέμπειν διά ('to send word by'). Given the unexpectedness of this construction and the similarity of διά ('through') and δύο ('two'), as well as other verses which refer to the sending of two disciples (Mark 11:1, 14:13; Luke 19:29), it is unsurprising to find δύο τῶν μαθητῶν ('[he sent] two of his disciples'; 04³ 019 f^1 etc.) in the majority of manuscripts. Two disciples are also seen here in the parallel at Luke 7:18–19: while this may have prompted assimilation in the present verse, it raises the slim possibility that Matthew also originally had δύο which was misread or otherwise changed to διά at a very early point. Some Latin witnesses just read 'disciples', which is likely to be a simplification of the construction in the editorial text.

11:15 ὦτα (ears) {B}

All instances of the formula 'anyone with ears' in Mark and Luke include both the infinitive and the imperative. In the three occurrences in Matthew (see also Matt. 13:9 and 13:43), a few key manuscripts lack the infinitive and simply read ὁ ἔχων ὦτα ἀκουέτω ('Let anyone with ears hear'; attested in this verse by 03 05 700 lat^{vl-pt} sy^s). The consistency of this in several witnesses within this gospel suggests that it is not due to eyeskip between ἀκούειν ('to hear') and ἀκουέτω ('let them hear'), but may be Matthew's deliberate modification of the Markan source, removing the redundancy within the expression. Nevertheless, the phrasing 'ears to hear' in the other gospels would have led to the reintroduction of ἀκούειν ('to hear'; 01 04 019 etc.) at an early point.

11:19 ἀπὸ τῶν ἔργων (by her deeds) {B}

The majority of manuscripts read ἀπὸ τῶν τέκνων ('by her children'; 03² 04 05 019 etc.). This is the key word in the parallel at Luke 7:35, to which ἀπὸ πάντων τῶν τέκνων ('by all her children'; 13 828 lat^{vl-pt}) is an even closer assimilation. The dissimilar text ἀπὸ τῶν ἔργων ('by her deeds'; 01 03* 032 sy^{pt} co^{mss}) is therefore the harder reading, but with early attestation. The expansion ἀπὸ πάντων τῶν ἔργων ('by all her works'; $f^{13\text{pt}}$) is another partial assimilation to the Lukan wording; the full range of readings in continuous-text Greek manuscripts is given in *TuT Matthew* (TS34).

11:23 μὴ ἕως οὐρανοῦ ὑψωθήσῃ; (will you be exalted to heaven?) {B}

The editorial text has strong external support: μὴ ἕως οὐρανοῦ ὑψωθήσῃ; (lit. 'will you not be exalted to heaven?'; 01 03* 05 032 etc. and most early versions). Most Byzantine manuscripts read ἡ ἕως τοῦ οὐρανοῦ ὑψωθεῖσα ('the one who was exalted to heaven'; 037 33 157 565 etc.: some witnesses lack τοῦ), while others read ἥ ἕως οὐρανοῦ ὑψώθης ('you who were exalted to heaven'; f^{13} etc.) and a couple of majuscules have ἥ ἕως οὐρανοῦ ὑψωθήσῃ ('you who will be exalted to heaven'; 03^2 019). This appears to reflect a two-stage alteration: the initial μ of μή was omitted by haplography after the μ at the end of the preceding word Καφαρναούμ ('Capernaum'), after which the verb was altered depending on whether the resulting η was interpreted as a definite article (ἡ, 'the one') or a relative pronoun (ἥ, 'who'). Although there remains a possibility that μή was created by dittography, the external evidence suggests that this is less likely. The combination of μή and the subjunctive means that this reading should be treated as a rhetorical question, as indicated by the punctuation: if one of the variant readings is followed (as in translations based on the *Textus Receptus*), the sense is ironic. See also the comment on Luke 10:15 below.

11:23 καταβήσῃ ('you will be brought down') {C}

The majority of Greek witnesses read καταβιβασθήσῃ ('you will be brought down'; 01 04 019 etc.). The literal translation of καταβήσῃ is 'you shall go down': this reading has early but slim attestation (03 05 032 lat sy$^{c, s}$ co^{sa} eth Irenaeus^{lat}), and is also read in the SBLGNT. A few minuscules read καταβληθήσῃ ('you will be thrown down'; see *TuT Matthew* TS35), which is likely to be a misreading of the majority text. While καταβήσῃ could be an early simplification, καταβιβασθήσῃ could be an expansion of this to match the passive verb in the preceding clause (see previous variation unit). The same variation is seen in the parallel at Luke 10:15. It has been observed that, in Greek more generally, καταβήσῃ is more common and is also seen in this construction in the Septuagint (e.g. Isaiah 14:15), which might favour καταβιβασθήσῃ as the harder form.[16] If the latter is adopted, as in the THGNT, it may be considered as a 'divine passive', which in some languages may need to be recast as an active verb with God as the subject. See also Luke 10:15 below.

12:4 ἔφαγον (they ate) {C}

Only two majuscule manuscripts support the editorial text ἔφαγον ('they ate'; 01 03). The majority reading is ἔφαγεν ('he ate'; 𝔓⁷⁰ 04 05 019 etc.). Of these, the plural seems to be the more difficult reading, as the previous verb with which it is co-ordinated is singular (εἰσῆλθεν, 'he entered') and the expected reading would be another singular. In addition, the synoptic parallels at Mark 2:26 and Luke 6:4 both read ἔφαγεν. On the other hand, the following phrase implies that David's companions also ate the bread, so an initial singular could have been changed to a plural in order to harmonise to this. The variant reading ἔλαβεν ('he took'; 892*) may be an editorial attempt to resolve the incongruity. If the plural is adopted (as here and in the SBLGNT), it is necessary to understand that David took the bread out of the Temple before the others ate it.

12:15 [ὄχλοι] πολλοί (many [crowds]) {C}

While a few witnesses just read πολλοί ('many people'; 01 03 lat^(vl-pt, vg) etc.) and others have ὄχλοι ('crowds'; 022* and some minuscules: see *TuT Matthew* TS37), the majority of Greek manuscripts have ὄχλοι πολλοί ('many crowds'; 04 05 019 032 etc.). Although the longer reading looks like a Byzantine conflation or an intensification (compare Matt. 8:18 above), the shorter readings may be mechanical errors. An editor might even have intervened here to avoid the risk that the following statement 'he cured all of them' was considered to be an overexaggeration.

---

[16] Metzger 1994: 25; Victor 2009: 73–74.

12:47 [εἶπεν δέ τις αὐτῷ· ἰδοὺ ἡ μήτηρ σου καὶ οἱ ἀδελφοί σου ἔξω ἑστήκασιν ζητοῦντές σοι λαλῆσαι.] (Someone told him, "Look, your mother and your brothers are standing outside, wanting to speak to you.") {C}

This entire verse is missing from a number of important witnesses (01* 03 019 579 597 lat^(vl-pt) sy^(c, s) co^(sa)). It seems that this is due to eyeskip from λαλῆσαι at the end of the previous verse, as seen in Codex Sinaiticus where it is supplied by the scriptorium corrector (01¹). However, there is also the possibility that it was added by an early editor in order to improve the continuity between the statement about Jesus' mother and brothers in Matt. 12:46 and the detail in Matt. 12:48 that Jesus 'replied … to the one who had told him': not only does most of the verse repeat the previous statement, but this is the only instance in Matthew of a sentence beginning with εἶπεν (apart from the quotation at Matt. 22:44). The early attestation of the shorter reading therefore deserves serious consideration, as currently represented by the editorial brackets. Nevertheless, both the SBLGNT and THGNT include the full verse; compare the missing text with similar attestation at Matt. 16:2–3, while secondary duplication of material is seen at Matt. 28:9 (both discussed below).

13:9 ὦτα (ears) {B}

As noted above at Matt. 11:15, in all three instances of the formula 'anyone with ears' in Matthew there is variation in the textual tradition regarding the presence of the infinitive ἀκούειν ('[ears] to hear'; see also Matt. 13:43 below). In this verse, two different Greek majuscules join Codex Vaticanus in reading ὁ ἔχων ὦτα ἀκουέτω ('Let anyone with ears hear'; 01* 03 019 lat^(vl-pt) sy^s), while Codex Bezae and GA 700 have the longer reading. Despite the possibility of eyeskip between ἀκούειν and ἀκουέτω, the consistency of the shorter reading across Matthew suggests that this is the earliest form. This verse is included in *ECM Parallel Pericopes*.

13:13 ὅτι βλέποντες οὐ βλέπουσιν καὶ ἀκούοντες οὐκ ἀκούουσιν οὐδὲ συνίουσιν (that 'seeing they do not perceive, and hearing they do not listen, nor do they understand.') {A}

Early witnesses and the majority of minuscules support the editorial text in this reference to Isaiah 6:9–10, which differs from that at Mark

4:12. A group of manuscripts have an alternative version which is much closer to the text of Mark and seems likely to be an editorial adjustment: ἵνα βλέποντες μὴ βλέπωσιν καὶ ἀκούοντες μὴ ἀκούσωσιν καὶ μὴ συνιῶσιν μήποτε ἐπιστρέψωσιν ('so that seeing they may not see, and hearing they may not hear, and they may not understand nor ever turn again'; 05 038 f^1 f^{13} lat$^{vl\text{-}pt}$ sy$^{c, s}$). A few witnesses have a shorter form which appears to be a hybrid version, ὅτι βλέποντες μὴ βλέπουσιν καὶ ἀκούοντες μὴ ἀκούσωσι μηδὲ συνῶσιν ('that "seeing they do not see, and hearing they may not hear nor understand"'; 1424 co$^{sa, mae}$). The full citation of these verses from Isaiah which follows in Matt. 13:14–15 indicates that the evangelist knew the Septuagint text, and thus had good reason to adjust this introductory phrase to portray Jesus' situation rather than reflect the fulfilment of the prophetic saying.

13:35   διά (through) {C}

The following quotation comes from Psalm 78:2 [77:2 LXX], and it is therefore surprising to find a strand of early tradition which precedes it with διὰ Ἠσαΐου ('through Isaiah [the prophet]'; 01* 038 f^1 f^{13} 33). Jerome mentions some manuscripts which read διὰ Ἀσάφ ('through Asaph'), which is likely to be an editorial correction to the author named at the beginning of Psalm 78. The majority of manuscripts, however, do not include a name, and simply read διά ('through [the prophet]'; 01^1 03 04 05 etc.). It is difficult to decide whether the error is authorial or scribal: was Isaiah the original reading, removed at an early point when the error was noticed, or was it inadvertently added by analogy with other references in Matthew (e.g. 12:17 and 13:14; see also the comment on Matt. 27:9 below)? It has been suggested that, if Asaph was the original reading, it could have been changed to the more common name Isaiah or simply deleted by a reader who did not consider Asaph to be a prophet.[17] However, the lack of surviving manuscripts with Asaph makes this very unlikely.

13:35   ἀπὸ καταβολῆς [κόσμου] (since the foundation [of the world])

The citation of Psalm 78:2 [77:2 LXX] does not correspond closely to the Septuagint, so the source cannot shed light on this variant. Most

---

[17] Metzger 1994: 27.

witnesses read ἀπὸ καταβολῆς κόσμου ('since the foundation of the world'; 01* 04 05 etc.), which is the form of this phrase on every other occasion in the New Testament (Matt. 25:34, Luke 11:50, Heb. 4:3 and 9:26, Rev. 13:8 and 17:8). The shorter reading, ἀπὸ καταβολῆς ('since the foundation'; 01² 03 f^1 lat^{vl-pt} Origen Eusebius) has early attestation and is the more difficult reading as it goes against the prevailing pattern. Even so, the omission of a single word could easily be an oversight, and only nine Greek manuscripts lack it (see *TuT Matthew* TS40). In translation, it may be necessary to supply a qualifier to explain 'the foundation' even if the shorter reading is adopted.

13:40   [κατα]καίεται (are burned up)

A few important witnesses read κατακαίεται ('are burned up'; 01 03 f^1 892 Cyril), but most Greek manuscripts have just καίεται ('are burned'; 04 017 019 etc.). Codex Bezae reads κατακαίονται ('they are burned up'; 05) which may be due to the influence of the Latin translation: Greek neuter plural nouns take a singular verb. The first part of the compound verb, κατά, could have been omitted through eyeskip to the following κα; alternatively κατά may have been added through assimilation to the previous phrase with the same subject a few verses earlier (Matt. 13:30), as a deliberate intensification of the image, or partially through dittography. The balance of internal and external evidence makes a decision difficult, although the shorter reading in the majority of witnesses is less common, and καίεται is adopted in both the SBLGNT and THGNT.

13:43   ὦτα (ears) {B}

This is the third instance of the formula 'anyone with ears' (cf. Matt. 11:15 and 13:9 above). This verse appears to have the best attestation of the shorter reading ὁ ἔχων ὦτα ἀκουέτω ('Let anyone with ears hear'; 01* 03 038 0242 700 lat^{vl-pt, vg}): if this is original, it may be that correctors had tired of adjusting it by this point. Nevertheless, the majority of witnesses still include ἀκούειν ('[ears] to hear'; 01² 04 05 019 etc.), which could have been omitted by accident in the others. As in the other verses, the overall pattern in Matthew suggests that the shorter reading is original, against the formula in Mark and Luke.

13:55   Ἰωσήφ (Joseph) {B}

The editorial text, Ἰωσήφ ('Joseph'; 01¹ 03 04 etc.) has been adopted on the basis of its external support and its dissimilarity from the parallel at Mark 6:3, which is reflected here in the alternatives Ἰωσῆς ('Joses'; 𝔓^103vid 019 032 and many minuscules) and Ἰωσῆ ('Jose'; 157 700* 1006 etc.). The Markan form of the name reflects the Galilaean pronunciation: Matthew appears to have replaced this with the standard Hebrew form.[18] A large number of Greek manuscripts instead have Ἰωάννης ('John'; 01*vid 05 07 011 etc.), which is likely to be a scribal error under the influence of the common pairing of 'James and John'. One witness not cited in UBS6 has a conflated form of the two most common readings, Ἰωάννης καὶ Ἰωσῆς ('John and Joses'; 1344), showing how variants were sometimes incorporated into the text.

14:3   [αὐτόν] (him²)

The majority of witnesses include the pronoun αὐτόν ('him'; 011 04 05 017 019 etc.). Its absence (from 01* 03 700 lat^vl-pt co^bo-mss) is a harder reading, although the preceding reference to John still supplies an object. However, the poor attestation suggests that this may be an error: in translation the verbs are likely to require an explicit object even if the shorter reading is adopted.

14:9   λυπηθεὶς ὁ βασιλεὺς διά (lit. the king was grieved because) {B}

The majority of manuscripts read ἐλυπήθη ὁ βασιλεύς· διὰ δέ ('the king was grieved, but because'; 01 04 019^c 032 etc.), yet important witnesses have λυπηθεὶς ὁ βασιλεὺς διά (lit. 'the king, having been grieved because [of his oaths]'; 03 05 038 ƒ¹ etc.). The latter reading is the more difficult, with its apparent sense that the oaths and the guests grieve the king rather than the request, but it is also possible to punctuate before διά and take it with ἐκέλευσεν ('[having been grieved], he ordered because [of his oaths]'), which is preferable in translation. It is hard to see how or why this ambiguity would have been introduced if the other form were original, whereas the majority text is an obvious clarification and improvement. The full range of readings in continuous-text Greek manuscripts is given in *TuT Matthew* (TS44).

---

[18] Thus Metzger 1994: 28.

14:10 [τὸν] Ἰωάννην (John)

The definite article is lacking from a few important witnesses (01* 03 035 f^1). The practice varies throughout Matthew, and it is possible that its absence here was influenced by the anarthrous Ἰωάννου two verses earlier. On the other hand, τόν could have been added in keeping with the common Greek treatment of proper nouns. Translation is unaffected.

14:12 αὐτό[ν] (lit. it)

A few witnesses read αὐτόν ('him'; 01* 03 0106 lat^{vl-pt} co^{bo-mss}), a construction which follows the sense and picks up αὐτοῦ earlier in the verse. The neuter αὐτό ('it'; 01^2 04 05 and the majority of manuscripts) is more grammatically accurate in agreeing with the previous noun τὸ πτῶμα ('the corpse'). It is unclear whether the looser construction was introduced or corrected during transmission.

14:16 [Ἰησοῦς] (Jesus)

The name Jesus is not required here for the sense, as the contrast with the disciples is unambiguous. Nevertheless, it appears here and in Matt. 14:14 in the majority of manuscripts, with slightly better support in this verse (where it is also present in 01^2 03 038 f^1 f^{13}). This leads to doubt as to whether it is part of the earliest text, or whether the shorter reading (attested by 01* 05 035^{vid} 579 1424 and most early translations) should be preferred. This verse is included in *ECM Parallel Pericopes*.

14:24 ἤδη σταδίους πολλοὺς ἀπὸ τῆς γῆς ἀπεῖχεν (was far from the land) {C}

The majority of manuscripts read ἤδη μέσον τῆς θαλάσσης ἦν ('was already in the middle of the sea'; 01 04 019 032 etc.), also supported by ἦν εἰς μέσον τῆς θαλάσσης ('was approaching the middle of the sea'; 05 lat^{vl-pt} etc.) and ἐκινδύνευεν ἤδη μέσον τῆς θαλάσσης ('was already in danger in the middle of the sea'; 1546, not cited in UBS6). There is comparatively little support for the alternatives ἤδη σταδίους πολλοὺς ἀπὸ τῆς γῆς ἀπεῖχεν (lit. 'was already many stades away from the land'; 03 f^{13} sy^c etc.), ἤδη ἀπεῖχεν ἀπὸ τῆς γῆς σταδίους ἱκανούς (lit. 'was already from the land several stades away'; 038: some Bohairic and Ethiopic texts read 'around twenty-five stades'), and ἤδη σταδίους τῆς γῆς ἀπεῖχεν ἱκανούς (lit. 'already several stades was away from the land'; 700).[19] Most of these differences reflect accounts in the other gospels: the reference to 'stades' corresponds to John 6:19; 'danger' comes from Luke 8:23; 'the middle of the sea' is seen in Mark 6:47. However, none of them offers an exact verbal match, suggesting that the variants were introduced from memory. The choice of the editorial text (also adopted in the SBLGNT) is based on the opinion that a harmonisation to Mark was more likely than one to John, and that the parallel with John is relatively slight.[20] The other references to 'stades' support this reading, with an adjustment of πολλούς ('many') to ἱκανούς ('several', 'sufficient') by an editor concerned with geographical accuracy. Although this is plausible, the extensive and early attestation of 'was in the middle of the sea' is consistent with this being the original reading (as preferred in the THGNT), and the reference to 'stades' being the work of an early editor.

14:27 [ὁ Ἰησοῦς] (Jesus)

As at Matt. 14:16 (see above), it is not clear whether Jesus was originally mentioned by name, as this is superfluous in context. The uncertainty is due both to the lack of the name from some important witnesses (01* 05 073 892 and most early translations) and to the appearance of the name in different places. The sequence ἐλάλησεν αὐτοῖς ὁ Ἰησοῦς ('Jesus said to them'; 04 017 019 etc.) is the majority reading: given the use of the nomen sacrum abbreviation (IC), it is easy to see why the name would have fallen out through haplography in AYTOICOIC. The variant ἐλάλησεν ὁ Ἰησοῦς αὐτοῖς ('said Jesus to them'; 01¹ 03) is unusual in separating the verb from the indirect object (cf. Matt. 13:3, 13:33, 28:18) and would not explain the omission of Jesus: however, it might have arisen from Jesus being (re)introduced from the shorter reading (as seen in Codex Sinaiticus). Even if the shorter reading is adopted, translators may wish to supply the subject of the verb.

---

[19] A Greek stade was a distance of around 185 metres (200 yards); some English translations use 'furlong' (around 201 metres/220 yards). In translation, it is simpler to state that the boat was 'some distance' or 'a great distance' depending on which reading is followed.

[20] Metzger 1994: 30.

14:29 [ὁ] Πέτρος (Peter)

The article before Peter is missing from some early witnesses (01 03 05 Eusebius). Although Matthean practice is generally to include the article before this name, this is not always the case (e.g. Matt. 8:14, 16:16) and it is possible that ὁ was introduced through assimilation to the previous verse.[21] In any case, translation is unaffected.

14:29 καὶ ἦλθεν (and came) {B}

The editorial text has slim but early support (03 04*vid 700 1010 sy^{c, s} [co^{sa}] Chrysostom), and is the most difficult reading in that it could be taken to suggest that Peter actually reached Jesus, in contrast with the following verse. The majority form, ἐλθεῖν ('[he walked] to come [to Jesus]'; 01² 04² 05 etc.) removes this possibility and therefore appears to be secondary. The first hand of Codex Sinaiticus reads ἐλθεῖν· ἦλθεν οὖν ('[he walked] to come; and so he went [to Jesus]'; 01*). This looks like a conflation of the two readings, but the presence of οὖν ('and so') has also led to it being described as an expansion by an editor.[22]

14:30 ἄνεμον [ἰσχυρόν] (strong wind) {C}

The shortest reading, ἄνεμον ('wind'; 01 03* 073 33 etc.) has early support, but could have arisen through eyeskip within the majority reading ἄνεμον ἰσχυρόν ('strong wind'; 03¹ 04 05 019 etc.), as may have been the case in Codex Vaticanus. The other possibility is that ἰσχυρός is a later intensification, beginning a trend seen in the other variant reading, ἄνεμον ἰσχυρὸν σφόδρα ('a very strong wind'; 032). Matthean usage and the other gospels do not provide much help in deciding between the readings; both the SBLGNT and THGNT follow the majority form, which also serves to provide an explanation for Peter's fear.[23]

15:2 [αὐτῶν] (their)

The pronoun αὐτῶν ('their') is superfluous and is missing from a range of early witnesses (01 03 037 073 f^1 etc.), but appears in the majority of

---

[21] Smit Sibinga 1981: 26–27 prefers the shorter reading.
[22] Metzger 1994: 30.
[23] Smit Sibinga 1981: 27–29 opts for the shortest text on the grounds of authorial style.

manuscripts (04 05 017 etc.). While Matthew normally follows χείρ ('hand') with a genitive, this is not the case in his other reference to washing hands (Matt. 27:24; cf. Mark 7:3) which might favour the shorter reading here.

15:4 εἶπεν (said) {B}

The early evidence favours εἶπεν ('said'; 01²ᵃ 03 05 038 etc.), even though the majority of manuscripts read ἐνετείλατο λέγων ('commanded, saying'; 01*, ²ᵇ 04 019 etc.). Matthew uses the latter phrase for formal commands (Matt. 17:9, 19:7, 28:20), so this is in keeping with the context. However, it seems to have been introduced by an early editor through analogy with such usage, prompted by the reference to the commandment (τὴν ἐντολήν) in the previous verse. The source text at Mark 7:10 simply reads Μωϋσῆς εἶπεν ('Moses said'), which supports εἶπεν here too: the attribution to Moses rather than God makes it less likely that εἶπεν is a later harmonisation to Mark.

15:6 τὸν πατέρα αὐτοῦ (their father)[24] {C}

Most witnesses include a reference to a mother as well, matching the previous verse: the majority of Greek manuscripts have τὸν πατέρα αὐτοῦ ἢ τὴν μητέρα αὐτοῦ ('their father or their mother'; 04 019 032 etc.), while others read τὸν πατέρα αὐτοῦ ἢ τὴν μητέρα ('their father or mother'; 073 f^{13} etc.) or τὸν πατέρα ἢ τὴν μητέρα αὐτοῦ ('their father or mother'; 038 f^1 etc.). The shortest reading, of just τὸν πατέρα αὐτοῦ ('their father'; 01 03 05 latᵛˡ⁻ᵖᵗ syᶜ coˢᵃ Origenˡᵃᵗ), could easily have arisen from eyeskip between the two instances of αὐτοῦ in the majority reading. However, it has early attestation, including multiple translations, leading to the suspicion that 'mother' was added later in order to match the previous verse. The variety of forms is also indicative of multiple subsequent additions, each supplying slightly different wording: this does not, however, rule out the possibility that a longer reading was original and the other forms are expansions following a subsequent omission. In any case, in translation, 'father' may be taken as standing here for both parents mentioned in the previous verse.

---

[24] In some English translations (NRSVue, Common English Bible), this phrase is treated as the final element of Matt. 15:5.

15:6 τὸν λόγον (the word) {B}

There is early support for τὸν λόγον ('the word'; 01²ᵃ 03 05 038 etc.), but most Greek manuscripts read τὴν ἐντολήν ('the commandment'; 019 032 [037] etc.) and a few have τὸν νόμον ('the law'; 01*, ²ᵇ 04 073 ƒ¹³ 1010; see *TuT Matthew* TS47). All three relate back to Matt. 15:3–4, and it is likely that the majority reading is assimilation to the phrase τὴν ἐντολήν τοῦ θεοῦ there. The source at Mark 7:13 reads τὸν λόγον, meaning that this could have been reintroduced through harmonisation. Although τὸν νόμον lacks a parallel, this may be too difficult a reading: there is no other instance of 'the law of God' in the rest of the New Testament. Furthermore, either 'law' or 'commandment' could have been introduced by an editor who felt that 'word' was too general here in the light of the quotation from the law in Matt. 15:4. The external evidence has led to the adoption of τὸν λόγον, which is also preferred in the SBLGNT and THGNT. Nevertheless, in translation it is still appropriate to translate this as 'God's command' to avoid confusion with the common use of 'God's word' to mean the Bible in general (or, indeed, the divine Word).

15:8 ὁ λαὸς οὗτος (this people) {B}

Most Greek manuscripts have a longer form at the beginning of this citation, ἐγγίζει μοι ὁ λαὸς οὗτος τῷ στόματι αὐτῶν καί ('this people draws near to me with their mouth and'; 04 032 037 etc.), corresponding more closely to Isaiah 29:13 in the Septuagint. Family 1 just reads ὁ λαὸς οὗτος ἐγγίζει μοι ('this people draws near to me'). There is strong external evidence for the shortest form, ὁ λαὸς οὗτος ('this people'; 01 03 05 019 038 etc. and early translations and writers). This is unlikely to be an accidental abbreviation of the longer reading, yet it is possible that it was introduced under the influence of the parallel at Mark 7:6. However, as this is not an exact match (most manuscripts in Mark have the word order οὗτος ὁ λαός), it seems most probable that a later editor expanded the beginning of the quotation to make it closer to its Septuagintal source.

15:14 τυφλοί εἰσιν ὁδηγοὶ [τυφλῶν] (they are blind guides of the blind) {C}

A variety of sequences is found at this point. Most Greek manuscripts have ὁδηγοί εἰσιν τυφλοὶ τυφλῶν ('they are blind guides of the blind'; 04 032 037 etc.), and there is also good support for τυφλοὶ εἰσιν ὁδηγοί τυφλῶν ('blind are the guides of the blind'; 01²ᵃ 019 035 038 *f* ¹ etc.). Other witnesses lack the complement τυφλῶν, reading τυφλοί εἰσιν ὁδηγοί ('they are blind guides'; 03 05 0237 lat^(vl-pt)) or ὁδηγοί εἰσιν τυφλοί ('the guides are blind'; 01*, ²ᵇ co^(sa, bo, fa-vid)). It would have been very easy to omit τυφλῶν at the end of this phrase through eyeskip as it is immediately followed by τυφλός (the majority text has no fewer than four instances of the same noun in succession, separated by just one δέ). Equally, an editor could have deliberately removed the word τυφλῶν in order to focus on the Pharisees and not condemn other Jews. However, it is also possible that τυφλῶν was introduced in order to make this condemnation a better fit with the following phrase, where the person being guided is blind—even though the responsibility is that of the guide. While the decision is difficult on both internal and external grounds (and the parallel at Luke 6:39 does not offer clarification), the shorter readings are attractive for their economy and Codex Vaticanus and Codex Bezae offer a strong combination. Nevertheless, τυφλοί εἰσιν ὁδηγοὶ τυφλῶν is adopted in the SBLGNT and THGNT.

15:15 τὴν παραβολὴν [ταύτην] (this parable) {C}

The majority of Greek manuscripts include ταύτην ('this'; 04 05 019 032 etc.), but it is missing from a range of important witnesses (01 03 035^(vid) *f* ¹ etc., early translations, Origen Cyril). Although the phrase 'this parable' is relatively common in Luke, it hardly ever appears in Matthew and Mark (Mark 4:13; cf. the plural at Matt. 13:53), and the Markan parallel for this verse also lacks the demonstrative (Mark 7:17). This suggests that the shorter reading is original, yet the possibility of harmonisation to Mark cannot be ruled out. Despite a suggestion that the distance between the original parable in Matt. 15:11 and this explanation has led scrupulous scribes to delete the demonstrative, inadvertent assimilation to the Lukan phrasing is more plausible.[25] In translation, it may be worth indicating that the parable refers to the earlier saying about the body rather than the blind guides of Matt. 15:14 by rendering it as 'what you said to the people'.[26]

15:17   οὐ (not) {C}

Most manuscripts read οὔπω ('not yet'; 01 04 019 032 etc.), but there is good support for οὐ ('not'; 03 05 035 038 f^{13} and most early translations). The latter matches the parallel at Mark 7:18, which favours the shorter reading here (although harmonisation cannot be ruled out): οὔπω is an easy assimilation to the same phrase at Matt. 16:9 (or Mark 8:17). While a case might be made for a deliberate change by an editor trying to present the disciples in a more favourable light (cf. Matt. 17:20, Mark 4:40), the unmitigated criticism of the previous verse and the presence of οὔπω elsewhere make a mechanical explanation far more plausible.

15:39   Μαγαδάν (Magadan) {C}

Place names are of significance in reconstructing the geographical location of the events narrated, but have often been altered to correspond to more common forms or more likely settings. There is early support for Μαγαδάν ('Magadan'; 01* 03 05) or Μαγεδάν ('Magedan'; 01² lat^{vl-pt, vg} co^{sa} eth Eusebius), but there does not appear to be any match for this name in other sources. Most manuscripts have Μαγδαλά ('Magdala'; 019 037 038 etc.) or Μαγδαλάν ('Magdalan'; 04 022 023 etc.), which looks like substitution with a better known place-name, although there remains a possibility that Magadan is a misreading of one of these given their similarity in majuscule script (ΜΑΓΑΔΑΝ and ΜΑΓΔΑΛΑΝ). The parallel at Mark 8:10 appears to read Dalmanutha, another unknown place, which has led to adjustments there including the options from this verse (see comment below). Magadan is adopted here (and in the SBLGNT and THGNT) on the basis of the external evidence. This verse is included in *ECM Parallel Pericopes*.

---

[25] For the suggestion, Metzger 1994: 32.
[26] See Omanson 2006: 24.

16:2–3 [Ὀψίας γενομένης … οὐ δύνασθε;] (When it is evening … the signs of the times.) {C}

The majority of Matt. 16:2 and all of Matt. 16:3 is missing from a range of early and important witnesses (01 03 036 f^{13} etc., sy$^{c,\,s}$ co$^{sa,\,bo\text{-}pt,\,mae}$ Origen). There is no obvious mechanical reason for this, and the idea in the longer text has a parallel at Luke 12:54–56 even though the wording there is very different. On the other hand, the narrative flows very smoothly without this passage and some of the uses are not paralleled elsewhere in Matthew (e.g. διακρίνειν as 'interpret' in contrast to Matt. 21:21, and γινώσκειν with the infinitive), suggesting that it might be a later addition. Some have argued that the words were deleted in places where red sky in the morning is not a sign of rain (e.g. Egypt).[27] However, the external evidence indicates that there is a strong possibility that this is a saying from a separate collection which was inserted at a suitable point in the narrative. Given this range of probabilities, the words have been presented in brackets for the time being, although these verses are given in full in the SBLGNT and THGNT.[28] Compare also the text missing at Matt. 12:47 above. The final clause can be read either as a rhetorical question or a statement.

16:13 τίνα (who) {B}

After this interrogative, the majority of manuscripts include με ('me'; 05 019 037 038 etc.), while a couple have it after the following word (04 032). The meaning of both is the same, 'who do people say that I, the Son of Man, am?', with Jesus identifying himself as the Son of Man. In contrast, there is good external evidence for the absence of με ('who do people say that the Son of Man is?'; 01 03 579 700 lat$^{vl\text{-}pt,\,vg}$ co eth Origen Cyril^{pt}). Both the parallel passages—which lack the reference to the Son of Man—include με (Mark 8:27, Luke 9:18), as does the more direct question two verses later, which strengthens the likelihood that the pronoun was introduced by assimilation. However, the awkwardness of the reading with με, in which Jesus appears to answer his own question ('who do people say that I am, the Son of Man?') could be taken to support it as the more difficult version.

---

[27] See Metzger 1994. 33.

[28] See further Hirunuma 1981 and Quarles 2020: the latter considers the longer reading to be original.

16:20   ὁ χριστός (the Messiah) {B}

There is early attestation of just ὁ χριστός ('the Messiah'; 01* 03 019 etc. and several translations), which matches the parallels at Mark 8:29 and Luke 9:20. The inclusion of 'Jesus' appears to be an inadvertent scribal error prompted by the presence of the noun 'Christ': it makes no sense in context for Jesus to prohibit the disciples from telling people his name. However, it is seen in the majority of manuscripts as Ἰησοῦς ὁ χριστός ('Jesus the Messiah'; 01² 04 032 etc.), while Codex Bezae has ὁ χριστὸς Ἰησοῦς ('the Messiah, Jesus'; 05 lat^(vl-pt)). As in the previous unit, the difficulty of the majority reading is the main reason that it might be considered as the most ancient text. Whichever reading is preferred, translators should render χριστός as a title ('Messiah') rather than a proper noun, as indicated by the lower-case initial letter.

17:4   ποιήσω (I will make) {B}

Most witnesses read ποιήσωμεν ('let us make'; 04³ 05 019 032 etc.), but there is also support for ποιήσομεν ('we will make'; *f*¹ 565 etc.) and ποιήσω ('I will make'; 01 03 04* etc.). The most difficult of these is the singular ποιήσω, which contrasts with the preceding plural ἡμᾶς ('us') and both parallel passages (Mark 9:5 and Luke 9:33, which both read ποιήσωμεν): combined with its early attestation, this has been adopted as the editorial text and is also preferred in the SBLGNT and THGNT. If this is the original reading, it is interesting to note how it affects the characterisation of Peter, who speaks on behalf of the other disciples in the Markan source but here makes himself solely responsible.

17:20   ὀλιγοπιστίαν (little faith) {A}

There is good evidence for ὀλιγοπιστίαν ('little faith'; 01 03 038 etc.), which matches the use of ὀλιγόπιστοι ('people of little faith') of the disciples on four other occasions in Matthew. The variant reading ἀπιστίαν ('lack of faith'; 04 05 019 032 etc.; see further *TuT Matthew* TS52), seen in most witnesses, is even harsher on the disciples, although it is the more common term in Mark and Luke. The only occasions on which ἀπιστία or ἄπιστος appear in Matthew are 13:58 and 17:17 (both reflecting Markan parallels) and it is very likely that assimilation to the latter verse has led to the variant reading here.

17:21   *omit verse* {A}

After Matt. 17:20, the majority of Greek manuscripts read τοῦτο δὲ τὸ γένος οὐκ ἐκπορεύεται εἰ μὴ ἐν προσευχῇ καὶ νηστείᾳ ('but this kind does not come out except by prayer and fasting'; 01² 04 05 019 etc.). This is lacking from ten Greek manuscripts, most of them considered to be important, and witnesses to each early translation (01* 03 038 0281 33 579 788 892* 1604 2680 [see *TuT Matthew* TS53]; lat^{vl-pt} sy^{c, s} cpa co^{sa, bo-pt} eth^{ms}). There is no obvious reason for a mechanical omission, and the extra text is close to the parallel at Mark 9:29, where it fits the context better: an early reader may have felt that Jesus' answer to the disciples was incomplete and therefore added the more direct response from memory (including the variant with the last two words; see Mark 9:29 below). This is one of three additional verses in the Byzantine tradition of Matthew (see also Matt. 18:11 and 23:14), which are also excluded from the editorial text of the SBLGNT and THGNT.

17:22   συστρεφομένων (as they were gathering) {B}

The editorial reading συστρεφομένων ('as they were gathering'; 01 03 f^1 etc.) is a rare word which only otherwise occurs in the New Testament at Acts 28:3. In context, its sense is unexpected because the previous episode also involved Jesus and the disciples, so there is no obvious need to gather. This explains why it might be replaced by a similar but more common term, such as ἀναστρεφομένων ('as they were dwelling'; 04 05 019 and the majority of minuscules) or ὑποστρεφόντων ('as they were returning'; 579). Nevertheless, the majority reading may be of interest for its historical implication that the disciples were living in Galilee.

17:24   [τὰ] δίδραχμα (the temple tax)

The definite article is missing from two majuscules (01* 05) and written as the singular τό in another (032), with Coptic support in both cases. The phrase τὰ δίδραχμα appears without variation earlier in the verse, and despite the importance of these witnesses and the greater difficulty of their readings, these variants may simply be errors.

18:11   *omit verse* {A}

After Matt. 18:10, the majority of Greek manuscripts include the line ἦλθεν γὰρ ὁ υἱὸς τοῦ ἀνθρώπου σῶσαι τὸ ἀπολωλός ('for the Son of

Man came to save the lost'; 05 032 037 etc.), while others have the form ἦλθεν γὰρ ὁ υἱὸς τοῦ ἀνθρώπου ζητῆσαι καὶ σῶσαι τὸ ἀπολωλός ('for the Son of Man came to seek and save the lost'; 011 019[mg] 157 etc.; see *TuT Matthew* TS54). There is no obvious reason for its accidental omission from a range of early and important witnesses (01 03 019[txt] 038* f^1 etc. and several early translations and Christian writers). Instead, it appears that a phrase resembling Luke 19:10 was added by a reader or editor who felt that it formed an appropriate link between the teaching on children and the parable of the lost sheep (despite the conclusion to both episodes provided in 18:14); later, ζητῆσαι καί ('to seek and') was added to assimilate it fully to the source. For the other additional verses in the Byzantine tradition of Matthew, see Matt. 17:21 and 23:14.

18:14   ὑμῶν (your) {C}

The textual tradition is evenly split between ὑμῶν ('your [Father]'; 01 05[c] 019 032 etc.) and μου ('my [Father]'; 03 09 013 022 etc.); ἡμῶν ('our [Father]'; 05*) is an error probably due to itacism, while the Christian Palestinian Aramaic has no pronoun. Both of the main forms are found in Matthew, with a slight predominance of μου, making ὑμῶν the less common reading. In addition, the occurrence of the same phrase with μου in Matt. 18:10 (and 18:19) could easily have resulted in assimilation here. Still, it remains possible that all three of these verses could originally have read μου.

18:15   ἁμαρτήσῃ [εἰς σέ] (sins against you) {C}

Most witnesses support ἁμαρτήσῃ εἰς σέ ('sins against you'; 05 019 037 038 etc.), with others reading ἁμάρτῃ εἰς σέ ('should sin against you'; 032 33 180 etc.). The complement is lacking from a few important witnesses with ἁμαρτήσῃ ('sins'; 01 03 f^1 etc.) or ἁμάρτῃ ('should sin'; Origen[lem] Basil[pt]). This makes for a significant theological and ethical change: is sin general or against individuals, and in which cases should it be raised with the perpetrator? The only other instance of the same verb 'to sin' in Matthew, six verses later, has the complement εἰς ἐμέ ('against me'; Matt. 18:21): this could represent the expected usage, or have prompted assimilation here. The same variation is seen in the parallel at Luke 17:3–4, where there is stronger external evidence for the shorter reading: if Luke used Matthew, this is further support for the lack of a complement here. Luke 17:3 also has the present subjunctive, ἁμάρτῃ, which might have influenced some readings here. On the other hand, the similarity in sound and spelling of the syllables THCH EIC CE could have led to the erroneous omission of εἰς σέ. The SBLGNT and THGNT both prefer ἁμαρτήσῃ εἰς σέ here in full. In some languages, even if the shorter reading is adopted, it may be necessary to provide a complement for the verb 'to sin'.

18:19 [ἀμήν] (truly) {C}

The reading ἀμήν ('truly'; 03 058 f^{13} etc.) is supported by the majority of Greek manuscripts. The *Textus Receptus*, however, along with several early manuscripts, lacks it (01 05 019 f^1 etc.), while a small number instead have δὲ ('but'; 022 [032] 037 etc.). Among the numerous other instances of ἀμὴν λέγω ὑμῖν ('truly I say to you') in Matthew, there is no other example of ἀμήν not coming first in its clause. The most recent occurrence of this formula is in the previous verse, and it is not clear whether the present unit is an authorial exception or whether ἀμήν was introduced after πάλιν ('again') through assimilation to the preceding sentence. If ἀμήν were originally present, as preferred by the SBLGNT and THGNT, it may have been deliberately deleted to give a smoother reading or even accidentally overlooked (ΠΑΛΙΝ and ΑΜΗΝ have a similarity of shape in some scripts). The external evidence suggests that δέ is a development from the shortest form, on the model of Matt. 19:24.

18:26 λέγων (saying) {B}

Most manuscripts begin the direct speech with Κύριε ('Lord'; 01 019 032 etc.), a word which evokes the context of prayer even though the 'Lord' in this instance is the master of the slave. The vocative is absent from a range of important witnesses (03 05 038 700 lat sy[c, s] Origen Chrysostom), which indicates that it may be a later addition. On the other hand, it would be easy to overlook the vocative if it were written as a *nomen sacrum* (ΚΕ), and there is also the possibility that the passage was deliberately assimilated to the plea of the fellow slave in Matt. 18:29. Adopting the shorter reading here (as in the SBLGNT) makes it deliberate authorial irony that the unforgiving slave is addressed with precisely the same words that he has just uttered. The THGNT, however, has the longer reading: it is also possible that κύριε was deleted by an editor because this plea was not addressed to Jesus.

19:7 ἀπολῦσαι [αὐτήν] (to divorce her)

The pronoun αὐτήν ('her') is missing from a variety of early witnesses (01 05 019 035 038 f^1 lat), even though the other three instances of ἀπολῦσαι ('to divorce') in Matthew all have a direct object. The shorter reading here matches the source at Mark 10:4, which is an argument for its originality: an editor could easily have supplied an object. On the other hand, the pronoun is ambivalent, as it could be taken with the generic wife in the quotation at Matt. 19:5 or the original wife back in Matt. 19:3 (also the object of ἀπολῦσαι), and it might therefore have been deleted. There is also the possibility of assimilation to the Markan source. The range of possibilities and the division of the external evidence leads to αὐτήν being placed in brackets, although it is included in both the SBLGNT and THGNT. In translation it may be necessary to provide an object even if the shorter reading is adopted.

19:9 μὴ ἐπὶ πορνείᾳ καὶ γαμήσῃ ἄλλην μοιχᾶται (except for sexual immorality, and marries another commits adultery) {B}

The editorial text corresponds to the reading of Greek manuscripts (01 04³ 019 [032] etc.), but Codex Vaticanus and others have παρεκτὸς λόγου πορνείας ποιεῖ αὐτὴν μοιχευθῆναι ('outside of the reason of sexual immorality, causes her to commit adultery'; 03 0233 f^1 lat^{vl-pt} [cpa] co^{bo} eth^{TH} etc.). The latter is identical to the prohibition at Matt. 5:32, suggesting that this verse has been harmonised to the earlier instance by an editor: the dissimilar text in the majority of witnesses is the harder reading. There are also instances of partial assimilation: Codex Bezae and others combine the first clause from Matt. 5:32 with the majority ending, παρεκτὸς λόγου πορνείας καὶ γαμήσῃ ἄλλην μοιχᾶται ('outside of the reason of sexual immorality, and marries another, commits adultery'; 05 f^{13} 33 [597] etc.), while the first hand of Codex Ephraemi Rescriptus has the opposite combination, μὴ ἐπὶ πορνείᾳ καὶ γαμήσῃ ἄλλην ποιεῖ αὐτὴν μοιχευθῆναι ('except for sexual immorality, and marries another causes her to commit adultery'; 04*). The impact of this prohibition on Christian life may provide a reason why users were keen to ensure the consistency of the teaching: the variation in the final verb provides a contrast between these two Matthean sayings.[29] A similar harmonisation is seen in the following unit.

19:9   μοιχᾶται (commits adultery) {C}

At the end of this verse, the majority of witnesses include the phrase καὶ ὁ ἀπολελυμένην γαμήσας μοιχᾶται ('and the one who marries a divorced woman commits adultery'; 03 28 157 etc.); other witnesses have the present-tense γαμῶν for the aorist γαμήσας (04* 022 023 etc.), while yet others have the formulation ὡσαύτως καὶ ὁ γαμῶν ἀπολελυμένην μοιχᾶται ('likewise too the one marrying a divorced woman commits adultery'; 𝔓[25] [co[mae]]). This observation is missing from a few early witnesses (01 04[3] 05 019 etc.; lat[vl-pt, vg-ms] sy[c, s] co[sa, bo-ms] Origen), which suggests that it may be a later addition. On the other hand, the entire phrase could have been omitted due to eyeskip between the two instances of μοιχᾶται. There are significant parallels with Matt. 5:32 (cf. Mark 10:11): if the shorter reading were original, an editor or reader would be likely to supply the second part of the teaching from 5:32 (compare the previous unit), and the slight textual variation might reflect this being provided from memory. On the other hand, this earlier verse shows that there could still have been eyeskip between μοιχευθῆναι and μοιχᾶται, or even deliberate deletion (Codex Bezae and some Old Latin manuscripts lack this stipulation in both places). While the external evidence here seems to justify the shorter reading, the reasons for omission mean that a case can also be made for a longer form, which is adopted by the SBLGNT and THGNT and also included in the NRSVue. Compare the duplication of Matthean text at Matt. 20:16 below.

19:10   μαθηταὶ [αὐτοῦ] (his disciples)

The pronoun αὐτοῦ ('his') is missing from a few important witnesses (𝔓[71vid] 01 03 038 lat[vl-pt] etc.). Both forms are found in Matthew, and parallels elsewhere would lead copyists to include αὐτοῦ if it were absent (see also Matt. 8:21 above). Conversely, the preceding αὐτῷ ('to him') might have prompted an editor to delete the second pronoun for

---

[29] On this variant, and the topic in general, see Holmes 1990 and Parker 1997: 85–89; Crouzel 1972 considers the patristic evidence in detail.

euphony. In context, there is minimal difference in sense whichever reading is adopted, although it is important to distinguish this reference to the disciples from the Pharisees who were the previous interlocutors.[30]

19:11 τὸν λόγον [τοῦτον] (this teaching)

The demonstrative τοῦτον ('this') is missing from a few manuscripts (03 f^1 892*). This is likely to be an error due to eyeskip from the end of λόγον ('teaching'), although it has been suggested that it was deliberately deleted due to a lack of clarity as to whether it refers to Jesus' original observations or the disciples' response.[31] This same ambiguity makes it unlikely that it was a later editorial addition.

19:17 τί με ἐρωτᾷς περὶ τοῦ ἀγαθοῦ; εἷς ἐστιν ὁ ἀγαθός (Why do you ask me about what is good? There is one who is good.) {A}

The editorial text is supported by a range of Greek manuscripts and early versions (01 03 05 019 038 etc., with some minor variations). Some of the ancient translations also include the equivalent of ὁ θεός ('God') at the end, to make the referent clear. The majority of manuscripts, however, have a different phrasing: τί με λέγεις ἀγαθόν; οὐδεὶς ἀγαθὸς εἰ μὴ εἷς ὁ θεός ('why do you call me good? No-one is good but God alone'; 04 032 037 etc.). This corresponds exactly to the parallels at Mark 10:18 and Luke 18:19. The external evidence indicates that this conformity was introduced by a later editor; the divergent form is the harder reading, too, since it would be very unexpected for the text to be altered away from the parallels. A few witnesses alternate between the two forms, with some reading τί με ἐρωτᾷς περὶ τοῦ ἀγαθοῦ; οὐδεὶς ἀγαθὸς εἰ μὴ εἷς ὁ θεός ('why do you ask me about what is good? No-one is good but God alone'; 892[c] lat[vl-pt] Eusebius) and certain writers quoting it as τί με λέγεις ἀγαθόν; εἷς ἐστιν ἀγαθός, ὁ πατήρ μου ὁ ἐν τοῖς οὐρανοῖς ('why do you call me good? There is only one who is good, my Father in heaven'; Marcus[acc. to Irenaeus] Justin): despite the antiquity of this reference and the Matthean phrasing of 'my Father in heaven', these

---

[30] On this phrase, see also Elliott 1979.
[31] Metzger 1994: 39.

appear to be loose quotations. This verse is included in *ECM Parallel Pericopes* and the full range of readings in continuous-text Greek manuscripts is given in *TuT Matthew* (TS55).[32]

19:21 [τοῖς] πτωχοῖς (to the poor)

Very few witnesses include the definite article in τοῖς πτωχοῖς ('to the poor'; 03 05 038 co). The same variation is found in the parallel at Mark 10:21, where the ECM has a split guiding line although there is more support for the longer reading, while the parallel at Luke 18:11 just reads πτωχοῖς ('to poor people'). It is possible that τοῖς was overlooked after δός because of the similarity of the two words, or that there was assimilation between the different parallels. In any case, there is little difference in meaning. This verse is included in *ECM Parallel Pericopes*.

19:29 πατέρα ἢ μητέρα (father or mother) {C}

Variation in lists is commonplace, reflecting omissions due to oversight of a term and the addition of elements which were thought to be lacking. The majority of manuscripts read πατέρα ἢ μητέρα ἢ γυναῖκα ('father or mother or wife'; 01 04 019 032 etc.). This is present in the parallel at Luke 18:29 and in the majority of manuscripts at Mark 10:29 (see below), and accordingly may be original: it is adopted in the SBLGNT and THGNT (as well as the NRSVue). Nevertheless, *ECM Mark* lacks ἢ γυναῖκα, and this shorter reading has also been adopted here despite its very slim attestation (03 lat[vl-pt] cpa Chrysostom). Codex Bezae and some early versions just read μητέρα ('mother'; 05 lat[vl-pt] sy[s]), presumably due to oversight of the similar preceding term in the list. The replacement of πατέρα ἢ μητέρα with γονεῖς ('parents'; f^1 etc.) is likely to be assimilation to the Lukan parallel. If ἢ γυναῖκα is not read in this list in Mark or Matthew, it may be noted that the result makes no assumptions about the gender of the believer, and contemporary translations may choose to follow this lead even if the longer reading is followed.

---

[32] For a discussion with particular emphasis on early Christian authors, see Strutwolf 2011: 32–39.

20:5 πάλιν [δέ] (again)

The connective δέ ('but') is missing from the majority of Greek manuscripts (03 032 037 f^1 etc.) but present in some early witnesses (01 04 05 etc.). Given the presence of δέ in the preceding and following sentences, it may have been deleted by an editor to give a smoother reading. On the other hand, the occurrence of πάλιν δέ a few verses earlier, at Matt. 19:24, may have led to its introduction here as well. There is little difference in translation between the two readings (see also Matt. 23:23 below).

20:10 [τὸ] ἀνὰ δηνάριον (a denarius)

The definite article τό ('the') is only present in a few manuscripts (01 019 035 038 085). This is the harder reading, because ἀνὰ δηνάριον (lit. 'a denarius apiece') is used without the article in the previous verse: τό could have been added either by the author or an early editor to emphasise that it was the same amount as the previous workers, but it would easily have been lost through assimilation to the preceding sentence. There is also variation in word order in this phrase, but little impact on translation.

20:15 [ἢ] οὐκ ([or] am I not)

The first word of this verse is missing from some important manuscripts (03 05 019 035 700 sy[c, s]). As a single letter, it could easily have been overlooked (particularly as it would have been pronounced the same as the previous vowel in σοι), or it may have been deliberately deleted to avoid the possibility that, in conjunction with the following clause, it could be understood as 'either'. On the other hand, its inclusion indicates that it is an alternative to the previous clause and a later editor could have added it to clarify that this is a question. It is adopted by the THGNT but lacking from the SBLGNT. Principally, this is a difference of style, and translators should handle it as appropriate in the target language: several modern translations do not have anything reflecting this particle.

20:16 ἔσχατοι (last) {B}

At the end of this verse, the majority of manuscripts include the phrase πολλοὶ γάρ εἰσιν κλητοί, ὀλίγοι δὲ ἐκλεκτοί ('for many are called, but few are chosen'; 04 05 032 etc.). This is the text of Matt. 22:14, but here is absent from some important witnesses (01 03 019 035 085 etc.; see further *TuT Matthew* TS56), suggesting that it may have been added later (compare Matt. 19:9 above). Given the repetition of some phrases in Matthew (e.g. 'wailing and gnashing of teeth') it is possible that this is authorial, but was omitted through eyeskip from TOI to TOI. However, the external evidence makes it more likely that the text was supplied by a later reader as a similar saying which matches the sentiments of the rest of the verse. It is not adopted in the SBLGNT or the THGNT.

20:17 τοὺς δώδεκα [μαθητάς] (the twelve disciples)

The shorter reading, τοὺς δώδεκα ('the twelve'; 01 05 019 038 f^1 f^{13} etc.) is used later in Matthew to refer to the apostles (e.g. Matt. 26:14, 26:20 etc.). The majority of manuscripts in this instance have τοὺς δώδεκα μαθητάς ('the twelve disciples'; 03 04 022 037 etc.), as has been the evangelist's practice up to this point. The parallels at Mark 10:32 and Luke 18:31 both lack μαθητάς, which might have led to assimilation here or might correspond to the original reading. In translation it may be helpful to expand the expression if the shorter reading is followed.

20:22 πίνειν (I am about to drink) {A}

At the end of Jesus' question, the majority of manuscripts include the line ἢ τὸ βάπτισμα ὃ ἐγὼ βαπτίζομαι βαπτισθῆναι ('or be baptised with the baptism that I am baptised with'; 04 032 037 etc.), while others read καὶ τὸ βάπτισμα ὁ ἐγὼ βαπτίζομαι βαπτισθῆναι ('and be baptised with the baptism that I am baptised with'; 157 [180] 892 1071 *TR* etc.). There is no obvious reason for its omission, and the extensive early attestation of its absence (01 03 05 019 etc. and most of the ancient translations) suggests that it was introduced through assimilation to the parallel at Mark 10:38 (see also the following unit). The variation in the preceding infinitive between the aorist πιεῖν ('to drink'; 03 085) and the present πίνειν (lit. 'to be drinking'; 01 05 019 etc.) is less significant. As πιεῖν has already occurred six words previously, the present is the harder reading and is found in almost all manuscripts.

20:23 πίεσθε (you will drink) {A}

In keeping with the addition in the previous unit, most Greek manuscripts also include in Jesus' response καὶ τὸ βάπτισμα ὃ ἐγὼ βαπτίζομαι βαπτισθήσεσθε ('and you will be baptised with the baptism that I am baptised with'; 04 032 037 etc.; 892 just reads καὶ τὸ βάπτισμα βαπτισθήσεσθε, 'and you will be baptised with the baptism'). Despite the possibility of accidental omission through eyeskip from ΕΣΘΕ to ΕΣΘΕ, the strong external evidence for the absence of this phrase (01 03 05 019 etc.) indicates that it is a later harmonisation to the preceding verse or Mark 10:39.

20:23 οὐκ ἔστιν ἐμὸν [τοῦτο] δοῦναι (this is not mine to grant)

The demonstrative τοῦτο ('this') is missing from the majority of manuscripts (01 03 019 022 035 036 etc.) and is only present in relatively few witnesses (04 05 032 037 085 33 etc.). However, as its inclusion differs from the source at Mark 10:40, a case could be made for its being original and the shorter reading an assimilation to the parallel. Against the suggestion that τοῦτο was added later by an editor who felt that δοῦναι ('to give') needed a direct object is the lack of a direct object in the previous occurrence of the same infinitive at Matt. 20:14. Nevertheless, τοῦτο is not included by the SBLGNT or THGNT, probably on the basis of the strong external evidence.

20:30 ἐλέησον ἡμᾶς, [κύριε] (Lord, have mercy on us) {C}

Most manuscripts have ἐλέησον ἡμᾶς, κύριε ('have mercy on us, Lord'; 𝔓[45vid] 04 032 037 etc.), matching their text of the following verse. This is a more unusual sequence than κύριε, ἐλέησον ἡμᾶς ('Lord, have mercy on us'; 03 035[vid] 085 lat[vl-pt, vg] etc.), where the initial vocative is in the customary position, also matching the liturgical norm. The external evidence for ἐλέησον ἡμᾶς, Ἰησοῦ ('have mercy on us, Jesus'; 01 038 f^{13} etc.) or just ἐλέησον ἡμᾶς ('have mercy on us'; 05 13 157 etc.) raises the question as to whether κύριε was originally present. The former is the reading of the synoptic parallels at both Mark 10:47 and Luke 18:38, while the latter is the cry of the two blind men at Matt. 9:27.[33] In both cases, then, assimilation is a possibility—although assimilation to the

---

[33] See *ECM Parallel Pericopes*.

following verse would result in the majority reading. There is also the possibility that κύριε could have been omitted through oversight, especially in manuscripts in which the following word is the vocative υἱέ: the likelihood of this would increase if κύριε was written as the *nomen sacrum* KE. The external evidence for ἐλέησον ἡμᾶς, κύριε Ἰησοῦ ('have mercy on us, Lord Jesus'; 022 042) and κύριε, ἐλέησον ἡμᾶς, Ἰησοῦ ('Lord, have mercy on us, Jesus'; 019 892 etc.) suggests that these are later developments. The spread of variants here demonstrates the effect of assimilation, conflation and other editorial or scribal alteration, and it is difficult to be confident which form is earliest. The SBLGNT has κύριε, ἐλέησον ἡμᾶς while the THGNT opts for ἐλέησον ἡμᾶς, Ἰησοῦ.[34]

21:12   ἱερόν (temple) {B}

The majority of manuscripts read ἱερὸν τοῦ θεοῦ ('temple of God'; 04 05 032 037 etc.), but there is early evidence for just ἱερόν ('temple'; 01 03 019 038 etc.; see *TuT Matthew* TS57). Both parallels have the shorter reading (Mark 11:15, Luke 19:45), and the other instances of 'temple' in Matthew are unqualified (Matt. 4:5, 12:5–6, 21:23, 24:1 etc.). Although this may suggest that the shorter reading arose through assimilation, the departure from the author's usual practice raises questions: while there is no obvious reason for the deletion of τοῦ θεοῦ, the qualification could have been added either to draw attention to the holiness of the place, or to provide the context for the quotation in the following verse (where there is no explanation that the pronoun μου ['my'] refers to God). The external evidence suggests that this clarification was the work of a later editor.

21:29–31   οὐ θέλω, ὕστερον δὲ μεταμεληθεὶς ἀπῆλθεν. ... ἑτέρῳ ... ἐγώ, κύριε· καὶ οὐκ ἀπῆλθεν. ... ὁ πρῶτος ("I will not"; but later he changed his mind and went. ... to the second ... "I go, sir," but he did not go. ... the first) {C}

The editorial text matches the *Textus Receptus*: Byzantine tradition is split between this and the same text but with δευτέρῳ ('to the second'; 01[2] 04[2] 019 etc.) rather than ἑτέρῳ ('to the other'; 01* 04* 032 etc.). The situation is reversed in a few early witnesses, in which the first son does

---

[34] Min 2005: 209–213, 298–299 offers a fuller discussion, preferring ἐλέησον ἡμᾶς as the earliest reading.

not go and it is the second son who is commended for changing his mind. Codex Vaticanus, supported by some translations, reads ἐγώ, κύριε· καὶ οὐκ ἀπῆλθεν. ... δευτέρῳ ... οὐ θέλω· ὕστερον μεταμεληθεὶς ἀπῆλθεν. ... ὁ ὕστερος ("'I, Lord" yet he did not go. ... to the second ... "I will not"; but later he changed his mind and went. ... the latter'; 03 [cpa^pt] [co^bo] eth^ms). Similarly, the Koridethi Codex has ὑπάγω, καὶ οὐκ ἀπῆλθεν. ... ἑτέρῳ ... οὐ θέλω· ὕστερον δὲ μεταμεληθεὶς ἀπῆλθεν. ... ὁ ἔσχατος ("'I am going," yet he did not go. ... to the other ... "I will not"; but later he changed his mind and went. ... the last'; 038 [0233] [*f*^13] etc.). The most surprising form is seen in Codex Bezae, with Old Latin and Old Syriac support, in which the first changes his mind, and yet the second son who did not go receives the commendation: οὐ θέλω, ὕστερον δὲ μεταμεληθεὶς ἀπῆλθεν εἰς τὸν ἀμπελῶνα ... ἑτέρῳ ... ἐγώ, κύριε, ὑπάγω· καὶ οὐκ ἀπῆλθεν. ... ὁ ἔσχατος ("'I will not"; but later he changed his mind and went to the vineyard. ... to the other ... "I, Lord, am going"; yet he did not go. ... the last'; 05 lat^vl-pt, vg [sy^c, s]). As the hardest reading by far, some have argued that this is the original form: it was known to Jerome, who explained it as Jesus' interlocutors deliberately giving the wrong answer in order to frustrate the parable which was being spoken against them. A simpler explanation is that this variant, which features a couple of expansions, originates from a partial adjustment of editorial text in the light of another manuscript reflecting the Koridethi text without full attention being given to the significance of making this change when the phrases were not transposed. In terms of the sense, this reading is too difficult to adopt and the Byzantine tradition is preferable to the other majuscules: if the first son had agreed to go, there would have been no need to ask the second. The disobedience of the first son also makes for an obvious supersessionist interpretation, identifying the Jews as the first son: these alternatives therefore appear to be secondary, despite their early attestation, indicating that editorial adjustment of this saying to try to bring out the perceived interpretation happened in antiquity. However, the variety of readings makes for doubt as to the oldest form: the most common reading with ἑτέρῳ has been adopted on the basis of the external evidence.[35]

---

[35] For extended considerations of this variant, see Aland & Aland 1989: 312–316, Foster 2001 (who argues in favour of the reading in Codex Vaticanus) and Elliott 2002.

21:44 [καὶ ὁ πεσὼν ἐπὶ τὸν λίθον τοῦτον συνθλασθήσεται· ἐφ' ὃν δ' ἂν πέσῃ λικμήσει αὐτόν.] (The one who falls on this stone will be broken to pieces; and it will crush anyone on whom it falls.) {C}

The entire verse is missing from Codex Bezae, GA 33, the Old Latin and Sinaitic Syriac, but is present in other early majuscules and the majority of minuscules (01 03 04 019 etc.). It is possible that it was omitted due to eyeskip from καί at the beginning of this verse to καί at the beginning of Matt. 21:45. However, as the absence of the sentence is clearly early and its text is very similar in form to Luke 20:18, which ends the parallel account, it may be a later addition: whereas in Luke it follows the quotation directly, here it seems more of an afterthought. This placing could be seen as making the longer reading more difficult, although if this had led to intervention by a later editor, then an obvious solution would have been to change the sequence to match that of Luke rather than total deletion. Because the slim attestation for the shorter reading is consistent with accidental omission, it is very difficult to determine the earliest form, yet the verse is included in both the SBLGNT and THGNT.[36]

22:23 Σαδδουκαῖοι, λέγοντες (Sadducees ... saying) {C}

There is extensive early support for the editorial text (01* 03 05 032 etc.), also seen in the SBLGNT and THGNT, but the majority of Greek manuscripts read Σαδδουκαῖοι οἱ λέγοντες ('Sadducees, who say'; 01² 019 038 etc.), and some minuscules have οἱ Σαδδουκαῖοι οἱ λέγοντες ('the Sadducees, who say'; f^{13} co^sa). The significance of the relative is the historical question of whether the denial of the resurrection is characteristic of all Sadducees (as implied by the majority reading) or whether it may have been peculiar to this particular group: while both Mark 12:18 and Luke 20:27 can only be interpreted in the former sense, a deliberate change by Matthew could be important. On the other hand, it would be very easy for οἱ to be omitted by haplography after Σαδδουκαῖοι or, indeed, to be produced by dittography of the last two letters. While the shorter reading seems more likely to be original on

---

[36] Min 2005: 294–295 prefers the longer text as authorial, while Lanier 2016 argues in favour of the shorter reading which he also detects in Papyrus 104.

the basis of its external attestation and dissimilarity from the parallels, it may still have arisen through a copying error.

22:30   ἄγγελοι (angels) {C}

Most manuscripts read ἄγγελοι τοῦ θεοῦ ('angels of God'; 032 037 0102 etc.), while others have ἄγγελοι θεοῦ ('angels of God'; 01 019 042 f^{13} etc.). There is limited support for οἱ ἄγγελοι ('the angels'; 038 f^1 etc.) and ἄγγελοι ('angels'; 03 05 0233 etc.), and it is not always possible to determine whether early translations reflect the Greek article or not. The addition of 'God' could be an expansion, as nowhere else does Matthew have the phrase 'angel of God', preferring the 'angel of the Lord', although there are references to the angels of individuals (Matt. 18:10) and of the devil (Matt. 25:41). If one of the longer readings were original, it may have been shortened through assimilation to the parallel at Mark 12:25, or oversight involving the *nomen sacrum* ΘΥ. The Markan source text, however, might also support the shorter reading here: conversely, the appearance of θεοῦ in a few witnesses in Mark may be due to the influence of the longer readings in the present unit. Both the SBLGNT and THGNT read ἄγγελοι θεοῦ, probably on the basis of the external evidence.

22:35   [νομικός] (an expert in the law)

The word νομικός ('an expert in the law') is only absent from Family 1, the Old Latin Codex Palatinus and the Sinaitic Syriac. Its position is unexpected, without a following τις, which would be consistent with its being a marginal gloss later incorporated into the text: nowhere else does Matthew have a substantive following the partitive ἐξ αὐτῶν ('of them'). While νομικός is common in Luke, including the parallel at Luke 10:25, this is the only time that Matthew refers to a lawyer or uses the term. On the other hand, the external evidence for the presence of the word is very strong and it is clearly stylistically the harder reading while still suited to the context of a question about the Law. Accordingly, it has been retained in the text with some doubt. The word is included in both the SBLGNT and THGNT; this verse appears in *ECM Parallel Pericopes*.

23:4 βαρέα [καὶ δυσβάστακτα] (heavy and hard to bear)

The majority of manuscripts read βαρέα καὶ δυσβάστακτα ('heavy and hard to bear'; 03 05 032 etc.), yet there are variants in some important witnesses: several read only βαρέα ('heavy'; 019 f^1 892 lat^vl sy^{c, s, p}), Codex Sinaiticus has μεγάλα βαρέα ('great [and] heavy'; 01) and one minuscule δυσβάστακτα ('hard to bear'; 700). Although δυσβάστακτα could be assimilation to the parallel at Luke 11:46 (which lacks βαρέα), the omission of this phrase through eyeskip from καί to καί is highly likely. Early translators may have chosen simply to render one of two words which seemed synonymous in context, which would accord with the external evidence for the shorter reading.

23:8 διδάσκαλος (teacher) {B}

There is very slim support for the editorial reading διδάσκαλος ('teacher'; 01^{2a} 03 33 892*). All other witnesses have καθηγητής ('instructor'; 01^{*, 2b} 05 019 etc.), the word which is seen in the plural at Matt. 23:10. The translation of 'Rabbi' by 'teacher' is seen in John (1:38, 20:16), but Jesus' Jewish interlocutors frequently address him as διδάσκαλε ('teacher') in Matthew. The only occurrence of καθηγητής in the New Testament is two verses later, where the similar phrasing could have led to the introduction of καθηγητής in the present verse: the conjunction μηδέ ('nor') at the beginning of Matt. 23:10 makes little sense if the prohibition on being called 'instructor' had already been issued two verses previously. Despite the limited external evidence and the possibility of assimilation to John, it appears that διδάσκαλος is the correct reading, also adopted in the SBLGNT and THGNT, and should be distinguished from καθηγητής in translation.

23:14 *omit verse* {B}

The majority of Greek witnesses include an extra element in this list of woes, reading οὐαὶ δὲ ὑμῖν, γραμματεῖς καὶ Φαρισαῖοι ὑποκριταί, ὅτι κατεσθίετε τὰς οἰκίας τῶν χηρῶν καὶ προφάσει μακρὰ προσευχόμενοι· διὰ τοῦτο λήμψεσθε περισσότερον κρίμα ('Woe to you, scribes and Pharisees, hypocrites! For you devour widows' houses and for the sake of appearance you make long prayers; therefore you will receive the greater condemnation; 032 037 0102 0107 etc.). In most manuscripts, this appears at the beginning of the list, after Matt. 23:12, but as it is found after 23:13 in Erasmus' 1516 edition (and in 0233 f^{13} lat^(vl-pt, vg-ms) etc.), it is traditionally numbered as 23:14.[37] Although eyeskip from one instance of οὐαί to the next could easily have led to the omission of one of the elements, the extensive evidence in favour of the shorter reading (01 03 05 019 035 038 f^1 etc.) indicates that it is a later addition. The text has been adjusted from Mark 12:40 or Luke 20:47, both of which are individual episodes rather than a long list of condemnations. Similar additional verses in the Byzantine tradition of Matthew are seen at Matt. 17:21 and 18:11.

23:23 ταῦτα [δέ] (it is these)

External evidence is evenly split between the inclusion of δέ ('but'; 03 04 019 032 037 etc.) and its absence (01 05 036 038 f^1 etc.). The connective is present in the parallel at Luke 11:42, and so could have been introduced by assimilation; equally, it could have been omitted before ἔδει through confusion with the same letters. As at Matt. 20:5 (see above), there is little difference in meaning between the two forms.

23:25 ἀκρασίας (self-indulgence) {A}

The majority of manuscripts read ἀκρασίας (lit. 'lack of control'; 01 03 05 019 etc.), which could even be a play on words because inside the aforementioned cup one would expect to find κρᾶσις ('mixed wine'). Because this word is comparatively rare, however, and 'lack of control' may have seemed far less worthy of condemnation than ἁρπαγῆς ('taking by violence'), alternatives were introduced into the tradition, often with a similar form: ἀδικίας ('injustice'; 04 28 157 579 etc.), ἀκαθαρσίας ('uncleanness'; 023 042 etc.), the conflation ἀκρασίας ἀδικίας ('lack of control, injustice'; 032) and, from assimilation to the parallel at Luke 11:39, πονηρίας ('wickedness'; 180). In translation, it may work best to treat ἁρπαγῆς καὶ ἀκρασίας as sins of consumption (e.g. 'greed and self-indulgence').

---

[37] Despite the claim of Metzger 1994: 50 that the *Textus Receptus* has the addition after Matt. 23:13, both Stephanus' edition of 1550 and the Oxford printing of 1873 have it after Matt. 23:12.

23:26 τοῦ ποτηρίου … τὸ ἐκτὸς αὐτοῦ (of the cup … the outside) {D}

Given the reference to the two vessels in the previous verse, it is unsurprising to find τοῦ ποτηρίου καὶ τῆς παροψίδος ('of the cup and of the plate') in the majority of witnesses here. The external evidence is weak for τοῦ ποτηρίου alone ('of the cup'; 05 038 f^1 etc.). However, while the shorter reading might have been expanded later, there is also a strong possibility, supported by its attestation, that an editor deleted the reference to the plate, on the grounds that to clean the inside of a plate seemed impossible. The number of vessels also affects the final pronoun: the plural τὸ ἐκτὸς αὐτῶν ('the outside of them'; 01^2 03^2 04 019 032) is the obvious form for the longer reading, seen in most Greek manuscripts, while references only to a single vessel only have a singular pronoun, as τὸ ἐκτὸς αὐτοῦ ('the outside of it'; 038 f^1 etc.) or τὸ ἔξωθεν αὐτοῦ ('the external part of it'; 05). The most difficult reading is one with two vessels but only one outside: τοῦ ποτηρίου καὶ τῆς παροψίδος … τὸ ἐκτὸς αὐτοῦ ('of the cup and of the plate … the outside of it'; 03* 07* 011 f^{13} etc.), adopted in the SBLGNT. This does not seem impossible if the singular is understood as distributive (each has only one outside): if it is taken as the earliest form, both the plural αὐτῶν and witnesses which lack the pronoun entirely (lat[vl-pt, vg] co[mae] Origen[lat]) can be seen as different ways of resolving the apparent inconsistency. The THGNT follows the majority reading: the choice of the reading of GA 038 for the UBS editorial text makes for good sense, but its attestation is slim and consistent with a deliberate alteration.

23:38 ἔρημος (desolate) {B}

The majority of manuscripts include ἔρημος ('desolate'; 01 04 05 032 etc.), but it is lacking from some important witnesses ($\mathfrak{P}^{77vid}$ 03 019 sy[s] co[sa, bo-pt] etc.). The shorter reading could be a harmonisation to the parallel at Luke 13:35, where the lack of ἔρημος is more strongly attested even though the adjective appears in other witnesses (presumably from the variant reading here). Alternatively, ἔρημος might have been added as a later clarification, or perhaps to bring the saying into closer agreement with Jer. 22:5 (although there is minimal overlap with the wording of the Septuagint). The strength of the attestation of ἔρημος leads to its adoption here and in both the SBLGNT and THGNT. In translation, ὁ οἶκος (lit. 'the house') may be taken to mean the Temple in Jerusalem and ἀφίεται ('is left') treated as a divine passive ('God has left …'): in such a context, translators may combine ἔρημος with the verb (e.g. 'deserted') or it may even be considered superfluous (which could explain some instances of the shorter reading here in Greek).[38]

24:7   λιμοὶ καὶ σεισμοί (famines and earthquakes) {C}

The longest readings are λιμοὶ καὶ λοιμοὶ καὶ σεισμοί ('famines and plagues and earthquakes'; 04 037 038 0102 f^1 and the majority of minuscules) and λοιμοὶ καὶ λιμοὶ καὶ σεισμοί ('plagues and famines and earthquakes'; 019 032 13 33 etc.). The shared sequences of letters provide plenty of opportunity for accidental omission due to eyeskip, as seen in the absence of καὶ σεισμοί from 565: in addition, λιμοί and λοιμοί would have been almost identical in pronunciation, hence the uncertainty regarding the sequence of 579 and 828*. Nevertheless, there is good external evidence for λιμοὶ καὶ σεισμοί ('famines and earthquakes'; 03 05 07* 892 and several early versions) and also σεισμοὶ καὶ λιμοί ('earthquakes and famines'; 01). The latter is likely to be assimilation to the order in the parallel at Mark 13:8 (on which see below) or Luke 21:11. Both λιμοί and λοιμοί are established in the text of Luke, but it is not clear whether the introduction of λοιμοί is a Lukan innovation (which has influenced the majority of manuscripts in Matthew) or whether it was taken over from Matthew. The choice of λιμοὶ καὶ σεισμοί as the editorial text is based on its attestation, but the range of variants indicates how unstable all these readings are.

24:31   [τῶν] ἄκρων (the other)

The definite article τῶν ('the') is missing from the majority of manuscripts (01 05 019 032 etc.) and only present in a few (03 038 f^1 f^{13} etc.). Matthew's practice elsewhere after ἕως ('up to') is variable but, as the previous instance of ἕως four verses earlier is followed by an anarthrous noun and the preceding ἄκρων (lit. 'the ends') in this verse lacks an article, the inclusion of τῶν is the harder reading. Translation is unaffected in any case.

---

[38] See Omanson 2006: 42.

24:36 οὐδὲ ὁ υἱός (nor the Son) {B}

This theologically significant phrase is absent from the majority of witnesses (01[2a] 019 032 037 etc., lat[vl-pt, vg] sy co). However, all the oldest Greek manuscripts include οὐδὲ ὁ υἱός ('nor the Son'; 01[*, 2b] 03 05 038 etc.), along with almost one hundred minuscules (see *TuT Matthew* TS60) and the variation was known to Jerome in the fourth century. Accidental omission due to eyeskip is unlikely: it would have to involve jumping from the *nomen sacrum* for οὐρανῶν ('heavens') to the *nomen sacrum* for υἱός ('son'). At the parallel in Mark 13:32, the same phrase is clearly present (apart from a few minor exceptions), and Matthew's addition of the emphatic μόνος ('alone') after ὁ πατήρ ('the Father') would not be in keeping with his deletion of the clause relating to the Son. Nevertheless, it has been noted that the co-ordination of οὐδέ ... οὐδέ ('neither ... nor') is only rarely used in Matthew (Matt. 6:28 and 12:19; the latter is a quotation from the Septuagint).[39] The external evidence suggests that an early editor removed the detail of the son's ignorance from this gospel, presumably on doctrinal grounds, but failed to notice it in Mark where it was left for a handful of others to make the same change at a later point.[40]

24:38 ἡμέραις [ἐκείναις] ([those] days)

The word ἐκείναις ('those') is lacking from the majority of manuscripts (01 019 032 037 038 etc.), but present in a few early witnesses (03 05 579 lat[vl] co[sa]). While it may have dropped out through eyeskip, there is no other instance of this phrase in Matthew, and this verse could easily have been assimilated to the Septuagintal formula adopted in the Lukan writings (e.g. Luke 2:1, 4:2; Acts 2:18, 7:41 etc.). Both the SBLGNT and THGNT omit the bracketed word, as does the NRSVue.

24:39 ἔσται [καί] (too will be)

The situation is reversed here, with καί ('also') absent from early witnesses (03 05 lat[vl] sy[s] co[sa] etc.), but present in the majority. The same phrase occurs two verses earlier, where again the Byzantine tradition includes καί but it has been excluded from the editorial text due to the

---

[39] Wallace 2015: 196, which offers other arguments in favour of the shorter reading as the earliest form.
[40] See further Ehrman 2011: 107–108.

slightly larger number of manuscripts which lack it. In both cases, καί is not required for the sense and could easily have been omitted by eyeskip after ἔσται. Although the phrase is unstable elsewhere in Matthew (see Matt. 6:21 and 12:40) and καί could have been added through assimilation to Matt. 12:45, the more likely direction of assimilation is its removal following Matt. 24:27. In both Matt. 24:37 and 39, then, there is good reason to prefer the longer reading, as seen in the SBLGNT and THGNT.

24:42   ἡμέρᾳ (day) {B}

There is very strong early evidence for ἡμέρᾳ ('day'; 01 03 04 05 etc.), which suggests that the majority reading ὥρᾳ ('hour'; 019 28 180 etc.) is an anticipation of the same word two verses later: compare also the partial parallels at Luke 12:39 and the use of both words at Matt. 24:50 and 25:13, seen here in some translations and ancient writers. There may have been a preference for the more specific term; similarly, while the concept of a 'day of judgment' is already present in the New Testament, an editor may have observed that no guidance is given about the hour.[41] In any case, the sense is simply 'at what time'.

25:1   τοῦ νυμφίου (the bridegroom) {B}

The editorial text has excellent support, including the majority of manuscripts (01 03 019 032 etc.). A couple of poorly attested variants have little claim to be original: the dative τῷ νυμφίῳ ('the bridegroom'; 04 157) provides the case expected for the verb ὑπαντᾶν ('to meet') rather than the genitive following the noun ('a meeting with'; see also the next unit); the plural τῶν νυμφίων ('the bridegrooms'; 892*) may simply be a slip occasioned by the number of women, but it could be understood as 'the married couple'. The latter is also seen in τοῦ νυμφίου καὶ τῆς νύμφης ('the bridegroom and the bride'; 05 038 042 f^1 lat sy co^mae). There is no obvious reason for the accidental omission of 'and the bride', although the interpretative association of Christ and the Church as bridegroom and bride may have led to the removal of this phrase by an editor on the grounds that this was yet to happen. The shorter reading implies that the wedding is taking place at the bride's house, whereas

---

[41] See Metzger 1994: 52.

the mention of the couple locates it at the house of the bridegroom.[42] As the latter was more customary in antiquity, this may have been the reason for the addition of the bride. Alternatively, an editor may have felt it inappropriate for ten virgins to be meeting the bridegroom independently of the bride (even though five of them were wise), and so ensured that she was present too for the sake of propriety. The secondary nature of the longer reading is consistent with its attestation.

25:6 [αὐτοῦ] (him)

The pronoun is missing from a few manuscripts (01 03 035 700): as these include Codex Sinaiticus and Codex Vaticanus, there is a possibility that the shorter reading is original. Alternatively, it may simply be an oversight, as the word is not necessary for the sense. It may be noted in passing that Codex Ephraemi Rescriptus again has the dative, αὐτῷ ('to him'; 04), matching the usual case of the verb rather than the noun derived from it (see previous unit).

25:13 ὥραν (hour) {A}

At the end of the verse, the majority of manuscripts include the phrase ἐν ᾗ ὁ υἱὸς τοῦ ἀνθρώπου ἔρχεται ('in which the Son of Man is coming'; 04³ *f*¹³ etc.; see *TuT Matthew* TS61). The very strong early evidence for the shorter reading (𝔓³⁵ 01 02 03 04* 05 etc.), which can stand by itself even though it may seem to be a rather abrupt ending, indicates that the additional text is an expansion based on Matt. 24:44 by someone seeking to emphasise the allegorical nature of the parable. In translation, a similar clarification may be required.

25:15–16 ἀπεδήμησεν. εὐθέως πορευθείς (he went away. At once … went off) {B}

Without punctuation, the editorial text is ambiguous: did the master go abroad at once, as the modern division of verses suggests, or did the first slave immediately set off with the five talents? The addition of the postpositive δέ in much of the manuscript tradition resolves the question. The majority of Greek manuscripts read ἀπεδήμησεν εὐθέως. πορευθεὶς δέ ('he immediately went abroad. Then [the one who had

---

[42] Metzger 1994: 52–53.

five talents] set off'; 01² 02 04 05 019 etc.), while another group of witnesses has ἀπεδήμησεν. εὐθέως δὲ πορευθείς ('he went abroad. Immediately, then, [the one who had five talents] set off'; 038 *f*¹ 205 700 etc.). The existence of these two forms, each removing the ambiguity, indicates that the witnesses without δέ are likely to preserve the earliest form of text: ἀπεδήμησεν εὐθέως πορευθείς ('he went abroad immediately having set off'; 01* 03 lat^(vl-pt) Origen^(lat)), even though they are very few in number. Matthew's consistency elsewhere in always placing εὐθέως or εὐθύς before the verb shows that, despite the verse division, the punctuation should come after ἀπεδήμησεν ('he went abroad'): this is also followed by both the SBLGNT and THGNT.

25:22 προσελθὼν [δέ] (came forward)

The connective δέ ('and', 'then', 'but') is only missing from a few witnesses, but they are all early and important (01* 03 co^(sa)). While this is likely to be due to an accidental omission, it could be that the rest of the tradition represents an early assimilation to the identical phrase two verses later, in which these witnesses also read δέ. It is possible that Papyrus 35 also supports the shorter reading.[43]

25:41 [οἱ] κατηραμένοι (you who are accursed)

The definite article οἱ ('the'), which makes no difference to the sense, is absent from some important witnesses (01 03 019 0128 0281 33). The same construction, with the definite article before a participle, is found in a quotation at Matt. 7:23, but the version of this quotation at Luke 13:27 lacks the definite article. While the Matthean parallel makes the longer reading attractive, assimilation could have happened in either direction.

26:27 ποτήριον (a cup) {B}

The textual tradition is split between ποτήριον ('a cup'; 01 03 019 032 etc.) and τὸ ποτήριον ('the cup'; 𝔓³⁷ᵛⁱᵈ 𝔓⁴⁵ 02 04 05 etc.). The parallels at Mark 14:23 and Luke 22:17 have a similar variation. Given the importance of the cup in the Eucharistic liturgy pointing back to this episode, it is more likely that the definite article was added later (cf.

---

[43] See Min 2005: 294.

1 Cor. 11:25–27): there would be no reason to remove it if it were present. As this is the first reference to a cup in Matthew's narrative, the shorter form (which has good early attestation) is preferable and is also adopted in the SBLGNT and THGNT.

26:28   διαθήκης (of the covenant) {B}

Both here and in the parallel at Mark 14:24 (see below), the majority of manuscripts read καινῆς διαθήκης ('of the new covenant'; 02 04 05 032 etc.). The adjective 'new' is clearly present in the institution narratives at Luke 22:20 and 1 Cor. 11:25, which would easily have led to its insertion here: accidental omission of καινῆς following τῆς is possible, but less likely. The strong external evidence for the shorter reading διαθήκης ('of the covenant'; $\mathfrak{P}^{37}$ $\mathfrak{P}^{45vid}$ 01 03 019 etc.) leads to its adoption here and in the other hand editions.

26:36   ἕως [οὗ] (while)

The textual tradition is split between ἕως ('until'; 01 04 0281 33 700 etc.), ἕως ἄν ('until'; 05 019 032 037 etc.), ἕως οὗ ('until when'; 03 036 067 and the majority of minuscules) and ἕως οὗ ἄν ('until when'; $\mathfrak{P}^{53vid}$ 02). All forms apart from the last one are paralleled elsewhere in Matthew, albeit often with textual variation omitting a following οὗ or ἄν which may be indicative of later changes in the Greek language (see also the next unit). For this reason, one of the longer readings is preferable. The context suggests that the sense of ἕως here is, unusually for Matthew, 'while' or 'during' rather than 'until': the choice of οὗ may support this (cf. Matt. 14:22), and is also seen in the SBLGNT and THGNT.

26:45   [τὸ] λοιπόν (still)

The definite article τό is not needed for the sense, and is missing from several important witnesses (03 04 019 032 892 1241). There is also the same variation in the parallel at Mark 14:41 and elsewhere in the New Testament (e.g. 1 Cor. 7:29). As in the previous unit, this may reflect linguistic changes in Greek, with an apparent tendency to remove the definite article: as τό is present in the majority of manuscripts here (and could also have been omitted by accident), this may favour the longer reading.

26:71 οὗτος (this man) {B}

The majority of manuscripts read καὶ οὗτος ('this man also'; 02 04 019 032 037 etc.), but there is early evidence for just οὗτος ('this man'; 01 03 05 sy^s co^{sa, mae}). The latter is preferable in context: no other companion of Jesus has been identified, and there is a strong possibility that καί was added through assimilation to the accusation of the other female servant two verses earlier, καὶ σύ ('you also'). It may also be noted that the shorter reading is found in the source at Mark 14:69. On the other hand, the deletion of καί might have been an editorial improvement. The parallel at Luke 22:59 has καὶ οὗτος, which offers support for either scenario: the longer reading could have been introduced by assimilation to Luke, or Luke may reflect the original Matthean form.

27:2 Πιλάτῳ (to Pilate) {B}

Most Greek manuscripts read Ποντίῳ Πιλάτῳ ('Pontius Pilate'; 02 04 032 etc.), but several important witnesses only have Πιλάτῳ ('Pilate'; 01 03 019 etc., sy^{s, p} cpa^{pt} co Origen). The same variation is seen in the parallel at Mark 15:1. Although 'Pilate' is used by itself in the rest of the narrative, the longer form might have seemed appropriate on this first instance (cf. Luke 3:1), along with his designation as τῷ ἡγεμόνι ('the governor'). Accidental omission is a possibility, but the external evidence suggests that, as in Mark, the expansion is secondary. Nevertheless, in translation it may be appropriate to follow the convention of giving the full name for this first mention of the governor, whichever reading is followed.

27:9 Ἰερεμίου (Jeremiah) {A}

The following quotation appears to derive from Zech. 11:12–13, yet most manuscripts attribute it to Jeremiah, with a variety of spellings (Ἰερεμίου 03 019 and most minuscules, Ἰηρεμίου 01 02 04* etc., Ἰερημίου 04² 205 1292). Only Origen's commentary and the margin of the Harklean Syriac have the correct identification, while the omission of the name (043 33 157 etc.) is likely to be another means of fixing the error. One Old Latin manuscript replaces Jeremiah with the standard prophet Isaiah (as does GA 21, not cited in UBS6). The early and thoroughgoing attestation of Jeremiah indicates that this is the earliest form and probably an authorial error, although it may derive from the use of an intermediate source such as a collection of *testimonia*. Compare the comments above on Matt. 1:7–8, 1:10 and 13:35.

27:16 ['Ἰησοῦν] Βαραββᾶν (Jesus Barabbas) {C}

The name Ἰησοῦν ('Jesus'; 038 f^1 700* sy^s cpa^{pt}) is unexpected, not least as it is not mentioned in any of the other three gospels, yet it occurs consistently in some important witnesses both here and in the following verse. Did Matthew know an alternative source in which Barabbas was also named Jesus, or was this a later Christian tradition which was introduced by an editor? If 'Jesus Barabbas' were the earliest reading, it could easily have been removed through assimilation to the other gospels, perhaps coupled with a desire not to profane the name of Jesus by also having it attached to a 'notorious prisoner' (as expressed by Origen in his comment on the passage). There is no obvious motivation for accidental addition or omission here, but see the following entry.

27:17 ['Ἰησοῦν τὸν] Βαραββᾶν (Jesus Barabbas) {C}

Exactly the same witnesses read 'Jesus Barabbas' here as in the previous verse. Some witnesses have the definite article, τὸν Βαραββᾶν (03 f^1 Origen etc.), but most manuscripts just read the name by itself, Βαραββᾶν (01 02 05 etc.). The key to the reading may be in the extended description of 'Jesus who is called the Messiah': if another 'Jesus' were not present, an early reader may have felt that this double identification required something to balance it in the previous clause. The word preceding 'Barabbas', ὑμῖν ('for you') ends with the letters IN, the *nomen sacrum* for Ἰησοῦν, which through dittography (or the suspicion of haplography) could have led to the insertion of Ἰησοῦν here. The inclusion of the definite article would then match the structure of the following clause and serve to distinguish the two men named Jesus. This might be the origin of the tradition of Barabbas' name also being Jesus, through a variant only preserved in some manuscripts of Matthew: there is a marginal note referring to this in GA 028 and several minuscules, which is often attributed to Anastasius of Antioch as well as better known writers such as Chrysostom and Origen.[44] The appearance of the definite article without Ἰησοῦν is a difficult reading, as it was not

---

[44] See Metzger 1994: 56. On the variation more broadly, see Moses 2012.

used with the name in the previous verse nor in the following clause, and may therefore be indirect evidence for the longer text. On the other hand, if τὸν Βαραββᾶν were original here, it could have prompted the insertion of Ἰησοῦν in the manner just described. Despite the strong external evidence for Barabbas by itself in this and the previous verse (which is preferred in the THGNT), it cannot be excluded that the inclusion of Jesus reflects a tradition known to the evangelist which other Christians found problematic. The SBLGNT text includes the words in brackets, and they are represented in many modern translations.

27:24   τούτου (this man's) {C}

The shorter reading, adopted as the editorial text here and in the SBLGNT, is supported by early and important witnesses (03 05 038 lat[vl-pt] sy[s] etc.). However, it is ambiguous: does it mean 'of the blood of this man' or 'of this blood'? Most Greek manuscripts have τοῦ δικαίου τούτου ('of this righteous man'; 01 019 032 f^1 etc.), but others have the order τούτου τοῦ δικαίου (also 'of this righteous man'; 02 037 lat[vl-pt, vg-ms]) and one minuscule just reads τοῦ δικαίου ('of the righteous man'; 1010). The last of these is clearly due to eyeskip: although it is possible that τούτου by itself arose in the same way, the external evidence (along with the differing sequences) suggests that τοῦ δικαίου was a later addition, possibly to resolve the ambiguity mentioned above. If τοῦ δικαίου τούτου were original, as preferred in the THGNT, the following phrase could be taken as enhancing Pilate's culpability rather than his intended abnegation of responsibility, so this reading also has its difficulties.[45]

27:29   ἐνέπαιξαν (they mocked) {B}

The majority of Greek manuscripts have the imperfect-tense ἐνέπαιζον ('they began to mock'; 02 032 037 038 etc.), but early and important witnesses have the aorist ἐνέπαιξαν ('they mocked'; 01 03 05 019 etc.). The source passage at Mark 15:18 is ambivalent, with an inchoative, ἤρξαντο ἀσπάζεσθαι ('they began to hail'), followed by the aorist ἐνέπαιξαν ('they mocked') two verses later, corresponding to

---

[45] Elliott 1975: 144 also prefers τοῦ δικαίου τούτου on the grounds of its unusual word order. See too Wettlaufer 2007.

Matt. 27:31. These could have prompted assimilation in either direction, and the same variation is seen in the parallel at Luke 23:36. The adoption of the aorist both here and in Luke is based on the external evidence. This verse is included in *ECM Parallel Pericopes*.

27:34   οἶνον (wine) {A}

Most of the oldest witnesses, including a range of early translations, read οἶνον ('wine'; 01 03 05 019 etc.). This differs from the parallels at Mark 15:36 and Luke 23:35, the source at Psalm 69:21 [68:22 LXX], and the majority of manuscripts here, all in support of the reading ὄξος ('vinegar' or perhaps 'poor wine'; 02 032 037 etc.). This makes 'wine' the more difficult reading, although only Matthew has the detail that it is 'mixed with gall'. This was perhaps to accentuate the parallel with the first half of the psalm verse, which would also have the effect of making the wine sour and thus represent the source text.

27:35   κλῆρον (lots) {A}

A few manuscripts read κλῆρον ἐπ' αὐτά ('a lot for them'; 042 892* sy^s), which is an assimilation to the parallel at Mark 15:24. The shorter reading, κλῆρον (lit. 'a lot'; 01 02 03 05 etc.) is attested by the majority of manuscripts, including the oldest witnesses. After this, some later manuscripts include ἵνα πληρωθῇ τὸ ῥηθὲν διὰ τοῦ προφήτου· διεμερίσαντο τὰ ἱμάτιά μου ἑαυτοῖς καὶ ἐπὶ τὸν ἱματισμόν μου ἔβαλον κλῆρον ('in order that what had been spoken through the prophet might be fulfilled, "They divided my clothes among themselves, and for my clothing they cast lots."'; 037 038 0233 etc.). Although it is possible that this was omitted due to eyeskip between the two instances of κλῆρον, the evidence for the shorter reading in the majority of manuscripts is decisive. The additional text, repeating the allusion already made in this verse to Psalm 22:18/19 [21:19 LXX], therefore came from the subsequent introduction of the verbatim text of that psalm or its quotation at John 19:24 (compare also the introduction of Johannine material at Matt. 27:49 below). Nevertheless, it is striking that, in contrast to the quotation formula at that point in John, the form of introduction unique to Matthew (τὸ ῥηθὲν διὰ τοῦ προφήτου, 'what was spoken through the prophet') is used here. This may, however, simply have been reproduced from the previous quotation at Matt. 27:9.

27:40 [καὶ] κατάβηθι (come down) {C}

Only a few witnesses preserve the connective καί ('and'; 01* 02 05 lat$^{vl\text{-}pt}$ sy$^{(s), p}$ etc.) before κατάβηθι ('come down'), but their antiquity means that this reading is worthy of consideration. If it is lacking, there is a question of punctuation: should 'if you are the Son of God' be taken with the preceding command ('save yourself'), the following one ('come down from the cross'), or both? The parallels at Luke 23:37 and 39 suggest the first of these, whereas Mark offers a closer match for the middle option (at Mark 15:32) or the last one (at Mark 15:30). It is possible that καί was added to resolve this problem, but it could also have been overlooked due to its similarity to the following three letters. If the shorter reading is preferred, the tendency in Matthew for conditional clauses to precede imperatives (e.g. Matt. 4:3 and 4:6, 5:29–30, 8:31 etc.) favours punctuating before 'if you are the Son of God'. This is adopted in both the SBLGNT and THGNT. Otherwise, some form of connective is likely to be required in order to co-ordinate the two imperatives.

27:42 βασιλεύς (king) {B}

The majority of manuscripts read εἰ βασιλεύς ('if [he is] king'; 02 032 037 038 etc.), but several of the earliest witnesses just have βασιλεύς ('[he is] king'; 01 03 05 019 etc.). The latter, stating that Jesus is king of Israel, should be interpreted as mockery by the chief priests, as seen clearly in the source parallel at Mark 15:32. It appears, however, that an early reader did not appreciate this, and so added εἰ ('if'), in order to resolve the inconsistency that, despite this statement, the priests did not yet believe in him. This may have been influenced by the conditional clause two verses earlier and it also matches the structure of the following verse. There remains a slight possibility that an original εἰ was omitted by accident, but the wider context and external attestation favour the shorter reading.

27:49 αὐτόν (him) {B}

At the end of this verse, a number of early manuscripts include the text ἄλλος δὲ λαβὼν λόγχην ἔνυξεν αὐτοῦ τὴν πλευράν, καὶ ἐξῆλθεν ὕδωρ καὶ αἷμα ('and another took a spear and pierced his side, and out came water and blood'; 01 03 04 019 and some early translations). This is based on John 19:34, but with a number of differences which are consistent with it having been supplied from memory: strikingly, in John, this episode is after Jesus has died. Its absence from the majority of manuscripts (02 05 032 037 etc.) is not obviously due to accidental omission, but it may have been deleted by an editor because it did not match the expected sequence of events: it also makes Jesus' cry in the following verse appear to be the result of being pierced by the spear. Nonetheless, it would be very odd if Matthew here abandoned his normal correspondence with Mark to include text reminiscent of a detail only found in John, with no hint of it in Luke. The unusual situation of a shorter, non-harmonistic reading being supported by the majority of Greek manuscripts leads to its adoption here, and raises questions about how the early tradition developed: this variant was considered as one of the nine probable 'Western non-interpolations', in which Codex Bezae and other witnesses appear to preserve an original shorter text.[46] The full range of readings in continuous-text Greek manuscripts is given in *TuT Matthew* (TS63); for another instance of Johannine material introduced into Matthew's passion narrative, see Matt. 27:35 above.[47]

27:59 [ἐν] σινδόνι (in a linen cloth)

The preposition ἐν ('in'; 03 05 038 lat[vl-pt] co[sa-mss, bo]) is only present in a few witnesses. It is not required for the sense, and is lacking from the parallels at Mark 15:46 and Luke 23:53, so this is probably an early addition for clarification. Equally, it may have been added by Matthew but then overlooked or omitted through assimilation. Translation is unaffected.

28:6 ἔκειτο (he lay) {A}

The majority of manuscripts read ἔκειτο ὁ κύριος ('the Lord lay'; 02 04 05 019 etc.), and one minuscule even has ἔκειτο τὸ σῶμα τοῦ κυρίου ('the body of the Lord lay'; 1424). Although ἔκειτο ('he lay'; 01 03 038 33 etc.) is only attested by a few witnesses and early translations, it is superior to the others: no subject is needed, as Jesus has already been

---

[46] The others are all in Luke 22–24; see the Overview for Luke and individual discussions below.

[47] On the secondary nature of the longer reading, see also Schmid 2011: 60–61. The attestation of the variant is described in detail in Gurtner 2015.

supplied from the context for the previous verbs. In addition, while Christian readers would naturally think of him as 'the Lord', not only might this seem unusual on the lips of an angel, but Matthew never uses κύριος of Jesus (except for the vocative in direct speech).[48] Both external and internal evidence favour the shorter reading.

28:9   καὶ ἰδού (suddenly) {A}

At the beginning of this verse, most Greek manuscripts include ὡς δὲ ἐπορεύοντο ἀπαγγεῖλαι τοῖς μαθηταῖς αὐτοῦ ('but when they were journeying to tell his disciples'; 02 04 019 037 etc.), but it is absent from several early codices as well around two hundred minuscules and most translations (01 03 05 032 etc.; see *TuT Matthew* TS64). While it is possible that the phrase was omitted through eyeskip between any of its final four words, this repetition could also be indicative of a subsequent intervention to make it clear that that the women had not yet reached the disciples (as anticipated in the previous verse) in order that Jesus' words should not appear redundant (cf. the adjustment in Matt. 14:29 above; see also the repetition discussed at Matt. 12:47). The external evidence is consistent with this being an alteration by a later editor.

28:14   [αὐτόν] (him)

The pronoun αὐτόν ('him'; 02 04 05 019 032 and the majority of minuscules) is missing from some important witnesses (01 03 038 33 etc.). Its absence is the harder reading, as it leaves the verb πείσομεν ('we will persuade') without a formal object, even though it can be understood from the context. While it might be the case that the emphatic preceding ἡμεῖς ('we ourselves') could have led the evangelist to omit the object, it may have fallen out by accident and in translation it will probably be necessary to supply it.

28:15   [ἡμέρας] (day)

The word ἡμέρας ('day') is implicit in τῆς σήμερον ('the present day') and therefore not required for the sense. At both other instances of the phrase in this gospel (Matt. 11:23 and 27:8), ἡμέρας is not included. This makes it likely that, despite the slimness of the evidence for its

---

[48] See Kilpatrick 1968: 65–66.

absence (01* 03* 032 0234), the presence of ἡμέρας in the majority of Greek manuscripts is a later expansion.

28:18   [τῆς] γῆς (earth)

The vast majority of witnesses lack the definite article here ('on earth'), and ἐπὶ τῆς γῆς ('on the earth'; 03 05) is only read in Codex Vaticanus and Codex Bezae. The preference elsewhere in Matthew is for the longer form of the phrase, except in the formula at the end of the Lord's Prayer (Matt. 6:10), although there too most manuscripts include the definite article. Even though it follows the anarthrous 'in heaven', the shorter form is probably the harder reading and so may be preferred here. In any case, there is no significant difference in meaning.

28:20   αἰῶνος (age) {A}

As at the end of most books of the New Testament, the majority of manuscripts include a final Amen.[49] If this were original to Matthew, it would be difficult to account for its absence from a range of important witnesses (01 02* 03 05 032 f^1 33 etc, including many translations). Rather, it seems that this was added in early editions: while no Amen is preferable, it may be justified in a translation which chooses to follow this later practice.

---

[49] On the 'Liturgical Amen', see Wasserman 2023: 60–62.

THE GOSPEL ACCORDING TO MARK

Overview

The main sources for the text of Mark are the same majuscule codices as in Matthew (see above).[1] The principal papyrus is the third-century Papyrus 45 ($\mathfrak{P}^{45}$), which is only extant for parts of Mark 4–12; the sixth-century Papyrus 84 ($\mathfrak{P}^{84}$) contains part of Mark 2 and 6, while the fourth-century Papyrus 88 ($\mathfrak{P}^{88}$) transmits almost all of Mark 2. Two instances of 'block mixture' in majuscule manuscripts are worth noting: both Codex Washingtonianus (032) and the ninth-century Codex Sangallensis (037) preserve an earlier text in Mark than they do in Matthew. In addition to the four regular early biblical translations, UBS6 includes information in Mark from the Gothic version (got).

Despite being the first of the canonical gospels to be written, Mark was largely neglected in antiquity, and was often considered to be an abbreviation of Matthew. There are no major commentaries by early Christian writers, and in the 'Western' order of the gospels (seen in Codex Bezae, Codex Washingtonianus and the Old Latin tradition) it comes last in sequence. Nevertheless, the use of Mark by both Matthew and Luke can be of text-critical significance when shared passages are compared.

The most famous textual variation in Mark concerns its ending (see Mark 16:8 below). Other variants which are often discussed include the presence or absence of 'Son of God' in Mark 1:1, the question of whether Jesus was moved by pity or anger at Mark 1:41, the single or double cock-crow in Mark 14, and Jesus' cry on the cross at Mark 15:34. Alongside the Short Addition and Long Addition at the end of the gospel, there are four verses in the Byzantine tradition of Mark which are not considered part of the earliest text: Mark 7:16, 9:43, 11:26 and 15:27.

---

[1] Note that in the ECM and UBS6, Codex Alexandrinus (02) is considered to be a Byzantine witness and is therefore only cited in Mark when it differs from the majority of manuscripts or the Byzantine tradition is divided. The same is true of $\mathfrak{P}^{84}$ and several other majuscules listed in the introduction of UBS6.

The *Editio Critica Maior* of Mark (*ECM Mark*) was published in 2021 and its editorial text has been adopted in UBS6, leading to several changes from previous editions. There are no longer any brackets in the text: the equivalent in the ECM is a 'split guiding line' where the editorial committee could not decide on the earliest reading. Not all of these are reported in UBS6, but when this does affect a variation unit it is shown by a diamond (◆). *ECM Mark* does not indicate Family 1 and Family 13 in its apparatus, but only the individual members. Alongside the printed volumes of the ECM, the apparatus for Mark is available online along with the presentation of the data used for the Coherence-Based Genealogical Method (CBGM).[2] These resources also feature a textual commentary with notes on some of the ECM editorial decisions, noted at relevant points in the discussion below.[3]

1:1 Χριστοῦ υἱοῦ τοῦ θεοῦ (lit. Christ the Son of God) {C}

The way in which Jesus is characterised in the first verse of the gospel has a significant bearing on how the following narrative is understood: is he identified as 'Son of God' from the first verse or not? The text adopted in the ECM has the support of the majority of Greek manuscripts, Χριστοῦ υἱοῦ τοῦ θεοῦ ('Christ the Son of God'; 037 f^1 f^{13} etc.). Earlier hand editions employed brackets to indicate uncertainty as to whether the earliest reading was Χριστοῦ υἱοῦ θεοῦ ('Christ the Son of God'; 01¹ 03 05 019 032) or just Χριστοῦ ('Christ'; 01* 038 and some early versions). The long string of *nomina sacra* abbreviations, ΙΥ ΧΥ ΥΥ (ΤΟΥ) ΘΥ, could easily have led to oversights or errors (as seen in 1241, which reads Χριστοῦ υἱοῦ τοῦ κυρίου, 'Christ the Son of the Lord'). Alternatively, a shorter original first line could have been expanded by an editor who wished to make it more substantial. The fact that this is the first line of the gospel does not preclude the possibility of scribal error. The CBGM analysis indicates that, despite their early attestation, the two shorter forms emerged independently several times, a situation consistent with one or more words being overlooked

---

[2] See https://ntvmr.uni-muenster.de/ecm and https://ntg.uni-muenster.de/.

[3] This is available online at https://ntvmr.uni-muenster.de/forum/-/message_boards/category/1582011.

by a copyist.[4] In contrast, the coherence of the Byzantine reading has led to its adoption here, even though important witnesses support Χριστοῦ υἱοῦ θεοῦ. The latter formulation is only paralleled in Mark in the affirmation of the centurion at Mark 15:39 (in contrast to Mark 3:11 and 5:7): the absence of the article there could be translated as 'a son of a god', appropriately for the context, whereas in this verse the customary English rendering of 'Son of God' can apply whether or not τοῦ is present. Overall, however, the question remains open: the SBLGNT just reads Χριστοῦ, while the THGNT has υἱοῦ θεοῦ.[5] The suggestion that Mark 1:1–3 is a later addition to the gospel may also be borne in mind.[6] The full attestation for this variant in Greek continuous-text manuscripts is given in *TuT Mark* TS1.

1:2 ἐν τῷ Ἠσαΐᾳ τῷ προφήτῃ (in the prophet Isaiah) {A}

The problem here is that the quotation actually consists of Exodus 23:20 and Malachi 3:1 followed by Isaiah 40:3. The strong early support for the most difficult reading, ἐν τῷ Ἠσαΐᾳ τῷ προφήτῃ ('in the prophet Isaiah'; 01 03 019 037 etc.), which identifies only Isaiah as the source, leads to its adoption here (contrast Matt. 13:35 above). Other important manuscripts lack the first definite article, reading ἐν Ἠσαΐᾳ τῷ προφήτῃ ('in Isaiah the prophet'; 05 038 f^1 etc.). The majority form, ἐν τοῖς προφήταις ('in the prophets'; 032 f^{13} 1342 etc.: see *TuT Mark* TS2) appears to have been introduced by an editor seeking to correct the apparent inaccuracy.

1:4 βαπτίζων ἐν τῇ ἐρήμῳ καί (lit. baptising in the wilderness and) {C}

As at Mark 1:1, the ECM has adopted the reading of the majority of manuscripts, βαπτίζων ἐν τῇ ἐρήμῳ καί ('baptising in the wilderness and'; 032 f^1 f^{13} etc.: see *TuT Mark* TS4). The alternative ὁ βαπτίζων ἐν τῇ ἐρήμῳ ('the baptiser in the wilderness'; 03 33 892*) makes the parti-

---

[4] This is presented in Wasserman and Gurry 2017: 43–50; see also Wasserman 2015a and the *ECM Mark* Textual Commentary.
[5] For further discussion, see Head 1991, Ehrman 2006: 149–154, Wasserman 2011, and the literature cited therein; Strutwolf 2021: 76–80 is important for the evidence in early Christian writers.
[6] Elliott 2000.

ciple into a title, on the model of Ἰωάννης ὁ βαπτιστής (John the Baptist): although ὁ βαπτίζων is the editorial text at Mark 6:14, the correlation here with the participle κηρύσσων and its very poor attestation tell against its adoption in this verse. Similarly, the reading ὁ βαπτίζων ἐν τῇ ἐρήμῳ καί ('who baptises in the wilderness and'; 01 019 037 1342) appears to be an adjustment towards the expected title, but the antiquity of manuscripts with the definite article means that it deserve consideration. The group of witnesses which read ἐν τῇ ἐρήμῳ βαπτίζων καί ('[appeared] in the desert baptising'; 05 038 700 lat^(vl-pt, vg) sy^p etc.) represent an editorial change to focus on John's appearance in the desert rather than the implication that his baptism took place there. The appearance of ὁ βαπτιστής at Mark 6:25 and 8:28 (but not 6:14) offers some support against the use of ὁ βαπτίζων as a title: however, if ὁ βαπτίζων is adopted as a possible earlier form of title (as in SBLGNT and THGNT), it might be worth distinguishing its translation from that of the standard 'John the Baptist'.[7]

1:14 εὐαγγέλιον (the good news) {A}

The majority of manuscripts read εὐαγγέλιον τῆς βασιλείας ('the good news of the kingdom [of God]'; 02 05 032 037 etc.). There is nothing in context which would explain the omission of τῆς βασιλείας, whereas its addition turns an unusual form ('the good news of God') into a standard phrase involving 'the kingdom of God', which is also present in the next verse. The strong attestation of the more difficult, shorter reading εὐαγγέλιον ('the good news'; 01 03 019 038 etc.) leads to its adoption here. The full attestation for this variant in Greek continuous-text manuscripts is given in *TuT Mark* (TS11).

1:27 τί ἐστιν τοῦτο; διδαχὴ καινὴ κατ' ἐξουσίαν· καί (What is this? A new teaching – with authority! … even) {B}

Several forms are found of this phrase. The majority of manuscripts offer a text with two questions: τί ἐστιν τοῦτο; τίς ἡ διδαχὴ ἡ καινὴ αὕτη; ὅτι κατ' ἐξουσίαν καί ('What is this? What is this teaching which itself is new? Because with authority [he commands] even' 04 037 etc.). Other

---

[7] Strutwolf 2021: 80–81 notes that no early Christian authors who cite this verse treat it as a title; in favour of ὁ βαπτίζων see also Elliott 1981b: 49–50. This unit is also discussed in the *ECM Mark* Textual Commentary.

witnesses lack the first question, perhaps by eyeskip from τί to τίς in the majority text. The simplest form is τίς ἡ διδαχὴ ἡ καινὴ αὕτη; ὅτι κατ' ἐξουσίαν καί ('What is this teaching which itself is new? Because with authority [he commands] even'; 1342 Lect[pt]); Codex Bezae appears to be a corruption of this: τίς ἡ διδαχὴ ἐκείνη ἡ καινὴ αὕτη ἡ ἐξουσία ὅτι καί ('What is that teaching? It is new authority itself. Because [he commands] even'; 05 lat[vl·pt]) features a partial repetition (ἐκείνη ἡ καινή) and the loss of the preposition before ἐξουσία. Codex Washingtonianus has an unusual adjective which seems to be an expansion: τίς ἡ διδαχὴ ἡ καινὴ αὕτη ἡ ἐξουσιαστικὴ αὐτοῦ καὶ ὅτι ('What is this teaching which itself is new, his authoritative nature? Because he also [commands]'; 032 lat[vl·pt]). The abrupt reading adopted as the editorial text has early if limited attestation (01 03 019 etc.), and suggests that the majority form is a smoother, expanded version which still led to some confusion among individual copyists. Nevertheless, the double question of the Byzantine tradition has been claimed to be typical of Markan style.[8] Various forms of punctuation can be applied to some of these readings, such as a break after καινή rather than ἐξουσίαν ('a new teaching. With authority he even' as seen in SBLGNT): the connection of ἐξουσίαν with διδάσκων in Mark 1:22 supports the punctuation adopted in UBS6, although the alternative is reflected in the parallel passage at Luke 4:36.

1:34 αὐτόν (him) {A}

The shortest text, adopted here, is found in the *Textus Receptus* and many minuscules (01* 02 05 037 etc.). The rest of Byzantine tradition has an expansion which is also attested in early witnesses, αὐτὸν Χριστὸν εἶναι ('[they knew] him to be Christ'; 03 019 032 *f*[1] etc.); other manuscripts read τὸν Χριστὸν αὐτὸν εἶναι ('[they knew] him to be the Christ'; 01[2] 011 *f*[13] etc.; a different word order is found in 04 0233 892), which matches the parallel at Luke 4:41. These longer forms appear to have been motivated by a desire to clarify the way in which the demons 'know' Jesus, in line with the treatment in Luke. Ten different variants are listed here in *TuT Mark* (TS20).

---

[8] Kilpatrick 1969: 198–201; Elliott 1981b: 50–52. On the versional evidence for this verse, see Williams in Hill & Kruger 2012: 248–249.

1:40 καὶ γονυπετῶν (and kneeling) {C}

The majority of manuscripts read καὶ γονυπετῶν αὐτόν ('and kneeling before him'; 04 037 f^{13} etc.). However, there is strong early evidence for an intransitive use of the participle, καὶ γονυπετῶν ('and kneeling'; 01 019 038 f^1 etc.), which may have felt incomplete (cf. Mark 10:17; Matt. 17:14, 27:29). Some early witnesses lack this phrase altogether (03 05 011 032 0104 lat^(vl-pt) co^(sa); see further *TuT Mark* TS23). Although the shortest form could be original, with the detail about kneeling added later by someone concerned to present Jesus as divine, the parallel at Mark 10:17 shows that this combination of actions was already established at the time the gospel was written. It is therefore more likely that καὶ γονυπετῶν before καὶ λέγων was overlooked in these witnesses.

1:41 σπλαγχνισθείς (moved with pity) {B}

Almost all Greek witnesses read σπλαγχνισθείς ('moved with pity'; 01 03 04 019 etc.: see *TuT Mark* TS24). Only Codex Bezae reads ὀργισθείς ('moved with anger'; 05 lat^(vl-pt)), which is reflected in early Latin manuscripts and adopted in the SBLGNT.[9] This variant has given rise to much discussion, with the suggestion that 'anger' was the earliest reading which was later tempered to 'pity' by those who either found it inconsistent with their image of Jesus or felt that it did not fit the context.[10] However, the similarity between the two words in Latin (*miseratus* 'moved with pity', *iratus* 'moved with anger') provides a means by which the word 'anger' may have been introduced into the Greek side of a bilingual manuscript, as reflected in Codex Bezae (compare Mark 15:34 below).[11] The strength of the attestation of σπλαγχνισθείς leads to its adoption here, and it may also be noted that no similar variants are associated with the descriptions of Jesus' anger

---

[9] *Text und Textwert* is wrong in citing 1358 as a second witness to ὀργισθείς: it has the following, omissive reading.

[10] For ὀργισθείς as the original reading, see Turner 1926: 157, Ehrman 2003 [2006: 120–141] and Haelewyck 2013; these are countered by Williams 2012.

[11] Omanson 2006: 61–62 observes similarities between the Aramaic words for 'to have pity' and 'to be enraged'. Further consideration of the versional evidence is provided by Johnson 2017. It may also be noted that the Greek noun σπλάγχνα can mean 'anger' as well as 'pity', which may have misled an early translator unaware that the cognate verb is only used in the latter sense.

at Mark 3:5 or 10:14. The latter has led to the suggestion that ὀργισθείς is more characteristic of Markan style, and that the absence of this word from the parallels at Matt. 8:3 and Luke 5:13 may be due to deliberate omission.[12] As σπλαγχνισθείς appears several times of Jesus elsewhere (e.g. Matt. 15:32, 20:34), this term would not have been problematic if it were in Matthew's text of Mark.

2:5 ἀφίενται (are forgiven) {B}

The majority of manuscripts have the perfect-tense ἀφέωνται ('have been forgiven'; $\mathfrak{P}^{88}$ 01 04 05 019 etc.). This matches the version of this account found at Luke 5:20 (see also Luke 7:47–48; John 20:23; 1 John 2:12) and is adopted in the THGNT. In contrast, several witnesses have a present tense, ἀφίενται ('are forgiven'; 03 [037] [038] 33 565 1342), which corresponds to the wording of the saying at Matt. 9:2. The latter form is less common, which favours it as original: it may have been present here initially, from where it was adopted by Matthew, but was then changed to the form which occurs elsewhere in the New Testament. However, it remains possible that the present tense was introduced here in a limited number of witnesses under the influence of the parallel in Matthew. The reading of the following unit (Mark 2:9) could support either scenario. The tense may be considered to have theological significance, in order to determine when the forgiveness took place: translators should note that in both readings this action is complete rather than ongoing.

2:9 ἀφίενται (are forgiven) {B}

The variation here is the same as Mark 2:5, of which this is a quotation. Here, a slightly different selection of witnesses has the present-tense ἀφίενται ('are forgiven'; 01 03 565 1342 lat[vl-pt, vg] eth), showing how copyists might reproduce a reading despite its inconsistency with that appearing four verses previously. The other Synoptic Gospels are consistent with their text in the earlier verse (ἀφίενται at Matt. 9:5, ἀφέωνται at Luke 5:23), and so the same form has been adopted here as at Mark 2:5.

---

[12] Elliott 1981b: 52–53.

2:14 Λευίν (Levi) {A}

Most Greek manuscripts have Levi here, either as an indeclinable Hebrew noun Λευί (01* 02 037 etc.) or with Greek accusative morphology in Λευίν (𝔓⁸⁸ 01² 03 04 019 032 etc.: see *TuT Mark* TS29). A group of early witnesses instead read Ἰάκωβον ('James'; 05 038 f^{13} 565 lat^vl sy^f). This is an accommodation to 'James son of Alphaeus' in the list of disciples at Mark 3:18; the parallel passage at Luke 5:27 also has Λευίν.

2:15–16 αὐτῷ. καὶ οἱ γραμματεῖς τῶν Φαρισαίων ἰδόντες (him. When the scribes of the Pharisees saw) {C}

The editorial text, found in just four Greek manuscripts (03 032 28 124) and some Christian Palestinian Aramaic, includes the unusual phrase 'the scribes of the Pharisees'. This is also seen in other witnesses which punctuate it so as to place the scribes among those who followed Jesus: αὐτῷ καὶ γραμματεῖς τῶν Φαρισαίων. καὶ ἰδόντες ('him also the scribes of the Pharisees. And seeing'; [𝔓⁸⁸ᵛⁱᵈ] 01 019 [037] 33). However, as the verb 'follow' is normally used to indicate discipleship, this does not fit the context. The majority of manuscripts have both the regular punctuation and the more customary double grouping: αὐτῷ. καὶ οἱ γραμματεῖς καὶ οἱ Φαρισαῖοι ἰδόντες ('him. And the scribes and the Pharisees, seeing'; 04 05 038 f^1 etc.). A few witnesses agree with this, but read οἱ δὲ γραμματεῖς ('but the scribes'; 042 700 lat^vl-pt) rather than καὶ οἱ γραμματεῖς. The editorial text has been chosen as the form which best explains the other developments, and is also adopted in the SBLGNT and THGNT. The full attestation for this variant in Greek continuous-text manuscripts is given in *TuT Mark* (TS30).

2:16 ἐσθίει² (does he eat) {B}

The majority of Greek manuscripts have ἐσθίει καὶ πίνει ('does he eat and drink'; 𝔓⁸⁸ᵛⁱᵈ f^1 33 etc.). Early witnesses read only ἐσθίει ('does he eat'; 03 05 032 lat^vl-pt): this could be the earliest form, or an omission through oversight, or an accommodation to the earlier part of the verse which only has ἐσθίει. One majuscule appears to support a second-person plural, matching the address to the disciples: ἐσθίετε ('do you eat'; 038). This is also seen in ἐσθίετε καὶ πίνετε ('do you eat and drink'; 011 042 565 700 cpa), which matches the parallel passage at Luke 5:30. The other variants both include ὁ διδάσκαλος ὑμῶν ('your teacher') as seen in the parallel at Matt. 9:11 (which lacks καὶ πίνει): ἐσθίει ὁ διδάσκαλος ὑμῶν ('does your teacher eat'; 01 1342) and ἐσθίει καὶ πίνει ὁ διδάσκαλος ὑμῶν ('does your teacher eat and drink'; 019 037 f^{13} etc.; 04 has a different word order). The choice of the shortest reading, even though it could be due to omission, is the best way of explaining the readings in Matthew and Luke which, in turn, have led to assimilation here (see also Mark 2:22). The full attestation for this variant in Greek continuous-text manuscripts is given in *TuT Mark* (TS34). This and the following unit are included as examples of harmonisation between the Synoptic Gospels in the textual tradition.

2:22 ἀπόλλυται καὶ οἱ ἀσκοί (is lost and so are the skins) {C}

Most witnesses read ἐκχεῖται καὶ οἱ ἀσκοὶ ἀπολοῦνται ('pours out and the skins will be destroyed'; 01 02 04 [019] etc.), which is very close to the parallel at Matt. 9:17. This, or Luke 5:37, may be behind the reading of Codex Bezae, καὶ οἱ ἀσκοὶ ἀπολοῦνται ('and the skins will be destroyed'; 05 lat^{vl}). The shortest reading has been chosen despite its limited attestation, ἀπόλλυται καὶ οἱ ἀσκοί ('is destroyed and so are the skins'; 𝔓^{88vid} 03 892 co^{bo}), given the likelihood of harmonisation to the parallels which feature two verbs as a natural expansion. While the SBLGNT also has this text, the THGNT adopts the majority reading. It may be noted that Codex Bezae and a few early translations omit the next sentence (ἀλλ' οἶνον νέον εἰς ἀσκοὺς καινούς, 'but one puts new wine into fresh wineskins'; om. 05 lat$^{vl\text{-}pt}$), either through the editorial deletion of a superfluous observation or simply through oversight.

3:14 δώδεκα ἵνα ὦσιν μετ' αὐτοῦ (twelve to be with him) {B}

A longer reading has strong external support: δώδεκα, οὓς καὶ ἀποστόλους ὠνόμασεν, ἵνα ὦσιν μετ' αὐτοῦ ('twelve, whom he also named apostles, to be with him'; 01 03 [04*^{vid}] etc.; 032 and 037 have a different word order and 032 includes μαθητάς, 'disciples'). However, the middle phrase is missing from the majority of manuscripts, which have δώδεκα ἵνα ὦσιν μετ' αὐτοῦ ('twelve to be with him'; 02 04^{2} 019 f^1 etc., with a different word order in 05 lat$^{vl\text{-}pt,\,vg}$). The reference to the apostles is present at the parallel in Luke 6:13, a gospel which has the word 'apostle' on several occasions, but in Mark it is only otherwise found at Mark 6:20 where it refers specifically to those sent out on that particular task. Accordingly, the shorter reading is more compelling and it has been adopted in the ECM as well as the SBLGNT and THGNT. In earlier hand editions, the extra phrase was included in brackets. The full attestation for this unit in Greek continuous-text manuscripts is given in *TuT Mark* (TS45); see also the discussion in the *ECM Mark* Textual Commentary, which observes that ἐποίησεν preceding this clause must be understood as 'determine' or 'appoint'.

3:16 καὶ ἐπέθηκεν ὄνομα (Simon … he gave the name) {C}

Before this phrase, a number of important manuscripts include καὶ ἐποίησεν τοὺς δώδεκα ('And he appointed the twelve'; 01 03 04* 037 565 [1342] co^(sa-ms)). As at Mark 3:14, the ECM prefers the shorter reading found in the majority of Greek manuscripts (04² 05 019 etc.; see *TuT Mark* TS46), as does the THGNT. The additional phrase is an expanded repetition of the beginning of Mark 3:14: it is not required in this context, but serves formally to introduce the list of disciples by name. It is possible that it could have fallen out through eyeskip of a single line, or between the two instances of ΚΑΙΕΠ. Nevertheless, as this kind of resumptive repetition is not a feature elsewhere in Mark, the words may have been introduced by an editor. The difficulty in deciding meant that these words were enclosed in brackets in earlier editions; the SBLGNT (and NRSVue) has the longer text. Other variants are also found in individual witnesses, relating to the end of the previous verse: Codex Washingtonianus, cited here in support of the shorter reading, actually has καὶ περιάγοντας κηρύσσειν τὸ εὐαγγέλιον. καὶ ἐπέθηκεν ὄνομα ('and going around to proclaim the good news. And he gave the name'; 032 lat^(vl-pt)), while Family 13 and Sahidic read πρῶτον Σίμωνα καὶ ἐπέθηκεν ὄνομα ('especially Simon. And he gave the name'; f^{13} co^(sa)). The latter may be an instance of an editor enhancing the prestige of Peter, assimilating to Matt. 10:2, or simply smoothing the transition between the previous verse and the list of disciples.

3:18 Καναναῖον (Cananaean) {A}

The majority of Greek manuscripts describe Simon as Κανανίτην ('the Cananite'; 038 f^1 f^{13} etc.), as they also do at Matt. 10:4. However, in both cases, there is strong external evidence for Καναναῖον ('the Zealot'; 01 03 04 05 019 etc.), which prompts its adoption here. If it is not simply a harmonisation, the Byzantine form may stem from the understanding of Καναναῖον as 'Cananaean' rather than deriving from the Aramaic word for 'zealot'. The CBGM shows an incoherent attestation for Καναναῖον, suggesting that it was reintroduced into the tradition at a later point. Translators have the option of either rendering.

3:29 ἁμαρτήματος (sin) {B}

The reference to an 'eternal sin' is a difficult reading, but with strong early support (01 03 019 037 038 etc.). The majority of manuscripts have κρίσεως ('judgment'; 04^2 f^1 etc.), the noun which is also found after ἔνοχος ('guilty of') in Matt. 5:21–22, even though there is no other instance of 'eternal judgment' elsewhere in the New Testament. Another parallel, Matt. 25:46, is likely to have prompted κολάσεως ('punishment'; see *TuT Mark* TS52). Other witnesses have the standard word for 'sin', ἁμαρτίας (04^{*vid} 05 032 f^{13} Athanasius), even though ἁμάρτημα also appears in the previous verse. The strength of attestation for 'sin' and the lack of parallel elsewhere leads to the choice of ἁμαρτήματος, although it is possible that this was introduced as a replacement for ἁμαρτίας under the influence of the previous verse.

3:32 οἱ ἀδελφοί σου (your brothers) {C}

The manuscript tradition is split between those which include καὶ αἱ ἀδελφαί σου ('and your sisters'; 05 700 Byz etc.) after this phrase, and those which lack it (01 03 04 011 019 etc.: see *TuT Mark* TS55). The shorter reading could have arisen through the accidental omission of the similar phrase, or assimilation to the previous verse or the parallels at Matt. 12:47 and Luke 8:20. The longer reading seems more difficult, given the lack of reference to sisters in the previous verse, but it might have been introduced in anticipation of the mention of a sister in Mark 3:35 or the reference to sisters in Mark 6:3. The CBGM indicates that within Byzantine tradition καὶ αἱ ἀδελφαί σου was omitted on several occasions due to eyeskip, whereas the attestation of the longer reading is entirely coherent (see also the *ECM Mark* Textual Commentary). Earlier versions of the hand edition included καὶ αἱ ἀδελφαί σου in brackets, but the external evidence for the shorter reading as well as the lack of a reference to sisters in the synoptic parallels lead to its adoption in the ECM, as well as the SBLGNT and THGNT.

4:8 ἕν ... ἕν ... ἕν (lit. one ... one ... one) ◆

As the earliest manuscripts of the New Testament lack accents and breathing marks, where the context is ambivalent it can be difficult to decide whether EN represents ἕν ('one') or ἐν ('in'), while EIC could be εἷς ('one') or εἰς ('into'). The majority of minuscules read ἐν ... ἐν ... ἐν ('in [thirty], in [sixty], in [a hundred]'; f^1 33^{vid} 565 892 etc.), but the *Textus Receptus* and some versions support ἕν ... ἕν ... ἕν ('one [thirty], one [sixty], one [a hundred]'; f^{13} *TR* lat got, cf. 032). Some majuscules have EN throughout (02 04² 05 011 038 042), while others have EIC on each occasion (01 04*^{vid} 037). As the subject is neuter, the latter should be expanded as εἰς ('into [thirty], into [sixty], into [a hundred]'). Most surprising are two manuscripts which have a mixture of terms: EIC ... EN ... EN appears in Codex Vaticanus, where a later hand has added the accents εἰς ... ἐν ... ἐν ('into [thirty], in [sixty], in [a hundred]'; 03), while in Codex Regius the accentuation is εἰς ... ἕν ... ἕν ('into [thirty], one [sixty], one [a hundred]'; 019).[13] The reading ἕν, contrasting with the following numbers and giving a new subject for the verb ἔφερεν, is attractive: the construal of this as a preposition ('in') may have led to its replacement by a more appropriate preposition, εἰς ('into'), with 03 and 019 deriving from a source in which the change had only been introduced on the first occasion. On the other hand, the accentuation for ἕν is relatively poorly attested and the *ECM Mark* Textual Commentary considers ἐν the harder reading. Accordingly, the ECM has a split guiding line, allowing that threefold ἕν or ἐν are equally likely: SBLGNT has the former and THGNT the latter. A consideration adduced in favour of 'one' is that the Aramaic number for 'one' is also used as the sign of multiplication ('-times' or '-fold').[14] See also Mark 4:20 below.

4:15 ἐν αὐτοῖς (in them) {C}

The ECM provides a new editorial text, ἐν αὐτοῖς ('in them'; 01 04 019 037 892 lat$^{vl\text{-}pt}$), also seen in the THGNT. Previous editions read εἰς αὐτούς (lit. 'into them'; 03 032 f^1 f^{13}: also the SBLGNT), which conveys more precisely the action of sowing. The majority of Greek manuscripts

---

[13] In *ECM Mark*, the breathings in 019 have been regularised to those of 03².
[14] Metzger 1994: 71.

have ἐν ταῖς καρδίαις αὐτῶν ('in their hearts'; 05 038 33 565 700 etc.). Although it begins with the same preposition as the editorial text, this appears to be an expansion motivated by a desire to emphasise the spiritual interpretation. The variant ἀπὸ τῆς καρδίας αὐτῶν ('from their heart'; 02 eth) is an editorial adjustment of this which construes the complement with the main verb αἴρει ('takes away') rather than the immediately preceding participle ('sown'); it also matches the parallel at Luke 8:12.

4:20 ἕν ... ἕν ... ἕν (lit. one ... one ... one) ◆

The variation here is the same as at Mark 4:8 (see above). Despite the likelihood that the text is the same as that previous instance, the manuscripts which there read EIC here all have EN throughout (including 01 and 019): Codex Vaticanus (03) only has EN as the first term, and lacks both subsequent repetitions. As at Mark 4:20, the ECM has a split guiding line, judging that triple ἕν or ἐν are equally likely.

4:24 καὶ προστεθήσεται ὑμῖν (and it will be added to you) {A}

Several manuscripts lack this phrase (05 032 565 lat^(vl-pt) co^(sa-ms)), presumably through eyeskip from the previous ὑμῖν: there is no obvious reason for its removal, unless it is a harmonisation to the parallel at Matt. 7:2, where it is also absent. In addition, at the end of the phrase the majority of manuscripts include τοῖς ἀκούουσιν ('and it will be added to you who hear'; 02 038 f^1 f^{13} etc.). The strong external evidence for its absence (01 03 04 019 037 etc.) suggests that this is a later expansion. A number of witnesses which lack καὶ προστεθήσεται ὑμῖν but have τοῖς ἀκούουσιν ('to those who hear'; 011 etc.: see *TuT Mark* TS60) suggests that the eyeskip from -θήσεται ὑμῖν to -θήσεται ὑμῖν happened on more than one occasion.

4:40 δειλοί ἐστε; οὔπω (are you afraid? ... still) {A}

There is good external evidence for the editorial text, δειλοί ἐστε; οὔπω ('[Why] are you afraid? Do you not yet [have faith]?'; 01 03 05 019 037 etc.). The form in the majority of manuscripts, δειλοί ἐστε οὕτως; πῶς οὐκ ('[Why] are you so afraid? How is it that you do not [have faith]?'; 04 33 etc.), may be interpreted as a softening of the criticism of the disciples seen in the shorter reading, introduced by an editor: the phrase πῶς οὐ is not otherwise found in Mark.[15] An intermediate form attested by some important witnesses is seen in οὕτως δειλοί ἐστε; οὔπω ('[Why] are you so afraid? Do you not yet [have faith]?'; 𝔓⁴⁵ᵛⁱᵈ? *f*¹ *f*¹³). There is no obvious reason for οὕτως to have fallen out if it were original and it is missing from the parallel at Matt. 8:26: in contrast, the addition of this modifier permits the expectation of some fear rather than none at all. The shortest reading, δειλοί ἐστε οὕτως; ('[Why] are you so afraid? [Have faith!]'; 032) also seems to be a diminution of the criticism, perhaps inspired by Mark 11:22. Some minuscules, with δειλοί ἐστε, ὀλιγόπιστοι; οὔπω ('[Why] are you afraid, you of little faith? Do you not yet [have faith]?'; 579 892ᶜ: see further *TuT Mark* TS62), introduce the characteristically Matthean term from the synoptic parallel.

5:1   Γερασηνῶν (Gerasenes) {C}

Most Greek manuscripts read Γαδαρηνῶν ('Gadarenes'; 04 *f*¹³ 1342 etc.), matching the editorial text of the parallel at Matt. 8:28—although the majority reading there is Γεργεσηνῶν ('Gergesenes'). There is also strong evidence here for Γεργεσηνῶν ('Gergesenes'; 01² 019 037 038 *f*¹ etc.). Both Lukan parallels (Luke 8:26 and 8:37) have Γερασηνῶν ('Gerasenes'), albeit with both variants well attested. This is found in just four Greek manuscripts here (01* 03 05 1282 lat coˢᵃ), and has been adopted on the basis of the external evidence (as in the SBLGNT and THGNT). It is possible that 'Gergesenes' was a correction proposed by Origen, on the basis of his geographical enquiries: Gerasa seems to have been thirty-five miles away from the shore of Lake Galilee, yet it could have been used of the area in general. The incoherent attestation of 'Gergesenes' here, replacing 'Gadarenes' on several occasions, may provide an indication of multiple editors correcting the biblical text with a commentary. While it is difficult to decide between these alternatives, it is clear that Γεργυστηνῶν ('Gergustenes'; 032) and other variations (all reported at *TuT Mark* TS64) are anomalies typical of the transmission of foreign names.[16]

---

[15] Ross 2003: 211 prefers the majority reading, suggesting that it is the editorial text which is softened.

[16] See further Baarda 1969.

5:36 παρακούσας (overhearing) {B}

This is the only instance of this participle in the New Testament, but there is early support for παρακούσας ('overhearing' or 'ignoring'; 01*, 1, 2b 03 019 032 037 892* lat^(vl-pt)). The more common reading, ἀκούσας ('hearing'; 01^(2a) 05 038 f^1 etc.) matches the parallel at Luke 8:50. The majority of manuscripts, however, have a longer form, εὐθέως ἀκούσας ('immediately hearing'; 04 [042] f^{13} 33 etc.). This seems to be an expansion, introducing a typically Markan word, in order to emphasise Jesus' command of the situation. However, the more haphazard activity indicated by the ambiguous word παρακούσας, together with its attestation, leads to its adoption here.

6:3 ὁ τέκτων, ὁ υἱός (the carpenter, the son) {A}

The majority of manuscripts, including many ancient witnesses, read ὁ τέκτων, ὁ υἱός ('the carpenter, the son [of Mary]'; 01 03 04 05 019 032 etc.). A small group instead have ὁ τοῦ τέκτονος υἱὸς καί ('the son of the carpenter and [Mary]'; [𝔓^45 042*^vid 565] f^{13} 33 700 etc.). This is an assimilation to the parallel at Matt. 13:55: it is possible that it was motivated by dissatisfaction at the description of Jesus as a carpenter, but harmonisation is sufficient to explain the variation here. Those who prefer the alternative reading cite a tendency to minimise references to Joseph as Jesus' father.[17]

6:11 μαρτύριον αὐτοῖς (testimony against them) {A}

At the end of this verse, the majority of Greek witnesses have a lengthy extra observation matching the text of Matt. 10:15: ἀμὴν λέγω ὑμῖν, ἀνεκτότερον ἔσται Σοδόμοις ἢ Γομόρροις ἐν ἡμέρᾳ κρίσεως ἢ τῇ πόλει ἐκείνῃ ('truly I tell you, it will be more tolerable for the inhabitants of Sodom and Gomorrah on the day of judgment than for that town'; f^1 f^{13} etc.). The very strong early evidence for the shorter reading (01 03 04 05 019 032 etc. and several versions) and the lack of obvious motivation for an omission means that it has been adopted as the editorial text, with the longer reading considered a harmonisation.[18]

---

[17] Thus Elliott 1981b: 54–55. For the use of this verse in ancient apologetics, see Kannaday 2004: 19–22.

[18] For an example of how a long parallel text could have been added in a margin and later incorporated in the text, see Schmid 2008.

6:14 καὶ ἔλεγον (some were saying) {B}

Most witnesses here have a singular, καὶ ἔλεγεν ('and he was saying'; 01 04 019 etc.), co-ordinating this verb with ἤκουσεν ('he heard') earlier in the sentence. However, there is early evidence for καὶ ἔλεγον (lit. 'and they were saying'; 03 [05] 032 0167? lat^(vl-pt, vg-ms) co^(sa-ms)), which matches the two instances of this verb in the following verse. The plural is preferable, both because of the contrasting clauses in Mark 6:15 and because Herod's own opinion is set out in Mark 6:16. The alteration of ἔλεγον to ἔλεγεν under the influence of the previous verb is much easier to explain than a change in the opposite direction. Nevertheless, it cannot be ruled out that an original singular here was then repeated in Mark 6:16 (as seen in translations based on the Byzantine text or Vulgate, and adopted in the THGNT). The full attestation for this unit in Greek continuous-text manuscripts is given in *TuT Mark* (TS75).

6:20 πολλὰ ἠπόρει (he was greatly perplexed) {C}

The majority of witnesses read πολλὰ ἐποίει ('he did many things'; 04 05 f^1 etc.; see further *TuT Mark* TS80), which has been characterised as a Semitism equivalent to πολλάκις ('often').[19] The variant πολλὰ ἃ ἐποίει ('the many things that he did'; f^{13} eth) is either a deliberate attempt to improve the sense or dittography of the last letter of πολλά. One majuscule reads only πολλά ('many things'; 037 co^(bo-ms)) which seems to be an error. The early witnesses which have πολλὰ ἠπόρει ('he was greatly perplexed'; 01 03 019 038) cannot be easily dismissed: the verb makes better sense in context, even though this is the only time it occurs in Mark. However, it is used of Herod on another occasion at Luke 9:7, which may have led to its introduction here. Either this or the majority reading (which has a parallel at Mark 7:13) could have derived from the other as copying errors (ΗΠΟΡΕΙ and ΕΠΟΙΕΙ): ἠπόρει has been preferred with hesitation on the basis of the external evidence and the consideration that the majority reading results in a tautology which duplicates the following phrase.[20]

---

[19] Blass, Debrunner & Funk 1961: 214 (§414.5). I am grateful to Tommy Wasserman for this reference.

[20] Black 1988a offers arguments in favour of the majority reading.

6:22 θυγατρὸς αὐτοῦ Ἡρῳδιάδος (his daughter Herodias) {D}

Most manuscripts have θυγατρὸς αὐτῆς τῆς Ἡρῳδιάδος ('the daughter of Herodias herself'; 04 [032] 038 f^{13} etc.), or θυγατρὸς τῆς Ἡρῳδιάδος ('the daughter of Herodias'; f^1 etc.: see *TuT Mark* TS81). These match the description of Herodias as Herod's wife at Mark 6:17–19, the mention of the daughter's mother at 6:24 and the parallel at Matt. 14:6. In context, then, the masculine pronoun in θυγατρὸς αὐτοῦ ('his daughter'; 01 03 05 019 037 565), which means that Ἡρῳδιάδος has to be taken as the daughter's name, appears to be an error (or another word has dropped out, such as διά ['by'] or ἀπό ['from'] before Ἡρῳδιάδος). Nonetheless, this reading has strong early attestation and is clearly the most difficult form, which has led to its adoption in the text. The question, however, is whether this reading is too difficult: SBLGNT and THGNT prefer the better sense given by the majority reading.[21] The *ECM Mark* Textual Commentary indicates some inconsistencies in the coherence, including a change from αὐτῆς to αὐτοῦ (predominantly in catena manuscripts) and a possible instance of the editorial text being reintroduced from the majority reading.

6:33 ἐκεῖ καὶ προῆλθον αὐτούς (there … and arrived ahead of them) {B}

The editorial text has early attestation (01 03 892 1342 lat$^{\text{vl-pt, vg}}$) and is indirectly supported by manuscripts which read just καὶ προσῆλθον αὐτούς ('and went over to them'; 0187^{vid}) or ἐκεῖ καὶ προσῆλθον αὐτούς ('there and went over to them'; 019 [037] [038]), in which the verb has been altered to a more common form less appropriate in context. In contrast, a different verb is seen in ἐκεῖ καὶ συνῆλθον αὐτοῦ ('there and went together with him'; 05 [565 700]), which may have been influenced by the preceding word συνέδραμον ('they hurried there'). The majority of manuscripts have a combination of the two forms, ἐκεῖ καὶ προῆλθον αὐτοὺς καὶ συνῆλθον πρὸς αὐτόν ('there and arrived ahead of them and went together towards him'; 𝔓$^{84\text{vid}}$ [02] [022] [042] [f^{13}] etc.).[22] Family 1 reads only καὶ ἦλθον ἐκεῖ ('and went there'; f^1), while

---

[21] Thus also Elliott 1981b: 55–56.

[22] Note that 𝔓^{84} is considered a Byzantine witness and not cited in the ECM or UBS6 when it agrees with the majority of manuscripts: the majuscules are listed here because of their slight differences from the Byzantine reading.

Codex Washingtonianus (032) lacks the entire phrase after ἐκεῖ, probably through eyeskip to the beginning of the next verse. One minuscule also has what seems to be a shorter version of the majority reading, πρὸς αὐτοὺς καὶ συνῆλθον πρὸς αὐτόν ('to them and went together towards him'; 33). It remains possible that all the shorter variants derive from a misreading of the longest form, but the external evidence for the short reading indicates that this is most likely to be the earliest text and the Byzantine reading a conflation.

6:45   εἰς τὸ πέραν (to the other side) {A}

Although almost all manuscripts include this phrase, it is absent from some early witnesses ($\mathfrak{P}^{45}$ 032 f^1 lat$^{vl\text{-}pt}$ sy^s). This may have been an alteration in order better to correspond to the geography of the region, as the town most commonly identified as Bethsaida is east of the river Jordan.[23] However, it is possible that the evangelist was referring to a different settlement on the west side of the lake. This variant has been included to show the way in which considerations of geography may have affected the text: the editorial reading is not in doubt.

7:2   τοὺς ἄρτους (lit. the bread) {A}

At the end of this verse, a very large number of manuscripts include the verb ἐμέμψαντο ('they found fault [with them]'; 022 032 038 042 etc., including *TR*), even though the Byzantine tradition is split between this verb and its absence. Codex Bezae at this point has κατέγνωσαν ('they condemned [them]'; 05). Without a finite verb here, the sentence is grammatically incomplete until ἐπερωτῶσιν ('they asked') in Mark 7:5. Given the length of the intervening explanation, it is unsurprising if it was felt necessary to add a verb at this point. There is no obvious reason why an original verb would have been overlooked, and the fact that two different verbs are present in the tradition also suggests they are later additions: the external evidence for the shorter reading in the editorial text is very strong (01 02 03 011 019 etc.).

---

[23] Metzger 1994: 79. For a more detailed investigation of this verse, see Vaganay 1940.

7:3 πυγμῇ (lit. thoroughly) {A}

The editorial text is attested by almost all Greek manuscripts, but it is unclear how πυγμῇ, literally 'with a fist', is to be understood in context: is it some reference to the process of ritual handwashing which has otherwise been lost? Or does it indicate the completeness of the action, hence the translation 'thoroughly'? It seems that this difficulty—or perhaps a simple misreading—led to the alternative πυκνά ('frequently'; 01 032), which appears to be supported by multiple translations. Other translational forms (e.g. 'first' on the Latin side of Codex Bezae) seem to be a gloss with an expected word. The absence of the word from Codex Sangallensis and the Sinaitic Syriac (037 sy^s) is probably due to eyeskip from MH to MH, although it cannot be ruled out that the word was omitted because of its difficulty: it may be worth adding a note to translations to explain the situation.[24]

7:4 βαπτίσωνται (they wash) {B}

Most Greek manuscripts have the aorist subjunctive βαπτίσωνται ('they wash'; 𝔓⁴⁵? 05 032 038 etc.), which as a single action is a better fit for the context than the poorly-attested present subjunctive βαπτίζωνται ('they are washing'; 037). Vowel isochrony between ω and ο means that some witnesses have a different tense (βαπτίσονται, 'they will wash'; 022 042 1342, and βαπτίζονται, 'they are washing'; 019), while Papyrus 45 might support καταβαπτίσωνται ('they wash completely'). More intriguing is the variant ῥαντίσωνται ('they sprinkle'; 01 03 co^{sa} and over fifty minuscules: see *TuT Mark* TS92). This could be seen as a technical term for ritual washing which was replaced by a more common word (compare Mark 7:3). It is unlikely that an early editor deliberately introduced this word in place of βαπτίζειν because they considered the latter to be distinctively Christian, given the presence of βαπτισμούς later in the verse. The possibility of visual error involving the first three letters cannot be ruled out, especially given the context. Alternatively, the variation may depend on the way in which the sentence structure is interpreted: is the verb reflexive ('they wash/purify themselves') or

---

[24] A survey of possible meanings of πυγμῇ is given by Hengel 1969; Skeat 1990 suggests that the word is a scribal error and may be omitted in translation. Elliott 1981b:73 considers πυκνά original on the grounds that it was more likely to have been replaced by an Atticising editor.

transitive, taking its object as ἀπ' ἀγορᾶς ('[food] from the market')? The stronger attestation of βαπτίσωνται leads to its adoption here, as well as in the SBLGNT and THGNT.

7:4 καὶ κλινῶν (and beds) {C}

The words καὶ κλινῶν ('and beds'; 05 032 038 etc.) are present in the majority of witnesses, an element which is unexpected at the end of a list of kitchen vessels although it could be translated as 'dining couches'.[25] There is early evidence for the absence of this phrase ($\mathfrak{P}^{45\text{vid}}$ 01 03 019 037^c 1342 sy^s co$^{\text{sa-ms, bo}}$), but it may simply be eyeskip (from the initial καί or the previous -ων). While lists often get longer in a textual tradition, deletion due to perceived irrelevance is also a possibility. However, the likelihood of accidental omission is strongest here, so the longer reading is retained in the editorial text. The full attestation for this variant in Greek continuous-text manuscripts is given in *TuT Mark* (TS93). The THGNT prefers the shorter reading.

7:8 ἀφέντες ... ἀνθρώπων. (You abandon ... human tradition) {A}

An additional phrase occurs in the tradition at different points in this verse. In the majority of manuscripts, βαπτισμοὺς ξεστῶν καὶ ποτηρίων καὶ ἄλλα παρόμοια τοιαῦτα πολλὰ ποιεῖτε ('you carry out washings of pots and cups and many other such similar things'; [02] f^{13} 33 700 etc.) appears at the end of the verse. Other witnesses have it at the beginning of the verse, with minor textual variations (05 038 565 lat$^{\text{vl-pt}}$). The Sinaitic Syriac omits the entire verse, due to eyeskip between the two instances of ἀνθρώπων ('of humans'). The longer text is a partial repetition of Mark 7:4, providing specific examples of 'human precepts' or 'human tradition': its absence from many important witnesses ($\mathfrak{P}^{45}$ 01 03 019 032 etc.), combined with its appearance in two different places, is a strong indication that it is a later editorial addition. A full list of variant forms is provided in *TuT Mark* (TS94).

7:9 τηρήσητε (to keep) {B}

Almost all Greek manuscripts have τηρήσητε ('you keep'; 01 03 [which just has τηρῆτε] 019 etc.), while just twelve have στήσητε ('you estab-

---

[25] Cf. BDAG s. v. κλίνη 2, referring only to this verse.

lish'; 05 032 038 f^1 etc.: see *TuT Mark* TS95). Elsewhere in the New Testament, the idea of preserving a tradition (παράδοσις) is expressed by κρατεῖν ('maintain'; Mark 7:3, 7:8; 2 Thess. 2:15: cf. 0211 etc.) or κατέχειν ('hold onto'; 1 Cor. 11:2). Both verbs in this verse appear to be a deliberate variation from the previous one, suggesting that τηρήσητε is the initial text because it is more similar in meaning to κρατεῖτε ('you maintain'). The preceding ἀθετεῖτε ('you reject') may have led an editor to change τηρήσητε to στήσητε in order to improve the logical sequence: such an intervention is often seen in the manuscripts in which στήσητε is found, and the attestation of this reading is incoherent, meaning that this may have happened on more than one occasion. The choice of τηρήσητε in the ECM is a change from earlier editions, but matches the SBLGNT and THGNT.

7:16   *omit verse* {A}

The vast majority of manuscripts include this verse as εἴ τις ἔχει ὦτα ἀκούειν ἀκουέτω ('Let anyone with ears to hear listen'; 05 032 037ᶜ 038 etc.; see *TuT Mark* TS97). This matches Mark 4:23 (see also 4:9), yet here is absent from some early witnesses (01 03 019 037* 0274 etc.). There is no obvious stimulus for eyeskip, although an entire line could have been overlooked in an exemplar. However, given the similarity with the context of Mark 4:9, where Jesus concludes a parable before explaining it to his disciples, it is quite possible that an editor or reader noted the parallel and introduced the same text here as well. The appeal to the crowd to listen and understand in Mark 7:14 renders this command superfluous, and it is not present in the parallel at Matt. 15:11. This and the external evidence led the editors to prefer the shorter reading. The *ECM Mark* Textual Commentary suggests that the verse may be a liturgical addition, as it closes the passage read on Tuesday in the sixteenth week after Pentecost but is absent from that on the following day: the surviving lectionary tradition is split at this point.

7:19   καθαρίζων (he declared clean) {A}

The strongest external evidence has the masculine participle, καθαρίζων (lit. 'making clean'; 01 02 03 011 019 032 etc.), which must have Jesus as its implied subject and thus be taken as a metaphor ('declaring clean' rather than actually 'making clean'). The Byzantine tradition has a neuter singular καθαρίζον ('making clean'; 33^vid 700 etc.), whose subject is the same as that of the four previous verbs, πᾶν τὸ ἔξωθεν ('whatever ... from outside'). Despite being the easier reading grammatically, the literal understanding of food itself making all foods clean offers less good sense, unless the meaning is 'purging' (as in the KJV). The poorly-attested finite verb καθαρίζει ('he/it declares/makes clean'; 05 lat^vl-pt got) is probably a translational variant attempting to improve this final participle. Both the meaning and attestation of καθαρίζων lead to its adoption here.

7:24   Τύρου (of Tyre) ◆

The majority of witnesses, including the earliest manuscripts, read Τύρου καὶ Σιδῶνος ('of Tyre and Sidon'; 01 03 f^1 f^{13} etc.). The shorter reading—which would be the only time that Tyre appears in the gospels without Sidon—has significant support (05 019 032 037 038 565 lat^vl-pt sy^s cpa Origen). Accidental omission, through jumping between the two instances of καί, seems unlikely across such a broad range of witnesses, while the addition of Sidon in keeping with the other eight instances (including Mark 3:8 and the parallel at Matt. 15:21) would be an expected assimilation. On the other hand, the shorter form could be an emendation in the light of the further reference to the mountains of Tyre in Mark 7:31 (see below): this may have caused one or more editors to delete the reference to Sidon here in order to avoid a contradiction with the contrast in the later verse. The CBGM indicates that most of the potential ancestors of manuscripts with the short form have the longer reading, which is in keeping with this explanation and has led to the diamond reading here in the ECM; the SBLGNT prefers just Τύρου, while the THGNT has the majority text. Another shorter reading in several of the same witnesses appears in the following entry on Mark 7:28.

7:28   κύριε (Sir) {B}

Before this address, most manuscripts include the affirmative ναί ('yes'; 01 03 019 037 etc.), which makes it clear that the woman has accepted Jesus' words rather than completely opposing him. The absence of this word from some important sources ($\mathfrak{P}^{45}$ 05 032 038 0274 f^{13} 565 700 lat^vl-pt sy^s) renders the tone of the response ambiguous, suggesting that this may later have been clarified by the addition of ναί. What is more, this would be the only time that ναί appears in Mark, adding weight to the likelihood that it was introduced through assimilation to the parallel at Matt. 15:27. The attestation of the shorter text adopted here and in the SBLGNT has some overlap with that seen in Mark 7:24; again, the THGNT follows the majority.

7:31 ἦλθεν διὰ Σιδῶνος (he went by way of Sidon) {A}

There is strong external evidence for the reading ἦλθεν διὰ Σιδῶνος ('he went by way of Sidon'; 01 03 05 019 037 etc.), which is also the less expected form in that it involves a contrast between Tyre and Sidon (see the comment on Mark 7:24 above). The majority of manuscripts have καὶ Σιδῶνος ἦλθεν ('and Sidon, he went'; 𝔓^{45vid} 032 0131^{vid} f^1 etc.: see *TuT Mark* TS98), which has the standard pairing of 'Tyre and Sidon' rather than the contrast. It is likely that this was introduced through harmonisation, perhaps to ensure consistency with the observation seven verses earlier. There is also a possibility that an editor adjusted the text to simplify Jesus' route: the editorial text implies that he first went north from Tyre to Sidon before heading southeast towards the Sea of Galilee, although no reason for this doubling-back is given in the text. The variant is therefore also of interest in mapping the narrative onto the geography of the land (cf. Mark 8:10).

7:35 καὶ ἠνοίγησαν (And … were opened) {B}

After the initial καί ('and'), the majority of manuscripts include εὐθέως ('immediately'; 𝔓^{45} 032 038 etc.). It is missing from a number of early witnesses (01 03 05 019 037 etc.), yet some of these include εὐθύς after the next καί ('and immediately [his tongue was released]'; 01 019 037 0274 892: see *TuT Mark* TS100). The adverb εὐθύς ('immediately'), usually written as εὐθέως in Byzantine tradition, is very frequently used by Mark, occurring some forty times in the gospel. In addition to the early external evidence for the lack of the adverb here, there is only one instance of εὐθύς (GA 719) among all the manuscripts reported in the ECM. This strongly suggests that it was added at a later point in the tradition, perhaps under the influence of the healing miracle at Mark 5:41 where εὐθύς also follows the translation of an Aramaic term. Although the word was included in brackets in earlier editions (as the only instance of εὐθέως in Mark), it has now been removed from the editorial text on the basis of its attestation (see the *ECM Mark* Textual Commentary). It is also absent from the SBLGNT and THGNT.

8:7   εὐλογήσας αὐτά (after blessing them) {B}

The Byzantine tradition lacks a pronoun, just reading εὐλογήσας ('after blessing'; 33 700 etc.). However, one is present in many manuscripts, as either εὐλογήσας αὐτά (01 03 04 019 037 etc.), or αὐτὰ εὐλογήσας ([02] 022 032 042 etc.). A few witnesses read εὐχαριστήσας ('after giving thanks'; 05 lat[vl-pt]), which seems to be assimilation to the use of this verb in the previous verse. The external evidence is strongest for εὐλογήσας αὐτά, and the change in word order to αὐτὰ εὐλογήσας can be seen as a simple improvement which moves the pronoun away from the main verb (εἶπεν) and closer to the original noun. The absence of the pronoun may be harmonisation to the previous verse, in which 'giving thanks' has no direct object, but it could also have been motivated by theological concerns, to avoid presenting Jesus as blessing the actual fish rather than blessing God for the fish. In some languages, the verb 'to bless' may customarily only take God as subject or object. The full attestation for this unit in Greek continuous-text manuscripts is given in *TuT Mark* (TS102).

8:10   Δαλμανουθά (the district of Dalmanutha) {B}

The name of this place varies: some manuscripts have Μαγεδά ('Mageda'; 05[c] 565 lat[vl] cpa) or Μαγδαλά ('Magdala'; 038 *f*[1] *f*[13] got), while the first hand of Codex Bezae has Μελεγαδά ('Melegada'; 05). The difficulty appears to be that the place Dalmanutha is not otherwise attested, so some editors sought to resolve the difficulty by replacing it with the place name from the parallel at Matt. 15:39 (Magdala in the majority of manuscripts, Magadan or Magedan elsewhere). The full range of variants is given in *TuT Mark* (TS104).

8:16   ἔχουσιν (lit. they have) {B}

Most witnesses here read ἔχομεν ('we have [no bread]'; 01 04 019 037 038 etc.). According to this reading, the disciples interpret Jesus' warning as directed to them, reflected in Jesus' use of the second-person plural in the following verse, ἄρτους οὐκ ἔχετε ('you have no bread'), although a few manuscripts also have ἔχομεν there, making it a quotation. The alternative reading ἔχουσιν ('they have [no bread]'; 𝔓⁴⁵ 03 032 f^1 etc.) is difficult. It could be taken as direct speech (as implied by Mark 8:17) but directed against the Pharisees and Herod, yet this makes poor sense in the light of the earlier observation in Mark 8:14 that the disciples themselves 'had no more than one piece of bread'. If it is a statement (treating ὅτι as 'because'), the sequence of tenses does not seem to match: this appears to have prompted the variant εἶχαν ('they had'; 05). It is possible that the third-person form was introduced inadvertently by assimilation to the third person in the similar phrase in Mark 8:14 or to διελογίζοντο ('they said') at the beginning of this verse; alternatively, ἔχομεν could have been a correction to the sense of the passage or harmonisation to the parallel at Matt. 16:7 with ἐλάβομεν ('we have brought'). As the harder reading but with early attestation, ἔχουσιν has been preferred in the editorial text (as in the SBLGNT and THGNT), but its genealogical coherence is imperfect and it may have been reintroduced at some point. The challenges of rendering ἔχουσιν in translation may mean that either the tense or the person has to be adjusted in order to make good sense in the target language.

8:26 μηδὲ εἰς τὴν κώμην εἰσέλθῃς (do not even go into the village) {B}

Support for the shortest reading, adopted here, is early but relatively slight ([01*] 01² 03 019 [032] 037* f^1 sy^s co$^{sa, bo\text{-}mss, fa}$). The majority of manuscripts have μηδὲ εἰς τὴν κώμην εἰσέλθῃς μηδὲ εἴπῃς τινὶ ἐν τῇ κώμῃ ('neither go into the village, nor speak to anyone in the village'; [02] 04 037^c etc.). Codex Bezae alone reads ὕπαγε εἰς τὸν οἶκόν σου καὶ μηδενὶ εἴπῃς εἰς τὴν κώμην ('go off into your house and do not speak to anybody into the village'; 05), while some other witnesses present the longest form: ὕπαγε εἰς οἶκόν σου καὶ ἐὰν εἰς τὴν κώμην εἰσέλθῃς μηδενὶ εἴπῃς ἐν τῇ κώμῃ ('go off into your house and if you go into the village do not speak to anybody in the village'; 038 [f^{13} 565] lat$^{vl\text{-}pt, vg}$). These appear to be editorial attempts to resolve the apparent contradiction between Jesus' sending the man to his house at the beginning of the verse and the command not to enter the village (where, presumably, the house was), although the version in Codex Bezae may be a garbled version of the longer text. The main question is whether the shortest reading is an omissive form of the majority reading, or whether the latter is an expansion, perhaps through assimilation to similar commands at Mark 2:11 and 5:19 (cf. Matt. 8:4). According to the CBGM, neither form is fully coherent, suggesting that they were (re)introduced on more than one occasion. Given the difficulties which this verse clearly posed (the ECM reports no fewer than twenty-six variants here, and an even longer list appears in *TuT Mark* TS116), the shortest and earliest reading has been preferred, with the additional material in the majority text considered an explanation of the shorter command. It may likewise be necessary for translators to find a way of explaining the implication of the prohibition.[26]

9:14 ἐλθόντες ... εἶδον (when they came ... they saw) {B}

The majority of witnesses have two singular forms, ἐλθὼν ... εἶδεν ('when he came ... he saw'; 04 05 038 etc.). Although this fits the singular reference to 'him' in the following verse and features the customary distinction between Jesus and his disciples, the group coming down the mountain consists of Jesus, Peter, James and John. While an editor may have corrected a singular in order better to reflect the context, the external evidence for ἐλθόντες ... εἶδον ('when they came ... they saw'; 01 03 019 032 037 044 892 1342 lat[vl-pt] co[sa]) suggests that this is original, and that the singular was introduced following the focus on Jesus in the previous two verses (compare Mark 11:18 below). Translators may wish to indicate that the object τοὺς μαθητάς refers to 'the other disciples', especially if the plural is adopted.

9:16 ἐπηρώτησεν αὐτούς (he asked them) {A}

There is strong support for αὐτούς ('them'; 01 03 05 019 032 etc.), although it leaves it unclear whether Jesus is addressing the disciples, the crowd or the scribes—as well as who the other 'them' is in Jesus' question. The reading in the majority of Greek manuscripts, ἐπηρώτησεν τοὺς γραμματεῖς ('he asked the scribes'; 04 *f*[13] 33 700 etc.) appears to be an attempt to provide some clarification through repeating the construction of Mark 9:14: it results in the only instance in Mark when Jesus

---

[26] For a fuller examination, which prefers the reading μὴ εἰς τὴν κώμην εἰσέλθῃς (01* 032), see Miller 1986.

addresses the scribes rather than the disciples. This would be an unusual feature in terms of Jesus' practice and is unlikely to be authorial.

9:23 τὸ εἰ δύνῃ ('if you are able') {B}

This is a reference back to ἀλλ' εἴ τι δύνῃ ('but if you are able to do anything') in the previous verse, indicated as a quotation by the neuter definite article τό. The oldest extant witness just has εἰ δύνῃ ('if you are able'; $\mathfrak{P}^{45}$), while another important manuscript has τοῦτο εἰ δύνῃ ('this if you are able'; 032), but these are errors or simplifications. The brevity of the quotation has led to its expansion. The majority of Greek manuscripts have τὸ εἰ δύνασαι πιστεῦσαι (04³ [022ᶜ] 044 33 etc.): δύνασαι is a later form of δύνῃ also seen in the majority reading in Mark 9:22, while πιστεῦσαι could be an infinitive ('if you are able to believe') or imperative ('"if you are able?" Believe!'). The presence of the final verb appears to be an assimilation to the following clause, especially when the quotation was not observed: other witnesses read εἰ δύνῃ πιστεῦσαι ('if you are able to believe'; 05 038 565 etc.) or εἰ δύνασαι πιστεῦσαι (also 'if you are able to believe'; f^{13} 700ᶜ). It is unlikely that πιστεῦσαι would have been omitted if it was originally present, and there is significant early support for τὸ εἰ δύνῃ ('"if you are able"'; 01* 03 [04*] [019] 022* 037 etc.).

9:24 παιδίου (of the child) {A}

The difference between the diminutives παιδίου and παιδαρίου (both 'of the little child') and the regular παιδός ('of the child'; f^1 etc.) is negligible. The principal variation here is the presence or absence of μετὰ δακρύων ('with tears'). There is very strong external evidence for the shorter form of text ($\mathfrak{P}^{45}$ 01 02* 03 04* 019 032 037 etc.), suggesting that the longer form in the majority of Greek manuscripts stems from a later intervention to heighten the narrative: there is no other instance of tears in Mark. It is also notable that in some manuscripts the phrase is added earlier in the verse (see *TuT Mark* TS121).

9:29 προσευχῇ (prayer) ◆

The most widespread form by far is the longer text, προσευχῇ καὶ νηστείᾳ ('prayer and fasting'; $\mathfrak{P}^{45\text{vid}}$ 01² 04 05 019 etc.). By contrast, only three Greek majuscules have προσευχῇ ('prayer'; 01* 03 0274 lat^(vl-pt).²⁷ The ubiquity of the phrase 'prayer and fasting' in Christian discourse may have led to the addition of the second element here (cf. Matt. 17:20, 1 Cor. 7:5, and the discussion of Mark 13:33 below). On the other hand, the shorter reading is poorly attested, and could have been accidentally skipped because the next word also begins with κα. For this reason, the ECM has a diamond reading indicating that either form is equally likely. The editorial text here follows the shorter reading adopted both in previous editions and the SBLGNT; the THGNT has the longer form.

9:41   ἐν ὀνόματι (because) {A}

The reading ἐν ὀνόματι (01² 02 03 04* 019 etc.). has good early support: although it involves the Greek word for 'name' (ὄνομα), the meaning of this construction is 'on the grounds', 'for the reason'. The majority of manuscripts, however, read ἐν ὀνόματί μου ('in my name'; 01* 04³ 032 etc.), while numerous others have ἐν τῷ ὀνόματί μου ('in my name'; 05 037 038 f^{13} etc.: see *TuT Mark* TS127). It is easy to see why ὄνομα would be taken literally and supplemented by μου ('my'), given the parallels in Mark 9:37 and 9:39. However, nowhere else in the gospels is this noun followed by ὅτι ('that'): this unusual idiomatic use is therefore adopted as the earliest text. Translators will need to take account of this: the NRSVue tries to get the best of both worlds by transferring 'name' to the following genitive ('because you bear the name of Christ').

9:44   *omit verse* {A}

The majority of manuscripts include ὅπου ὁ σκώληξ αὐτῶν οὐ τελευτᾷ καὶ τὸ πῦρ οὐ σβέννυται ('where their worm never dies and the fire is never quenched'; 05 038 f^{13} etc.) both after Mark 9:43 and 9:45 (see below). However, its absence from numerous early witnesses (01 03 04 019 032 037 etc.) indicates that this is a later addition from Mark 9:48 (based on Isaiah 66:24) to reinforce the formulaic nature of these utterances.

---

²⁷ The inclusion of 706 at this point in the ECM is erroneous; the only minuscule with this reading is 2427, which is a copy of a printed edition based on Codex Vaticanus: see *Text und Textwert* Mark (TS123).

9:45 εἰς τὴν γέενναν (to hell) {A}

The shorter reading adopted as the editorial text has strong external support (01 03 04 019 032 037 etc.). The majority reading, εἰς τὴν γέενναν εἰς τὸ πῦρ τὸ ἄσβεστον ('into hell, into the unquenchable fire'; 05 [022] 038 [f^{13}] etc.) assimilates this verse to the fuller form at the end of Mark 9:43. While the editorial text is unlikely to have arisen by eyeskip, the variant εἰς τὸ πῦρ τὸ ἄσβεστον ('into the unquenchable fire'; 700) is an omission due to jumping between the two instances of εἰς ('into').

9:46 *omit verse* {A}

This variant consists of the introduction of the quotation from Isaiah 66:24 in Mark 9:48 after Mark 9:45 by exactly the same manuscripts which add it at Mark 9:44 (see above). It is noteworthy that these are also the same witnesses which have the longer reading at Mark 9:45 (see previous unit), indicating a sustained editorial reworking of this passage at an early point.

9:49 πᾶς γὰρ πυρὶ ἁλισθήσεται (for everyone will be salted with fire) {B}

The reading unique to Codex Bezae, πᾶσα γὰρ θυσία ἁλὶ ἁλισθήσεται ('for every sacrifice will be salted with salt'; 05 lat$^{vl\text{-}pt}$) not only brings this verse into closer connection with the mention of salt in the following verse but is also a quotation of Lev. 2:13 (following the quotation from Isaiah in the previous verse). If this were original, it is difficult to explain how the alternative metaphorical reading arose, πᾶς γὰρ πυρὶ ἁλισθήσεται ('for everyone will be salted with fire'; [01] 03 019 [032] 037 etc.); rather, it seems that Codex Bezae features a correction which brings the original reading closer to the Septuagint. This was clearly introduced at an early stage, perhaps initially as a marginal annotation, because the majority of manuscripts combine the two readings: πᾶς γὰρ πυρὶ ἁλισθήσεται καὶ πᾶσα θυσία ἁλὶ ἁλισθήσεται ('for everyone will be salted with fire and every sacrifice will be salted with salt'; [04] [038] [044] etc.). Although it is theoretically possible that the two shorter readings are omissive forms of this longer one, the external evidence indicates that this is most likely to be a conflation of the others, as is typical of the Byzantine text. The full attestation for this unit in Greek continuous-text manuscripts is given in *TuT Mark* (TS129). Some Latin witnesses support the form πᾶσα δὲ οὐσία ἀναλίσκεται ('but all substance is used up'; lat[vl-pt]), which appears to be a misreading of the Greek text of Codex Bezae, confusing Θ with Ο and ΛΙ with Ν yet still arriving at something which could make sense in context: it is not clear whether this ever circulated in Greek or was simply a translator's error. Modern translations may need to provide further explanation of the complex metaphor in the editorial text based on the idea of fire and salt as purifying elements.

10:1   καὶ πέραν (and beyond) ◆

The geographical implications of this unit appear to have given rise to the different variants. The shortest form, πέραν ('beyond'; 04² 05 011 032 037 etc.) implies that the region of Judea is beyond the Jordan, the same reading as at the parallel in Matt. 19:1. There is early evidence for καὶ πέραν ('and beyond'; 01 03 04* 019 etc.), which presents the two areas in the opposite order to the expected one. The majority of manuscripts read διὰ τοῦ πέραν ('along the far side'; 700 etc.), which seems to be a correction to make sense of the topography.[28] However, the CBGM indicates that several instances of πέραν arose from this Byzantine reading, suggesting that assimilation to the Matthean form was the principal influence on later copyists. Both πέραν and καὶ πέραν appear in a split guiding line in the ECM, but the external attestation of the latter and its difference from the synoptic parallel favour καὶ πέραν here, as seen in the SBLGNT and THGNT. The full attestation for this unit in Greek continuous-text manuscripts is given in *TuT Mark* (TS130).

10:7   καὶ προσκολληθήσεται πρὸς τὴν γυναῖκα αὐτοῦ (and be joined to his wife) ◆

This text is completely lacking from some important witnesses (01 03 044 892* sy[s] got). This is a hard reading, since it leaves the identification of οἱ δύο ('the two') in the next verse to be determined from the broader context. While it is possible that the other readings are later additions

---

[28] For the translational implications of each of these readings, see Omanson 2006: 86.

either with reference to the original source (Gen. 2:24) or the parallel at Matt. 19:5, the possibility of eyeskip between two clauses beginning with καί (or the two instances of αὐτοῦ καί in certain manuscripts) would explain their omission. The diamond reading in the ECM concerns the inability to decide between these longer forms. Either καὶ προσκολληθήσεται πρὸς τὴν γυναῖκα αὐτοῦ ('and be joined to his wife'; 05 019? 032 038 f^{13} and the majority of minuscules, also the SBLGNT and THGNT), matching the Septuagintal text of Genesis, or καὶ προσκολληθήσεται τῇ γυναικὶ αὐτοῦ (also 'and be joined to his wife'; 02 04 019 022 037 f^1 etc.), corresponding to the parallel in many manuscripts of Matthew, could be the earliest form. There is no significant difference in meaning between them: the change in case is a minor stylistic alteration.

10:19 μὴ ἀποστερήσῃς (you shall not defraud) {A}

This clause is present in the majority of manuscripts, including early witnesses (01 03¹ 04 05 038 0274 etc.). However, it is absent from a large proportion of the tradition (03* 032 037ᶜ 042 etc.: see *TuT Mark* TS135). While eyeskip between the two instances of -ρήσῃς would provide a very likely reason for its omission, it may have been deliberately deleted by an editor: these words are not present in the parallels at Matt. 19:18 and Luke 18:20 and, unlike the other five elements of this quotation, are not found among the Ten Commandments (instead, they reflect Exod. 20:17 or Deut. 24:14). The well-attested longer reading is clearly more difficult, and provides an indication of how the other evangelists edited their source.

10:21 δεῦρο ἀκολούθει μοι (come, follow me) {A}

There is strong external support for the short form adopted in the editorial text (01 03 04 05 etc.). Other witnesses add an element from the similar command to follow at Mark 8:34, with ἄρας τὸν σταυρόν ('having taken up the cross'; 700 and the majority of minuscules: see *TuT Mark* TS138) after this phrase, or ἄρας τὸν σταυρόν σου ('having taken up your cross'; [011] 032 [f^1] f^{13} etc.) before it. The appearance of the additional material in two locations and the slight differences between them indicate that it is a later addition: it does not appear in the parallels at Matt. 19:21 and Luke 18:22.

10:24 ἐστιν (it is) {B}

The reading ἐστιν ('[how hard] it is'; 01 03 037 044* lat^vl-pt co^sa) presents an uncompromising saying about the difficulty of entering the kingdom of God. The alternatives restrict this to rich people: one witness anticipates Mark 10:25 and adds πλούσιον ('a rich man'; 032) at the end of the verse; others repeat the text of Mark 10:23, οἱ τὰ χρήματα ἔχοντες ('those who have money'; lat^vl-pt); the majority of manuscripts read ἐστιν τοὺς πεποιθότας ἐπὶ χρήμασιν ('it is for those who trust in riches'; 04 [05] [038] [*f*¹] etc.). The variety of additions suggest that they are secondary, although there remains a possibility that, as this verse is essentially a repetition of the previous one, a restriction to the wealthy was originally present. The full attestation for this unit in Greek continuous-text manuscripts is given in *TuT Mark* (TS139).

10:29 τέκνα (children) {A}

Before τέκνα ('children'), the majority of Greek manuscripts include ἢ γυναῖκα ('or wife'; 04 044 *f*¹³ etc.), but there is strong external evidence for its absence (01 03 05 032 038 etc.) and both elements are missing from Codex Sangallensis (037). The full attestation is given in *TuT Mark* (TS141). While it could have been omitted through eyeskip, it is more likely that ἢ γυναῖκα was added for the sake of completeness, perhaps through assimilation to the parallel at Matt. 19:29 where, despite its absence from the editorial text, there is even fuller attestation of γυναῖκα. This element is missing from the corresponding list in Mark 10:30 (apart from a handful of minuscules, several of which have the plural, 'wives'!). The ethical implications of the inclusion of γυναῖκα in this list contrast with the Pauline teaching at 1 Cor. 7:12; as noted in the comment above on Matt. 19:29, the absence of ἢ γυναῖκα means that no assumptions are made at this point about the gender of believers.

10:34 μετὰ τρεῖς ἡμέρας (after three days) {A}

There is strong external evidence for μετὰ τρεῖς ἡμέρας ('after three days'; 01 03 04 05 019 etc.), which matches the references to the resurrection at Mark 8:31 and 9:31. In contrast, the majority reading τῇ τρίτῃ ἡμέρᾳ ('on the third day'; 032 038 0233 *f*¹ etc.; see *TuT Mark* TS142) is not otherwise attested in Mark. It seems that this more common phrase has been introduced on the basis of the parallel passages at Matt. 20:19

and Luke 18:33: it is also attested here in Origen, indicating that it entered the tradition very early.[29] The inclusive system of counting means that both readings are likely to have the same meaning, although some suggest that 'after three days' could be taken to mean 'on the fourth day', making Mark differ from the other Synoptic Gospels.[30]

11:3   αὐτὸν ἀποστέλλει πάλιν (will send it back) ◆

Many Greek manuscripts lack πάλιν ('back'), with the majority reading αὐτὸν ἀποστέλλει (lit. 'he sends it'; 04² f^{13} 565 1342 etc.) and others αὐτὸν ἀποστελεῖ ('he will send it'; 011 032 044 f^1 etc.). At issue is the punctuation of the passage: is this phrase part of what the disciples should say, or is Jesus informing them of the expected outcome? The reading αὐτὸν ἀποστέλλει πάλιν (lit. 'he sends it back'; 01 03 04*vid 05 019 etc.) supports the former interpretation that 'the Lord' who 'has need' (ὁ κύριος ... χρείαν ἔχει) promises to return the colt, but πάλιν does not sit well with the following εὐθύς ('immediately'). The others are ambiguous, because either τις ('someone') or 'the Lord' could be the subject depending on where the quoted speech ends. The first of these options raises an additional discontinuity, because τις initially appears to be a bystander yet then turns out to be a person with the authority to send the colt. In this case, πάλιν could have been added as confirmation that direct speech runs until the end of the verse. The future ἀποστελεῖ is likely to be an adjustment to the expected tense. Although the external evidence may favour αὐτὸν ἀποστέλλει πάλιν, adopted in both the SBLGNT and THGNT, the difficulties of αὐτὸν ἀποστέλλει alone lend it strong internal support and πάλιν is also lacking from the parallel at Matt. 21:3. The ECM has a diamond reading indicating that either is equally likely to be the initial text. In some cases, however, the synoptic parallel may have led to the removal of πάλιν (compare Mark 10:1).

11:19   ἐξεπορεύοντο ἔξω τῆς πόλεως (went out of the city) ◆

The majority of manuscripts have a singular, ἐξεπορεύετο ἔξω τῆς πόλεως ('he went out of the city'; 01 04 [05] 038 [f^1] etc.). This matches

---

[29] See Strutwolf 2021: 91.
[30] See further Omanson 2006: 90.

the previous emphasis on Jesus in Mark 11:17–18, but contrasts with the plural in the following verse and, more significantly, the plural in Mark 11:15 describing the entrance of several people to the city. The reading ἐξεπορεύοντο ἔξω τῆς πόλεως ('they went out of the city'; 02 03 [032] 037 044 etc.) would be consistent with this, yet it is somewhat ambiguous because it could be taken with the preceding subject, the chief priests and scribes, or even the crowd as a sense construction. While the plural is preferable from an internal point of view, the external evidence is stronger for the singular. A diamond reading in the ECM signifies that either could have been the initial text. The THGNT adopts the singular (cf. Mark 6:14 above); if the plural is chosen, it may be advisable to specify that the subject is 'Jesus and his disciples' (as in the NRSVue).

11:22   ἔχετε (have) {B}

The majority reading ἔχετε ('have'; 03 04 019 032 037 etc.) could be interpreted as an imperative ('have faith!'), an indicative ('you have faith') or a question ('do you have faith?'). A significant group of manuscripts have a conditional clause, εἰ ἔχετε ('if you have [faith]'; 01 05 038 0233 f^{13} etc.), which could also be translated as a question. Although this offers some clarification, it contrasts with all other instances in the gospels of ἀμὴν λέγω ὑμῖν ('truly I tell you'), which only appears at the beginning of a statement. For this reason, ἔχετε by itself is the more likely reading, and the corresponding instructions in Mark 11:24–25 indicate that the imperative is to be preferred in translation. The introduction of εἰ may be through assimilation to Luke 17:6 (cf. ἐάν in the closer parallel at Matt. 21:21).

11:24   ἐλάβετε (you have received) {A}

There is strong external evidence in favour of the aorist ἐλάβετε ('you received'; 01 03 04 019 032 etc.). Even though this tense appears to contrast with what is known in the present situation, it has been described as 'the Semitic usage of the prophetic perfect (which expresses the certainty of a future action)'.[31] The majority reading, λαμβάνετε ('you are receiving'; 0233^{vid} f^{13} 33 etc.: see *TuT Mark* TS151) seems to be a simple

---

[31] Metzger 1994: 93.

assimilation to the present tense of the three preceding verbs in the clause, although it is preferred by some on the basis of Mark's preference for the present tense.[32] The future λήμψεσθε ('you will receive'; 05 038 f^1 etc.) is an editorial adjustment to the expected tense, as seen in the following verb and the parallel at Matt. 21:22. In translation, it may be necessary to use a different tense to express this future action, or add a word such as 'already'.

11:26   *omit verse* {B}

After Mark 11:25, the majority of manuscripts include, with minor variations, the text εἰ δὲ ὑμεῖς οὐκ ἀφίετε, οὐδὲ ὁ πατὴρ ὑμῶν ὁ ἐν τοῖς οὐρανοῖς ἀφήσει τὰ παραπτώματα ὑμῶν ('but if you do not forgive, neither will your Father in heaven forgive your trespasses'; 04 05 038 f^1 f^{13} etc.). This matches the positive and negative aspects in the parallel at Matt. 6:14–15, while reflecting the phrasing of the previous verse. This could easily have been accidentally omitted due to eyeskip between the two instances of τὰ παραπτώματα ὑμῶν, but the external evidence in favour of the shorter reading (01 03 019 032 etc., including some early translations) suggests that it is likely to be original. The ECM shows that a few minuscules and lectionaries have an even longer text here, supplementing the warning with two sentences corresponding to Matt. 7:7–8 or Luke 11:9–10.

12:36   ὑποκάτω (under) {C}

The preposition ὑποκάτω ('under'; 03 05 032 0233 sy^s) differs from the Septuagintal form of this quotation of Psalm 110:1 [109 LXX]. The latter reads ὑποπόδιον ('a footstool'; 01 019 037 038 etc.), as seen in the majority of manuscripts both in this verse and in the synoptic parallels (Matt. 22:44 and Luke 20:43). Despite very strong evidence for ὑποπόδιον in Luke, the editorial text of Matthew is ὑποκάτω. Either of the other gospels could, therefore, have influenced the reading in Mark: the reading differing from the Septuagint has been adopted here on the basis that it is less common, especially as Codex Bezae often tends to match the original form of such quotations (cf. Mark 9:49 and 10:7

---

[32] Elliott 1981b: 59–60.

above).³³ While the SBLGNT agrees with the editorial text, the THGNT has ὑποπόδιον.

13:8   ἔσονται λιμοί (there will be famines) {B}

The majority of witnesses read καὶ ἔσονται λιμοὶ καὶ ταραχαί ('and there will be famines and disturbances'; 037 f^1 f^{13} etc.: see *TuT Mark* TS167). Codex Bezae has just καὶ λιμοί ('and famines'; 05 etc.), while Codex Washingtonianus reads λιμοὶ ταραχαί ('famines, disturbances'; 032), other witnesses have καὶ λιμοὶ καὶ ταραχαί ('and famines and disturbances'; [038] 565 700 etc.), also with no verb, and a few minuscules read καὶ ἔσονται λιμοὶ καὶ λοιμοὶ καὶ ταραχαί ('and there will be famines and plagues and disturbances'; 042 1342 etc.) probably through assimilation to the parallels at Matt. 24:7 (in the majority text) or Luke 21:11. There is fairly strong external evidence for ἔσονται λιμοί ('there will be famines'; 01² 03 019 044 etc.; see also 05 above). Although it is possible that καὶ ταραχαί was omitted through confusion with the following word, which is ἀρχαί in the majority text, the fact that these witnesses have it as ἀρχή makes this less likely. The fact that there is no other instance of ταραχή ('disturbance') in the New Testament, and nothing corresponding to it in the synoptic parallels, also suggests that this is a later expansion (cf. Mark 9:24 above).

13:33   ἀγρυπνεῖτε (keep alert) {C}

Most Greek manuscripts read ἀγρυπνεῖτε καὶ προσεύχεσθε ('keep alert and pray'; 01 04 019 032 037 etc.). The evidence for the short reading of ἀγρυπνεῖτε alone ('keep alert'; 03 05 lat^{vl-pt} co^{fa}) is relatively slight, but the addition could have arisen from the common association of staying awake and praying (cf. Mark 14:38, Luke 21:36, Eph. 6:18 etc. and the similar variation at Mark 9:29 discussed above). It is possible that the shorter form is the result of assimilation to Mark 13:35, where the verb 'keep awake' is followed by a similar construction. Considering expansion more likely on internal grounds, ἀγρυπνεῖτε has been preferred in the ECM, whereas the THGNT follows the much stronger external ev-

---

³³ It is striking that Codex Bezae also reads ὑποκάτω in Luke 20:43, but this may be a harmonisation to its text of Matt. 22:44.

idence for the longer reading. The full attestation for this unit in Greek continuous-text manuscripts is given in *TuT Mark* (TS170).

14:20   τὸ τρύβλιον (the bowl) {B}

The editorial text here follows the majority reading (01 04ᶜ 05 019 032 etc.; see further *TuT Mark* TS172). Four important witnesses read τὸ ἓν τρύβλιον (lit. 'the one bowl'; 03 04* 038 565). Clearly, this is a more emphatic reading, perhaps reflecting later theological reflection on the unity of the elements at the eucharist. If it were original, it could provide specific information about the Last Supper. However, it is not reflected in the synoptic parallels and is restricted in its attestation. While it is unusual to see a longer reading in Codex Vaticanus than the majority of witnesses, the better attested reading has been preferred.

14:24   τῆς διαθήκης (of the covenant) {A}

Most Greek manuscripts read τὸ τῆς καινῆς διαθήκης ('which is of the new covenant'; 037 f^1 f^{13} etc.), matching the form of the institution narrative at Luke 22:20 and 1 Cor. 11:25. A few witnesses lack the repeated article, with τῆς καινῆς διαθήκης ('of the new covenant'; 892 and multiple early translations. There is strong external evidence in Mark for the absence of καινῆς ('new'), as seen in τῆς διαθήκης ('of the covenant'; 01 03 04 05¹ 019 etc.) and τὸ τῆς διαθήκης ('which is of the covenant'; 05* 032 lat$^{vl\text{-}pt}$). Although it is possible that καινῆς was overlooked through eyeskip from the previous τῆς, the expected direction of change is towards the longer, harmonising reading. A couple of versional manuscripts lack the entire phrase, presumably through a copying error. The full attestation for this unit in Greek continuous-text manuscripts is given in *TuT Mark* (TS173); see also the comment above on Matt. 26:28.

14:30   δὶς ἀλέκτορα φωνῆσαι (the cock crows twice) {B}

The appearance of the adverb δίς ('twice') in the editorial text is problematic: it is separated from the verb which it appears to qualify (φωνῆσαι, 'crows') and in the quotation of this verse at Mark 14:72b it occurs in a different position. What is more, unlike the parallel passages (Matt. 26:34, Luke 22:34, John 13:38), Mark is the only gospel which relates a double cock crow. This appears to have given rise to several editorial attempts to assimilate Mark to the other accounts (see the entries on Mark 14:68 and 14:72a below). The external evidence for the connection of δίς with φωνῆσαι in the present verse is very strong: the editorial text corresponds to the majority of Greek witnesses (03 019 037 044 083 etc.), and the variant ἀλέκτορα δίς φωνῆσαι ('the cock twice crows'; 038 f^{13} 565 etc.) moves the adverb to a more expected place. The other two readings are less well attested and appear to be harmonisations: ἀλέκτορα φωνῆσαι δίς ('the cock crows twice'; 04²) matches the sequence of Mark 14:72b, while the witnesses which only have ἀλέκτορα φωνῆσαι ('the cock crows'; 01 04* 05 032 etc.) assimilate Mark to the other gospels.

14:41 ἀπέχει· ἦλθεν (enough! ... has come) {B}

The majority of manuscripts read ἀπέχει· ἦλθεν ('enough! [The hour] has come'; 01 03 04 019 037 etc.). However, this features an unusual impersonal use of ἀπέχει, meaning 'it is enough'. Several early variants involve alternatives to this, although it is unclear whether in these ἀπέχει is understood to mean 'is lacking', 'is far off' or 'has fully come':[34] Codex Bezae reads ἀπέχει τὸ τέλος καί ('the end and [the hour] are far off'; 05 lat^{vl-pt}); others have ἀπέχει τὸ τέλος· ἦλθεν ('the end is far off: [the hour] has come'; [032] 038 0233 f^{13} etc.); another majuscule just reads ὅτι ἦλθεν ('because [the hour] has come'; 044 [892 lat^{vl-pt}]). The introduction of τὸ τέλος appears to derive from the parallel at Luke 22:37, but the meaning there is clearer. While the additions may colour in some way the portrayal of Jesus here, the shorter majority reading is most like to be original. Discussions of the meaning of ἀπέχει are found in commentaries.[35]

14:68 καὶ ἀλέκτωρ ἐφώνησεν (then the cock crowed) ◆

This phrase is lacking from several important witnesses (01 03 019 032 044* etc.) and a range of early translations, but is present in the majority of manuscripts (04^{vid} 05 037 038 etc.: see *TuT Mark* TS179). Its absence corresponds to the other gospels which have no reference to a cock crowing at this point (Matt. 26:72, Luke 22:57, John 18:25): omission

---

[34] For the last, see Metzger 1994: 96.
[35] See references in Omanson 2006: 98, as well as Müller 1986.

due to harmonisation appears more likely than eyeskip to καί at the beginning of the next verse, although that remains a possibility. Conversely, the detail could have been added by an editor to ensure the literal fulfilment of the prophecy at Mark 14:30 by providing a clear first cockcrow before Mark 14:72a. The ECM marks this with a diamond, indicating that a choice cannot be made between the two readings, although the editorial text of UBS6 continues to print the longer form because this was present in earlier hand editions (albeit in brackets). The tendency of several witnesses with the shorter text to harmonise to the other gospels in this passage (compare Mark 14:30 above and the following entry) provides a reason to prefer the majority reading, which is adopted in the SBLGNT and THGNT.

14:72   ἐκ δευτέρου (for the second time) {B}

Four Greek manuscripts in the ECM do not have this phrase (01 04* 019 579): three of these (01 04* and 579) lack the reference to the double crow in Mark 14:30 (see above), while 01 019 and 579 do not include the first cock crow at Mark 14:68 (see previous unit). Although the possibility that this is the earliest form cannot be ruled out, it is more likely that they reflect an editorial intervention to make the Markan account consistent. One minuscule instead of ἐκ δευτέρου reads δίς ('twice'; 1342), which is likely to be assimilation to Mark 14:30 or the latter part of this verse (see Mark 14:72b). However, the extensive attestation of ἐκ δευτέρου in the majority of manuscripts and most early witnesses leads to its adoption here. The split guiding line in the ECM relates to the presence or absence of the preceding εὐθύς ('immediately').

14:72   ὅτι πρὶν ἀλέκτορα φωνῆσαι δὶς τρίς με ἀπαρνήσῃ (that … before the cock crows twice, you will deny me three times) {C}

The editorial text is only attested by a few witnesses (04[2vid] 019 044 892). The preference for this form, shared by SBLGNT and THGNT, is because the juxtaposition of δίς τρίς ('twice … three times') is considered the most difficult reading.[36] Codex Vaticanus is similar but with an

---

[36] There is a typographical error in the first printing of *ECM Mark*, in which a comma appears before δίς rather than afterwards.

easier order: ὅτι πρὶν ἀλέκτορα δὶς φωνῆσαι τρίς με ἀπαρνήσῃ ('that before the cock twice crows three times me you will deny'; 03 [1342]). The majority of Greek manuscripts read ὅτι πρὶν ἀλέκτορα φωνῆσαι δὶς ἀπαρνήσῃ με τρίς ('that before the cock crows twice you will deny me three times'; f^1 f^{13} 33 etc.), where each verb is qualified by a following adverb; a few witnesses have the order δὶς φωνῆσαι ('twice crows'; 038 565 700). Given the variants earlier in the chapter and the parallels in other gospels (Matt. 26:75, Luke 22:62), it is not surprising to find a number of manuscripts which lack the word δίς ('twice'): ὅτι πρὶν ἀλέκτορα φωνῆσαι τρίς με ἀπαρνήσῃ ('that before the cock crows three times you will deny me'; 01 04* 032 037 etc.). The entire variation unit is missing from Codex Bezae (05 lat[vl-pt]), which seems to be an alternative editorial solution to resolve the inconsistencies.

15:8   ἀναβὰς ὁ ὄχλος (the crowd came) ◆

The majority of manuscripts read ἀναβοήσας ὁ ὄχλος ('the crowd shouted out'; 01² 04 032 037 038 etc.). There is early attestation of ἀναβὰς ὁ ὄχλος ('the crowd went up'; 01* 03 892 etc.), including witnesses which support ἀναβὰς ὅλος ὁ ὄχλος ('the whole crowd went up'; 05 lat[vl-pt] got). Septuagint manuscripts feature several instances of the confusion of ἀναβοῆσαι ('shout out') and ἀναβῆναι ('go up'): the former is not found elsewhere in Mark, whereas ἀναβῆναι appears on nine occasions.[37] While ἀναβοήσας is the less common verb, ἀναβάς may be a more difficult reading given that πάλιν ἔκραξαν ('they cried again') in Mark 15:13 presupposes an earlier shout (unless πάλιν is translated as 'back'). As either could be an error for the other and both are genealogically coherent, the ECM marks both readings with a diamond. The SBLGNT and THGNT both prefer ἀναβάς, which suits the initial arrival of the crowd and may later have been adjusted in the light of Mark 15:13 to a verb which differs from Mark's customary usage. As for the additional adjective, Mark uses πᾶς ('all') or πολύς ('great') to qualify ὄχλος ('crowd'), but never ὅλος ('the whole'): the closest example of this intensifier is ὅλον τὸ συνέδριον ('the whole Sanhedrin') at Mark 14:55 and 15:1, which may have led to its introduction here.

---

[37] See further Metzger 1994: 98.

15:12 ποιήσω (lit. should I do) {C}

There is good external support for just ποιήσω ('[what] shall I do'; 01 03 04 032 037 044 etc.). The majority reading θέλετε ποιήσω ('do you want me to do'; 02 05 038 etc.) could be assimilation to Pilate's previous question in Mark 15:9: the additional verb is missing from the parallel at Matt. 27:22. The CBGM indicates that both readings are inconsistent, suggesting that harmonisation happened repeatedly. It is striking that several of the earlier witnesses which include θέλετε here lack λέγετε in the following unit, suggesting that it could have been part of an editorial rearrangement. Some versional witnesses support θέλετε ἵνα ποιήσω ('do you wish that I do'; lat[vl-pt] sy[h, s]), conforming to later Greek grammar. The THGNT matches the editorial text here, while the SBLGNT has θέλετε ποιήσω (also seen in the NRSVue). The latter reading may be of theological importance because it emphasises the culpability of the crowd.

15:12 ὃν λέγετε (you call) {B}

The majority of witnesses include the phrase ὃν λέγετε ('whom you call'; 01 04 037 044 etc.), which is a difference from Pilate's previous statement in Mark 15:9, where he simply refers to Jesus as 'the King of the Jews'. If the phrase had been introduced here by an editor to indicate some doubt on the part of Pilate, then it should also be present on the earlier occasion. Its absence here, despite significant attestation (02 05 032 038 f^1 etc.) appears to be assimilation to Mark 15:9, although note the observation in the previous unit. Codex Vaticanus lacks ὅν, 'whom', in keeping with its propensity to omit small words. Further evidence in support of the presence of ὃν λέγετε is the parallel at Matt. 27:22, which reads τὸν λεγόμενον Χριστόν ('the one who is called Christ'). The full attestation for this unit in Greek continuous-text manuscripts is given in *TuT Mark* (TS182).

15:28 *omit verse* {A}

After Mark 15:27, the majority of manuscripts include καὶ ἐπληρώθη ἡ γραφὴ ἡ λέγουσα· καὶ μετὰ ἀνόμων ἐλογίσθη ('and the scripture was fulfilled that says: And he was counted among the lawless'; 019 037 038 083 f^1 f^{13} etc.), usually numbered as verse 28. There are no other fulfilment sayings in Mark beginning with this formula (which matches

James 2:23), and the quotation from Isaiah 53:12 corresponds to the form at Luke 22:37 rather than the Septuagint. Extensive early evidence supports the absence of this verse (01 02 03 04 05 044 0184 lat[vl-pt] sy[s] co[sa, bo-mss]) and it is also missing from the parallel at Matt. 27:38. There is no obvious reason for its omission or oversight: eyeskip from the initial καί in such a range of witnesses seems unlikely. It appears rather that the quotation was added from Luke by a later reader, prompted by the mention of bandits in the narrative. The variety of forms in which the extra text is found is provided in *TuT Mark* (TS184).

15:34 ἐγκατέλιπές με (have you forsaken me) ◆

Most Greek manuscripts have the word order με ἐγκατέλιπες ('me have you forsaken'; 04 037 038 f^1 f^{13} etc.), which corresponds to the parallel at Matt. 27:46. In contrast, ἐγκατέλιπές με (01 03 044 etc., adopted in the SBLGNT and THGNT) matches the source of the quotation, Psalm 22:2 [21:2 LXX]. Either of these forms could have been assimilated to the other, and the ECM has a diamond reading allowing that each has an equal claim to be the initial text. The variant ἐγκατέλειπες is an itacistic form which corresponds to the imperfect, 'were you forsaking', although this makes no sense in context. Codex Bezae and some Old Latin manuscripts support ὠνείδισάς με ('have you reproached me'; 05 lat[vl-pt]). It has been suggested that this change was theologically motivated, in order to remove the implication that Jesus was abandoned by God, yet no comparable variation is found for the same word at Matt. 27:46.[38] The preceding Aramaic *sabachthani* clearly corresponds to 'forsaken' rather than 'reproach'. It is possible that ὠνείδισας is a retranslation from a Latin version which interpreted the word as 'abuse' (ἐγκακεῖν)—compare Mark 1:41 above—yet the Latin side of Codex Bezae has *dereliquisti* corresponding to ἐγκατέλιπες. Alternatively, the variant may have arisen through conflating the Septuagint quotation with one from another psalm (e.g. Psalm 35:7 [34:7 LXX], 42:10 [41:11 LXX], cf. 2 Kings 19:22), or assimilation to the context (cf. ὠνείδιζον in 15:32).[39]

---

[38] Ehrman 2011: 168–171.

[39] For more detailed considerations of this variant, see Ehrman 2011: 168–171 and Wasserman 2020: 323–326.

15:39 ὅτι οὕτως ἐξέπνευσεν (that in this way he breathed his last) ◆

There are two forms of shorter text attested in early witnesses: ὅτι οὕτως ἐξέπνευσεν ('that in this way he breathed his last'; 01 03 019 044 892 co[sa, fa]) and ὅτι κράξας ἐξέπνευσεν ('that having cried out he breathed his last'; 032 038 565 sy[s] Origen[lat]). The majority of manuscripts have what looks like a conflation, ὅτι οὕτως κράξας ἐξέπνευσεν ('that in this way having cried out he breathed his last'; 04 037 f^1 f^{13} etc.; see *TuT Mark* TS186), similar to οὕτως αὐτὸν κράξαντα καὶ ἐξέπνευσεν ('him crying out in this way, and he breathed his last'; 05, which lacks the following εἶπεν). The participle κράξας ('having cried out') appears several times elsewhere in Mark, but in Matthew is only present in the parallel passage (Matt. 27:50). It is therefore possible that the majority reading preserves the earliest form of Mark and explains the other readings: the ECM marks it with a diamond to indicate that either this or ὅτι οὕτως ἐξέπνευσεν (as adopted in the SBLGNT and THGNT) could be the initial text. The *ECM Mark* Textual Commentary observes that οὕτως ('in this way') by itself refers back to the previous six verses, whereas with κράξας it indicates a previous cry: perhaps the latter was added to reflect Mark 15:34 or 15:37, or this ambiguity may have led to its deliberate deletion.

15:44 εἰ πάλαι (whether ... for some time) {B}

Almost all witnesses support the reading εἰ πάλαι (01 04 019 044 etc.: see *TuT Mark* TS188): this could mean 'if for a long time' or 'if already'.[40] Some manuscripts read εἰ ἤδη ('if already'; 03 05 032 038 etc.), which matches the previous clause. Although it is possible that πάλαι was introduced to avoid repetition, it is much more likely that it was replaced by ἤδη through assimilation or an editorial intervention to remove the ambiguity. One manuscript reads καὶ εἶπεν ('and he said'; 037), which may be a misreading of εἰ πάλαι or simply a replacement with an expected form. The Sinaitic Syriac corresponds just to εἰ ('if', sy[s]).

16:8 ἐφοβοῦντο γάρ (for they were afraid) {A}

Several forms of the ending of Mark are found in the manuscript tradition: an overall view of all Greek continuous-text manuscripts is given

---

[40] BDAG s. v. πάλαι 3 gives the meaning 'already' with regard to this verse.

in *TuT Mark* (TS190). The 'Short Ending' is attested by the two oldest surviving manuscripts, Codex Vaticanus and Codex Sinaiticus. In these, the gospel ends abruptly at ἐφοβοῦντο γάρ ('for they were afraid'; 01 03). In both cases, this is clearly the end of the text, marked with a *coronis*. Further evidence in favour of the Short Ending is the Sinaitic Syriac, the oldest Sahidic manuscript, the Christian Palestinian Aramaic, and observations in early Christian writers including Eusebius of Caesarea, Severus of Antioch and Jerome. The variety in the other endings suggests that this abrupt form is the initial text, underlying all subsequent forms: the unexpected conclusion with the connective γάρ ('for'), even though this is not entirely unparalleled, has led to the hypothesis that one or more pages was lost from the autograph of the gospel.[41]

The 'Short Addition' is sometimes called the 'Intermediate Ending' or 'Shorter Ending'. It is translated as 'And all that had been commanded them they told briefly to those around Peter. And afterward Jesus himself sent out through them, from east to west, the sacred and imperishable proclamation of eternal salvation. Amen' (NRSVue). This is attested by itself, as an extension to Mark 16:8, only in one of the oldest Latin manuscripts (Codex Bobiensis). However, several Greek manuscripts have both the Short Addition and the Long Addition (019 044 083[vid] [099[vid]] etc.) and there is also versional evidence for this combination as well as patristic testimony to the Short Addition and comments in the margins of manuscripts (e.g. the Harklean Syriac [sy[hmg]]). The linguistic form of the Short Addition (for example, the word συντόμως ['briefly'], found nowhere else in the gospels), and its surprising inconsistency with the first part of Mark 16:8, indicates that it was added to the Short Ending by an early editor who was dissatisfied with its abruptness, and from there became part of wider tradition.

The 'Long Addition', sometimes called the 'Longer Ending', comprises Mark 16:9–20. This material is present in the majority of witnesses (04 05 037 038 f^1 f^{13} etc.). Again, there are linguistic features which, along with the external evidence, suggest that it was not part of the original text of Mark but was composed by an editor as a more suitable conclu-

---

[41] For instances in Classical and later Greek of sentences consisting solely of a verb followed by γάρ, see BDAG s. v. γάρ 1.a.

sion for the gospel than the abrupt ending.[42] At any rate, correspondences with the Long Addition in the Diatessaron and Irenaeus of Lyons suggest that it was in circulation in the second century. Some manuscripts have notes before the Long Addition (e.g. f^1) or marginal symbols which may indicate that its status is dubious (compare John 7:53–8:11). An extended form of the Long Addition in 032 includes the text of the Freer Logion (see Mark 16:14–15 below).

Numerous publications have been dedicated to the question of the ending of Mark and its treatment in the textual tradition, including surveys in most handbooks and commentaries.[43] From a translational point of view, it may be advisable to include translations of each of the different elements as they are presented in the edition, along with a note explaining the situation. The THGNT reproduces the heading in Family 1 before the Long Addition.

It should be noted that the expressions of certainty in the following variation units are to be understood within the context of the confident editorial opinion that the 'Short Ending' is the earliest attainable form.

Short addition Ἰησοῦς (Jesus) {B}

Some manuscripts, including the Old Latin Codex Bobiensis and other early translations, support a longer text such as Ἰησοῦς ἐφάνη ('Jesus appeared'; 044) or Ἰησοῦς ἐφάνη αὐτοῖς ('Jesus appeared to them'; 099). It is easy to see why it was considered appropriate to introduce a verb at this point, given the distance between 'Jesus' and the verb ἐξαπέστειλεν ('sent out'), yet it introduces problems in determining which parts of the rest of the sentence relate to which of the verbs. The shortest reading, Ἰησοῦς ('Jesus'; 019 083 etc.), appears to be the best explanation of the other variants, although there is a faint possibility that ἐφάνη αὐτοῖς could have been omitted though eyeskip after the *nomen sacrum* IC.

---

[42] Metzger 1994: 105 suggests that it may consist of extracts from another early Christian writing which has not been transmitted.
[43] Among these are Aland 1969, Parker 1997: 124–147 and Black 2008. A consideration of the evidence in early biblical quotations is offered by Kiel in the *ECM Mark* Studies volume; for other witnesses see Clivaz, Monier and Batovici 2022.

Short addition σωτηρίας. ἀμήν (salvation. Amen) ◆

The final Amen in the Short Addition is only attested in Codex Regius (019) and a Bohairic manuscript. All other witnesses lack it (044 083 099 etc.). If this were the conclusion of the book, a final 'Amen' might have been expected by copyists and supplied if it were lacking (see also Mark 16:20 below). In contrast, when the Short Addition is followed by the Long Addition, a final 'Amen' could have been removed in the light of the following text. Given the balance of the limited evidence, the diamond reading in the ECM allows that either form may be original. As Codex Bobiensis, the only witness with the Short Addition alone, lacks the 'Amen', this may favour the shorter reading. The SBLGNT includes 'Amen' here, also seen in the THGNT apparatus.

Long addition
16:14–15 ἐπίστευσαν. καὶ εἶπεν αὐτοῖς (believed ... and he said to them) {A}

The extra passage in Codex Washingtonianus (the Freer Gospels) is also known as the Freer Logion. It reads κἀκεῖνοι ἀπελογοῦντο λέγοντες ὅτι ὁ αἰὼν οὗτος τῆς ἀνομίας καὶ τῆς ἀπιστίας ὑπὸ τὸν Σατανᾶν ἐστιν, ὁ μὴ ἐῶν τὰ ὑπὸ τῶν πνευμάτων ἀκάθαρτα τὴν ἀλήθειαν τοῦ θεοῦ καταλαβέσθαι δύναμιν· διὰ τοῦτο ἀποκάλυψον σοῦ τὴν δικαιοσύνην ἤδη. ἐκεῖνοι ἔλεγον τῷ Χριστῷ, καὶ ὁ Χριστὸς ἐκείνοις προσέλεγεν ὅτι πεπλήρωται ὁ ὅρος τῶν ἐτῶν τῆς ἐξουσίας τοῦ Σατανᾶ, ἀλλὰ ἐγγίζει ἄλλα δεινά· καὶ ὑπὲρ ὧν ἐγὼ ἁμαρτησάντων παρεδόθην εἰς θάνατον ἵνα ὑποστρέψωσιν εἰς τὴν ἀλήθειαν καὶ μηκέτι ἁμαρτήσωσιν· ἵνα τὴν ἐν τῷ οὐρανῷ πνευματικὴν καὶ ἄφθαρτον τῆς δικαιοσύνης δόξαν κληρονομήσωσιν. ἀλλά ('And they excused themselves, saying, "This age of lawlessness and unbelief is under Satan, who does not allow the truth and power of God to prevail over the unclean things of the spirits. Therefore reveal your righteousness now"—thus they spoke to Christ. And Christ replied to them, "The term of years of Satan's power has been fulfilled, but other terrible things draw near. And for those who have sinned I was handed over to death, that they may return to the truth and sin no more, that they may inherit the spiritual and imperishable glory of righteousness that is in heaven. But [go into all the world]"; 032, translation from NRSVue). Part of this is also quoted by Jerome, showing that it was present in Latin witnesses in the fourth century, but its origin is unclear. The very slim attestation means that it is highly unlikely that this text was originally part of the Long Addition: it is of interest in that it shows that someone chose to expand this ending at some point, but may not be considered relevant to include in a translation.

16:20   σημείων. (signs) ◆

The majority of Greek manuscripts include a final 'Amen' (04* 019 032 037 038 etc.). The external evidence for the absence of 'Amen' is also early, but relatively slim (02 04² 33 and several versions: see further *TuT Mark* TS196). It is particularly notable that Amen was deleted in Codex Ephraemi Rescriptus, against the prevailing tendency to add it as a formulaic conclusion to a biblical book. The ECM has a diamond reading, indicating that either form may be the earliest text: the SBLGNT lacks 'Amen', while the THGNT includes it.

The Gospel according to Luke

Overview

Luke is preserved in six papyri which were probably copied in the third century. Only four pages survive of Papyrus 4 ($\mathfrak{P}^4$), with portions of Luke 1–6; Papyrus 7 ($\mathfrak{P}^7$) has three verses from Luke 4; Papyrus 45 ($\mathfrak{P}^{45}$) is extant for much of Luke 6–14, but with some large lacunae; Papyrus 69 ($\mathfrak{P}^{69}$) is a single sheet with verses from Luke 21; Papyrus 75 ($\mathfrak{P}^{75}$) is fragmentary for Luke 3–9, but fairly complete from Luke 10 to the end of the gospel; Papyrus 111 ($\mathfrak{P}^{111}$) has a few verses from Luke 17. The earliest complete witnesses are the fourth-century majuscules already listed for Matthew (see the Overview above): the text of Papyrus 75 is very close to that of Codex Vaticanus (03). Among the later majuscules, the palimpsest Codex Zacynthius (040) has an important text of much of the first half of the gospel, while Codex Washingtonianus (032) preserves an ancient form until the middle of Luke 8, after which it corresponds to Byzantine tradition. In addition to the other early translations, a third Coptic version is partly extant in the Achmimic dialect (co^{ach}).

Luke and Acts appear to have been composed by the same author, with stylistic consistency between the two books. At the beginning of the gospel, the author refers to having used multiple sources: it is generally agreed that these include the Gospel according to Mark; some consider the extensive material common to Luke and Matthew to indicate Luke's use of Matthew as well, while others attribute this to a hypothetical shared source designated as Q. Comparing readings in Luke with both Mark and Matthew may thus reveal changes characteristic of the author. It appears that Luke was the source for an abbreviated gospel produced in the first half of the second century by Marcion of Sinope.[1] This has not been transmitted directly, but has to be reconstructed from comments

---

[1] Claims that Marcion's gospel preceded that of Luke fail to take into account the relationship between the Synoptic Gospels. However, Marcion would have been using a copy of Luke which preceded all the surviving documents and may have differed from these in key respects.

in early Christian writers, especially Tertullian, Epiphanius of Salamis and a dialogue known by the name of Adamantius.[2] It is not clear whether Marcion's work has affected the transmission of the canonical Luke. In addition, Luke is included with the other gospels in Tatian's *Diatessaron* (see the Overview for Matthew). There are few extant ancient commentaries on Luke: Origen's homilies on Luke are transmitted in a Latin version, while the commentary by the fifth-century Cyril of Alexandria is largely known only through a Syriac translation.

In keeping with the distinctive 'Western' text of Acts (see the Overview for Acts), there are several readings in Luke which are restricted to 'Western' witnesses, principally Codex Bezae (05) and the Old Latin version (lat^{vl}), The best-known of these are eight shorter readings in the last three chapters (Luke 22:19–20, 24:3, 24:6, 24:12, 24:36, 24:40, 24:51 and 24:52), traditionally described as 'Western non-interpolations', where the majority text resembles one of the other gospels. Opinions are still divided as to whether the shorter form is original or abbreviated by an editor.[3] Codex Bezae is also the sole witness to a saying of Jesus at the end of Luke 6:4, known as the 'Cambridge pericope'. The mention of the angel and drops of blood at Luke 22:43–44 additionally appears to be a later insertion into the gospel, along with Luke 23:17 and 23:34a. In contrast, Luke 17:36 is present in early witnesses but not Byzantine tradition. Other well-known points of variation in Luke are the reference to the 'second-first sabbath' (Luke 6:1), the number of seventy or seventy-two disciples (Luke 10:1, 10:17) and the differences in the Lukan version of the Lord's Prayer (Luke 11:2–4).

The *Editio Critica Maior* of Luke is still in preparation (see the links given in the Overview for Matthew). In addition to the collations in *Text und Textwert*, the International Greek New Testament project provides an extensive apparatus of witnesses to the whole gospel.[4] The text of UBS6 is identical to the two previous editions. Wasserman's

---

[2] See Roth 2015.

[3] The term originally comes from Westcott & Hort. For an overview of the position taken by the editors of UBS4, see the 'Note on Western Non-interpolations' at Metzger 1994: 164–166 and, updated, at Omanson 2006: 160–161. Other studies include Snodgrass 1972, Parker 1997: 148–174, Martin 2005 and Hernández in Hill & Kruger 2012: 133–138.

[4] IGNTP 1984, 1987.

textual commentary on the Lukan travel narrative is cited below in Luke 10–19.

1:15 [τοῦ] κυρίου (of the Lord)

The textual tradition is split mostly between manuscripts which just have κυρίου ('Lord'; 01 02 04 019* f^1 etc.) and those which read τοῦ κυρίου ('the Lord'; 03 05 019ᶜ 032 etc.). In the Septuagint the formula ἐνώπιον κυρίου ('in the sight of the Lord') commonly lacks the article, as seen in the quotation at Luke 1:76 which is the only other instance in this Gospel. Elsewhere, Luke has ἐνώπιον τοῦ θεοῦ ('in the sight of God': Luke 1:19, 12:6, 16:15; cf. 038 044 etc. here). The balance of internal and external evidence makes a decision difficult, although the longer reading may be more unexpected given the parallels elsewhere. Translation is unaffected.

1:28 σοῦ. (you) {A}

At the end of this verse, the majority of manuscripts include the phrase εὐλογημένη σὺ ἐν γυναιξίν ('blessed are you among women'; 02 04 05 037 etc.), which is found in Elizabeth's acclamation at Luke 1:42. The words are absent from most early witnesses (01 03 019 032 etc.) and there is no obvious reason for their accidental omission. This strongly suggests that they were added by an early editor, perhaps conforming this greeting to the liturgical form of the *Ave Maria* ('Hail Mary'). This is seen in a minuscule which reads εὐλογημένη σὺ ἐν γυναιξίν καὶ εὐλογημένος ὁ καρπὸς τῆς κοιλίας σου ('blessed are you among women and blessed is the fruit of your womb'; 1071): wider attestation of this might allow for the possibility of omission through eyeskip from σου to σου, but as a one-off it is clearly an addition.

1:29 ἡ δε (but she) {A}

Most Greek manuscripts here include ἰδοῦσα ('seeing [him]'; 02 04 037 038 etc.). This appears to be assimilation to Zechariah's response at Luke 1:12, which is the previous instance of ἐταράχθη ('was perplexed'). Not only is it missing from most early manuscripts (01 03 05 019 032 etc.), with no obvious grounds for an oversight, but Luke normally puts the participle ἰδών ('seeing') at the beginning of the phrase (e.g. Luke 2:17, 5:8, 8:47 etc.).

1:35 γεννώμενον (the child to be born) {A}

A few witnesses read γεννώμενον ἐκ σοῦ ('the child to be born from you'; 04* 038 f^1 33 lat$^{vl\text{-}pt}$ etc.). The Syriac Peshitta may support γεννώμενον ἐν σοί ('the child to be born in you'; sy^p). The prepositional phrase appears to have been introduced through parallelism with the two previous clauses, which both end with 'you': as the majority of manuscripts have the shorter reading, this has been preferred as the editorial text.

1:46 Μαριάμ (Mary) {B}

Some early Latin manuscripts and ancient writers preserve a tradition in which Elizabeth rather than Mary spoke the *Magnificat* (Luke 1:46–55). These are Codex Vercellensis, Codex Veronensis, the first hand of Codex Rehdigeranus, Irenaeus (on one of two occasions) and Nicetas of Remesiana; Origen was also aware of manuscripts with this reading. The wider context supports this: the previous words are spoken by John the Baptist's mother and there is no contrastive particle; the emphasis of the canticle on God's overturning of human situations suits conception by a barren woman (compare the similar wording of the Song of Hannah at 1 Sam. 2:1–10); the other canticle in this account is pronounced by John's father (the *Benedictus* at Luke 1:68–79); after the *Magnificat* at Luke 1:56, the pronoun αὐτῇ ('Mary remained with *her*') is used for Elizabeth rather than Mary, in keeping with her being the previous subject. It has also been conjectured that the name was originally absent, with different editors expanding the phrase according to different traditions.[5] Nevertheless, the universal Greek support for 'Mary' means that it has been adopted as the editorial text.

1:78 ἐπισκέψεται (will break upon) {B}

The majority of Greek manuscripts have the aorist tense, ἐπεσκέψατο ('has broken upon'; 01^2 02 04 05 037 etc.), but early and important witnesses have the future ἐπισκέψεται ('will break upon'; 01* 03 [019] 032 etc.). This external evidence suggests that the future is original, and the aorist is assimilation to the occurrence of ἐπεσκέψατο earlier

---

[5] *Amsterdam Database* cj10069 [Loisy 1894]. For a full discussion of this variant, see Kloha 2014.

in the canticle at Luke 1:68. On the other hand, there remains a possibility that the evangelist used the aorist, which was then changed under the influence of the two preceding future verbs in Luke 1:76. The interpretation of the phrase may also have affected the tense: if the new dawn (ἀνατολή) is interpreted as referring to John the Baptist then the aorist is appropriate following his birth, whereas if it is Jesus the future offers a better reading because his birth is yet to be described.

2:14 ἐν ἀνθρώποις εὐδοκίας (among those whom he favours) {B}

Most Greek manuscripts read ἐν ἀνθρώποις εὐδοκία ('good will among people'; 01² 03² 019 037 etc.; see further *TuT Luke* TS1), which matches the structure of the previous clause ('peace on earth'). A few witnesses have an even closer parallel, καὶ ἐν ἀνθρώποις εὐδοκία ('and good will among people'; sy⁽ˢ⁾, ⁽ᵖ⁾, ʰ Origen^pt). Several early manuscripts, however, read ἐν ἀνθρώποις εὐδοκίας ('among people of good will'; 01* 02 03* 05 032 etc.). This changes the whole structure from three clauses to two, in which God is contrasted with humans. Both readings are plausible, although the three-clause one is slightly easier and more likely to result from the omission of a single letter than the other way around. The Old Latin reading *hominibus bonae voluntatis* ('to people of good will') offers further support for the editorial text even though it does not obviously include the initial preposition. Exegetically, the phrase 'people of good will', with the qualification implying God as subject ('of God's good will', or 'among those whom he favours' [NRSVue]) had been considered unusual until the discovery of the same construction in the Dead Sea Scrolls, even though the other New Testament instances of εὐδοκία ('good will') are consistent with this (e.g. Luke 10:21, Eph. 1:5 and 9, Phil. 2:13).[6]

2:26 πρὶν [ἤ] (before)

A few important manuscripts lack ἤ (01* 03 032 038 etc.) amidst a variety of wordings for this phrase. The only other instance of πρίν in this gospel is at Luke 22:61, where the additional ἤ is absent from all witnesses apart from Codex Vaticanus and 044, but the shorter reading

---

[6] See further Metzger 1994: 111.

matches the synoptic parallels. It is therefore difficult to be sure as to the original form of this phrase, although translation is the same whichever reading is adopted.

2:33 ὁ πατὴρ αὐτοῦ καὶ ἡ μήτηρ (the child's father and mother) {B}

The oldest manuscripts and early translations provide strong support for the editorial text (01 03 05 032 etc.). The reading of the majority of Greek tradition, Ἰωσὴφ καὶ ἡ μήτηρ αὐτοῦ ('Joseph and his mother'; 02 037 038 044 f^{13} etc.), appears to be an editorial adjustment. This was probably to avoid explicitly identifying Joseph as the father of Jesus at this point in the light of the statement at Luke 2:49, even though some references to the 'parents' of Jesus in this passage were not altered (Luke 2:27, 2:41). Ehrman suggests that this is part of a wider scheme of theologically-motivated changes, while Wasserman argues that the variations are primary stylistic because they are not systematically carried out (see also Luke 2:43 below).[7] A few minuscules have a conflation of the two readings, with Ἰωσὴφ ὁ πατὴρ αὐτοῦ καὶ ἡ μήτηρ αὐτοῦ ('Joseph his father and his mother'; 157 etc.), while part of the Christian Palestinian Aramaic tradition has 'Joseph' but then erroneously lacks 'the mother' despite the following plural participle. The full attestation of this variant in Greek continuous-text manuscripts is given in *TuT Luke* (TS3). It is unnecessary to add 'Joseph' in translation, given the clear references to Mary and Joseph as Jesus' parents (cf. Luke 2:16).

2:35 [δέ] (lit. but)

The particle δέ is missing from some important witnesses (03 019 032 044 lat sy^s). Coming after καὶ σοῦ ('and your') the inclusion of a further conjunction, especially in this position, is a very difficult reading. However, it is attested in the majority of Greek manuscripts and may have been added later to signal that this phrase is a parenthesis. As this is now indicated by punctuation in most editions, sometimes with a change in sequence in translations (e.g. NIV, NRSVue), the presence or absence of the particle has little effect on the meaning.

---

[7] See Ehrman 2011: 65; Wasserman 2012: 329–333.

2:38 Ἰερουσαλήμ (of Jerusalem) {B}

The editorial text is supported by the oldest manuscripts and most early translations (01 03 032 040 etc.), and involves treating this word as an indeclinable noun in the genitive or dative ('of Jerusalem' or 'for Jerusalem'). The majority reading, ἐν Ἰερουσαλήμ ('in Jerusalem'; 02 05 019 037 etc.) seems to have been introduced as a clarification, even though it changes the meaning by describing τοῖς προσδεχομένοις ('those who were expecting') rather than λύτρωσιν ('redemption'). It is, however, possible that an original ἐν was omitted by accident after the previous word ending in ιν. There is some versional support for τῷ Ἰσραήλ ('for Israel'; lat[vl-pt, vg-ms] co[bo-ms] etc.): this is probably because the expected complement of the noun 'redemption' was 'Israel' (cf. Luke 1:68, 24:21), although it may simply have been a misreading of the *nomen sacrum* for Jerusalem (usually ΙΛΗΜ) as that for Israel (ΙΗΛ). The same is true of minuscules which read ἐν Ἰσραήλ ('in Israel'; 1071 1243), a separate secondary development from the majority form. In any case, Jerusalem is used here as a synonym for Israel in general.[8]

2:40 ἐκραταιοῦτο (became strong) {B}

After this verb, the majority of Greek witnesses include πνεύματι ('in spirit'; 02 022 037 038 044 etc.), but it is lacking from the oldest manuscripts and translations (01 03 05 019 032 etc.). It is possible that this word, written as the *nomen sacrum* ΠΝΙ, was accidentally omitted before the following word πληρούμενον ('filled'), but it is more likely that the phrase has been assimilated to the form at Luke 1:80. This variant is of interest for the development of a theology of the Spirit.[9]

2:43 ἔγνωσαν οἱ γονεῖς αὐτοῦ (his parents did [not] know) {A}

There is extensive early support for ἔγνωσαν οἱ γονεῖς αὐτοῦ ('his parents knew'; 01 03 05 019 032 etc.), but Byzantine tradition reads ἔγνω Ἰωσὴφ καὶ ἡ μήτηρ αὐτοῦ ('Joseph knew and his mother'; 02 04 022 [037] 044 etc.). This is similar to the variant at Luke 2:33 (see above), as well as the Old Latin version at Luke 2:41 which replaces 'his parents' with 'Joseph and Mary'. While some have considered these to be theo-

---

[8] Thus Omanson 2006: 112.
[9] For the claim that the longer reading is original, see Ehrman 2011: 108–109.

logically motivated alterations, reflecting unease with the implication that Joseph was Jesus' father, the lack of variation in the same phrase in the Greek text of Luke 2:27 and 2:41 tells against this.[10] Instead, the majority reading seems to have been introduced by the editor responsible for inserting the same phrase at Luke 2:33: this is the last mention of Jesus' parents prior to his statement about his father's house at Luke 2:49, making it appropriate to distinguish Joseph at this point.

2:52 [ἐν τῇ] σοφίᾳ (in wisdom)

Most Greek manuscripts only have σοφίᾳ ('wisdom'; 02 04 05 037 044 etc.), treating it as an instrumental dative matching ἡλικίᾳ ('in age') two words later. A couple precede it with a preposition, ἐν τῇ σοφίᾳ ('in wisdom'; 01 019), while others just have an initial article τῇ σοφίᾳ ('wisdom'; 03 032 579). Although a shorter Byzantine reading is uncommon, the possibility that here it results from assimilation to the following term or, possibly, the dative σοφίᾳ at Luke 2:40 makes for some doubt as to the earliest text. Both the SBLGNT and THGNT prefer the shortest reading. In any case, all three forms are comparable in translation.

3:3 [τὴν] περίχωρον (the region around)

The definite article τὴν is missing from a range of early manuscripts (01 03 019 022 032 044 etc.). Lukan practice elsewhere is not to include the article in such geographical indications (see Luke 4:37 and 10:1), although that would more naturally result in the sense of 'every region' rather than 'all the region'. As only a single region seems to be intended here, the majority reading with the article may be preferable, yet both the SBLGNT and THGNT adopt περίχωρον alone.

3:20 [καί] (lit. and)

The earliest manuscripts lack the connective καί ('and'; 𝔓[75] 01* 03 05 040 lat[vl-pt]). Given that the act of locking John up in prison is already indicated by καὶ τοῦτο ('this too') this may be an editorial deletion, or the accidental omission of καί before κατέκλεισεν. On the other hand the shorter form could be original, with καί being added later by some-

---

[10] See Metzger 1994: 112, Ehrman 2011: 65, Wasserman 2012: 329–333.

one seeking to co-ordinate the two verbs but not realising that the second phrase was dependent on the first. The external evidence and context favour the shorter reading: if this is adopted, punctuation such as a colon will need to be added before this clause or the verb κατέκλεισεν ('he locked up') should be treated as subordinate.

3:22 σὺ εἶ ὁ υἱός μου ὁ ἀγαπητός, ἐν σοὶ εὐδόκησα (You are my Son, the Beloved; with you I am well pleased) {B}

The editorial text is supported by the majority of Greek witnesses, including early manuscripts ($\mathfrak{P}^4$ 01 02 03 019 etc.). This is identical to the parallel at Mark 1:11. One minuscule has the Matthean form, οὗτός ἐστιν ὁ υἱός μου ὁ ἀγαπητός, ἐν ᾧ εὐδόκησα ('this is my Son, the Beloved, in whom I am well pleased'; 1574 co[bo-ms]: see Matt. 3:17 and 17:5), while a few other witnesses have a hybrid, σὺ εἶ ὁ υἱός μου ὁ ἀγαπητός, ἐν ᾧ εὐδόκησα ('You are my Son, the Beloved, in whom I am well pleased'; 033 1253 lat[vl-pt] co[bo-pt]): both of these are clearly assimilations. Most striking, however, is an early form seen in Codex Bezae, Old Latin witnesses and ancient writers: υἱός μου εἶ σύ, ἐγὼ σήμερον γεγέννηκά σε ('My son are you, I have this day begotten you'; 05 lat[vl-pt] Justin). This is an exact match for the Septuagintal text of Psalm 2:7. Was this the authorial text, which was soon conformed to the Markan parallel? Doble notes the use of the same quotation at Acts 13:33, which could support its use here by Luke, while Ehrman suggests that the statement 'I have this day begotten you' could have been taken to support an adoptionist Christology and this resulted in its replacement.[11] While the relatively weak attestation is consistent with the introduction of the Septuagint parallel by an early editor as seen elsewhere (compare especially Mark 9:49, as well as Matt. 2:18, 15:8; Mark 10:7, 12:36 etc.), one may wonder why the same change does not seem to have been introduced in the other Synoptic Gospels.[12] The lack of other examples of Luke preferring quotations from the Septuagint rather than the text of synoptic sources and the very strong external evidence lead to the preference for the Markan text here.

---

[11] Doble 2014, Ehrman 2011: 73–79; see further Wasserman 2012: 334–337 and Wasserman 2020: 308–311.

[12] Compare *ECM Parallel Pericopes* (Strutwolf & Wachtel 2011: 5).

3:32 Σαλά (Sala) {B}

The Lukan genealogy (Luke 3:23/24–38) is missing entirely from two manuscripts (032 579), possibly to avoid duplication with Matthew, while in Codex Bezae it is replaced by the Matthean genealogy in reverse order. In this verse, most Greek manuscripts have Σαλμών ('Salmon'; 01² 02 05 019 etc.), while the two families of minuscules read Σαλμάν ('Salman'; f^1 f^{13}). The first of these matches the parallels at both Matt. 1:4–5 and 1 Chr. 2:11, while 'Salman' is found in this place in the genealogy at Ruth 4:20–21. The most difficult reading is that of the oldest Greek manuscripts and translations, Σαλά ('Sala'; $\mathfrak{P}^4$ 01* 03 sy^s cpa co$^{sa, bo-mss}$). This name is found in a different genealogy which has no obvious connection with the present one ('Shelah', Gen. 10:24, 11:13–15). The external evidence suggests that this is the earliest form, which was later corrected to readings from the parallels. It is possible that Luke drew the genealogy from a separate source (see comment above on Matt. 1:7–8): as noted previously, the principle of consistency means that translators may prefer to read 'Salmon' here in order to match the lists in Matthew and 1 Chronicles.

3:33 τοῦ Ἀμιναδὰβ τοῦ Ἀδμὶν τοῦ Ἀρνί (son of Amminadab, son of Admin, son of Arni) {D}

This section of the Lukan genealogy is beset by variants. The Byzantine tradition is split between τοῦ Ἀμιναδάβ τοῦ Ἀράμ τοῦ Ἰωράμ ('son of Amminadab, son of Aram, son of Joram'; 037 044 [180] 597 700 etc., with some minuscules reading Ἀμιναδάμ) and τοῦ Ἀμιναδὰβ τοῦ Ἀράμ ('son of Amminadab, son of Aram'; 02 05 33 565 etc.). The latter is followed in the Latin Vulgate and *Textus Receptus* and matches the parallel at Matt. 1:3–4: if it was not a deliberate editorial replacement, it may have arisen from the other Byzantine reading through eyeskip between the end of Ἀράμ and Ἰωράμ. The oldest attested reading appears to be τοῦ Ἀδὰμ τοῦ Ἀδμὶν τοῦ Ἀρνί ('son of Adam, son of Admin, son of Arni'; $\mathfrak{P}^{4vid}$ 01* [03] 1241 co^{sa}); Codex Vaticanus lacks the first term, probably due to eyeskip from Ἀδάμ to Ἀδμίν. The appearance of another Adam in the genealogy is problematic, however, and none of these names obviously matches any kings in the Septuagint. The choice of τοῦ Ἀμιναδὰβ τοῦ Ἀδμὶν τοῦ Ἀρνί ('son of Amminadab, son of Admin, son of Arni'; 01² 019 f^{13} etc.) as the editorial text here and in both the SBLGNT and THGNT (with itacistic spelling) seems to be based on its being the next most difficult reading. Other majuscule readings, such as τοῦ Ἀμιναδὰβ τοῦ Ἀδμὶν τοῦ Ἀράμ ('son of Amminadab, son of Admin, son of Aram'; 0102) and τοῦ Ἀμιναδὰβ τοῦ Ἀράμ τοῦ Ἀδμὶ τοῦ Ἀρνί ('son of Amminadab, son of Aram, son of Admi, son of Arni'; 038), appear to be different attempts to introduce correspondence between different genealogies. The unfamiliar names and the similarity between several of them lead to further variants. It has been observed that a reading with three names here leads to a symbolic construction with eleven sets of seven generations, which seems to have been further divided into corresponding subgroups.[13] Nevertheless, the exact reading at this point is very difficult to determine.

4:4 ἄνθρωπος (one) {B}

At the end of this verse, the majority of manuscripts include the text ἀλλ' ἐπὶ παντὶ ῥήματι θεοῦ ('but by every word of God'; 02 [05] 037 038 etc.), with over one hundred minuscules reading ἀλλ' ἐπὶ παντὶ ῥήματι ἐκπορευομένῳ διὰ στόματος θεοῦ ('but by every word that proceeds from the mouth of God'; 157 [205] etc.; the full attestation is given in *TuT Luke* TS4). Both forms are found in the tradition of Matt. 4:4, with the second text offering a closer match to the source at Deut. 8:3. Several of the earliest witnesses lack this phrase (01 03 019 032 1241 sy^s co$^{sa, bo-pt}$ Origen), which suggests that its inclusion is likely to be an assimilation to the parallel in Matthew: there is no obvious reason for it to have been omitted by accident apart, perhaps, from eyeskip between *nomina sacra* if ἄνθρωπος was written as an abbreviation. However, Luke does not shorten any of the other biblical quotations in this episode in comparison with Matthew: at Luke 4:10–11, in fact, the extract from Psalm 91 [90 LXX] has been extended and brought closer to the Septuagint. This makes for some doubt in accepting the shorter reading as the earliest form.

4:17 ἀναπτύξας (he unrolled) {C}

Some of the earliest manuscripts have ἀνοίξας ('opening up'; 02 03 019 032 040 etc.), whereas the majority of the tradition reads ἀναπτύξας

---

[13] Metzger 1994: 166 note 6; this variation unit is also examined in Heater 1986.

('unrolling'; 01 05 037 038 etc.). The latter specifically relates to the use of a scroll, and is co-ordinated with πτύξας ('rolling up') at Luke 4:20 following this quotation: this verb only appears here in the New Testament. It appears that the term ἀνοίξας, also used with τὸ βιβλίον ('the book') in Revelation (e.g. Rev. 5:2–5), is a later introduction, either under the influence of Revelation or reflecting the general adoption of books in codex form. Both participles are similar in appearance and sound, which would promote the substitution of an unusual term by a more common word. On the other hand, no adjustment was made to πτύξας τὸ βιβλίον ('rolling up the book') at Luke 4:20, and it is possible that an original ἀνοίξας was changed to ἀναπτύξας in order to correspond to this. The SBLGNT and THGNT both adopt ἀναπτύξας here. In translation, the rendering of βιβλίον may affect that of this verb: if it is translated as 'scroll', then 'unrolling' is appropriate; if it is rendered by 'book', then 'opening' is likely to make better sense regardless of the reading which is followed.

4:18   ἀπέσταλκέν με (he has sent me) {A}

After the reference to bringing 'good news to the poor', most Greek manuscripts read ἀπέσταλκέν με ἰάσασθαι τοὺς συντετριμμένους τὴν καρδίαν ('he has sent me to heal the brokenhearted'; 02 037 038 044 etc.). This makes the quotation conform to its source, Isaiah 61:1. As a large range of early witnesses and the oldest translations only read ἀπέσταλκέν με ('he has sent me'; 01 03 05 019 032 etc.) and there are no similarities which would prompt omission through eyeskip, it is very likely that this expansion was introduced by an early editor.

4:41   κρ[αυγ]άζοντα (shouting)

The textual tradition is split between κράζοντα ('screaming'; 01 03 04 019 038 etc.) and κραυγάζοντα ('baying'; 02 05 032 037 etc.), with extensive numbers of Byzantine minuscules on either side. Both words, reflecting animal sounds, are appropriate in context. In favour of κράζοντα is the early attestation and the use of this verb at Luke 9:39 and 18:39. Equally, as κραυγάζω does not otherwise appear in Luke (although it is used at Acts 22:23) it might be considered the harder reading, but it could have been introduced through assimilation to the numerous uses of this verb in John.

4:41 σὺ εἶ (you are) {B}

The majority of Greek manuscripts here include ὁ χριστός ('the Messiah', 'Christ'; 02 022 026 037 etc.), making this acclamation correspond to others in the gospels with an explicit statement that Jesus was the Christ (e.g. Matt. 16:16, 26:63; John 11:27 etc.). The extensive attestation for its absence from early manuscripts and most ancient translations (01 03 04 05 etc.) indicates that it is likely to be a later addition. However, it is possible—especially if both were written as *nomina sacra*—that ὁ χριστός was overlooked before ὁ υἱός. Nevertheless, the final clause of the verse, which states that 'they knew him to be the Christ', makes good sense without the extra term and may actually have prompted an early editor to insert it in order to make this explicit in what the demons said.

4:44 τῆς Ἰουδαίας (of Judea) {B}

There is good early evidence for τῆς Ἰουδαίας ('of Judea'; $\mathfrak{P}^{75}$ 01 03 04 019 etc.), but this is a hard reading: the previous section beginning with Luke 4:14 has all taken place in Galilee, which is the logical setting for the 'other cities' mentioned in Luke 4:43 and is found in the parallel at Mark 1:39 (cf. Matt. 4:23), and the following episode is set at the Sea of Galilee. Accordingly, most Greek manuscripts here have τῆς Γαλιλαίας ('of Galilee'; 02 05 037 038 etc.). It remains possible that Ἰουδαίας was an early copying error, but the external attestation suggests that it is the earliest reading. This seems to be confirmed by the presence of two other variants which also resolve the inconsistency, αὐτῶν ('their [synagogues]'; 1424) which introduces the complement from Matt. 4:23, and τῶν Ἰουδαίων ('of the Jews'; 032); the full list of variants is given in *TuT Luke* (TS5). It therefore seems that Luke has introduced an additional element in the geography of Jesus' early ministry, although some interpreters suggest that 'Judea' in Luke does not indicate only the southern district but the whole of Palestine, including Galilee.[14]

5:17 αὐτόν (him) {A}

The oldest witnesses and some ancient translations have the singular αὐτόν ('him'; 01 03 019 032 040 etc.), but the majority of Greek manu-

---

[14] See Omanson 2006: 114–115.

scripts read αὐτούς ('them'; 02 04 05 037 etc.) and other witnesses support πάντας ('all people'; cpa Cyril^pt); for the full list of variants see *TuT Luke* (TS6). The variation appears to be due to the ambiguity of the verb: despite being passive in form, in the present tense ἰᾶσθαι can be active or passive in meaning. In the context of the following episode, the accusative and infinitive εἰς τὸ ἰᾶσθαι αὐτόν makes good sense with αὐτόν as the subject of an active verb ('for him to heal'). However, the more common use of the accusative to indicate the object, in combination with the passive appearance of ἰᾶσθαι, means that this could also be understood as 'for him to be healed'. The variants were introduced by those who read this sentence in the latter way but decided it needed adjustment because Jesus did not need to be healed: while αὐτούς ('[for] them [to be healed]') is only a minor intervention, its reference to the Pharisees and teachers of the Law in context does not make good sense; πάντας ('[for] all [to be healed]') offers better sense yet is very poorly attested. The evidence thus points strongly towards the reading adopted in the editorial text.

5:18 θεῖναι [αὐτόν] (lay him)

Almost all Greek manuscripts lack the pronoun; there are merely four which have αὐτόν ('him'; 03 019 038 040), but these majuscules are often important. The word itself is not required in context, as the previous instance of αὐτόν earlier in the sentence can provide an object for both verbs. However, because this structure makes it seem that θεῖναι ('to lay') lacks a direct object, an additional pronoun may have been supplied in these witnesses. Alternatively, given that two words later the pronoun αὐτοῦ ('[before] him') refers to Jesus, an editor may have deleted αὐτόν to minimise ambiguity and repetition. The pronoun is not adopted in either the SBLGNT or THGNT. In translation, the verb will need an object and the pronouns must be disambiguated.

5:33 οἱ μαθηταί (disciples¹) {B}

In most Greek manuscripts, this is treated as a question as shown by an initial διὰ τί ('why [do John's disciples]…?'; 01*, 2b 02 04 05 etc.). This interrogative is missing from a range of early witnesses (𝔓⁴ 01^2a 03 019 032 etc.), which means that this must be taken as a formal statement ('John's disciples often fast') even if a question is implicit. Given that the parallels at Matt. 9:14 and Mark 2:18 both begin with διὰ τί ('why?'), the dissimilar shorter reading in Luke is more likely to be the most ancient form which was later brought into agreement with the other Synoptic Gospels.

5:39 [καί] (and)

A few witnesses lack the conjunction ($\mathfrak{P}^4$ 01² 03 579 700 892 1241). It is difficult to decide whether it was a later addition, through assimilation to the beginning of Luke 5:37, or removed by an editor seeking to ensure the separation of this comment from the previous parable on a related topic. The whole verse is lacking from Codex Bezae and the Old Latin tradition, possibly because it does not appear in the synoptic parallels (Matt. 9:17, Mark 2:22), and does not sit well with the preceding parable. Although it has been suggested that the verse may have been deleted by Marcion because it could be read in support of the Hebrew Scriptures, this is difficult to substantiate.[15]

5:39 χρηστός (good) {A}

Most witnesses have the comparative adjective χρηστότερος ('better'; 02 04 037 038 etc.). In the context of the judgment between the two different types of wine, this is the more expected reading. The regular form χρηστός ('good'; $\mathfrak{P}^4$ 01 03 019 032 etc.) has strong early attestation and may even work better in context: there is no indication that the drinkers of the old wine have actually tasted the new wine, but instead they prefer to stick with their existing opinion.

6:1 ἐν σαββάτῳ (one sabbath) {B}

The shortest reading, ἐν σαββάτῳ ('on a sabbath'; $\mathfrak{P}^4$ 01 03 019 032 etc.) has good support in early manuscripts and ancient translations. Part of the Coptic Bohairic tradition reflects ἐν τοῖς σάββασιν ('on the sabbaths'; co^(bo-pt)), which may have been influenced by synoptic parallels at Matt. 12:1 or Mark 2:23, or the use of the plural at Luke 4:31, 6:2 or 13:10. The majority of Greek manuscripts have a unique word (*hapax legomenon*) in ἐν σαββάτῳ δευτεροπρώτῳ ('on a second-first sabbath'; 02 04 05 037 038 etc.). Much has been written on this. It has been sug-

---

[15] Metzger 1994: 116; compare Roth 2015: 414.

gested that it arose through two subsequent adjustments: one reader, noting a reference to 'another sabbath' at Luke 6:6, added 'the first sabbath' here; a later editor, seeing the activity on the sabbaths at Luke 4:31 sought to change this to 'the second sabbath', but the two words were combined rather than replaced.[16] As it has just been noted, Luke 4:31 has the plural which makes the idea of a 'second sabbath' unlikely. An alternative explanation is that the last four letters of the word were duplicated and reinterpreted as numerals, β for 'second' and α for 'first', with the dative ending indicated by τῳ (which, although unnecessary, is paralleled in scribal practice).[17] Such an account has the merit of explaining why 'first sabbath' and 'second sabbath' are not attested in early witnesses, unless *sabbato mane* ('early on the Sabbath') in the Old Latin Codex Palatinus reflects 'first sabbath'. The full list of variants in *TuT Luke* (TS8) shows that there is one minuscule with σαββάτῳ πρώτῳ (GA 382), and just one in which the terms are written as numerals (GA 2796). In any case, while it remains unclear how this early variant arose, the external attestation for the shorter reading suggests that it is likely to be the earliest form. If δευτεροπρώτῳ is followed, as in translations based on the *Textus Receptus*, a choice must be made as to the meaning of this unparalleled term.

6:3 [ὄντες] (were)

The participle ὄντες makes no difference to the sense, and the manuscript tradition is split: it is missing from most of the early witnesses (𝔓⁴ 01 02 05 019 032 etc.), but is typical of Byzantine tradition (02 04 037 044 etc.). It is likely that it was added later in order to make it clear that 'and those with him' refers to the previous verb ('he was hungry') rather than the following one ('he went in'), although this is not seen in the parallels at Matt. 12:3 or Mark 2:25.

6:4 [ὡς] (how)

A few ancient manuscripts lack any conjunction here (𝔓⁴ 03 05). This is appealing in that the following clause provides the answer to the preceding question. Most manuscripts have ὡς ('as', 'how', 'when'; 01* 02

---
[16] Metzger 1994: 116.
[17] This was first advanced by Burkitt and is enthusiastically promoted in Skeat 1988.

04 032 037 044 etc.), while others read πῶς ('how'; 01² 019 038 f^1 f^{13} etc.). Both of these reinforce the initial question, as in the parallels at Matt. 12:4 and Mark 2:26 to which the latter is likely to be assimilation. It is striking that at Mark 2:26 both Codex Vaticanus and Codex Bezae also have no conjunction, suggesting that the short reading is the result of an early editorial intervention in both cases. The result is that ὡς appears to be the most compelling reading because of its dissimilarity, and it is also adopted in the SBLGNT and THGNT.

6:4 μόνους τοὺς ἱερεῖς; (but the priests) {A}

At the end of this verse, there is a unique addition in Codex Bezae. Known as the 'Cambridge pericope', it reads τῇ αὐτῇ ἡμέρᾳ θεασάμενός τινα ἐργαζόμενον τῷ σαββάτῳ εἶπεν αὐτῷ· ἄνθρωπε, εἰ μὲν οἶδας τί ποιεῖς, μακάριος εἶ· εἰ δὲ μὴ οἶδας, ἐπικατάρατος καὶ παραβάτης εἶ τοῦ νόμου ('On the same day, having seen someone working on the Sabbath, he said to him, "Man, if you know what you are doing, you are blessed; but if you do not know, you are accursed and a transgressor of the Law."'). As noted in the following unit, in this manuscript the summary statement of Luke 6:5 is moved to after Luke 6:10, making it the conclusion of three episodes involving Jesus and the Sabbath. While this is likely to be an editorial reworking, the possibility remains that this saying is an *agraphon* preserving Jesus tradition not otherwise attested in the gospels. A few manuscripts (including Codex Bezae) have a dative, μόνοις τοῖς ἱερεῦσιν ('to the priests alone'; 05 157 1505), which is a grammatical correction to the expected case of the object of the verb ἔξεστιν ('it is permitted').

6:5 κύριός ἐστιν τοῦ σαββάτου ὁ υἱὸς τοῦ ἀνθρώπου (the Son of Man is lord of the Sabbath) {B}

The word order adopted in the editorial text is unexpected, giving prominence to 'the sabbath', but has early support (01 03 032 etc.) and matches the parallel at Matt. 12:8. The majority of manuscripts have a more customary sequence with an additional καί, reading κύριός ἐστιν ὁ υἱὸς τοῦ ἀνθρώπου καὶ τοῦ σαββάτου ('the Son of Man is also lord of the sabbath'; 02 05 019 037 etc.). This corresponds to the text of the parallel at Mark 2:28. Either form could have been Luke's source or led to assimilation. The preference for the Matthean text, also adopted in the SBLGNT and THGNT, is based on it being the more difficult reading. Although Codex Bezae also witnesses to the majority form, as noted in the previous unit, this is displaced until the end of Luke 6:10, following the next episode of teaching about the sabbath, as part of a clear editorial restructuring.

6:10 εἶπεν (he said) {A}

Some manuscripts read ἐν ὀργῇ εἶπεν ('in anger, he said'; [05] 038 f^1 etc.) or μετ' ὀργῆς εἶπεν ('with anger, he said'; f^{13} 157). The parallel at Mark 3:5 includes the words μετ' ὀργῆς, so this appears to be an assimilation to that verse: if it were original, wider attestation would be expected. As it is, the support of Byzantine tradition as well as early witnesses for the shorter reading of just εἶπεν ('he said'; $\mathfrak{P}^4$ 01 02 03 019 etc.) leads to its adoption. The portrayal of Jesus as angry in part of the textual tradition may be significant (cf. the comment on Mark 1:41 above).

6:33 καὶ [γὰρ] ἐάν (if) {C}

The vast majority of witnesses lack the connective γάρ ('for'), but it is present in the three oldest surviving manuscripts ($\mathfrak{P}^{75}$ 01* 03). This makes for some doubt as to whether it was originally lacking. It could have been added through assimilation to the previous clause, or deleted in order to match the verses on either side. Arguably, the presence of γάρ here is the more difficult reading, as it means that this verse does not match the structure of those on either side: this may pose an issue for translators, even though the effect on meaning is limited. See also the following unit.

6:33 καὶ οἱ (even) {C}

In contrast with the previous unit, the majority of manuscripts include γάρ ('for'; 02 05 019 022 etc.) in this phrase. There is strong early evidence for its absence (01 03 07 032 etc. with some Old Latin and Old Syriac), although the first two of these witnesses do have it in the preceding clause (see above; $\mathfrak{P}^{75}$ is lacunose here but the number of characters on each line suggest that it probably also lacked γάρ). At issue is the difference in structure between this verse and those on either side: were they originally identical, or were they subsequently brought into a closer parallelism? The variation in the previous and following units suggests that the tendency towards assimilation may have introduced confusion: this offers a reason to prefer the shorter reading throughout.

6:34 [ἐστίν] (is)

In both Luke 6:32 and 6:33 this phrase ends with ἐστίν, and it is not surprising to find it in the majority of manuscripts here (01 02 05 019 032 etc.). However, several of the oldest manuscripts lack it ($\mathfrak{P}^{45}$ $\mathfrak{P}^{75}$ 03 700 and the Old Latin Codex Palatinus). Given that the dissimilarity is the harder reading, this may be a deliberate authorial variation: equally, it could reflect an early oversight in copying. In translation, the verb is likely to be necessary.

6:36 καθὼς [καί] (just as)

A range of early witnesses read καθὼς ὁ πατὴρ ὑμῶν ('just as your father'; 01 03 019 032 040 etc. lat^{vl} sy^s co). The majority of Greek manuscripts, however, have καθὼς καὶ ὁ πατὴρ ὑμῶν ('just as your father too'; 02 05 037 038 etc.). The only other instances of the collocation καθὼς καί ('just as also') in the gospels are also seen in Luke (11:1 and 24:24); a similar construction at Matt. 5:48 lacks the intensifier. While the older documents support the shorter reading, it is possible that this is secondary, either through assimilation or to enable this phrase to stand separately: in context, καί reflects the description of God as χρηστός ('kind') in the previous verse. This balance of external and internal evidence leads to the inclusion of the variant in brackets: while the THGNT includes καί here, it is absent from the SBLGNT.

6:48 διὰ τὸ καλῶς οἰκοδομῆσθαι αὐτήν (because it had been well built) {A}

The majority of manuscripts read τεθεμελίωτο γὰρ ἐπὶ τὴν πέτραν ('for it had been founded on rock'; 02 04 05 037 038 etc.). This is the same phrase as seen in the parallel at Matt. 7:25: if it were original to Luke, it would be hard to explain why διὰ τὸ καλῶς οἰκοδομῆσθαι αὐτήν ('because it had been well built'; $\mathfrak{P}^{75vid}$ 01 03 019 032 etc.) is so widely attested in early witnesses. Instead, it appears that Luke adjusted this saying to focus on the overall quality of the building rather than the nature of the foundation (there is no mention of sand in the following verse, and the building process is described in greater detail here), but the more memorable Matthean phrase was reintroduced at an early point. The dissimilar reading can also explain the absence of this phrase from a few important witnesses ($\mathfrak{P}^{45\text{vid}}$ 700* sy^s) as being due to eyeskip between the two instances of the word αὐτήν ('it').

7:11   ἐν τῷ ἑξῆς (soon afterwards) {B}

The Byzantine tradition is split between ἐν τῷ ἑξῆς (lit. 'in the following [time]'; $\mathfrak{P}^{75}$ 01² 03 019 etc.), with the masculine article presupposing the word χρόνῳ ('time'), and ἐν τῇ ἑξῆς (lit. 'on the following [day]'; 01* 04 28 565 etc.), with the feminine article indicating ἡμέρᾳ ('day'). The latter is found in the *Textus Receptus*. Two early majuscules just have τῇ ἑξῆς ('the following [day]'; 05 032). In the New Testament, the adverbs ἑξῆς ('following') and καθεξῆς ('in sequence') are only found in the Lukan writings: the other four instances of ἑξῆς all have the feminine article and lack the preposition ἐν ('in', 'on'; Luke 9:37, Acts 21:1, 25:17, 27:18). On the other hand, the phrase ἐν τῷ καθεξῆς ('soon afterwards') is used to introduce the new section at Luke 8:1, and the only occurrence of the feminine in the gospel also has the word ἡμέρᾳ ('day'; Luke 9:37). These internal considerations, also supported by the distribution of witnesses, suggest that the masculine is the earliest text here and was altered during transmission to match the more common feminine phrase, with or without the preposition. In translation, the masculine is better rendered by an expression of sequence (e.g. 'soon afterwards') rather than time.

7:11   οἱ μαθηταὶ αὐτοῦ (his disciples) {B}

The majority of Greek manuscripts read οἱ μαθηταὶ αὐτοῦ ἱκανοί ('a number of his disciples'; 02 04 037 038 etc.). The oldest witnesses have only οἱ μαθηταὶ αὐτοῦ ('his disciples'; $\mathfrak{P}^{75}$ 01 03 05 019 etc.), and a few read μαθηταὶ ἱκανοί ('a few disciples'; f^1 205). The full attestation in Greek continuous-text manuscripts is given in *TuT Luke* (TS12). The word ἱκανός ('sufficient', 'enough') is characteristic of Luke, even though it is rarely applied to people and never to the disciples (making this the harder reading), so it could be original: it is possible that the sequence of letters IKANOIKAIO could have led to its omission through eyeskip.[18] An alternative scenario may be suggested by the following verse, with the phrase ὄχλος τῆς πόλεως ἱκανός ('a sizeable crowd from the town'): this contrasts with ὄχλος πολύς ('a great crowd') at the end of this sentence, and it may be that an early reader noted the difference between the two and wrote ἱκανός alongside the present verse, which a copyist then inserted but applied it to the disciples rather than the crowd. This is only a conjecture, but is in conformity with the superior external evidence for the shorter reading which has led to its adoption here, as well as in both the SBLGNT and THGNT.

7:28 Ἰωάννου (than John) {B}

This variation unit demonstrates the way in which texts increase over time. Most of the earliest manuscripts just read Ἰωάννου ('than John'; 𝔓⁷⁵ 01 03 019 032 etc.). A few witnesses read προφήτης Ἰωάννου ('a [greater] prophet than John'; 044 700 [892] sy^s): it is plausible that this was motivated by a concern that this might exclude Jesus from 'those born of women', despite his being the speaker (and no similar variation is seen in the parallel at Matt. 11:11). Other manuscripts have Ἰωάννου τοῦ βαπτιστοῦ ('John the Baptist'; 033 33 565 597 etc.): as this is clear from the context, the extra designation is probably assimilation to the Matthean parallel. Although this reading could in theory have given rise to the shortest reading through eyeskip, the other variants and the limited attestation indicate that this is unlikely. Finally, the majority of minuscules as well as majuscules with a Byzantine text conflate the two variants with προφήτης Ἰωάννου τοῦ βαπτιστοῦ ('a [greater] prophet than John the Baptist'; 02 [05] [037] 038 *f*¹³ etc.). As noted in the apparatus, in this verse Codex Bezae and an Old Latin manuscript lack the text from μείζων to ἐστιν ('among those … than John') at this point but instead have it at the end of Luke 7:26, in what appears to be a deliberate redistribution of the material by an early editor.

8:3 αὐτοῖς (to them) {B}

The textual tradition is split between the plural αὐτοῖς ('to them'; 03 05 032 etc.) and the singular αὐτῷ ('to him'; 01 02 019 044 etc.), with no clear Byzantine reading. The plural is slightly ambiguous, in that it

---

[18] As suggested by Metzger 1994: 119.

could include the named women even though the intended referent is probably Jesus and the disciples. It is unlikely that this would have been introduced as a deliberate replacement for αὐτῷ. In contrast, the singular may be assimilation to the the previous pronoun (αὐτῷ at the end of Luke 8:1) or a deliberate alteration to focus on Jesus. Compare also the singular pronoun after the same verb (διακονεῖν, 'to minister') in Matt. 27:55 and Mark 15:41.

8:26 Γερασηνῶν (Gerasenes) {C}

This variation unit has already been extensively discussed at Matt. 8:28 and Mark 5:1. The same variants are found here. Support for the editorial choice of Γερασηνῶν ('Gerasenes'; 𝔓⁷⁵ 03 05 lat sy^hmg co^(sa, bo-mss)) is early but comparatively slim, although this matches the reading adopted in Mark (see also Luke 8:37 below). There is early attestation too of the similar noun Γεργεσηνῶν ('Gergasenes'; 01 019 038 040 etc.), the majority reading in Matthew which may derive from a correction proposed by Origen. In this verse, most Greek manuscripts read Γαδαρηνῶν ('Gadarenes'; 02 032 037 044 etc.), which is preferred as the editorial text in Matt. 8:28. The similarities between all these readings, their geographical implications and assimilation between synoptic traditions make it difficult to be confident as to the earliest form: the antiquity and difficulty of 'Gerasenes' lead to its adoption here and in both the SBLGNT and THGNT, suggesting that, unlike Matthew, Luke did not change the Markan source here.

8:27 καὶ χρόνῳ ἱκανῷ (for a long time) {B}

The majority of Greek manuscripts read ἐκ χρόνων ἱκανῶν, καί ('[had demons] for a long time, and [had not worn]'; 01²ᵃ 02 032 037 etc.). Many of the oldest witnesses support καὶ χρόνῳ ἱκανῷ ('and for a long time [he had not worn]'; 𝔓⁷⁵ᵛⁱᵈ 01*, ²ᵇ 03 019 040 etc.), although there are a couple of other readings: ἀπὸ χρόνων ἱκανῶν ὅς ('[had demons] for a long time, who [had not worn]'; 05 [lat^(vl-pt)]) and καὶ χρόνων πολλῷ ('and for much time [he had not worn]'; ƒ¹). The full list of variants in Greek continuous-text manuscripts is given in *TuT Luke* (TS13). The difficulty of the editorial text, as well as its early attestation, leads to its adoption: the majority reading provides the more expected connection of the 'long time' with the demon possession rather than its specific manifestations, and if this text had been original there would be no obvious reason for the other variants. While the plural is the preferred form of this phrase elsewhere in the gospel (Luke 20:9, 23:8), the singular is standard in Acts (8:11, 14:3 and 27:9).

8:37 Γερασηνῶν (Gerasenes) {C}

The distribution of variants here is similar to Luke 8:26 (see above). A few more Greek manuscripts support Γερασηνῶν ('Gerasenes'; 𝔓⁷⁵ 03 04* 05 579 lat sy^hmg co^sa): 579 differs here from 'Gergasenes' in the earlier verse, while the others are not extant on the previous occasion. There is also early support for Γεργεσηνῶν ('Gergasenes'; 01*, 2b [04²] 019 024 etc.), while the majority reading continues to be Γαδαρηνῶν ('Gadarenes'; 01²ᵃ 02 032 037 044 etc.). The overall consistency indicates that the editors responsible for introducing the changes were thorough: the evangelist, too, is likely to have been consistent and the editorial text matches that at Luke 8:26.

8:41 [τοῦ] Ἰησοῦ (Jesus's)

The definite article τοῦ is only missing from four Greek manuscripts, but all of them are early (𝔓⁷⁵ᵛⁱᵈ 01* 03 024). Although it may seem unusual to find the name 'Jesus' without a definite article, there are other instances in Luke, with a close parallel at Luke 5:8. More influential for the present verse is the identical phrase at Luke 8:35, where Papyrus 75 and Codex Vaticanus once again lack τοῦ. This makes it very difficult to decide whether the absence of the article from both these verses is an early editorial deletion or oversight, or whether this is an original harder reading which was later brought into line with standard practice. In any case, translation is unaffected.

8:43 ἥτις [ἰατροῖς προσαναλώσασα ὅλον τὸν βίον] (she had spent all she had on physicians) {C}

Some early witnesses here read only ἥτις ('who'; 𝔓⁷⁵ 03 [05] 0279 [lat^vl-pt] sy^s cpa^pt co^sa Origen). The longer form, ἥτις ἰατροῖς προσαναλώσασα ὅλον τὸν βίον ('who had spent all her livelihood on doctors'; 01* 02 019 032 etc.) appears in the majority of manuscripts; at the end, others include the pronoun αὐτῆς ('her [livelihood]'; 04 044 etc.) or ἑαυτῆς ('her own [livelihood]'; 01* 1071). There is no obvious reason for the omission of the extra text (a leap from ἥτις to αὐτῆς through homophony is unlikely), and its resemblance to Mark 5:26 as well as the external evidence suggest that it is a later addition. Unlike most additions, however, it does not use any of the vocabulary from the Markan source: instead, it includes the only instance of the verb προσαναλίσκω, 'to consume/waste' in the New Testament. Even though this particularly elegant summary would not be beyond the capacity of an early reader or editor, the skill of the writing has led to the suggestion that this is the work of the evangelist.[19] Both the SBLGNT and the THGNT adopt a longer form, with the THGNT also including αὐτῆς at the end.

8:45   Πέτρος (Peter) {B}

The majority of Greek manuscripts read Πέτρος καὶ οἱ μετ' αὐτοῦ ('Peter and those with him'; 04³ 037 044 etc.), while there is also extensive support for Πέτρος καὶ οἱ σὺν αὐτῷ (also 'Peter and those with him'; 01 02 04* 05 019 etc.). The shortest reading, just Πέτρος ('Peter'; 𝔓⁷⁵ 03 700* sy^{c, s} cpa co^{sa} Origen^{vid}), has limited but early support. Of the two longer forms, οἱ σὺν αὐτῷ is the more common phrasing in Luke, and is found in the same formulation at Luke 9:32: it is possible that this was an original, harder reading because of the singular verb εἶπεν ('he said') and was later corrected by an editor, although one might expect the verb to have been made plural instead (cf. Luke 9:32). While οἱ σὺν αὐτῷ is adopted in the THGNT, the editorial preference here and in the SBLGNT is that the shortest text came first and was expanded in two different forms, perhaps through assimilation to the parallel at Mark 5:31 where this criticism is attributed to all the disciples (see also the following unit).

8:45   καὶ ἀποθλίβουσιν (and pressing against you) {B}

At the end of this verse, most Greek manuscripts include καὶ λέγεις· τίς ὁ ἁψάμενός μου ('and you say, "Who is the one who touched me?"'; 02 04 024 032 etc.). Some majuscules instead add καὶ λέγεις· τίς μου ἥψατο ('and you say, "Who touched me?"'; 05 044 28 etc.). The shorter reading adopted as the editorial text has the earliest support (𝔓⁷⁵ 01 03 019 𝑓¹ etc.), and there is no obvious cause for accidental omission. In-

---

[19] Metzger 1994: 121.

stead, it seems that, as in the previous unit, the two alternatives are later assimilation to Mark 5:31 (the first with the Lukan phrasing of Jesus' initial question). The variant reading which lacks καὶ ἀποθλίβουσιν and instead only has καὶ λέγεις· τίς μου ἥψατο ('and you say, "Who touched me?"'; 1071 lat^(vl-pt)) is likely to be due to eyeskip between the two instances of καί.

9:1   δώδεκα (twelve) {B}

The disciples have already been referred to as 'the twelve' at Luke 8:1. The shorter text found in both the majority of minuscules and several early witnesses, δώδεκα ('twelve'; 𝔓⁷⁵ 02 03 05 etc.), therefore has a strong claim to be original. Elsewhere, Luke never uses the phrases δώδεκα ἀποστόλους ('the twelve apostles'; 01 04* 019 038 etc.) or δώδεκα μαθητὰς αὐτοῦ ('his twelve disciples'; 04³ 07 09 etc.), which suggests that these are both later expansions. The latter appears to be an assimilation to the parallel at Matt. 10:1. Nevertheless, there remains a possibility that the shorter reading arose through assimilation to Mark 6:7. In translation, it may still be necessary to indicate that these are the disciples.

9:2   ἰᾶσθαι [τοὺς ἀσθενεῖς] (to heal [the sick])

The verb ἰᾶσθαι ('to heal') has no complement in Codex Vaticanus or the two Old Syriac manuscripts. If this were original, it would explain why three different objects are found in the tradition: other majuscules have τοὺς ἀσθενεῖς ('the sick'; 01 02 05 019 040 etc.), the majority of minuscules read τοὺς ἀσθενοῦντας ('the ailing'; 04 032 037 038 etc.) and one manuscript even has τοὺς νοσοῦντας ('the diseased'; 2542). The first two words are both found in Luke (cf. the parallel at Luke 10:9), whereas the verb νοσεῖν ('to be diseased') only occurs once in the New Testament (1 Tim. 6:4). However, the other three active instances of ἰᾶσθαι in Luke all have a direct object: this might make the shortest form too difficult a reading, although the more frequent θεραπεύειν ('to cure') appears with and without a direct object. The very slim evidence for the shorter reading, including the propensity for omissions in Codex Vaticanus, makes it hard to adopt, hence the inclusion of the better attested early complement in both the SBLGNT and THGNT as well as here in brackets. Even if the shorter reading is followed, the verb may require a direct object in translation. The full attestation of this variant in Greek continuous-text manuscripts is given in *TuT Luke* (TS15).

9:3 [ἀνὰ] δύο (an extra)

A range of early witnesses just read δύο ('two [tunics]'; 01 03 04* 019 040 etc.), but the majority of manuscripts have ἀνὰ δύο ('up to two [tunics]' or '[tunics] in twos'; 02 04³ 05 032 037 etc.; see further *TuT Luke* TS16). There are other instances of ἀνά with numerals at Luke 9:14 and 10:1, but the synoptic parallels both only read δύο (Matt. 10:10, Mark 6:9). However, as the shorter reading might be taken to mean that the disciples only had one coat between them, it is possible that either Luke or a copyist added ἀνά for clarification. In translation, whichever reading is followed, the implication should be that each disciple should only take one coat.

9:10 εἰς πόλιν καλουμένην Βηθσαϊδά (to a city called Bethsaida)
{B}

The editorial text is supported by a small range of early witnesses ([𝔓⁷⁵] 01²ᵃ 03 019 040 etc.), but appears to provide the best explanation of the numerous variants in the textual tradition. Codex Bezae reads εἰς κώμην λεγομένην Βηθσαϊδά ('to a village called Bethsaida'; 05 [latᵛˡ⁻ᵖᵗ]), perhaps as an editorial adjustment because a city seemed too large a place to which to withdraw privately. The greater inconsistency is the statement in Luke 9:12 that the disciples are 'in a deserted place' (ἐν ἐρήμῳ τόπῳ). This is seen in the parallels at Matt. 14:13 and Mark 6:35, and is read in the present verse in a few witnesses: εἰς τόπον ἔρημον ('to a deserted place'; 01*,²ᵇ 157 [1241] syᶜ). One majuscule has a conflation of this with the reading of Codex Bezae: εἰς κώμην λεγομένην Βηθσαϊδὰν εἰς τόπον ἔρημον ('to a village called Bethsaida to a deserted place'; 038 [1342] latᵛˡ⁻ᵖᵗ]). The majority of Greek manuscripts also combine the two readings but with an adjustment: εἰς τόπον ἔρημον πόλεως καλουμένης Βηθσαϊδά(ν) ('to a deserted place of a city called Bethsaida'; [02] 04 032 037 etc.). Other readings include εἰς τόπον καλούμενον Βηθσαϊδά ('to a place called Bethsaida'; 044 [latᵛˡ⁻ᵖᵗ, ᵛᵍ coᵇᵒ⁻ᵐˢˢ]) and the absence of the entire phrase from two minuscules (579 1010), probably due to eyeskip from the end of the preceding ἰδίαν to the end of Βηθσαϊδάν. The reference to Bethsaida is clearly the harder reading, apparently introduced by Luke because it had some significance in connection with the feeding of the five thousand: the reversion to 'a deserted place' two verses later, as seen in both parallels, may be an example of editorial fatigue, in which the evangelist does not consistently carry through changes to the source text.[20] Most of the variants here can be understood as attempts by earlier editors to remedy this inconsistency, influenced by the synoptic parallels. This verse is included in *ECM Parallel Pericopes*.

9:14 [ὡσεί] (about)

Most early witnesses include the word ὡσεί ('about'; 01 03 04 05 019 040 etc., lat$^{vl\text{-}pt}$ co^{sa}), but it is missing from the majority of Greek manuscripts. This term is largely superfluous before ἀνά ('up to'), and could have been repeated erroneously from the beginning of the verse where it occurs before the same letters (ὡσεὶ ἄνδρες). While it is unusual to find a shorter reading in Byzantine tradition, the repetition and redundancy may have led to its deletion by an early editor. The combination of the external evidence and a harder reading tend to support the adoption of ὡσεί (as seen in both the SBLGNT and THGNT), a word which is largely restricted to Luke and Acts in the New Testament. This verse is included in *ECM Parallel Pericopes*.

9:28 [καὶ] παραλαβών (took with him)

The majority of manuscripts include the conjunction καί ('and [taking]'; 01^2 02 04 05 019 etc.), separating this clause from the indication of time at the beginning of the verse. However, it is absent from some of the oldest Greek codices and translations ($\mathfrak{P}^{45vid}$ 01* 03 579 lat^{vl} sy$^{p, h}$ co). This more elegant structure parallels other instances in Luke (e.g. Luke 1:5, 2:1, 9:37, 11:27) but there are also counterexamples (e.g. Luke 6:1, 6:6, 6:12 etc.). The relatively slim attestation makes it difficult to decide whether the shorter reading is the earliest form (as in the THGNT) or a later omission or editorial deletion (as in the SBLGNT).

---

[20] See further Goodacre 2002: 40–43. Another example may occur at Luke 19:25, which has been eliminated from certain witnesses.

9:35 ἐκλελεγμένος (chosen) {B}

There is strong support among the earliest witnesses for ἐκλελεγμένος ('chosen'; 𝔓⁴⁵ 𝔓⁷⁵ 01 03 019 etc. and several translations). This is the harder reading, as it differs from other parallel passages. The majority of manuscripts have ἀγαπητός ('beloved'; 02 04* 032 037 etc.), matching Mark 9:7 and the baptism narrative at Matt. 3:17, Mark 1:11 and Luke 3:22. Some majuscules have ἀγαπητὸς ἐν ᾧ εὐδόκησα ('beloved with whom I am well pleased'; 04³ 05 044 etc.), corresponding to the parallel at Matt. 17:5 and the baptism passages, while a few manuscripts have ἐκλεκτός ('chosen'; 038 *f*¹) which may reflect Luke 23:35 or the alternative at John 1:34. Given the variety of parallel passages and the presence of ἐκλεκτός elsewhere in Luke, the variants are much more likely to have arisen through assimilation rather than a theological concern that describing Jesus as 'chosen' might support a position such as adoptionism.

9:54 αὐτούς (them) {B}

At the end of this verse, the majority of Greek manuscripts include ὡς καὶ Ἠλίας ἐποίησεν ('as Elijah also did'; 02 04 05 032 037 etc.), with a few supporting ὡς Ἠλίας ἐποίησεν ('as Elijah did'; 892 lat^(vl-pt, vg-ms): see further *TuT Luke* TS17). This reference to 2 Kings 1:10 and 12 serves to explain the disciples' thinking. Nevertheless, it is lacking from most of the earliest manuscripts and translations (𝔓⁴⁵ 𝔓⁷⁵ 01 03 019 etc.) and as there is no obvious mechanical or theological reason for omission, the shorter reading is adopted as the editorial text. The addition may have originated as a marginal note.

9:55-56 αὐτοῖς (them) {A}

There is extensive support in the earliest witnesses as well as part of Byzantine tradition for a short version of these two verses, reading ἐπετίμησεν αὐτοῖς. ⁵⁶ καὶ ἐπορεύθησαν ('he rebuked them. Then they went'; 𝔓⁴⁵ 𝔓⁷⁵ 01 02 03 04 etc.). Codex Bezae has a longer text at the end of verse 55: ἐπετίμησεν αὐτοῖς καὶ εἶπεν· οὐκ οἴδατε ποίου πνεύματός ἐστε ('he rebuked them and said, "You do not know of what sort of spirit you are."'; 05 lat^(vl-pt) Chrysostom). This forms the basis of an expansion in numerous Byzantine witnesses, including the *Textus Receptus*, reading ἐπετίμησεν αὐτοῖς καὶ εἶπεν· οὐκ οἴδατε οἵου πνεύματός ἐστε ὑμεῖς. ⁵⁶ ὁ γὰρ υἱὸς τοῦ ἀνθρώπου οὐκ ἦλθεν ψυχὰς ἀνθρώπων ἀπολέσαι ἀλλὰ σῶσαι ('he rebuked them and said, "You do not know of what spirit you are. For the Son of Man did not come to destroy but to save the souls of humans."'; 038 f^1 f^{13} etc.). The second part appears to be an expansion based on Luke 19:10, supplied by an early editor who was troubled by the disciples' suggestion (compare the addition of the precedent of Elijah in the previous unit). The clarifications offered in the longer texts and the external support indicate that the shortest reading is very likely to be the earliest. The full list of variants in Greek continuous-text manuscripts in these two verses is given in *TuT Luke* (TS18–19).

9:62 [πρὸς αὐτόν] (to him)

The words πρὸς αὐτόν ('to him') are absent from the oldest Greek manuscripts ($\mathfrak{P}^{45}$ $\mathfrak{P}^{75}$ 03 0181; also 700 co^{sa-mss}), while in Byzantine tradition they come after ὁ Ἰησοῦς ('Jesus'). This raises a doubt as to whether they were part of the earliest text: the phrase could easily have been added through assimilation to parallels (e.g. Luke 7:40, 9:50 etc.). On the other hand, the removal of this contextual detail could be secondary, in order to turn Jesus' words into a more general saying. Noting the appearance of an object for each occurrence of εἶπεν ('he said') with Jesus as subject in the four preceding verses, Wasserman prefers the shorter reading, in common with the SBLGNT, whereas the THGNT has the longer form.[21]

10:1 ἑβδομήκοντα [δύο] (seventy [two]) {D}

The majority of manuscripts read only ἑβδομήκοντα ('seventy'; 01 02 04 019 etc.), matching their reading at the end of the pericope (Luke 10:17; see below). Several early witnesses, however, have ἑβδομήκοντα δύο ('seventy-two'; $\mathfrak{P}^{75}$ 03 05 0181 lat^{vl-pt, vg} sy^{c, s} co^{sa, bo-ms}) in both verses. This consistency makes it unlikely that the difference is accidental. Instead, the numbers appear to be symbolic. While seventy-two is a multiple of the main group of apostles (and half of the 144 at Rev. 7:4 and 14:1), there are numerous instances of seventy in Jewish tradition (e.g. Exod. 15:27, 24:1; Num. 11:16–25, 33:9; Deut. 10:22; Ezek. 8:11)—as well as the eponymous number of translators of the Septuagint itself

---

[21] Wasserman 2017: 94–95.

(although the Letter of Aristeas gives the total as seventy-two). Similarly, the number of nations in the world listed in Genesis 10 is seventy in Hebrew but seventy-two in the Septuagint.[22] This makes it very difficult to decide between the two numbers on external or internal grounds. Aland considers that there would have been a strong drive to normalise to seventy, as the more common number in the Jewish Scriptures, making seventy-two the more difficult reading.[23] The Greek lectionary tradition reads ἑβδομήκοντα μαθητάς ('seventy disciples'). Other editions are also split, with 'seventy-two' in the SBLGNT and 'seventy' in the THGNT. Wasserman considers the two variants 'of equal value for establishing the initial text', while another recent detailed study suggests that the balance might favour the longer reading.[24]

10:1 ἀνὰ δύο [δύο] (in pairs)

Only a few witnesses have the repetitive ἀνὰ δύο δύο ('two by two'; 03 038 f^{13} 565 sy^h Eusebius). The simplification of this to ἀνὰ δύο ('in twos'; 01 02 04 05 019 etc.), as seen in the majority of manuscripts, would be an easy error with no significant change to the sense. On the other hand, the longer reading could have arisen through an erroneous repetition of δύο ('two'). The other uses of ἀνὰ with numerals in Luke might support a single number (cf. Luke 9:3 above, 9:14), but the Septuagintal phrasing δύο δύο ('two by two') at Gen. 6:19ff. could also have been influential even though there is no clear parallel to the present verse. While it is difficult to be confident about the earliest form in Greek (the SBLGNT prefers the longer text, and the THGNT the shorter), the alternatives have minimal effect on translation.

10:15 μὴ ἕως οὐρανοῦ ὑψωθήσῃ; (will you be exalted to heaven?) {B}

The majority of manuscripts read ἡ ἕως τοῦ οὐρανοῦ ὑψωθεῖσα ('the one who has been exalted to heaven'; 02 [03²] 04 022 etc.), while the earliest witnesses have μὴ ἕως οὐρανοῦ ὑψωθήσῃ; (lit. 'will you not be exalted to heaven?'; 𝔓⁴⁵ 𝔓⁷⁵ 01 03* 05 etc.). The same variation has already been discussed at Matt. 11:23, where it was noted that the first

---

[22] Omanson 2006: 127.
[23] See Metzger 1994: 127.
[24] Wasserman 2017: 97; Cole 2017.

letter of μή was probably omitted by accident after the preceding Καφαρναούμ ('Capernaum'). As there are fewer variants in Luke, the differences here are probably due to assimilation towards the Matthean parallel. Although the external evidence suggests that the rhetorical question is the older reading, with the majority reading from Matt. 11:23 being introduced later, a very slight possibility remains that the assimilation could have happened in the opposite direction.

10:15   καταβήσῃ (you will be brought down) {C}

As with the previous unit, the same variation appears at Matt. 11:23 (see above). There is slim but early attestation here for καταβήσῃ (lit. 'you shall go down'; 𝔓⁷⁵ 03 05 579 1342 lat^{vl-pt} sy^{c, s} eth) and much broader support for καταβιβασθήσῃ ('you will be brought down'; 𝔓⁴⁵ 01 02 04 019 etc.). It was observed in the parallel passage that καταβήσῃ is more common in Greek and occurs on multiple occasions in the Septuagint, which may make καταβιβασθήσῃ the harder reading, as preferred by the SBLGNT and THGNT.[25] It could be that Luke introduced a different term to that in Matthew, which led to the confusion, but the similar attestation in both places suggests that the variation could be the result of the same editorial intervention. The direction of this, however, is hard to establish. There is relatively little difference in meaning between the two verbs: in translation, as noted above, even if καταβιβασθήσῃ is adopted it may be necessary to render the 'divine passive' as an active verb with God as subject.

10:17   ἑβδομήκοντα [δύο] (seventy [two]) {D}

The same variant readings are found here as at Luke 10:1, with almost the same attestation. On this occasion, 𝔓⁴⁵ is partly extant and supports ἑβδομήκοντα ('seventy'; 𝔓^{45vid} 01 02 04 019 etc.) although the numeral occurs at the end of a fragmentary line.[26] The Curetonian Syriac changes from 'seventy-two' in 10:1 to 'seventy' in the present verse. Nevertheless, the original reading should be identical to the beginning of the pericope, with the same editorial intervention made in both places. Some Greek minuscules also have ἑβδομήκοντα μαθηταί ('sev-

---

[25] Also Wasserman 2017: 97–98.
[26] For confirmation of this, see Cole 2017 and Wasserman 2017: 96.

enty disciples'; 1243) in this verse, matching the lectionary tradition in the earlier verse.

10:21 [ἐν] τῷ πνεύματι τῷ ἁγίῳ (in the Holy Spirit) {C}

The majority of manuscripts read τῷ πνεύματι ὁ Ἰησοῦς ('Jesus [rejoiced in] the spirit'; 02 032 037 044 etc.), which could either mean 'within himself' or 'in the Holy Spirit'. The other readings have limited attestation: early witnesses cluster around ἐν τῷ πνεύματι τῷ ἁγίῳ ('[he rejoiced] in the Holy Spirit'; 01 05 040 1241 etc.) or τῷ πνεύματι τῷ ἁγίῳ ('[he rejoiced in] the Holy Spirit'; 𝔓⁷⁵ 03), while two have just ἐν τῷ πνεύματι ('[he rejoiced] in the spirit'; 𝔓⁴⁵ᵛⁱᵈ 157). Other manuscripts have a longer form with all three elements, such as τῷ πνεύματι τῷ ἁγίῳ ὁ Ἰησοῦς ('Jesus [rejoiced in] the Holy Spirit'; 04 f^1 syʰ) or ὁ Ἰησοῦς τῷ πνεύματι τῷ ἁγίῳ ('Jesus [rejoiced in] the Holy Spirit'; [019] 038 [33] 579 etc.): the full attestation in Greek continuous-text manuscripts is given in *TuT Luke* (TS20). Of the variants, 'Jesus' appears to be a later addition for clarification before the discourse: there is no reason for it to have been omitted and it does not change the sense in context. It is more difficult to decide whether ἐν ('in') and ἁγίῳ ('holy') are original. The problem appears to be the ambiguity of the construction: is 'spirit' the reason or the means of Jesus' rejoicing? At John 5:35 and 1 Pet. 1:6, ἀγαλλιαθῆναι ('to rejoice') clearly takes ἐν, but at Luke 1:47 it is followed by ἐπί ('at') although a few manuscripts have ἐν: the dative alone is seen at 1 Pet. 1:8. Analogies for an instrumental use are seen elsewhere in the gospels (e.g. Mark 2:8, 8:12; Luke 2:27, 4:1; John 11:33, 13:21). Few of these, however, refer to the 'Holy Spirit', making this the more difficult reading, even though it is also possible that ἁγίῳ was a later addition deemed appropriate before the following theological discourse. It may also be observed that references to 'the' Holy Spirit are comparatively rare in Luke (cf. Luke 1:15, 1:41, 4:1, 11:13 etc.). The distribution of the readings makes it difficult to be confident about the earliest form, and the exact meaning here. The SBLGNT and THGNT both adopt the oldest attested text (τῷ πνεύματι τῷ ἁγίῳ).

10:22 πάντα (all things) {A}

At the beginning of this verse, the majority of manuscripts include the line καὶ στραφεὶς πρὸς τοὺς μαθητὰς εἶπεν ('and turning towards the disciples, he said'; 02 04 032 037 etc.). This is clearly a later addition in order to make sense of the change from addressing the Father in the second person to speaking about him in the third person: it anticipates the same text at the beginning of verse 23, which thus becomes redundant. The shorter reading has extensive early support ($\mathfrak{P}^{45}$ $\mathfrak{P}^{75}$ 01 03 05 etc.). The full range of variants is given in *TuT Luke* (TS21), many only attested in one or two manuscripts, and these illustrate the way in which readings could be supplemented, replaced or expanded in minor ways during copying. If the shorter reading is followed, it may be necessary in translation to indicate that this verse continues to be part of Jesus' prayer.

10:27 [τῆς] καρδίας (heart)

The definite article is missing before καρδίας ('heart') in four early manuscripts ($\mathfrak{P}^{75}$ 03 040 070). Codex Vaticanus also lacks the definite article in the parallels at Matt. 22:37 (with numerous other witnesses) and Mark 12:30 and 12:33. This consistency suggests that the shorter reading may be the work of an editor. On the other hand, there are several other instances of καρδία without the definite article in this gospel (Luke 1:17, 1:51, 6:45, 8:15) which, with the slightly wider early attestation, allows the possibility that this may be authorial. The source text, Deut. 6:5, reads τῆς καρδίας in the Septuagint, and the expected direction of change would be to conform the gospel accounts to this. Translation is unaffected. This verse is included in *ECM Parallel Pericopes*.

10:32 [γενόμενος] (lit. arriving)

The participle γενόμενος ('arriving') is superfluous with the following ἐλθών ('coming'), although both appear in Byzantine tradition. While γενομενος is absent from a range of early manuscripts ($\mathfrak{P}^{75}$ 01² 03 019 040 etc.), other ancient witnesses lack ἐλθών instead ($\mathfrak{P}^{45}$ 05 etc.). Elsewhere in Luke, this sort of construction usually involves ἐλθών (e.g. Luke 8:51, 11:25, 12:37 etc.), but there is a very close parallel for γενομενος at Luke 22:40. While the external evidence suggests that γενομενος is a later addition, and the longer majority reading the result of conflation, its difficulty means that both of the shorter forms could be later editorial improvements. Nevertheless, both the SBLGNT and THGNT omit γενομενος in keeping with the external evidence. If

10:38 αὐτόν (him) {B}

At the end of this verse, some early witnesses include the phrase εἰς τὴν οἰκίαν (αὐτῆς) ('into [her] home'; 𝔓³ᵛⁱᵈ 01 04 019 040 etc.), while the majority of manuscripts have εἰς τὸν οἶκον αὐτῆς ('into her house'; 02 05 032 037 etc.). Only four witnesses lack this phrase, but they are all early (𝔓⁴⁵ 𝔓⁷⁵ 03 coˢᵃ). There is no obvious reason for the omission of this phrase, which expands the verb ὑπεδέξατο ('received'): the only other instance of this in the New Testament is at Luke 19:6, where it stands by itself (although the previous verse provides the context). The presence of multiple forms suggests that the longer forms are secondary, introduced independently on at least two occasions, but the relatively slim attestation of the shorter form allows for some doubt: SBLGNT has the shortest reading, but the THGNT prefers εἰς τὴν οἰκίαν.[27] In translation, some expansion may in any case be required to convey the meaning of ὑπεδέξατο. The full list of variants in Greek continuous-text manuscripts is given in *TuT Luke* (TS22).

10:39 [ἣ] καί (who [also])

The relative pronoun ἣ ('who') is missing from a range of early witnesses (𝔓⁴⁵ 𝔓⁷⁵ 01* 03² 019 040 579). Although it could easily have been overlooked, it is noteworthy that it was deleted by a corrector of Codex Vaticanus. The presence of the pronoun might be seen as removing the ambiguity that the second part of the verse could apply to Martha instead of Mary (in contrast with the following verse), and THGNT prefers the shorter reading. However, it has been observed that the combination of the pronoun and the following καί ('also') implies that both women were 'sitting at the Lord's feet' (which may be taken as a metaphor for discipleship).[28] Wasserman considers this—the majority form, also adopted in the SBLGNT—to be the harder reading, meaning that an editor was more likely to delete the pronoun (as in Codex Vaticanus).[29] However, the balance of internal and external evidence means

---

[27] For arguments in favour of the longer reading, see also Wyant 2019.
[28] D'Angelo, cited in Wasserman 2018: 457.
[29] Wasserman 2018: 457.

that it is difficult to be confident about the earliest text, and it is possible that the pronoun was added (or omitted) on more than one occasion.

10:41–42 μεριμνᾷς καὶ θορυβάζῃ περὶ πολλά, ἑνὸς δέ ἐστιν χρεία (lit. you are worried and distracted by many things; but only one thing is needed) {C}

There is slim support for the editorial text (𝔓⁴⁵ 𝔓⁷⁵ 04* 032 038*), but the majority of manuscripts have a very similar text in which the rare word θορυβάζῃ is replaced by a slightly more common synonym τυρβάζῃ ('you are troubled'; 02 037 038ᶜ 𝑓¹³ etc.). A variety of early manuscripts read μεριμνᾷς καὶ θορυβάζῃ περὶ πολλά, ὀλίγων δέ ἐστιν χρεία ἢ ἑνός ('you are worried and troubled by many things, but there is need of few things, or of one'; 𝔓³ 01 [03] 04² 019 etc.). While some have seen this as a later expansion of the shorter reading, in order to soften the contrast between 'many things' and 'one thing', others argue that this opposition is secondary: the lack of clarity as to the significance of the 'few things', a reading attested as early as Origen, led to its deletion.[30] That this statement was seen as problematic in antiquity seems to be reflected in Codex Bezae, which simply reads θορυβάζῃ ('you are troubled'; 05 latᵛˡ⁻ᵖᵗ); the Sinaitic Syriac and some Old Latin witnesses lack the phrase completely. Although the attestation of a shorter form in Byzantine tradition is less usual, it can be claimed that this is a simpler reading and therefore secondary. Internal evidence from Luke is inconclusive: the natural opposition between πολύς ('much') and ὀλίγος ('little') is seen on several occasions (e.g. Luke 7:47, 10:2, 12:48), but there are also instances of 'many' and 'one' (cf. Luke 4:25–27, 16:10). While the THGNT agrees with the text adopted here, the longer reading is accepted in the SBLGNT and translated in the NRSVue as 'but few things are needed—indeed only one'.[31]

11:2 πάτερ (Father) {A}

The majority of manuscripts read πάτερ ἡμῶν ὁ ἐν τοῖς οὐρανοῖς ('Our Father in heaven'; 02 04 05 032 etc.), matching the parallel at Matt. 6:9. The short reading, of just πάτερ ('Father'; 𝔓⁷⁵ 01 03 etc.), has strong

---

[30] For the former view, Metzger 1994: 129; the latter is in Wasserman 2017: 98–102 and Wasserman 2018. See too Fee 1981.

[31] The longer reading is also preferred by Wasserman and Fee (see previous note).

support among early witnesses: there is no obvious reason for deliberate or accidental omission, whereas assimilation to the Matthean form is extremely likely. Origen explicitly comments on the differences between these two gospels, providing further early evidence in support of their divergent texts.[32]

11:2   ἐλθέτω ἡ βασιλεία σου· (Your kingdom come) {A}

On this occasion, the earliest witnesses align with Byzantine tradition in attesting to the shortest reading, ἐλθέτω ἡ βασιλεία σου ('your kingdom come'; 𝔓[75] 01 02 03 04 etc.). This strong external support leads to its adoption as the editorial text. The variant readings are intriguing but not sufficiently well supported to be taken as the earliest form. Codex Bezae reads ἐφ' ἡμᾶς ἐλθέτω σου ἡ βασιλεία ('upon us may your kingdom come'; 05 lat[vl·pt]), which appears to be an expansion matching the references to the first-person plural in the following clauses.[33] It is possible that this is loosely connected with an even more poorly attested form, ἐλθέτω τὸ πνεῦμά σου τὸ ἅγιον ἐφ' ἡμᾶς καὶ καθαρισάτω ἡμᾶς ('may your Holy Spirit come upon us and cleanse us'; 700 Tertullian[vid] Gregory-Nyssa). That form, in turn, could be linked to Marcion's text as reported by Tertullian, here reconstructed as: ἐλθάτω τὸ ἅγιον πνεῦμά σου, ἐλθάτω ἡ βασιλεία σου ('may your Holy Spirit come, may your kingdom come').[34] The evidence in early Christian writers confirms that a version of the Lord's Prayer referring to the Holy Spirit rather than the kingdom was circulating at least in the fourth century and possibly the end of the second century, even though direct evidence for this is much later. It is generally thought that the mention of the Spirit was introduced through liturgical influence.[35] Even so, the agreement between the majority reading and Matt. 6:10 means that the text adopted here could be a secondary assimilation despite its strong early support.

---

[32] This is quoted in Parker 1997: 62–63, as part of a chapter which illustrates and discusses the differences between the two forms of the Lord's Prayer.

[33] In fact, ἐφ' ἡμᾶς appears on the previous line in Codex Bezae, indicating that it should be taken with the preceding clause: 'may your name be hallowed upon us'. Metzger 1994: 131 notes that this is in keeping with references in the Hebrew Scriptures to the 'dwelling of the divine name' (e. g. Deut. 12:11, 14:23 etc.).

[34] For the complexities of this evidence, see Roth 2015: 138–140.

[35] See Metzger 1994: 131, Parker 1997: 67 and Strutwolf 2011: 25–32.

11:2 βασιλεία σου· (your kingdom) {A}

After this petition, the majority of Greek manuscripts read γενηθήτω τὸ θέλημά σου ὡς ἐν οὐρανῷ καὶ ἐπὶ τῆς γῆς ('your will be done on earth as in heaven'; 01 02 04 05 etc.), as seen at Matt. 6:10. Some early translations simply support γενηθήτω τὸ θέλημά σου ('your will be done'; lat[vl-pt, vg-ms] co[sa, bo-mss]). The shortest form, which entirely lacks the extra clause, is attested by several early witnesses (𝔓[75] 03 019 *f*[1] 1342 lat[vg] sy[c, s] Tertullian[vid] Origen). As at the beginning of the verse (see above) and in Luke 11:4, this attestation makes it highly probable that the longer readings arose through assimilation to the Matthean parallel.

11:4 πειρασμόν (the time of trial) {A}

The same early witnesses which support the shorter reading in the previous unit, joined by others, end the Lord's Prayer in Luke with πειρασμόν ('the time of trial'; 𝔓[75] 01[*, 2b] 03 019 *f*[1] 700 1342 lat[vg] sy[s] co[sa, bo-pt] Tertullian[vid] Origen Cyril). Although the majority of Greek manuscripts include ἀλλὰ ῥῦσαι ἡμᾶς ἀπὸ τοῦ πονηροῦ ('but rescue us from the evil one'; 02 04 05 032 etc.), this is very likely to be assimilation to Matt. 6:10. An example of how such additions, made by memory, can go wrong is seen in Codex Sinaiticus: a corrector first begain to add the Matthean phrase at the end of the prayer, but erased this before it was completed and instead wrote in the margin further up καὶ ῥῦσαι ἡμᾶς ἀπὸ τοῦ πονηροῦ ('and rescue us from the evil one'; 01[2a]), placing the insertion mark after ἐπὶ τῆς γῆς ('on earth') at the end of Luke 11:2.

11:10 ἀνοιγ[ήσ]εται (will be opened)

The Byzantine tradition is split between two different orthographic forms of the future tense, ἀνοιγήσεται ('will be opened'; 𝔓[45] 01 04 019 038 044 etc.) and ἀνοιχθήσεται ('will be opened'; 02 032 037 etc.). A few early witnesses read the present-tense ἀνοίγεται ('is opened'; 𝔓[75] 03 05). Although the future tense could be assimilation to the same verb in the previous verse, it is the harder reading in this verse where all the other verbs are in the present tense (yet with a future significance). This, and the future tense in the parallel at Matt. 7:8, suggests that ἀνοίγεται is an editorial correction (as is also seen in Codex Vaticanus in Matthew) or even a copying error: both SBLGNT and THGNT have ἀνοιγήσεται.[36]

11:11 ἰχθύν (for a fish) {B}

Most Greek manuscripts include a phrase corresponding to the parallel at Matt. 7:9, ἄρτον μὴ λίθον ἐπιδώσει αὐτῷ; ἢ καὶ ἰχθύν ('[asks for] bread will give them a stone? Or, too, for a fish'; 02 04 [05] 032 037 etc.); another group of witnesses also includes this text but without καί ('too'; 01 019 28 33 etc.). The support for the shortest reading of just ἰχθύν ('for a fish'; 𝔓⁴⁵ [𝔓⁷⁵] 03 1241 etc.) includes Origen, early translations, and possibly Marcion.[37] There is no obvious reason for accidental omission, and the short reading makes better sense of the additional clarification ἀντὶ ἰχθύος ('instead of a fish') appearing in the first unit: such a rewriting of the Matthean passage deliberately excludes 'bread' and 'stone', perhaps in order to remove the reminiscence of the Temptations (Luke 4:3), with the illustration of the egg and scorpion—corresponding more closely to the fish and snake—added instead. The reintroduction of the first phrase from Matthew makes less sense of Luke's changes (cf. Luke 17:35 below): only the relative scarcity of the shorter reading in Greek manuscripts gives cause for uncertainty. See also *ECM Parallel Pericopes*.

11:13 [ὁ] ἐξ οὐρανοῦ (heavenly) {C}

The majority of witnesses read ὁ ἐξ οὐρανοῦ ('who [is] from heaven' or 'who from heaven [will give]'; 02 03 05 032 037 etc.), while a group of early manuscripts have just ἐξ οὐρανοῦ ('from heaven'; 𝔓⁷⁵ 01 019 044 etc.) and a few others have ὑμῶν ὁ ἐξ οὐρανοῦ ('your [Father] who [is/will give] from heaven'; 04 [*f*¹³] etc.). Some read ὑμῶν ὁ οὐράνιος ('your heavenly [Father]'; 𝔓⁴⁵ 579 1424 etc.) and part of the Old Latin tradition supports ὑμῶν ('your [Father]'; lat^(vl-pt)). Fuller details of attestation are given in *ECM Parallel Pericopes*. If the text is interpreted as referring to a 'heavenly Father', this would be the only such reference in Luke (or Acts), but it does correspond to the parallel at Matt. 7:11: ὁ πατὴρ ὑμῶν ὁ ἐν τοῖς οὐρανοῖς ('your Father who is in the heavens').

---

[36] This is also supported by Wasserman 2017: 103. See in addition *ECM Parallel Pericopes* (Strutwolf & Wachtel 2011: 12–13).

[37] See further Roth 2015: 421.

On the other hand, any of the readings with ἐξ οὐρανοῦ can be taken with the following verb, 'will give from heaven'. The inclusion of ὑμῶν ('your') is likely to be due to the Matthean parallel or Lukan practice elsewhere, while οὐράνιος ('heavenly') is assimilation to other passages in Matthew. Of the other two forms ἐξ οὐρανοῦ diverges most from Matthew, but ὁ ἐξ οὐρανοῦ is the harder reading which highlights the exegetical ambiguity yet is widely attested. The latter is adopted in the SBLGNT and THGNT, but in either case translators will have to decide whether to interpret it as '[who is] from heaven' or '[who] will give from heaven'. The vast majority of English translations prefer the former, assimilating it to Matthew, but this may risk obscuring a possible theological difference in Luke.

11:13 πνεῦμα ἅγιον (Holy Spirit) {A}

The hardest reading in context, πνεῦμα ἅγιον ('Holy Spirit'; 𝔓[75] 01 02 03 04 etc.), has abundant support in Greek manuscripts. The readings ἀγαθὸν δόμα ('a good gift'; 05 lat[vl-pt] [eth]) and δόματα ἀγαθά ('good gifts'; 038) provide the expected object from the beginning of the verse: the singular in Codex Bezae presumably reflects the subject of the verb, in contrast to the previous plural. The variant ἀγαθά ('good things'; lat[vg-ms] sy[s]), only seen in early translations, is assimilation to Matt. 7:11. The curious reading πνεῦμα ἀγαθόν ('good spirit'; 𝔓[45] 019 lat[vl-pt, vg] sy[hmg] Cyril[pt]) may be a conflation of the others or simply a misreading of ἅγιον as ἀγαθόν.[38] Although ἅγιον ('holy') often follows πνεῦμα ('spirit'), the external evidence indicates that it is more likely that the expectation of 'good' from the previous clause led to its introduction here. In translation, it may be worth noting that this is a typically Lukan anarthrous use of 'Holy Spirit' (see Luke 10:21 above), so the article could be supplied in order to correspond with practice elsewhere.

11:14 [καὶ αὐτὸ ἦν] (that was)

The majority of Greek manuscripts include the phrase καὶ αὐτὸ ἦν ('and it was'; 02[c] 04 032 037 038 etc.), but it is lacking from the earliest witnesses (𝔓[45] 𝔓[75] 01 02* 03 019 etc., sy[c, s] co). The full list of variants in Greek continuous-text manuscripts is given in *TuT Luke* (TS23). The

---

[38] North 2005, however, prefers this as the earliest text.

shorter reading appears to be the smoother form, but its general sense is difficult: usually demons cause muteness rather than being mute themselves, as appears to be implied in the following sentence (compare also the parallel at Matt. 9:32). It is therefore possible that the additional words were supplied in an attempt to clarify this. Even if the shorter reading is followed, as in the SBLGNT and THGNT, some expansion may be required in translation.

11:20   [ἐγώ] (I)

Before ἐκβάλλω ('I cast out'), some early witnesses include the emphatic pronoun ἐγώ ('I'; 𝔓^{75} 01^{1} 03 04 [05] 019 etc., lat^{vl} co) but it is missing from the majority of manuscripts (𝔓^{45} 01* 02 032 037 etc.). It is possible that it was omitted through eyeskip, or added through assimilation to the previous verse or the parallel at Matt. 12:28. In any case, there is little difference in translation.

11:23   σκορπίζει (scatters) {B}

Although almost all Greek manuscripts and early translations just have σκορπίζει ('scatters'; 𝔓^{45} [𝔓^{75}] 01^{2a} 02 03 etc.), a group of witnesses reads σκορπίζει με ('scatters me'; 01*, ^{2b} 04^{2} 019 038 etc.). The sense of this is very difficult, unless it is taken to refer in some way to the theological understanding of Christians as members of the body of Christ, which is not obvious in context.[39] It is possible that με was simply added through inadvertence by a copyist influenced by 'me' as a complement of the three previous elements in the clause, but one would expect this to be in the form μετ' ἐμοῦ ('with me') or κατ' ἐμοῦ ('against me'). A copyist may have started writing μετ' ἐμοῦ and stopped after the first two letters, which were nonetheless incorporated in subsequent copies. If this were the case, however, it is surprising to see the breadth of its attestation, including the Sinaitic Syriac and Bohairic. Furthermore, the fact that με was added by two correctors (Codex Sinaiticus and Codex Ephraemi Rescriptus) suggests that it was not considered nonsensical: this is also evident in witnesses which read it in the parallel at Matt. 12:30 (01 33 sy^{h} co^{bo}), although that may simply be assimilation to the

---

[39] Ehrman 2011: 159–160 suggests that this sense underlies a deliberate later addition.

present verse. While the original, absolute use of σκορπίζει is extremely well attested and matches the Matthean source, this variant offers some insight into patterns of transmission.

11:24 [τότε] λέγει ([then] it says)

There is early support for the adverb τότε ('then'; 𝔓⁷⁵ 01² 03 019 038 040 etc.), but it is missing from the majority of manuscripts (𝔓⁴⁵ 01* 02 04 05 032 etc.). If it was original, it may have been deleted by an editor who considered that the true complement of the phrase beginning ὅταν ('whenever') was the τότε at the beginning of Luke 11:26—but there is no evidence for this in the parallel at Matt. 12:44. On the other hand, it could easily have been added by someone who felt that this clause was too distant from the initial ὅταν, or more likely through assimilation to the Matthean parallel. The appearance of this shorter reading both in early witnesses and in Byzantine tradition favours it as original, a Lukan improvement to Matthew which was nevertheless undone by the insertion of τότε at an early point in transmission (compare Luke 11:11 above).

11:33 [οὐδὲ ὑπὸ τὸν μόδιον] (or under a bushel basket) {C}

The phrase οὐδὲ ὑπὸ τὸν μόδιον ('nor under the bushel basket'; 01 02 03 04 05 etc.) appears in the majority of Greek manuscripts, but is missing from both papyri and other important witnesses (𝔓⁴⁵ 𝔓⁷⁵ 019 040 070 *f*¹ etc., sy^s co^sa). Although the bushel basket appears in the parallels (Matt. 5:15; see also Mark 4:21), it does not feature in the earlier instance of the same saying at Luke 8:16, where Luke prefers σκεύει ('jar'), and here it is made superfluous by Luke's reference to the lamp being put 'into a cellar' (εἰς κρύπτην). While this internal evidence suggests that the shorter reading is more likely to be original (as accepted by the THGNT and Wasserman), the strong external evidence in support of the extra phrase provides justification for its adoption in the SBLGNT.[40]

11:44 [οἱ] περιπατοῦντες (walk)

The definite article οἱ, which may here be translated as 'who [walk]', is found in several early majuscule manuscripts (01 03 04 019 [038] 044 etc.), but is missing from the majority of Greek witnesses (𝔓⁷⁵ 02 05 032

---

[40] See Wasserman 2017: 104.

037 etc.). As it follows the noun ἄνθρωποι ('people'), it would be easy for the article to be omitted through haplography or introduced through dittography. There are few direct parallels, but Lukan practice elsewhere appears to support the definite article before a participle (e.g. Luke 13:4), suggesting that the longer reading is preferable. There is minimal effect on translation.

12:22 [αὐτοῦ] (his)

A few early witnesses lack the pronoun ($\mathfrak{P}^{45\text{vid}}$ $\mathfrak{P}^{75}$ 03 1241 lat$^{\text{vl-pt}}$), which is present in the majority of Greek manuscripts (01 02 05 019 032 etc.) and early translations. Lukan usage does not provide a clear guide: αὐτοῦ is also lacking or unclear in the same context at Luke 16:1 and 17:22 (cf. 10:23, 22:45). Given that the pronoun in the phrase 'his disciples' would be expected from the many instances elsewhere, it is more likely that it would have been added rather than removed. The possibility of error (or, indeed, assimilation to the other shorter readings in Luke) cannot be ruled out.[41] The choice of reading makes little difference in translation, and in some languages the pronoun would be appropriate or necessary even if the shorter form is adopted. See also Luke 20:45 below.

12:39 οὐκ (not) {C}

Most manuscripts read ἐγρηγόρησεν ἄν καὶ οὐκ ('he would have watched and not'; [01¹] 01² 02 03 019 etc.), but the phrase is lacking from early witnesses which only support οὐκ ('not'; $\mathfrak{P}^{75}$ 01* [05] lat$^{\text{vl-pt}}$ sy$^{\text{c, s}}$ co$^{\text{sa-mss, ach}}$ Marcion). The former matches the parallel at Matt. 24:43, making the shorter reading the more difficult form and therefore more likely to be original: Luke could have removed it as incidental to the sense, and he uses the verb γρηγορεῖν ('to watch') much less frequently than Matthew or Mark. However, the phrase could also have fallen out accidentally through eyeskip between the end of ἔρχεται and καί. The very limited attestation of the shorter reading in Greek manuscripts would be consistent with such a copying error, leading to considerable

---

[41] On this phrase throughout the gospels see Elliott 1979, who prefers the longer reading here.

doubt as to the earliest text here. The SBLGNT also prefers the shorter form, whereas the THGNT follows the majority text.

12:42 [τὸ] σιτομέτριον (allowance of food)

The definite article τό is present in the majority of manuscripts (01 02 019 032 etc.) but missing from a few witnesses, some of which are early (𝔓⁷⁵ 03 05 *f*¹³ co^(bo-mss)). There are several other occasions where the object of διδόναι ('to give') lacks an article (e.g. Luke 7:44–45, 9:1, 11:13, 15:29, 18:43, 23:2 etc.), but it could have been overlooked. This is the only occurrence of σιτομέτριον in the New Testament, so there is no direct parallel. In any case, translation is unaffected.

12:54 [τὴν] νεφέλην (cloud)

A significant number of early manuscripts only read νεφέλην ('a cloud'; 𝔓⁷⁵ 01 02 03 019 037 etc.), whereas the majority have τὴν νεφέλην ('the cloud'; 𝔓⁴⁵ 05 032 038 etc.). The shorter reading makes better sense in context, matching the anarthrous νότον ('a south wind') in the next verse: similarly, Luke only uses the definite article elsewhere to refer to a cloud which has already been mentioned (Luke 9:34–35, 21:27, Acts 1:9). This strongly favours νεφέλην by itself: it is possible that the article arose through partial dittography of the end of ἴδητε and beginning of νεφέλην.

13:7 ἔκκοψον [οὖν] (cut)

The conjunction οὖν ('and so'; 𝔓⁷⁵ 02 019 038 070 etc.) is missing from the majority of manuscripts, including several early witnesses (01 03 05 032 037 etc.). There are multiple instances in Luke of οὖν following an imperative (Luke 3:8, 8:18, 10:2, 10:40, 11:35 etc.) and it is possible here that it was overlooked due to its similarity to the preceding aorist imperative ending. On the other hand, it may have been added through analogy to the other imperatives: it could be argued that the reason for cutting the tree is provided by the following clause rather than solely the preceding one. The external evidence appears to favour the shorter reading, although it is finely balanced. The SBLGNT lacks οὖν while it is included in the THGNT.[42]

---

[42] Wasserman 2017: 105 also supports οὖν.

13:9 εἰς τὸ μέλλον· εἰ δὲ μή γε (next year … but if not) {B}

The majority of manuscripts have these clauses in the sequence εἰ δὲ μή γε, εἰς τὸ μέλλον ('but if does not for the following [year]'; 𝔓⁴⁵ᵛⁱᵈ 02 05 032 037 etc.). This offers a smoother reading than the early witnesses which have εἰς τὸ μέλλον· εἰ δὲ μή γε, ('[bear fruit] for the following [year]; but if does not'; 𝔓⁷⁵ 01 03 019 etc.), which involves an unexpected break after 'the following year'. This harder reading has been adopted on the grounds of its difficulty and the external attestation, but in translation it may be thought appropriate to indicate the change of thought by an ellipsis ('and if it should bear fruit next year …') or a dash, or to supply the missing intention (e.g. 'well' in the KJV, 'fine' in the NIV, or 'well and good' in the NRSVue).

13:19 δένδρον (a tree) {B}

Most witnesses read δένδρον μέγα ('a big tree'; 𝔓⁴⁵ 02 032 037 etc.), but others have just δένδρον ('a tree'; 𝔓⁷⁵ 01 03 05 019 etc.; the full list of variants is given in *TuT Luke* TS28). There is no adjective in the parallel at Matt. 13:32 and, while there is at least one example of Luke adding this adjective to his sources (Luke 21:11; cf. Matt. 24:7 and Mark 13:8), the external evidence suggests that μέγα is a later addition in order to emphasise the difference in size between the seed and the tree. It remains possible, however, that it was removed through assimilation to the Matthean source.

13:27 ἐρεῖ λέγων ὑμῖν (he will say to you) {C}

Most manuscripts have ἐρεῖ· λέγω ὑμῖν ('he will say, "I say to you"'; 𝔓⁷⁵* 02 05 019 032 etc.). This differs by only a single letter from ἐρεῖ λέγων ὑμῖν ('he will say, speaking to you'; 𝔓⁷⁵ᶜ 03 205 892). Other witnesses have ἐρεῖ ὑμῖν ('he will say to you'; 01 579 latᵛˡ⁻ᵖᵗ, ᵛᵍ syᵖ coˢᵃ, ᵇᵒ⁻ᵖᵗ) or just ἐρεῖ ('he will say'; coᵇᵒ⁻ᵖᵗ). The full list of variants in Greek continuous-text manuscripts is given in *TuT Luke* (TS29). This is the second instance of this rebuke, following Luke 13:25, so the question is whether this is an exact repetition (see also the next unit). Adopting λέγων ὑμῖν would keep the direct speech the same, with λέγων corresponding to the participle before ἐρεῖ at Luke 13:25, but it is technically redundant and there is no other instance of this collocation in the New Testament (despite attempts to explain it as a Hebraic construction).[43] Its removal would explain the origin of the reading ἐρεῖ ὑμῖν. On the other hand, there are many instances in Luke of λέγω ὑμῖν as an intensifier, and this would be in keeping with the extension of the rebuke through the quotation of Ps. 6:8 [6:9 LXX]. Given that either of the longer readings could have arisen from the other by a simple copying error, it is difficult to be confident as to the earliest form. While λέγων is the hardest reading, and a copyist might have been primed by Luke 13:24 to introduce λέγω ὑμῖν here, the attestation of λέγων is very slim: even though Codex Sinaiticus might be considered as indirect support, ἐρεῖ ὑμῖν could still be an improvement of a secondary error rather than the most ancient form. The SBLGNT agrees with the editorial text here, while the THGNT prefers the majority reading. Even if λέγων is adopted, it may be simplest in translation to omit it as superfluous.

13:27 οἶδα [ὑμᾶς] (know ... you)

Although the inclusion of ὑμᾶς ('you'; 01 02 032 037 etc.) in the majority of Greek manuscripts matches the version of this rebuke two verses earlier, these are generally the witnesses which have already added λέγω ὑμῖν ('I say to you') at the beginning of the direct speech (see the previous unit). Conversely, a significant proportion of the sources which lack ὑμᾶς (𝔓⁷⁵ 03 019 070 1241 etc.) are those which preserve the same opening words as Luke 13:25. Even though the pronoun ὑμᾶς is redundant, there is no doubt about its inclusion in the earlier rebuke: the present unit is rather a question of style involving the extent to which variation is introduced into the second speech. The external and internal evidence are both evenly balanced, making a decision difficult. The THGNT has the longer reading and the SBLGNT the shorter one. In translation, the pronoun may be idiomatic in some languages but not in others.

13:35 ὑμῶν (to you) {B}

The Byzantine tradition is divided between just ὑμῶν ('to you'; 𝔓⁴⁵ᵛⁱᵈ 𝔓⁷⁵ 01 02 03 etc.) and ὑμῶν ἔρημος ('to you desolate'; 05 037 038 044 etc.), with the latter appearing in the *Textus Receptus*. The same variation appears at Matt. 23:38, where ἔρημος is adopted as the editorial text (see

---

[43] See Metzger 1994: 137.

above). As noted there, this additional word may be considered superfluous after the verb ἀφίεται ('is left'), and there is also the possibility that it was introduced in order to correspond more closely to the source (Jer. 22:5, although the verbal parallels with the Septuagint are limited). In this case, the strong early evidence for the shorter reading leads to its adoption here, but expansion may be appropriate in translation.

13:35   λέγω [δέ] (and I tell)

The connective δέ is absent from a few manuscripts ($\mathfrak{P}^{45}$ 01* 019) and apparently not supported by the earliest translations (lat^{vl} sy^c co^{sa}). This makes for some doubt as to whether it was present in the earliest text. However, as λέγω ὑμῖν ('I say to you') and λέγω δὲ ὑμῖν ('But I say to you') are both found throughout Luke and there is no obvious reason for its addition or deletion, on this occasion it is reasonable to follow the majority reading which also has extensive early support.

13:35   ἕως [ἥξει ὅτε] εἴπητε (until the time comes when you say) {C}

The Byzantine tradition is split between ἕως ἂν ἥξῃ ὅτε εἴπητε ('until [the time] might come when you say'; 044 180 565 597 etc., including the *Textus Receptus*) and ἕως ἂν ἥξει ὅτε εἴπητε ('until [the time] may come when you say'; 02 022 032 etc.). The difference is likely to be itacism resulting in the interchange of EI and H. Earlier witnesses present a variety of alternatives: ἕως ἥξει ὅτε εἴπητε ('until [the time] will come when you say'; 05: some early translations add ἡ ἡμέρα, 'until the day...'); ἕως εἴπητε ('until you say'; $\mathfrak{P}^{75}$ 03 019 892); ἕως ἂν εἴπητε ('until when you may say'; $\mathfrak{P}^{45}$ 01 f^1 etc); ἀπ' ἄρτι ἕως ἂν εἴπητε ('from now until when you may say'; 038 1241 etc.); ἀπ' ἄρτι ἕως ἂν ἥξει ὅτε εἴπητε ('from now until [the time] may come when you say'; 037). The reading of 038 matches the parallel at Matt. 23:39, but here this is too poorly attested to be the original form, while 037 has a conflation of both readings. The inclusion of a reference to 'the time coming' is a precision which may have been introduced by the evangelist, but the early attestation of ἕως ἂν εἴπητε (and ἕως εἴπητε, preferred in the THGNT) make it possible that Luke followed his source and the expansion is later (even though it is not found in the textual tradition in Matthew): the normal way of saying 'until the time when' in Luke is ἕως οὗ (e.g. Luke 13:21, 24:49) or ἕως ὅτου (e.g. Luke 12:20, 13:8, 22:16). The most difficult reading is that of Codex Bezae, where ἕως is followed directly by the future indicative and ὅτε by the subjunctive. This is the justification for its adoption in the editorial text and the SBLGNT despite its very slim attestation, although the lack of ἄν could simply be a scribal error. While considerable doubt remains about the earliest form of text, the meaning of all the variants is broadly similar, and expansion along similar lines may be required in translation.

14:1 [τῶν] Φαρισαίων (the Pharisees)

The definite article is missing from the four oldest Greek manuscripts (𝔓⁴⁵ 𝔓⁷⁵ 01 03). As it follows ἀρχόντων ('rulers'), it could easily have been omitted through haplography, or added later through dittography. Both constructions are unparalleled in Luke and the difference in their meaning is very slight. The external evidence may suggest that the longer reading is secondary and was perhaps prompted by the general tendency to include an article before Φαρισαίων.

14:5 υἱὸς ἢ βοῦς (a child or an ox) {B}

There is very strong external evidence for υἱὸς ἢ βοῦς ('a child or an ox'; 𝔓⁴⁵ 𝔓⁷⁵ [02] 03 032 etc.), attested by the earliest witnesses and the majority of manuscripts. A significant group, however, reads ὄνος ἢ βοῦς ('a donkey or an ox'; 01 019 044 *f*¹ etc.), while Codex Bezae has πρόβατον ἢ βοῦς ('a sheep or an ox'; 05). As the combination of 'ox' and 'donkey' appeared with regard to Sabbath observance at Luke 13:15, the majority reading with its unexpected pairing of 'child' and 'ox' is the hardest as well as the best attested form. Witnesses with all three terms (038 syᶜ) are the result of conflation: the more common readings cannot both be derived from these by eyeskip.

14:17 ἕτοιμά ἐστιν (is ready) {C}

The reading preferred in the editorial text and most other recent accounts is only attested in Greek by Codex Vaticanus and one minuscule not cited in UBS6 (GA 192).[44] There is early support for ἕτοιμά εἰσιν ('are ready'; 𝔓⁷⁵ 01*, ² 019 etc.), but this violates the grammatical con-

---

[44] It is also adopted by the SBLGNT, THGNT and Wasserman (2017: 106). Although *TuT Luke* (TS30) also lists 019, 027 and 038 in support of ἕτοιμά ἐστιν, they actually read ἕτοιμά εἰσιν.

vention that a neuter plural takes a singular verb: it was probably introduced during copying under the influence of the previous plural verb ἔρχεσθε ('come'). Such an error seems unlikely to be authorial (cf. Luke 15:31), although if it were then Codex Vaticanus would represent a later correction. The majority reading, ἕτοιμά ἐστιν πάντα ('everything is ready'; 02 032 037 etc.) and πάντα ἕτοιμά ἐστιν ('everything is ready'; 05 lat^(vl-pt)) are both likely to be assimilation to the parallel at Matt. 22:4. In translation, a similar expansion is likely to be necessary in order to represent the neuter plural.

15:16   χορτασθῆναι ἐκ (lit. to be fed from) {A}

The majority of Greek manuscripts read γεμίσαι τὴν κοιλίαν αὐτοῦ ἀπό ('to fill his belly from'; 02 037 038 044 etc.), but there is very strong early support for χορτασθῆναι ἐκ ('to be fed from'; 𝔓75 01 03 05 019 etc.). The latter corresponds to Lukan usage elsewhere (Luke 6:21, 16:21), in contrast with the rarity of γεμίσαι in the New Testament (and never of humans) and κοιλία only otherwise occurring in this gospel with the meaning 'womb'. Both internal and external evidence therefore suggest that the majority reading is the work of a later editor concerned that the text might misrepresent the nutritional properties of acorns.[45] Nevertheless, it is adopted in the SBLGNT and the NRSVue. Codex Washingtonianus has a conflation of the two readings: γεμίσαι τὴν κοιλίαν καὶ χορτασθῆναι ἀπό ('to fill [his] belly and be fed from'; 032). The full list of readings in Greek continuous-text manuscripts is given in *TuT Luke* (TS31).

15:21   υἱός σου. (your son) {B}

At the end of the verse, several of the earliest manuscripts along with around two hundred minuscules include ποίησόν με ὡς ἕνα τῶν μισθίων σου ('treat me as one of your hired servants'; 01 03 [05] 33 180 etc.). This repeats the final line of the son's planned speech in Luke 15:19, and it could well have been added through assimilation. On the other hand, the phrase may have been omitted at an early point through eyeskip between the two instances of σου.[46] Despite the force of the

---

[45] See further Westcott and Hort, quoted in Wasserman 2017: 107.
[46] IGNTP Luke (1987) shows that this is paralleled at Luke 15:19 by 032 and 713.

shorter reading appearing in the sole papyrus and the majority of manuscripts ($\mathfrak{P}^{75}$ 02 019 032 etc.), witnesses in which assimilation might be expected, the question remains as to whether the evangelist deliberately truncated the actual speech: if original, the shorter reading could convey a change of mind by the son, the recognition that events had overtaken him, or an interruption by his father. The full attestation in Greek continuous-text manuscripts is given in *TuT Luke* (TS32).

16:12 ὑμέτερον (your own) {B}

There is very strong external evidence for ὑμέτερον ('what is yours'; $\mathfrak{P}^{75}$ 01 02 05 032 etc.), attested in early manuscripts as well as the Byzantine tradition and which is the expected opposite of τῷ ἀλλοτρίῳ ('what belongs to another'). On the other hand, it might be perceived as contradictory to be given what is one's own. The variant ἡμέτερον ('what is ours'; 03 019 Origen[pt]) is probably an instance of the common variation between the first- and second-person plural due to the similar pronunciation of Υ and Η in later Greek. However, it was known as early as Origen and a case might be made for its originality: the first person could be considered the harder reading, understood as meaning something shared by Jesus and the disciples.[47] The two other variants seem to be simplifications. Tertullian reports Marcion as reading ἐμόν ('what is mine'; 157 lat[vl-pt]), but it is only transmitted in one Greek manuscript and may simply represent a scribal change to an expected reading. Two important minuscules have ἀληθινόν ('what is true'; 33[vid] 597*) which is likely to be assimilation to the previous verse.

16:21 τῶν πιπτόντων (what fell) {B}

The majority of witnesses read τῶν ψιχίων τῶν πιπτόντων ('the crumbs that fall'; 01² 02 [05] 032 037 etc.), matching the similar expression at Matt. 15:27. There is early support for τῶν πιπτόντων ('that which falls'; $\mathfrak{P}^{75}$ 01* 03 019 etc.). Although this could have arisen through eyeskip between the two instances of τῶν, the variant τῶν πιπτόντων ψιχίων ('the falling crumbs'; f^1 205) provides indirect support for the shorter reading, as it is an alternative way of assimilating it to the other gospels

---

[47] Metzger 1994: 140 notes that a theological interpretation of the first person plural as the Father and the Son is likely to have been a later development.

(cf. Mark 7:28). The oldest reading has therefore been preferred, but in translation it may require expansion. The full list of variants in Greek continuous-text manuscripts is given in *TuT Luke* (TS35).

17:3 ἁμάρτῃ (sins) {A}

There is strong early evidence for the short reading adopted in the text, ἁμάρτῃ ('should sin'; 01 02 03 019 032 etc. and most ancient translations). The majority reading, ἁμάρτῃ εἰς σέ ('should sin against you'; [05] [037] 044 [f^{13}] etc.) is likely to be the result of assimilation to the following verse or the parallel at Matt. 18:15 (in most manuscripts; see the fuller discussion above). Although there is an ethical difference between the two readings, with the shorter reading having broader implications (rebuke for any sin, not just sin 'against you'), this is minimised by the appearance of εἰς σέ in the next sentence.

17:6 [ταύτῃ] (this)

The demonstrative pronoun ταύτῃ ('this'; 02 03 032 037 038 etc.) is present in the majority of manuscripts but missing from a range of early witnesses ($\mathfrak{P}^{75}$ 01 05 019 579 sy^c), leading to doubt as to whether it is original. Even though Luke has changed the example from a mountain to a sycamore tree, there is a strong possibility that the demonstrative was added here through assimilation to Matt. 17:20. There is no obvious reason for accidental omission, and deliberate removal by an editor hardly makes the saying general in its application. While the THGNT has the shorter reading, the SBLGNT retains ταύτῃ.

17:9 διαταχθέντα (what was commanded) {B}

The shorter reading, with early attestation ($\mathfrak{P}^{75}$ 01^1 03 019 etc.), is a rhetorical question. In the majority of manuscripts, an answer is provided: οὐ δοκῶ ('I think not'; 02 05 032 037 [038] etc.: some of these, including the *Textus Receptus,* read διαταχθέντα αὐτῷ, 'what was commanded to him'). There is no parallel for this phrase elsewhere in the New Testament, and the provision of an answer to avoid any ambiguity is very likely to be secondary. Nevertheless, a possibility remains that it was accidentally omitted through eyeskip to the beginning of the following word (οὕτως). The full list of variants in Greek continuous-text manuscripts is given in *TuT Luke* (TS36). The external evidence indicates that the pronoun αὐτῷ ('to him') is unlikely be original, but it may be required or offer a smoother reading in certain languages (as seen in most early versions).

17:12 [αὐτῷ] (him)

The pronoun is attested in almost all manuscripts and is missing from just four early witnesses. Of these, Codex Bezae and Codex Regius (05 019) have different forms of the preceding verb, leaving just Papyrus 75 and Codex Vaticanus ($\mathfrak{P}^{75}$ 03) with the shorter reading. This is grammatically preferable, given the same pronoun in the genitive absolute at the beginning of the sentence, and fits well too with the following indication that they stood far off. The shorter reading could therefore be an editorial deletion, but it is also possible that it is original and αὐτῷ was added later by a reader who was uncomfortable with the lack of object following the verb ἀπήντησαν ('they met'). It may, in any case, be necessary to supply an object in translation.

17:23 [ἤ] (or)

The contrastive particle ἤ ('or') is attested in most manuscripts, but missing from some early witnesses (05 019 032 lat). Codex Sinaiticus and both Old Syriac manuscripts support καί ('and'; 01 etc.) instead. This leads to doubt as to whether ἤ was originally present at this point: it could have been introduced through assimilation to Luke 17:21, but as it is only a single letter, it may have been omitted through oversight or its similarity in sound to the preceding vowel (ἐκεῖ). In any case, as in the earlier verse, these are two separate exclamations which should be distinguished in translation.

17:24 ὁ υἱὸς τοῦ ἀνθρώπου [ἐν τῇ ἡμέρᾳ αὐτοῦ] (the Son of Man ... in his day) {C}

The majority of Greek manuscripts have the full text, ὁ υἱὸς τοῦ ἀνθρώπου ἐν τῇ ἡμέρᾳ αὐτοῦ ('the Son of Man in his day'; 01 02 019 [022] 032 etc.), whereas a few early witnesses read just ὁ υἱὸς τοῦ ἀνθρώπου ('the Son of Man'; $\mathfrak{P}^{75}$ 03 [05] lat^{vl-pt} co^{sa}). The longer reading may have arisen through assimilation to Luke 17:26, although that has the plural: the additional clause fits well with the following πρῶτον δέ ('but first'), yet this is adequately anticipated by the preceding future tense. There is also the possibility that ἐν τῇ ἡμέρᾳ αὐτοῦ was omitted through eyeskip after ἀνθρώπου. This makes it very difficult to be confident of the earliest form: both the SBLGNT and THGNT prefer the longer reading, while Wasserman inclines towards the shorter.[48] The alternative ἡ παρουσία τοῦ υἱοῦ τοῦ ἀνθρώπου ('the presence of the Son of Man') is only attested in translations, and is clearly assimilation to the parallel at Matt. 24:27.

17:33   περιποιήσασθαι (to make secure) {B}

There is slim but early support for the editorial text, περιποιήσασθαι ('to preserve'; $\mathfrak{P}^{75}$ 03 019 579). The majority of manuscripts have the more common verb σῶσαι ('to save'; 01 02 032 037 etc.), which is likely to have arisen through assimilation to the parallels at Mark 8:35, Matt. 16:25 and Luke 9:24 (cf. Luke 6:9 and 19:10). Codex Bezae and some early translations recast the whole phrase, including ζωογονῆσαι ('to make alive'; 05 lat$^{vl\text{-}pt}$ sy$^{c, s, p}$ co^{sa}), matching the verb of the following clause, which is a further case of assimilation. Both περιποιήσασθαι and ζωογονῆσει are only found in the New Testament in this verse, indicating Luke's distinctive reworking of this well-known saying.

17:36   *omit verse* {A}

The majority of Greek manuscripts lack the sentence which is traditionally numbered as Luke 17:36 and resembles Matt. 24:40 ($\mathfrak{P}^{75}$ 01 02 03 etc.). Codex Bezae and some minuscules have it in the form δύο ἐν τῷ ἀγρῷ· εἷς παραλημφθήσεται καὶ ὁ ἕτερος ἀφεθήσεται ('two [will be] in the field; one will be taken and the other will be left'; [05] [180] 579 [700] etc.), also supported by the Syriac and parts of the Latin and Ethiopic traditions, while Family 13 has a slightly different text: δύο ἔσονται ἐν τῷ ἀγρῷ· εἷς παραλημφθήσεται ἡ δὲ ἑτέρα ἀφεθήσεται ('two will be in the field; one man will be taken and the other woman will be left'; f^{13} [lat$^{vl\text{-}pt}$]). Although there is a slight possibility that a longer phrase was originally present but omitted through eyeskip from ἀφεθήσεται to ἀφεθήσεται (as happened in Codex Sinaiticus for Luke 17:35 itself), multiple considerations favour the originality of the shorter reading: the restricted attestation of the extra verse; the multiple text-forms of

---

[48] Wasserman 2017: 107–108.

the addition (with Family 13 partially assimilating to the feminine in Luke 17:35); the change in sequence from Matthew; other instances in which Luke has revised a Matthean list to something more appropriate for the context (e.g. Luke 11:11 above).

18:11 πρὸς ἑαυτὸν ταῦτα (by himself … thus) {C}

The earliest Greek manuscripts read ταῦτα πρὸς ἑαυτόν ('[standing, prayed] these things to himself'; 𝔓⁷⁵ 01² 03 [019] etc.), while most minuscules have πρὸς ἑαυτὸν ταῦτα (lit. '[standing] to himself [prayed] these things'; 02 032 037 f^{13} etc.). The latter is ambiguous: it is not clear whether 'to himself' refers to the posture or the prayer. (The same is true in the Sinaitic Syriac, which lacks a pronoun corresponding to ταῦτα.) The reading καθ' ἑαυτὸν ταῦτα ('[standing] by himself [prayed] these things'; 05 lat^{vl-pt}) is a clarification which provides the expected preposition when the complement is taken as the posture: the variant ταῦτα ('[standing, prayed] these things'; 01* lat^{vl-pt} co^{sa, ach}) or the omission of the phrase completely (828 1071 eth) may represent other attempts to resolve the ambivalence. The full list of variants in Greek continuous-text manuscripts is given in *TuT Luke* (TS37). Given that the majority reading is difficult, it could be the earliest form (as in the SBLGNT).[49] The sequence ταῦτα πρὸς ἑαυτόν may have been a later improvement to the syntax, even though it leaves unclear whether 'prayed to himself' means that he prayed privately or that his prayer was directed to himself rather than God. This latter ambiguity could alternatively justify ταῦτα πρὸς ἑαυτόν as the earliest reading (as in the THGNT): an editor might have moved ταῦτα to avoid the implication that this was a private prayer (which seems not to suit the context). Although the resulting collocation σταθεὶς πρὸς ἑαυτόν ('standing towards himself') appears strange, it has been suggested that it is an Aramaic idiom for 'taking his stand'.[50] It may also be noted that the structure of the majority reading corresponds more closely to the tax collector 'standing far off' in Luke 18:13. With such uncertainty about the text, translators may employ considerable freedom in interpreting the syntax.

---

[49] It is also preferred by Wasserman 2017: 108–109.
[50] See Omanson 2006: 142.

18:22 [τοῖς] οὐρανοῖς (heaven)

The definite article τοῖς ('the') is lacking from all manuscripts except Codex Vaticanus and Codex Bezae (03 05). However, ἐν οὐρανοῖς ('in heavens') does not otherwise appear in Luke or Acts, and ἐν οὐρανῷ ('in heaven') is only found in the quotation at Luke 19:38, in contrast to four instances of the phrase with a definite article (Luke 6:23, 10:20, 12:33, 15:7). As the synoptic parallels of this well known saying at Mark 10:21 and Matt. 19:21 both lack the article, it is plausible that the article was dropped through assimilation. Conversely, it remains possible that Luke followed his source and the article was later added by an editor in keeping with Lukan style: this is preferred by both the SBLGNT and THGNT. See also Luke 18:30 below.

18:24 αὐτὸν ὁ Ἰησοῦς [περίλυπον γενόμενον] εἶπεν (Jesus … him and said) {C}

The majority of manuscripts include the words περίλυπον γενόμενον ('[seeing that] he had become very sad'; 02 032 037 038), as does Codex Bezae in a different place (αὐτὸν περίλυπον γενόμενον εἶπεν ὁ Ἰησοῦς, '[seeing that] he had become very sad, Jesus said'; 05 etc.); see further *TuT Luke* (TS38). This phrase is lacking from the earliest witnesses (01 [03] 019 f^1 etc.), and repeats the detail from the previous verse that 'he became very sad'. This early evidence for the shorter reading, the lack of obvious reason for accidental or deliberate omission, and the differing word order in the longer variants all suggest that these words are a later addition. Two counterarguments, however, are that Luke often repeats phrases within the same passage and ἰδὼν δὲ αὐτόν ('but seeing him') makes poor sense without a further complement because the encounter began six verses earlier.[51] Nevertheless, Luke frequently uses ἰδών ('seeing') without fully specifying the object (e.g. Luke 1:15, 5:8, 7:39, 11:38, 17:14, 18:43 etc.), and in this instance the emotional state from the preceding sentence could be implicitly conveyed in the pronoun αὐτόν ('him'). If the shorter reading is followed (as in the SBLGNT, THGNT and Wasserman), this may require expansion in translation (ἰδών in Luke cannot usually be translated as 'looking'), just

---

[51] See Metzger 1994: 143, citing Cadbury for the former observation; also Wasserman 2017: 109–110.

as a later editor may have expanded the text because of the perceived inadequacy of the pronoun by itself.

18:30 [ἀπο]λάβῃ (get back)

Almost all witnesses have ἀπολάβῃ ('receive in return'; 01 02 019 032 etc.), with just Codex Vaticanus and Codex Bezae reading λάβῃ ('receive'; 03 05). Although the latter witnesses could preserve the earliest text in Luke 18:22 (see above), on this occasion the uncompounded form is not seen in the synoptic parallels (Matt. 19:29, Mark 10:30) and Luke uses ἀπολάβειν elsewhere (Luke 6:34, 15:27, 16:25). The shorter reading may therefore be due to accidental omission or assimilation in this instance.

19:15 τί διεπραγματεύσαντο (what they had gained by doing business) {B}

The majority of Greek manuscripts read τίς τί διεπραγματεύσατο ('who had gained what by doing business'; 02 038 f^1 etc.), with others reading τίς τί ἐπραγματεύσατο ('who had been busy with what'; 032 037 0233 etc.). Most early witnesses have just τί διεπραγματεύσαντο ('what they had gained by doing business'; 01 03 05 019 etc., lat[vl-pt] sy[c, s] co eth Origen). Although it is possible that one of the indefinite articles was omitted by accident and the verb was subsequently changed to the plural to compensate, it is more probable that the majority reading represents an editorial intervention in order to match the sense of the following verses and avoid the implication that they had been collaborating. The change in verb is likely to be due to the oversight of ΔΙ after ΤΙ, but it could be assimilation to Luke 19:13. The full list of variants in Greek continuous-text manuscripts is given in *TuT Luke* (TS39).

19:29 Βηθανία[ν] (Bethany)

Most manuscripts have the accusative Βηθανίαν ('Bethany'; 01[2] 02 05[1] 019 032 etc.), with regular Greek morphology in keeping with the other eleven occasions it appears in the New Testament. The three earliest manuscripts read Βηθανία ('Bethany'; 01* 03 05*), treating it as an indeclinable foreign proper noun. This is probably under the influence of the preceding Βηθφαγή ('Bethphage'), which is always indeclinable even though it also looks like a Greek first-declension feminine. It is likely that Βηθανία was a scribal error, hence the corrections in Codex Sinaiticus and Codex Bezae: Codex Vaticanus also has it in the parallel at Mark 11:1, where it seems to have been corrected.

19:38   ὁ ἐρχόμενος ὁ βασιλεύς (the king who comes) {C}

The editorial text is only supported by Codex Vaticanus: ὁ βασιλεύς ('the king') interrupts the quotation from Psalm 118:26 [117:26 LXX] and is not found in the parallels at Matt. 21:9, Mark 11:9 and John 12:13. Mark does, however, follow this quotation with εὐλογημένη ἡ ἐρχομένη βασιλεία ('blessed is the coming kingdom'), which could have inspired either Luke or a copyist to insert ὁ βασιλεύς here. Similarly, the next line in John includes a reference to 'the king of Israel'. There are a few manuscripts which read just ὁ ἐρχόμενος ('the one who comes'; 05 032 579 1505 etc.), although Codex Bezae then includes εὐλογημένος ὁ βασιλεύς ('blessed is the king') at the end of the clause. The limited attestation of the reading which matches the other gospels suggests that it is due to assimilation. The external evidence for the inclusion of 'king' in this verse is considerable: the majority of manuscripts read ὁ ἐρχόμενος βασιλεύς ('the coming king'; 01² 02 019 037 038 etc.), and there is early support for ὁ βασιλεύς ('the king'; 01* [013] 69^vid [1243] Origen). The latter could be due to eyeskip and thus provide indirect support for the editorial text: ὁ ἐρχόμενος ὁ βασιλεύς ('the one who comes, the king'; 03) is both the least expected construction (with the double article) and an explanation for the other readings. It has therefore been adopted with hesitation because of its preservation in only a single manuscript. Both the SBLGNT and THGNT, however, prefer the majority reading.

19:42   ἐν τῇ ἡμέρᾳ ταύτῃ καὶ σύ (even you ... on this day) {B}

The majority of manuscripts read καὶ σὺ καί γε ἐν τῇ ἡμέρᾳ σου ταύτῃ ('even you, indeed, on this your day'; 032 037 28 180 etc.), while earlier Byzantine witnesses have καὶ σὺ καί γε ἐν τῇ ἡμέρᾳ ταύτῃ ('even you, indeed, on this day'; 02 044 *f*¹ etc.). Most of the oldest testimony is for ἐν τῇ ἡμέρᾳ ταύτῃ καὶ σύ ('on this day, even you'; 01 03 019 etc., Origen), a harder reading because the intensifier καὶ σύ ('even you') is at some distance from the verb it qualifies. This is remedied in the early variant καὶ σὺ ἐν τῇ ἡμέρᾳ ταύτῃ ('even you, on this day'; 05 038 etc.)

and the other forms appear to be expansions of this (see also the next unit). It is worth observing too that there is no other use of καί γε ('indeed') in the New Testament apart from a quotation at Acts 2:18. The full list of variants in Greek continuous-text manuscripts is given in *TuT Luke* (TS41).

19:42   εἰρήνην (peace) {B}

Codex Bezae and other witnesses have εἰρήνην σοι ('peace for you'; 05 f^{13} etc.), while the majority reading is εἰρήνην σου ('your peace'; 02 032 037 044 etc.), matching 'your day' in the previous clause and 'your eyes' in the following one. The early attestation of the shortest reading, εἰρήνην ('peace'; 01 03 019 038 etc.) and the absence of any obvious prompt for an omission leads to its adoption as the editorial text.

20:9   ἄνθρωπός [τις] (a man)

Most manuscripts lack the indefinite article, although they display a variety in their word order (01 03 04 05 019 036 etc.), with some putting ἀμπελῶνα ('vineyard') first in order to highlight its importance. The phrase ἄνθρωπός τις ('a certain man'; 02 037 038 f^{13} etc., lat^{vg} sy) is the standard opening in Luke for such parables (Luke 10:30, 14:16, 15:11, 16:1, 19:12 etc.). This suggests that the shorter form is the harder reading, and τις was added through assimilation (thus also the SBLGNT and THGNT). Nevertheless, it remains possible that τις was overlooked at an early point.

20:27   [ἀντι]λέγοντες (say)

The majority of manuscripts read ἀντιλέγοντες ('contradicting'; 02 032 037 f^{13} etc.), whereas older witnesses just have λέγοντες ('saying'; 01 03 04 05 019 etc.; see further *TuT Luke* TS42). The more difficult reading is ἀντιλέγοντες, as it differs from the parallels at Matt. 22:23 and Mark 12:18 and a literal interpretation results in the opposite interpretation to that of the other gospels. Moreover, compound verbs with ἀντί are particularly common in Luke (e.g. Luke 2:34, 6:38, 10:31–32, 14:12, 21:15, 24:17), suggesting that this may be the earliest form. If ἀντιλέγοντες is adopted (as in the SBLGNT), it should be considered as a double negative and translated along the lines of 'contending'.

20:30   καὶ ὁ δεύτερος (then the second) {B}

Most witnesses have a longer form of this verse, reading καὶ ἔλαβεν ὁ δεύτερος τὴν γυναῖκα καὶ οὗτος ἀπέθανεν ἄτεκνος ('and the second married the wife and he too died childless'; 02 032 037 [038] etc.). Although this is reflected in Old Latin and Old Syriac tradition, the Coptic and earliest Greek manuscripts simply read καὶ ὁ δεύτερος ('and the second'; 01 03 05 019 0266 etc.). The longer text appears to reflect the parallel at Mark 12:21 but adapted using the Lukan wording of the previous verse, whereas the shorter form matches the parallel at Matt. 22:26. As the shorter form could not have arisen from the longer reading through eyeskip, it seems probable that this brief statement was later expanded on the basis of the previous verse. It could be, however, that the longer form, with its Lukan wording, was abbreviated under the influence of the Matthean parallel.

20:45   [αὐτοῦ] (lit. his)

The majority of manuscripts have τοῖς μαθηταῖς αὐτοῦ ('to his disciples'; 01 02 019 032 037 etc.), but a few read simply τοῖς μαθηταῖς ('to the disciples'; 03 05 1 2542). The same variation has already been discussed at Luke 12:22 (see above): it was suggested that there was a later tendency to drop αὐτοῦ, and the longer reading appears here to have the stronger early attestation.[52] The slim external evidence for τοῖς μαθηταῖς may be consistent with an accidental omission (cf. Luke 18:30).

21:4   δῶρα (contributed) {B}

The editorial text, δῶρα ('gifts'; 01 03 019 f^1 etc., sy$^{c, s}$ cpa [co]), is supported by multiple early witnesses, The other Greek manuscripts have δῶρα τοῦ θεοῦ ('gifts of God'; 02 05 032 037 etc.). This appears to be an explanatory addition for those unfamiliar with the system of offerings, as δῶρα is used in a slightly different way in this verse compared with Luke 21:1; it has been suggested that this instance might be translated as 'offering chest' rather than 'gifts'.[53] There is no obvious reason for the omission or deletion of τοῦ θεοῦ if these words were original.

---

[52] Metzger 1994: 146; the longer reading here is also preferred in Elliott 1979.
[53] Omanson 2006: 146.

21:35 ὡς παγίς· ἐπεισελεύσεται γάρ (like a trap. For it will come upon) {B}

Most Greek manuscripts read ὡς παγὶς γὰρ ἐπελεύσεται ('For like a trap it will come on'; 02 04 032 037 etc.). The placement of the postpositive γάρ in the oldest witnesses, however, indicates that the first two words are to be taken as the end of the previous clause: ὡς παγίς· ἐπεισελεύσεται γάρ ('[catch you] like a trap. For it will come upon'; 01 03 05 019 070 579 lat^vl-pt co). Luke never begins a sentence elsewhere with the comparative ὡς ('like'), and there are several examples of it coming at the end of a phrase (e.g. Luke 3:22, 17:6, 18:17, 22:31). The combination of this internal and external evidence justifies the choice of the editorial text: an early editor may have felt that the idea already conveyed by αἰφνίδιος ('unexpectedly') in the previous verse was not matched in the following sentence, and so rearranged the words to address this.

21:38 αὐτοῦ. (to him) {A}

At the end of this verse, the eight members of Family 13 (13, 69, 124, 346, 543, 788, 826, 983) add the story of the woman taken in adultery (John 7:53–8:11). This floating pericope is also found in different places in John, appearing at the end of that gospel in Family 1. It is possible that the similarity between the reference here to the crowds listening to Jesus 'early in the Temple' and John 8:2, together with the conclusion of the teaching in the Temple in Luke at this point, led the editor responsible for the source of Family 13 to insert the pericope at this point. This position may reflect the liturgical practice of including related lections near to each other, which also affects Luke 22:43–44 in the same witnesses (see below).[54]

22:7 [ἐν] ᾗ (on which)

The preposition ἐν ('in') is missing from early manuscripts ($\mathfrak{P}$^75vid 03 04 05 019 044 etc.), but is present in the majority (01 02 032 037 etc.). There are parallels elsewhere in Luke for the preposition being included (e.g. Luke 21:6, 23:29) and absent (e.g. Luke 12:46). Although it is possible that ἐν was omitted by accident, the attestation suggests that it was

---

[54] On both passages, see Knust and Wasserman 2018: 300–301.

added later for clarification. This shorter reading is also preferred in the SBLGNT and THGNT.

22:16   ὅτι οὐ μὴ φάγω (I will not eat) {B}

The majority of manuscripts read ὅτι οὐκέτι οὐ μὴ φάγω ('that no longer will I eat'; 04 [022] 032 037 etc.), while Codex Bezae has οὐκέτι μὴ φάγωμαι ('no longer will I eat for myself'; 05). The earliest witnesses support ὅτι οὐ μὴ φάγω ('that I will not eat'; 𝔓^{75vid} 01 02 03 etc.). It is possible that οὐκέτι was omitted by eyeskip before οὐ, or deleted in order to match Luke 22:18. However, the attestation suggests that it is more likely that it was added to correspond to the institution narrative at Mark 14:25, even though some early manuscripts lack οὐκέτι there (compare also Matt. 26.29 with ἀπ' ἄρτι, 'from now').

22:17–20   *verses 17, 18, 19, 20* {B}

These four verses appear in the traditional order in the majority of Greek manuscripts, including the oldest surviving copies and early translations (𝔓⁷⁵ 01 02 03 04 etc.). They present an unusual form of the institution narrative, with a cup of wine and bread before the meal followed by another cup after the meal. Although this strong external attestation for what seems to be a more difficult reading has led to its adoption in the editorial text, this has been questioned: some suggest that the second cup was the result of an attempt to bring Luke into correspondence with the other accounts of the Last Supper (1 Cor. 11:23–26, Mark 14:22–25, Matt. 26:26–29), not least because Luke 22:19b–20 corresponds closely to 1 Cor. 11:24b–25 and contrasts with Lukan style.[55] A shorter reading is seen in Codex Bezae and some Old Latin manuscripts, which lack the second half of Luke 22:19 and all of Luke 22:20 (τὸ ὑπὲρ ὑμῶν ... ἐκχυννόμενον, 'which is given for you ... poured out for you ... in my blood'), and with it the problematic description of a second cup: this is one of the 'Western non-interpolations' (see the Overview for Luke above). The SBLGNT includes these words in brackets. The most variant tradition is the Syriac: the Curetonian

---

[55] The literature on this passage is abundant. Earlier bibliography is presented in Petzer 1991 (see also Ehrman 1991b and Ehrman 2011: 231–245) and Billings 2006. The principal text forms are set out in English in Parker 1994: 151–157 and O'Loughlin 2018, while a table of Greek witnesses is given in Metzger 1994: 149.

Syriac has the verses in the order 19, 17, 18, resulting in the bread followed by a single cup (but with part of 1 Cor. 11:24 added to the first verse); the Sinaitic Syriac displays the same order with parts of verse 20 distributed in between; the Peshitta and some Coptic manuscripts only have verses 19 and 20 (the bread followed by a cup after the meal). Given that all the variants match the order of the other institution narratives, they are usually considered to be later corrections inspired by ecclesiastical practice. Nevertheless, the possibility that even the earliest attested text of Luke had also been subject to this sort of interference, leading to its peculiar form, cannot entirely be discounted. Further information about the attestation of variants in these verses is given in *ECM Parallel Pericopes*.

22:18 [ὅτι] (that)

The connective ὅτι ('that') is lacking from some of the earliest manuscripts ($\mathfrak{P}^{75\text{vid}}$ 03 04 05 019 f^1 etc.). This appears to be the harder reading, as it is present in most witnesses in the same phrase at Luke 22:16 (but not in 04* 05 022 and some Old Latin manuscripts). On the other hand, the similarity in structure may be an authorial feature, and the loss of ὅτι could be the result of assimilation to a biblical parallel (e.g. Matt. 26:29) or liturgical practice, or even accidental omission. See further *ECM Parallel Pericopes*.

22:43–44 *omit verses* {B}

These verses are lacking from a number of ancient witnesses ([$\mathfrak{P}^{69\text{vid}}$] $\mathfrak{P}^{75}$ 01^{2a} 02 03 022 etc., lat$^{\text{vl-pt}}$ sy^{s} co$^{\text{sa, bo-pt}}$), while in some majuscules and around forty minuscules they are accompanied by asterisks or obeli (037^{c} 0171^{vid} 892^{c} etc.); in Family 13 and some lectionaries they are not found here but in the corresponding place at the parallel passage, after Matt. 26:39 (compare the comment on Luke 21:38 above), and some witnesses have them in both places: see the full attestation in *TuT Luke* (TS45). There is no obvious reason for accidental omission, but the passage might have been removed on theological grounds, such as concerns that the presence of the angel diminished Jesus' agency at this point or the depiction of his anguish. Ancient writers make extensive references to this passage (e.g. Justin, Irenaeus, Hippolytus and possibly Origen) with some indicating that it was a source of controversy: the detail that Jesus sweated drops of blood, although it seems incidental at this point in Luke, was often cited in early debates as an illustration of his full humanity. While these verses are present in manuscripts as early as Codex Sinaiticus and Codex Bezae (01*, 2b 05 019 037* 038 etc.), the external evidence for their absence is consistent with their being added from another ancient Christian tradition at an early point. Accordingly, the UBS4 committee decided not to adopt this text, but because of its importance to keep it in its traditional place within double brackets to indicate that it is not considered to be part of the original form of the gospel (matching the *Pericope Adulterae* at John 7:53–8:11). Nevertheless, there is an ongoing debate over these verses, with a number of recent proponents in favour of their originality: they are included in both the SBLGNT and THGNT.[56] See also Luke 23:34 below.

22:68 ἀποκριθῆτε (answer) {B}

At the end of this verse, the majority of Greek manuscripts read ἀποκριθῆτε μοι ἢ ἀπολύσητε ('you will [not] answer me or let go'; 02 05 032 037 etc.). A few witnesses have ἀποκριθῆτε μοι ('you will [not] answer me'; 038 f^1 etc.), while the oldest evidence supports just ἀποκριθῆτε ('you will [not] answer'; $\mathfrak{P}^{75}$ 01 03 019 etc.).[57] Although there is a possibility that an original longer reading was omitted through eyeskip between ἀποκριθῆτε and ἀπολύσητε, this would not explain the reading ἀποκριθῆτε μοι. The external evidence suggests that both the longer texts are secondary. If the reading with ἀπολύσητε is followed, a direct object (such as 'me') may need to be supplied.

23:11 [καί] (even)

The majority of manuscripts (02 03 05 032 037 etc.) lack the intensifier καί. Its presence in some early witnesses ($\mathfrak{P}^{75}$ 01 019 044 f^{13} etc.) means that a case can be made for its originality: if the latter is the harder reading, καί may have been deleted because its significance was not clear.[58] On the other hand, the balance between the internal and external evi-

---

[56] Among numerous discussions, see Ehrman & Plunkett 1983; Head 1993: 123–126; Parker 1997: 157–159; Clivaz 2010; Ehrman 2011: 220–227; Blumell 2014; Wasserman 2020: 316–321 (and the literature cited in these).

[57] In *TuT Luke* (TS46), 038 and 044 should exchange places.

[58] Thus Metzger 1994: 152.

dence makes a final decision difficult. If it is adopted, as in the SBLGNT and THGNT, καί could be translated as 'also' or 'even'.

23:15 ἀνέπεμψεν γὰρ αὐτὸν πρὸς ἡμᾶς (for he sent him back to us) {A}

There is good early support for the editorial text ($\mathfrak{P}^{75}$ 01 03 019 etc.), which also makes the best sense in context and matches Luke 23:11. The reading ἀνέπεμψεν γὰρ αὐτὸν πρὸς ὑμᾶς ('for he sent him back to you'; f^{13} 579 sy^{hmg}) is probably due to the similar pronunciation of ἡμᾶς ('us') and ὑμᾶς ('you') in later Greek, although it may also have been influenced by the second person in the previous verse. The first-person verb in the preceding clause seems to have been extended to this phrase at some point, probably through scribal inadvertence, which then led to further adjustments to try to mitigate the confusion: the basic form ἀνέπεμψα γὰρ αὐτὸν πρὸς ὑμᾶς ('for I sent him back to you'; 788) does not fit the narrative; the Syriac ἀνέπεμψα γὰρ αὐτὸν πρὸς αὐτόν ('for I sent him back to him'; sy$^{c, s, p}$) is ambiguous; even the majority reading ἀνέπεμψα γὰρ ὑμᾶς πρὸς αὐτόν ('for I sent you back to him'; 02 05 032 037 etc.) misses the nuance of the compound verb and involves changing the referent of the pronoun from Jesus to Herod and back again to Jesus. As all these variants can be explained as minor slips in copying and attempts to repair them, matching the historical pattern of attestation, there is no need to invoke the criterion of the most difficult reading.

23:17 *omit verse* {B}

Although the majority of manuscripts include the text traditionally numbered as verse 17, ἀνάγκην δὲ εἶχεν ἀπολύειν αὐτοῖς κατὰ ἑορτὴν ἕνα ('He was obliged to release one person for them at the festival'; 01 032 037 038 etc.), it is missing from many of the earliest witnesses ($\mathfrak{P}^{75}$ 02 03 019 etc., lat$^{vl\text{-}pt}$ co$^{sa, bo\text{-}pt}$). The idea resembles the parallels at Mark 15:6 and Matt. 27:15, but its different phrasing includes features characteristic of the Lukan writings: the use of ἀνάγκη ('compulsion'; cf. Luke 14:18, 14:23 and 21:23) and ἕνα at the end of a sentence (Luke 17:12, Acts 1:24).[59] This raises the possibility that the text is authorial,

---

[59] *TuT Luke* (TS47) indicates that around 130 minuscules add δέσμιον after ἕνα, providing a closer match with the synoptic parallels.

but was omitted through eyeskip between ἀνάγκην and ἀνέκραγον at the beginning of the following verse. In Codex Bezae and the Old Syriac, however, the sentence appears at the end of Luke 23:19. While this is in keeping with a later addition being inserted at different points, it is possible that an omission through eyeskip had already happened and the line was reinserted in the wrong place. Nevertheless, the external evidence suggests that the extra text is secondary, inspired by the parallel passages due to the verb ἀπολύσω in Luke 23:16, and it is not included in the SBLGNT or the THGNT.

23:23 αὐτῶν (their) {B}

At the end of this verse, most Greek manuscripts include καὶ τῶν ἀρχιερέων ('and [those of] the chief priests'; 02 05 032 037 etc.), while one minuscule has καὶ τῶν ἀρχόντων καὶ τῶν ἀρχιερέων ('and [those of] the rulers and the chief priests'; 1424: for other variants see *TuT Luke* TS48). Although these longer phrases could have been overlooked by eyeskip after αὐτῶν, the early evidence for the shortest reading ($\mathfrak{P}^{75}$ 01 03 019 070 1241 lat$^{vl\text{-}pt,\,vg}$ co) indicates that it is likely to be original.

23:28 [ὁ] Ἰησοῦς (Jesus)

A few early witnesses lack the definite article ὁ ($\mathfrak{P}^{75}$ 01* 03 019). Both alternatives are paralleled elsewhere in Luke, but it may be noted that several of these witnesses—especially Codex Vaticanus—also lack ὁ before Ἰησοῦς elsewhere (e.g. Luke 5:10, 9:50, 9:58, 10:37, 18:24, 18:40). It is difficult to know whether this is a peculiarity of a scribe or editor or whether it transmits an authorial characteristic which has been eliminated in the majority of manuscripts. In any case, translation is unaffected.

23:34 *omit verse 34a*, ὁ δὲ ... ποιοῦσιν. (Then Jesus said ... they are doing) {B}

The first half of this verse is present in most Greek manuscripts but missing from many of the earliest witnesses ($\mathfrak{P}^{75}$ 01^{2a} 03 05* 032 etc., lat$^{vl\text{-}pt}$ sy^s co$^{sa,\,bo\text{-}pt}$) and is indicated with asterisks in Codex Basiliensis (07; compare Luke 22:43–44 above). A full list of the forms it takes in Greek continuous-text manuscripts is given in *TuT Luke* (TS49). Although a similar sentiment is expressed by Stephen at Acts 7:60, the wording is entirely different so assimilation is unlikely. The SBLGNT and THGNT consider the longer text to be original, but in the absence of any obvious reason for omission or deletion, the UBS4 committee decided it was an early tradition which was incorporated at an early point into the Lukan crucifixion narrative. Like Luke 22:43–44 and the *Pericope Adulterae* (John 7:53–8:11), it was therefore marked with double brackets to indicate the belief that it was not part of the earliest text.[60]

23:38 ἐπ' αὐτῷ (over him) {A}

The shortest reading, ἐπ' αὐτῷ ('over him'; 𝔓⁷⁵ 01²ᵃ 03 019 070 etc.) has the earliest attestation and its brevity explains the longer readings which all still include these two words. Other ancient witnesses support ἐπ' αὐτῷ γεγραμμένη ('written above him'; 04* [579*] [latᵛˡ⁻ᵖᵗ] [syᶜ⁻ ˢ] coˢᵃ⁻ᵐˢ), while Codex Sinaiticus incorporates a detail from John 19:20: ἐπ' αὐτῷ γράμμασιν Ἑλληνικοῖς Ῥωμαϊκοῖς Ἑβραϊκοῖς ('over him in Greek, Latin [and] Hebrew letters'; 01*, ²ᵇ). Codex Bezae combines both these readings with ἐπιγεγραμμένη ἐπ' αὐτῷ γράμμασιν Ἑλληνικοῖς Ῥωμαϊκοῖς Ἑβραϊκοῖς ('written above over him in Greek, Latin [and] Hebrew letters'; 05 latᵛˡ⁻ᵖᵗ), and a similar text is seen in the majority of Greek manuscripts: γεγραμμένη ἐπ' αὐτῷ γράμμασιν Ἑλληνικοῖς καὶ Ῥωμαϊκοῖς καὶ Ἑβραϊκοῖς ('written over him in Greek and Latin and Hebrew letters'; 04³ 032 037 038 etc.: some manuscripts have ἐπιγεγραμμένη ['written above'; 02 026 latᵛˡ⁻ᵖᵗ, ᵛᵍ]). The difference in sequence and phrasing from John (which has 'in Hebrew, Latin, Greek') serves not only to demonstrate that all these readings stem from the same intervention but also suggests that it originated as a note added from memory rather than through comparison with the other gospel.[61]

23:39 οὐχί (not) {A}

There is early support for οὐχί ('[are you] not [the Messiah?]'; 𝔓⁷⁵ 01 03 04* 019 etc.), indicating that this is a rhetorical question. Most Greek

---

[60] In favour of its originality, see most recently Eubank 2010; Gurry in Hixson & Gurry 2019: 202–205 offers a summary of the arguments on either side.

[61] IGNTP 1987 indicates that four minuscules reverse the order of Latin and Hebrew, while others overlook one of the languages through eyeskip, but the sequence is remarkably consistent in Greek tradition.

manuscripts have εἰ ('if [you are the Messiah]'; 02 04³ 026 032 037 etc.): such a conditional clause corresponds to the similar statements made about Jesus in Luke 23:35 and 23:37 and is likely to represent assimilation to those. Luke uses οὐχί more than any of the other evangelists (but not elsewhere in this chapter), so both internal and external evidence point towards its adoption here. The entire clause is absent from Codex Bezae, although it retains the speech of the other criminal in the following verse: perhaps an early editor felt it inappropriate to include the actual words described as 'blasphemy' (ἐβλασφήμει) in the gospel text.

23:42 εἰς τὴν βασιλείαν (lit. into [your] kingdom) {C}

The majority of Greek manuscripts read ἐν τῇ βασιλείᾳ ('in [your] kingdom/kingship'; 01 02 04 032 037 etc.), while a few early witnesses have εἰς τὴν βασιλείαν ('into [your] kingdom'; 𝔓⁷⁵ 03 019 lat^{vl-pt, vg} eth? Origen^{lat}). The question is whether this complement relates to the destination or the manner of Jesus' coming. The former is supported by the description of the Messiah 'entering into his glory' at Luke 24:26 (εἰσελθεῖν εἰς τὴν δόξαν αὐτοῦ), while the latter matches the phrase ὅταν ἔλθῃ ἐν τῇ δόξῃ ('when he comes in glory') at Luke 9:26. The preceding ὅταν ἔλθῃς ('when you come') in the current verse may have prompted assimilation to this second parallel, with βασιλεία understood as 'kingly glory'. On the other hand, an initial dative could have been adjusted by an editor who took βασιλεία to refer to a physical 'kingdom' (cf. Luke 13:29, 18:24–25, 22:30), an interpretation also seen in the variant in one manuscript and some ancient writers, where ἐν τῇ βασιλείᾳ follows μνήσθητί μου ('remember me in your kingdom'; 579 Gregory-Nyssa Chrysostom). In support of this understanding is Jesus' response in the following verse: although ἐν τῷ παραδείσῳ ('in paradise') is a dative phrase, its principal reference is to a location rather than a state. This suggests that the accusative εἰς τὴν βασιλείαν could be the earlier reading, matching its external evidence.[62] However, Codex Bezae substitutes the whole phrase with ἐν τῇ ἡμέρᾳ τῆς ἐπελεύσεως ('on the day of your coming'; 05 lat^{vl-pt}), using a noun which only otherwise appears in the New Testament at Acts 7:52. This total replacement may be an indication that the presented text was consid-

---

[62] In favour of this reading, see also the discussion at Ehrman 2011: 273–275.

ered too difficult: this would have been unlikely if it had the accusative, but plausible with a dative and a locational phrase. If ἐν τῇ βασιλείᾳ is adopted, as in the SBLGNT and THGNT, it might be better to translate it as 'kingly glory' rather than 'kingdom', yet the NRSVue, which does follow this reading, renders it as 'in your kingdom'.

23:45 τοῦ ἡλίου ἐκλιπόντος (while the sun's light failed) {B}

There is strong early support for a genitive phrase, whether in the form τοῦ ἡλίου ἐκλιπόντος ('when the sun had failed'; 𝔓⁷⁵* 01 04*vid 019 etc.) or τοῦ ἡλίου ἐκλείποντος ('while the sun was failing'; 𝔓⁷⁵c 03 597 Origen). Most Greek manuscripts, however, read καὶ ἐσκοτίσθη ὁ ἥλιος ('and the sun was darkened'; 02 04³ [05] 032 037 etc.). The latter is a simpler construction, even though it is less elegant in treating the darkness over the land as separate from the darkening of the sun, and the attestation also suggests that it is secondary. The other readings provide the implicit reason for the darkening of the land, but have elements of ambiguity: the phrase is best taken as a genitive absolute, but could be treated as qualifying the previous phrase ('until the ninth hour of the failing sun'); the verb ἐκλείπειν leaves it open as to whether the sun was eclipsed or failed of its own accord. Both of these provide motivation for editorial intervention. The difference between the two verb tenses (the present ἐκλείποντος and the aorist ἐκλιπόντος) is a matter of a single letter and may be due to itacism (compare Mark 15:34 above). Both are found in Origen: the aorist appears to have slightly stronger external support and provides a better fit as an explanation, and has therefore been preferred (thus also the SBLGNT and THGNT). The whole phrase is absent from a few witnesses (04² 33 etc.), perhaps because of confusion involving the different readings or because it was considered superfluous and unhelpful in its ambiguity: *TuT Luke* (TS50) also lists nineteen minuscules with a conflation of the two readings.[63]

23:50 [καί] (and)

The majority of manuscripts lack καί ('and') before ἀνήρ ('a man'; 02 03 05 032 037 etc.). Nevertheless, as it is present in some early witnesses

---

[63] For the addition in the Christian Palestinian Aramaic and other variants in this verse, see Parker 1997: 163–164.

($\mathfrak{P}^{75}$ 01 04 019 33) there is a possibility that it may be original: an argument can be made for either deletion or addition by an editor in order to improve the structure following ἀνήρ earlier in the sentence. In any case, there is little effect on translation.

24:6   οὐκ ἔστιν ὧδε, ἀλλ' ἠγέρθη (He is not here but has risen) {B}

The editorial text is found in many of the oldest witnesses and Byzantine tradition ($\mathfrak{P}^{75}$ 01 02 03 04³ etc.). There is some support for οὐκ ἔστιν ὧδε· ἠγέρθη ('he is not here: he has been raised'; 04* sy^p etc.), which is likely to be assimilation to the parallel at Matt. 28:6 (cf. Mark 16:6). According to Epiphanius, Marcion read only ἠγέρθη ('he has been raised'), and some Old Latin manuscripts support ἠγέρθη ἐκ νεκρῶν ('he has been raised from the dead'; lat$^{vl\text{-}pt}$), which may be an expansion of the same reading: both of these overlap with forms of Matt. 28:7, although the absence of οὐκ ἔστιν ὧδε ἀλλά ('he is not here but') is probably an editorial deletion. Codex Bezae and other Old Latin witnesses lack the entire phrase. There is no obvious explanation for this as an accidental omission, and it is usually considered a 'Western non-interpolation' (see the Overview for Luke above, as well as Matt. 27:49, Luke 24:12, 24:40 etc.). However, other phrases missing from these witnesses in this part of Luke and the synoptic parallels (e.g. Luke 23:50, 23:56, 24:3, 24:10, 24:17 etc.; Matt. 28:7) are indicative of sustained editorial revision of the narrative, making it less probable that this small group of witnesses transmits the original text (see also Luke 24:12 below). In addition, the difference between Luke and the other Synoptic Gospels here (the addition of ἀλλά) tells against the suggestion that the phrase was added through assimilation to the parallel passages. In some modern translations, these words are treated as the end of Luke 24:5 rather than the beginning of Luke 24:6.

24:10   ἦσαν δέ (it was) {B}

As in the previous unit, early sources and Byzantine tradition attest the editorial text, ἦσαν δέ ('And they were'; $\mathfrak{P}^{75}$ 01 03 019 etc.). A few manuscripts have the singular, ἦν δέ ('And it was'; 044 f^1 205 etc.), probably through assimilation to the standard phrase for setting a scene (especially in John): this does not suit the following list of nouns in the nominative, although it may serve to highlight Mary Magdalene (cf. Matt.

27:61). The whole phrase is absent from a range of manuscripts (02 05 032 180 etc.), including both Old Syriac codices: this could be through eyeskip (from ἦσαν to ἡ), or as part of an editorial adjustment to improve the flow by deleting this superfluous verb and making the women the subject only of ἔλεγον ('they said'). The wide support for the slightly harder reading leads to its adoption.

24:12 *include verse* {B}

This verse is present in almost all witnesses, but missing from Codex Bezae and part of Old Latin tradition. It is considered one of the 'Western non-interpolations' (see the Overview for Luke above and Matt. 27:49, Luke 22:19–20 etc.). Again, there are similarities to a parallel passage (in this case John 20:3–10), and in this case it is also possible that the text was added in order to correspond to Luke 24:24, especially as it contrasts with the disciples' reaction in the previous verse. Most instances of θαυμάζειν ('to be amazed') in Luke are followed by a prepositional phrase rather than the accusative complement seen here, but there is an exception at Luke 7:9; in addition, the only other instance of πρὸς ἑαυτόν in the New Testament is seen in Luke, albeit in a slightly different sense (see Luke 18:11 above). The very restricted attestation, especially given other omissions in these witnesses relating to the empty tomb (cf. Luke 24:6 above), tells against the adoption of the shortest reading here despite the other factors in its favour.[64]

24:13 σταδίους ἑξήκοντα (lit. sixty stades) {B}

There is widespread support for ἑξήκοντα ('sixty'; 𝔓75 02 03 05 019 etc.), but a few manuscripts have ἑκατὸν ἑξήκοντα ('one hundred and sixty'; 01 022vid 038 079vid etc.). The latter form may derive from a tradition which identified Emmaus with 'Amwâs, a town approximately this distance from Jerusalem mentioned by a number of ancient writers.[65] On the other hand, this reading is poorly attested and seems not to fit the assertion in Luke 24:33 that they travelled back from that village the same night, as this would be a round trip of thirty-seven miles. The reading ἑπτά ('seven') is only supported by one Old Latin manuscript,

---

[64] More detailed studies of this verse include Muddiman 1972 (in favour of the longer reading), and Ehrman 2011: 248–254 (who prefers the shorter reading).

[65] See Metzger 1994: 158.

although it is not clear how it emerged as there is no particular similarity between these numerals in either Greek or Latin. Given that most readers are unlikely to know the length of sixty stades, translators usually give equivalents such as 'about seven miles' or 'two hours' walk'.

24:17 καὶ ἐστάθησαν (they stood still) {B}

The majority of Greek manuscripts have καὶ ἐστέ ('and [why] are you [sad]?'; 02ᶜ 032 037 038 etc.). This extension of the previous question offers a much smoother reading than καὶ ἐστάθησαν ('and they stood [looking sad]'; 𝔓⁷⁵ 01 02* 03 [019] etc.): the ancient attestation of the latter also suggests that it is the oldest form. Codex Bezae and some other early witnesses lack the entire unit, resulting in 'while you walk along, sad?' (05 latᵛˡ⁻ᵖᵗ eth Cyril). This may represent an alternative editorial intervention prompted by the unexpectedness of καὶ ἐστάθησαν, or the removal of καὶ ἐστέ because of the lack of an appropriate preceding interrogative. In any case, it is consistent with the many shorter readings seen in these witnesses in this narrative (see further Luke 24:6 above).

24:32 [ἐν ἡμῖν] (within us)

The words ἐν ἡμῖν ('within us') are lacking from the oldest witnesses (𝔓⁷⁵ 03 05), as well as from two Old Latin codices and both Old Syriac manuscripts, but are present in the majority of Greek tradition (01 02 019 032 etc.). It is worth noting that several of the witnesses to the shorter text have a different preceding participle ('veiled' in 05, 'blinded' or 'destroyed' in the Old Latin manuscripts), which may have led to the deletion of ἐν ἡμῖν. In the other cases, an editor may have removed these words because they were superfluous or to simplify the many first-person plural pronouns. Accidental omission after ἦν (which would have sounded the same as the last syllable of ἡμῖν) is also a possible explanation: it is more difficult to account for why they would have been added, although accidental dittography of one of the following instances of ἡμῖν might explain this. Accordingly, the longer reading is adopted in the SBLGNT and the THGNT. However, because of the early evidence for the the shorter reading, the words are here enclosed within square brackets: they may feature in an idiomatic translation regardless of the text adopted.

24:36 καὶ λέγει αὐτοῖς· εἰρήνη ὑμῖν (and said to them, "Peace be with you.") {B}

There is excellent attestation of the editorial text ($\mathfrak{P}^{75}$ $\mathfrak{P}^{141\text{vid}}$ 01 02 03 etc.), which is also the Byzantine form. After ὑμῖν ('you'), some Greek manuscripts and early translations include ἐγώ εἰμι, μὴ φοβεῖσθε ('It is I, do not be afraid'; 011 024 [032] [579] 1241 etc.), which is likely to have been introduced from one of the other gospels (e.g. Matt. 14:27 or 28:10, Mark 6:50, John 6:20). Once again, however, the entire unit is lacking from Codex Bezae and some Old Latin witnesses, with no obvious reason for its absence. For that reason, it has been counted among the 'Western non-interpolations', with the suggestion that the greeting was inserted from John 20:19 (cf. Luke 24:12 above). This text is not included in the SBLGNT.[66] As in the other cases, however, the very restricted attestation and other evidence of editorial abbreviation of the text in these witnesses means that the shortest form has not been adopted here or in the THGNT (see also the following unit).

24:40 *include verse* {B}

This is yet another instance of an entire verse absent from Codex Bezae and some Old Latin witnesses, joined here by the Old Syriac. As before (e.g. Luke 24:12, 24:36), there is nothing which would prompt its accidental omission. The text is very similar to John 20:20, except for τοὺς πόδας ('his feet') rather than τὴν πλευράν ('his side'). On the other hand, the invitation to touch the risen Jesus in the previous verse is uncontested, even through it resembles John 20:27. In the light of this, it seems probable that an editor deleted Luke 24:40, perhaps deeming it to be redundant after the instruction to 'see my hands and my feet' at the beginning of Luke 24:39. Nevertheless, this is considered a 'Western non-interpolation' and the SBLGNT includes the text within brackets.[67]

24:42 μέρος (a piece) {B}

At the end of this verse, the majority of witnesses include καὶ ἀπὸ μελισσίου κηρίου ('and from a honeycomb'; 037 044 f^1 etc.), which oth-

---

[66] It is also considered an interpolation in Parker 1997: 168–169 and Ehrman 2011: 257–258.

[67] The shorter reading is also preferred by Ehrman 2011: 255–256, who considers all the 'Western non-interpolations' as anti-Docetic additions.

ers have in a simpler grammatical form as καὶ ἀπὸ μελισσίου κηρίον ('and honey from a comb'; 07* 038 f^{13} etc.; see further *TuT Luke* TS52). The shortest reading has very good early support in Greek manuscripts, early translations and ancient writers ($\mathfrak{P}^{75}$ 01 02 03 05 etc.): although it could have arisen from eyeskip between two instances of καί, it is more likely that the reference to honeycomb is secondary. Honey was used in some ancient Christian rituals and this may have been added to provide scriptural justification for this.[68]

24:47 μετάνοιαν εἰς (repentance and) {C}

Most Greek manuscripts read μετάνοιαν καί ('repentance and [forgiveness]'; 02 04 05 019 032 etc.), but a few early witnesses have μετάνοιαν εἰς ('repentance for [forgiveness]'; $\mathfrak{P}^{75}$ 01 03 sy^p co: see *TuT Luke* TS53). The latter is theologically preferable, in that it presents the two as a single concept. It also matches the previous instance of this phrase in the gospel (Luke 3:3), meaning that it could be the result of assimilation. On the other hand, the following εἰς (in a slightly different sense) and the polysyndeton of the earlier part of the sentence could have led to the deliberate or accidental introduction of καί as an easier reading. Although the UBS4 committee considered that the external evidence for εἰς is better, the SBLGNT and THGNT both prefer καί as the earliest form. The Latin version of Irenaeus lacks these words and simply has 'forgiveness of sins' as the object of the proclamation. The coupling of 'repentance' and 'forgiveness' elsewhere (e.g. Mark 1:4; Luke 3:3; Acts 2:38, 5:31) would be consistent with the introduction of 'repentance' by an editor seeking to underline their theological connectedness. However, given that quotations in ancient writers are frequently omissive and μετάνοιαν is universally attested in the Greek manuscript tradition, there is little justification for adopting the shortest form as the editorial text.

24:47 ἀρξάμενοι (beginning) {B}

This variation unit relates to the punctuation of this clause as well as the form of the participle. The majority reading, the neuter singular ἀρξάμενον ('it beginning'; $\mathfrak{P}^{75}$ 02 04^3 032 etc.), is an accusative absolute

---

[68] Metzger 1994: 161.

which treats this phrase as the continuation of the preceding sentence followed by a full stop at the end of the verse. In contrast, the masculine plural ἀρξάμενοι ('beginning'; 01 03 04* 019 etc.) could be preceded by punctuation in order for it to qualify ὑμεῖς ('you') in verse 48, but the possibility remains that it may be taken as a sense construction following 'all people'. The genitive plural ἀρξαμένων (05 037^c lat$^{vl\text{-}pt,\, vg}$) is ambivalent: it too might be considered a sense construction after τὰ ἔθνη ('for all peoples, of those who begin') or, with ὑμῶν or αὐτῶν implied, as a genitive absolute at the end of verse 47 ('as you/they begin'), yet it could instead qualify τούτων in the following verse ('of these things which begin'). The most difficult form to parse is the nominative singular, ἀρξάμενος ('beginning'; 038 044 and over fifty minuscules: see *TuT Luke* TS54), which only seems to go with εἶπεν ('he said') at the beginning of Luke 24:46. However, the attestation of this suggests that it is unlikely to be the earliest form. Instead, the adoption of ἀρξάμενοι, which has strong early support, may serve to explain the development of the others as attempts to improve the integration of the phrase into the preceding text. Nevertheless, although the punctuation in NA29 and UBS6 connects this clause with the following verse, the SBLGNT and THGNT (which also have the masculine plural) punctuate at the end of Luke 24:47. The latter is not only more difficult because of the discontinuity it involves (indicated by a dash in the SBLGNT), but it also matches the punctuation in some of the manuscripts with this reading (03 04* 019; the others are ambivalent), and the tendency of the emphatic ὑμεῖς ἐστε ('you are') to begin a sentence (e.g. Matt. 5:13–14, Luke 16:15, Acts 3:25). Despite the agreement on the form of the participle, then, considerable doubt remains as to how it relates to the wider structure.[69]

24:49 [ἰδού] (see)

While the majority of manuscripts read ἰδού ('see'; 02 03 04 032 037 etc.), it is missing from a range of early witnesses and most ancient translations ($\mathfrak{P}^{75}$ 01 05 019 33 etc.). There are several parallels for the phrase ἰδοὺ [ἐγὼ] ἀποστέλλω ('see I [myself] am sending'; Matt. 10:16, 11:10, 23:34; Luke 7:27, 10:3), which suggest that it was more likely to

---

[69] The comment on segmentation at Omanson 2006: 157 allows for either option.

have been introduced through assimilation than overlooked. On the other hand, given that the promise is not being delivered visibly at this moment, an early editor could have deleted this deictic word. This balance of internal and external evidence means that it has been included in brackets; it is adopted in the SBLGNT but lacking in the THGNT.

24:50   [ἔξω] (out)

Most Greek manuscripts read ἔξω ἕως ('out as far as'; 02 04³ 032 037 etc.), while earlier witnesses have just ἕως ('as far as'; 𝔓⁷⁵ 01 03 04* 019 etc.) or only ἔξω ('out [towards]'; 05 lat). It is easy to see how one of these words could have been omitted through eyeskip, and both are superfluous: 'out' is already present in the verb ἐξήγαγεν ('he led out') and ἕως is followed by another preposition. There are other instances in Luke of a compound verb combined with ἔξω (Luke 4:29, 13:28, 22:62), which may provide additional support for the longer reading. However, given the early evidence for ἕως alone (which is preferred by both the SBLGNT and THGNT), ἔξω has been put in brackets. Translation is unaffected.

24:51   καὶ ἀνεφέρετο εἰς τὸν οὐρανόν (and was carried up into heaven) {B}

This phrase is missing from the first hand of Codex Sinaiticus, Codex Bezae and part of Old Latin tradition. Although it is counted among the 'Western non-interpolations', suggesting that the shorter reading was original, the deliberate deletion of Jesus' ascension at this point in order to avoid overlap with Acts 1:9 provides a plausible reason for its removal by an early editor.[70] There is also the possibility of the omission of this clause by eyeskip from καί to καί, which may account for the first-hand reading in Codex Sinaiticus. The words are included in the THGNT, but marked in brackets in the SBLGNT. See too the following unit (Luke 24:52).

---

[70] The Sinaitic Syriac still refers to the ascension, even though it lacks the previous verb and the phrase 'into heaven': see Williams in Hill & Kruger 2012: 255–256. For further discussions of this and the following verse, see Epp 1981, Zwiep 1996, Parker 1997: 170–171, Ehrman 2011: 266–271.

24:52 προσκυνήσαντες αὐτόν (worshipped him) {B}

Again, Codex Bezae, some Old Latin witnesses and the Sinaitic Syriac lack these words (cf. Luke 24:40 above), although most manuscripts read προσκυνήσαντες αὐτόν ('worshipping him'; 𝔓⁷⁵ 01 02 03 04 etc.) and a few have just προσκυνήσαντες ('worshipping'; 700 lat^(vl-pt, vg)). The inclusion of this phrase offers support for the description of the ascension in the previous verse: without that, there would be no obvious reason for the disciples to respond to Jesus in this way. (The lack of αὐτόν would alleviate this, because 'God' could be taken as the object, but this appears to be a secondary development because it is an easier reading.) If the end of the previous sentence were deleted by an editor, it would also have made sense to remove this clause. In contrast, there is no reference to worship of Jesus following his ascension at Acts 1:9 which would have led to its inclusion here through assimilation. As in the previous verse, the words are included in brackets in the SBLGNT.[71]

24:53 εὐλογοῦντες (blessing) {B}

The majority of witnesses have αἰνοῦντες καὶ εὐλογοῦντες ('praising and blessing'; 02 04² 032 037 etc.). There is strong support in the oldest manuscripts for just εὐλογοῦντες ('blessing'; 𝔓⁷⁵ 01 03 04* 019 sy^s cpa co) while Codex Bezae and some Old Latin manuscripts have simply αἰνοῦντες ('praising'; 05 lat^(vl-pt)). The appearance of these two participles independently in early tradition makes it likely that the majority reading is a conflation: while αἰνοῦντες by itself could be explained as eyeskip, this would not account for the better attested εὐλογοῦντες. Both words are found elsewhere in the Lukan writings, but never in combination: it is plausible that, given the difference between the use of εὐλογεῖν ('to bless') here and in Luke 24:50–51, where Jesus is the agent, an editor chose to replace it with αἰνεῖν ('to praise'), which always has God as object (see Luke 2:13, 2:20, 18:43, 19:37 etc.).

24:53 θεόν. (God) {A}

Many early witnesses do not have a final Amen (𝔓⁷⁵ 01 04* 05 019 etc.), although it is present in the majority of Greek manuscripts (02 03 04² 037 etc.). As at the end of most other New Testament books, it is likely

---

[71] See also the literature cited in the previous note.

that this is a later addition, probably connected with their reading during Christian worship.[72] One minuscule includes the latter part of the *Pericope Adulterae* after the end of Luke, but as this is a liturgical lection on a supplementary leaf of GA 1333, this is not of great significance for the placing of this passage (see further Luke 21:38 above and John 7:53–8:11).

---

[72] See Wasserman 2023: 60–62, which has a discussion of this feature here in Codex Vaticanus.

The Gospel according to John

Overview

John is the gospel preserved most extensively in surviving papyri, including three substantial witnesses from the third century: Papyrus 66 ($\mathfrak{P}^{66}$) transmits almost the whole gospel; Papyrus 75 ($\mathfrak{P}^{75}$) contains most of John 1–15; Papyrus 45 ($\mathfrak{P}^{45}$) has portions of John 4–5 and 10–11. Among the numerous other fragments, Papyrus 6 ($\mathfrak{P}^{6}$) is a fourth-century Greek-Coptic bilingual with parts of John 10–13, while Papyrus 52 ($\mathfrak{P}^{52}$) with a few verses from John 18 is believed to be the oldest surviving New Testament manuscript, usually assigned to the second century. Among the major majuscules and families of minuscules listed in the Overview for Matthew, it is worth noting that Codex Sinaiticus (01) differs from its customary affiliation in John 1–8 and is often close to Codex Bezae (05). The first five chapters of Codex Washingtonianus are a supplement (032^{supp}) which, like the rest of the gospel, matches early witnesses. As with the other gospels, John is well attested by the principal early translations: Old Latin (lat^{vl}) and Vulgate (lat^{vg}); Coptic Sahidic (co^{sa}) and Bohairic (co^{bo}) as well as numerous minor Coptic versions, including the Lycopolitan (co^{ly}) and proto-Bohairic (co^{pbo}); the Old Syriac (sy^{c} and sy^{s}), as well as the Peshitta (sy^{p}), the Harklean Syriac (sy^{h}) and the Christian Palestinian Aramaic (cpa).

In the 'Western' order of the gospels (see the Overview for Mark), John comes second in the sequence probably because, like Matthew, it was believed to be written by one of the Apostles. Although John stands apart from the three Synoptic Gospels, there are still points of overlap. In addition, it shares a similar style with the three Epistles of John. Frequent repetitions in John, as well as the step-by-step progressions of thought, give rise to much textual variation: it is often difficult to decide whether the reading which matches Johannine style or a neighbouring verse is to be preferred to a dissimilar form. Variations in the presence or absence of the definite article and the tense of verbs are particularly common.

The most famous variant passage in John is that of the Woman Taken in Adultery (*Pericope Adulterae*, John 7:53–8:11) which, like the Angel at the Well (John 5:3b–4) does not appear to have been part of the original gospel. Two verses are absent from a few manuscripts (John 12:8, 14:14; see below), while some early witnesses include an extra sentence in John 21:6 which appears to be derived from Luke. Other well-known points of variation include the reading 'only-begotten God' at John 1:18, the description of Jesus as the 'Chosen One' at John 1:34, readings which suggest that Jesus' power was limited at John 6:15 and 7:1, and the sequence of the interrogations in John 18:13–27.

The *Editio Critica Maior* of John is in preparation: full transcriptions and an initial apparatus have been published online.[1] The published volume of *Text und Textwert* covers only John 1–10, yet it has a significant number of variation units (cf. John 21:11). The text of UBS6 remains identical to that of the two previous editions.

1:3–4 οὐδὲ ἕν. ὃ γέγονεν ἐν (not one thing … What has come into being in) {B}

The punctuation of these verses was a matter of debate at least as early as the fourth century. The oldest documents lack any punctuation, reading οὐδὲ ἕν ὃ γέγονεν ἐν (lit. 'not one thing what has come into being in [him]'; 𝔓⁶⁶ 𝔓⁷⁵* 01* 02 03 etc.). The next earliest manuscripts, along with the first translations and Christian authors, punctuate it as οὐδὲ ἕν. ὃ γέγονεν ἐν ('not one thing. What has come into being in [him]'; 𝔓⁷⁵ᶜ 04 [05] 019 032ˢᵘᵖᵖ etc.). Most of Greek tradition, however, has the punctuation οὐδὲ ἕν ὃ γέγονεν. ἐν ('not one thing which has come into being. In [him]'; 01² 038 044 050ᶜ etc.), while a few minuscules combine the two major forms and read οὐδὲ ἕν· ὃ γέγονεν· ἐν ('not one thing, that which has come into being, in [him]'; 28 205 1241). The majority reading explains the position of the modern verse division, and is preferred in the THGNT. The punctuation adopted in the editorial text (as well as the SBLGNT) reflects the antiquity of the break after οὐδὲ ἕν ('not one thing'); it is also arguable that taking ὃ γέγονεν as part of the next sentence is the more difficult reading, because of the contrast between the perfect tense of γέγονεν ('has come into being')

---

[1] See www.iohannes.com.

and the imperfect ἦν ('was') as well as the obscurity of the sense. (Compare, too, the change from ἦν to ἐστίν in the following unit.) Stylistically, arguments can be made for either reading: if the sentence ends with οὐδὲ ἕν, this results in a chiastic structure with πάντα at the beginning of the verse; conversely, there may be a preference in John for clauses starting with ἐν and a demonstrative pronoun, such as ἐν αὐτῷ ('in him').[2] It has also been suggested that the punctuation in the majority reading was a theologically-motivated reaction against the use of this verse to claim that the Holy Spirit was created.[3]

1:4 ἦν (was) {A}

Almost all Greek witnesses have the imperfect tense, ζωὴ ἦν ('[in him] was life'; 𝔓66 𝔓75 02 03 04 etc.: see *TuT John* TS1). Two early manuscripts and most of the ancient translations read ζωή ἐστιν ('[in him] is life'; 01 05 lat^vl sy^c co^sa eth etc.). The present tense seems likely to be an adjustment in order to make this verb correspond with the preceding perfect, γέγονεν ('has come into being'), when the two are read in the same sentence (see the previous unit). Although it might be argued that ζωή ἐστιν could have been changed to ζωὴ ἦν under the influence of the following clause, the imperfect tense there provides further support for adopting it here. The attestation of ἐστιν and for the absence of the verb (only 032^supp) is insufficient for considering either as original.

1:18 μονογενὴς θεός (the only Son, himself God) {B}

This is a very famous variation unit. The oldest witnesses read μονογενὴς θεός ('only-begotten God'; 𝔓66 01* 03 04* 019 etc.) or ὁ μονογενὴς θεός ('the only-begotten God'; 𝔓75 01² 33 co^bo and numerous Christian writers), while most Greek manuscripts have ὁ μονογενὴς υἱός ('the only-begotten Son'; 02 04³ 037 038 etc.). A few sources read εἰ μὴ ὁ μονογενὴς θεός ('except the only-begotten God'; 032^supp lat^vl-pt etc.). The full attestation in Greek continuous-text manuscripts is given in *TuT John* (TS2). While some Latin witnesses appear to support μονογενὴς υἱὸς θεοῦ ('only-begotten son of God'), this may

---
[2] Thus Metzger 1994: 168.
[3] See further Aland 1968 and Nässelqvist 2018.

be an expansion due to translation or assimilation to John 3:18. The most difficult reading is μονογενὴς θεός by itself, both for the lack of the definite article and the unexpected juxtaposition of these terms: elsewhere in the New Testament, μονογενής appears in conjunction with υἱός (John 3:16, 3:18; 1 John 4:9; Luke 7:12, 9:38; cf. Luke 8:42). The phrase 'only-begotten God' (or 'God the only Son', because μονογενής could itself convey the notion of sonship, as at John 1:14 and Heb. 11:17) would be a bold statement about the divinity of Christ at the beginning of the gospel, otherwise unparalleled. It is much more likely that θεός would be altered to the more common term υἱός. However, given that both were customarily abbreviated as *nomina sacra*, there remains a slight possibility that, at an early point, ΥC (with an overline) might have been misread as ΘC. This does not explain the lack of article in the earliest manuscripts: although this might be considered assimilation to John 1:14, this previous use of μονογενής by itself rather supports the shorter reading here. The reading ὁ μονογενὴς υἱός is adopted in the THGNT; the SBLGNT agrees with the UBS text.[4]

Even though UBS6 treats John 1:1-18 as a single unit, the division in manuscripts is less clear and it is advisable not to describe this section as a 'prologue'.[5] It is also possible to argue that the direct speech of John the Baptist which begins in John 1:15 could extend as far as the end of 1:18 (cf. John 1:19), but the customary practice in translations is to restrict it to 1:15 only.

1:19 [πρὸς αὐτόν] (lit. to him) {C}

The words πρὸς αὐτόν ('to him') are lacking from most Greek manuscripts, including both papyri ($\mathfrak{P}^{66*}$ $\mathfrak{P}^{75}$ 01 04³ 019 etc.). Nevertheless, they have early attestation after ἀπέστειλαν ('they sent to him'; 03 04* 33 892ᶜ etc., along with several ancient translations) or after Λευίτας ('[they sent ... priests and] Levites to him'; $\mathfrak{P}^{66cvid}$ 02 038 044 etc.). The

---

[4] Among numerous discussions, see further Ehrman 2011: 92-96, who prefers ὁ μονογενὴς υἱός on the basis of Johannine style, Wasserman 2012: 341-343 in response to Ehrman, and—especially on the evidence in early translations and Christian writers—McReynolds 1981. On the translation of μονογενὴς θεός, see Fennema 1985. Burkholder 2012 suggests that the variation is unlikely to be doctrinally motivated.

[5] See further Williams 2011.

appearance of the phrase in two different places in the textual tradition suggests that it is a later addition. On the other hand, as it is superfluous, it is possible that it was removed by an editor but then reintroduced elsewhere. It is unusual to find the shorter reading in the majority of Greek manuscripts, which is a further factor in favour of its originality, although the early attestation of both variants makes for doubt as to the earliest form. Internal evidence is ambivalent (e.g. John 7:32, 18:24), but it is notable that the only other use of ἀπέστειλαν πρὸς αὐτόν in the Gospel at John 11:3 has a slightly different sense ('they sent word to him').

1:27 ἐρχόμενος (coming) {A}

After ἐρχόμενος, the majority of witnesses include the phrase ὅς ἔμπροσθέν μου γέγονεν ('who ranks ahead of me'; 02 04³ 037 [038] etc.). This appears to have been introduced through assimilation to similar phrases at John 1:15 and 1:30. There is a possibility of eyeskip from ὅς to οὗ, but it is remote and the phrase is lacking from almost all the earliest manuscripts, including all four extant papyri and the oldest translations.

1:27 εἰμὶ [ἐγώ] (I am)

The pronoun ἐγώ is not required for the sense, and is lacking from a range of early witnesses which just read οὐκ εἰμὶ ('I am not'; 𝔓⁶⁶* 𝔓⁷⁵ 𝔓¹²⁰ 01 04 etc.). Although οὐκ εἰμὶ ἐγώ ('I am not'; 𝔓⁶⁶ᶜ 𝔓¹¹⁹ 03 032ˢᵘᵖᵖ 044) is found in early manuscripts, its attestation is limited: the majority of Greek manuscripts have the more common sequence ἐγὼ οὐκ εἰμί ('I am not'; 02 037 038 *f*¹ etc.). If ἐγώ were not originally present, it is hard to explain its appearance in the Byzantine reading: as it is absent from the synoptic parallels (Mark 1:7, Luke 3:16), this may have inspired the short reading here, leaving οὐκ εἰμὶ ἐγώ as the earliest form. The stronger external evidence for οὐκ εἰμὶ by itself, however, makes for doubt: the SBLGNT reads οὐκ εἰμί, while the THGNT has οὐκ εἰμὶ ἐγώ. Translation is unaffected. *TuT John* (TS4) shows that a number of manuscripts, including both papyri, read ἱκανός ('sufficient') rather than ἄξιος ('worthy') as the next word: this is assimilation to the synoptic parallels even in these early witnesses (Matt. 3:11, Mark 1:7, Luke 3:16).

1:28 ἐν Βηθανίᾳ ἐγένετο (took place in Bethany) {C}

The Byzantine tradition is split between the place names Bethany (ἐν Βηθανίᾳ) and Bethabara (ἐν Βηθαβαρᾷ). The former has the predominant early attestation ($\mathfrak{P}^{66}$ $\mathfrak{P}^{75}$ 01* 02 03 04* etc.), whereas the latter is found in the *Textus Receptus* (01² 04² 029^vid 044^c etc.). The variation was known to Origen, who preferred Bethabara both on etymological grounds ('House of Preparation') and because of local tradition on his visit to the area, when he was unable to identify a 'Bethany across the Jordan'. Given the predominance of the place name Bethany in the gospels, it is possible that a copyist substituted it for the less common Bethabara. Alternatively, Origen's choice may have influenced the later manuscripts (compare Matt. 8:28 above). The balance between these two possibilities makes for uncertainty, although the manuscript support for Bethany leads to its adoption.[6]

1:34 ὁ υἱός (lit. the Son) {C}

Almost all Greek manuscripts read ὁ υἱός ('the Son [of God]'; $\mathfrak{P}^{66}$ $\mathfrak{P}^{75}$ $\mathfrak{P}^{120}$ 01² 02 03 etc.). The alternative ὁ ἐκλεκτός ('the Chosen One [of God]'; $\mathfrak{P}^{106vid}$ 01* lat^{vl-pt} sy^{c, s}) is only found in the first hand of Codex Sinaiticus, part of the Old Latin tradition, the Old Syriac, four minuscules and, possibly, Papyrus 5 and Papyrus 106 (see *TuT John* TS7).[7] Other versional evidence supports ὁ ἐκλεκτὸς υἱός ('the Chosen Son'; lat^{vl-pt} cpa^{mss} co^{sa}) which appears to be a conflation of the two forms. There is no obvious reason for the introduction of ἐκλεκτός, as Luke 23:35 and the variant at Luke 9:35 seem too distant to be influential. It may therefore be the earliest text, as proposed in the SBLGNT (followed by the NRSVue). Another argument in its favour is the appearance of ὁ ἐκλεκτός in Isaiah 42:1, building on the citation of Isaiah 40:3 a few verses earlier.[8] The replacement of ἐκλεκτός by the more common phrase 'Son of God' could simply be assimilation to Johannine usage or other examples of the phrase οὗτός ἐστιν ὁ υἱός ('this is the Son'; e.g.

---

[6] For a recent discussion, see Hutton 2008.

[7] The ECM John transcription website (www.iohannes.com) prefers the reconstruction ὁ ἐκλεκτός for Papyrus 5, following the *editio princeps*, although Wasserman 2020: 312, following Barbara Aland, considers this reading too uncertain and only considers ὁ ἐκλεκτός likely in Papyrus 106.

[8] I am grateful to Tommy Wasserman for this observation.

Matt. 3:17, 12:23; 17:5; Acts 9:20): doubt has been cast on the suggestion that it was motivated by theological concerns against an adoptionist Christology given the early attestation of both readings.[9] Nevertheless, the very strong external attestation for ὁ υἱὸς τοῦ θεοῦ, which is also standard Christological terminology in this gospel (John 1:49, 3:18, 5:25, 10:36 etc.), led to its adoption by the UBS4 committee and the THGNT.

1:42 Ἰωάννου (of John) {B}

The majority of witnesses read Ἰωνᾶ ('of Jonah'; 02 03² 037 044 etc.), but the oldest manuscript evidence is for Ἰωάννου ('of John'; 𝔓⁶⁶ 𝔓⁷⁵ 𝔓¹⁰⁶ 01 03* etc.). There is very limited support for Ἰωαννᾶ ('of Joanna[s]'; 038 1241 lat^vg), which may be a conflation of the two forms. The full attestation in Greek continuous-text manuscripts is given in *TuT John* (TS11). The Old Latin reading *frater Andreae* ('brother of Andrew') is likely to be influenced by John 1:40. John is a more common name than Jonah in the New Testament, and there is a possibility too that Ἰωάννου could have been introduced from John 1:40. On the other hand, the same variation appears three times in John 21:15–17 (see below), suggesting that the majority reading is a deliberate editorial change: Jonah corresponds to the one mention of Simon's father outside this gospel, at Matt. 16:17. John, therefore, not only has superior early attestation but is also a more difficult reading in this broader context. In any case, both Ἰωάννης and Ἰωνᾶς could be Greek versions of the same Hebrew name.

1:46 [ὁ] Φίλιππος (Philip)

The definite article before Φίλιππος is only attested in a few manuscripts, but these are important witnesses (𝔓⁶⁶ᶜ 𝔓⁷⁵ᵛⁱᵈ 03 019 33 579). It is also the more difficult reading, given the absence of articles before names in the verses on either side (including Philip in John 1:45 and 1:48). This combination makes for doubt as to whether or not it should be included, although there is no effect on translation. This type of var-

---

[9] See further Quek 2009, Ehrman 2011: 81–82, Wasserman 2020: 311–314. Fee 1974: 453 is also in favour of ὁ ἐκλεκτός as the hardest reading. This verse is included, albeit with minimal attestation, in *ECM Parallel Pericopes* (Strutwolf & Wachtel 2011: 7).

iant appears on numerous occasions in John, and it may be noted that the THGNT usually prefers the shorter reading (cf. John 3:4, 4:5 and 6:7 below).

1:51 ὄψεσθε (you will see) {B}

Before this verb, the majority of Greek manuscripts read ἀπ' ἄρτι ('from now on [you will see]'; 02 037 038 044 f^1 etc.). This is lacking from the earliest witnesses ($\mathfrak{P}^{66}$ $\mathfrak{P}^{75}$ $\mathfrak{P}^{134}$ 01 03 etc.: see *TuT John* TS13). It is unlikely that it was omitted by accident. Rather, it seems to have been added through assimilation to a comparable saying about the Son of Man at Matt. 26:64. There is a theological significance in this vision happening now, at the beginning of Jesus' ministry, rather than at an unspecified point in the future.

2:4 [καί] (and)

The initial καί is lacking from the majority of Greek manuscripts, including some early ones ($\mathfrak{P}^{75}$ 01*, 2b 044 f^1 etc.), but present in a range of witnesses ($\mathfrak{P}^{66}$ 01²ᵃ 02 03 019 032ˢᵘᵖ etc.). Similar variation is seen throughout the passage, and because of the balance in both external and internal evidence the word is included in brackets.

2:12 οἱ ἀδελφοὶ [αὐτοῦ] (his brothers)

The possessive pronoun αὐτοῦ ('his') occurs several times in this phrase. Most Greek manuscripts and early translations have it on all three occasions, including οἱ ἀδελφοὶ αὐτοῦ ('the brothers of him'; $\mathfrak{P}^{66c}$ 02 037 038 f^1 etc.). It is lacking from some early witnesses ($\mathfrak{P}^{66*}$ $\mathfrak{P}^{75}$ 03 019 044 etc.), although there is no effect on translation as it persists from the previous phrase ('his mother and brothers'). Codex Sinaiticus and some early versions lack the following phrase completely due to eyeskip between the two instances of αὐτοῦ, thus supporting the longer reading. Deletion by an earlier editor, to avoid repetition, and addition by a copyist in order to match the rest of the list are equally plausible. While there is a possibility of assimilation to Mark 3:31, the double αὐτοῦ in John 19:25 might favour οἱ ἀδελφοὶ αὐτοῦ here, but both the SBLGNT and THGNT prefer the shorter reading. No fewer than fifteen variants of the longer phrase are listed in *TuT John* (TS15).

2:15 φραγέλλιον (a whip) {B}

Some early witnesses read ὡς φραγέλλιον ('a kind of whip'; 𝔓⁶⁶ 𝔓⁷⁵ 011 019 022 etc.), but the majority just have φραγέλλιον ('a whip'; 01 02 03 037 etc.; see *TuT John* TS16). It is possible that ὡς was omitted by eyeskip after ποιήσας, but also that it was added by an early editor seeking to avoid the implication that Jesus was using a weapon which was forbidden in the Temple precinct (cf. John 7:10 below; Rev. 14:3, 19:12). Although the presence of a shorter reading in the majority of manuscripts supports the text without ὡς (adopted in the SBLGNT and THGNT), the possibility of accidental omission and the presence of ὡς in the two papyri means that the longer form cannot be easily discounted. Part of the significance of this variant may involve determining whether πάντας ('all of them') refers to humans or just animals.[10]

3:4 [ὁ] Νικόδημος (Nicodemus)

The manuscript tradition is split between those which include the definite article ὁ (01 02 037 *f*¹ *f*¹³ etc.) and those which lack it (𝔓⁶⁶ 𝔓⁷⁵ 03 019 032^supp 038 etc.). Unless a pattern can be discerned in the evangelist's scheme of introducing a character, the context suggests that the shorter text is likely to be original (cf. John 3:9). However, the extensive attestation of ὁ means that it has been included in brackets. As with the variation above at John 1:46, translation is unaffected.

3:13 ἀνθρώπου (of Man) {B}

At the end of this verse, the majority of Greek manuscripts include the phrase ὁ ὢν ἐν τῷ οὐρανῷ ('who is in heaven'; 02 037 038 044 etc.), but it is missing from many of the earliest witnesses (𝔓⁶⁶ 𝔓⁷⁵ 01 03 019 etc.). It could have been omitted by accident, if a copyist jumped between the *nomina sacra* of ΑΝΟΥ and ΟΥΝΩ, or on purpose, if an editor felt that it was wrong to say at this point that the Son of Man was in heaven: there is no other instance of this in John, where the title Son of Man is usually connected with soteriological activity. On the other hand, the presence of this phrase seems to complement the two other references to heaven in this verse, so it may have been added subsequently. It is worth noting that, while there are several instances of ὁ ὤν in relation

---

[10] See further the extended discussion at Wasserman 2020: 314–316.

to Christ (John 1:18, 6:46, 8:47 etc.), none of these has the complement of 'in heaven'. The variant reading ὁ ὢν ἐκ τοῦ οὐρανοῦ ('who is from heaven'; 0141 sy⁸) is either a deliberate emendation to improve the meaning or assimilation to the previous clause. External evidence leads to the preference for the shorter reading here and in the SBLGNT and THGNT.[11] The full attestation in Greek continuous-text manuscripts is given in *TuT John* (TS23).

3:15 ἐν αὐτῷ (in him) {B}

The majority of witnesses read εἰς αὐτὸν μὴ ἀπόληται ἀλλ' (lit. '[believe] into him may not perish but [have eternal life]'; 𝔓⁶³ᵛⁱᵈ [02] 037 038 044 etc.). This matches the phrase at the end of the following verse, meaning that it may be due to assimilation. Older manuscripts are split between several shorter readings: ἐν αὐτῷ ('in him'; 𝔓⁷⁵ 03 029 032ˢᵘᵖᵖ etc.), ἐπ' αὐτῷ ('on him'; 𝔓⁶⁶ 019 Cyril) and εἰς αὐτόν ('into him'; 01 086 *f*¹ etc.: see further *TuT John* TS24). Elsewhere, John always follows πιστεύειν ('believe') with εἰς, making the other two readings more difficult: there is very little support elsewhere in the New Testament for ἐν after πιστεύειν (Mark 1:15) and only slightly more for ἐπί (Matt. 27:42, Luke 24:25, Acts 11:17 and 21 etc.). On the other hand, ἐν αὐτῷ could be taken with the following words (i.e. 'in him will have eternal life'), which has been noted as a feature of Johannine style (cf. John 5:39, 16:33, 20:31 and 1 John).[12] As this reading is found in some important early manuscripts, and would explain the other developments towards more common constructions, it has therefore been adopted as the editorial text, although the THGNT prefers εἰς αὐτόν. Translations which follow the shorter reading with ἐν αὐτῷ will have to decide whether it qualifies the previous participle or the next verb.

3:25 μετὰ Ἰουδαίου (and a Jew) {B}

The singular μετὰ Ἰουδαίου ('with a Jew'; 𝔓⁷⁵ 01² 02 03 019 etc.) is attested by the majority of manuscripts, including several early ones. Others, among which are the *Textus Receptus* and the Latin tradition, read μετὰ Ἰουδαίων ('with Jews'; 𝔓⁶⁶ 01* 011 038 0141 etc.: see *TuT John*

---

[11] In favour of the longer reading, see Black 1985.
[12] Metzger 1994: 175.

TS27). All the other references to unnamed Jews in John are in the plural, meaning that the singular is unusual and thus a harder reading. If the plural were original, Ἰουδαίου could have arisen as an error following the previous Ἰωάννου ('John'), but the strong external attestation of this less common form leads to its adoption.[13]

3:28 εἶπον [ὅτι] (I said)

The word ὅτι ('that') is missing from Papyrus 75, Codex Sinaiticus and numerous minuscules. The tendency in John is not to include ὅτι after εἶπον, but there are exceptions (e.g. John 1:50, 6:36, 8:24 etc.). This balance of internal and external evidence leads to doubt as to whether it is original, but translation is unaffected.

3:31 ἐκ τοῦ οὐρανοῦ ἐρχόμενος [ἐπάνω πάντων ἐστίν] (comes from heaven is above all) {C}

The phrase ἐπάνω πάντων ἐστίν ('is above all'; $\mathfrak{P}^{36\text{vid}}$ $\mathfrak{P}^{66}$ 01² 02 03 etc.), present in the majority of Greek manuscripts, also occurs at the beginning of the verse after 'the one who comes from above'. It is missing from a range of early witnesses ($\mathfrak{P}^{75}$ 01* 05 f^1 etc., lat$^{\text{vl-pt}}$ sy^c co^{sa} Tertullian$^{\text{pt?}}$ Origen^{pt}), which suggests that it may not originally have been present: it is easy to see how it could have been added after ἐρχόμενος through assimilation to the previous sentence. On the other hand, such repetition is also a feature of Johannine style: there is no obvious reason for its accidental omission, but it might have been deleted by an early editor who felt that it was superfluous here. Again, the balance of internal and external evidence means that the reading has been included in brackets, although it is adopted in both the SBLGNT and THGNT. The full attestation in Greek continuous-text manuscripts is given in *TuT John* (TS30).

3:34 τὸ πνεῦμα (the Spirit) {B}

Most witnesses read ὁ θεὸς τὸ πνεῦμα ('God [gives] the Spirit'; 02 04² 05 037 044 etc.), but the earliest manuscripts have only τὸ πνεῦμα ('[he gives] the Spirit'; $\mathfrak{P}^{66}$ $\mathfrak{P}^{75}$ 01 03² 04* etc.). The latter reading is ambiguous: it could have as implied subject 'God' or 'the one who speaks the

---

[13] The detailed discussion in Pryor 1997 also prefers the singular.

words of God', or the phrase could even be translated as 'the Spirit gives'. Even if ὁ θεός was added later it does not entirely remove this ambiguity, because even the majority reading might be translated as 'God the Spirit gives'. As both nouns and the following ὁ πατήρ may all have been written as *nomina sacra* abbreviations, it is also possible that one of them was overlooked. In theological terms, taking the Spirit as subject has parallels elsewhere in the Gospel (cf. John 3:8, 4:24, 6:63), although this is balanced by descriptions of the Spirit as a gift (John 14:26, 15:26, 20:22; see also John 7:39 and variants). The external evidence justifies the adoption of the shorter reading: in translation, it is probably simplest to take τὸ πνεῦμα as an object and understand the previous ὁ θεός as the subject.

4:1 Ἰησοῦς (Jesus) {C}

The majority of Greek manuscripts, including early ones, read κύριος ('the Lord'; 𝔓⁶⁶ᶜ 𝔓⁷⁵ 02 03 04 etc.), but there is also substantial support for Ἰησοῦς ('Jesus'; 𝔓⁶⁶* 01 05 038 etc.). The early translations are divided and a few later manuscripts lack any noun (see *TuT John* TS32). As both would have been written as *nomina sacra* (ΚΣ and ΙΣ), one could easily have been misread as the other or overlooked. Each is problematic on stylistic grounds: 'Jesus' appears twice in the rest of the sentence, making a third occurrence rather clumsy, but 'the Lord' is very rarely used by John to indicate Jesus in narratives before the Resurrection and is therefore more likely to have been added later.[14] It has been suggested that the shortest reading was the earliest, with both nouns being added subsequently to make the subject explicit, but the external evidence is too weak to support this.[15] Instead, Ἰησοῦς has been chosen as the editorial text on internal grounds (cf. John 16:19). The SBLGNT also has Ἰησοῦς, but the THGNT prefers κύριος.

4:3 πάλιν (back) {A}

The adverb πάλιν (lit. 'again'; 𝔓⁶⁶ 𝔓⁷⁵ 01 03² 04 etc.) is present in a wide range of early witnesses, including the earliest translations, but absent

---

[14] See Kilpatrick 1968: 68–69.
[15] It consists of GA 047, 6 21, 49 and twenty other minuscules (none of which has been selected for the ECM), meaning that the conjecture in Brown 1966: 164, also reported in the *Amsterdam Database* (cj14670), is actually an attested reading.

from the majority of manuscripts (02 03* 037 044 etc.: see *TuT John* TS34). Its inclusion seems to be the harder reading, as Jesus does not enter Galilee until two days later (John 4:43). There are two previous mentions of Galilee in this gospel (John 1:43 and 2:1), but as it is not said that Jesus left the area in the interim, an editor might have considered the literal force of πάλιν ('returning a second time') to be inaccurate and removed it. Alternatively, it may have been omitted through oversight, since the preceding word ends with the same letter. This variant is included because of the intrinsic interest in tracing New Testament itineraries, not least as this may have led to the change in antiquity.

4:5   [τῷ] Ἰωσήφ (Joseph)

The definite article τῷ is missing from almost all Greek manuscripts and is only present in the four oldest (𝔓⁶⁶ 𝔓⁷⁵ 01 03). It has the appearance of a later clarification, to indicate that the following indeclinable proper noun is in the dative. As this is clear from the context anyway and the early attestation is so striking, it could be original even though John often does not use articles before names. Translation is unaffected.

4:11   [ἡ γυνή] (the woman)

Most Greek manuscripts read ἡ γυνή ('the woman'; 𝔓⁶⁶ 01² 02 04 05 etc.), matching John 4:9 and 4:15 on either side, and it is adopted in the SBLGNT and THGNT. The first hand of Codex Sinaiticus has ἐκείνη ('that woman'; 01*), a pronoun which is not typical of Johannine style: although it makes sense in context, this may have arisen through visual or phonetic confusion.[16] The absence of the subject completely from four early witnesses (𝔓⁷⁵ 03 sy^s co^ly) and the fact that it is clear from the context leads to some doubt as to whether it was originally present: the variation in Codex Sinaiticus could provide further indirect support for this. It may be noted that, despite the signalling of each participant on most occasions in this dialogue, these and other witnesses also lack a subject in John 4:16 where the shorter reading is adopted as the editorial text. The evidence is thus evenly balanced, hence the brackets. The

---

[16] Phonetic confusion is proposed in Jongkind 2022: 149.

full attestation in Greek continuous-text manuscripts is given in *TuT John* (TS36). In translation, it may still be necessary to provide the subject of the verb if the shorter reading is followed.

4:25   οἶδα (I know) {C}

There is extensive manuscript support for the first-person singular, οἶδα ('I know'; 𝔓⁶⁶* 𝔓⁷⁵ 01* 02 03 etc. and the majority of minuscules). A few witnesses, however, including much of the Coptic tradition, have the plural οἴδαμεν ('we know'; 𝔓⁶⁶ᶜ 01² 011 019 etc.). This fits well with the following ἡμῖν ('[he will tell] us') and the preceding use of the plural in the discussion from John 4:20 onwards. It is possible that the last three letters of οἴδαμεν were overlooked or misinterpreted as οἶδα μέν ('while I know'), with the μέν then deleted because of the lack of a corresponding clause with δέ. On the other hand, the extensive evidence for the singular and its discontinuity with the rest of the clause favour its adoption: a move towards the plural is evident in the corrections in Papyrus 66 and Codex Sinaiticus (compare also Mark 1:24). The variant is also of theological interest: is the woman speaking only for herself, or as a Samaritan more generally? It may be noted that Nicodemus also uses the plural οἴδαμεν when he addresses Jesus (John 3:2; cf. 14:5), which has an effect on the portrayal of attitudes to Jesus (and the potential for irony): if translators follow the plural, they may need to decide whether it is inclusive or exclusive.

4:30   ἐξῆλθον (they left) {B}

Although there is wide attestation of the verb alone, ἐξῆλθον ('they left'; 𝔓⁷⁵ 02 03 037 038 etc.), other witnesses have a connective: ἐξῆλθον οὖν ('And so they left'; 𝔓⁶⁶ 01 032ˢᵘᵖᵖ *f*¹ etc. and numerous minuscules), καὶ ἐξῆλθον ('And they left'; 04 05 latᵛˡ⁻ᵖᵗ sy) or ἐξήρχοντο δέ ('But they were beginning to leave'; 1241 coˡʸ, ᵖᵇᵒ). The presence of a connective affects the way in which this activity is connected to the preceding declaration, and may be reflected in translation. While there is good support for οὖν, which might have been overlooked after ἐξῆλθον, this word is found in both John 4:28 and 4:33 and so could have been added through assimilation. The variety of connectives, however, suggests that the shortest reading is the earliest and was expanded in different ways.

4:35–36 θερισμόν. ἤδη ὁ (harvesting … already) {B}

In some of the earliest witnesses, no indication is given of how this phrase should be punctuated (𝔓⁶⁶ 01* 03). Others give it as θερισμόν. ἤδη ὁ θερίζων ('[ripe for] harvesting. Already the reaper'; 01ᶜ 04* 05 019 032ˢᵘᵖᵖ etc.), or θερισμὸν ἤδη. ὁ θερίζων ('already [ripe for] harvesting. The reaper'; 𝔓⁷⁵ 083 0141* etc.). The majority of Greek manuscripts follow the latter, with an additional conjunction: θερισμὸν ἤδη. καὶ ὁ θερίζων ('already [ripe for] harvesting. And the reaper'; 02 04³ 037 038 etc.). This explains why verse 36 begins after ἤδη, but it is likely to be secondary because the extra word eliminates the ambiguity. The choice of the editorial text (also adopted in the SBLGNT) is based on Johannine usage: there are several other examples of ἤδη beginning a sentence (e.g. John 4:51, 7:14, 9:22, 15:3 etc.) and no instances of it in final position. The THGNT, however, prefers the reading of Papyrus 75, which is the most difficult because it differs from the pattern elsewhere.

4:51 λέγοντες (and told him) {B}

The editorial text (also adopted in the SBLGNT and THGNT) is the shortest reading, with limited but early support: λέγοντες ('saying'; 𝔓⁷⁵ 03 019 022 etc.). Codex Sinaiticus reads καὶ ἤγγειλαν ('and they announced'; 01), while Codex Bezae has καὶ ἤγγειλαν αὐτῷ ('and they announced to him'; 05). The other readings appear to be conflations of these forms: the majority of manuscripts have καὶ ἀπήγγειλαν λέγοντες ('and they reported, saying'; 𝔓⁶⁶ 02 04 032ˢᵘᵖᵖ etc.), and others read καὶ ἀνήγγειλαν λέγοντες ('and they proclaimed, saying'; *f*¹ 33 565: see *TuT John* TS44). There is no obvious reason for the longer readings to have been abbreviated: instead, they appear to be intensifications, as shown by the compound verb (see also the next unit). However, the early attestation of the majority reading makes for some doubt as to the oldest form.

4:51 παῖς αὐτοῦ (his child) {B}

Many witnesses have a second-person pronoun, meaning that the announcement takes the form of direct speech. The majority of manuscripts read παῖς σου ('your child'; 037 038 044 etc.), while others have υἱός σου ('your son'; 𝔓⁶⁶ᶜ 05 019 022 0141 etc.). The latter was probably introduced through assimilation to Jesus' words in John 4:50 and 4:53 (compare also the Latin witnesses which support υἱός αὐτοῦ, 'his son'). The reading παῖς αὐτοῦ ('his child'; 𝔓⁶⁶* 𝔓⁷⁵ 01 02 03 04 032ˢᵘᵖᵖ) is the most dissimilar from the previous verse, with very strong early attestation, leading to its adoption here and in both the SBLGNT and THGNT. Nevertheless, it may be noted that this is the only occurrence of παῖς in John (the diminutive τὸ παιδίον is used elsewhere, as in John 4:49) and there is the possibility of influence from synoptic parallels (e.g. Matt. 8:13, 17:18; Luke 7:7). If the second person σου was not due to repetition, it is likely to have been introduced because the preceding ὅτι was taken as introducing direct speech: it is far less probable that it was replaced by αὐτοῦ. The reading of Family 13, παῖς σου ὁ υἱὸς αὐτοῦ ('your child, his son'; f^{13}) is a clear instance of nonsensical conflation produced by the combination of alternative readings. The full attestation in Greek continuous-text manuscripts is given in *TuT John* (TS45). Even if παῖς is adopted, translators may prefer to use 'son', as it has already been applied to this child in John 4:47 and 4:50.

4:53   [ἐν] ἐκείνῃ (this)

The preposition ἐν is lacking from a few manuscripts, some early (𝔓⁷⁵ 01* 03 04 029 1 892). It is not required in context, and was probably omitted through eyeskip before ἐκείνῃ. However, an original shorter reading could have been assimilated to the more common construction with ἐν (cf. John 5:9, 14:20, 16:23 etc.). Compare also John 6:39–40 below.

4:54   [δέ] (now)

There is very early but limited attestation of the connective δέ ('but'; 𝔓⁶⁶ 𝔓⁷⁵ 03 04* 029 032ˢᵘᵖᵖ 078ᶜ f^{13} 1241 Origen). In initial position in John, τοῦτο is normally followed by δέ (see John 13:28 below), which could have led to its insertion. Alternatively, a later editor may have removed it, considering that the following πάλιν ('again') was sufficient to connect this to the previous narrative or that the contrast was out of place. Despite the antiquity of witnesses with δέ, it is rare to find a shorter reading attested by the majority of manuscripts, which might support it here.

5:1 ἑορτή (a festival) {B}

A large number of manuscripts read ἡ ἑορτή ('the festival'; 01 04 019 037 etc.), but there is strong early support for just ἑορτή ('a festival'; 𝔓⁶⁶ 𝔓⁷⁵ 02 03 05 etc.) and the Byzantine tradition is split. The presence of the definite article in conjunction with the journey to Jerusalem may have been intended to identify the festival as Passover (cf. John 2:13, 6:4), although this is not clear from the narrative and there is disagreement among commentators over which feast is intended.[17] It is more likely that this would have been added to make the narrative more precise: among many instances of ἑορτή in John this is the only anarthrous example, which makes it the harder reading. The external evidence also supports the shorter text, although the possibility remains of accidental omission of a single letter.

5:2 Βηθζαθά (Beth-zatha) {C}

The majority of manuscripts have Βηθεσδά ('Bethesda'; 02 04 037 038 etc.), a place name which does not otherwise appear in the New Testament. Early witnesses are divided between Βηθζαθά ('Bethzatha'; 01 [019] 33 etc.), Βελζεθά ('Belzetha'; 05 lat^{vl-pt}) and Βηθσαϊδά ('Bethsaida'; 𝔓⁶⁶ 𝔓⁷⁵ 03 029 032^{supp} 044 etc.: see *TuT John* TS47). External evidence favours the last of these, but it is the most likely to reflect assimilation to a more common New Testament place (cf. John 1:44, 12:21; Mark 6:45, 8:22; Luke 9:10). Nevertheless, as the biblical Bethsaida is by the Sea of Galilee rather than in Jerusalem, this poses geographical problems: it could instead have developed as a misreading of Bethesda. The other variants seem to be related: Bethzatha and Belzetha look very similar, yet their meaning is unclear. In contrast, Bethesda can be interpreted as 'House of Mercy'—which led the earlier UBS committee to prefer the better attested alternative reading on the suspicion that Bethesda had been introduced on the basis of its etymology.[18] Even so, the latter is adopted by both the SBLGNT and THGNT. Although it has been suggested that a mention of a pool in the Copper Scroll from Qumran might relate to this verse, the latest scholarship indicates that

---

[17] See further Omanson 2006: 173.

[18] Metzger 1994: 178. A discussion of the textual and archaeological evidence is given in J. F. Strange 1992.

this does not provide a place name.[19] The original text is very uncertain, and in a translation it may be appropriate to indicate the alternatives in a footnote.

5:3   ξηρῶν (paralysed) {A}

Codex Bezae and part of the Old Latin tradition include the word παραλυτικῶν ('paralysed'; 05 lat[vl-pt]) after ξηρῶν: the latter literally means 'withered', but can also be rendered as 'paralysed'. The reason for adding this word appears to have been in order to include the paralysed man of this passage: that it is restricted to these witnesses may be because the literal Latin translation of ξηρῶν, *aridorum*, lacks the further meaning of 'paralysis', and so the connection was not evident. The word παραλυτικός, 'paralysed man' occurs in Matthew and Mark, but does not otherwise feature in John. At the end of the verse, the majority of manuscripts have ἐκδεχομένων τὴν τοῦ ὕδατος κίνησιν ('waiting for the movement of the water'; 02ᶜ 04³ 05 032ˢᵘᵖᵖ 037 etc.), before adding John 5:4. This is an anticipation of the detail in John 5:7, but uses two words which do not otherwise feature in the Gospels, ἐκδέχεσθαι ('to wait') and κίνησις ('movement'). The extra text is lacking from the earliest witnesses (𝔓⁶⁶ 𝔓⁷⁵ 01 02* 03 04* etc.), including ancient translations. As there is no obvious reason for its accidental omission it appears to be part of a later addition, yet not all manuscripts with this include John 5:4 (see the next unit). The full attestation in Greek continuous-text manuscripts is given in *TuT John* (TS48).

5:4   *omit verse* {A}

The majority of Greek manuscripts include the verse traditionally numbered as John 5:4, as in Codex Alexandrinus: ἄγγελος γὰρ κυρίου κατὰ καιρὸν ἐλούετο ἐν τῇ κολυμβήθρα καὶ ἐτάρασσε τὸ ὕδωρ· ὁ οὖν πρῶτος ἐμβὰς μετὰ τὴν ταραχὴν τοῦ ὕδατος ὑγιὴς ἐγίνετο οἵῳ δήποτ' οὖν κατείχετο νοσήματι ('for an angel of the Lord at certain times used to wash in the pool and disturb the water: accordingly, the first who went in after the disturbance of the water became healthy from whatever sort of sickness by which they were possessed'; 02, also in 04³ 019 037 038 etc. with several variations). This is lacking from most of the earliest

---

[19] Ceulemans 2007.

Greek manuscripts ($\mathfrak{P}^{66}$ $\mathfrak{P}^{75}$ 01 03 04* 05 etc.; see *TuT John* TS49) as well as the three oldest translations. As with the extra text in the previous unit, this features several words or expressions which do not otherwise appear in John (κατὰ καιρόν, ἐμβαίνειν [in this sense], δήποτε, κατέχεσθαι, νοσήμα). Most striking is the reference to an angel, which is rare in this gospel, only otherwise appearing in the narrative at John 20:12. This too therefore seems to be a later addition, perhaps incorporating an early tradition transmitted separately (cf. Luke 22:43–44 above). Its evident antiquity, with quotations in some of the earliest Christian authors, may justify including it in a translation as a footnote.[20]

5:5 τριάκοντα [καὶ] ὀκτώ (thirty-eight)

In the papyri, this number is written as a numeral (λη', '38'), and a large number of manuscripts just read τριάκοντα ὀκτώ ('thirty-eight'; 03 036 038 892 1424 etc.). There is also extensive support for τριάκοντα καὶ ὀκτώ ('thirty-eight'; 01 02 04 05 019 f^1 etc.) and it is hard to be sure of the earliest form.

5:17 ὁ δὲ [Ἰησοῦς] (but Jesus)

Some early and important witnesses just read ὁ δέ ('but he'; $\mathfrak{P}^{75}$ 01 03 032 892 1241), but the rest have ὁ δέ Ἰησοῦς ('but Jesus'; $\mathfrak{P}^{66}$ 02 05 019 037 038 044 etc., and most early translations). It is possible that the name was overlooked, especially as it is likely to have been written as a *nomen sacrum* (IC), yet it could also have been added for clarity and to ensure that the formerly paralysed man was not taken as the subject. It may also be appropriate to supply 'Jesus' in translation whichever reading is followed.

5:44 θεοῦ (God) {C}

The noun θεοῦ ('God') is missing from some of the earliest witnesses ($\mathfrak{P}^{66}$ $\mathfrak{P}^{75}$ 03 032 etc.), which refer to 'the glory that comes from the one'. There is no parallel for this as a title for God in John or in the New Testament more broadly, making this the harder reading in contrast to formulations such as τὸν μόνον ἀληθινὸν θεόν ('the one true God') in

---

[20] For further studies, see Fee 1982; Parker 1997: 175–176.

John 17:3. On the other hand, the shorter reading could be explained as accidental omission of the *nomen sacrum* ΘΥ through eyeskip after ΜΟΝΟΥ or before the following ΟΥ. The full attestation is given in *TuT John* (TS56), which shows that only six manuscripts have the shorter reading.[21] While eyeskip of this sort may be more likely to occur in majuscule script, it would be surprising if it happened on more than one occasion affecting these four important witnesses but no others, especially as the *nomen sacrum* would have been indicated by a line above the letters. As a result, there is considerable doubt about the earliest text here, although the longer text is adopted in both the SBLGNT and THGNT.

6:1 τῆς Γαλιλαίας τῆς Τιβεριάδος (lit. of Galilee of Tiberias) {A}

This verse is included in *ECM Parallel Pericopes*. There is strong attestation of the majority reading τῆς Γαλιλαίας τῆς Τιβεριάδος ('of Galilee of Tiberias'; 𝔓⁶⁶ᶜ 𝔓⁷⁵ᵛⁱᵈ 01 02 03 etc.), which is adopted as the editorial text. Nevertheless, the double genitive looks like a conflation or error (cf. John 21:1, where only the latter term is used), so it is not surprising to find alternative readings. Some early witnesses have τῆς Γαλιλαίας εἰς τὰ μέρη τῆς Τιβεριάδος ('of Galilee into the region of Tiberias'; 05 038 597 892 etc.), which appears to be an editorial expansion to make sense of the two terms. The first hand of Papyrus 66 just reads τῆς Γαλιλαίας ('of Galilee'; 𝔓⁶⁶*), which may be harmonisation to the Synoptic Gospels (e.g. Matt. 4:8, 15:29 etc.). Some later manuscripts have only τῆς Τιβεριάδος ('of Tiberias'; 011 022 0210 etc.: see *TuT John* TS57), perhaps through eyeskip between the two instances of τῆς or, less likely, assimilation to John 21:1. The simplest explanation for all these variants is the editorial text, which may require expansion in translation to explain the double form (e.g. 'the Sea of Galilee, also called the Sea of Tiberias' as in the NRSVue). It is possible that this stems from an error or gloss in a very early copy.

6:7 [ὁ] Φίλιππος (Philip)

The majority of Greek manuscripts lack the definite article before Φίλιππος ('Philip'; 𝔓⁷⁵ 02 03 05 037 etc.), in keeping with the previous

---

[21] It may also be noted that the first hand of GA 821 reads τούτου in place of θεοῦ.

occurrence of this name two verses earlier. The reading ὁ Φίλιππος is perhaps harder, but has early support (𝔓⁶⁶ 01 019 022 032 892).[22] As before (see John 1:46 above), translation is unaffected.

6:7 βραχύ [τι] (a little)

This is the only occurrence of βραχύ ('small') in John. Although the majority of manuscripts have the common phrase βραχύ τι ('something small'; 𝔓⁶⁶ 01 02 019 032 037 etc., cf. Heb. 2:7), τι is missing from a few of the earliest witnesses (𝔓⁷⁵ 03 05 lat^{vl}), leading to doubt as to whether it was originally present. If the shorter reading is followed, βραχύ must be interpreted as a neuter substantive ('a small thing'), which is effectively the same as the alternative form.

6:11 διέδωκεν (distributed) {B}

The majority of Greek manuscripts include an additional stage in the distribution, reading διέδωκεν τοῖς μαθηταῖς, οἱ δὲ μαθηταί ('he distributed them to the disciples, and the disciples [to those who were seated]'; 01² 05 037 038 etc.). The shorter reading, διέδωκεν ('he distributed them [to those who were seated]'; 𝔓²⁸ᵛⁱᵈ 𝔓⁶⁶ 𝔓⁷⁵ 01* 02 03 etc.) has strong ancient support, including most of the early translations. It is possible that this arose from eyeskip between the two occurrences of τοῖς, but the external evidence makes it more likely that this is a later expansion harmonising to Matt. 14:19. This verse is included in *ECM Parallel Pericopes*, which gives fuller details of the variant readings. It has been suggested that, even if the shorter reading is adopted, translators may need to add a similar phrase for clarity.[23]

6:14 ὃ ἐποίησεν σημεῖον (the sign that he had done) {B}

The singular, ὃ ἐποίησεν σημεῖον ('the sign that he had done'; 01 02 05 019 etc.) is found in most Greek manuscripts and early translations. There is early evidence too for the plural, ἃ ἐποίησεν σημεῖα ('the signs that he had done'; 𝔓⁷⁵ 03 091 lat^{vl-pt} co^{bo}: see *TuT John* TS62). Both forms are found throughout John: in the present context, it is likely that the singular was assimilated to the plural σημεῖα in John 6:2 and 6:26

---

[22] *ECM Parallel Pericopes* (2011: 67) is inaccurate in citing 𝔓⁷⁵ in support of ὁ.
[23] See King 2017: 24–25.

(cf. John 2:23). On the other hand, it remains possible that an early editor changed an initial plural to the singular in order to reflect the specific sign of the miraculous feeding witnessed by these people. See also *ECM Parallel Pericopes*.

6:15 ἀνεχώρησεν (withdrew) {A}

Almost all Greek manuscripts have ἀνεχώρησεν ('he withdrew'; 𝔓⁷⁵ 01² 02 03 05 etc.). The first hand of Codex Sinaiticus instead reads φεύγει ('he flees'; 01* [lat^(vl-pt, vg)] [sy^c] Tertullian).[24] The present tense is surprising, given the aorist tense of the narrative throughout: it is possible that it derives from Latin, because *fugit* is both the present and perfect form. However, the normal Latin rendering of ἀνεχώρησεν, which only appears here in John, is *secessit* or *recessit* (cf. Matt. 2:14). The variant changes the portrayal of Jesus, suggesting that he was forced to depart, which an early editor may have felt was inappropriate and changed (cf. John 10:12), substituting it with a verb common in Matthew. However, the attestation of φεύγει is too slim to justify taking it as the earliest text and it seems instead to be a loose ancient translation which had a minor influence on other traditions. Compare also John 7:1 below.

6:22 ἕν (one) {A}

There is good early support for the reading ἕν ('[no other boat except] one'; 𝔓⁷⁵ 01² 02 03 019 etc. and several translations). The majority of Greek manuscripts have ἓν ἐκεῖνο εἰς ὃ ἐνέβησαν οἱ μαθηταὶ αὐτοῦ ('one, that into which his disciples embarked'; [01*] [037] 038 0141 etc.), with a similar reading in Codex Bezae: ἓν εἰς ὃ ἐνέβησαν οἱ μαθηταὶ αὐτοῦ ('one into which his disciples embarked'; 05 33 1071 sy^s etc.). There is nothing to prompt the omission or deletion of this phrase, which instead seems to be a subsequent editorial expansion for the clarification of a confusing aspect of the narrative: Codex Bezae seems to represent an intermediate form to which ἐκεῖνο was subsequently added, although it could have been overlooked. The full attestation in Greek continuous-text manuscripts is given in *TuT John* (TS66).

---

[24] The Curetonian Syriac has a conflation: "he left them and fled again".

6:23 πλοιά[ρια] (boats)

The diminutive πλοιάρια ('little boats'; 02 05 019 037 038 etc.) is found in the majority of manuscripts, while πλοῖα ('boats'; 𝔓⁷⁵ 01 02 032 044 etc.) has significant early support (see further *TuT John* TS67). Both words occur in the previous verse, with πλοιάρια in the following verse as well. Although πλοῖα could have arisen through eyeskip between the two instances of ια, the longer reading may be assimilation: the internal evidence is evenly balanced but the attestation seems to support πλοῖα as the earliest form. The size of the boats does not seem to be particularly relevant for translation.[25] The lack of accents in the earliest manuscripts could make for ambiguity between ἄλλα ('other [boats]') and ἀλλά ('but [boats]'): the latter, however, was often written as ἀλλ', and several textual variants as well as the first translations make it clear that the first word of the verse was taken as an adjective rather than a conjunction in antiquity, hence its adoption in modern editions.

6:23 εὐχαριστήσαντος τοῦ κυρίου (after the Lord had given thanks) {B}

Most witnesses support the editorial text, εὐχαριστήσαντος τοῦ κυρίου ('after the Lord had given thanks'; 𝔓⁷⁵ 01 02 03 019 etc.). As noted above at John 4:1, the use of κύριος ('Lord') for Jesus in the narrative is rare in John except after the Resurrection.[26] Some Syriac and Coptic versions have εὐχαριστήσαντος τοῦ Ἰησοῦ ('after Jesus had given thanks'), but this is not found in Greek despite the similarity of the two *nomina sacra* (ΚΥ and ΙΥ). A few early witnesses lack the entire phrase (05 091 lat^{vl-pt} sy^{c, s}; see further *TuT John* TS68). This is an attractive reading, comparable to some of the 'Western non-interpolations' observed in the Synoptic Gospels (e.g. Matt. 27:49, Luke 24:6 etc.): there is no obvious reason for its deletion or omission, whereas the clarification could easily have been added to make it clear that this referred to the previous feeding miracle rather than some unspecified bread. However, its restricted attestation was considered insufficient to displace the majority reading, and there is the possibility that a line was overlooked in an ancestor in the 'Western' tradition.

---

[25] See further BDAG s.v. πλοιάριον. Elliott 1975: 143 suggests that diminutive endings were replaced by Atticist editors.
[26] See Kilpatrick 1968: 68–69.

6:29 [ὁ] Ἰησοῦς (Jesus)

The definite article is absent from most Greek manuscripts ($\mathfrak{P}^{75}$ 01 032 037 044 etc.) but present in other early witnesses (02 03 05 019 038 etc.). There appears to be a consistent pattern throughout John not to include an article in the phrase ἀπεκρίθη Ἰησοῦς ('Jesus answered'), notwithstanding manuscript variation, unless αὐτοῖς ('them') comes between the two words (see John 7:16 and 10:34 below). This suggests that the shorter reading should be preferred here, and the article was introduced through assimilation to John 6:26.

6:36 [με] (me)

Almost all the Greek tradition includes με ('me'), but it is lacking from two early majuscules (01 02), both Old Syriac manuscripts and some Old Latin witnesses. This could be accidental omission after the previous two letters (τε) or a deliberate deletion, perhaps to bring it into line with John 6:26 or through assimilation to the second half of John 20:29 (see also John 6:47 below). The preceding verse shows that in context, even if the shorter reading is adopted, the object is still Jesus.

6:39–40 [ἐν] τῇ ἐσχάτῃ ἡμέρᾳ (on the last day)

Elsewhere in John, the full form of this phrase is preferred (John 7:37, 11:24, 12:48). In this passage, there is considerable variation: the preposition ἐν ('in' or 'on') is in brackets in both John 6:39 and 6:40, included in 6:44 and absent from 6:54, reflecting considerable variation between manuscripts. It is lacking from numerous minuscules in 6:39 and the majority of witnesses in 6:40; Papyrus 66 and Papyrus 75 both lack it in 6:39, but Papyrus 66 includes it in 6:40 (and 6:44); Codices Sinaiticus, Alexandrinus and Bezae (01 02 and 05) have it in both verses but Codices Vaticanus and Ephraemi Rescriptus (03 and 04) do not. Given the probable tendency of copyists to conform the phrase to whatever was considered standard, especially in these well-known passages, it is very difficult to determine the earliest form and it is possible that the author was inconsistent. Translation, however, is unaffected.

6:42 νῦν (now) {B}

Most Greek manuscripts read οὖν ('then'; $\mathfrak{P}^{66}$ 01 02 05 019 etc.), which is a common conjunction after πῶς ('how'; see Matt. 12:29, 22:43, 26:54;

John 9:19 etc.). It is unlikely that this would have been changed to νῦν ('now'; 𝔓⁷⁵ 03 04 032 038 etc.), which has strong early support. John has more instances of νῦν than the other three gospels combined, which supports its originality here: assimilation to the question in John 9:21 is very improbable. A few witnesses have neither word (579 lat^{vl-pt} sy^{c, s} co^{sa-mss, ly}). This is likely to reflect eyeskip from οὖν to the following word οὕτως, or translational freedom in the early versions. The full attestation in Greek continuous-text manuscripts is given in *TuT John* (TS71).

6:47 πιστεύων (believes) {A}

The majority of witnesses read πιστεύων εἰς ἐμέ ('believes in me'; 02 04² 05 037 etc.), but the oldest manuscripts have only πιστεύων ('believes'; 𝔓⁶⁶ 𝔓^{75vid} 01 03 04* etc.; see *TuT John* TS74). There is a slight possibility of omission through eyeskip to the following word (ἔχει), but the external evidence indicates that εἰς ἐμέ is likely to be assimilation to the many other instances of this phrase (e.g. John 6:35, 7:38, 11:25–26 etc.). The variant in the Old Syriac indirectly supports the shorter reading: πιστεύων εἰς τὸν θεόν ('believes in God'; sy^{c, s}) could be assimilation to John 14:1 or an independent expansion. The object of belief is clearly of theological importance, and translations into languages which require an object for this verb may choose to follow the majority text.

6:52 [αὐτοῦ] (his) {C}

The pronoun αὐτοῦ ('his') is absent from the majority of manuscripts (𝔓^{75vid} 01 04 05 019 etc.) but present in a range of early Greek witnesses (𝔓⁶⁶ 03 029 etc. and most translations). There is no obvious reason for its omission or deletion, whereas it could easily have been added to remove the possibility of interpreting the reference as 'meat' in general.[27] In context, however, the verses on either side suggest that the meaning is 'his flesh', which is a valid translation even without the pronoun. In some languages, it will be necessary or more natural to include the possessive 'his'.

---

[27] However, see Ferda 2019 on the interpretative possibilities of the shorter reading.

6:55 ἀληθής (true) {B}

On both occasions in this verse, there is variation between the adjective ἀληθής ('true') and the adverb ἀληθῶς ('truly'). There is slight variation in the attestation (due partly to omissions through eyeskip), but the majority of minuscules along with Codex Bezae and the first hand of Papyrus 66 have the adverb whereas the other oldest manuscripts have the adjective: the full attestation in Greek continuous-text manuscripts is given in *TuT John* (TS76). Both forms are found elsewhere in John, but the adjective seems to be a slightly harder reading because it is separated from the noun it qualifies by the verb ἐστιν ('is'). This and the external evidence lead to its adoption. In translation, a difference could be made between the alternatives ('my flesh is true food' versus 'my flesh is truly food'), with potential theological implications, although it may not be possible to reflect this in all languages.

6:58 οἱ πατέρες (the ancestors) {A}

The majority of Greek manuscripts read οἱ πατέρες ὑμῶν τὸ μάννα ('your ancestors [ate] the manna'; 037 038 044 etc.). Most early witnesses just have οἱ πατέρες ('the ancestors'; 𝔓⁶⁶ 𝔓⁷⁵ 01 03 04 etc.), while some have οἱ πατέρες ὑμῶν ('your ancestors'; 05 0141 33 597 etc.) and a number of minuscules read οἱ πατέρες ἡμῶν ('our ancestors'; see *TuT John* TS79) due to the identical pronunciation of ὑμῶν and ἡμῶν through itacism (compare John 11:50 below). The reference to manna is clearly a gloss to explain the heavenly bread, perhaps through assimilation to John 6:31 or 6:49: the even longer phrase οἱ πατέρες ὑμῶν τὸ μάννα ἐν τῇ ἐρήμῳ ('your ancestors [ate] the manna in the wilderness'; lat^{vl-pt} cpa^{ms} [co^{bo-mss}]) clearly derives from these verses. The external evidence indicates that the pronoun ὑμῶν ('your') is also likely to be assimilation or a later clarification, perhaps to distance Jesus from his audience. In context, the inclusion of a possessive pronoun may be more natural in translation even when the shorter reading is followed (compare John 6:52 above).

6:66 [ἐκ] τῶν μαθητῶν (of the disciples)

The preposition ἐκ ('out of') is absent from most Greek manuscripts (01 04 05 019 etc.) and attested by relatively few witnesses (𝔓⁶⁶ 03 029 *f*¹ 33 565: see *TuT John* TS82). This could be assimilation to John 6:60.

However, the phrase πολλοὶ τῶν μαθητῶν ('many of the disciples') does not otherwise occur in the gospels, and John has a clear preference for the construction ἐκ τῶν μαθητῶν ('out of the disciples'): it could be that an early editor removed the second instance of ἐκ in this verse as a stylistic improvement. In any case, translation is unaffected. See also John 12:4 below.

6:69 ὁ ἅγιος τοῦ θεοῦ (the Holy One of God) {A}

There is extensive early attestation of ὁ ἅγιος τοῦ θεοῦ ('the Holy One of God'; 𝔓⁷⁵ 01 03 04* 05 etc.). All the other readings include ὁ χριστός ('the Christ'), found by itself in Tertullian, which appears to be assimilation to Peter's confession in Mark 8:29. A conflation of these two readings is seen in ὁ χριστὸς ὁ ἅγιος τοῦ θεοῦ ('the Christ, the Holy One of God'; 𝔓⁶⁶ co^(sa-mss, bo, ly) Cyril). The majority reading, ὁ χριστὸς ὁ υἱὸς τοῦ θεοῦ τοῦ ζῶντος ('the Christ, the Son of the living God'; [037] 038ᶜ 044 etc.) is assimilation to the Matthean form of Peter's confession (Matt. 16:16): both this and ὁ χριστὸς ὁ υἱὸς τοῦ θεοῦ ('the Christ, the Son of God'; 04³ 038* 0141 f^1 etc.) are found as variants to Mark 8:29 and the latter could be assimilation to John 11:27. Although the phrase ὁ ἅγιος τοῦ θεοῦ ('the Holy One of God') is present in the Synoptic Gospels (Mark 1:24, Luke 4:34), this is on the lips of demons and there would be no reason to interpolate it into Peter's confession here, unlike the other forms of text. The full attestation in Greek continuous-text manuscripts is given in *TuT John* (TS83).

6:71 Ἰσκαριώτου (Iscariot) {A}

Most Greek manuscripts read Ἰσκαριώτην ('Iscariot'; 037 f^1 565 etc.), a first-declension accusative singular agreeing with Ἰούδαν ('Judas'), resulting in 'Judas Iscariot, son of Simon'. The earliest witnesses have a genitive singular, Ἰσκαριώτου ('Iscariot'; 𝔓⁶⁶ 𝔓⁷⁵ 01² 03 04 etc.), giving 'Judas, son of Simon Iscariot'. The latter is consistent with John 13:2 and 13:26, but is clearly the more difficult form in comparison with references to 'Judas Iscariot' (e.g. Matt. 10:4, 26:14; Luke 22:3; John 12:4 and 14:22); there is no mention of Judas' father outside John. This strongly attested harder reading is therefore adopted as the earliest form. The variant Σκαριώθ ('Scarioth'; 05 lat^(vl)) seems to be assimilation to the Markan form of this name (Ἰσκαριώθ; Mark 3:19, 14:10; see also Luke

6:16). Most interesting is ἀπὸ Καρυώτου ('from Karyot'; 01* 038 f^{13} sy^{hmg}). This has been explained as an etymologising rendering of the Hebrew אִישׁ קְרִיּוֹת *(ish Qᵉriyyoth*, 'man of Kerioth') referring to a town in southern Judaea.[28] The same reading appears in Codex Bezae in the four other instances of this name in John (12:4, 13:2, 13:26 and 14:22; see below), demonstrating that it was an early interpretative tradition. In translation, however, it is best to keep Iscariot as a proper noun. The full attestation in Greek continuous-text manuscripts is given in *TuT John* (TS85).

7:1 ἤθελεν (wish) {A}

Almost all manuscripts have ἤθελεν ('did [not] wish'; 𝔓^{66} 𝔓^{75} 01 03 04 etc.). A few diverse witnesses, however, support εἶχεν ἐξουσίαν (lit. 'did [not] have authority'; 032 lat$^{vl\text{-}pt}$ sy^c Chrysostom). The latter phrase is seen at John 10:18 and 19:10, as well as in the other gospels, but this instance is different with the implication that Jesus was constrained by factors outside his control. It is clearly the more difficult reading, but the attestation is not sufficient to justify its adoption. Although it is difficult to explain its origin, it may be noted that one Old Latin manuscript has a rendering of ἤθελεν as *habebat uoluntatem* ('had a wish'), a misreading of which seems to have led to *habebat potestatem* ('had power') attested in other Old Latin sources. This could then have been introduced into other traditions, similar to the variation at John 6:15 discussed above.

7:8 οὐκ (not) {C}

The majority of witnesses support οὔπω ('not yet'; 𝔓^{66} 𝔓^{75} 03 019 etc.), but there is some early evidence for οὐκ ('not'; 01 05 1071 1241 and multiple translations). The latter is the harder reading, given that Jesus does later attend the festival. An editor could therefore have introduced οὔπω to avoid the inconsistency, or it could have been assimilated to οὔπω later in the verse: a change in the other direction is much harder to explain. However, the limited attestation for οὐκ (preferred in the SBLGNT) and the earlier evidence for οὔπω (adopted in the THGNT) make a decision difficult. It may be significant that the external evi-

---

[28] Metzger 1994: 184.

dence for the two variants in this verse is very similar to those in John 7:10 (see below), suggesting that these two interventions could be related.

7:9   αὐτός (he) {C}

There is a difference of one letter between the readings αὐτός ('he himself'; 𝔓⁶⁶ 01 05* 019 032 etc.) and αὐτοῖς ('to them'; 𝔓⁷⁵ 03 05¹ 029 037 etc.; see *TuT John* TS88). The latter is the easier reading, as the indirect object would be expected after a verb of speech (e.g. John 6:61, 6:67, 7:21 etc.). Nevertheless, the subject αὐτός by itself is in accordance with Johannine style (e.g. John 2:25, 6:6, 18:1) and suits the context well: it has been adopted despite the possibility that it could have been introduced through analogy to the following verse. Two variants only found in Old Latin tradition can be easily dismissed: αὐτοῖς αὐτός ('to them, he himself') is a conflation of the two readings, while the absence of the pronoun is due to freedom in translation, probably because αὐτός was superfluous with a third-person verb.

7:10   ἀλλ' [ὡς] (but, as it were) {C}

The majority of manuscripts, including early witnesses, contain the qualifier ὡς ('as if'; 𝔓⁶⁶ 𝔓⁷⁵ 03 019 etc.), yet it is lacking from others (01 05 205 1424 and early translations); as noted above, this is similar to the distribution of the two readings in John 7:8. Although on the face of it an editor is more likely to insert a qualifier to mitigate an expression (compare John 2:15 above and John 11:33 below), the poor attestation of the shorter reading leads to uncertainty. In the contrast with οὐ φανερῶς ('not publicly') ὡς might have been overlooked or removed in order to simplify the construction: confusion as to its significance could also explain its absence from the Old Latin, Old Syriac and early Coptic translations. Its semantic difficulty, especially following a different use of ὡς at the beginning of the sentence, could make ὡς the harder reading: it is included in both the SBLGNT and THGNT.

7:12   ἄλλοι [δέ] (others)

The evidence for the particle δέ is early but limited (𝔓⁷⁵ᵛⁱᵈ 03 022 029 032 038 *f*¹ etc.) and it is missing from the majority of manuscripts (𝔓⁶⁶ 01 05 019 037 etc.). The preceding μέν means that δέ would be expected: the shorter reading is more difficult but not impossible if the semantics of οἱ μέν ... ἄλλοι ('some ... others') are seen as equivalent to οἱ μέν ... οἱ δέ ('some ... others'). An editor may therefore have supplied δέ for formal reasons: it is difficult to explain its omission if it were originally present, and the rarity of the shorter reading in Byzantine tradition also supports it. Even though the textual decision is difficult, the meaning of both variants is the same. See also John 9:16 below.

7:34, 36   [με] (me)

In both these verses, a few witnesses read εὑρήσετέ με ('you will find me'; 𝔓⁷⁵ 04 022 029 565 sy; 0105 has με in 7:34 but not 7:36, whereas Family 1 only has it in 7:36). The shorter majority reading also has early support (𝔓⁶⁶ 01 05 019 etc.). It is difficult to determine whether με was added by analogy with the previous verb in this saying (ζητήσετέ με, 'you will seek me'), or whether it was deleted as a stylistic improvement. There is no other instance of εὑρίσκειν ('to find') in John without a direct object, but this construction is paralleled in the other gospels (e.g. Matt. 12:43, Luke 13:6–7). In any case, the same object is implicit from the previous verb if the shorter reading is adopted and there is minimal difference in translation.

7:36   *add* 7:53–8:11 {A}

After John 7:36, one minuscule manuscript (GA 225, copied in the year 1192) has the *Pericope Adulterae* (John 7:53–8:11, see below). This location provides a good context for this contested passage, with its reference to Jesus withdrawing to the Mount of Olives and then returning to the Temple before the last day of the festival in John 7:37: clearly this is a intervention by an editor aware of the difficulties with this piece of floating tradition. It is also worth noting that the Byzantine liturgical lection for Pentecost consisted of John 7:37–52 and 8:12, so placing this passage here does not interrupt this reading.[29]

7:39   οἱ πιστεύσαντες (believers) {B}

The majority of Greek manuscripts have the present participle, οἱ πιστεύοντες ('those who believe'; 01 05 037 038 044 etc.). Early wit-

---

[29] See Knust and Wasserman 2018: 286–300.

nesses have an aorist, οἱ πιστεύσαντες ('those who believed'; 𝔓⁶⁶ 03 019 029 032 etc.), while some early translations support a future, οἱ πιστεύσοντες ('those who would believe'; lat^{vl-pt} co^{sa-mss}). The tense is of theological significance: is belief a single action (aorist) or an ongoing state (present), and how is this connected with the gift of the Spirit? The future is clearly an accommodation to the context, with its observation that the Spirit was not yet given. The early attestation supports οἱ πιστεύσαντες, perhaps with the sense of 'those who have come to belief' (cf. John 20:29): the present participle is more frequently used in the New Testament, and is therefore more likely to have been introduced than the aorist. See also John 19:35 below.

7:39 πνεῦμα (Spirit) {B}

Most Greek witnesses have πνεῦμα ἅγιον ('Holy Spirit'; 𝔓⁶⁶* 019 032 037 etc.), while there is early support for just πνεῦμα ('Spirit'; 𝔓⁶⁶ᶜ 𝔓⁷⁵ 01 022* 029 038 etc.). Although 'Holy Spirit' is likely to be an expansion to the standard expression (seen at John 1:33, 14:26 and 20:22), there is also a possibility that this longer form was assimilated to 'Spirit' by itself earlier in the verse. In both cases, the use of ἦν is slightly unexpected: 'there was not yet [Holy] Spirit', or 'the [Holy] Spirit was not yet'. This may also have been seen as theologically problematic, if it was taken to mean that the Spirit did not exist before Jesus was glorified. This is resolved in the three longer readings: πνεῦμα δεδομένον ('the Spirit [was not yet] given'; lat^{vl-pt, vg-mss} sy^{c, s, p} Eusebius), πνεῦμα ἅγιον δεδομένον ('the Holy Spirit [was not yet] given'; 03 lat^{vl-pt, vg-ms} cpa etc.) and τὸ πνεῦμα ἅγιον ἐπ' αὐτοῖς ('the Holy Spirit [was not yet] upon them'; 05 lat^{vl-pt}). The very limited attestation of these is a further indication that they are secondary, and that the shorter texts were difficult for translators. Some form of expansion may also be advisable in modern languages, and many English versions read 'the Spirit had not yet been given'. The full attestation in Greek continuous-text manuscripts is given in *TuT John* (TS90).

7:40 ἐκ τοῦ ὄχλου οὖν (some in the crowd) {A}

Early witnesses have ἐκ τοῦ ὄχλου οὖν ('And so [some] from the crowd'; 𝔓⁶⁶ᶜ 𝔓⁷⁵ 01 03 05 etc.), but the first hand of Papyrus 66 has πολλοὶ ἐκ τοῦ ὄχλου οἱ ('Many from the crowd who'; 𝔓⁶⁶*) and the majority of manuscripts read πολλοὶ οὖν ἐκ τοῦ ὄχλου ('And so many from the crowd'; 037 [038] 044 0105 etc.) The last of these is a stylistic improvement, matching the reorganisation of the similar phrase at John 7:31. The addition of πολλοί ('many') may simply be due to assimilation to the earlier verse, but it illustrates a tendency to enhance the narrative by increasing the numbers involved (cf. Matt. 8:18, 12:15).

7:46   ἐλάλησεν οὕτως ἄνθρωπος (has anyone spoken like this) {B}

The meaning of this phrase is clear, but it is transmitted in a variety of forms. The majority of Greek manuscripts read οὕτως ἐλάλησεν ἄνθρωπος ὡς οὗτος ὁ ἄνθρωπος ('[never] thus has spoken a person like this person'; [022] 037 038 [044] etc.). An even longer form is seen in οὕτως ἄνθρωπος ἐλάλησεν ὡς οὗτος λαλεῖ ὁ ἄνθρωπος ('[never] thus has a person spoken like this person speaks'; 𝔓⁶⁶* 01* [05] etc.). With the repeated words and sequences of characters, is not surprising that there are several instances of eyeskip in the tradition. However, the editorial text ἐλάλησεν οὕτως ἄνθρωπος ('has a person spoken thus'; 𝔓⁶⁶ᶜ 𝔓⁷⁵ 01² 03 019 etc.) cannot be an omissive form of any of the longer forms and has extensive early attestation. It therefore appears that the other readings reflect editorial attempts to expand and emphasise this statement; see the full list in *TuT John* (TS94).

7:50   πρὸς αὐτὸν [τὸ] πρότερον (to him before) {B}

The earliest witnesses are divided between πρὸς αὐτὸν τὸ πρότερον ('to him earlier on'; 𝔓⁶⁶ 019 032) and πρὸς αὐτὸν πρότερον ('to him earlier'; 𝔓⁷⁵ 01² 03 029), hence the inclusion of the definite article in brackets. The other variants all include the word νυκτός ('by night'), reflecting John 3:2 and the other reference to this episode at John 19:39. Most Greek minuscules read νυκτὸς πρὸς αὐτόν ('by night to him'; 579 700 1424 etc.), while some Byzantine majuscules have πρὸς αὐτὸν νυκτός ('to him by night'; 022 037 044 etc.). The reading νυκτὸς πρὸς αὐτὸν τὸ πρότερον ('by night to him earlier on'; 038 *f*¹ *f*¹³ etc.) could be seen as a conflation of two other forms, although it is possible that the majority reading arose from it through eyeskip. Codex Bezae has πρὸς αὐτὸν νυκτὸς τὸ πρῶτον ('to him by night at first'; 05 syʰ), which seems to be assimilation to John 19:39. The full attestation in Greek continuous-text manuscripts is given in *TuT John* (TS97). If νυκτός had originally been present, there is no obvious reason for its omission: the fact that it appears in different places is a further indication that all these variants are secondary.

7:53–8:11   *omit* 7:53–8:11 {A}

The story of the Woman Caught in Adultery (the *Pericope Adulterae*) was not part of the original text of the Gospel according to John. Although it is present in the majority of Greek minuscules, it is lacking from most early witnesses and treated by others in an unusual manner (see the list in *TuT John* TS100). It has been noted above that this passage is found after Luke 21:38 (Family 13), at the end of Luke (GA 1333), after John 7:36 (GA 225), as well as at the end of John preceded by an editorial note (Family 1). In multiple manuscripts, it is accompanied by marginal symbols (asterisks or obeli) similar to those which are found alongside other textually contested passages (Luke 22:43–44, Luke 23:34, John 5:4), but it should be noted that here these are often found only alongside John 8:2–11 and appear to relate to the use of this portion in the lectionary rather than indicating uncertainty about its authenticity. The absence of the passage from the two papyri, most majuscules and the first translations (as well as later versions such as Gothic and Old Georgian) provides clear external evidence that it was not originally present. Several early Christian writers do not quote it in discussions of adultery or other relevant places, while others (such as Jerome and Augustine) observe that it is missing from manuscripts known to them. The vocabulary and style also suggest that these verses were written by a different author to the rest of this Gospel. The presence of the passage here in Codex Bezae and the Vulgate demonstrates that it had been incorporated at this point by the end of the fourth century. It continues to be printed here in recognition of its longstanding acceptance as part of Christian scripture, but in double brackets to indicate its secondary status (cf. Mark 16:8b, 9–20 and Luke 22:43–44): both the SBLGNT and THGNT relegate it to the apparatus. It is likely that this was an early tradition about Jesus which circulated separately outside the biblical canon (an *agraphon*), until editors inserted it at different places in the gospels. In addition to discussions in commentaries, numerous publications have been devoted to this passage which continues to excite considerable interest.[30]

It should be noted that the confidence rating in the following seven units, all within this passage, should be understood with reference to the tradition of the *Pericope Adulterae* rather than the gospel in general (cf. Mark 16:8). The division of witnesses means that in this passage it is often not possible to establish a majority Byzantine reading: the *Textus Receptus* is therefore indicated for reference in the apparatus.

8:6 τοῦτο ... κατηγορεῖν αὐτοῦ (they said this ... some charge to bring against him) {A}

The first sentence of this verse is present in the majority of manuscripts, but is missing at this point in a few witnesses, all of which have it elsewhere. In Codex Bezae, 1071 and part of the Old Latin tradition, it occurs at the end of John 8:4, while in GA 021 it occurs—bizarrely—at the end of John 8:11. Neither of these locations fits the narrative as well as the present verse, where it follows the question of Jesus' interlocutors. Instead, the variation appears to be an indication of fluidity within the tradition of this floating passage, represented by distinctive groups of witnesses (see also the following units).

8:7 αὐτοῖς (to them) {B}

Most witnesses, including Codex Bezae, have αὐτοῖς ('to them'; 05 028 039 f^1 etc.), but other majuscules and the *Textus Receptus* read πρὸς αὐτούς (lit. 'towards them'; 07 011 013 180 etc.) and the complement is entirely absent from GA 021. In the Gospels, the use of the preposition πρός after εἶπεν ('he said') is almost entirely restricted to Luke, in which it is very common indeed. Although there are several stylistic features in this passage which are closer to Luke than John, αὐτοῖς has been preferred on the basis of its external support. It may also be noted that this construction does not occur with any of the three other verbs of speaking in this passage.

---

[30] An extensive account of the reception history of the passage is provided in Knust and Wasserman 2018; see also Ehrman 1988b, Parker 1997: 95–102, and Keith 2009 as well as the classic study of Becker 1963.

8:9 οἱ δὲ ἀκούσαντες ἐξήρχοντο εἷς καθ' εἷς (when they heard it they went away, one by one) {B}

A large number of manuscripts, along with the *Textus Receptus*, read οἱ δὲ ἀκούσαντες καὶ ὑπὸ τῆς συνειδήσεως ἐλεγχόμενοι ἐξήρχοντο εἷς καθ' εἷς ('but they, having heard and being convicted by their conscience, began to go away one by one'; 07 011 013 180 etc.). Other witnesses have a similar and slightly shorter form, οἱ δὲ ἀκούσαντες ἐξήρχοντο εἷς καθ' εἷς ('but they, having heard, began to go away one by one'; [021] 028 28 597 700 etc.). Family 1 reads ἀκούσαντες δὲ ἐξήρχοντο εἷς ἕκαστος αὐτῶν ('But, having heard, each one of them began to go away'; f^1), while Codex Bezae has ἕκαστος δὲ τῶν Ἰουδαίων ἐξήρχετο ('but each of the Jews began to go away'; 05 1071 lat^{vl-pt}) and some other manuscripts have καὶ ἐξῆλθεν εἷς καθ' εἷς ('and one by one went away'; 039 [f^{13}] 1424^{mg} cpa). The shorter of the two most widely attested readings has been chosen as the editorial text: the inclusion of the detail about 'their conscience' (a word which does not otherwise appear in the Gospels) is likely to be a subsequent clarification and there is no obvious reason for its omission. The introduction of 'the Jews', not otherwise mentioned in this passage, corresponds to an anti-Jewish tendency noted elsewhere in the text of Codex Bezae.[31]

8:9 πρεσβυτέρων (elders) {B}

The shortest reading πρεσβυτέρων ('elders'; 07 011 013 etc.) has good external attestation, as does the form in the *Textus Receptus* which follows it with ἕως τῶν ἐσχάτων ('up to the youngest'; 028 039 f^{13} etc.). Other witnesses include ὥστε πάντας ἐξελθεῖν ('until all went out'; 05 1071 lat^{vl-pt}) or πάντες ἀνεχώρησαν ('all withdrew'; lat^{vl-pt} cop^{bo-ms}). Again, there is no obvious reason for omission and the variety of alternatives suggests that the longer forms are all expansions.

8:10 Ἰησοῦς (Jesus) {B}

After this word, the *Textus Receptus* has καὶ μηδένα θεασάμενος πλὴν τῆς γυναικός ('and seeing no-one except the woman'; 07 09^{vid} 011 etc.), and other witnesses include εἶδεν αὐτὴν καί ('saw her and'; 039 f^{13} 180 etc.). There is good support for just Ἰησοῦς ('Jesus'; 05 021 028 f^1 etc.),

---

[31] See further Epp 1966.

which would explain the others as two different types of expansion. Nevertheless it is worth noting that there is a slight possibility that the shorter reading could have arisen through eyeskip from εἶδεν to εἶπεν.

8:10 ποῦ εἰσιν (where are they) {B}

The readings ποῦ εἰσιν οἱ κατήγοροί σου ('where are your accusers?'; 013 028 f^{13} etc.) and ποῦ εἰσιν ἐκεῖνοι οἱ κατήγοροί σου ('where are those people, your accusers?'; 07 09 011 579 etc.) both appear to be expansions of ποῦ εἰσιν ('where are they?'; 05 021 039 f^1 etc.). There is no obvious reason for omission or deletion. It is not clear why GA 205 lacks the whole clause, unless it is due to eyeskip between εἶπεν and εἰσιν.

8:11 [καὶ] ἀπό (and from)

The conjunction καί ('and') is present in all witnesses apart from Codex Bezae, f^{13} and some Latin and Bohairic manuscripts. It could have been added by an editor to avoid taking ἀπὸ τοῦ νῦν ('from now on') with πορεύου ('go'), or deleted to improve the style, with the two imperatives matching the double question of the previous verse. Although καί has been included in brackets, the external evidence suggests that it should probably be adopted. If the shorter reading is followed in translation, care should be taken not to overemphasise πορεύου ('go your way') because in context the following command is the more important.

8:25 ὅ τι (why) {B}

The words of Jesus in this verse have been described as 'the most obscure sentence in the Gospel and the most uncertain how to translate'.[32] There are three key elements: τὴν ἀρχήν, which can be read as a noun ('the beginning', perhaps as an accusative of time), or an adverb ('primarily'); the punctuation of the verse as a statement, question, or exclamation; and the division of the letters OTI as one word, ὅτι ('because', 'why', 'that') or two, ὅ τι ('that which', 'what'). The oldest manuscripts lack both word division and the full range of punctuation, because the question mark was only introduced in Greek in later centuries. This means that it is impossible to be clear how OTI is to be divided and how

---

[32] Beasley-Murray quoted in Omanson 2006: 185.

the words are punctuated in most early witnesses ($\mathfrak{P}^{66}$ 01 03 019 022 etc.); although $\mathfrak{P}^{75}$ reads O TI, this could be a question or a statement. The ninth-century GA 565 confirms that the phrase with ὅ τι was understood by some as a question, yet the *Textus Receptus* treats it as a statement. The majority of Greek manuscripts have a single word, ὅτι, followed by a full stop (05 038 044 0141 etc.). Options for translation include 'Why do I speak to you at all?' or 'That I speak to you at all!', both of which are negative in tone, and 'What I am telling you from the beginning'.[33] A correction in Papyrus 66 gives an expanded form of the phrase, which may be translated as 'I told you at the beginning what I am also telling you'. Early Latin translations take τὴν ἀρχήν as an attribute of Jesus (because the Latin equivalent is neuter), leading to renderings such as '[I am] the beginning, who speak to you' (qui, lat$^{vl\text{-}pt}$). Most modern translations prefer a statement, supplying a verb: 'I am from the beginning what I am telling you' or 'Primarily I am what I am telling you'.[34] While the THGNT has ὅ τι followed by a full stop, both the SBLGNT and UBS6 punctuate this phrase as a question.

8:28 [αὐτοῖς] (lit. to them)

The pronoun αὐτοῖς ('to them') is lacking from some early witnesses ($\mathfrak{P}^{66*}$ 03 019 029 032 f^1 etc.), but also has ancient support ($\mathfrak{P}^{66c}$ $\mathfrak{P}^{75}$ 01 05 etc. and the oldest translations; see the full attestation at *TuT John* TS108). Both constructions are paralleled elsewhere in this gospel. It could be that αὐτοῖς was introduced through assimilation to John 8:25, or removed because it was seen as repetitious following αὐτοῖς in the previous verse. In context, there is little difference in meaning.

8:34 τῆς ἁμαρτίας (to sin) {A}

A few early witnesses, mostly translations, lack the last two words of this verse, resulting in the reading 'everyone who commits sin is a slave' (05 lat$^{vl\text{-}pt}$ sy^s co$^{bo\text{-}mss}$). This may be because a second reference to sin within the verse was seen as unnecessary and therefore omitted by a translator or removed by an editor. In terms of Johannine style, the

---

[33] See further the discussion in Metzger 1994: 191.

[34] On the translation of τὴν ἀρχήν, see also Caragounis 2007 and Förster 2017 (who proposes translating it as 'immediately'). A lengthy consideration of the text of this verse is given in Rico 2006.

repetition of ἁμαρτία ('sin') in the longer reading is counterbalanced by the proximity of the two instances of δοῦλος ('slave') in the shorter text. The external evidence, however, is overwhelmingly in favour of the presence of τῆς ἁμαρτίας (lit. '[a slave] of sin').

8:38 παρὰ τῷ πατρί (in the Father's presence) {B}

In the first clause, the majority of Greek manuscripts read παρὰ τῷ πατρί μου ('in my Father's presence'; 01 037 038 044 etc.), and the first-person pronoun is also seen in παρὰ τῷ πατρί μου, ταῦτα ('in my Father's presence, these things [I say]'; 05 33 892 etc.). Codex Washingtonianus alone has ἀπὸ τοῦ πατρός, ταῦτα ('from my Father, these things [I say]'; 032). There is strong early support for the shortest reading, παρὰ τῷ πατρί ('in the Father's presence'; $\mathfrak{P}^{66}$ $\mathfrak{P}^{75}$ 03 04 019 etc.), which is likely to be original: although ὁ πατήρ ('father') is found with and without the qualifier μου ('my') in John, there is no reason for its removal if it were originally present here. It was probably added in order to enhance the contrast with the rest of the verse and to make the identity of the father less ambiguous (see the following unit). Similarly, ταῦτα ('these things') is likely to have been inserted to correspond to ἅ ('the things') at the beginning of the sentence. The full attestation in Greek continuous-text manuscripts is given in *TuT John* (TS111–112). In translation, it may be more natural to say 'my Father' even if the shorter reading is followed.

8:38 ἠκούσατε παρὰ τοῦ πατρὸς ποιεῖτε (you should do what you have heard from the Father) {B}

There are four readings in this unit: ἠκούσατε παρὰ τοῦ πατρὸς ποιεῖτε ('you do what you have heard from the Father'; [$\mathfrak{P}^{75}$] 03 019 032 etc.); ἠκούσατε παρὰ τοῦ πατρὸς ὑμῶν ποιεῖτε ('you do what you have heard from your Father'; 01² 04 038 etc.); ἑωράκατε παρὰ τοῦ πατρὸς ποιεῖτε ('you do what you have seen from the Father'; $\mathfrak{P}^{66}$ [01*] 070); ἑωράκατε παρὰ τῷ πατρὶ ὑμῶν ποιεῖτε ('you do what you have seen in your Father's presence'; [05] 037 044 and the majority of minuscules; see further *TuT John* TS113–115). The difference from the previous clause makes ἠκούσατε ('you have heard') preferable to ἑωράκατε ('you have seen'), while the dative phrase παρὰ τῷ πατρί ('in the Father's presence') is assimilation to earlier in the verse. As in the previous variation unit, the inclusion of the pronoun ὑμῶν ('your') after τοῦ πατρός ('the Father') appears to be secondary in order to heighten the contrast. These considerations and the external attestation lead to the choice of the editorial text. It is possible, however, that ὑμῶν was initially present but deleted in order to match the first half of the verse: the pronoun in the following verse could support its inclusion here. It is not clear whether the distinction between a single, shared, 'Father' and differing 'fathers', as seen in the next few verses, was also intended here. Either way, the identification of τοῦ πατρός is of theological significance and is reflected in translation. If the two instances in this verse relate to the same father, then ποιεῖτε is likely to be imperative ('do!') rather than indicative ('you are doing') because of the contrast with Jesus' response.

8:39 ἐστε (you are) {A}

Most Greek manuscripts have the present subjunctive ἦτε ('[if] you were'; 04 032 037 038 etc.), which corresponds to the imperfect in the second part of this conditional clause (see the following unit). The indicative ἐστε ('[if] you are'; 𝔓⁶⁶ 𝔓⁷⁵ 01 03 05 etc.) is the more difficult reading grammatically but has very strong early attestation and has therefore been adopted. While the subjunctive implies that the conditional clause is counterfactual, and thus that the Jews are not Abraham's children, a present indicative is usually positive in this context. This verb may require expansion in translation to make its implication clear.[35]

8:39 ἐποιεῖτε (you would do) {B}

The majority of manuscripts are split between ἐποιεῖτε ('you would do'; 𝔓⁷⁵ 01* 03² 05 032 etc.) and ἐποιεῖτε ἄν (also 'you would do'; 01² 04 019 022 etc.). The latter is a grammatical improvement; while ἄν could have been overlooked before the following νῦν it is more likely that it is a later addition, even though it is only necessary in Classical Greek. The combination of a present tense in the protasis and an imperfect in the apodosis results in a 'mixed' conditional clause (see the

---

[35] A more detailed discussion of this and the following variation unit is given in Mees 1981.

previous unit): the early reading ποιεῖτε ('do'; 𝔓⁶⁶ 03* [700] lat Origen) may be an attempt to provide a more expected construction, although it could simply be assimilation to the previous verse. See also John 14:7 below.

8:41 [οὖν] (lit. and so)

The conjunction οὖν ('and so') is missing from several early manuscripts (01 03 019 032 070 and several translations). The same variation after εἰπεῖν ('to say') is found in the following verse, demonstrating the tendency to add connectives. While it is not so well attested there, its appearance here in both papyri and most minuscules (𝔓⁶⁶ 𝔓⁷⁵ 04 05 037 etc.) suggests that it might be original. See also the following unit.

8:52 [οὖν] (lit. and so)

On this occasion, οὖν ('and so') is once again lacking from some of the oldest witnesses (𝔓⁶⁶ 01 03 04 032 and the early translations). Nevertheless, the external evidence in favour of its inclusion here is stronger than in other verses in this passage (compare the previous unit, as well as John 8:48), meaning that it could have been part of the earliest text. Even so, neither the SBLGNT nor THGNT has it here or at John 8:41.

8:54 θεὸς ἡμῶν (our God) {B}

Most witnesses read θεὸς ἡμῶν ('our God'; 𝔓⁷⁵ 02 03² 04 032 etc.). There is also early evidence for ὁ θεὸς ἡμῶν (lit. 'the God of us'; 𝔓⁶⁶ᶜ 019) and θεὸς ὑμῶν ('your God'; 01 03* 05 09 044 etc., including the *Textus Receptus*), while some translations support θεὸς ἀληθής ('true God'; lat^vl-pt) or only θεός ('God'; co^ly). In later Greek, ἡμῶν and ὑμῶν were pronounced identically due to itacism, leading to confusion in manuscripts. The preceding ὑμεῖς ('you') could have influenced copyists to write ὑμῶν here: ἡμῶν may therefore be the more difficult reading, as well as better attested. A direct quotation by Jesus here would parallel the Jews' repetition of his words in John 8:52. On the other hand, a change from indirect to direct speech was noted above at John 4:51, and the THGNT adopts θεὸς ὑμῶν here. Compare also John 11:50 below. If the first-person plural is adopted, in some languages it will be necessary to decide whether this includes or excludes Jesus.

8:59 τοῦ ἱεροῦ (the temple) {A}

There is strong early evidence for the ending of the verse with τοῦ ἱεροῦ ('the temple'; 𝔓⁶⁶ 𝔓⁷⁵ 01* 03 05 032 etc., as well as the first translations and Christian writers). Other witnesses have longer forms of text which appear to be based on Luke 4:30. The majority of manuscripts follow τοῦ ἱεροῦ with διελθὼν διὰ μέσου αὐτῶν καὶ παρῆγεν οὕτως ('crossing through the middle of them, and he passed along in this way'; 02 037 038ᶜ *f*¹ etc.). There is also good support for a longer form which includes the main verb of Luke 4:30, καὶ διελθὼν διὰ μέσου αὐτῶν ἐπορεύετο καὶ παρῆγεν οὕτως ('and crossing through the middle of them, he went on his way and he passed along in this way'; 01²ᵃ 04 019 022 044 etc.). The second correction to Codex Sinaiticus (01²ᵇ) is an erasure of the last four words of this, which means that the remaining text would have to be taken with the following verse: this appears to be an error. Although there is a very slight possibility that the longest text is original and the shortest form arose from eyeskip between the two instances of καί ('and'), this does not correspond to the external attestation. Rather, it appears that one or more editors expanded the text, drawing on a similar occasion elsewhere, to emphasise the miraculous nature of Jesus' escape. The full attestation in Greek continuous-text manuscripts is given in *TuT John* (TS119).

9:4 ἡμᾶς δεῖ … πέμψαντός με (we must … of him who sent me) {B}

The majority of Greek manuscripts read ἐμὲ δεῖ … πέμψαντός με ('I must [work the works] of him who sent me'; 01¹ 02 04 037 038 etc.), while the papyri and other early witnesses have ἡμᾶς δεῖ … πέμψαντος ἡμᾶς ('We must [work the works] of him who sent us'; 𝔓⁶⁶ 𝔓⁷⁵ 01* 019 032 Cyril: see further *TuT John* TS120–121). The first-person singular is the easier reading, given its appearance in the following verse and the frequency of με following πέμψας throughout this gospel; the plural is not in keeping with the application of this verb to Jesus alone elsewhere in John. A few witnesses are inconsistent, reading ἡμᾶς δεῖ … πέμψαντός με ('We must [work the works] of him who sent me'; 03 [05] 070 [latᵛˡ⁻ᵖᵗ] cpa). This combines the unexpected plural with Jesus alone as the one who is sent. It is possible that με was accidentally substituted for ἡμᾶς through assimilation to this collocation elsewhere in John.

Nevertheless, the inconsistency makes for the hardest reading, leading to its adoption as the editorial text here and in both the SBLGNT and THGNT.

9:8   προσαίτης ἦν (as a beggar) {B}

The majority of manuscripts read τυφλὸς ἦν ('he was blind'; 04³ 037 f^{13} etc.), but there is very strong early support for προσαίτης ἦν ('he was a beggar'; 𝔓⁶⁶ 𝔓⁷⁵ 01 02 03 etc.). The latter is the more difficult reading on internal grounds, as the man has not previously been described as a beggar. While the majority reading could have been assimilated to προσαιτῶν ('begging') at the end of the verse, the external evidence suggests that it is a later editorial improvement. Some witnesses have a conflation of the two readings, τυφλὸς ἦν καὶ προσαίτης ('he was blind and a beggar'; 69 lat^(vl-pt)); the antiquity of some of the Old Latin manuscripts which attest this indicates that 'blind' was circulating at an earlier stage than the surviving Greek evidence suggests.

9:10   [οὖν] (then)

The conjunction οὖν ('then') is missing from most Greek manuscripts (𝔓⁷⁵ 02 03 032 etc.) as well as some ancient translations. Although it is present in other early witnesses (𝔓⁶⁶ 01 04 05 019 etc.), it may have been added through assimilation to other instances of πῶς οὖν ('how then'; e.g. Matt. 12:26, 22:43, 26:54 etc.). Equally, as οὖν has already appeared as the second word in the verse, this repetition may have been removed by an editor. It is difficult to decide: there is only one firm instance of πῶς οὖν in John, but it is part of this pericope (at John 9:19; see also John 6:42 above).

9:16   [δέ] (lit. but)

The situation is very similar to the previous unit: a few early manuscripts have δέ ('on the other hand'; 01 03 05 032 070 etc.), but most lack it (𝔓⁶⁶ 𝔓⁷⁵ 02 019 037 etc.). There is no obvious reason for its omission, apart from the accidental oversight of a small word, whereas the phrase ἄλλοι δέ ('but others') is common elsewhere and may have led to its introduction here (cf. John 7:12 above). There is no significant difference in translation.

9:26 αὐτῷ (to him) {B}

The majority of manuscripts read αὐτῷ πάλιν ('to him again'; 𝔓⁶⁶ 01² 02 019 037 etc.), but early witnesses have just αὐτῷ ('to him'; 𝔓⁷⁵ 01* 03 05 032 etc.). The absence of πάλιν could be due to an editorial deletion, as this exact question has not been put to the man previously, or a stylistic improvement in the light of πάλιν in the following verse. On the other hand, the external evidence suggests that it was added later, perhaps because this is the second time that the questioners speak to the man.

9:35 ἀνθρώπου (of Man) {B}

Seven Greek manuscripts read ἀνθρώπου ('[Son] of Man'; 𝔓⁶⁶ 𝔓⁷⁵ 01 03 05 032 397; see *TuT John* TS129): its strong early support also includes multiple translations and Origen. Most Greek manuscripts have θεοῦ ('[Son] of God'; 02 019 037 038 etc.). Both words would probably have been written as *nomina sacra* (ΑΝΟΥ and ΘΥ), but confusion between these seems unlikely. The two appellations are well attested in John, and this is the only instance with significant textual variation. The most plausible explanation for the change is that the preceding πιστεύεις εἰς ('believe in') led a copyist to substitute θεοῦ because of the predominance of 'Son of God' in credal formulae (cf. 1 John 5:10). This direction of change is far more likely than the alternative, and matches the attestation.

9:38–39 ὁ δὲ ἔφη ... καὶ εἶπεν ὁ Ἰησοῦς (he said ... Jesus said) {C}

The whole of John 9:38 and the first phrase of John 9:39 are absent from some important Greek manuscripts and early translations (𝔓⁷⁵ 01* 032 lat^{vl-pt} co^{sa-ms, ly, cw}; see *TuT John* TS130). This has the effect of removing the man's statement of faith and act of reverence, and bringing Jesus' words into a single longer speech. There is no obvious reason for accidental omission, nor evidence for this in later Greek tradition. It could be that an editor deleted them out of a concern that such worship of Jesus before his ascension was not appropriate (cf. Luke 24:52 above), although simply excising καὶ προσεκύνησεν αὐτῷ ('and worshipped him') would have been sufficient. The age of the witnesses makes it possible that the shorter reading is original—compare the attestation of the editorial text in the previous unit—and the proclamation of belief was inserted by an early editor who felt that the questions of John 9:35–36 required a formal response (the variation at Acts 8:37 may provide a loose parallel) or that the narrative lacked a suitable conclusion regarding the outcome of the encounter. This is the only occasion in John when Jesus is the object of προσκύνησις ('homage') and it may also be noted that there is only one other firm instance in John of ἔφη ('he said'; John 1:23). The attestation of the shorter reading suggests that it is not related to the 'Western non-interpolations' (see the Overview for Luke). Even so, the strong external support for the longer reading has led to its adoption as the earliest text here and in both the SBLGNT and THGNT.[36]

9:40   ἤκουσαν (they heard) {B}

A range of connectives are found in the textual tradition, which affect the way in which the Pharisees' response is characterised. The majority of manuscripts read καὶ ἤκουσαν ('And they heard'; 02 037 f^{13} 700 etc.), while a few minuscules have the imperfect καὶ ἤκουον ('And they begin to hear'; 892 1424). Codex Bezae has ἤκουσαν δέ ('but they heard'; 05 co[sa-ms, bo-mss]), and Family 1 reads ἤκουσαν οὖν ('And so they heard'; f^1 565 1241). The range of early witnesses which just have ἤκουσαν ('they heard'; $\mathfrak{P}^{66}$ $\mathfrak{P}^{75}$ 01 03 019 032 etc.) offers the best explanation of the variety in the rest of the tradition (compare also John 10:39 below). This leaves open the relationship of this to the preceding speech and also allows it to be taken as the beginning of a new section. Nevertheless, there is a remote possibility that an initial καί was omitted following the previous word which ends with the same two letters.

10:8   ἦλθον [πρὸ ἐμοῦ] (came before me) {C}

The manuscript tradition is fairly evenly split between the presence of πρὸ ἐμοῦ ('before me'; $\mathfrak{P}^{66}$ 01[2a] 02 03 05 etc.) and its absence ($\mathfrak{P}^{45\text{vid}}$ $\mathfrak{P}^{75}$ 01[*, 2b] 037 etc.). In a few witnesses, it appears before the verb (038 f^1 etc.): such variation can be typical of an addition and it is possible that an editor inserted these words to ensure that Jesus does not inadvertently condemn himself (cf. John 10:10) or later Christian leaders. Al-

---

[36] The shorter reading is preferred by Brown 1966: 375 and Porter 1967, who both claim that the insertion was due to liturgical influence.

ternatively, πρὸ ἐμοῦ may originally have been present after the verb but was subsequently moved before ἦλθον for clarity or emphasis (cf. John 5:7): its absence could be due to a partial correction. It might even be that these words were deleted because they do not fit well with the image of the gate in the neighbouring verses. Given this balance of evidence the phrase was placed in brackets in UBS4, although it is adopted in both the SBLGNT and THGNT.

10:11 τίθησιν (lays down) {B}

There is very strong attestation for the majority reading τίθησιν ('lays down'; $\mathfrak{P}^{66}$ $\mathfrak{P}^{75}$ 01² 02 03 etc.), while a few early manuscripts and translations have δίδωσιν ('gives'; $\mathfrak{P}^{45}$ 01* 05 lat$^{vl\text{-}pt,\ vg}$ sy^s cpa co$^{bo,\ pbo}$). The latter is found in the Synoptic Gospels but the former is characteristic of John (10:15, 17; 13:37, 38; 15:13; 1 John 3:16). The external evidence suggests that the possibility that δίδωσιν has been assimilated to Johannine usage is less likely than consistency within this gospel. See also John 10:15 below.

10:13 ὅτι (because) {B}

Most Greek manuscripts begin this verse with ὁ δὲ μισθωτὸς φεύγει ὅτι ('the hired hand flees because'; 02^c 037 044 f^{13} etc.), repeating information from the previous verse. The early evidence only has ὅτι ('because'; $\mathfrak{P}^{44\text{vid}}$ $\mathfrak{P}^{45}$ $\mathfrak{P}^{66}$ $\mathfrak{P}^{75}$ 01 etc.), which involves reading the preceding clause as a parenthesis and understanding this ὅτι as relating to the previous instance of φεύγει. This is a more difficult reading, but still makes good sense. Even though there is a possibility that the shorter form is due to eyeskip from the end of σκορπίζει to φεύγει, it has been adopted on the basis of its attestation. In translation, it may be appropriate to repeat the subject if the parenthesis cannot be adequately expressed.

10:15 τίθημι (I lay down) {B}

There is slightly more support here for δίδωμι ('I give'; $\mathfrak{P}^{45}$ $\mathfrak{P}^{66}$ 01* 05 032: see *TuT John* TS133) than in John 10:11 (see above), although both the Latin Vulgate and the Old Syriac join the majority of manuscripts with τίθημι ('I lay down'; 01² 02 03 019 etc.). Again, it seems most likely that Johannine usage has been assimilated to the construction in the Synoptic Gospels, but the early attestation of δίδωμι raises some doubts.

10:16 γενήσονται (there will be) {C}

Most Greek manuscripts have the singular, γενήσεται ('it will become'; 𝔓⁶⁶ 01* 02 037 etc.), but numerous early witnesses read the plural γενήσονται ('they will become'; 𝔓⁴⁵ 01² 03 05 19 etc.; see *TuT John* TS135). The plural matches the previous verb, ἀκούσουσιν ('they will hear'), which does not seem to be attested here in the singular even though the preceding noun is a neuter plural, πρόβατα ('sheep'). Instead, the singular appears to relate to the following μία ποίμνη ('one flock'). On the other hand, the plural would also be appropriate because μία ποίμνη is followed by εἷς ποιμήν ('one shepherd'), which is technically two complements. The balance within both the internal and external evidence makes a decision difficult: while the singular might be a slightly harder reading in context, it could also be a stylistic alteration. If γενήσεται is adopted, it would be best to treat it as an impersonal verb ('there will be'). Nevertheless, the plural is preferred in the SBLGNT and THGNT.

10:19 πάλιν (again) {B}

There is much early evidence for just πάλιν ('again'; 𝔓⁷⁵ 01 03 019 032 etc.), while Codex Bezae and some witnesses have οὖν ('and so'; 05 0233 1241 etc.). The majority of manuscripts read οὖν πάλιν ('and so ... again'; 𝔓⁶⁶ 02 037 038 etc.), which looks like a conflation of the two forms. The full attestation in Greek continuous-text manuscripts is given in *TuT John* (TS136). There are two previous instances in the narrative of σχίσμα ('division'; John 7:43, 9:16), which makes πάλιν appropriate, even though neither relates specifically to 'these words': οὖν could therefore be a pedantic editorial correction or simply assimilation to John 7:43. In the absence of a connective, this could be taken as the beginning of a new section.

10:22 τότε (at that time) {B}

The majority of witnesses read δέ ('but'; 𝔓⁶⁶* 01 02 05 037 etc.), but there is early support for τότε ('at that time'; 𝔓⁶⁶ᶜ 𝔓⁷⁵ 03 019 032 etc.). Some Coptic versions combine both as δὲ τότε ('but at that time'). There is no other instance of ἐγένετο τότε ('it came to pass at that time') in the New Testament, which makes it the harder reading but with good attestation. In contrast, ἐγένετο δέ ('but it came to pass') is very common in Luke and Acts, which is likely to have led to assimilation here, perhaps assisted by eyeskip following the last two letters of the verb (ΕΓΕΝΕΤΟΤΟΤΕ and ΕΓΕΝΕΤΟΔΕ). Manuscripts which lack any conjunction here (f^1 205 565 1010 etc.) may also represent eyeskip to the following ΤΑ.

10:26 ἐμῶν (my) {B}

At the end of the verse, most Greek manuscripts include καθὼς εἶπον ὑμῖν ('as I said to you'; [𝔓⁶⁶*] 02 05 037 044 etc.), yet these words are missing from the earliest witnesses (𝔓⁶⁶ᶜ 𝔓⁷⁵ 01 03 019 etc.; see *TuT John* TS137). There is no obvious reason for their omission, but they could have been deleted by an editor who observed that Jesus does not make the preceding statement anywhere else in John. On the other hand, καθώς is more common in John than in all three Synoptic Gospels combined, and is sometimes found in initial position or preceding the comparison: if this phrase were taken with the following verse, it would plausibly refer to John 10:3. However, although the first hand of Papyrus 66 (which includes ὅτι at the end of the phrase) connects it with what comes next, Codex Bezae, 037 and 0233 are ambivalent, while in Codex Alexandrinus, 044 and Family 1 the punctuation clearly indicates that these words are considered part of John 10:26. The attestation of these words suggests that they are an addition, yet the reason remains unclear: perhaps an editor decided to emphasise εἶπον ὑμῖν ('I said to you') in the previous verse with a phrase reminiscent of John 13:33.

10:29 ὃ δέδωκέν μοι πάντων μεῖζόν ἐστιν (lit. what he has given me is greater than all else) {D}

The majority of Greek manuscripts read ὃς δέδωκέν μοι μείζων πάντων ἐστίν ('who has given to me is greater than all'; [𝔓⁶⁶] 037 [0141] f^1 etc.), but there are numerous minor variations: some early witnesses have the neuter μεῖζον for μείζων ('a greater thing'; 02 [03²] 038 sy), while after μοι Family 13 includes the direct object αὐτά ('[who has given] them [to me...]'; f^{13} 1243 eth). The other readings begin with a neuter pronoun: ὃ δέδωκέν μοι πάντων μεῖζόν ἐστιν ('what he has given me is greater than all things'; 03* lat^{vl-pt, vg} co^{bo} Tertullian) and ὃ δέδωκέν μοι πάντων μείζων ἐστίν ('what he has given me of all things, he is greater' or 'what he has given me, he is greater than all'; 01 [05] 019 032 044). Either μεῖζον or μείζων could have arisen from the other in an attempt to match other elements of the phrase, and the loss of distinction between o and ω through vowel isochrony in later Greek may have contributed to the confusion. The variants with both ὅς and μείζων are much simpler grammatically and therefore likely to be secondary. It has been claimed that ὅ followed by μείζων was 'impossible Greek', hence the preference for ὅ ... μεῖζον in the editorial text despite its poor attestation and the resultant hanging nominative (ὁ πατήρ μου, 'my father') which has no connection to the rest of the sentence apart from the verb δέδωκεν.[37] Nevertheless, others have not found the alternative reading so problematic, and ὅ ... μείζων is adopted in the SBLGNT and the THGNT, as well appearing in translations such as: 'My Father, in regard to what he has given me, is greater than all' (NRSVue).[38] The full attestation in Greek continuous-text manuscripts is given in *TuT John* (TS139–140).

10:34 [ὁ] Ἰησοῦς (Jesus)

The definite article is missing from a few early witnesses ($\mathfrak{P}^{45}$ $\mathfrak{P}^{66}$ 03 032; see further *TuT John* TS146). As noted at John 6:29 and 7:16 above, while the phrase ἀπεκρίθη Ἰησοῦς ('Jesus answered') in John normally lacks the article, it appears that ὁ is included when this verb and noun are separated by the indirect object αὐτοῖς ('them'; see John 6:26, 6:70, 8:34, 10:25, 10:32 as well as 1:23). The only exception to this longer reading in the editorial text is John 16:31. While it is possible that the author was inconsistent, and the present verse was assimilated to John 10:32, the relatively slim attestation of the shorter reading and the general pattern favours the inclusion of the article here.

10:38 καὶ γινώσκητε (and understand) {B}

There is extensive early support for γνῶτε καὶ γινώσκητε ('you may know and understand'; $\mathfrak{P}^{45}$ $\mathfrak{P}^{66}$ $\mathfrak{P}^{75}$ 03 019 etc., lat^vl-pt cpa co eth), with the aorist and present subjunctive of the same verb. The majority of manuscripts read γνῶτε καὶ πιστεύσητε ('you may know and believe';

---

[37] Metzger 1994: 198.
[38] See Omanson 2006: 191; ὅ ... μείζων is also preferred in the discussion at Birdsall 1960.

[01] 02 037 044 etc.), while others just have γνῶτε ('you may know'; 05 28 157 1424 lat^{vl-pt} sy^s Tertullian Cyril: see further *TuT John* TS149). Although the duplication of the verb could be a copying error, the possibility of different meanings being conveyed by the two tenses and the ancient attestation suggests that it is the earliest text, with the other variants being attempts to remove the overlap or—in the case of the shortest form—omission due to eyeskip.

10:39 ἐζήτουν [οὖν] (then they tried)

Byzantine tradition is split between ἐζήτουν ('they tried'; 𝔓^{75vid} 03 038 700 etc.) and ἐζήτουν οὖν ('and so they tried'; 𝔓^{66} 01 02 019 032 etc.). Papyrus 45 and some early versions support ἐζήτουν δέ ('but they tried'), while Codex Bezae has καὶ ἐζήτουν ('and they tried'). The full attestation in Greek continuous-text manuscripts is given in *TuT John* (TS150). It would have been an easy copying error to add οὖν through dittography of the last three letters of the preceding verb (along with possible assimilation to John 7:30 and 11:56), or to omit it by haplography. The presence of other connectives might support ἐζήτουν alone (cf. John 9:40 above), but their very limited attestation makes for considerable doubt as to the earliest text: it could be that they were added in order to provide an expected particle after an original οὖν had been accidentally omitted.

11:2 Μαριάμ (Mary) {B}

A few witnesses have the Semitic form of the name Mary, Μαριάμ ('Mariam'; 𝔓^{6vid} 03 33 sy^h) instead of the regular Greek Μαρία ('Maria'; 𝔓^{66} 01 02 05 etc.). This appears throughout this chapter with differing attestation (e.g. John 11:19, 20, 28), and is also seen later in the gospel with regard to Mary Magdalene (see John 19:25 and 20:1ff. below). There is similar variation in the other gospels (e.g. Matt. 27:56, 28:1; Mark 15:40, 15:47; Luke 2:19, 10:39, 10:42 etc.). Although it may be tempting to imagine that the Semitic name was original but fell out of use as the New Testament was transmitted in the broader Greek context, the varying external support makes it very difficult to establish whether even a single evangelist was consistent throughout their writing. Accordingly, the most likely reading has to be established at each point; in translation, however, the principle of consistency means that the same form of name should be used for the same person throughout the text (cf. Matt. 1:7–8 above).[39]

11:19   πρὸς τήν ([come] to) {B}

The majority of Greek manuscripts read πρὸς τὰς περί ('to the women around [Martha and Mary]'; 𝔓⁴⁵ᵛⁱᵈ 02 04³ 037 038 etc.), but the earliest witnesses agree on πρὸς τήν ('to [Martha and Mary]'; 𝔓⁶⁶ 𝔓⁷⁵ᵛⁱᵈ 01 03 04* etc.) with Codex Bezae reading just πρός ('to'; 05). The plural is unexpected, as there is no other reference in the narrative to a group of people and later in the verse the majority reading is 'to console them about their brother'. On the other hand, a group of mourners would have been expected, and in John 11:28 there is a reference to Martha speaking to Mary λάθρᾳ ('in private'). It is possible that the variation is a mechnical error, accidentally incorporating τὰς περί from later in the sentence, perhaps because a line was initially skipped. In any case, while the reason for the majority reading is unclear, the attestation favours the singular article.

11:22   [ἀλλά] (but)

The word ἀλλά ('but') is absent from a few important witnesses (𝔓⁷⁵ 01* 03 04* 1 33 1241 etc.). It is possible that it was deleted by an editor who felt that, without a preceding οὐ μόνον ('not only'), the combination of conjunctions in ἀλλὰ καί ('but also') was excessive (cf. John 5:18, 13:9, 17:20). Alternatively, it may have been added to emphasise the contrast between the two parts of Martha's statement. The balance of external evidence, with no obvious internal factors, makes it difficult to decide whether ἀλλά is original or not: it is adopted in the THGNT but not the SBLGNT.

11:25   καὶ ἡ ζωή (and the life) {A}

It is hard to account for the absence of this famous phrase from Papyrus 45, part of the Old Latin tradition (including the third-century writer Cyprian) and the only extant Old Syriac manuscript. There is no obvious reason for mechanical omission, but as ἀνάστασις ('resurrection')

---

[39] Bryan 2021 is the most recent overview of the forms by manuscript. For other variants involving the names in this passage, see Schrader 2016 and Fellows 2023.

is the key word here, which also informs the statement in the latter part of the verse, it is possible that these short words were overlooked in order to focus on the main topic. The attestation of this shorter reading is not sufficiently strong for there to be much likelihood that it is original and that the extra words were added later in anticipation of the verb ζῆν ('to live') in the following two phrases (or even through assimilation to John 14:6).

11:31 δόξαντες (because they thought) {B}

Most Greek manuscripts read λέγοντες ('saying'; 𝔓⁶⁶ 02 04² 037 038 etc.), but there is extensive support for δόξαντες ('thinking'; 01 03 04* 05 019 etc.). The word δοξάζοντες ('glorifying'; 𝔓⁷⁵ 33) is a clear replacement of δόξαντες by a more common word with a similar appearance. Although δοκεῖν ('to think') is rare in John, making it the harder reading, the only other instance of the participle is in a similar context (John 20:15). The external evidence suggests that it is the earliest reading. It has been proposed, however, that an editor might have introduced λέγοντες on the grounds that the author could not have known what the Jews were thinking: the same variation is also seen in a few witnesses at John 11:13.[40]

11:33 ἐνεβριμήσατο τῷ πνεύματι καὶ ἐτάραξεν ἑαυτόν (he was greatly disturbed in spirit and deeply moved) {A}

Almost all Greek evidence corresponds to the editorial text, but a selection of early witnesses has a different form: ἐταράχθη τῷ πνεύματι ὡς ἐμβριμούμενος (𝔓⁴⁵ᵛⁱᵈ 05 latᵛˡ⁻ᵖᵗ coˢᵃ, ˡʸ; 𝔓⁶⁶ᶜ 038 ƒ¹ give the last word in the form ἐμβριμώμενος). This alternative may have been prompted by the construction with ἐμβριμᾶσθαι in the majority reading: in the Septuagint and the Synoptic Gospels, this verb with a dative object means 'rebuke' (cf. Dan. 11:30, Matt. 9:30, Mark 1:34 and 14:5). In order to avoid the interpretation that Jesus was 'rebuking the spirit', an early editor appears to have rearranged this verse, introducing ἐταράχθη τῷ πνεύματι from John 13:21 (the only other use of ταράσσειν of Jesus in the Gospels, yet with the same dative object), and treating the difficult ἐμβριμούμενος as an absolute: the variant may thus be translated with

---

[40] Metzger 1994: 199.

the standard meaning of this verb, 'he was troubled in spirit as if giving a rebuke'. This explanation seems more plausible than the suggestion that an editor was trying to minimise Jesus' distress out of reverence: despite the introduction of ὡς, which can often be secondary (cf. John 2:15 and 7:10 above), there is no attempt to reduce the force of ἐμβριμώμενος five verses later. The majority reading is clearly more difficult, yet very strongly attested: ἐνεβριμήσατο as the editorial text is usually translated in a similar manner to ἐμβριμώμενος at John 11:38, such as 'deeply moved', even though the latter has a preposition rather than the dative alone.[41]

11:50 ὑμῖν (for you) {B}

In later Greek, the identical pronunciation of the vowels *eta* and *upsilon* through itacism meant that it was impossible to distinguish between first-person and second-person plural pronouns except by context (cf. John 8:54 above). Here, the majority of manuscripts have ἡμῖν ('[it is better] for us'; 02 032 037 038 etc.), but most of the oldest witnesses read ὑμῖν ('for you'; 𝔓⁴⁵ 𝔓⁶⁶ 03 05 019 etc.) and a few lack any pronoun (01 co^(sa-ms, pbo) Chrysostom Cyril^(pt)). The last of these may be assimilation to the reference to this verse at John 18:14, which lacks any pronoun: it does not seem sufficiently well attested to be original. Of the two pronouns, the preceding second-person plural verbs make ὑμῖν the expected reading, and are also in keeping with Caiaphas distancing himself from the other Jews in the previous verse. An editor could have substituted the first-person form in order for the High Priest to be included among those who benefitted from Jesus' death. While internal considerations are thus divided, the second person has been preferred here and in the SBLGNT and THGNT on the basis of its attestation.

12:4 Ἰούδας ὁ Ἰσκαριώτης (Judas Iscariot) {A}

The majority of Greek manuscripts read Ἰούδας Σίμωνος Ἰσκαριώτης ('Judas Iscariot, son of Simon'; 02 026 037 038 etc.), with Ἰούδας Σίμωνος ὁ Ἰσκαριώτης ('Judas son of Simon, the Iscariot'; f^1 565) in others. The oldest manuscripts mostly read Ἰούδας ὁ Ἰσκαριώτης

---

[41] For an alternative proposal, suggesting that the use of this verb in John is related to an Aramaic term, see Black 1967: 240–243.

('Judas the Iscariot'; 𝔓⁶⁶ 𝔓⁷⁵ᵛⁱᵈ 01 03 019 etc.), although Codex Bezae has Ἰούδας ἀπὸ Καρυώτου ('Judas from Karyot'; 05), an etymological rendering which has already been discussed at John 6:71 (see above). There is no obvious reason for the omission of 'Simon' if it was original: rather, it seems to be assimilation to the longer form at John 6:71, the first occasion on which Judas is mentioned in this gospel. There is no need to render the definite article in translation: although it indicates that 'Iscariot' was originally a title, its significance is not obvious and 'Judas Iscariot' has become established as a form.[42] Consistency with the name elsewhere is more important.

12:4   εἷς [ἐκ] τῶν μαθητῶν (one of his disciples)

The preposition ἐκ ('out of') is unnecessary for the sense, and missing from several of the oldest witnesses (𝔓⁶⁶ 𝔓⁷⁵ᵛⁱᵈ 03 019 032 33 579). Nevertheless, the construction εἷς ἐκ τῶν ('one out of the') occurs on multiple occasions in John, usually with reference to the disciples, against only one instance of the partitive genitive εἷς τῶν ('one of the'; John 19:34). Internal evidence thus strongly favours the longer, more angular reading, despite the early support for the shorter text, adopted in the SBLGNT and THGNT. In either case, there is little difference in translation. Compare also John 6:66 above.

12:8   *include verse* {B}

The saying of Jesus in John 12:8 matches the text of Matt. 26:11, an abbreviated form of Mark 14:7, and is present in most Greek manuscripts (𝔓⁶⁶ 01 02 03 [019] etc.), albeit with a few minor variations. The repeated verb means that it is unsurprising that the second half of the verse is occasionally missing due to eyeskip (𝔓⁷⁵ 892ˢᵘᵖᵖ*). More striking is the absence of the whole of John 12:8 from Codex Bezae and some versional witnesses (05 latᵛˡ⁻ᵖᵗ syˢ), and John 12:7–8 from 0250. The latter could be due to eyeskip between ΕΙΠΕΝΟΥΝ and ΕΓΝΩΟΥΝ. However, the presence of the material in other gospels (John 12:7 resembles Matt. 26:11 and Mark 14:8) raises the possibility that one or both of these verses is a later insertion (cf. Luke 24:12, 24:36 etc.).

---

[42] Omanson 2006: 196 notes that Iscariot could mean 'dagger bearer', 'deceiver' or 'betrayer', as well as its connection with the place name Kerioth.

Against this are the observations that the whole story corresponds to synoptic parallels and that John appears to have rearranged the sequence in John 12:7–8 in order to end with this general saying, along with the very slim external evidence for the shorter reading. It remains unclear whether the lack of this verse in Codex Bezae is to be explained as deliberate editorial removal or accidental omission (compare the 'Western non-interpolations' in the last chapters of Luke).

12:9   [ὁ] ὄχλος πολύς (the great crowd)

The definite article is absent from the majority of Greek manuscripts, but attested in some important witnesses (01* 03* 019 579 700 892). Both these readings could easily have arisen through scribal error involving the two *omicrons*, whether haplography or dittography. The initial article makes for much more difficult Greek, however, and it seems that the variant ὁ ὄχλος ὁ πολύς (also 'the great crowd'; 𝔓66c 032 0250) is an attempt to improve this. The question is whether ὁ ὄχλος πολύς, as the subject of the verb but with πολύς in the predicate position, is such a hard construction that it could not be original: it is also found at John 12:12, based on slightly different attestation, and it is adopted here in the THGNT. In any case, translations should provide a natural construction in the target language: this is the first mention of this crowd, which is also referred to in John 12:17, but the 'great crowd' of John 12:12 and 12:18 is a different group of people.[43]

12:13   [καί] (lit. and [the king])

There is limited but early attestation of καί ('and'; 01*, 2b 03 019 032 044 579): along with ὁ, which is also lacking from the majority of manuscripts, it is an interpolation into the quotation of Psalm 118:26 [117:26 LXX]. The variation already discussed above in Luke 19:38 suggests that different forms of this text were circulating in the early Church. There is no obvious reason for the addition of καί if it is not original, whereas its absence could be assimilation to the Lukan form. It seems clear that the same person is intended in both clauses, and if καί is adopted it could be translated as an intensifier ('even the king').

---

[43] Omanson 2006: 194.

12:18 [καί] (also)

The majority of witnesses include καί here ($\mathfrak{P}^{66c}$ 01 02 [03] 019 etc.), but it is absent from both papyri and some early translations ($\mathfrak{P}^{66*}$ $\mathfrak{P}^{75}$ 037 lat^{vl} co^{pbo}). It may have been added by an editor who felt that a closer connection with the previous verse was required, or simply omitted by accident. The relatively small number of witnesses suggests that an oversight is more likely.

12:28 σου τὸ ὄνομα (your name) {A}

Most Greek manuscripts, including early ones, attest the text adopted as the editorial reading ('your name'; $\mathfrak{P}^{66}$ $\mathfrak{P}^{75}$ 01 02 032 etc.), but there are several variant readings which demonstrate a range of alterations. Codex Vaticanus alone reads μου τὸ ὄνομα ('my name'; 03), a difference of one letter, which presumably reflects the pronoun expected by the copyist after the first-person singular in the previous verse. There is relatively extensive support for σου τὸν υἱόν ('your Son'; 019 0233 f^1 f^{13} etc.), in which the continued reference to Jesus makes this an easier reading in context: however, it is extremely likely that this has been assimilated to the same phrase at John 17:1. Codex Bezae expands the majority reading with material taken from a similar passage at John 17:5: σου τὸ ὄνομα ἐν τῇ δόξῃ ᾗ εἶχον παρὰ σοὶ πρὸ τοῦ τὸν κόσμον γενέσθαι ('your name in the glory which I had in your presence before the world existed'; 05 lat$^{vl\cdot pt}$). As the source of the additional text can be identified, this is clearly a secondary form and it appears to involve an inconsistency between ὄνομα ('name') and the first-person verb εἶχον ('I had'). The editorial reading is not only the most widespread but also the least expected in context, and so is adopted with confidence.

12:47 φυλάξῃ (keep) {A}

There is strong support in the oldest witnesses for φυλάξῃ ('keep'; $\mathfrak{P}^{66}$ $\mathfrak{P}^{75}$ 01 02 03 etc., lat$^{vl\cdot pt,\ vg}$ sy co), even though this is the only reference in John to 'keeping words'. Perhaps because of this unusual collation, later Greek manuscripts instead have πιστεύσῃ ('believe'; 037 and the majority of minuscules), which is an easier reading. It may have been prompted by the frequent appearance of πιστεύειν ('believe') in the three preceding verses, or the same phrase at John 5.47. The expression 'taking words' (λαμβάνων τὰ ῥήματα) in the parallel construction in the next verse (again, the only instance of this in John) provides internal evidence which corroborates the unusual construction here.

13:2 γινομένου (during) {B}

The majority of Greek manuscripts have an aorist participle, γενομένου ('[when supper] had happened'; 𝔓⁶⁶ 01² 02 05 037 etc.), but several early witnesses have the present participle γινομένου ('[when supper] was happening'; 01* 03 019 032 etc.). The rest of the narrative (e.g. John 13:26) suggests that the present tense is more suitable, as the meal appears to continue. Although this might point to the aorist as the harder reading, there is a very strong transcriptional probability that it would be substituted for the present: there are over thirty genitive absolute constructions in the Gospels and Acts with this verb in the aorist, but only two in the present (here and Acts 23:10), both of which are also aorist in the majority of manuscripts. The adoption of the aorist would imply that Jesus' actions took place after they had eaten, yet it could be translated as 'when supper had been served'. The external attestation of the present, however, supports it as the earliest form, placing the subsequent events in the context of the meal.

13:2 Ἰούδας Σίμωνος Ἰσκαριώτου (Judas son of Simon Iscariot) {C}

Variation in the name of Judas has already been encountered at John 6:71 and 12:4 (see above) and occurs again later in the chapter (John 13:26). Here, most manuscripts put this phrase before the preceding clause, reading Ἰούδα Σίμωνος Ἰσκαριώτου ('[into the heart] of Judas, son of Simon, Iscariot; 02 037 038 0141 etc.): this genitive means that 'Iscariot' could be applied to Judas or Simon, but the word order favours the latter. Two other readings have the genitive, the etymological Ἰούδα Σίμωνος ἀπὸ Καρυώτου ('Judas, son of Simon, from Karyot'; 05 lat^vl-pt, see John 6:71) and Σίμωνος Ἰσκαριώτου ('of Simon Iscariot'; ƒ¹³ 1505 lat^vl-pt co^pbo) which seems to involve an accidental omission. The oldest manuscripts have the name in the nominative at the end of the verse, and are split between Ἰούδας Σίμωνος Ἰσκαριώτου ('Judas, son of Simon Iscariot'; 𝔓⁷⁵? 019 044 070 1241) and Ἰούδας Σίμωνος Ἰσκαριώτης ('Judas Iscariot, son of Simon'; 𝔓⁶⁶ 𝔓⁷⁵? 01 02 [032] etc.). The identification of Judas as 'Iscariot' in John 12:4 and the other gospels suggests that 'Judas, son of Simon Iscariot' is the more likely reading (as adopted at John 6:71 and 13:26, where it is better attested). Nevertheless, the stronger external support for 'Judas Iscariot, son of Simon' (preferred in the THGNT) makes it difficult to decide.

13:10 εἰ μὴ τοὺς πόδας νίψασθαι (**to wash except for the feet**) {C}

The simplest reading is the shortest, νίψασθαι ('to wash'; 01 [579] lat^{vl-pt, vg} Tertullian^{vid} Origen). If this were the earliest form, the others could be explained as stemming from an early interpolation in order to reflect the context of footwashing. Its attestation is ancient but is not strong enough to justify its adoption as the editorial text, especially as quotations often elide incidental details. Instead this seems to be an abbreviated form of one of the other readings, removing the exception of the feet in order to make this observation consistent with the subsequent declaration ἀλλ᾽ ἔστιν καθαρὸς ὅλος ('but is clean all over'). The alternative forms also have early support: εἰ μὴ τοὺς πόδας νίψασθαι ('to wash except the feet'; 03 04* 019 032 etc.), εἰ μὴ τοὺς πόδας μόνον νίψασθαι ('to wash except the feet only'; 𝔓⁶⁶ 038 [1424] etc.), ἢ τοὺς πόδας νίψασθαι ('than to wash the feet'; 𝔓⁷⁵ 02 04³ 037 0141 and the majority of minuscules), and τὴν κεφαλὴν νίψασθαι εἰ μὴ τοὺς πόδας μόνον ('to wash the head except the feet only'; 05 lat^{vl-pt}). The last of these is an accommodation to Peter's reference to his head in the previous verse, while the other reading with μόνον ('only') is also likely to be an expansion. It is more difficult to decide between the other two: unlike the text of Codex Vaticanus, chosen as the editorial form here and in the SBLGNT, the majority reading is slightly elliptical and would have lent itself to expansion. Some witnesses have the order of the preceding words as χρείαν ἔχει ('has need'), which could have resulted in the omission of a following εἰ through haplography, but this is poorly attested in the earliest witnesses. Alternatively, εἰ μὴ may have been replaced by an editor who interpreted it as 'unless' and felt that was not suitable. Whichever text is adopted, it may be necessary to expand the phrase and adjust the word order in translation.[44]

---

[44] A more detailed consideration of this unit is seen in Thomas 1987; O'Neill 1994 prefers the shortest reading of all, that of GA 579, which just reads οὐ χρείαν ἔχει.

13:18   μου (my) {C}

This is a quotation of Psalm 41:9 [40:10 LXX], which refers to 'my bread'. This reading is reflected by manuscripts with μου ('my'; 03 04 019 892 etc.), even though they are relatively few in number. The majority have μετ' ἐμοῦ ('with me'; 𝔓⁶⁶ 01 02 05 032 etc.): this seems to be an easier reading in context, especially given its position in the sentence, and could be assimilation to the same context in Mark 14:18. While it remains possible that μου might have been a later adjustment towards the Septuagint, the different phrasing there makes this less likely.[45] It has therefore been adopted as the editorial text here. Some early translations conflate both readings, with μετ' ἐμοῦ τὸν ἄρτον μου ('with me my bread'; lat^{vl-pt} co^{bo-pt, ly, pbo}).

13:21   [ὁ] Ἰησοῦς (Jesus)

The name 'Jesus' often appears without a definite article in John, but it is not always possible to identify consistent patterns (see also the following unit). Here, all Greek manuscripts include the article except for four important witnesses (𝔓⁶⁶* 01 03 019). The only other instance of this particular phrase in the gospels is at John 18:1, where the same witnesses extant there again lack ὁ and this shorter reading has been adopted. This may suggest that the article here should be rejected, but it is very difficult to be confident. Translation is unaffected.

13:26   [ὁ] Ἰησοῦς (Jesus)

It was noted at John 6:29 above that ἀπεκρίθη Ἰησοῦς ('Jesus answered') in John usually lacks an article unless the words are separated by a pronoun. There are only two instances of the present-tense form, here (where the article is missing from 𝔓⁶⁶ 03 032 579^{vid}) and John 13:38 (where there is stronger evidence for the shorter reading). The tradition in this verse is further confused by the appearance of οὖν ('and so') or αὐτῷ ('to him') in some witnesses. This makes it very hard to be confident of the earliest form, although translation is unaffected.

---

[45] There are, however, two fourth-century papyri of the Psalms which read ὁ ἐσθίων ἄρτους μου μετ' ἐμοῦ ('who eats my breads with me'; Rahlfs 2013 and 2050); I am grateful to Tommy Wasserman for this observation.

13:26 βάψας οὖν τὸ ψωμίον [λαμβάνει καὶ] δίδωσιν (so when he had dipped the piece of bread, he gave it) {C}

Most Greek manuscripts read καὶ ἐμβάψας τὸ ψωμίον δίδωσιν ('and having dipped in the piece of bread, he gives it'; 𝔓⁶⁶ 02 [05] 032 037 etc.), while the others are split between βάψας οὖν τὸ ψωμίον δίδωσιν ('And so, having dipped the piece of bread, he gives it'; 01*,²ᵇ [0141] latᵛˡ⁻ᵖᵗ Cyrilˡᵉᵐ) and βάψας οὖν τὸ ψωμίον λαμβάνει καὶ δίδωσιν ('And so, having dipped the piece of bread, he takes and gives it'; 01²ᵃ [03] 04 019 etc.). The readings without λαμβάνει correspond to the words of Jesus immediately preceding this phrase, meaning that it could have been removed in order to match more closely. On the other hand, the presence of this verb as the first element in numerous other parallels involving bread (e.g. Matt. 15:36, 26:26; Mark 8:6, 14:22; Luke 9:16, 22:19; John 6:11; 1 Cor. 11:23) may have provided an impetus to add it here. As for the variation between βάψας οὖν and καὶ ἐμβάψας, the latter may reflect assimilation to Matt. 26:23 (perhaps mediated through the compound verb in some witnesses earlier in this present verse), but βάψας could be a correction towards the standard form of Jesus' words. Both the external and internal evidence are divided, making a decision difficult; despite its slim attestation both the SBLGNT and THGNT adopt βάψας οὖν τὸ ψωμίον δίδωσιν.

13:32 [εἰ ὁ θεὸς ἐδοξάσθη ἐν αὐτῷ] (if God has been glorified in him) {C}

Most witnesses include εἰ ὁ θεὸς ἐδοξάσθη ἐν αὐτῷ ('if God has been glorified in him'; 01² 02 04² 037 038 etc.), but it is lacking from the oldest manuscripts (𝔓⁶⁶ 01* 03 04* 05 etc.). Given that the last five words of this clause are identical to the preceding one, there is a very strong likelihood of its omission through eyeskip. Nevertheless, without this clause, the speech still makes sense and consists of four balanced elements, the first two with the aorist passive ἐδοξάσθη ('has been glorified') and the second two with the future active δοξάσει ('will glorify'): it is possible that an early editor found the disjunction between these too stark and therefore added the conditional clause in order to make the progression easier. However, there is also good reason to consider it as authorial, given the frequency of repetition and conditional constructions in this Gospel (e.g. John 3:12, 8:19, 8:42, 10:38, 13:14, 14:7 etc.).

This makes it very difficult to decide whether this phrase is part of the earliest text: it is included in the SBLGNT but absent from the THGNT.

13:36 ἀπεκρίθη [αὐτῷ] (answered)

The pronoun αὐτῷ ('him') is absent from a few majuscules and early translations (03 04* 019 lat co^(sa-ms, pbo, bo)). This may have been a deliberate deletion, given the appearance of αὐτῷ in the introduction to Peter's preceding and following speech. However, it could have been added through assimilation: the majority of manuscripts also have αὐτῷ before Jesus' next response in John 13:38. In any case, there is minimal effect on translation. Compare also John 19:11 below.

14:2 ὅτι (that) {B}

This word is missing from the majority of Greek manuscripts ($\mathfrak{P}^{66*}$ 04² 037 038 etc.), but is found in most early witnesses ($\mathfrak{P}^{66c}$ 01 02 03 04* etc.). It may be interpreted as causal ('because [I go]') or as introducing direct speech (ὅτι *recitativum*). Without ὅτι, the following phrase could be a new statement, although the conditional in the next verse works against this. The external evidence indicates that the longer reading is likely to be the earliest, and it is plausible that ὅτι was omitted as unnecessary before direct speech or perhaps removed by an editor because of its ambiguity. The punctuation between ὑμῖν and ὅτι in the THGNT encourages the rendering of the latter as 'because', supported by the full stop at the end of the phrase. In contrast, the UBS6 editorial text presents it as a question and the SBLGNT has a colon.

14:4 [ἐγὼ] ὑπάγω (I am going)

The emphatic pronoun ἐγώ ('I'; 01 02 03 04 037 etc.) is not required for the sense and is absent from a range of manuscripts ($\mathfrak{P}^{66}$ 05 019 032 038 and most minuscules). There is no obvious reason for accidental omission, but an editor may have removed it for stylistic reasons given that the same pronoun appears in John 14:3 and 14:6. The meaning is unaffected.

14:4 τὴν ὁδόν (the way) {B}

Most Greek manuscripts read καὶ τὴν ὁδὸν οἴδατε ('and you know the way'; $\mathfrak{P}^{66*}$ 02 04³ 05 037 etc.). The shorter reading, τὴν ὁδόν ('the way';

𝔓⁶⁶ᶜ 01 03 04* 019 etc.), involves unusual word order, especially because the preceding clause with ὅπου could be taken as the complement of οἴδατε ('you know [where I am going]'). It would therefore be unsurprising if the sentence had been expanded to remove this confusing construction and give two separate phrases, matching the following verse. Conversely, it is very hard to see how τὴν ὁδόν alone would have arisen if it were not the earliest reading.

14:7 ἐγνώκατέ με (you know me) {C}

The most widespread reading is the pluperfect ἐγνώκειτέ με ('if you had come to know me'; [02] 03 04 [05¹] 019 etc.), implying that the disciples do not currently know Jesus. The perfect-tense ἐγνώκατέ με ('if you have come to know me'; 𝔓⁶⁶ [01] [05*] 579 latᵛˡ⁻ᵖᵗ Irenaeusˡᵃᵗ Tertullianᵖᵗ) is a positive statement which provides the basis for the knowledge of the Father (see next unit; compare also John 8:39 above). It is very difficult to determine the relationship of these readings. The pluperfect could have been introduced through assimilation to the criticism of the Pharisees at John 8:19 (cf. John 8:54–55), or because there is a clear statement of the disciples' lack of knowledge at John 14:9. The latter makes it unlikely that an early editor changed this reading in order to present the disciples in a favourable light. However, the positive statement in the latter half of this verse could have led to the adjustment of the previous sentence to remove a possible contradiction. The perfect has early but limited attestation, which does not rule out an editorial adjustment; the strong external support for the pluperfect makes it equally likely to be original, and it is adopted in both the SBLGNT and THGNT.

14:7 γνώσεσθε (you will know) {C}

Matching the pluperfect in the previous unit, the majority of manuscripts read ἐγνώκειτε ἄν ('you would have come to know'; 02 04³ 037 [038] etc.), while others have the same tense but a different verb: ἄν ᾔδειτε ('you would have known'; 03 04* [019] 026 etc.). The witnesses with the perfect in the first clause have the future here, γνώσεσθε ('you will come to know'; 𝔓⁶⁶ 01 05 032 [579] etc.), but a few Latin sources support another perfect, ἐγνώκατε ('you have come to know'; latᵛˡ⁻ᵖᵗ Tertullianᵖᵗ). The choice of reading here is connected to the preceding unit. The future is unexpected: an editor would probably have introduced another perfect or a present tense, although there is the possibility of the influence of another verse (e.g. John 14:20). Likewise, the change of verb from ἐγνώκειτε to ἤδειτε is surprising, but in keeping with variation elsewhere (as in the following sentence). Each of these has a good claim to be the earliest reading, depending on the tense chosen for the first part of the conditional clause. The SBLGNT and THGNT both prefer ἤδειτε, which appears to be the most difficult reading because of its dissimilarity, yet it is possible that this word was introduced through assimilation to one of its many other occurrences in this gospel (cf. John 8:19).

14:14   *include verse* {A}

The entire verse is missing from a few witnesses (f^1 157 565 lat$^{vl\text{-}pt}$ sy^s cpa). Although an editor might have removed it because of its overlap with the previous verse (or possibly to avoid contradiction with John 16:23), the attestation indicates that it is more likely that its omission is due to eyeskip between the two instances of ἐάν ('if'); early translators may have left it out as unnecessary duplication. Other manuscripts lack both this verse and the latter half of the previous verse, through skipping from one ποιήσω ('I will do') to the next (0141 205). The witness which includes verse 14 after ποιήσω of verse 13 is likely to reflect a partial correction of this longer omission (1010). The possibility that this entire verse originated as dittography may be discounted: while a copyist could have gone back from ἐάν in verse 15 to ἄν in verse 13 (ἐάν in some manuscripts), and there are early variants in verse 14 which bring it closer to verse 13, the absence of the final phrase of verse 13 cannot be explained by this scenario and the variation appears to have been introduced by the evangelist (see next unit).

14:14   με (me) {B}

There is strong early support for με ('me'; 𝔓^{66} 𝔓^{75vid} 01 02 032 etc.), which is the hardest reading as it differs from the previous verse and makes for an unusual expression. This pronoun also matches the emphatic ἐγώ ('I') in the next clause, another variation from John 14:13. The lack of any complement here (02 05 019 044 etc.) is assimilation to that verse; a few witnesses, not cited in UBS6, read τὸν πατέρα ('the father'), through assimilation to John 15:16 and 16:23.

14:15 τηρήσετε (you will keep) {C}

Most manuscripts have an aorist imperative, τηρήσατε ('keep'; 02 05 032 037 038 etc.). Others are split between the aorist subjunctive τηρήσητε ('may you keep'; 𝔓⁶⁶ 01 060 0141 etc.) and the future τηρήσετε ('you shall keep'; 03 019 044 etc.). The imperative and subjunctive are paralleled both in conditional clauses with ἐάν in John (7:37, 8:52, 9:22, 12:26) and in phrases with τὰς ἐντολάς ('the commandments'; see Matt. 19:17). Nevertheless, the future matches the construction of the previous verse and corresponds to the tense of the next verse. In addition, there is a preference in John for the future in the result clause following ἐάν (compare the close parallels at John 14:23 and 15:10). It is difficult, but not impossible, to explain how the other readings arose if the future were original: τηρήσατε could have been influenced by the preceding ἀγαπᾶτε ('you love'), while the subjunctive may be an attempt to make this clause part of the initial condition before the double future in the following verse. Accordingly, τηρήσετε has been adopted here and in the SBLGNT and THGNT, despite some hesitation because of its relatively slim attestation.

14:17 μένει ... ἔσται (he abides ... he will be) {C}

It is impossible to tell whether the first verb is in the present tense (μένει, 'he abides') or the future (μενεῖ, 'he will abide') in the early manuscripts which lack accents. All of the later Greek witnesses, however, treat it as present, matching the preceding verb and the first part of the verse. The second verb is present-tense in a few manuscripts, ἐστιν ('he is'; 𝔓⁶⁶* 03* 05* 032 f^1 etc.), but in the oldest of these it is corrected to the future which is also the majority reading, ἔσται ('he will be'; 𝔓⁶⁶ᶜ 𝔓⁷⁵ᵛⁱᵈ 01 02 03² 05¹ etc.). The hardest reading seems to be the present followed by the future, which has been adopted as the editorial text here as well as in the SBLGNT and THGNT. Although the Latin and Coptic translations unambiguously have two futures, (μενεῖ ... ἔσται, 'will abide and will be'; latᵛˡ⁻ᵖᵗ, ᵛᵍ coˢᵃ, ˡʸ, ᵖᵇᵒ), this may well be under the influence of the second verb, while the reading with both verbs in the present tense is also likely to be assimilation.

14:22 [καί] (lit. and)

The connective καί ('and') preceding the interrogative τί ('what') at the beginning of a question is an unusual construction, despite being found in the majority of manuscripts ($\mathfrak{P}^{66c}$ 01 032 037 044 etc.). There is early support for a shorter reading without καί, which is much easier ($\mathfrak{P}^{66*}$ $\mathfrak{P}^{75}$ 02 03 05 019 etc.). This balance of internal and external considerations makes a decision difficult. Given that κύριε ('Lord') would have been written as a *nomen sacrum* (KE) and sound changes meant that καί was sometimes pronounced as κέ, it is possible that the majority reading arose through dittography and its more difficult form is simply an error. The shorter text is preferred by the SBLGNT and THGNT.

14:26 [ἐγώ] (I)

The emphatic pronoun ἐγώ ('I'; 03 019 0141 [33]) is not needed for the sense and appears in an unexpected position.[46] Both of these reasons, as well as the possibility of eyeskip to the next word which also begins with ε, could have led to its omission. It is difficult to explain why it was added if it was not originally present: assimilation to the beginning of John 14:28 may be a possibility. In any case, its attestation is slim: there is also good early evidence for its absence ($\mathfrak{P}^{75}$ 01 02 05 037 etc.), on the basis of which the shorter reading is preferred in the SBLGNT and THGNT.

14:28 ὅτι² (lit. that) {B}

The majority of Greek manuscripts read ὅτι εἶπον ('that I said [I am going]'; 037 700 892^{supp} etc.), while a few witnesses have ὅτι ἐγώ ('that I myself [am going]'; f^1 lat$^{vl\text{-}pt}$ co$^{sa\text{-}mss}$). The earliest sources, however, just have ὅτι ('that [I am going]'; $\mathfrak{P}^{75vid}$ 01 02 03 05 etc.). Both longer readings could be assimilation to the beginning of the verse (ὅτι ἐγὼ εἶπον, 'that I myself said'), but an editor could have removed εἶπον, either to ensure that the rejoicing was in the journey rather than the speech or to avoid discontinuity with the following verse in which the journey has not yet happened. In any case, the shortest form has compelling support. In translation, ὅτι could also be rendered as 'because' whichever reading is adopted.

---

[46] The punctuation of the manuscripts precludes taking it as the first word of the following sentence.

15:8 γένησθε (become) {C}

Most witnesses have the future γενήσεσθε ('you will become'; 01 02 037 044 etc.), but there is early evidence for the aorist subjunctive γένησθε ('you may become'; 𝔓⁶⁶ᵛⁱᵈ 03 05 019 038 etc.) and one manuscript has a present, γίνεσθε ('you are becoming', or the imperative 'become'; 579). The last of these seems to be a misreading. Although γένησθε could have arisen from γενήσεσθε through the omission of two letters, the subjunctive can be taken as connected to the preceding ἵνα ('so that'). Conversely, the future may have been assimilation to γενήσεται ('it will become') in John 15:7: given the discrepancy with the subjunctive φέρητε ('you may bear'), it is best to understand γενήσεσθε as part of a separate clause, matching that at the end of the preceding verse (compare too the parallel at John 13:35 with an additional idea after the end of the main clause). The possibility of change in either direction and the division of external evidence makes a decision difficult: the subjunctive has been adopted here and in the SBLGNT and THGNT on the basis of its attestation. There is minimal difference in meaning.

15:11 ἐν ὑμῖν ᾖ (may be in you) {B}

There is a difference in meaning between ᾖ ('may be [in you]'; 02 03 05 038 etc.) and the majority reading μείνῃ ('may remain [in you]'; 01 019 037 etc.), raising the question as to whether Jesus already has joy in the disciples or not. Either reading could have arisen as an error following ὑμῖν, whose final syllable would have been pronounced the same as the first syllable of μείνῃ: haplography would result in ᾖ, while dittography would give μ[ε]ίνῃ. The predominance of μένω ('remain') in the previous verses, however, makes ᾖ the harder reading, which also has early support. As εἶναι ('to be') is semantically weak and could present the disciples in a negative light, it would also be a candidate for adjustment by an early editor.

16:4 ὥρα αὐτῶν μνημονεύητε αὐτῶν (their hour ... you may remember) {B}

Most Greek manuscripts read ὥρα μνημονεύητε αὐτῶν ('the hour [comes] you may remember them'; 01* 044 0141 f^1 etc.), with other Byzantine support for ὥρα μνημονεύετε αὐτῶν ('the hour [comes], remember them'; 037 565 1006 etc.). The other readings are ὥρα αὐτῶν μνημονεύητε αὐτῶν ('their hour [comes] you may remember them'; 𝔓⁶⁶ᵛⁱᵈ 01²ᵇ 02 03 038 etc.), ὥρα αὐτῶν μνημονεύητε ('their hour [comes] you may remember'; 01²ᵃ [019] [*f*¹³] etc.), and ὥρα μνημονεύετε ('the hour [comes] remember'; 05 latᵛˡ⁻ᵖᵗ syˢ co). The last of these is the easiest reading, reflected in its appearance in early translations. In contrast, both appearances of αὐτῶν ('them') are more difficult, especially as the protagonists are not identified. Although the other instances of μνημονεύειν ('to remember') in John both have a genitive object, here the following ὅτι could be taken as the complement ('remember that') instead of introducing an explanation ('remember ... because'). The pronoun might easily have dropped out after ὥρα, through assimilation to John 16:2. There is good early support for the longest reading, ὥρα αὐτῶν μνημονεύητε αὐτῶν, which also explains the others: the double αὐτῶν could have arisen from conflation of the other readings, but it is also likely that one or both of these pronouns were removed to improve the style and sense. The phrase ὥρα αὐτῶν ('their hour') may be a reminiscence of Luke 22:53.

16:13 ὁδηγήσει ὑμᾶς ἐν τῇ ἀληθείᾳ πάσῃ (he will guide you into all the truth) {B}

The majority of Greek manuscripts read ὁδηγήσει ὑμᾶς εἰς πᾶσαν τὴν ἀλήθειαν ('he will guide you into all the truth'; [02] [03] 037 044 etc.), while others have ὁδηγήσει ὑμᾶς ἐν τῇ ἀληθείᾳ πάσῃ ('he will guide you in all truth'; 01 019 032 [038] etc.). A longer form of the latter reading is found in Codex Bezae, ἐκεῖνος ὑμᾶς ὁδηγήσει ἐν τῇ ἀληθείᾳ πάσῃ ('that one will guide you in all truth'; 05 latᵛˡ⁻ᵖᵗ), repeating the demonstrative from the previous line. The fourth reading, διηγήσεται ὑμῖν τὴν ἀλήθειαν πᾶσαν ('he will recount to you the whole truth'; latᵛˡ⁻ᵖᵗ, ᵛᵍ⁻ᵐˢˢ Eusebius Cyril-Jerusalem) only appears in early Christian writers and Latin translations. No support is given from Johannine usage because neither verb occurs elsewhere in this gospel, but διηγήσεται may have arisen from a corruption or misreading of ὁδηγήσει and the rest of the phrase adjusted accordingly. The dative ἐν ('in') seems less suitable than εἰς ('into') as a complement to the verb ὁδηγήσει ('he will guide'), and has therefore been adopted here and in the SBLGNT as a harder reading with early attestation: it may be taken to indicate the realm of the Paraclete's activity rather than the specific destination. The THGNT prefers the reading of Codex Alexandrinus and Codex Vaticanus, ὁδηγήσει ὑμᾶς εἰς τὴν ἀλήθειαν πᾶσαν ('he will guide you into all truth').

16:16 ὄψεσθέ με (you will see me) {A}

At the end of this verse, most Greek manuscripts include ὅτι ὑπάγω πρὸς τὸν πατέρα ('because I am going to the Father'; 02 [022] 037 038 etc.), some in the form ὅτι ἐγὼ ὑπάγω πρὸς τὸν πατέρα ('because I myself am going to the Father'; [28] [33] 892^supp etc.) and occasionally with an initial καί ('and'). This line is missing from most early witnesses (𝔓⁵ 𝔓⁶⁶ 01 03 05 etc.). There is nothing to prompt accidental omission, but in the following verse three statements are attributed to Jesus. As only the first two are found here, it appears that an editor has added the third in for consistency, not noticing that this phrase had already been spoken by Jesus at John 16:10. Nevertheless, the SBLGNT prefers the longer text.

16:18 [ὃ λέγει] (lit. which he says) {C}

The words ὃ λέγει ('which he says'; 01² 02 03 05² 019 etc.) are missing from some early manuscripts and translations (𝔓⁵ 𝔓⁶⁶ 01* 05* 032 etc.). The shorter reading makes good sense and it could easily have been supplemented by ὃ λέγει through assimilation to the previous verse or to clarify that this is a quotation. On the other hand, it is possible that this phrase was deleted by an editor in order to reduce repetition: the sense is covered by τί λαλεῖ ('what he speaks') at the end of the verse. Accidental omission through eyeskip between τοῦτο and τό is unlikely because ὃ λέγει is present in witnesses which lack the latter article (τό). Both the SBLGNT and THGNT prefer the longer reading, but the evidence in favour of the shorter reading is also strong.

16:23 ἐν τῷ ὀνόματί μου δώσει ὑμῖν (in my name he will give it to you) {C}

The majority of manuscripts have the word order ἐν τῷ ὀνόματί μου δώσει ὑμῖν ('[ask] in my name he will give to you'; 𝔓²²vid 02 04³ 05 032 etc.), but others have δώσει ὑμῖν ἐν τῷ ὀνόματί μου ('he will give to you in my name'; 𝔓⁵vid 01 03 04* 019 etc.). The latter is the harder reading because it differs from the many other occasions on which Jesus invites the disciples to 'ask in my name' (John 14:13, 14:14, 15:16, 16:24 and

16:26). As it also has good early support, this would normally be adopted as the editorial text (as it is in the SBLGNT and THGNT). However, the UBS4 committee chose the other form based on the range of early witnesses for the other reading and the strength of the parallels. The harder reading might have been introduced through assimilation to John 14:26, where the Father acts 'in my name', but assimilation to the predominant form is more likely. One minuscule just reads δώσει ὑμῖν ('he will give to you'; 205), perhaps reflecting a partial correction or eyeskip from ἐν to ἕως.

16:27   [τοῦ] θεοῦ (God) {C}

Most Greek manuscripts read παρὰ τοῦ θεοῦ ('from God'; 04³ 032 037 044 etc.), while earlier witnesses have παρὰ θεοῦ (also 'from God'; 𝔓⁵ 01*, 2b 02 022 etc.) or παρὰ τοῦ πατρός ('from the Father'; [01²ᵃ] 03 04* 05 019 etc.). All three constructions are paralleled elsewhere in John, but there is an overall preference for παρὰ τοῦ πατρός ('from the Father'). The latter is the easiest reading here, given the previous occurrence of 'Father' as well as the matching phrase in the following verse. It is more difficult to explain how θεοῦ would have been introduced, although the parallel at John 8:42 could have prompted assimilation. Despite the external support for παρὰ τοῦ πατρός, a form with θεοῦ has been preferred: similarly, the SBLGNT has παρὰ τοῦ θεοῦ and the THGNT παρὰ θεοῦ. Other Johannine references to coming 'from God' support the lack of a definite article (e.g. John 1:6, 9:16, 9:33).

17:11   ᾧ δέδωκάς μοι (that you have given me) {B}

There is early support for the majority reading ᾧ δέδωκάς μοι ('[the name] that you have given me'; 𝔓⁶⁰ 02 03 04 037 etc.). In context, οὓς δέδωκάς μοι ('those whom you have given me'; 05¹ [022ᶜ] 205 1505 etc.), which appears in the *Textus Receptus* and translations based on that edition, is an easier reading in that it identifies the object more clearly and could have been inspired by John 17:6 (see also the following unit and John 17:24 below). The reading ὃ δέδωκάς μοι ('that you have given me'; 05* 157 1424 etc.) appears to be a grammatical correction: while ὅ is the expected form, in the majority reading this relative pronoun has been attracted to the preceding dative. The same pronoun is seen with the aorist in ᾧ ἔδωκάς μοι ('[the name] that you gave me';

𝔓⁶⁶ᵛⁱᵈ 𝔓¹⁰⁷ 01 019 032). It is difficult to decide between this and the majority reading, given the various preceding occurrences of both δέδωκάς μοι (John 17:4, 17:7, 17:9) and ἔδωκάς μοι (John 17:6, 17:8): the stronger attestation of the perfect tense in the same phrase in the next verse (see the next unit) has been taken in support of the perfect here, although anticipatory assimilation remains a possibility. The omission of the end of the verse from some early translations (lat^{vl-pt} sy^s co^{ly}; cf. 𝔓⁶⁶*) may represent independent attempts to simplify the two verses and remove duplicate material.

17:12 ᾧ δέδωκάς μοι, καί (that you have given me and) {C}

This resembles the previous variation unit. Here, however, the majority of manuscripts read οὓς δέδωκάς μοι ('those whom you have given me'; 02 [04³] 05 [022ᶜ] 037 etc.), while there are only a few witnesses for ᾧ δέδωκάς μοι ('[the name] that you have given me'; [01²] 03 [04*] 019 [032] etc.) and less support for the aorist. The phrase is missing from the first hand of Papyrus 66 and Codex Sinaiticus, perhaps through a deliberate decision to remove repetition. The difference from the previous unit is surprising, suggesting that οὓς ('those') here might be the harder reading. On the other hand, οὓς could have been introduced by an editor in order to provide a clearer object for the following verb ἐφύλαξα ('I guarded'), which does not refer back to the noun ὀνόματι ('name'). Despite the possibility of assimilation to the preceding sentence, the early support for ᾧ and the difficulty it poses for ἐφύλαξα have led to its adoption.

17:21 ἐν ἡμῖν ὦσιν (may they ... be in us) {B}

Most manuscripts have ἐν ἡμῖν ἓν ὦσιν ('in us they may be one'; 01 02 04³ 019 037 etc.), but other early witnesses, including several translations, read ἐν ἡμῖν ὦσιν ('they may be in us'; 𝔓⁶⁶ᵛⁱᵈ 03 04* 05 032 etc.). It is possible that ἕν ('one') was overlooked because the previous word also ends in ν or through confusion with the previous ἐν, yet the introduction of the word by assimilation to the first phrase of this verse is very likely.[47] The preceding clauses with ἐν and the dative indicate that

---

[47] Croy 2022 favours the longer reading, but minimises considerations of external evidence and transcriptional probability.

the pattern of construction has changed in this part of the verse and it is not simply a repetition of the initial purpose clause. In fact, some translations start a new sentence with καθώς ('just as'), which also begins the sentence at John 17:18 (compare also John 10:26 above).

17:24 ὃ δέδωκάς μοι (whom you have given me) {B}

The majority reading, οὓς δέδωκάς μοι ('those whom you have given me'; [02] 04 019 037 etc.) is much easier than ὃ δέδωκάς μοι ('that which you have given me'; 𝔓⁶⁰ 01 03 05 032 etc.) where it is not clear to what the relative refers. The strong early attestation of the neuter singular, however, has led to its adoption. Because this seems to be coordinated with κἀκεῖνοι ('they also') later in the verse, it may be simpler in translation to render the relative pronoun with a plural whichever reading is followed.

18:1 τοῦ Κεδρών (Kidron) {B}

The best attested form is τῶν Κεδρών ('[the valley] of the cedars'; 01² 03 04 019 038 etc.), preferred in the THGNT. However, this would not explain either of the other readings, τοῦ Κεδροῦ ('of the cedar'; 01* 05 032 lat^{vl-pt}) and τοῦ Κεδρών ('of Kidron'; 02 037 lat^{vg}). Despite its very slim attestation, the proper noun—misinterpreted as the Greek word for 'cedar' and adjusted accordingly—is most likely to be the earliest reading. This variant provides information about the geography of the narrative.

18:5 ἐγώ εἰμι (I am) {C}

The shortest reading, ἐγώ εἰμι ('I am'; 𝔓⁶⁰ 05 lat^{vl-pt} sy^s cpa^{ms} co^{pbo} Origen), has early but restricted support. The majority of manuscripts read ὁ Ἰησοῦς ἐγώ εἰμι ('Jesus [said to them], "I am"'; [01] 02 04 019 032 etc.), specifying the subject of the verb. Although this is clear from the context, in the repetition of this exchange two verses later Jesus is named as the speaker, suggesting that this longer reading may be original or have been added through assimilation. The fact that ὁ Ἰησοῦς would have been written as the *nomen sacrum* Ο ΙC following αὐτοῖς ('to them') means that it could easily have been overlooked through haplography in ΑΥΤΟΙCΟΙC (cf. John 20:21 and 21:5 below). Most surprising is the reading of Codex Vaticanus, ἐγώ εἰμι Ἰησοῦς ('I am Jesus';

03 lat$^{vl\text{-}pt?}$). The presence of Jesus in the direct speech affects the theological significance of this response: rather than 'I am', invoking the name of God in the Hebrew Scriptures, 'I am Jesus' is a far more prosaic answer. Despite fitting the soldiers' preceding words, this neither matches the quotation in the following verse (cf. also John 18:8) nor explains their shocked reaction. Instead, it seems to be accidental: the *nomen sacrum* may have arisen through dittography of the first two letters of the following word εἰστήκει ('was standing'), often written as ἰστήκει ($\mathfrak{P}^{66}$ 01 03 05 etc., thus ICICTHKEI).[48] Codex Vaticanus offers indirect support for the shortest reading, but the limited external evidence and possibility of haplography leads to considerable doubt as to whether this is the earliest form.

18:13–27   *verses 13–27 in this sequence* {A}

It is the High Priest who questions Jesus in John 18:19, but Annas is implied to be Jesus' interlocutor at John 18:13 and John 18:24: in the latter, he sends Jesus to Caiaphas the High Priest, yet nothing is reported of that encounter. For this reason, several different sequences of these verses are found in the textual tradition, all of which have John 18:24 in an earlier position in order to resolve this inconsistency. The most complex is found in the Sinaitic Syriac, where Peter's two denials are also brought into a single block of text: one suggestion is that this may reflect Tatian's Diatessaron.[49] In some witnesses, John 18:24 appears twice, once in its normal position and once either after John 18:13 (1195 sy^{hmg} cpa^{ms} Cyril^{comm}) or in the middle of John 18:13 (225): both these minuscules are dated to the twelfth century. The overwhelming attestation of the traditional sequence indicates that this is the earliest attainable text, with these variations later editorial attempts to correct the problematic narrative. Some modern commentators believe that Annas is to be identified as the High Priest in the first encounter, thereby resolving the problem.[50] Nevertheless, it remains

---

[48] Thus Metzger 1994: 215, although this verb begins a new sentence. Tommy Wasserman, however, has pointed out to me that the lacuna in Papyrus 60 means that it might have had the same reading as Codex Vaticanus and the first hand of GA 2561 seems to have written ἐγώ εἰμι ὁ Ἰησοῦς.

[49] Metzger 1994: 215.

[50] See Omanson 2006: 208.

possible that the original order of these verses was corrupted at a very early point.[51]

18:20 πάντες (all) {B}

There is strong early evidence for πάντες ('all [the Jews]'; 01 02 03 04* 019 etc.), which reflects the Temple as the focal point for Jewish observance. The majority reading πάντοτε ('[the Jews] always'; 04³ 05^supp 037 044 etc.) is either an accidental repetition of this word from the previous clause or an alteration by an editor concerned that there was no occasion on which literally 'all the Jews' would gather in the Temple, even if it were large enough.

18:29 [κατά] (against)

Most manuscripts include the preposition κατά ('against'; $\mathfrak{P}^{66}$ 01¹ 02 04 05^supp etc.) but it is absent from a few early witnesses (01* 03 087^vid 579 lat^vl-pt). The shorter reading is a less expected construction, in which the genitive must qualify κατηγορίαν ('accusation'). This may be too hard a reading, but it is difficult to explain how it arose in multiple witnesses: it could be that the similarity of words ending with a sequence of a τ between two identical vowels (ΦΕΡΕΤΕ ΚΑΤΑ) led to omission, but this is not a standard form of eyeskip. While the word is presented here in brackets on the basis of the external attestation, it is included in the SBLGNT and THGNT.

18:30 κακὸν ποιῶν (criminal) {B}

There is slim but early evidence for κακὸν ποιῶν ('one who does evil'; 01² 03 019 032 lat^vl-pt), which would explain the other two readings, κακοποιῶν ('doing evil'; 04* 044 33 lat^vl-pt Cyril^pt) and κακοποιός ('an evildoer'; 02 04³ 05^supp 037 038 etc.). The compound words appear to be more typical of later Greek (cf. 1 Pet. 2:12, 2:14, 4:15), and κακοποιός is a technical term, which might be expected in a formal accusation. The first hand of Codex Sinaiticus has an aorist participle, κακὸν ποιήσας ('one who did an evil thing'; 01*), probably through assimilation to

---

[51] Multiple conjectures are recorded in the *Amsterdam Database* (Krans, Lietaert Peerbolte et al. 2016). For further editorial attempts to resolve the inconsistencies within the Latin tradition, see Houghton 2018: 15.

Pilate's question in the Synoptic Gospels (Matt. 27:23, Mark 15:14, Luke 23:22).

18:36   ἠγωνίζοντο [ἄν] (would be fighting)

Although the majority of manuscripts have an unusual word order, with ἄν coming after ὑπηρέται ('followers') rather than next to the verb, this particle is only lacking from the first hand of Codex Vaticanus. It is included in brackets because an original shorter reading would explain the two different sequences, especially as the more customary placing is found in several early witnesses ($\mathfrak{P}^{60\text{vid}}$ $\mathfrak{P}^{90\text{vid}}$ 01 019 032 etc.). However, its omission through a copying oversight could also have led to the variation here. There is no effect on translation.

18:40   πάλιν (in reply) {B}

The oldest manuscripts are divided between πάλιν ('again'; $\mathfrak{P}^{60}$ 01 03 019 etc.) and πάντες ('all'; $\mathfrak{P}^{66\text{vid}}$ 022 044 f^1 etc.). The majority reading, πάλιν πάντες ('again all'; 02 [05^{supp}] 037 038 etc.) could be a conflation of the two, but it is also plausible that πάντες by itself arose from eyeskip within this longer reading. The introduction of πάντες might have been intended to heighten the narrative or to emphasise the culpability of all the Jews, although it is not found at John 19:15 where this effect would have been greater. It is also possible that πάντες stems from a copying error, combining the beginning of πάλιν and end of λέγοντες, which may be reflected in the first hand of Papyrus 66. In any case, πάλιν offers a harder reading, because the crowd has not used these words before, with strong early attestation: in translation, it may be better to represent its sense as 'back' rather than 'again'.

19:11   [αὐτῷ] (him)

A range of early manuscripts have the pronoun αὐτῷ ('to him'; $\mathfrak{P}^{60\text{vid}}$ 01 03 05^{supp} 019 032 044 etc.) but it is absent from the majority of witnesses ($\mathfrak{P}^{66}$ 02 037 038 etc.). As noted at John 6:29 above, the phrase ἀπεκρίθη Ἰησοῦς ('Jesus answered') is very common in John but it rarely includes the pronoun. It is possible that it was originally included or added here later because of its occurrence in the previous introductions to direct speech (John 19.7, 19:10 etc.). The situation here is thus very similar to John 13:36 (see above): while the external evidence may favour the inclusion of the pronoun (as seen in the SBLGNT and THGNT), internal considerations lead to doubt.

19:16   Παρέλαβον οὖν τὸν Ἰησοῦν (So they took Jesus) {C}

The majority of manuscripts read Παρέλαβον οὖν τὸν Ἰησοῦν καὶ ἤγαγον ('and so they took Jesus and they led him'; 05^supp 037 038 etc.), although Codex Alexandrinus, Latin tradition and the *Textus Receptus* give the last verb as ἀπήγαγον ('they led him away'; 02 *TR* lat^vl-pt, vg). Others have a shorter text, Παρέλαβον οὖν τὸν Ἰησοῦν ('and so they took Jesus'; 03 019 044 0141 etc.), while several variants feature a participle: Οἱ δὲ παραλαβόντες τὸν Ἰησοῦν ἀπήγαγον ('But they, having taken Jesus, led him away'; 𝔓^60vid [𝔓^66vid] [01] 022 032 etc.), Οἱ δὲ παραλαβόντες αὐτὸν ἤγαγον καὶ ἐπέθηκαν αὐτῷ τὸν σταυρόν ('But they, having taken him, led him and laid on him the cross'; *f*^13 [Origen]) and παραλαβόντες οὖν τὸν Ἰησοῦν ἀπήγαγον εἰς τὸ πραιτώριον ('And so, having taken Jesus, they led him away into the headquarters'; 700 1006 [*Lect*] [cpa^mss]). The principal issue here seems to be the subject (compare John 19:29 below): the preceding plural agent is the chief priests in the previous verse, but in John 19:18 it is implied to be Roman soldiers. The readings beginning οἱ δέ ('but they') could mark a change of subject and even be translated as 'others'. Similarly, the reference to the headquarters, reminiscent of John 18:28, restores Jesus to the oversight of the soldiers. These are less ambiguous than the readings which begin παρέλαβον ('they took him away'), and therefore likely to be secondary. The reading with only one verb appears to be the most difficult, as there is no option for a change of subject: in those with καὶ ἤγαγον or καὶ ἀπήγαγον, the second verb clarifies the meaning of the first and might even be attributed to a different subject, yet this is not obvious. These phrases could have been omitted through eyeskip to the following καί, but it is worth noting that ἤγαγον occurs earlier in this passage (John 18:13, 19:13) and ἀπήγαγον appears in the parallel accounts (Matt. 27:31, Luke 23:26), which is consistent with their introduction through assimilation. The attestation for the shortest text is not particularly extensive, but seems to be the best of this type of reading and it has therefore been adopted here, as well as in the SBLGNT and THGNT.

19:24 [ἡ λέγουσα] (lit. which says)

Most witnesses include ἡ λέγουσα ('which says'; 02 05^supp 019 032 037 etc.) but this is lacking from Codex Sinaiticus, Codex Vaticanus and some early translations. The phrase is not found in other quotations in John involving the fulfilment of prophecy, but the participial formula appears frequently in Matthew (e.g. Matt. 1:22, 2:15, 4:14, 8:17, 12:17, 13:14 etc.; cf. James 2:23) and so could have been introduced here. Alternatively, the words could have been omitted through assimilation to other instances in John, (e.g. John 13:18, 19:36; cf. 17:12).[52] Given the balance of evidence, brackets have been placed around the longer text, which is adopted in both the SBLGNT and THGNT. If the shorter reading is preferred, a translation may need to indicate in some other way that the following words are a quotation.

19:25 Μαρία ... Μαρία (Mary) {B}

Both instances of the name Mary are written as Μαριάμ in four manuscripts (01 044 33 565) and Family 1; an additional witness has this Semitic form for the second occurrence, referring to Mary Magdalene (019). As noted at John 11:2 above, this may reflect a local custom or tradition—a further witness to 'Mariam' is the Harklean Syriac on both occasions—but there remains a possibility that this form of the name was originally widespread and later adjusted to the Greek spelling. The principle of consistency means that translations will use the same name for each individual throughout the Bible. See also John 20:1 below.

19:29 σπόγγον οὖν μεστὸν τοῦ ὄξους ὑσσώπῳ περιθέντες (they put a sponge full of the wine on a branch of hyssop) {A}

Most Greek manuscripts read οἱ δὲ πλήσαντες σπόγγον ὄξους καὶ ὑσσώπῳ περιθέντες ('but they, having filled a sponge of sour wine and having put it around some hyssop'; 02 05^supp 0141 28^supp etc.), while others have a longer form: οἱ δὲ πλήσαντες σπόγγον ὄξους μετὰ χολῆς καὶ ὑσσώπῳ περιθέντες ('but they, having filled a sponge of sour wine with gall and having put it around some hyssop'; f^{13} 1342 etc.) or οἱ δὲ πλήσαντες σπόγγον τοῦ ὄξους μετὰ χολῆς καὶ ὑσσώπῳ περιθέντες

---

[52] There is a parallel at John 12:38, where Papyrus 75 lacks a similar relative clause (I am grateful to Tommy Wasserman for this observation).

καλάμῳ ('but they, having filled a sponge of sour wine with gall and having put it around some hyssop on a stick'; 038 [892^supp] [1243]). There is strong early support for σπόγγον οὖν μεστὸν τοῦ ὄξους ὑσσώπῳ περιθέντες ('And so having put a sponge full of the sour wine around some hyssop'; 𝔓^66vid 01 03 019 032 etc.). This last reading is the most difficult, because the lack of the contrastive δέ to indicate a different subject could suggest that this activity is done by the last two other people mentioned in the text, the disciple and Jesus' mother (cf. John 19:16 above). Likewise, the repetition of μεστόν from the previous clause is inelegant. The additional elements in the other readings are likely to be assimilations to the synoptic parallels: Matt. 27:48 and Mark 15:36 both mention 'filling' and a 'stick', while Matt. 27:34 features the mixture of wine with gall. This combination of internal and external evidence leads to confidence in the adoption of the editorial text. Exegetes have sometimes noted that hyssop does not have long branches, leading to interest in a variant reading in one Greek manuscript, ὑσσῷ ('a javelin'; 476*, not cited in UBS6), possibly reflected in some Old Latin manuscripts with *perticae* ('a pole').[53] However, this reading probably arose from eyeskip between the two instances of ω in the word ὑσσώπῳ: hyssop is symbolically significant (e.g. Ex. 12:22), and there is a possibility that the plant in antiquity may have been more substantial than its modern equivalent (e.g. 1 Kings 4:33). The reading 'hyssop' thus seems assured, and it should be translated in such a way that the parallels with the Hebrew Scriptures are made clear.

19:35 πιστεύ[σ]ητε (you may believe)[54]

Most witnesses read the aorist subjunctive πιστεύσητε ('you may believe' or 'you may come to believe'; 01¹ 02 05^supp 019 032 etc.), while there is ancient support for the present subjunctive πιστεύητε ('you may be believing' or 'you may continue to believe'; 01* 03 044 Origen). The difference is one of verbal aspect: the aorist subjunctive of this word, denoting a single action, is much more common in John, but there are several examples of the present, which has a continuous meaning (John

---

[53] For further details, see Parker 1997: 176–177.

[54] The NRSVue appears to translate this verb twice, as 'so that you also may believe' in the middle of the verse, and 'so that you also may continue to believe' (following πιστεύσητε) at the end of the verse.

6:29, 10:38 and 17:21; see also John 7:39 above). Even in these, however, the majority of manuscripts usually have an aorist, indicating the general direction of change. The present is therefore the harder reading, and is adopted in the SBLGNT and THGNT. An identical variation is found with similar support at John 20:31 (see below) and consistency suggests preferring the same tense in both places. The reading chosen may have a bearing on whether this Gospel was written for a Christian audience or not.

19:38 Ἰωσὴφ [ὁ] (Joseph)

Several early manuscripts lack the definite article after Ἰωσὴφ ('Joseph'; 𝔓66vid 02 03 05supp 019 044 579), making 'Joseph from Arimathea' more of a title rather than a description ('Joseph, who was from Arimathea'). The same variation is seen at Mark 15:43, where the longer majority reading is preferred in the ECM. In the present verse, this could be assimilation to Mark or a stylistic improvement, making it difficult to be confident as to which form is earliest.

20:1 Μαρία (Mary) {C}

In this passage, as in John 11 (see John 11:2 above), the textual tradition transmits two forms of the proper name 'Mary': the Greek Μαρία and the Semitic Μαριάμ. The majority of manuscripts have Μαρία throughout. On this occasion, the presence of Μαρία in Codex Vaticanus leads to its adoption despite early support for Μαριάμ ('Mariam'; 01 02 019 032 etc.), giving the same phrase as in John 19:25 (see above). For other variations, however, see the following units. It is unfortunate that Papyrus 66 is not extant for some of these verses.

20:11 Μαρία (Mary) {C}

Although the variation is the same as in the previous unit, the attestation is weaker for Μαριάμ ('Mariam'; 𝔓66c 01 044 050 etc.). The presence of Μαρία in the first hand of Papyrus 66 and Codex Alexandrinus, as well as Codex Vaticanus, supports its adoption.

20:16 Μαριάμ (Mary) {C}

The majority of manuscripts continue to read Μαρία ('Maria'; 02 05 037 etc.), but there is a shift in Codex Vaticanus which now joins those which in John 20:1 read Μαριάμ ('Mariam'; 01 03 019 022 032 050 etc.). This is the only instance on which the name appears in direct speech, and the Semitic form is appropriate on the lips of Jesus. The manuscript attestation indicates that it is unlikely that copyists or editors were concerned with such considerations, making the variation in Codex Vaticanus all the more significant. Given the principle of consistency in translation, this would normally be translated the same way as other instances of this name. However, the reference to Hebrew in this verse may justify the use of the Semitic form of the name on this occasion (i.e. Mariam): if so, it would be appropriate to provide a gloss to match that of the following Hebrew word.

20:18 Μαριάμ (Mary) {C}

This is the most difficult of the four instances of Mary in this chapter. The phrase, 'Mary (the) Magdalene' is the same as John 20:1, but the attestation of the alternatives is different. Whereas Codex Alexandrinus and Codex Washingtonianus read Μαριάμ in the earlier verse, here they have the majority reading Μαρία ('Maria'; 02 05 032 037 038 etc.). In contrast, Papyrus 66 and Codex Vaticanus join Codex Sinaiticus, Family 1 witnesses and other minuscules with Μαριάμ ('Mariam'; $\mathfrak{P}^{66}$ 01 03 019 1 33 etc.). On the basis of this external evidence, the reading has been adopted as the editorial text, but there is a possibility that Μαριάμ two verses earlier has led to assimilation here. The principle of consistency, however, means that translators should use the same form of the name as John 20:1 whichever reading is chosen here. The SBLGNT and THGNT adopt the same pattern as the UBS text in these four variation units.

20:19 μαθηταί (disciples) {A}

The majority of manuscripts read μαθηταὶ συνηγμένοι ('the disciples [were] gathered'; 01¹ 038 0141 etc.), while others have μαθηταὶ αὐτοῦ συνηγμένοι ('his disciples [were] gathered'; 019 037 044 33 etc.). The earliest witnesses have the shortest reading, just μαθηταί ('the disciples [were]'; 01* 02 03 05 032 etc.). Eyeskip from the end of μαθηταί to συνηγμένοι is just about possible but the external evidence indicates that this is less likely than the addition of συνηγμένοι ('gathered') from other New Testament parallels (Acts 4:31, 20:8; possibly Matt. 18:20).

20:21 [ὁ Ἰησοῦς] (Jesus)

Several early witnesses lack this indication of the speaker, which is the same as that of the last direct speech two verses earlier (01 05 019 032 044 050 and multiple early translations). As the *nomen sacrum* abbreviation for ὁ Ἰησοῦς ('Jesus'; 02 03 037 038 and most minuscules) is written as O IC, the name could easily have been accidentally added or omitted after AYTOIC. This balance of evidence makes it difficult to decide whether or not it was originally present: as the name is not needed in context and omission is more common than addition, this may favour the longer reading (compare John 19:30 above and 21:5 below).

20:23 ἀφέωνται (they are forgiven) {C}

Most Greek manuscripts have the present tense, ἀφίενται ('they are forgiven'; 03² 032 037 038 etc.), but there is also good support for the perfect, ἀφέωνται ('they have been forgiven'; 01² 02 05 [019] 050 etc.). The first hand of Codex Vaticanus has ἀφείονται, which may be a misreading of the perfect (compare ἀφέονται in 019 and ἀφίωνται in 044). A future tense, ἀφεθήσεται ('it will be forgiven'; 01* lat[vl-pt] cpa co[sa, ly, pbo] etc.), is likely to be an example of replacement with an expected form (cf. Matt. 12:31–32, Mark 3:28; James 5:15 etc). The perfect corresponds to the structure of the following clause: this could support it as original or have led to assimilation: compare other instances of ἀφέωνται in the same context (e.g. Luke 5:20, 7:47; 1 John 2:12). There is also the possibility that the present tense was assimilated to synoptic parallels (Matt. 9:2; Mark 2:5) or the verbs in Jesus' preceding words. While both internal and external evidence are evenly balanced, the attestation might tip the balance in favour of the perfect, which is also adopted in the SBLGNT; the THGNT prefers ἀφίενται. A perfect tense in this part of a conditional clause can have a future reference, the implication being that the resulting state will continue.[55] In translation, then, a present tense is appropriate even when following the editorial text.

---

[55] Brown 1970: 1024; see also Cadbury 1939 and Blass, Debrunner & Funk 1961: 177 (§344).

20:30 μαθητῶν [αὐτοῦ] (of his disciples) {C}

The pronoun is missing from a number of early manuscripts (μαθητῶν, 'of the disciples'; 02 03 07 011 037 etc.), but the majority of witnesses read μαθητῶν αὐτοῦ ('of his disciples'; 𝔓⁶⁶ 01 04 05 019 etc.). Most occurrences of the word 'disciples' in John are followed by αὐτοῦ, although there are several instances of this word without a qualifier in the present chapter.[56] There is also the possibility of accidental omission through homoeoarcton between αὐτοῦ and ἃ οὐκ. The balance within both the internal and external evidence makes it hard to be confident as to the earliest reading: even if the shorter reading is adopted, the phrase may still be translated as 'his disciples'.

20:31 πιστεύ[σ]ητε (you may continue to believe) {C}

Unlike the same variation at John 19:35 (see above), here the majority of manuscripts attest the aorist subjunctive πιστεύσητε ('you may [come to] believe'; 01² 02 04 05 19 etc.). There is early evidence for the present subjunctive πιστεύητε ('you may [continue to] believe'; 𝔓⁶⁶ᵛⁱᵈ 01* 03 038 etc.), but it is not clear whether this is sufficient to adopt this as the earliest text (as in the SBLGNT and THGNT): the possibility of assimilation to the present-tense verbs earlier in the verse or, in particular, the following present subjunctive leads to hesitation. The aorist subjunctive is the more common form of this verb in John and the discrepancy it makes with the subsequent clause may lead to its being preferred here. The difference between the tenses could indicate whether the evangelist was addressing those who were already Christians (with the present tense) or those who were not (with the aorist). However, this may be reading too much into it, especially given the uncontested present subjunctive ἔχητε ('you may [continue to] have') at the end of the verse. In some languages it may not anyway be possible to reproduce such a distinction. Although this verse gives the impression of being the conclusion of the gospel, there is no surviving manuscript which provides clear evidence for the end of the book at this point and, in contrast to the endings of Mark (see Mark 16:8 above), the language of the final verses is consistent with that of the preceding text.

---

[56] This is also seen in John 21. On the phrase in general, see Elliott 1979, who prefers the longer reading here.

21:3 τὸ πλοῖον (the boat) {A}

Most Greek manuscripts include the word εὐθύς ('immediately'; 02 04³ 024 037 etc.) after τὸ πλοῖον ('the boat'), but it is absent from most early witnesses (01 03 04² 05 019 etc., lat sy^{s, p} co). This strong external attestation leads to the adoption of the shorter reading as the editorial text. John does not use εὐθύς as frequently as the other gospels: it may have been introduced through assimilation to a previous instance when the disciples board a boat immediately (e.g. Matt. 14:22; Mark 6:45, 8:10 etc.), or to enhance the authority of Peter among the disciples after the crucifixion.

21:5 [ὁ] Ἰησοῦς (Jesus)

This is a further example of ὁ Ἰησοῦς ('Jesus') following αὐτοῖς ('to them'), as seen at John 20:21 above. It is not surprising that a few witnesses (02*^{vid} 032 lat^{vl-pt} sy^s) lack ὁ Ἰησοῦς entirely, which is likely to be due to eyeskip of the *nomen sacrum* (AYTOICOIC). Codex Sinaiticus and Vaticanus do not have ὁ but only Ἰησοῦς ('Jesus'; 01 03), reflecting the instability of the definite article in this position (cf. John 13:29 and 14:6 above). Their antiquity leads to some hesitation as whether it was originally present, but there is also early evidence for the majority reading, ὁ Ἰησοῦς ('Jesus'; 02^c 04 05 019 037 etc.).

21:6 εὑρήσετε (you will find some) {A}

After this word, some witnesses read οἱ δὲ εἶπον· δι' ὅλης νυκτὸς ἐκοπιάσαμεν καὶ οὐδὲν ἐλάβομεν· ἐπὶ δὲ τῷ σῷ ῥήματι βαλοῦμεν ('But they said, "We worked all night long and we caught nothing. But on your word, we will cast."'; 𝔓^{66} 01¹ 044 lat^{vl-pt} co^{sa}, with minor variants: for ῥήματι, 𝔓^{66vid} and co^{sa} have ὀνόματι ['for your sake']). This is a reworking of Simon's response to Jesus at Luke 5:5, which an early editor appears to have inserted at this point to bring the two accounts closer together. There is nothing in most manuscripts which would prompt accidental omission, although it may be noted that three read οἱ δὲ ἔβαλον ('but they cast'; 01* 05 032) rather than ἔβαλον οὖν ('and so they cast') as the following words. Even so, the presence of the shorter reading in Byzantine tradition as well as the major majuscules (01* 02 03 04 05 etc.) leads to its adoption as the earliest text.

21:15 Ἰωάννου (son of John) {B}

In this and the following three verses, the majority of Greek manuscripts read Ἰωνᾶ ('son of Jonah'; 02 04² 037 038 etc.) but the earliest witnesses have Ἰωάννου ('son of John'; 01¹ 03 04* 05 019 etc.). The former is likely to be harmonisation to the name of Peter as given in Matt. 16:17, which also appears as a variant at John 1:42 (see above). While 'John' is a more common name than 'Jonah', the latter is not so unusual that it would be replaced. The external evidence suggests that Ἰωάννου is the earliest reading. On this occasion, the name was omitted by the first hand of Codex Sinaiticus, one of several errors in this chapter (see also John 21:23 and 21:25 below).

21:16 Ἰωάννου (son of John) {B}

The attestation of 'son of John' and 'son of Jonah' is the same as the previous verse, with the exception of Ἰωάννου in the first hand of Codex Sinaiticus and the absence of Codex Regius (019), which has lost the final page of the gospel.

21:17 Ἰωάννου (son of John) {B}

Although there is variation elsewhere in these three questions and answers, the name is consistent. The witnesses for Ἰωάννου ('son of John') from John 21:16 seem to be joined in this verse by Papyrus 59, according to a reconstruction based on the number of characters per line. Conversely, Origen's only citation of this passage has Ἰωνᾶ ('son of Jonah') in this verse. This offers early support for the majority reading, but the consistency of Ἰωάννου in direct tradition again leads to its adoption here.

21:17 [ὁ Ἰησοῦς] (Jesus)

Before the final command, most manuscripts include the indication that the speaker is ὁ Ἰησοῦς ('Jesus'; 02 037 038 044 etc.), but early witnesses have just Ἰησοῦς ('Jesus'; 03 04) or nothing at all (01 05 032 f^1 33 565 lat sy^s co$^{pbo, bo}$). The last of these could be assimilation to the equivalent phrase in the two previous verses. Elsewhere in this passage, the predominant form of the name includes the article, suggesting that Ἰησοῦς is the harder reading, but it is not widely attested and there appears to be a preference for the anarthrous form in Codex Vaticanus.

The division of the external evidence makes it very hard to be confident of the earliest text.

21:23 ἔρχομαι[, τί πρὸς σέ] (I come, what is that to you) {C}

The majority of Greek manuscripts read ἔρχομαι τί πρὸς σέ ('[until] I come, what is that to you'; 01¹ 02 03 04* 032 etc.), but the question is missing from a few witnesses with just ἔρχομαι ('[until] I come'; 01* 04^{2vid} *f*¹ 565 lat^{vl-pt} sy^s cpa^{mss}) and Codex Bezae reads ἔρχομαι πρὸς σέ ('[until] I come to you'; 05). There is no obvious reason for the accidental omission of τί πρὸς σέ and the shortest reading is grammatically more difficult because the conditional clause has no conclusion. It is possible that the form in Codex Bezae is an attempt to provide this, but it seems more likely that it reflects the longer reading from which τί was omitted through eyeskip, either following the final letter of ἔρχομαι or the similarity of ΤΙ to the following Π. While it is possible that an editor or copyist may have added the question from the previous verse, this verse still lacks the final clause: if the desire was to make the two verses match, the repetition of the full text would be expected. Conversely, τί πρὸς σέ could have been deleted because it is not directly relevant to the contrast with οὐκ ἀποθνῄσκει ('he would not die'). The very limited attestation of the shorter reading does not rule out scribal error (compare Codex Sinaiticus in John 21:15 and the following unit), or the omission of superfluous material by translators. The longer reading, which also has early support, may therefore be preferred as in the SBLGNT and THGNT.

21:25 βιβλία (books that would be written) {A}

Most early witnesses end the gospel with βιβλία ('books'; 01 02 03 04*, ³ 05 etc.). There is no contextual reason for a final ἀμήν ('Amen'; 04² 037 038 044 etc.), but it appears in Byzantine tradition in keeping with the custom of ending each book with a liturgical Amen.[57] Multispectral imaging of Codex Sinaiticus has shown that the copyist initially ended the gospel at the end of John 21:24 and drew the final coronis at that point, before erasing it and writing the remaining text. This is in keeping with the other first-hand errors noted in this manuscript in

---

[57] See Wasserman 2023: 60–62.

preceding units, confirming that copyists may become less accurate when the end of a book is in sight. There is no evidence that the final verse was an addition.

After the end of John, manuscripts of Family 1 (whose text derives from an early source) include an editorial note introducing the *Pericope Adulterae* (see John 7:53–8:11 above). This observes that, because the passage is missing from many copies of John and is not quoted by early Christian writers, the editor of this text omitted it from its customary position at the end of John 7 (Eusebian section 86), and instead provided it separately at the end of the gospel.[58]

---

[58] According to Metzger 1994: 221 this is also the case in Armenian manuscripts.

The Acts of the Apostles

Overview

The Acts of the Apostles appears in fifteen Greek papyri. Of these, the most significant are the third-century Papyrus 45 ($\mathfrak{P}^{45}$), which contains portions of Acts 4–17, the seventh-century Papyrus 74 ($\mathfrak{P}^{74}$), extant for the whole book, and the fifth-century Papyrus 127 ($\mathfrak{P}^{127}$), with parts of Acts 10–12 and 15–17. It also appears in the major fourth- and fifth-century majuscules, mentioned above for the gospels: Codex Sinaiticus (01), Codex Alexandrinus (02), Codex Vaticanus (03), Codex Ephraemi Rescriptus (04) and Codex Bezae (05). To these is added the sixth-century Laudian Acts (08), a Greek-Latin bilingual written in very short sense lines and various fragmentary majuscules. The most important minuscule witnesses are GA 33, 81, and 1739, which were copied in the ninth or tenth century from much earlier documents and preserve readings which agree with the early majuscules. The principal Old Latin witnesses (lat^{vl}) are the Latin side of Codex Bezae and the fifth-century Fleury palimpsest, supplemented by the thirteenth-century Codex Gigas; the Vulgate (lat^{vg}) is therefore an important early versional source. There is no surviving Old Syriac manuscript, although Acts is transmitted in the Peshitta (sy^p) and Harklean (sy^h) versions as well as Christian Palestinian Aramaic (cpa) and Ethiopic (eth). In Coptic, the fifth-century Glazier Codex (co^{mae}) is a Middle Egyptian translation of Acts 1–15; the whole book is available in both Sahidic (co^{sa}) and Bohairic (co^{bo}) dialects. No Gothic witness is known to survive.

The text of Acts is notable for being transmitted in multiple forms. The 'Western' readings represent an extensive reworking which is around 6.5% to 8% longer than the standard editorial text: its characteristics include an expansion of the narrative with historical details, an emphasis on the role of the Holy Spirit and other theological tendencies.[1] The principal witnesses to 'Western' forms are Codex Bezae (05), some fragmentary papyri ($\mathfrak{P}^{38}$, $\mathfrak{P}^{48}$), the Old Latin (lat^{vl}), the Middle

---

[1] See further Epp 1966 and Black 1981.

Egyptian (co^{mae}) and the marginal readings in the Harklean Syriac (sy^{hmg}).[2] Another longer form of text is seen in Papyrus 127, with some expansions similar to 'Western' readings but notable differences. The standard, shorter text is attested by the other papyri and early majuscules. This forms the basis of the Byzantine tradition transmitted in the majority of minuscules, although the latter appears also to incorporate some 'Western' expansions (e.g. Acts 24:7–8, 28:16, 28:29). The history of the text is complicated, leading to a variety of theories explaining the relationship between the two, but it seems clear that the 'Western' readings (which are not always present in witnesses typically described as 'Western') are usually secondary.[3] For this reason, only a small representative selection of these variants is included in the UBS6 apparatus (e.g. Acts 8:37, 15:24, 19;1, 19:9). English versions of many of the 'Western' readings are given in Metzger 1994, which has a particular focus on the text of Acts.

The majority of well-known variations in Acts involve the 'Western' readings. These include the distinctive form of the Apostolic Decree in Acts 15:20, 15:29 and 21:25, and possibly also the addition of Acts 15:34. Among other notable variants are the introduction to the quotation at Acts 4:25, the conflation of two episodes from the Hebrew Scriptures at Acts 7:16, the variation between 'house' and 'God' at Acts 7:46, the recipients of the promise at Acts 13:33, the description of Philippi at Acts 16:12, the source of the blood at Acts 20:28 and Agrippa's response at Acts 26:28.

The *Editio Critica Maior* of Acts (*ECM Acts*) was published in 2017. This provides the basis for the text and apparatus of Acts in UBS6, with several changes from previous editions. As noted above in the Overview for Mark, only some of the variants with a 'split guiding line' in the ECM where the editors were unable to decide on the earliest reading are reported in the apparatus, indicated by a diamond (♦). The apparatus and presentation of the data for the Coherence-Based Genealogical Method are available online, along with a textual commentary with

---

[2] Papyrus 29 has sometimes also been considered a 'Western' witness: see further Tuckett in Hill & Kruger 2012: 160–162.

[3] A summary is offered in Parker 2008: 293–301; see also the studies volume of *ECM Acts*.

notes on some of the variants, including all those with a split guiding line.[4] These are referred to in the discussions below when relevant.

1:2 ἡμέρας ... ἀνελήμφθη (the day when he was taken up to heaven) {A}

Codex Bezae, supported by some early translations (lat[vl-pt] sy[hmg] co[sa, mae]) moves the final verb of this verse to after ἡμέρας ('the day') and adds in its place after ἐξελέξατο ('had chosen') the phrase καὶ ἐκέλευσεν κηρύσσειν τὸ εὐαγγέλιον ('and ordered to proclaim the gospel'). This poses a problem of how to understand the sequence of the main verbs: despite their position in the verse, 'he ordered' presumably preceded 'he was taken up'. Some Latin sources have the same addition at the end of the verse but do not include a phrase corresponding to ἄχρι ... ἀνελήμφθη ('until ... he was taken up'). This has the effect of removing this reference to the Ascension and instead connects this verse with the final clause of Acts 1:1, describing the choice and instruction of the disciples as part of Jesus' ministry in the first book. The result is to minimise the double reference to the Ascension at the end of Luke and in Acts 1:9. Thus, even at the beginning of this book, the editorial adjustments characteristic of 'Western' readings, their potential theological or exegetical significance, and the variety of their textual form in different witnesses are evident. At the same time, the lack of any obvious reason for the omission or deletion of the text which is absent from the majority of manuscripts supports their reading as the earliest form.[5]

1:15 ἀδελφῶν (brothers and sisters) {B}

The majority of Greek manuscripts read μαθητῶν ('disciples'; 04³ 05 08 044 etc.), but this appears to be an adjustment to an expected form, probably to avoid identifying this set of ἀδελφοί (lit. 'brothers') with those mentioned at the end of the previous verse. The same is true of the other variant, ἀποστόλων ('apostles'; 𝔓[74vid]), which might be thought to conflict with the number of 120 people in the crowd. Not

---

[4] See https://ntvmr.uni-muenster.de/ecm and https://ntg.uni-muenster.de/. The direct link to the textual commentary for *ECM Acts* is https://ntvmr.uni-muenster.de/forum/-/message_boards/category/1136044.

[5] For further discussions of this variation unit see Epp 1981, Parsons 1988, Zwiep 1996: 234–238, De Jonge 2013 and Gäbel 2021.

only is ἀδελφῶν the hardest reading here, but it also has strong external support (01 02 03 04* 33 etc.). There remains a slight possibility that this form might have arisen through assimilation to the ἀδελφοί addressed at the beginning of the following verse. It is also worth noting that the word μαθητής ('disciple') does not otherwise appear in the first five chapters of Acts.

1:26   κλήρους αὐτῶν (lit. their lots) {B}

The ECM adopts the genitive rather than the dative pronoun: κλήρους αὐτῶν ('their lots'; 05* 08 044 etc.) is present in the majority of manuscripts and its attestation is coherent. In contrast, the dative appears to have emerged several times, despite strong early support for κλήρους αὐτοῖς ('lots for them'; 01 02 03 04 05[1] etc.). The dative is ambiguous: it could be interpreted as an indirect object ('they gave lots to them' [i.e. the believers]) or an ethical dative ('they cast lots for them' [i.e. Joseph and Matthias]). However, the CBGM suggests that it was introduced on multiple occasions, probably through an expectation that ἔδωκαν ('they gave') would be followed by an indirect object. As the *ECM Acts* Textual Commentary observes, the technical term would be βάλλειν κλήρους ('to cast lots'), and so 'they gave their lots' is not necessarily an easier reading.[6]

2:30   καθίσαι (that he would put) {B}

There is no direct object for the verb καθίσαι ('to set'), which must be understood as represented by ἐκ καρποῦ τῆς ὀσφύος αὐτοῦ ('from the fruit of his loins'). This is a Hebrew idiom, but to clarify the structure in Greek several variants provide a direct object before this verb, perhaps inspired by the use of ἀναστήσω ('I will raise up') in a similar context at 2 Sam. 7:12. The majority of Greek manuscripts read τὸ κατὰ σάρκα ἀναστήσειν τὸν Χριστὸν καθίσαι ('that he should raise up [from the fruit of his loins] what was according to the flesh, to put the Messiah'; [044] [33] [181] 614 etc. with minor variations). This could be a development from, or the inspiration for, κατὰ σάρκα ἀναστῆσαι τὸν Χριστὸν καὶ καθίσαι τε ('that he would raise up the Messiah according

---

[6] A full explanation of this variation unit in the CBGM is provided by Wasserman & Gurry 2017: 80–86.

to the flesh and put him both'; [05*] 307 [1642*] co^mae). Simpler expansions are seen in ἀναστῆσαι τὸν Χριστὸν καὶ καθίσαι ('that he would raise up the Messiah and set him'; 08 lat^(vl-pt)) and ἀναστήσειν τὸν Χριστὸν καθίσαι ('that he should raise up the Messiah to set him'; 1739). The strong external support for the shortest reading καθίσαι ('to put'; 01 02 03 04 [051] etc.) justifies its adoption as the editorial text. The full attestation in Greek continuous-text manuscripts is given in *TuT Acts* (TS7).

2:31 οὔτε ἐγκατελείφθη (was not abandoned) {A}

The majority of Greek manuscripts add an explicit subject after this verb, ἡ ψυχὴ αὐτοῦ ('his soul'; 04³ 08 044 etc.: see further *TuT Acts* TS8), which is a repetition from the quotation of Ps. 16:10 [15:10 LXX] in Acts 2:27 and also introduces parallelism with 'his flesh' in the next phrase. However, there is no obvious reason for the omission of this if it were originally present and the shorter reading without a noun has excellent attestation ($\mathfrak{P}^{74}$ 01 02 03 04* 05 etc.).

2:41 ἀποδεξάμενοι (who welcomed) {A}

Although the participle already indicates a positive reception, the majority of Greek manuscripts include an adverb before it, ἀσμένως ἀποδεξάμενοι ('gladly welcoming'; 08 044 33 181 etc.). This is likely to be assimilation to its use before the same verb in Acts 21:17, the only other instance of this adverb in the New Testament. The strong early support for the shorter reading of just ἀποδεξάμενοι ('welcoming'; $\mathfrak{P}^{74}$ 01 02 03 04 etc.) indicates that it is unlikely that it was omitted through an oversight. The reading of Codex Bezae, πιστεύσαντες ('who believed'; 05) appears to reflect an editor's concern that faith, rather than merely acceptance, should be seen as necessary in order to receive baptism (see also Acts 8:37 below). The participle ὑποδεξάμενοι ('welcomed'; 1642) is synonymous with ἀποδεξάμενοι and is a simple misreading of the majority form.

2:43 ἐγίνετο² (were being done) {A}

The shorter reading adopted in the editorial text, ἐγίνετο ('were being done'; 03 05 81 etc.), is supported by early witnesses as well as the majority of Greek manuscripts. The four variants are all expansions. Some witnesses have ἐγίνετο ἐν Ἰερουσαλήμ ('were being done in Jerusalem'; [08] 33 181* etc.), an addition found in Codex Bezae in the previous verse. A significant group of witnesses, including several early translations, reads ἐγίνετο ἐν Ἰερουσαλήμ· φόβος τε ἦν μέγας ἐπὶ πάντας ('were being done in Jerusalem, and there was also great awe upon all'; 𝔓⁷⁴? 01 02 04 1175 etc.). Other forms are minor variations on this, such as the absence of μέγας ('great'; 𝔓⁷⁴? 181ᶜ) or the insertion of αὐτούς ('[all of] them'; 044 [307]). Despite their early attestation, these readings appear to be assimilation to other passages (e.g. Acts 5:5, 19:17). The external evidence in favour of the shortest form suggests that it was the earliest, and it is also adopted in SBLGNT and THGNT. The full attestation in Greek manuscripts is seen in *TuT Acts* (TS10).[7]

2:47–3:1   ἐπὶ τὸ αὐτό. Πέτρος δέ (to their number ... Peter) {B}

The phrase ἐπὶ τὸ αὐτό developed a technical Christian meaning signifying 'the union of the Christian body' or 'in church fellowship' (cf. Acts 1:15, 2:1; 1 Cor. 11:20, 14:23).[8] Here, however, this appears to have posed a problem for later readers, perhaps because ἐπὶ τὸ αὐτό in Acts 2:44 may not be used in this specialised way, or because the phrase seems superfluous here following that preceding instance. The majority of manuscripts end Acts 2:47 with τῇ ἐκκλησίᾳ ('in the church') and take this phrase in a non-technical sense as the beginning of the following verse, Ἐπὶ τὸ αὐτὸ δὲ Πέτρος ('Together, Peter ...'; 08 044 33 etc.). Others have the addition but a different sentence division: τῇ ἐκκλησίᾳ ἐπὶ τὸ αὐτό. Πέτρος δέ ('in the church for fellowship. Peter ...'; 1642 1739). The longest form is a 'Western' reading: ἐπὶ τὸ αὐτὸ ἐν τῇ ἐκκλησίᾳ. Ἐν δὲ ταῖς ἡμέραις ταύταις Πέτρος ('for fellowship in the church. In those days, Peter ...'; 05 latᵛˡ⁻ᵖᵗ coᵐᵃᵉ). In contrast, some witnesses lack the problematic phrase and have τῇ ἐκκλησίᾳ. Πέτρος δέ ('in the church. Peter ...'; 1409 syᵖ). There is strong external support for the editorial text (𝔓⁷⁴ᵛⁱᵈ 𝔓⁹¹ᵛⁱᵈ 01 02 03 04 etc.) which also explains the origin of the other readings: thirteen variants are recorded here in *TuT Acts* (TS12).

---

[7] For a longer discussion of this unit, see Strutwolf 2014: 256–259.
[8] Metzger 1994: 265.

3:6 ἔγειρε καὶ περιπάτει (stand up and walk) ◆

The first two words are absent from a few important early witnesses, which have just περιπάτει ('walk'; 01 03 05 lat[vl-pt] co[sa]). Given the use of the full phrase in healing miracles elsewhere (e.g. Matt. 9:5, Mark, 2:9, Luke 5:23, John 5:8), it is possible that they were added later. Conversely, because the following verse describes Peter raising the lame man by the hand, an editor could have deleted the first verb. The CBGM does not assist in the determination of the earlier reading, so the ECM has a split guiding line. The SBLGNT reads only περιπάτει, while THGNT has the longer text. Even if translators include both terms, exegetes should be wary of claiming that Peter's words parallel those of Jesus in the Gospels (cf. Matt. 9:5 etc.).

3:13 καὶ Ἰσαὰκ καὶ Ἰακώβ (and of Isaac and Jacob) {A}

The majority of witnesses do not have the repetition of ὁ θεός ('God') but read καὶ Ἰσαὰκ καὶ Ἰακώβ ('and of Isaac and of Jacob'; 03 08 044 0236 etc.). It seems unlikely that an editor would have deleted this if it had been originally present. Rather, manuscripts which read καὶ ὁ θεὸς Ἰσαὰκ καὶ ὁ θεὸς Ἰακώβ ('and the God of Isaac and the God of Jacob'; 𝔓[74] 01 04 307 etc.) harmonise this citation of Exod. 3:6/3:15 to other New Testament examples (e.g. Matt. 22:32, Mark 12:26, Luke 20:37). Those which have καὶ θεὸς Ἰσαὰκ καὶ θεὸς Ἰακώβ ('and God of Isaac and God of Jacob'; 02 05) harmonise it to the Septuagint, where definite articles are lacking. The CBGM indicates that the harmonisation was introduced on multiple occasions, while the majority attestation of the shorter reading is coherent and goes against the tendency of Byzantine tradition to harmonise.[9] Compare also Acts 7:32 below.

3:22 εἶπεν (said) {B}

There is strong early attestation of the shorter reading adopted in the editorial text, εἶπεν ('said'; 𝔓[74] 01 02 03 04 etc.). The appearance of extra text in different places is typical of a later insertion: the majority of manuscripts have γὰρ πρὸς τοὺς πατέρας εἶπεν ('for to the ancestors [Moses] said'; [35] 181 [424] 614 etc.), while others read εἶπεν πρὸς

---

[9] See further Wachtel 2020: 58–62; this unit is also discussed in Epp 1966: 51–54 and Strange 1992a: 120–122.

τοὺς πατέρας ('said to the ancestors'; 044 33? 1642 1739), or εἶπεν πρὸς τοὺς πατέρας ἡμῶν ('said to our ancestors'; 05 [08] 33? etc.: see further *TuT Acts* TS15). For a parallel to the longer reading, see Acts 3:25.

3:22   ὁ θεὸς ὑμῶν (your God) {C}

The Byzantine tradition is split between ὁ θεὸς ὑμῶν ('your God'; 01² 02 05 1 81 etc.) and ὁ θεὸς ἡμῶν ('our God'; 01* 04 08 044 etc.). These would have sounded identical through itacism. The source of the quotation, Deut. 18:15, has the singular second-person pronoun σοῦ ('your') in the Septuagint, which supports the second-person here. Although ἡμῶν ('our') seems to be the harder reading as it comes between other instances of the second-person plural, the sound change and the formulaic nature of the phrase 'the Lord our God' (cf. Acts 2:39 and Deut. 6:4) would have made this a very easy substitution. The Peshitta (syᵖ) lacks the phrase completely, perhaps considering it superfluous after κύριος ('the Lord'), while the pronoun is absent from Codex Vaticanus and some secondary sources (ὁ θεός, 'God'; 03 etc.): this is likely to be an oversight or possibly editorial deletion in the light of the numerous surrounding pronouns. See also the following unit.

3:25   τοὺς πατέρας ὑμῶν (your ancestors) ◆

As in the previous unit, the alternation between the first-person and second-person plural pronouns reflects their identical pronunciation in later Greek. In the context of numerous second-person plurals, the first-person τοὺς πατέρας ἡμῶν ('our ancestors'; 01* 04 05 044 0165 etc.) may seem to be the harder reading despite appearing in the majority of witnesses. However, the first-person version of this phrase is far more common in the New Testament (e.g. Acts 3:13, seven occurrences in Acts 7) and is therefore the form to which assimilation is more likely, especially given the frequency of itacism. There is strong early support for τοὺς πατέρας ὑμῶν ('your ancestors'; 𝔓⁷⁴ 01² 02 03 08 etc.). In the ECM there is a split guiding line, indicating that either reading could be original, although SBLGNT and THGNT both prefer ὑμῶν here.

4:8   πρεσβύτεροι (elders) {B}

The majority of witnesses read πρεσβύτεροι τοῦ Ἰσραήλ ('elders of Israel'; 05 08 044 33 614 etc.: see further *TuT Acts* TS16). This appears to have been introduced in order to balance the previous unit, 'rulers of the people' (which contains the customary complement for 'elders' seen in Matt. 21:23, 26:3, 27:1 etc.). There is no obvious reason for its omission or deletion, and good early attestation of the shorter reading πρεσβύτεροι ('elders'; 𝔓⁷⁴ 01 02 03 etc., lat^{vl-pt, vg} co^{sa, bo} eth Cyril).

4:25 ὁ τοῦ πατρὸς ἡμῶν διὰ πνεύματος ἁγίου στόματος Δαυὶδ παιδός σου εἰπών (**who said by the Holy Spirit through our ancestor David, your servant**) {C}

Unusually, the majority of Greek manuscripts have the shortest reading, ὁ διὰ στόματος Δαυὶδ παιδός σου εἰπών ('who said through the mouth of David your servant'; [18] 181 [330] 614 etc.: a significant proportion of Byzantine witnesses include τοῦ before παιδός, as indicated in *TuT Acts* TS17). Codex Bezae reads ὃς διὰ πνεύματος ἁγίου διὰ τοῦ στόματος λαλήσας Δαυὶδ παιδός σου ('who, through the Holy Spirit, spoke through the mouth of David your servant'; 05 lat^{vl-pt} sy^p). Both these forms are far smoother than the text found in most majuscules, ὁ τοῦ πατρὸς ἡμῶν διὰ πνεύματος ἁγίου στόματος Δαυὶδ παιδός σου εἰπών (lit. 'you of our father who spoke through the Holy Spirit of the mouth of David your servant'; 𝔓⁷⁴ 01 02 03 08 044 etc.). There are several problems with this: the syntax is confusing, as it is unclear whether τοῦ goes with πατρός ('father') or is part of a longer construction and whether διά ('through') only qualifies πνεύματος ἁγίου ('holy spirit') or is also connected to στόματος ('mouth'). Furthermore, the concept of God speaking 'through' rather than 'as' the Holy Spirit is only found here in the New Testament (cf. Heb. 3:7, 10:15) and raises a theological question. It is unlikely that such confusing additions were introduced into the shorter text, and surprising that this difficult form is consistently transmitted by excellent sources. Various explanations have been proposed (including an Aramaic source and an authorial revision misinterpreted by copyists), but the CBGM has been unable to shed further light on this complicated verse.[10] Westcott and Hort marked this verse as a 'primitive error' and it has been described as 'one of the most impossible clauses in the entire Book of Acts':[11] it will be necessary to sup-

---

[10] See further the *ECM Acts* Textual Commentary and Strutwolf 2014: 260–267; other explanations in Metzger 1994: 279–281.

[11] Dibelius quoted in Fitzmyer 1998: 308.

ply words or rearrange the text in order to make sense in translation, although most translations agree on the basic meaning of this phrase.

5:3   ἐπλήρωσεν (filled) {B}

The overwhelming external evidence is for the reading ἐπλήρωσεν ('filled [your heart]'; $\mathfrak{P}^8$ 01² 02 03 05 etc.). There are several poorly-attested alternatives, such as ἐπείρασεν ('tempted'; $\mathfrak{P}^{74}$ lat[vl-pt, vg]) and ἐπήρωσεν ('maimed'; 01* 330) which may be a misreading of ἐπλήρωσεν. All of these appear to be later developments which reflect the negative context of the phrase. Even so, the editorial text (with Satan as agent) makes sufficiently good sense, even without the suggestion that 'to fill the heart' is a Hebrew idiom for 'to dare'.[12] Translators, however, may prefer to render 'filled your heart' with a more common idiom such as 'put it into your mind'.

5:24   ὅ τε στρατηγός (the captain) {B}

The majority of Greek manuscripts read ὅ τε ἱερεὺς καὶ ὁ στρατηγός ('the priest and the captain'; 044 33 181 etc.), while the Laudian Acts and some Old Latin witnesses have οἵ τε ἱερεῖς καὶ ὁ στρατηγός ('the priests and the captain'; 08 lat[vl-pt]). The introduction of another person seems to be assimilation to Acts 5:17 and 21, where the high priest comes first in the list: whoever was responsible for this appears to have overlooked the mention of 'the chief priests' in this verse after 'the captain of the temple'. Not only does the shorter reading ὅ τε στρατηγός ('the captain') avoid repetition but it also has strong attestation ($\mathfrak{P}^{74}$ 01 02 03 05 etc.). The *ECM Acts* Textual Commentary notes that despite the better coherence of the majority reading, transcriptional probability supports the shorter text; the full attestation in Greek manuscripts is seen in *TuT Acts* (TS21).

5:28   οὐ παραγγελίᾳ παρηγγείλαμεν (lit. did we not give you strict orders) ◆

This direct speech appears as a question in the majority of manuscripts, with an initial οὐ ('did we not [give you strict orders]?'; 01² 05 08 [044] 181 etc.). However, the interrogative is missing from some early wit-

---

[12] Metzger 1994: 285–286.

nesses ($\mathfrak{P}^{74}$ 01* 02 03 1175 etc.). This could be an oversight, but it makes for a harder reading following the verb ἐπηρώτησεν ('he questioned') in the previous verse. In the ECM, there is a split guiding line, indicating that either form may be original. Nevertheless, a number of commentators consider οὐ as a later addition (see the *ECM Acts* Textual Commentary) and it is absent from the SBLGNT and THGNT. The longer text continues to be printed here as it was the form found in UBS5. If οὐ is not included, then the speech must be translated as a rebuke ('we gave you strict orders…'); there is a corresponding split line of punctuation in the ECM at the end of the clause.

5:32 ἐσμεν μάρτυρες (we are witnesses) ◆

A few witnesses reverse the order of these words, reading μάρτυρές ἐσμεν (lit. 'witnesses are we'; 02 1409 lat$^{vl\text{-}pt,\,vg\text{-}ms}$) but translation is unaffected. More significant is the inclusion of the pronoun in ἐσμεν αὐτοῦ μάρτυρες ('we are his witnesses'; 05² 08 [044] and the majority of minuscules). In context, this is an unwieldy double genitive (lit. 'we are his witnesses of these words'). The reading ἐν αὐτῷ ἐσμεν μάρτυρες ('in him we are witnesses'; 1739 co$^{bo\text{-}ms}$) may be an attempt to improve this: Codex Vaticanus is related to this but omits ἐσμεν ('we are') through oversight. Similarly, ἐσμεν μάρτυρες ('we are witnesses'; $\mathfrak{P}^{74vid}$ 01 05* 181 614 etc.) could be a deletion leading to a smoother reading, but has strong external attestation. If this were the original reading, the addition of αὐτοῦ would be assimilation to earlier instances of μάρτυρες preceded by a genitive (e.g. Acts 1:8, 2:32, 3:15). A split guiding line in the ECM indicates that either ἐσμεν μάρτυρες or ἐσμεν αὐτοῦ μάρτυρες could be the initial text (see also the *ECM Acts* Textual Commentary).

5:33 ἐβουλεύοντο (lit. were plotting) {B}

The majority of manuscripts read ἐβουλεύοντο ('were plotting'; 01 05 33? 181 307 etc.), which has been adopted as the initial text in the ECM. The principal alternative is ἐβούλοντο ('wanted'; 02 03 08 044 etc.), which is also widely attested among minuscules, while a few manuscripts have the aorist ἐβουλεύσαντο ('plotted' or 'decided'; 33? 1175 1241 1409; the reading of $\mathfrak{P}^{74}$ is unclear). The verb βουλεύω ('plot') is used elsewhere in the context of killing (ἐβουλεύσαντο in John 11:53,

12:10), which might have prompted its introduction here: βούλομαι ('wish') is semantically weaker, but more frequently used in Acts. The deciding factor is the genealogical coherence in the CBGM for ἐβουλεύοντο, whose attestation is entirely coherent in contrast to that of ἐβούλοντο, which appears to have arisen from the other reading on several occasions. This may have been through assimilation to the more common verb or simply the accidental omission of the two letters which distinguish the two forms.

5:37 λαόν (people) {A}

There is strong early support for the shortest form adopted in the editorial text, λαόν ('people'; 𝔓⁷⁴ 01 02* 03 etc.). The alternative readings include an adjective in different places, which is typical of later additions to enhance the narrative. The majority of Greek manuscripts read λαὸν ἱκανόν ('numerous people'; 02ᶜ 0140 307 1409 etc.); others have ἱκανὸν λαόν (also 'numerous people'; 08 044 33 181 etc.) or λαὸν πολύν ('many people'; 04 05 [coˢᵃ⁻ᵐˢˢ, ᵐᵃᵉ] [eth]).

5:39 αὐτούς (them) {A}

The variation reported here is between αὐτούς ('them'; 𝔓⁷⁴ 01 02 03 04² etc.) and the majority reading αὐτό ('it'; 04*ᵛⁱᵈ 623 1409 1739ᶜ etc.). The former has to be taken with ἀνθρώπων ('humans') towards the beginning of the previous verse; the latter appears to be a grammatical improvement in order to match the immediately preceding singular subject. Although there is a possibility that αὐτούς was introduced through assimilation to verse 38 ('let them alone'), the internal considerations and external attestation lead to its adoption as the editorial text. It is worth observing that this term is followed by a 'Western' reading which appears to combine material from Wisdom 12:13 with a repetition of the previous warning. Codex Bezae reads οὔτε ὑμεῖς οὔτε βασιλεῖς οὔτε τύραννοι· ἀπέχεσθε οὖν ἀπὸ τῶν ἀνθρώπων τούτων ('neither you, nor kings, nor tyrants; so keep away from these people'; 05 latᵛˡ⁻ᵖᵗ [syʰ* coᵐᵃᵉ]). Other manuscripts only have one of these elements, demonstrating the flexibility with which such expansions were handled. The Laudian Acts read οὔτε ὑμεῖς οὔτε οἱ ἄρχοντες ὑμῶν ('neither you nor your leaders'; 08 latᵛˡ⁻ᵖᵗ), replacing τύραννοι (a word not found in the New Testament) with ἄρχοντες, even though this speech is being addressed to the Jewish leaders (cf. Acts 5:34). One minuscule has ἀπόσχεσθε οὖν ἀπὸ τῶν ἀνδρῶν τούτων ('so keep away from these men'; 614), providing the expected imperative before the following μήποτε ('in case') by rephrasing the command in Acts 5:38 (cf. 1 Tim. 6:5).[13]

6:8 χάριτος (grace) {A}

Instead of χάριτος ('grace'; 𝔓[8] 𝔓[45] 𝔓[74] 01 02 03 05 etc.), the majority of Greek manuscripts read πίστεως ('faith'; 424* *Byz* sy[h] etc.). This is a simple assimilation to the phrase πλήρης πίστεως ('full of faith') in the description of Stephen three verses earlier. Two conflated forms are found in majuscule manuscripts: χάριτος καὶ πίστεως ('grace and faith'; 08 lat[vl-pt]) and πίστεως χάριτος πνεύματος ('faith, grace, spirit' [cf. Acts 6:5]; 044). The full attestation in Greek manuscripts is seen in *TuT Acts* (TS23).[14]

7:16 ἐν Συχέμ (in Shechem) {C}

The narrative has conflated two episodes from the Jewish Scriptures: Jacob and his relatives were buried in a tomb purchased by Abraham, but in Machpelah (Gen. 23:3–20, 49:31, 50:13), while Joseph was buried in a plot purchased by Jacob from the sons of Hamor, the father of Shechem, in Shechem (Gen. 33:19, Josh. 24:32). The majority of Greek manuscripts read τοῦ Συχέμ ('of Shechem'; 𝔓[74] 05 044 etc.), reflecting the description in the Septuagint, although as Hamor was Shechem's father it is preferable to take this as a geographical indication rather than a patronymic. The reading ἐν Συχέμ ('in Shechem'; 𝔓[33] 01* 03 04 etc.) is looser, corresponding to the standard use of Shechem as a place name both in the Jewish Scriptures and earlier in the verse. It is difficult to decide whether this is an early adjustment towards the more common use, or part of the original looseness of the narrative which was corrected by a later editor. The reading τοῦ ἐν Συχέμ ('who was in Shechem'; 01[2] 02 08 etc.) appears to be a simple conflation of the two forms and could support either reading. The continued preference for ἐν Συχέμ in the ECM is because all the texts with τοῦ Συχέμ are

---

[13] Hyytiäinen 2019: 12–17 offers an analysis of this variant with reference to the CBGM, suggesting that the reading in Codex Bezae is a combination of the shorter additions.

[14] This variant is discussed at greater length in Metzger & Ehrman 2005: 317–319.

posterior to those with ἐν Συχέμ, even though the coherence of the latter is not perfect: it seems that it was reintroduced into the tradition from the conflated form. It is also adopted in the SBLGNT and THGNT.

7:17 ὡμολόγησεν (made) {B}

The majority of Greek manuscripts read ὤμοσεν ('swore'; 044 81 181 614 etc.), but this makes for an unusual collocation with ἐπαγγελία ('promise') rather than ὅρκος ('oath'; cf. Acts 2:30, Luke 1:73). Early witnesses support ὡμολόγησεν (lit. 'agreed'; 𝔓⁷⁴ 01 02 03 04 etc., lat^{vl-pt, vg} co^{sa}), but this too sits oddly with 'promise'. The alternative ἐπηγγείλατο ('promised'; 𝔓⁴⁵ 05 08 lat^{vl-pt, vg-ms} sy^{p, hmg} co^{mae} eth), reproducing the same root as the noun, indicates that there was early dissatisfaction with the verb and thereby implies that one of the two other readings is original. The priority of ὡμολόγησεν is supported both by internal and external evidence, because it is more likely that the verb 'swear' would have been introduced in the context of God and Abraham (cf. Luke 1:73, Heb. 6:13), perhaps through inattention given the initial similarity of the two words. Alternatively, the technical Christian use of ὁμολογεῖν to mean 'make a confession' may have led to its replacement here. The full attestation in Greek manuscripts is seen in *TuT Acts* (TS25).

7:18 ἐπ' Αἴγυπτον (over Egypt) ◆

These two words are present in the source of this quotation at Exod. 1:8 in the Septuagint, but, surprisingly, are missing from most Greek manuscripts here (05 08 81 424* etc.). If the shorter form were the original reading, it would be unsurprising if an early editor had supplemented it with ἐπ' Αἴγυπτον ('over Egypt'; 𝔓³³vid 𝔓⁷⁴ 01 02 03 04 etc.). On the other hand, despite the verbatim agreement with the Septuagint, it is not obvious from the context that this is a quotation: given the explicit mention of Egypt as the location at the end of the previous verse, it is possible that this instance was deleted as repetition. The ECM has a split guiding line between these two variants, observing in the *ECM Acts* Textual Commentary that the attestation of the shorter reading is coherent but the longer reading has more support in early witnesses. The longer form is adopted by the SBLGNT and THGNT.

7:38 ἡμῖν (to us) {B}

As at Acts 3:22 and 3:25, both first- and second-person pronouns are attested here and would have sounded identical through itacism. The majority of external evidence supports the first-person ἡμῖν ('to us'; 02 04 05 08 044 etc.), but there is early and weighty support for ὑμῖν ('to you'; 𝔓⁷⁴ 01 03 307 1409 etc.). The latter is the more difficult reading after the preceding first person: in context, too, it seems to conflict with Stephen's rhetorical strategy of identifying with his Jewish audience (except, of course, in Acts 7:51–53). In contrast, the CBGM indicates that more changes occurred here from ἡμῖν to ὑμῖν than in the opposite direction, which has been taken to support the first person here.

7:46 οἴκῳ (house) ◆

The reading οἴκῳ ('house'; 𝔓⁷⁴ 01* 03 05 lat^{vl-pt} co^{sa-ms}) is by far the harder form. Not only is this verse a reference to Psalm 132:5 [131:5 LXX], which reads 'find a dwelling place for the God of Jacob' (εὕρω ... σκήνωμα τῷ θεῷ Ἰακώβ), but the idea of finding a 'dwelling place' for a house is problematic, not least because the following verse has a literal use of οἶκος preceded by the pronoun αὐτῷ ('for him', although 'for it' is also possible). Furthermore, the contrast to this statement two verses later has God as the subject ('the Most High'). According to the CBGM, the attestation for θεῷ ('God'; 01² 02 04 08 044 etc.) is perfectly coherent, as noted in the *ECM Acts* Textual Commentary. Nevertheless, the ECM has a split guiding line, indicating uncertainty as to the earliest form: οἴκῳ is much more likely to have been corrected towards θεῷ. It is possible that οἴκῳ was introduced through inattention, given the frequency in the Greek Bible of the formula 'house of Jacob' (cf. Luke 1:33; Ps. 114:1 [113:1 LXX]; Is. 14:1, 46:3, 48:1; Jer. 5:20). The similarity between the two words in majuscule script, especially if a *nomen sacrum* abbreviation were not used for God (ΟΙΚΩ and ΘΕΩ), could have contributed to their interchange; another factor might have been the presence of οἶκος or οἰκέω in each of the next three verses.[15] Both the SBLGNT and THGNT prefer the more plausible reading θεῷ.

---

[15] See Strutwolf 2014: 268–270.

8:5 τὴν πόλιν (the city) ◆

The majority of Greek manuscripts lack the definite article τήν, reading just πόλιν ('a city'; 04 05 08 044 etc.). This reading is historically preferable because, following the renaming of Samaria as Sebaste by Herod the Great, Samaria in the New Testament refers to a region rather than a city. It also fits with the description ἐν τῇ πόλει ἐκείνῃ ('in that city') three verses later. The longer phrase, τὴν πόλιν ('the city [of Samaria]'; 𝔓⁷⁴ 01 02 03 181 1175 Eusebius) is an anachronism or possibly a way of indicating 'the main city of Samaria' without naming it. Several potential cities are identified in commentaries. The CBGM indicates that there are several cases of the article being supplied independently, suggesting that copyists felt that an article was required: there is no other instance in Acts of εἰς πόλιν. The ECM has a split guiding line, allowing for either reading as original (see further the *ECM Acts* Textual Commentary).

8:10 καλουμένη (called) {A}

There is strong external support for the editorial text καλουμένη ('named'; 𝔓⁷⁴ 01 02ᵛⁱᵈ 03 04 05 08 etc.) even though it is unusual: the standard term λεγομένη ('called'; 614 syʰ) is likely to be a replacement for this. The majority of witnesses simply omit the word (044 307 etc.), which is an easier reading. As the participle καλούμενος is only used with proper nouns on the other twelve occasions it appears in Acts, μεγάλη too should be treated in this way (such as the capital on 'Great' in the NRSVue). It has been suggested that Μεγάλη was a transliteration of a Samaritan term meaning 'Revealer'.[16] The full attestation in Greek manuscripts is seen in *TuT Acts* (TS26).

8:37 *omit verse* {A}

The entire verse is lacking from the majority of manuscripts, although there is no obvious reason for accidental omission. It appears to be a 'Western' reading, motivated by a theological concern that baptism should be preceded by an explicit statement of faith (cf. Acts 2:41 above). The most widely attested form is εἶπεν δὲ αὐτῷ· εἰ πιστεύεις ἐξ ὅλης τῆς καρδίας σου, ἔξεστιν. ἀποκριθεὶς δὲ εἶπεν· πιστεύω τὸν υἱὸν τοῦ θεοῦ εἶναι Ἰησοῦν Χριστόν ('He said to him, "If you believe with all

---

[16] Klostermann 1883: 15–20.

your heart, you may." And he replied, "I believe that Jesus Christ is the Son of God."'; 307 1642 1739 *TR* lat[vl-pt, vg-mss] sy[h with *] co[mae]). It is worth noting that this reference to Jesus Christ departs from the standard practice in Acts of preceding this full name with 'in the name of' or 'Lord', although a baptismal confession could be a reasonable exception. The Laudian Acts have a different form, with a number of simplifications which are likely to be secondary: εἶπεν δὲ αὐτῷ ὁ Φίλιππος· ἐὰν πιστεύῃς ἐξ ὅλης τῆς καρδίας σου, σωθήσει. ἀποκριθεὶς δὲ εἶπεν· πιστεύω εἰς τὸν Χριστὸν τὸν υἱὸν τοῦ θεοῦ ('Philip said to him, "If you were to believe with all your heart, you will be saved." And he said in reply, "I believe in the Christ, the Son of God."'; 08 lat[vl-pt]). Other minor variations are noted in the ECM and *TuT Acts* (TS28). The early patristic evidence for the Ethiopian's confession of faith (Irenaeus, Cyprian) suggests that this variant goes back as far as the second century. Even though the verse is only present in a few witnesses and was lacking from Erasmus' main source, he inserted it in his text from the margin of another manuscript because he thought it had been omitted through oversight. This verse is therefore included in the *Textus Receptus* even though it is not part of the majority text.[17] See also the discussion of the next unit.

8:39 πνεῦμα κυρίου (the Spirit of the Lord) {A}

Most of the witnesses which include Acts 8:37 also have a longer reading here: πνεῦμα ἅγιον ἐπέπεσεν ἐπὶ τὸν εὐνοῦχον, ἄγγελος δὲ κυρίου ('the Holy Spirit fell upon the eunuch, while an angel of the Lord …'; 02[c] 307 1642 1739 lat[vl-pt] sy[h with *] co[mae]). Again the motivation for the expansion appears to be a theological concern to demonstrate the effectiveness of baptism: it also introduces a parallel with the intervention of 'the angel of the Lord' at the beginning of this episode (Acts 8:26). Although it is possible that the words were omitted by skipping from one *nomen sacrum* abbreviation to the next (ΠΝΑ to ΚΥ), or even deleted to avoid a conflict with Acts 8:15–18 where the gift of the Holy Spirit is connected with the laying-on of hands by the apostles, the external attestation confirms that it is secondary. The *Textus Receptus* and

---

[17] See further Metzger 1994: 315–316 and Wasserman 2023: 70–71, who considers it an addition due to liturgical influence. For the suggestion that the longer reading was deleted by a copyist, see Strange 1992a: 69–77.

the majority of manuscripts also support the short reading, πνεῦμα κυρίου ('the Spirit of the Lord'; 𝔓⁴⁵ 𝔓⁷⁴ 01 03 04 etc.; the full attestation is seen in *TuT Acts* TS29).

9:12 ἄνδρα (a man) {C}

There is early evidence for the shortest form, ἄνδρα ('a man'; 𝔓⁷⁴ 01 02 81 lat^{vl-pt, vg} co^{sa, bo} eth), while one manuscript reads only ἐν ὁράματι ('in a vision'; 044). The longer readings with their difference in sequence thus have the appearance of conflations, ἄνδρα ἐν ὁράματι ('a man in a vision'; 03 04 1175) and ἐν ὁράματι ἄνδρα ('in a vision a man'; 08 33 181 307 and the majority of minuscules). The former offers the more difficult sequence, with the noun separating the verb from its qualifier. If one of the longer readings was original, there would be the potential for ἄνδρα to be overlooked because of its initial similarity to Ἀνανίαν ('Ananias') and even for ὁράματι to be confused with the following ὀνόματι ('name'): accordingly, both SBLGNT and THGNT adopt ἄνδρα ἐν ὁράματι. Nevertheless, the ECM prefers the shortest reading, deeming that ἐν ὁράματι is more likely to have been added than omitted in the context of a vision (see the *ECM Acts* Textual Commentary). It is possible that an editor introduced it to qualify the use of εἶδεν ('he has seen') at a time when Saul was blind.

9:31 ἡ ... ἐκκλησία ... εἶχεν εἰρήνην οἰκοδομουμένη καὶ πορευομένη ... ἐπληθύνετο (the church ... had peace and was built up. Living ... it increased) {A}

The majority of Greek manuscripts have a plural throughout this verse, reading 'the churches' rather than 'the church' (αἱ ... ἐκκλησίαι ... εἶχον εἰρήνην οἰκοδομούμεναι καὶ πορευόμεναι ... ἐπληθύνοντο: 35^c 614 1409 etc.; see further *TuT Acts* TS31). As in Acts 8:37, there are numerous minor differences in the Laudian Acts, which emphasise the plural by reading 'all the churches' (αἱ ... ἐκκλησίαι πᾶσαι etc., 08: the masculine participles must be taken as a sense construction related to the members of the churches). This plurality of churches contrasts with the strong attestation of the singular ἡ ... ἐκκλησία ('the church ...' etc.; 𝔓⁷⁴ 01 02 03 04 etc.). While there might be a theological motivation behind a change describing the church as singular rather than plural, this variation is not seen at Acts 15:41 or 16:5. Rather, in the light of those later plurals and the multiple locations mentioned in this verse, it appears that the plural here was a subsequent alteration in order to reflect this multiplicity.

10:19 τρεῖς (three) {B}

The majority of Greek manuscripts do not specify the number of men searching for Peter (05 044 424* 614 623 etc.), even though three people are mentioned in Acts 10:7 and 11:11. There is good support for the inclusion of τρεῖς ('three'; 𝔓⁷⁴ 01 02 04 08 etc., along with most early translations). The external evidence suggests that τρεῖς was omitted, perhaps through homoeoteleuton with the preceding ἄνδρες ('men'), but the CBGM indicates that it was reintroduced on multiple occasions, perhaps in order to assimilate to the other verses. An intriguing variant, δύο ('two'; 03), appears in Codex Vaticanus alone. Commentators favouring this difficult reading have suggested that it refers just to the two servants mentioned in Acts 10:7 and not the soldier.[18] Alternatively, it could be that the numeral for three, Γ (with a line above to indicate that it was a number) was misread as Β ('2').

10:30 τὴν ἐνάτην (at three o'clock) {B}

The frequent collocation of 'fasting and prayer' (see also 1 Cor. 7:5) appears to have led to the majority reading νηστεύων καὶ τὴν ἐνάτην ὥραν (lit. 'fasting [and praying at] the ninth hour'; 044 307 614 etc.), from which some witnesses lack the final word (𝔓⁵⁰ 02ᶜ [05] [08] [181] etc.). This longer text makes more sense of the preceding phrase μέχρι ταύτης τῆς ὥρας (lit. 'until this very hour'). It is also possible that the detail about fasting was added to reflect Christian practice before baptism (cf. Acts 10:47 and the variant at Acts 8:37 above). There is good external evidence in favour of the shorter reading τὴν ἐνάτην ('[at] the ninth'; 𝔓⁷⁴ 01 02*ᵛⁱᵈ 03 04 81 1642* 1739 latᵛˡ⁻ᵖᵗ, ᵛᵍ coᵇᵒ eth) and no obvious reason for the omission of the additional words. Translators will probably need to clarify the expressions of time in this sentence.[19] The full attestation in Greek manuscripts is seen in *TuT Acts* (TS37).

---

[18] e.g. Ropes 1926. Elliott 1975: 145 prefers the shortest reading on the grounds that later tradition tended 'to make indefinite groups definite'.

[19] On the various challenges here (including the unexpected use of μέχρι), see Metzger 1994: 330–331 and Strutwolf 2014: 271–273.

10:32 θάλασσαν (the sea) {B}

The majority of witnesses include an extra phrase at the end of this verse, ὃς παραγενόμενος λαλήσει σοι ('who when he arrives will speak to you'; 𝔓127vid 04 05 08 044 etc.; the full attestation is seen in *TuT Acts* TS38). With strong support for the shorter reading (𝔓45 𝔓74 01 02 03 81 307 lat^(vl-pt, vg) co^(bo)) and no obvious cause for an omission, this has the better claim to be earlier: the longer text may be an anticipation of Acts 11:14. However, it remains possible that it might have been deleted by an earlier editor, perhaps because the relative ὅς technically relates to the preceding 'Simon the tanner' rather than Simon Peter.

10:36 ὅν (lit. which) {C}

The relative pronoun ὅν ('[the message] which'; 𝔓74 01* 04 05 08 044 and the majority of minuscules) is difficult to construe in context: it has to be taken in apposition to τὸ γενόμενον ῥῆμα in the following verse, which could be interpreted as 'the word which spread' or 'the event which happened' (cf. Luke 2:15). The shorter reading is attested by some important witnesses (01¹ 02 03 81 614 etc.), and it is easy to see how the unusual syntax, with the accusative object standing first, could have prompted the addition of the relative. At the same time, the transcriptional probability of a change in either direction is high: dittography of the last two letters of the preceding λόγον would lead to its insertion, while haplography would result in omission. The ECM prefers the longer reading because of its grammatical difficulty, as do the SBLGNT and THGNT.[20] With the relative pronoun, however, the verse has been described as 'so difficult as to be untranslateable'.[21] One possibility is that, after the interjection 'he is Lord of all', the author lost track of the originally intended construction. In translation, this may be resolved by providing the main verb from the next verse and transferring the relative to that clause (compare the NRSVue) or repeating the main verb; there is a further accusative at the beginning of Acts 10:38 ('Jesus of Nazareth') which could also form part of the same construction.

---

[20] The *ECM Acts* Textual Commentary on this variation unit is only available in the online interface; see also Strutwolf 2014: 273–275.

[21] Barrett 1994–98: 521.

10:40 τῇ τρίτῃ ἡμέρᾳ (on the third day) {C}

The editorial text, τῇ τρίτῃ ἡμέρᾳ ('on the third day'; 𝔓⁷⁴ 01² 02 03 05² etc.), is present in the majority of witnesses and is the more common form of this phrase in the New Testament (see *ECM Acts* Textual Commentary). A few manuscripts have ἐν τῇ τρίτῃ ἡμέρᾳ ('on the third day'; 01* 04): not only is the preposition unnecessary, but it could simply have arisen through dittography of the last two letters of the preceding word (ἤγειρεν, 'raised'): the multiple emergence of this reading indicated by the CBGM is consistent with this scenario. Codex Bezae has μετὰ τὴν τρίτην ἡμέραν ('after the third day'; 05* lat^vl-pt): this could be a literal reflection of the Latin *post tertium diem* or assimilation to the more common form of this phrase in the Gospels (e.g. Matt. 27:63).

11:20 Ἑλληνιστάς (Hellenists) {B}

Acts appears to be the first work in which the noun Ἑλληνιστής ('Hellenist') is found, and there are debates as to its meaning: it could signify 'Greek-speaking', 'Greek converts' or 'those following Greek practices'. In later Christian literature, it has the meaning of 'pagan', but it clearly refers to members of the Church at Acts 6:1 where it is contrasted with Ἑβραῖοι ('Hebrews'). The word Ἑλληνιστάς is well attested both at Acts 9:29 and here ([01*] 03 05² 08 044 and the majority of minuscules), although on these two occasions it does not refer to believers in Christ. The variant Ἕλληνας ('Greeks'; 𝔓⁷⁴ 01² 02 05* Chrysostom^ms) seems to be a replacement with a more common form, possibly through inattention: the CBGM indicates that it happened at least twice independently. The visual appearance of the word also gave rise to a copying error by the first hand of Codex Sinaiticus, with the reading εὐαγγελίστας ('evangelists'), probably also influenced by the following participle. If the technical 'Hellenists' is seen as too specialist a term in translation, then 'Greeks' or 'gentiles' would be adequate.[22]

12:25 εἰς Ἰερουσαλήμ (to Jerusalem) {C}

The majority of Greek manuscripts have εἰς Ἰερουσαλήμ ('to Jerusalem'; 01 03 81 623ᶜ etc.) even though this is the hardest reading in context:

---

[22] See the lengthy discussion at Metzger 1994: 340–342.

Barnabas and Saul arrived in Jerusalem in Acts 11:30, so at this point they should be leaving it. The expected direction is seen in ἀπὸ Ἰερουσαλήμ ('from Jerusalem'; 05 044 181 307 etc.) and ἐξ Ἰερουσαλήμ ('out of Jerusalem'; 𝔓⁷⁴ 02 33 etc.): some witnesses with these prepositions also include εἰς Ἀντιόχειαν ('to Antioch'; 08 424ᶜ 1175 1739 etc.). The full attestation in Greek manuscripts is seen in *TuT Acts* (TS42), which shows the large groupings for the different readings. Not only does the presence of two synonymous alternatives suggest that they are secondary, but these readings also contrast with the use of ὑποστρέφειν ('return') elsewhere in Acts: the place of departure is only specified at Acts 1:12 (contrast Acts 8:25, 13:13, 14:21, 22:17 etc.). One way of making sense of the majority reading is to construe it with the following clause rather than the previous verb, thus referring to 'the ministry to Jerusalem'. This could be achieved by conjecturing an initial τήν before εἰς or simply inserting a comma in the same place.[23] The unexpected presence of ἐξ Ἰερουσαλήμ in the *Textus Receptus* explains the use of 'from Jerusalem' in many translations despite its difference from the majority of manuscripts.

13:18 ἐτροποφόρησεν (he put up with) {B}

While most witnesses read ἐτροποφόρησεν ('he put up with'; 01 03 04² 05 etc.), a significant minority have ἐτροφοφόρησεν ('he cared for'; 𝔓⁷⁴ 02 04* 08 etc.). The same variation is found in the Septuagint at Deut. 1:31, to which this passage refers. In the context of Paul's positive presentation of God's relationship with the Israelites, ἐτροποφόρησεν is the harder reading, yet it is present in the majority of manuscripts and is also coherently attested (unlike the multiple emergence of ἐτροφοφόρησεν). For this reason, it has been adopted as the initial text (see also the *ECM Acts* Textual Commentary).

13:20 ὡς ἔτεσιν τετρακοσίοις καὶ πεντήκοντα. καὶ μετὰ ταῦτα (for about four hundred and fifty years. After that) {B}

The reading of the majority of manuscripts, καὶ μετὰ ταῦτα ὡς ἔτεσιν τετρακοσίοις καὶ πεντήκοντα ('And after that, for about four hundred

---

[23] *Amsterdam Database* cj10635 [Westcott & Hort 1881] and the SBLGNT respectively. Further discussion is available in the *ECM Acts* Textual Commentary, a lengthy note in Metzger 1994: 350–352 and Strutwolf 2014: 275–277.

and fifty years'; 05² 08 044 623 etc.) expresses the period as that of the judges, corresponding to the reckoning in Josephus (*Antiquities* 8.3.1). There is strong early support for the reading adopted in the editorial text, ὡς ἔτεσιν τετρακοσίοις καὶ πεντήκοντα. καὶ μετὰ ταῦτα ('for about four hundred and fifty years. And after that'; 𝔓⁷⁴ 01 02 03 04 33 etc.): this is also more difficult in that, by setting the time as Israel's presence in Canaan, the calculation only makes sense if it includes the events already mentioned in Acts 13:17–18. The majority reading appears to have been introduced in order to avoid the superficial (and erroneous) interpretation of the span of four hundred and fifty years as the time it took Joshua to divide the land (i.e. Acts 13:19 only), which would be nonsensical. The same concern seems to underlie the text of Codex Bezae, καὶ ἕως ἔτεσιν τετρακοσίοις καὶ πεντήκοντα ('and for four hundred and fifty years'; 05* lat^{vl-pt}). The poorly-attested ἔτεσιν τετρακοσίοις καὶ πεντήκοντα καί ('for four hundred and fifty years, and'; 614 sy^p co^{sa-ms}) probably arose through misinterpreting a correction of μετὰ ταῦτα between the two principal variants. The full attestation in Greek manuscripts is seen in *TuT Acts* (TS43). Translators who divide this long sentence into smaller units should be careful to avoid the implication that the temporal cause only relates to Acts 13:19.

13:26 ἡμῖν (to us) ◆

As noted above (Acts 3:22, 7:38), the sound change known as itacism resulted in the first- and second-person plural pronouns being pronounced identically, leading to their interchange in the textual tradition. The balance of early evidence favours ἡμῖν ('to us'; 𝔓⁷⁴ 01 02 03 05 etc.), while the majority of Greek manuscripts have ὑμῖν ('to you'; 𝔓⁴⁵ 04 08 181 307 etc.). It is possible that the first person was assimilated to the second person following ἐν ὑμῖν in the previous clause, but the change could have been made in the opposite direction in order to avoid separating Paul from his audience: the attestation of ἡμῖν is incoherent. For this reason, the ECM has a split guiding line, indicating that either pronoun could be the initial text, although in context ἡμῖν seems preferable (thus also the SBLGNT and THGNT). If this is adopted, translators may need to decide whether this is an exclusive or inclusive use of the first-person plural: its appearance in Acts 13:32 (which also supports the adoption of the first person here) suggests that it was intended exclusively.[24]

13:33   ἡμῖν (for us) {D}

There is very strong early support for ἡμῶν ('[for] our [children]'; 𝔓[74] 01 02 03 04* 05 etc.), yet it is a difficult reading in context: if the promise was made to the fathers (Acts 13:32), then its fulfilment to 'our children' (rather than 'their children') is unexpected. The majority of Greek manuscripts read αὐτῶν ἡμῖν ('for us, their [children]'; 04[3] 08 33 81 181 etc.), and there is also some support for αὐτῶν by itself ('[for] their [children]'; 1175 lat[vl-pt] co[bo]). These are both smoother readings which are likely to be secondary, not least as it is hard to see how either could have given rise to ἡμῶν. Dissatisfaction with the sense given by ἡμῶν has led to numerous conjectures, including ἡμῖν, the text adopted in the ECM ('for us [children]'), which gives the more expected sense of Paul's self-identification with the inheritors of the promise (cf. Acts 2:39).[25] In earlier hand editions, the brackets in [αὐτῶν] ἡμῖν obscured the fact that there was no manuscript support for ἡμῖν by itself; claims that αὐτῶν ἡμῖν represents a conflation of two early readings are not supported by any evidence (see the full attestation in *TuT Acts* TS44). Nonetheless, an early scribal error which turned the ethic dative ἡμῖν ('for us [children]') into a more expected genitive ἡμῶν ('for our [children]') is plausible. Another conjecture is that no pronoun was originally present (matching 'fathers' in the previous verse, attested here by co[bo-pt] eth), and scribal inattentiveness led to the introduction of ἡμῶν through assimilation to Acts 2:39.[26] If ἡμῖν is adopted (with or without αὐτῶν), it is also possible to read it as an indirect object of the following clause: 'by raising Jesus for us'. On the other hand, ἡμῶν by itself is not completely implausible, given the reference to 'my son' in the following Psalm quotation: there are few parallels to this observation in Acts, and the skipping of a generation could be seen as a rhetorical device to provoke the audience into a decision (cf. Acts 13:40). Although THGNT has the majority reading αὐτῶν ἡμῖν, the adoption of ἡμῶν in the

---

[24] However, Omanson 2006: 251 prefers an inclusive form in the present verse.

[25] *Amsterdam Database* cj10092 [Bornemann 1848]; see also Westcott and Hort 1896: II.95.

[26] *Amsterdam Database* cj10863 [van de Sande Bakhuyzen 1880].

SBLGNT suggests that the objections raised in commentaries (including the *ECM Acts* Textual Commentary) are not insuperable.[27]

13:42 αὐτῶν (lit. they) {A}

The shortest reading, adopted in the editorial text as part of the genitive absolute ἐξιόντων δὲ αὐτῶν ('as they went out'), has excellent external support ($\mathfrak{P}^{74}$ 01 02 03 04 05 08 etc. and all early versions). However, as neither the subject of this clause nor the subject of the main verb is made explicit, the Byzantine tradition is split between two expansions intended to clarify this (see also the next variation unit). The pronoun αὐτῶν by itself refers to Paul and Barnabas (cf. Acts 13:16, 46), who are differentiated from their audience in the reading αὐτῶν ἐκ τῆς συναγωγῆς τῶν Ἰουδαίων ('[as] they [went] out of the synagogue of the Jews'; 623^c 1241 1409 etc.). However, many manuscripts as well as the *Textus Receptus* lack the pronoun, resulting in a change of subject: ἐκ τῆς συναγωγῆς τῶν Ἰουδαίων ('[as] the Jews [went] out of the synagogue'; 1 18 35^c 330 398 etc.; see *TuT Acts* TS46). This has to be read in conjunction with the alternative subject of παρεκάλουν (see below). Translators will need to expand the pronoun to resolve the confusion; its omission (1642*) is a nonsense reading.

13:42 παρεκάλουν εἰς τὸ μεταξὺ σάββατον (they urged … the next Sabbath) {B}

The majority of minuscules include an explicit subject for the main verb, reading παρεκάλουν τὰ ἔθνη εἰς τὸ μεταξὺ σάββατον ('the gentiles urged [them to speak] on the next Sabbath'; 35^c 424* 623^c 1409 etc.). This is clearly secondary, and largely depends on identifying the subject of the preceding genitive absolute as 'the Jews' (see the previous unit), although it is supported by Acts 13:44–45. There is good external evidence for the reading adopted as the editorial text, παρεκάλουν εἰς τὸ μεταξὺ σάββατον ('they urged [them to speak] on the next Sabbath'; $\mathfrak{P}^{74}$ 01 02 04 044 etc.), but two early majuscules have synonyms: in Codex Bezae, μεταξύ ('between', but commonly understood as 'next') is replaced by the more correct word ἑξῆς ('following'; 05); in Codex Vaticanus, the verb παρεκάλουν ('they urged') is absent and instead ἠξίουν

---

[27] See also the extensive discussion in Glover 2020.

('they requested'; 03 co^bo) is found after σάββατον, possibly because the original verb had been omitted through oversight (as in 08 lat^vl-pt). As the subject of παρεκάλουν in Greek is clearly different to that of the preceding genitive absolute, it will be helpful to supply a noun in translation.

13:44 τὸν λόγον τοῦ κυρίου (the word of the Lord) {C}

The majority of witnesses have τὸν λόγον τοῦ θεοῦ ('the word of God'; 03* 04 08 044 etc.). However, there is strong support for τὸν λόγον τοῦ κυρίου ('the word of the Lord'; 𝔓^74 01 02 03^2 33 etc.). Both phrases occur frequently in Acts, often with textual variation, which could also be prompted by misreading the *nomen sacrum* (ΘΥ or ΚΥ; see also the following unit). The CBGM indicates that, whichever reading is preferred, the variant arose more than once: κυρίου is preferred here on the basis of its attestation in witnesses related to the initial text, and also adopted in SBLGNT and THGNT. There is also a 'Western' reading which offers a pedantic correction: to avoid the possible interpretation that the speaker was 'the Lord', it reads Παύλου πολύν τε λόγον ποιησαμένου περὶ τοῦ κυρίου ('[to hear] Paul making a great speech about the Lord'; 05 lat^vl-pt co^mae).

13:48 τὸν λόγον τοῦ κυρίου (the word of the Lord) {B}

On this occasion, most Greek manuscripts support τὸν λόγον τοῦ κυρίου ('the word of the Lord'; 𝔓^45 𝔓^74 01 02 04 etc.). The alternative, τὸν λόγον τοῦ θεοῦ ('the word of God'; 03 05 08 lat^vl-pt co^sa-ms, bo, mae) may seem to be harder in context, given the use of 'Lord' before the previous quotation and in the following verse, but it is also possible that it was introduced because the scriptural quotation was understood generically as 'the word of God'. Not only is there good early evidence for the majority reading, but its attestation is coherent, unlike the alternative, which seems to have emerged on several occasions. This is the only occurrence in the New Testament of the phrase 'to praise the word of the Lord/God', and its rarity prompted a few adjustments to more common forms: Codex Bezae has ἐδέξαντο ('they received') rather than ἐδόξαζον ('they began to praise'), while other witnesses simply read τὸν θεόν ('[they began to praise] God'; 614 sy) or τὸν κύριον ('the Lord'; lat^vl-pt).

14:25   τὸν λόγον (the word) {B}

Unusually, the majority of manuscripts have the shortest reading, with just τὸν λόγον ('the word'; 03 05 307 1175 1739 etc.). Other early witnesses have τὸν λόγον τοῦ κυρίου ('the word of the Lord'; 01 02 04 044 etc.) or τὸν λόγον τοῦ θεοῦ ('the word of God'; 𝔓[74] 08 lat[vl-pt] co[bo-ms]). The expansions to the fuller forms found elsewhere (see Acts 13:44 and 48 above) are an obvious secondary development, with nothing in context which would have prompted an omission leading to the shorter reading. In translation, it may be necessary to expand the noun to make its reference clear.

15:17-18   ταῦτα γνωστὰ ἀπ' αἰῶνος (these things known from long ago) {B}

The quotation from Amos 9:11-12 ends with ταῦτα ('these things'), and it is not clear whether the rest of the text is intended to be a broader scriptural reference (possibly inspired by Isaiah 45:21) which continues the quotation, or an addition by the speaker. There is strong external evidence for the shortest form, adopted as the editorial text, ταῦτα γνωστὰ ἀπ' αἰῶνος ('these things known from long ago'; 01 03 04 044 33 81 1175 co). The brevity of this text, and perhaps an awareness that it was not part of the Old Testament source, appears to have led to several expansions. Two manuscripts read ταῦτα πάντα γνωστὰ ἀπ' αἰῶνος ('all these things known from long ago'; 307 1739). A similar explanation of the sense of γνωστά, but with the addition separated from the quotation, is seen in both ταῦτα· γνωστὸν ἀπ' αἰῶνος τῷ κυρίῳ τὸ ἔργον αὐτοῦ ('these things. Known to the Lord from long ago is his work'; 𝔓[74] 02 [05] 1642 etc.) and ταῦτα· γνωστὰ ἀπ' αἰῶνος τῷ κυρίῳ πάντα τὰ ἔργα ('these things. Known to the Lord from long ago are all the works'; 1409). The majority of manuscripts have the longest text, combining elements from each other variant: ταῦτα πάντα· γνωστὰ ἀπ' αἰῶνός ἐστιν τῷ θεῷ πάντα τὰ ἔργα αὐτοῦ ('all these things. Known from long ago to God are all his works'; [08 181] 614 623 etc.). This verse therefore serves as an illustration of the tendency to expand the text in various ways, with no fewer than twenty-three different forms of Acts 15:18 in the ECM and twenty-four alternatives (with further subdivisions) in *TuT Acts* (TS50).

15:20 τῆς πορνείας καὶ τοῦ πνικτοῦ καὶ τοῦ αἵματος (from sexual immorality and from whatever has been strangled and from blood) {B}

This is the first instance of the Apostolic Decree, which is formally given at Acts 15:29 and also set out at Acts 21:25 (see below). On all three occasions, the editorial text comprises four elements, but in a different sequence. However, manuscripts contain a variety of readings, either reflecting differences in Christian practice or simply caused by eyeskip between the individual elements. There is strong external evidence for the editorial text, supported by early witnesses as well as the majority of minuscules: the absence in some of these of the definite article before πνικτοῦ ('whatever has been strangled': 𝔓⁷⁴ 02 03 044 33 etc.) may be assimilation to the other instances of the list. Papyrus 45 lacks the second element in this verse, καὶ τῆς πορνείας ('from sexual immorality'): this appears simply to be an oversight, although in the context of instructions about dietary laws it may have been considered superfluous. The most obvious variation is the inclusion of a negative version of the so-called 'Golden Rule'. In GA 1739, this is combined with a reordering of the preceding elements, probably through assimilation to Acts 15:29 and 21:25: τοῦ αἵματος καὶ τοῦ πνικτοῦ καὶ τῆς πορνείας καὶ ὅσα ἂν μὴ θέλωσιν αὐτοῖς γίνεσθαι ἑτέροις μὴ ποιεῖν ('from blood and whatever has been strangled and from sexual immorality, and whatsoever they do not wish to happen to them, not to do to others'; 1739 [co^sa]). This is also seen in Codex Bezae, which reads τῆς πορνείας καὶ τοῦ αἵματος καὶ ὅσα μὴ θέλουσιν ἑαυτοῖς γίνεσθαι ἑτέροις μὴ ποιεῖτε ('from sexual immorality and from blood and what they do not wish to happen to themselves, do not do to others'; 05 lat^{vl-pt} Irenaeus^{lat}). The lack of reference to strangulation is consistent in these witnesses for all three instances of the Apostolic Decree (compare also some Old Latin witnesses which here support just the first five words). Although this might reflect an alteration by a Christian community in which there was no objection to eating animals killed by strangulation, the combination of this omission and the 'Golden Rule' turns the decree from a dietary law into a moral code: while strangulation can only be understood in terms of food, the references to idols, sexual immorality and blood may all be taken in a broader context.[28] There is nothing in context to prompt the omission or deletion of the negative rule, whose limited attestation is indicative of its being a later addition. The reference of πορνείας could be to sexual immorality in general or to forms of marriage forbidden under Jewish Law (e.g. Lev. 18). While the original sense of αἵματος here is likely to be eating blood (cf. Lev. 3:17), the Greek could also be understood as 'bloodshed': the latter seems to be the case in the reading of this as a moral code, yet it is possible that the consumption of blood was considered already to have been covered under the term πνικτοῦ ('whatever has been strangled').

15:23   ἀδελφοί (brothers[1]) {B}

The majority of Greek manuscripts read καὶ οἱ ἀδελφοί ('and the brothers'; [𝔓45] 01[2] 08 044 181 etc.), taking it as the third element in a list, following the apostles and elders. Even so, the identification of the separate group constituted by such 'brothers' is not obvious. The shorter reading, ἀδελφοί ('brothers'; 𝔓33 𝔓74 01* 02 03 etc.) has excellent external support and is also grammatically more difficult: it is in the wrong place to be qualified by πρεσβύτεροι ('the elder brothers', an adjectival use of πρεσβύτερος which is not seen elsewhere in Acts), so it has to be taken in apposition to the two previous terms as an indication of their shared faith ('the apostles and the elders, brothers [i.e. fellow believers] …'). The hardness of this reading (or possibly eyeskip) seems to have led to the omission of ἀδελφοί from some witnesses (co[sa] Origen[lat]).

15:24   τὰς ψυχὰς ὑμῶν (your minds) {A}

After these words, the majority of Greek manuscripts include an additional explanatory phrase, λέγοντες περιτέμνεσθαι καὶ τηρεῖν τὸν νόμον ('saying "You must be circumcised and keep the law"'; 04 [08] 044 181 307 etc.); one minuscule just has the addition of τηρεῖν τὸν νόμον at the end of the verse ('[we did not instruct] to keep the law'; 1175). The longest reading appears to be a typical 'Western' expansion, with content derived from Acts 15:1 and 15:5: the strong external evidence for the shorter reading (𝔓33 vid 𝔓45vid 𝔓74 01 02 03 05 33 81

---

[28] See further Epp 1966: 107–112, Strange 1992a: 87–105; Metzger 1994: 379–383; Barrett 1994–98: 730–736.

lat^(vl-pt, vg) co eth)—including, unusually, Codex Bezae—supports its authenticity.

15:29 καὶ πνικτῶν (and from what is strangled) ◆

The sequence of the elements in this formal declaration of the Apostolic Decree, quoted from the letter, differs from Acts 15:20 (see above) but is the same as Acts 21:25. As in those verses, this reference to strangled animals is absent from Codex Bezae and some Latin witnesses apparently as part of a deliberate reshaping of the dietary instructions into a moral code. Despite the singular noun in both other verses, also seen here in the majority of manuscripts as καὶ πνικτοῦ ('and from what is strangled'; $\mathfrak{P}^{74}$ 01² 02² 08 044 etc.), there are some important witnesses with the plural καὶ πνικτῶν ('and from things strangled'; 01* 02*vid 03 04 81 etc.). This seems to be the harder reading, although it may just be an assimilation to the genitive plural in the preceding εἰδωλοθύτων ('things sacrificed to idols'), possibly prompted by the lack of definite articles in this verse (unlike the two parallels). As the plural (adopted by SBLGNT and THGNT) has an incoherent attestation, the ECM has a split guiding line, allowing that either reading may be original.

15:29 καὶ πορνείας (and from sexual immorality) {A}

As at Acts 15:20 (see above) and 21:25, Codex Bezae and some other witnesses include a negative version of the 'Golden Rule' after the final element: καὶ ὅσα μὴ θέλετε ἑαυτοῖς γίνεσθαι ἑτέροις μὴ ποιεῖν ('and whatever you do not wish to happen to yourselves, do not do to others'; 05* [614 1739 lat^(vl-pt) sy^(h with *) co^(sa) eth Irenaeus^(lat)]). This is an early editorial expansion, as has been discussed above.

15:29 εὖ πράξετε (you will do well) {A}

The majority of manuscripts have the future indicative, εὖ πράξετε ('you will do well'; $\mathfrak{P}^{33}$ 01 02 03 044 etc.). Some witnesses have an aorist imperative, εὖ πράξατε ('do well'; $\mathfrak{P}^{74}$ 04 05 etc.) and others an aorist subjunctive, εὖ πράξητε ('may you do well'; 08 623), but these may have been introduced through assimilation to general epistolary formulae because they do not fit the context as well as the future. Codex Bezae and some Latin witnesses include an additional phrase after this, φερόμενοι ἐν τῷ ἁγίῳ πνεύματι ('carried in the Holy Spirit'; 05 lat^{vl-pt} etc.). The purpose of this is not clear, but it is clearly secondary.[29]

15:34   omit verse {A}

This sentence is absent from the majority of manuscripts, including many early witnesses ($\mathfrak{P}^{74}$ 01 02 03 08 etc.). It appears to have been added by an editor concerned with the discrepancy between Acts 15:32–33, in which Judas and Silas leave Antioch, and Acts 15:40, where Paul and Silas leave Antioch. The shorter form reads either ἔδοξεν δὲ τῷ Σιλᾷ ἐπιμεῖναι αὐτούς ('But it seemed good to Silas that they should stay'; 04) or ἔδοξεν δὲ τῷ Σιλᾷ ἐπιμεῖναι αὐτοῦ ('But it seemed good to Silas to stay there'; 33 [181] 307 614 etc.). The latter is also found in the *Textus Receptus*, hence its inclusion in a number of translations. A longer text is found in a few witnesses, ἔδοξε δὲ τῷ Σιλᾷ ἐπιμεῖναι αὐτοῦ, μόνος δὲ Ἰούδας ἐπορεύθη ('but it seemed good to Silas to stay there and only Judas set off'; $\mathfrak{P}^{127vid}$ [05] lat^{vl-pt}). There is no obvious reason for the omission of the reference to Judas, so this appears to be a later expansion of the other text. In any case, the verse is clearly secondary. The full attestation in Greek manuscripts is seen in *TuT Acts* (TS53).

15:40   κυρίου (of the Lord) ◆

The phrase 'the grace of God' is more frequent than 'the grace of the Lord' in the New Testament (apart from the closing formulae in the Pauline Epistles), and the majority of manuscripts here read θεοῦ ('of God'; $\mathfrak{P}^{45}$ 04 08 044 etc.). There is strong external evidence for κυρίου ('of the Lord'; $\mathfrak{P}^{74}$ 01 02 03 05 etc.), which is the less common reading. As the previous occurrence of χάρις is in the form 'the grace of the Lord Jesus' at Acts 15:11, however, this may have influenced the reading here: conversely, the only other instance of παραδίδωμι τῇ χάριτι 'commended to the grace') occurs at Acts 14:26 with θεοῦ ('of God'). The ECM has a split guiding line, allowing that either κυρίου or θεοῦ may be the initial text. The attestation of κυρίου contains a larger core of early witnesses but is incoherent in the CBGM, suggesting

---

[29] Metzger 1994: 387 suggests that it may be a misplaced gloss on ἀπολυθέντες in the next verse, or a pious expansion.

that the reading was independently changed from θεοῦ on multiple occasions either under the influence of the other verses or through misreading of the *nomina sacra*. Both SBLGNT and THGNT adopt κυρίου.[30]

16:7   Ἰησοῦ (of Jesus) {A}

The phrase 'the Spirit of Jesus' only appears here in the New Testament, but has good attestation (τὸ πνεῦμα Ἰησοῦ: 𝔓⁷⁴ 01 02 03 04² 05 etc.). There is very limited support for the more expected form τὸ πνεῦμα κυρίου ('the Spirit of the Lord'; 04* lat^{vl-pt} sy^{p-ms} co^{bo-mss}), suggesting that this is a substitution. The majority of manuscripts, however, just read τὸ πνεῦμα ('the Spirit'; 81^c 1642 etc.): if this were original, there is no obvious reason for the addition of the unexpected word. Nevertheless, the CBGM indicates that both Ἰησοῦ and the shorter reading were reintroduced into the tradition on more than one occasion, probably through comparison with other manuscripts.

16:10   θεός (God) {B}

Most Greek manuscripts read κύριος ('the Lord'; 05 614 623 1409 etc.), but there is excellent support for θεός ('God'; 𝔓⁷⁴ 01 02 03 04 08 etc.). Either reading suits the context and there is no direct parallel elsewhere (cf. Acts 13:2). Although the external evidence justifies the adoption of θεός, the CBGM indicates that each reading emerged more than once—probably because of the similarity of the *nomina sacra* (ΚC and ΘC).

16:12   πρώτη τῆς μερίδος Μακεδονίας πόλις (a leading city of the district of Macedonia) {B}

The Byzantine tradition is split between πρώτη τῆς μερίδος (lit. 'first of the district'; 𝔓⁷⁴ 01 02 04 044 etc.) and πρώτη τῆς μερίδος τῆς ('first of the district of'; 623 etc.), while two witnesses have πρώτη μερίδος τῆς ('first of a district of'; 03 35^c). In all these cases, the syntax is slightly unusual and the historical context is problematic: πρώτη ('first') qualifies πόλις ('city') which stands in apposition to κολωνία ('colony') at the end of the clause, yet Thessalonica not Philippi was the principal

---

[30] Elliott 1988: 253, however, opts for θεοῦ.

city of Macedonia, and even within the district (μερίς) in which Philippi is located, the city of Amphipolis had precedence.[31] It has been conjectured that the original reading was πρώτης μερίδος τῆς ('[a city] of the first district [of Macedonia]'), which makes better sense, but there is no extant Greek evidence for this form: however, it would serve to explain the readings with πρώτη τῆς as arising from dittography of ΤΗ in ΠΡΩΤΗC.[32] A number of minuscules read πρώτη τῆς ('the first [city of Macedonia]'; 35* 614 1241 1409 etc.), which is also historically inaccurate and probably derived from eyeskip between the two instances of τῆς in the longer Byzantine reading. A variant on this is κεφαλὴ τῆς ('the head [city of Macedonia]'; 05 lat^(vl-pt)) which seems to be a retranslation of *caput* ('head', as in 'capital') as seen in the Latin side of Codex Bezae. The reading πρώτη μερίς ('the first district'; 08 lat^(vl-pt)) is likewise problematic, as Philippi was not a district. The ECM adopts πρώτη τῆς μερίδος in the light of its strong attestation, as do the SBLGNT and THGNT: the reason why the narrative includes the detail that this was a 'first' city and how this is to be understood remains unclear.[33]

16:13 ἐνομίζετο προσευχή (lit. according to custom there was a place of prayer) {C}

The verb is found in the first-person plural ἐνομίζομεν ('we thought'; 02^c 03 04 044 etc.), the third-person singular active ἐνόμιζεν ('he thought'; 𝔓^74 01), and the passive or impersonal ἐνομίζετο ('[it] was thought'; 02* 08 307 614 623 and the majority of minuscules). Codex Bezae also has a passive or impersonal, ἐδόκει ('it seemed'; 05), a synonym which again may be derived from Latin (see the previous unit). The case of the noun partly depends on the main verb: an active form is followed by the accusative and infinitive (ἐνομίζομεν/ἐνόμιζεν προσευχήν, 'we/he thought [there was] a place of prayer': 01 02^c 04 044 etc.), while the nominative provides a subject for the passive verb

---

[31] See the extensive discussion of this verse in BDAG s.v. μερίς 1; the suggestion is advanced that πρώτη πόλις could refer to the first city on a journey. I am grateful to Tommy Wasserman for this reference.

[32] *Amsterdam Database* cj10084 [Clericus 1714].

[33] For further discussion, see Wikgren 1981, Ascough 1998, Metzger 1994: 393–395 and the *ECM Acts* Textual Commentary.

(ἐνομίζετο προσευχή, 'a place of prayer was thought [to be]': 02* [05] 08 and the majority of minuscules). If ἐνομίζετο is taken as an impersonal verb, however, then its complement is an accusative and infinitive (ἐνομίζετο προσευχήν, 'it was thought [there was] a place of prayer': 307 623 1642). Confusion between the readings seems to underlie ἐνόμιζεν προσευχή in Papyrus 74 and ἐνομίζομεν προσευχή in Codex Vaticanus, although in majuscule script, ΠΡΟΣΕΥΧΗ could also represent the dative προσεύχῃ (e.g. 'we thought [they were] at prayer'). In context, the first-person plural is the easiest reading, while the lack of subject for the third-person singular suggests this is an error. While ἐνομίζετο is a more unexpected construction, the coherent attestation of ἐνομίζετο προσευχή is one reason which has led to its adoption (see the *ECM Acts* Textual Commentary). Both THGNT and SBLGNT have ἐνομίζομεν προσευχήν, which is reflected in the NRSVue.

16:17 ὑμῖν (to you) {B}

The majority of Greek manuscripts read ἡμῖν ('to us'; 𝔓¹²⁷* 02 04 044 etc.). As noted above (Acts 13:26 etc.), through itacism this would have sounded identical to ὑμῖν ('to you'; 𝔓⁷⁴ 𝔓¹²⁷ᶜ 01 03 05 etc.). It is difficult to decide between the two in context: does the woman (or the evil spirit) identify with the crowd or not? The first person might be considered the harder reading if includes the evil spirit. The CBGM shows that the two readings emerged on several occasions, as is expected in the case of sound changes. Despite this incoherence, there is a coherent core of witnesses related to the initial text which read ὑμῖν, leading to its adoption here.

17:4 Ἑλλήνων (of the Greeks) {B}

Some early witnesses have καὶ Ἑλλήνων ('and of the Greeks'; 𝔓⁷⁴ 02 05 33 81 181 lat^(vl-pt, vg) co^(bo)), leading to two groups of people ('of the devout [i.e. Jews] and of the Greeks'). The majority support for the shorter reading with just Ἑλλήνων ('of the Greeks'; 𝔓¹²⁷ 01 03 08 044 etc.) and the unparalleled collocation which results from this, 'the devout Greeks', suggest that it is original. At least one minuscule lacks Ἑλλήνων completely (307), but this is likely to be an error prompted by homoeoteleuton.

17:13 καὶ ταράσσοντες τοὺς ὄχλους (and incite the crowds) {B}

The majority of manuscripts only read τοὺς ὄχλους ('the crowds'; 𝔓⁴⁵ 08 etc.), apparently through homoeoteleuton between σαλεύοντες and ταράσσοντες: there is strong attestation for both participles ('to stir up and incite'; 𝔓⁷⁴ 01 02 03 05 etc.) even though they are largely synonymous. At the end of the verse, Codex Bezae includes οὐ διελίμπανον ('and they did not leave off'; 05 lat^{vl-pt} sy^p), a later Greek form which is only attested in this manuscript (cf. Acts 8:24). This creates a chiasmus which balances the sentence, but there is no other obvious reason for the addition. The full attestation in Greek manuscripts is seen in *TuT Acts* (TS57).

17:26 ἐξ ἑνός (from one ancestor) {B}

There is strong attestation for the shorter reading ἐξ ἑνός ('from one [person]'; 𝔓⁷⁴ᵛⁱᵈ 01 02 03 etc.). The majority of manuscripts include a noun, ἐξ ἑνὸς αἵματος ('from one blood'; 05 08 35c 307 etc.); ἐξ ἑνὸς στόματος ('from one mouth'; 044) appears to be a misreading of this. The full attestation in Greek manuscripts is seen in *TuT Acts* (TS59). If the longer reading is an expansion, the use of αἵματος ('blood') is unexpected: not only would a less specific noun such as 'person' or 'ancestor' be more appropriate, but if this reflects Gen. 2:7 the reference should be to 'dust' rather than 'blood'. The shorter reading is not only easier but could also have arisen through homoeoteleuton: this is reflected by the multiple emergence in the CBGM, in contrast to the coherent attestation of the longer reading. Nevertheless, the attestation of αἵματος suggests that it may have been introduced by an editor as a 'Western' reading which was subsequently adopted in broader tradition (cf. Acts 15:24, 18:21) and ἐξ ἑνός has been preferred on the basis of the external evidence.

17:27 ζητεῖν τὸν θεόν (search for God) {A}

Byzantine tradition is split between ζητεῖν τὸν κύριον ('search for the Lord'; 08 1 18 35 623 etc.) and ζητεῖν τὸν θεόν ('search for God'; 𝔓⁷⁴ 01 02 03 044 etc.). The latter has stronger early attestation and may be the harder reading, because God is already the subject of the sentence. On the other hand, the following idea of 'touching' might have been felt to be more difficult if the object was 'the Lord' (whose ascension had already taken place). Alternatively, the variant could have arisen as a misreading of the *nomen sacrum* (KN for ΘN): the CBGM indicates that, whichever reading is adopted as initial, the change also happened in the other direction. Codex Bezae has a longer text, μάλιστα ζητεῖν τὸ θεῖόν ἐστιν ('especially to search for what is divine'; 05 etc.), which is clearly a subsequent expansion and appears to draw on τὸ θεῖον ('the divine') in Acts 17:29.

18:5   λόγῳ (word) {B}

There is very strong evidence for the phrase συνείχετο τῷ λόγῳ ('was gripped by the word'; 𝔓⁷⁴ 01 02 03 05 08 etc.), despite the unusual collocation which has to be understood as 'was occupied with preaching'. The majority of minuscules have συνείχετο τῷ πνεύματι ('was gripped by the Spirit'; 307 623ᶜ 1175 1642 etc.), an easier reading which is based on the literal sense of συνείχετο and therefore likely to be secondary. The full attestation in Greek manuscripts is seen in *TuT Acts* (TS62). The CBGM for this variant is interesting: the majority reading is entirely coherent, indicating that all instances derive from a single change, but the editorial text is not, suggesting that the original reading was reintroduced on more than one occasion.

18:7   Τίτου Ἰούστου (lit. Titus Justus) {C}

The hardest reading is Τιτίου Ἰούστου ('Titius Justus', 03* 05¹ syʰ), which presents a non-standard form of the Latin first name seen in Τίτου Ἰούστου ('Titus Justus'; 𝔓⁷⁴ᵛⁱᵈ 01 08 307 etc.). The majority of Greek manuscripts only read Ἰούστου ('Justus'; 02 03² 05* 044 etc.), but it seems unlikely that this is an assimilation to the instances of this name at Acts 1:23 or Col. 4:11. Instead, all of the readings can be ascribed to copying errors. Τιτίου, which is very poorly attested, may be explained as the repetition of TI (which also occurs at the end of the previous word, ὀνόματι) or the duplication of IOY from the beginning of Ἰούστου. In the context of these repeated syllables, the majority reading is likely to have omitted Τίτου due to eyeskip, although it has been argued that Τίτου was introduced through dittography.[34] The ECM adopts Τίτου Ἰούστου because of its stronger attestation (see *ECM Acts*

---

[34] See Ropes 1926.

Textual Commentary), whereas the SBLGNT prefers Τιτίου Ἰούστου and the THGNT has just Ἰούστου. According to the CBGM, the two main readings arose more than once, in keeping with the suggestion that copyists were confused by the repeated letters.³⁵

18:17 πάντες (all of them) ◆

The presence of two different longer readings could indicate that πάντες ('all'; 𝔓⁷⁴ 01 02 03 lat^{vl-pt, vg} co^{bo}) is the earliest text, but its attestation is comparatively slight. Part of the motivation for the majority reading, πάντες οἱ Ἕλληνες ('all the Greeks'; 05 08 044 33 181 etc.) may have been to exclude Paul, or to avoid the implication that the Jews were responsible for beating the official of the synagogue. Nevertheless, a few manuscripts have πάντες οἱ Ἰουδαῖοι ('all the Jews'; 307; for others see *TuT Acts* TS63), which reflects Acts 18:14. The ECM has a split guiding line, indicating that either πάντες or πάντες οἱ Ἕλληνες could be the initial text: the former is preferred by SBLGNT and THGNT.³⁶

18:21 εἰπών (he said) {A}

The majority of Greek manuscripts feature an additional sentence at the beginning of Paul's speech, reading Δεῖ με πάντως τὴν ἑορτὴν τὴν ἐρχομένην ποιῆσαι εἰς Ἱεροσόλυμα ('I must at all costs keep the approaching festival in Jerusalem'; 044 181 614 623 etc.). Codex Bezae has a slightly different form, with δέ for μέ and an additional noun in τὴν ἑορτὴν ἡμέραν ('the festival day'), plausibly on the model of its Latin reading *sollemnem diem*. There is no reason for the omission or deletion of this sentence if it were original, and strong attestation for its absence (𝔓⁷⁴ 01 02 03 08 etc.). It therefore appears that a 'Western' expansion, reflecting the contents of Acts 20:16 (and the 'Western' reading at Acts 19:1), has become more widely adopted (cf. Acts 15:24, 17:26).³⁷

---

³⁵ The reference in the *ECM Acts* Textual Commentary to 'inconsistencies in the *b* attestation' is incorrect, however, because this is only represented in the CBGM by Codex Vaticanus.

³⁶ On this variant see also Hüffmeier 2015: 4–12.

³⁷ Ross 1992, however, considers the longer text to be 'pre-Western' and possibly authorial.

19:1 Ἐγένετο δὲ ἐν τῷ τὸν Ἀπολλῶ εἶναι ἐν Κορίνθῳ Παῦλον διελθόντα τὰ ἀνωτερικὰ μέρη κατελθεῖν εἰς Ἔφεσον (While Apollos was in Corinth, Paul passed through the interior regions and came to Ephesus) {A}

The editorial text is supported by almost all witnesses, apart from the insignificant variation between κατελθεῖν ('came down') and ἐλθεῖν ('came') for which the ECM has a split guiding line. The interest of this variation unit is a substantial 'Western' reading present not just in Codex Bezae, but also Papyrus 38 and the margin of the Harklean Syriac version: Θέλοντος δὲ τοῦ Παύλου κατὰ τὴν ἰδίαν βουλὴν πορεύεσθαι εἰς Ἱεροσόλυμα εἶπεν αὐτῷ τὸ πνεῦμα ὑποστρέφειν εἰς τὴν Ἀσίαν· διελθὼν δὲ τὰ ἀνωτερικὰ μέρη ἔρχεται εἰς Ἔφεσον ('But when Paul wished according to his own plan to journey to Jerusalem, the Spirit told him to turn back into Asia. Passing through the interior regions, he comes to Ephesus'; $\mathfrak{P}^{38\text{vid}}$ 05 lat$^{\text{vl-pt}}$ sy^{hmg}). This expansion contains several features which are noteworthy as characteristics associated with the 'Western' revision. First, there is a concern with motivation, replacing a bland statement with a more colourful narrative. The introduction of the Holy Spirit is significant both for the understanding of the role of the divine in matters as mundane as travel plans and for its effect on the portrayal of Paul, with the diminution of his autonomy (as emphasised by the inclusion of κατὰ τὴν ἰδίαν βουλήν, 'according to his own plan'). The significance of recasting this introductory clause is presumably to highlight the theological significance of the discussion about the Holy Spirit in the subsequent verses, yet it results in a distinction between the human and divine which contrasts with the depiction of Paul elsewhere in Acts and in his own Epistles. Furthermore, in the adjustment of the existing text as the original narrative resumes, the use of the vivid present-tense ἔρχεται ('he comes') in place of (κατ)ελθεῖν introduces a grammatical inconsistency with the following aorist verb εἶπεν ('he said'), even though the overall sentence structure is slightly simpler. The extent and detail of this editorial reworking is striking for the insight it provides into the aims and nature of the 'Western' revision, not least because nothing actually changes in the narrative and the key dialogue between Paul and the believers remains unaltered.[38] See also the following unit (Acts 19:9) and Acts 20:4 below.

19:9 Τυράννου (of Tyrannus) {B}

The majority of Greek manuscripts have Τυράννου/Τυραννίου τινός ('of a certain Tyrannus/Tyrannius'; 08 044 181 307 etc.), in which the indefinite indicates that this individual is not mentioned elsewhere and may therefore have been added for clarification. There is early attestation of simply Τυράννου ('Tyrannus'; 𝔓[74] 01 02 03 1739 etc.) although this could have arisen through oversight. A 'Western' expansion reads Τυράννου τινὸς ἀπὸ ὥρας πέμπτης ἕως δεκάτης ('of a certain Tyrann[i]us, from the fifth hour to the tenth [hour]'; 05 [614 1409] lat^vl-pt sy^h with *). This time period of 11am to 4pm may indicate that Paul taught during the heat of the day, when no one else wished to teach.[39] Acts 19:7–10 contains several numerals ('twelve people', 'three months', 'two years') and so the detail of the time could have been added by an editor for symbolic purposes, or to increase the apparent precision of the account. While the suggestion that it 'may represent an accurate piece of information, preserved in oral tradition'[40] cannot be entirely ruled out, it is implausible that such an apparently incidental detail introduced among the 'Western' readings has any greater claim to veracity than the other expansions characteristic of these additions.

19:33 συνεβίβασαν (gave instructions to) {A}

The verb συμβιβάζω appears elsewhere in Acts with the meaning 'prove' or 'convince' (Acts 9:22, 16:10): perhaps the latter sense is intended here, yet in the Septuagint it has the meaning 'instruct' (e.g. Exod. 4:15, Deut. 4:9) and the literal sense is 'press together' or 'unite'. The strong early attestation of συνεβίβασαν (𝔓[74] 01 02 03 08 etc.) justifies its adoption here as a difficult reading. The two alternatives are simpler reflexes of the same root verb: the majority of Greek manuscripts have προεβίβασαν ('pushed forward'; 05[2] 044 181 307 etc.), while the first hand of Codex Bezae has κατεβίβασαν ('made to come down'; 05* lat).

---

[38] Strange 1992b discusses this variant, although his suggestion that it stems from an authorial annotation has not found wide acceptance.

[39] See further Epp 1966: 94.

[40] Metzger 1994: 417.

19:37 ἡμῶν (our) {B}

The frequent interchange between 'your' and 'our' due to itacism has been noted several times (Acts 3:22, 13:26 etc.). Many Greek manuscripts, along with the *Textus Receptus*, read ὑμῶν ('your'; 08* 1 18 35 398 etc.), which corresponds to the preceding second-person plural verb. However, there is also extensive support for ἡμῶν ('our'; 𝔓⁷⁴ 01 02 03 05 08ᶜ etc.) and this is rhetorically more effective in identifying the speaker with his listeners: compare too the first-person κινδυνεύομεν and δυνησόμεθα in Acts 19:40. It is unclear, however, whether the speaker is the 'town clerk' (γραμματεύς) of Acts 19:35, or Alexander the Jew of Acts 19:33 and it might have been considered inappropriate for the latter to call Artemis 'our goddess'. Although the internal evidence is finely balanced, the *ECM Acts* Textual Commentary suggests that, sound changes aside, the direction of change is more likely to be towards the second-person plural and accordingly adopts ἡμῶν. Given the context, translators should use an inclusive first-person pronoun.

19:40 οὐ δυνησόμεθα (lit. 'we will be unable') {B}

The difficulties of both readings have led to the suggestion that this verse features a 'primitive error' and there is a detailed discussion in the *ECM Acts* Textual Commentary.[41] The majority of manuscripts include οὐ before δυνησόμεθα ('we will be unable'; 01 02 03 044 etc.), resulting in a double negative which suggests a concessive use of the genitive absolute: 'although there is no cause for which we will be unable to give an account'. Several important witnesses—as well as the *Textus Receptus*—only have δυνησόμεθα ('we will be able'; 𝔓⁷⁴ 05 08 33 35* etc.), which leads to a causal significance for the absolute: 'since there is no cause for which we will be able to give an account'. The preceding περὶ οὗ ('for which') could have prompted the insertion of οὐ through dittography, or its omission through haplography. However, the inclusion of οὐ gives the more difficult sense that the threat runs contrary to the actual situation, and the external evidence in its favour has led to its adoption as the editorial text here and in both the SBLGNT and THGNT.

---

[41] See also Westcott and Hort 1896: 97.

20:4 συνείπετο δὲ αὐτῷ (he was accompanied) {B}

The vast majority of Greek manuscripts read συνείπετο δὲ αὐτῷ ἄχρι τῆς Ἀσίας ('he was accompanied as far as Asia'; 02 08 [044] 181 307 etc.; see the full attestation in *TuT Acts* TS71). There is no obvious reason for the omission of the last three words, so the early attestation of just συνείπετο δὲ αὐτῷ ('he was accompanied'; $\mathfrak{P}^{74}$ 01 03 33 lat[vl-pt, vg] co eth) has led to its adoption as the editorial text.[42] The longer text seems to be the partial incorporation of a 'Western' expansion seen in Codex Bezae, which replaces the words above with μέλλοντος οὖν ἐξιέναι αὐτοῦ μέχρι τῆς Ἀσίας ('And so, when he was intending to set out as far as Asia'; 05). This introduces an element of Paul's own intention (cf. Acts 19:1 above; a 'Western' variant also inserts a direction from the Holy Spirit in Acts 20:3) as well as a grammatical discontinuity: there is no main verb in Codex Bezae for the following list of names, but this may simply be a copying error.

20:4 Πύρρου (son of Pyrrhus) {B}

This detail is absent from the majority of Greek manuscripts (424* 614 1642 etc.), either because it was overlooked or deliberately deleted on the grounds that all the other names in the list are identified by location rather than patronymics. The external evidence for Πύρρου ('son of Pyrrhus'; $\mathfrak{P}^{74}$ 01 02 03 05 08 etc.) justifies its adoption in the editorial text.

20:15 τῇ δὲ ἐχομένῃ (and the day after that) {B}

After the reference to Samos, the majority of Greek manuscripts include an extra detail: καὶ μείναντες ἐν Τρωγυλλίῳ τῇ ἐχομένῃ ('and after waiting at Trogyllium, on the day after that'; [05] 181 614 623ᶜ etc.; the reading εἰς τὸ Γύλλιον in 044 appears to be a corruption). The external evidence for this reading, along with that for just τῇ δὲ ἐχομένῃ ('and the day after that'; $\mathfrak{P}^{41}$ $\mathfrak{P}^{74}$ 01 02 03 04 etc.), suggests that the longer form is another 'Western' expansion incorporated into Byzantine tradition (cf. Acts 15:24, 17:26 etc.). Although the extra geograph-

---

[42] The shorter form is also seen in GA 629 (not cited here in UBS6), which the CBGM suggests was introduced separately. This is in keeping with what is known of the accommodation of the Greek text to the Latin side of this manuscript: see further the comments below on James 4:4, 1 John 5:7–8 and Phlm 2.

ical information is plausible and could have been inserted by a reviser who felt that an uninterrupted journey from Samos to Miletus was too far, there is no obvious reason for its omission or deletion. There are some different forms of the shorter reading, καὶ τῇ ἐχομένῃ ('and the day after that'; 623* lat^vl-pt, vg) or τῇ ἐχομένῃ ('the day after that'; lat^vl-pt co^bo): the full attestation in Greek manuscripts is seen in *TuT Acts* (TS72).

20:21   εἰς τὸν κύριον ἡμῶν Ἰησοῦν Χριστόν (lit. towards our Lord Jesus Christ) {B}

The Byzantine tradition is split between εἰς τὸν κύριον ἡμῶν Ἰησοῦν ('to our Lord Jesus'; 03 044 1 18 35^c etc.) and εἰς τὸν κύριον ἡμῶν Ἰησοῦν Χριστόν ('to our Lord Jesus Christ'; 𝔓^74 01 02 04 [08] etc.). The tendency to expand divine titles led previous editions to prefer the shorter reading (as do the SBLGNT and THGNT). However, genealogical coherence leads the ECM to adopt the longer form, explaining the other as an oversight of one of the *nomina sacra* (ΙΝ ΧΝ), an error which is common in Codex Vaticanus (see the *ECM Acts* Textual Commentary). Codex Bezae has a different preposition, reading διὰ τοῦ κυρίου ἡμῶν Ἰησοῦ Χριστοῦ ('through our Lord Jesus Christ'; 05 lat). This has theological significance in describing faith as 'through Christ' rather than 'in Christ': there are several other instances of the latter in this book (e.g. Acts 10:43, 16:41, 19:4, 24:24).

20:28   θεοῦ (of God) {C}

This is the only time in Acts that ἐκκλησία ('church') is qualified by a genitive noun. The editorial reading θεοῦ ('of God'; 01 03 35* 614 etc.), also seen in the *Textus Receptus*, is the complement found elsewhere in the New Testament (e.g. 1 Cor. 1:2, 2 Cor. 1:1, Gal. 1:13, 1 Th. 2:14). Other important witnesses read κυρίου ('of the Lord'; 𝔓^41 𝔓^74 02 04* 05 08 etc.). This is a more unusual collocation, but parallels in the Septuagint could have led to its introduction here. The majority of manuscripts have what seems to be a conflation, κυρίου καὶ θεοῦ ('of the Lord and God'; 04^3 35^c 623^c etc.). While this is likely to be secondary, it is a hard reading given the singular 'his own blood' at the end of the verse: the other readings in the next variation unit could also have prompted an editor to adjust the noun here. The CBGM indicates that θεοῦ emerged from the majority reading on several occasions, perhaps due to eyeskip between the *nomina sacra*). Although the attestation of each reading is incoherent, consistent with misreading of a *nomen sacrum* (ΘΥ and ΚΥ), coherence and the proportion of witnesses close to the initial text offer strong support for κύριου, making it difficult to decide on the earliest reading.[43]

20:28 τοῦ αἵματος τοῦ ἰδίου (the blood of his own Son) {A}

The majority of Greek manuscripts read τοῦ ἰδίου αἵματος ('his own blood'; 614 1409 1642 etc.). The rest of the tradition has τοῦ αἵματος τοῦ ἰδίου (𝔓[41] 𝔓[74] 01 02 03 04 05 etc.), whose attestation strongly suggests that this is the earliest form. This can be translated either as 'his own blood' too (with ἴδιος as an adjective, 'his blood, his very own'), or 'the blood of his own' (with ἴδιος as a noun). It has been suggested that ὁ ἴδιος ('his Own') may have been an early Christian term for Christ, which was later misunderstood and simply read as an adjective, hence the change to the corresponding standard word order in Byzantine tradition (cf. Heb. 9:12).[44] If it is taken as a noun, translations may need to supply another noun for clarification, such as 'Son'. The choice of reading in the previous variation unit (as to whether 'his' refers to 'God' or 'the Lord') may also affect the choice of interpretation here: taking this phrase to mean '[God's] own blood' could have prompted the introduction of κύριος in the previous variation unit.[45]

21:8 ἤλθομεν (we came) {A}

There is strong external evidence for the shortest reading, ἤλθομεν ('we came'; 𝔓[74] 01 02 03 04 08 etc.), leading to its adoption as the editorial text. Other manuscripts include a subject, as seen in one of the two Byzantine readings οἱ περὶ τὸν Παῦλον ἤλθομεν ('we who were with Paul came'; 35[v.r.] 623[c] 1642 etc.). This clarification may have been added at the beginning of a liturgical lection: the lectionary tradition here reads οἱ ἀπόστολοι ἀπὸ Τύρου ἦλθον ('the apostles came from Tyre'), based

---

[43] A consideration of the CBGM data for this variation unit is given in Wasserman & Gurry 2017: 86–91; the variants are also treated in Metzger & Ehrman 2005: 331–333 and King 2017: 32–36.

[44] Metzger 1994: 426–427.

[45] See further Ehrman 2011: 103–104.

on the previous verse. In the other Byzantine reading, the additional subject results in the change of the verb to the third person, οἱ περὶ τὸν Παῦλον ἦλθον ('those who were with Paul came'; 1 330 398 1241 etc.), despite the conflict with the first-person verb at the end of the sentence (ἐμείναμεν, 'we stayed'): compare also Acts 28:1 below. The full attestation in Greek manuscripts is seen in *TuT Acts* (TS77).

21:22   ἀκούσονται (they will hear) {B}

A group of Greek manuscripts read δεῖ συνελθεῖν πλῆθος· ἀκούσονται γάρ ('a multitude must assemble: for they will hear'; $\mathfrak{P}^{74}$ 01 02 04² 08 etc.). This longer form is also present in the majority of witnesses, with a slightly different word order: δεῖ πλῆθος συνελθεῖν· ἀκούσονται γάρ ('a multitude must assemble: for they will hear'; 05 044 623 1642 etc.). This appears to be an editorial insertion, perhaps in order to remove the implication that the 'thousands of believers' of Acts 21:20 would all hear of Paul's arrival. It may have been a 'Western' addition that became part of Byzantine tradition (cf. Acts 20:15, 21:25 etc.). It is not clear whether πλῆθος should be taken to refer to the 'multitude' of the whole church, or to a mob. The shortest reading, adopted as the editorial text, is just ἀκούσονται ('they will hear'; 03 04* 307 etc., sy co eth). Despite its limited attestation, its early support includes several ancient translations.

21:25   κρίναντες φυλάσσεσθαι αὐτούς (with our judgment that they should abstain) {B}

As in the previous variation unit, a 'Western' expansion seems to have become more widely adopted, taking the form κρίναντες μηδὲν τοιοῦτο τηρεῖν αὐτοὺς ἀλλὰ φυλάσσεσθαι ('with our judgment that they should not observe anything of this sort, but should abstain'; 1739) or the majority reading κρίναντες μηδὲν τοιοῦτον τηρεῖν αὐτοὺς εἰ μὴ φυλάσσεσθαι αὐτούς ('with our judgment that they should observe nothing of this sort, apart from abstaining'; [04] 05 [08 044 181] etc.). External evidence supports the adoption of the shortest form, κρίναντες φυλάσσεσθαι αὐτούς ('with our judgment that they should abstain'; $\mathfrak{P}^{74}$ 01 02 03 etc., lat^{vl-pt, vg} sy^p cpa co eth), although there remains a slight possibility that the longer text was deleted because it did not form part of the Apostolic

Decree in Acts 15:29. The full attestation in Greek manuscripts is seen in *TuT Acts* (TS80).⁴⁶

21:25 τό τε εἰδωλόθυτον καὶ αἷμα καὶ πνικτὸν καὶ πορνείαν (what has been sacrificed to idols and from blood and from what is strangled and from sexual immorality) {B}

The editorial text has early support ([𝔓⁷⁴] 01 02 03 04 etc.) and is very close to the majority reading, which inserts the definite article before αἷμα ('blood'; [044 181 614] 1409 1642 etc.). The Laudian Acts have this phrase in the genitive, which reinforces the sense of 'abstain from' (ἀπὸ εἰδωλοθύτων καὶ αἵματος καὶ πνικτοῦ καὶ πορνείας, 08). The plural εἰδωλοθύτων ('things sacrificed to idols') corresponds to a variant in the same lists at Acts 15:20 and 15:29 (see above), as does the absence from one minuscule of καὶ πορνείαν ('and from sexual immorality'; *cf.* 1175), although this may be an accidental omission. In keeping with those two earlier lists, it is striking that Codex Bezae and part of the Old Latin tradition again lack καὶ πνικτόν ('and what is strangled'). It may be noted that the negative version of the 'Golden Rule' included by some 'Western' witnesses in Acts 15:20 and 15:29 is not present on this occasion.

22:9 ἐθεάσαντο (saw) {B}

After this verb, the majority of manuscripts include a further detail, καὶ ἔμφοβοι ἐγένοντο ('and they became afraid'; 05 08 044 [307] 614 etc.; see the full listing in *TuT Acts* TS81). This could have been omitted by eyeskip between the two plural verbs, but the attestation of the shorter reading ἐθεάσαντο ('they saw'; 𝔓⁷⁴ 01 02 03 33 etc.) suggests that the longer text is a 'Western' expansion which became part of later tradition (cf. Acts 21:22 etc.).

23:9 ἢ ἄγγελος (or an angel) {A}

At the end of the verse, the majority of witnesses have the injunction μὴ θεομαχῶμεν ('let us not fight against God'; 307 614 623ᶜ 1409 1642 etc.: the full attestation is given in *TuT Acts* TS85). This is the only instance of this verb in the New Testament (cf. Acts 5:39), and it seems to have

---

⁴⁶ For further discussion see Epp 1966: 107–112; Strange 1992a: 87–105.

been added to provide a complement to the preceding clause (beginning εἰ δέ, 'but if'), which otherwise is left hanging. There is no obvious reason for its omission and the strong external support for the shorter reading of just ἢ ἄγγελος ('or an angel'; 𝔓⁷⁴ 01 02 03 04 etc.) indicates that is likely to be original. The sentence may be punctuated as a question ('What if…?') or a statement ('Perhaps … .').

23:12 ποιήσαντες συστροφὴν οἱ Ἰουδαῖοι (the Jews joined in a conspiracy) {B}

The earliest witnesses have ποιήσαντες συστροφὴν οἱ Ἰουδαῖοι ('the Jews joined in a conspiracy'; 𝔓⁷⁴ 01 02 03 04 etc.). This is mitigated in Byzantine tradition, which reads ποιήσαντές τινες τῶν Ἰουδαίων συστροφήν ('some of the Jews joined in a conspiracy'; [623] 1409 1642 etc.): the reason for this may be seen in the following verse, when it is revealed that the number was 'more than forty'. Papyrus 48, which contains a number of 'Western' readings, has an odd text: καιτ[…] βοήθειαν συστραφέντες τινὲς τῶν Ἰουδαίων ('although […] having gathered help, some of the Jews'; 𝔓⁴⁸). This suggests that the majority reading may have derived from a 'Western' editorial intervention. It is worth noting that Codex Bezae, the principal source of 'Western' readings, is not extant in the last six chapters of Acts.

23:30 ἐπὶ σοῦ (before you) ◆

At the end of the letter, the majority of manuscripts have a concluding greeting, either the singular ἔρρωσο ('Farewell'; 01 08 044 18 35 etc.) or the plural ἔρρωσθε ('Farewell'; 1 330 1241 etc. etc.). The latter is seen at the end of the apostles' letter in Acts 15:29, indicating that elsewhere the author of Acts was prepared to include this feature of a letter. The lack of a greeting is only attested by a few witnesses, yet they are early and important (𝔓⁷⁴ 02 03 33 lat^{vl-pt, vg} co eth). The ECM has a split guiding line, indicating that it is impossible to decide between this shortest reading (thus SBLGNT) and the presence of ἔρρωσο (thus THGNT). It could be that ἔρρωσο was omitted as an oversight following ἐπὶ σοῦ: the incoherencies in the attestation of the text without a greeting suggest that it may be an accidental omission which happened more than once (as noted in the *ECM Acts* Textual Commentary).

24:6–8 ἐκρατήσαμεν (we seized him) {B}

At the end of Acts 24:6, a significant number of Greek manuscripts and the *Textus Receptus* have a lengthy additional text which includes the whole of verse 7 as well as part of verse 8: ἐκρατήσαμεν καὶ κατὰ τὸν ἡμέτερον νόμον ἠθελήσαμεν κρῖναι.⁷ παρελθὼν δὲ Λυσίας ὁ χιλίαρχος μετὰ πολλῆς βίας ἐκ τῶν χειρῶν ἡμῶν ἀπήγαγε,⁸ κελεύσας τοὺς κατηγόρους αὐτοῦ ἔρχεσθαι ἐπὶ σέ ('we seized him and we would have judged him according to our law.⁷ But the chief captain Lysias came and with great violence took him out of our hands,⁸ commanding his accusers to come before you.'; 08 044 33 35* 181 etc.: the full attestation of the various forms of text found here in Greek are given in *TuT Acts* TS91). There is no obvious reason for the absence of this text from numerous manuscripts, including most of the earliest witnesses ($\mathfrak{P}^{74}$ 01 02 03 18 etc.). Instead, it appears to be a 'Western' expansion intended partly to harmonise Tertullus' statement with Lysias' own account at Acts 23:26, although it may be noted that it does not repeat Lysias' claim that the Jews were about to kill Paul but instead attributes the violence to the Romans. Technically, if the longer form is read, the following παρ' οὗ ('from whom') in verse 8 refers to Lysias rather than Paul, even though αὐτοῦ ('him') at the end of the verse is clearly Paul.

25:18 πονηράν (lit. crime) {C}

Unusually, the Byzantine tradition has the shortest reading, omitting this noun and simply relying on the earlier relative pronoun ('any of the things that I was expecting'; 1642 etc.). The variety of alternatives have the appearance of later glosses: πονηράν ('[no] criminal [charge]'; $\mathfrak{P}^{74}$ 02 04* 044 etc.), πονηρῶν ('[any] of the crimes'; 01² 03 08 81 1409 lat^{vl-pt}), and πονηρά ('crimes [of those which I was expecting]'; 01* 04² lat^{vl-pt}, although this is treated by the ECM as a scribal error for πονηράν). Nonetheless, the weight of external evidence leads the ECM to adopt πονηράν, which seems to have been changed in some witnesses to πονηρῶν under the influence of the relative pronoun and was omitted elsewhere: coming at the end of a phrase which is complete in itself and separated from its corresponding noun (αἰτίαν) by some distance, it probably seemed superfluous. The CBGM indicates that the Byzantine reading developed from manuscripts with πονηράν (see the *ECM Acts* Textual Commentary).

26:16 εἰδές με (you have seen me) ◆

Some important witnesses include the pronoun με ('me'; 03 614 1175 1739 sy co^sa), which might have been introduced to match σοι ('you') in the next phrase. The shorter reading is, unusually, attested by the majority of manuscripts ($\mathfrak{P}^{74}$ 01 02 04² 08 etc.). The ECM has a split guiding line, allowing that either could be the initial text: the *ECM Acts Textual Commentary* notes that the incoherent attestation of με indicates that it was added more than once. Even so, the presence of με (preferred by SBLGNT and THGNT) is difficult to incorporate in translation, as is σοι in the next phrase: the NRSVue translates ὧν ... ὧν as 'the things in which ... those in which' in order to include the pronouns.

26:28 Χριστιανὸν ποιῆσαι (lit. to act the Christian) {A}

The earliest manuscripts read ποιῆσαι ('to act [the Christian]'; $\mathfrak{P}^{74}$ 01 02 03 048 etc.), but the sense of the phrase is difficult: does it mean 'to be a Christian' or only to appear so? The alternative γενέσθαι ('to become [Christian]'; 08 044 307 614 etc.), attested in the vast majority of witnesses (see *TuT Acts* TS99), is much more straightforward and therefore secondary: the introduction of this verb may have been prompted by γενέσθαι in Paul's response in the following verse.

27:14 Εὐρακύλων (northeaster) {B}

There is good external support for Εὐρακύλων ('northeaster'; $\mathfrak{P}^{74}$ 01 02 03* lat), even though the word is not found elsewhere and appears to be a hybrid of the Greek Εὖρος ('east wind') and Latin *Aquilo* ('north wind'). The majority of manuscripts, however, read Εὐροκλύδων or Εὐρυκλύδων ('southeaster'; 03² 044 [33] 81 181 etc.); the full attestation is given in *TuT Acts* (TS101). The direction of the wind is significant for the reconstruction of Paul's itinerary.

27:16 Καῦδα (Cauda) {B}

The majority of manuscripts have Κλαύδην ('Clauda'; 307 1409 1642 etc.), which seems to be a development from Κλαῦδα ('Clauda'; 01* 33 81 181 614 1739 sy^h eth; Κλαῦδαν is read in 623). One majuscule has Γαύδην ('Gauda'; 044), which is close to the modern name of the island (Gaudonisi or Gaudos). It has been suggested that Καῦδα ('Cauda'; $\mathfrak{P}^{74}$

01² 03 1175 sy^p) is a Latin form of the same word.[47] As with the previous unit, the identification of the island is important in determining Paul's route.

28:1   ἐπέγνωμεν (we learned) {C}

The textual tradition is split between ἐπέγνωμεν ('we learned'; 𝔓⁷⁴ 01 02 03 04 etc.) and the majority form ἐπέγνωσαν ('they learned'; 044 35* 307 623 etc.). This may reflect the narrative variation between the first person and third person (cf. Acts 27:36–37). A number of manuscripts cited in the ECM have an insertion here reading οἱ περὶ τὸν Παῦλον ('those around Paul'), which may reflect adjustment at the beginning of a liturgical lection (cf. Acts 21:8) to a text which already read ἐπέγνωσαν. The first-person pronouns in the following verse are not contested, and the first person has accordingly been adopted here.

28:13   περιελόντες (we weighed anchor) ◆

The majority of Greek manuscripts read περιελθόντες ('having made a circuit'; 𝔓⁷⁴ 01² 02 04 066 etc.). The less frequent word περιελόντες (lit. 'having cast off'; 01* 03 044 398 lat^vl-pt) might have resulted from the accidental omission of Θ before Ο, but the occurrence of the same word in a similar context at Acts 27:40 suggests that it may have been used here as a nautical term which, in the absence of τὰς ἀγκύρας ('the anchors'), was not understood and accordingly replaced. If this is adopted, it will probably be necessary to supply this noun in translation.[48] The split guiding line in the ECM indicates that either of these readings may have been the initial text (see further the *ECM Acts* Textual Commentary): SBLGNT has περιελόντες, but THGNT prefers περιελθόντες. The variant παρελθόντες ('passing'; 623) is an example of substitution with a more common term.

28:16   ἐπετράπη τῷ Παύλῳ (Paul was allowed) {A}

A 'Western' reading has become incorporated into Byzantine tradition (cf. Acts 17:26 etc.), characteristically expanding the narrative to include an additional practical detail: ὁ ἑκατόνταρχος παρέδωκεν τοὺς

---

[47] See the authorities quoted in Metzger 1994: 440–441.
[48] See BDAG s. v. περιαιρέω 1, with an extensive discussion of this reading.

δεσμίους τῷ στρατοπεδάρχῳ, τῷ δὲ Παύλῳ ἐπετράπη ('the centurion handed the prisoners over to the captain of the guard, but Paul was allowed'; 307 [330] 614 [623] etc.). There is no obvious reason for its omission if it were original, and the external support for the shorter reading (01 02 03 044 048 etc.) justifies its adoption as the editorial text. The full attestation in Greek manuscripts is seen in *TuT Acts* (TS103).

28:25 ὑμῶν (your) {B}

As noted above (e.g. Acts 3:25, 19:37), the first-person and second-person plural pronouns were frequently interchanged due to itacism. Despite ἡμῶν ('our [ancestors]'; 1 18 35 307 330 etc.) in part of the Byzantine tradition, including the *Textus Receptus*, both the external evidence and the negative tone of Paul's speech favour the adoption of ὑμῶν ('your [ancestors]'; 𝔓⁷⁴ 01 02 03 044 etc.).

28:29 *omit verse* {A}

Acts 28:29 appears to be another instance of a 'Western' expansion which has become part of Byzantine tradition (cf. Acts 24:6–8, 28:16 etc.). The most widely attested text is καὶ ταῦτα αὐτοῦ εἰπόντος ἀπῆλθον οἱ Ἰουδαῖοι, πολλὴν ἔχοντες ἐν ἑαυτοῖς συζήτησιν ('and once he had said this, the Jews went away and held a great discussion among themselves'; 307 614 623 1409 etc.); other forms are indicated in *TuT Acts* (TS104). The addition appears to have been introduced to provide a smoother transition at the end of Paul's speech than the shorter, more abrupt reading, which has strong early attestation (𝔓⁷⁴ 01 02 03 08 etc., lat^{vl-pt, vg} sy co eth).

28:31 ἀκωλύτως (without hindrance) {A}

At the end of the book, a few later witnesses include ἀμήν ('Amen'; 044 181 307 398 614 etc.). This was presumably thought to be a fitting conclusion for a scriptural book, as at the end of many of the Pauline Epistles, although in the absence of an invocation or liturgical formula its appearance is unexpected. This is missing from the main Byzantine tradition, in which it is unusual not to have Amen at the end of a book. This shorter reading also has early support (𝔓⁷⁴ 01 02 03 08 etc.). Some Old Latin manuscripts and the Harklean Syriac attest a longer ending which was perhaps deemed more fitting to the end of the book: εἰπὼν ὅτι οὗτός ἐστιν ὁ Χριστὸς Ἰησοῦς ὁ υἱὸς τοῦ θεοῦ δι' οὗ μέλλει πᾶς ὁ κόσμος κρίνεσθαι. ἀμήν ('saying that this is the Messiah [or Christ], Jesus the Son of God through whom all the world will be judged. Amen'; lat[vl-pt] sy[h]).

The Catholic Epistles

Overview

In the oldest surviving copies of the whole Greek New Testament, the Catholic Epistles follow the Acts of the Apostles, a sequence which has been adopted in the ECM followed by UBS6 and NA29: it is also seen in the THGNT. These manuscripts are the fourth-century Codex Sinaiticus (01) and Codex Vaticanus (03), the fifth-century Codex Alexandrinus (02) and Codex Ephraemi Rescriptus (04). This order is also seen in the seventh-century Papyrus 74 ($\mathfrak{P}^{74}$), the only papyrus with all the Catholic Epistles. Among the eight papyri from the third or fourth century, Papyrus 20 ($\mathfrak{P}^{20}$), Papyrus 23 ($\mathfrak{P}^{23}$) and Papyrus 100 ($\mathfrak{P}^{100}$) are fragments of James, Papyrus 9 ($\mathfrak{P}^9$) is a page of 1 John, and Papyrus 72 ($\mathfrak{P}^{72}$) is a composite manuscript with both letters of Peter and Jude. Although Codex Bezae (05) may have included the other Catholic Epistles, only the final page of 3 John is extant (in Latin). The text of the ninth-century majuscules GA 025 and 044 often agrees with the older codices. The principal minuscule witnesses with an early form of these letters are GA 5, 6, 81, 436, 1175, 1243, 1739, 1852 and 1881 (some of which have already been mentioned in the Overview for Acts above). Most other Greek witnesses form the majority which makes up the Byzantine tradition.

Early translations transmit the Catholic Epistles in a variety of sequences and combinations. There is no complete Old Latin manuscript with all seven epistles: the fifth-century Fleury palimpsest (VL 55; see the Overview for Acts above) ends with portions of the two letters of Peter and 1 John, while the ninth-century Corbey St James (VL 66) transmits a fifth-century text of James with some non-canonical writings. The unknown reviser of the Vulgate (lat^{vg}) changed the sequence by putting James first, in order to match Greek witnesses. In the Sahidic Coptic (co^{sa}), the Johannine letters precede James. If there was an Old Syriac translation, it has been lost: the Peshitta (sy^p) only contains James, 1 Peter and 1 John. The full set of letters probably appeared in the sixth-century Philoxenian version (sy^{ph}) and is seen in the Harklean (sy^h).

The best-known variation unit in the Catholic Epistles is the Johannine Comma (1 John 5:7–8), referring to three witnesses in heaven, which is one of a number of glosses which arose in the Latin tradition. Other noteworthy variants include 'name' or 'part' at 1 Pet. 4:16, 'love feasts' or 'tricks' at 2 Pet. 2:13 and the question of what will happen on the earth at 2 Pet. 3:10, spirits which 'confess' or 'dissolve' Jesus at 1 John 4:3, and the subject of Jude 5.

The second edition of the *Editio Critica Maior* of the Catholic Epistles (*ECM Catholic Epistles*) provided the text and apparatus which appeared in UBS5. The selection of variants has been revised in UBS6. The CBGM data, including the textual flow diagrams, is available online.[1] Although no textual commentary has accompanied *ECM Catholic Epistles*, an analysis of all the test passages in *Text und Textwert* is provided in Wachtel 1995. Wasserman's edition of Jude (2006) based on all surviving Greek continuous-text manuscripts offers a detailed commentary on that letter.

---

[1] http://intf.uni-muenster.de/cbgm/GenQ.html

The Letter of James

1:12 ἐπηγγείλατο (has promised) {A}

In the editorial text (supported by 𝔓⁷⁴ 01 02 03 044 etc.), this verb stands without a subject, perhaps reflecting the Jewish tradition of not explicitly mentioning a divine agent. The majority of Greek manuscripts include ὁ κύριος ('the Lord'; [04] 025 5 307 436 etc.) after the verb, while other witnesses have ὁ θεός ('God'; 1175 1243 1735 1739 etc.). There is no obvious reason for the omission of either of these nouns, indicating that the shorter reading is likely to be original and was expanded in two different ways (although one of the *nomina sacra* KC and ΘC could have been misread for the other). The full attestation is given in *TuT Cath.* (TS2). In translation, it will normally be necessary to provide a subject.

1:17 παραλλαγὴ ἢ τροπῆς ἀποσκίασμα (variation or shadow due to change) {B}

There is strong external support for the editorial text, including the majority of minuscules (01² 02 04 025 etc.). A number of minor variations reflect difficulties in understanding this phrase. Codex Vaticanus and the first hand of Codex Sinaiticus have παραλλαγὴ ἢ (or ἡ) τροπῆς ἀποσκιάσματος ('variation which [ἢ] is due to a shadow of turning'; 01* 03). Although a later hand has marked η as ἢ ('or') in Codex Vaticanus, this leaves the second element without a subject; in Codex Sinaiticus, the previous ἐστίν means that this reading could be translated as '[there is no] variation or [ἢ] anything of a shadow of turning'). The one extant papyrus reads παραλλαγῆς ἢ τροπῆς ἀποσκιάσματος ('[not one thing] of variation or of the turning of the shadow'; 𝔓²³), while some witnesses replace ἢ ('or') in the majority reading with οὐδέ ('nor'; 044 lat^vg sy^p). Some Old Latin evidence appears to reflect παραλλαγὴ ἢ ῥοπὴ ἀποσκιάσματος ('variation or hint of shadow'; lat^vl-pt), which is probably a misreading. The slim attestation of these alternatives has led to the adoption of the majority reading.[1]

1:19 ἴστε, ἀδελφοί μου ἀγαπητοί· ἔστω δὲ πᾶς (You must understand this, my beloved brothers and sisters: let everyone be) {B}

The majority of Greek manuscripts read ὥστε, ἀδελφοί μου ἀγαπητοί, ἔστω πᾶς ('for this reason, my beloved brothers, everyone may be'; 025ᶜ 044 5 307 442 etc.). This is smoother than the rather abrupt command in the editorial text, where the first word is not ὥστε but ἴστε (lit. 'know'; 01 03 04 81 436 etc.). Further support for this is seen in manuscripts which begin the verse with ἴστε δέ ('but know'; 𝔓⁷⁴ᵛⁱᵈ 02), and most early translations also attest this verb. Greek lectionary tradition omits the first word entirely, reading ἀδελφοί μου ἀγαπητοί, ἔστω πᾶς ('my beloved brothers, let everyone be'). Nevertheless, there are similar examples of abrupt commands elsewhere in this epistle (e.g. James 2:5, 4:11) and the external evidence suggests that ἴστε is the earliest reading here. Some translations take ἴστε as indicative rather than imperative, but this requires an object to be supplied, e.g. 'You know this …'.

2:3 ἢ κάθου ἐκεῖ (lit. or sit there) {C}

The editorial text, following a change introduced by the ECM, has relatively slim support ('[stand] or sit there'; 03 1175 1243 1739 etc.). This is also the case for ἐκεῖ ἢ κάθου ('[stand] there or sit'; 02 044 33 81 etc.), which is preferred in THGNT and UBS4. The majority of Greek manuscripts read ἐκεῖ ἢ κάθου ὧδε ('[stand] there or sit here'; 01 025 5 307 436 etc.: see further *TuT Cath.* TS8); the form ἐκεῖ καὶ κάθου ὧδε ('[stand] there and sit here'; 04² coˢᵃ⁻ᵐˢ) is an error. The CBGM indicates that only the Byzantine reading and ἢ κάθου ἐκεῖ are coherently attested if adopted as the initial text, yet the introduction of ὧδε ('here') in the former is likely to be assimilation to the earlier part of the verse.[2] The latter reading has therefore been adopted, not least as it is more difficult in combining the two locations rather than providing a separate loca-

---

[1] See further the attestation in *TuT Cath.* (TS3) and the discussion at Wachtel 1995: 210–214.

[2] For a detailed discussion of this variant, see Wasserman and Gurry 2019; the position of ὧδε in the local stemma is also treated in Wachtel 2012: 131–136.

tion for each command. Many translations punctuate this speech as two separate commands ('"You stand" or "Sit there …"'), although the emphatic pronoun tells against this. The force of the saying is in the poor person being told to sit closer to the speaker than the rich person, which may need to be brought out in translation: because of the misunderstanding of ὑπὸ τὸ ὑποπόδιόν μου as 'under my footstool', in several witnesses the preposition has been changed to ἐπί ('beside [my footstool]') or some other adjustment.[3]

2:20 ἀργή (worthless) {B}

The adjective ἀργή (lit. 'barren'; 03 04* 1175 1243 1739 lat^{vg} co^{sa}) is the only variant to feature a word not already present in the context. Κενή ('empty/senseless'; 𝔓^{74} lat^{vl-pt}) appears to be a repetition of κενέ earlier in the verse, while the majority reading νεκρά ('dead'; 01 02 04^2 025 044 etc.: see *TuT Cath*. TS13) is assimilation to the similar statements at James 2:17 and 2:26.[4] Supported by some key witnesses, the editorial text could also be seen as a play on words due to the similarity of ἀργή and the preceding ἔργα ('works'), matching the other instances of assonance or wordplay in this passage.

3:3 εἰ δέ (if) {C}

Through the sound change known as itacism, the forms εἰ δέ ('but if'; 03^2 044 5 33 307 etc.) and ἴδε ('see'; 81 442 642 1175 1448 etc.) were pronounced identically and therefore often confused in copying (see also James 4:5). The Byzantine tradition is split between the two readings. The first hand of Codex Sinaiticus reads ΕΙΔΕΓΑΡ (without accents) which must be understood as ἴδε γάρ ('for see'; 01* sy$^{p, h-ms}$), as the two postpositive connectives δέ and γάρ cannot stand next to each other; the majuscule reading ΕΙΔΕ without accents (01^2 02 03*) could support either form. This variant comes between a conditional clause with εἰ ('if') in James 3:2 and a deictic clause with ἰδοὺ καί ('see too') in the next verse, either of which could have influenced its interpretation. Despite the latter, the form ἰδού in James 3:4 and 3:5 tells against the reading ἴδε here, which is not found elsewhere in James. In fact, the *Textus Receptus*

---

[3] Omanson 2006: 471; see also Wachtel 1995. 222.
[4] Elliott 1992: 70 suggests that νεκρά may have been introduced by an editor who preferred 'proper' forms ('Atticism').

has ἰδού ('see') at this point, matching the following verses but with minimal manuscript support. As the present verse is a continuation of the previous idea about the bridle and the body in James 3:2 rather than a new observation, the conditional has been preferred.

3:8 ἀκατάστατον (restless) {B}

There is good external support for ἀκατάστατον ('restless'; 01 02 03 025 etc.), a word which also appears at James 1:8 (cf. 3:16). The alternative, ἀκατάσχετον ('uncontrollable'; 04 044 5 81 307 etc.: see *TuT Cath.* TS17), attested in the majority of manuscripts, offers a more expected match for the noun κακόν ('evil') and therefore appears to be a later replacement with an easier reading involving the substitution of just two letters. Nevertheless, it is possible that ἀκατάστατον was introduced at an early point through assimilation to the other instances of this root in this letter: the incoherence in its attestation whichever reading is taken as the initial text suggests that this did happen during transmission.

3:9 κύριον (Lord) {A}

The majority of witnesses read θεόν ('God'; 307 436 442 642 etc.), assimilating this to the standard phrase 'the God and Father' (cf. Rom. 15:6, 2 Cor. 1:3, James 1:27, 1 Pet. 1:3 etc.). A form with κύριον ('Lord [and Father]'; 𝔓[20] 01 02 03 04 etc.) is only found here in the New Testament, but has very strong external attestation. Despite the possibility for scribal confusion between the two *nomina sacra* abbreviations (ΘΝ and ΚΝ), the combination of κύριον and εὐλογεῖν ('to bless') is found throughout the Septuagint and stands in opposition to θεοῦ ('God') at the end of the verse, supporting its adoption here.

3:12 οὔτε ἁλυκόν (no more ... salt) {B}

There is slim but early attestation for the shortest reading, οὔτε ἁλυκόν ('no more ... salt'; 02 03 04* 1175 1852). This displays the assonance typical of the epistle in the juxtaposition of ἁλυκὸν γλυκύ ('salt ... fresh'; cf. the possible wordplay in James 2:20) but it is somewhat telegraphic. Some important witnesses read οὕτως οὐδὲ ἁλυκόν ('thus nor [can] salt [water]'; 01 [04² 044] 33 81 etc.). There is a slight possibility that the shortest reading arose through eyeskip between οὕτως and οὐδέ, but it is more likely that the alternative was an expansion to give a smoother text. The longest reading is found in the majority of manuscripts, οὕτως οὐδεμία πηγὴ ἁλυκὸν καί ('thus no spring [can make] salt and [fresh water]'; 5 307 436 442 642 etc.); for οὐδεμία one majuscule has οὔτε μία ('neither [can] one [spring]'; 025). The majority form repeats both the idea and the word πηγή from James 3:11, but there is no obvious way in which it could have led to the shorter form in the oldest manuscripts. Instead, the shorter form continues the idea in the first half of the verse that one thing does not come from the other.

4:4   μοιχαλίδες (adulterers) {A}

The majority of Greek manuscripts read μοιχοὶ καὶ μοιχαλίδες (lit. 'adulterers and adulteresses'; 01² 025 044 5 307 etc., see *TuT Cath.* TS18), ensuring that both men and women are included in this address. The oldest witnesses, including the Latin and Syriac translations, only have the feminine μοιχαλίδες (lit. 'adulteresses'; 𝔓¹⁰⁰ 01* 02 03 33 etc.). This could have arisen through eyeskip, but the strong external attestation suggests that the feminine alone is likely to be the earliest reading.[5] This draws on the characterisation of Israel in the Septuagint as God's faithless wife (cf. Is. 54:5, Jer. 3:20, Ez. 16) even though the word μοιχαλίς appears there relatively rarely (e.g. Hos. 3:1), while in Matt. 12:39, 16:4 and Mark 8:38 it is feminine because it qualifies the noun γενεά ('generation'). In translation, an inclusive term will be preferable: the word is normally understood as figurative, but a literal reference to marriage (understood in terms of faithfulness) is also possible.

4:5   κατῴκισεν (caused to dwell) {B}

This variant provides a further case of itacism (see also James 3:3), with all three readings being pronounced identically. The editorial text, κατῴκισεν (from κατοικίζω), has the earliest attestation (𝔓⁷⁴ 01 03 044 1739) and is causative ('he made to dwell'). The majority reading, κατῴκησεν (025 5 33 307 436 etc., from κατοικέω) is intransitive, mean-

---

[5] The incoherence in the attestation for the editorial text in the CBGM is due to the difficulty of determining the original reading of GA 629, a manuscript which has been influenced by its Latin column: the ECM reconstructs this differently to *Text und Textwert;* for the latter see Wachtel 1995: 232–233.

ing 'it has settled' or 'it dwells'. Some manuscripts have an orthographic alternative which could support either reading, κατῴκεισεν (02 81 1175). The source of this quotation cannot be identified, and there are various ways of parsing it: τὸ πνεῦμα ('the spirit') could be the subject or object of ἐπιποθεῖ ('desires'). Still, God is the subject of the quotation from Prov. 3:34 in the following verse, and the transitive verbs there as well as the external evidence support the choice of κατῴκισεν in this verse. The identity of the subject of ἐπιποθεῖ ('desires') and the nuance of πρὸς φθόνον ('for envy') make this a complex verse to translate and it is discussed in many commentaries.

4:14 ἀτμὶς γάρ ἐστε (for you are a mist) {B}

Another sound change is reflected in two of the variants in this verse: ἐστέ ('you are') and ἔσται ('it will be') were pronounced identically. Witnesses with ἀτμὶς γάρ ἐστε ('for you are a mist'; 03 81 642 1175 1243 etc.) reflect the second-person plural earlier in this verse and in the next one. The Byzantine tradition is split between ἀτμὶς γάρ ἔσται ('for it will be a mist'; 025 044 307 436 442 etc.) and ἀτμὶς γάρ ἐστιν ('for it is a mist'; 5 etc., including the *Textus Receptus*). Some of its members also have ἡ ζωὴ ἡμῶν ('our life') immediately before this phrase, so the more general wording is suited to that broader context. Manuscripts which lack the connective γάρ ('for'; 02 33 1735 2344) further increase the applicability of the saying. The entire phrase is absent from Codex Sinaiticus, presumably as an error (it has around the same number of letters as a single line of this manuscript) but the resultant text still makes sense with ἡ ζωή ('life') as the subject. The local stemma for the CBGM reconstructs the sequence of variants as follows: ἐστέ ('you are') is the initial reading, which became the future tense ἔσται ('it will be') through sound change or accommodation to the preceding αὔριον ('tomorrow'); this was later replaced by the more standard third-person present ἐστίν ('it is'), perhaps encouraged by the alteration of the preceding ὑμῶν ('your [life]') to ἡμῶν ('our [life]'), again as a sound change; γάρ ('for') was omitted on more than one occasion. Although this is plausible, the incoherent attestation of ἐστέ suggests that it arose on multiple occasions (perhaps through sound change or the influence of the second person in context) and a different explanation cannot be entirely ruled out.

5:7 λάβῃ (it receives) {B}

The shorter reading, λάβῃ ('it receives [the early and the late]'; 𝔓⁷⁴ 03 048 1739 lat^vg co^sa) has early support and its brevity explains the addition of two different nouns for clarification. The majority of manuscripts include ὑετόν ('[the early and the late] rain'; 02 025 044 5 33 etc.), reflecting a Septuagintal phrase (Deut. 11:14, Hos. 6:3, Joel 2:23 etc.), but a few witnesses repeat the word καρπόν ('[the early and the late] fruit'; 01 1175 lat^vl-pt sy^hmg co^bo) from earlier in the verse. The full attestation is given in *TuT Cath.* (TS21).[6] In translation, a noun will need to be supplied unless the receptor language has terms for 'early rain' and 'late rain'.

5:20 γινωσκέτω ὅτι (lit. let him know that) {B}

The vast majority of witnesses have the third-person singular imperative γινωσκέτω ὅτι ('let him know that'; 01 02 025 5 81 etc.). The second-person plural, γινώσκετε ὅτι ('you know that'; 03 sy^h) seems to have been introduced because the vocative ἀδελφοί in the previous verse otherwise has no complement, although it is possible that the third person is an accommodation to the preceding τις ('someone'). Nevertheless, it is unclear whether the third person relates to the 'wanderer' or the one who 'brings back'. This ambiguity may be why the phrase is entirely missing from Papyrus 74, one Old Latin manuscript (VL 66) and Sahidic, while some witnesses simply have ὅτι ('because'; 044 Origen^lat). It is less likely that the phrase was originally absent, because there is no obvious reason why it would have been expanded. Accordingly, the ambivalent majority reading has been adopted which, unlike the others, is genealogically coherent.

5:20 ψυχὴν αὐτοῦ ἐκ θανάτου (his soul from death) {C}

Unusually, the majority of manuscripts have a shorter form than the editorial text, simply reading ἐκ θανάτου ('from death'; 044 81 442 642 1175 etc., see *TuT Cath.* TS25). This may reflect confusion around the placing of αὐτοῦ: alongside the editorial text αὐτοῦ ἐκ θανάτου ('his [soul] from death'; 01 02 025 048^vid 5 etc.) is found ἐκ θανάτου αὐτοῦ

---

[6] See the discussion in Wachtel 1995: 235–237.

('from death itself'; $\mathfrak{P}^{74\text{vid}}$ 03 1611 lat$^{\text{vl-pt}}$).[7] There is good external support for both readings, but only the adoption of the editorial text as the initial reading provides genealogical coherence for all variants. It is also worth noting that this form is ambiguous: 'his' could refer to the 'sinner' or the one who 'brings back' (compare the previous variation unit). It may be possible to reflect the ambiguity in translation, or translators may choose a particular interpretation and supply a note indicating the alternative meaning.

---

[7] Although Wachtel 1995: 241 plausibly suggests that the majority reading arose from eyeskip of θανάτου αὐτοῦ, the ECM local stemma differs in deriving it from αὐτοῦ ἐκ θανάτου.

The First Letter of Peter

1:22 ἀληθείας (truth) {A}

After this word, the majority of manuscripts include διὰ πνεύματος ('through the Spirit'; 025 5 307 442 642 etc.). The strong external evidence for the shorter reading ($\mathfrak{P}^{72}$ 01 02 03 04 etc.) suggests that this is the earliest form. It is possible that πνεύματος was introduced as a reminiscence of 1 Pet. 1:2. Instead of ἀληθείας ('truth'), some Latin witnesses appear to reflect ἀγάπης ('love', *caritatis*) or πίστεως ('faith', *fidei*), perhaps under the influence of parallel passages (e.g. Rom. 1:5, 16:26) or a misreading. The full attestation in Greek continuous-text manuscripts is given in *TuT Cath.* (TS26).[1]

1:22 ἐκ καθαρᾶς καρδίας (lit. from a pure heart) ♦

The word καθαρᾶς ('pure') is missing from some early witnesses, which just have ἐκ καρδίας ('from the heart'; 02 03 1852 lat^{vg}). While this could be due to eyeskip owing to the similarity of the two words, it is also possible that the adjective was added later through assimilation to 1 Tim. 1:5 or 2 Tim. 2:22 (cf. Matt. 5:8). This appears to be the case in Codex Sinaiticus, where a corrector has written ἐκ καρδίας ἀληθινῆς ('from a true heart'; 01² lat^{vl-pt}), providing indirect support for the shorter reading. There is no other attestation of these variants (see *TuT Cath.* TS27). As the CBGM does not enable a decision to be made between the two principal readings, they have been presented as a split guiding line in the ECM. The THGNT has ἐκ καθαρᾶς καρδίας, while the SBLGNT just reads ἐκ καρδίας.

2:2 εἰς σωτηρίαν (into salvation) {A}

The phrase εἰς σωτηρίαν ('into salvation') is missing from part of the Byzantine tradition (642 etc.). Although it is possible that there was a theological concern about 'growing into salvation', it is more likely that the words were omitted by eyeskip from εἰς to εἰ at the beginning of the

---

[1] See also Wachtel 1995: 242–243.

next verse. Their absence from the *Textus Receptus* is reflected in a number of older translations.

2:19 θεοῦ (of God) {B}

Elsewhere in 1 Peter, the noun συνείδησις ('knowledge') is always qualified by the adjective ἀγαθή ('good'; 1 Pet. 3:16 and 3:21, compare also 1 Tim. 1:5 and 1:19). This would explain its introduction here, either as ἀγαθήν alone (also 'good [knowledge]'; 04 044 307 442 etc.) or in the conflated forms ἀγαθὴν θεοῦ ('good [knowledge] of God'; 𝔓⁷² 81) and θεοῦ ἀγαθήν (also 'good [knowledge] of God'; 02* 33 2344). The unusual phrase συνείδησις θεοῦ ('knowledge of God'; 01 02ᶜ 03 025 etc.) occurs only here in the New Testament, but is attested by the majority of manuscripts as well as the Latin and Coptic traditions and explains the development of the other readings.

2:21 ἔπαθεν (suffered) {A}

A few witnesses read ἀπέθανεν ('died'; 𝔓⁸¹ 01 044 5 307 syᵖ Cyril). This appears to be an early editorial alteration making it explicit that Christ's suffering involved death, in contrast to the majority reading ἔπαθεν ('suffered'; 𝔓⁷² 02 03 04 etc.).[2] Suffering is a particular theme of this letter, which is unique in the New Testament in its statement that 'Christ suffered' (compare Heb. 13:12). The same alternative reading is found for this phrase at both 1 Pet. 3:18 and 4:1, bringing them into line with the standard affirmation that Christ died for us (e.g. Rom. 5:6–8, 14:9; 1 Cor. 15:3; Gal. 2:21; Col. 2:20 etc.).

2:21 ὑμῶν ὑμῖν (for you ... you) {A}

As noted on many occasions (cf. 1 Pet. 3:18), the sound change known as itacism meant that the two pronouns ἡμεῖς ('we') and ὑμεῖς ('you') were pronounced identically. Here, the preceding and following second-person plural verbs support both second-person pronouns in context, which have good early attestation (ὑμῶν ὑμῖν, 𝔓⁷² 01 02 03 04 etc.) and have accordingly been adopted as the editorial text. The reading of the majority of manuscripts, ἡμῶν ὑμῖν ('[suffered] for us [leaving] you [an example]'; 025 33 307 436 etc.) results in a curious switch,

---

[2] See further Ehrman 2011: 181.

in which the author first is identified with and then separated from the recipients: it is possible that the use of ὑπὲρ ἡμῶν ('for us') in credal formulae elsewhere may have inspired its introduction here (cf. Rom. 5:8, 8:31–32; Eph. 5:2; 1 Thess. 5:10; Titus 2:14). A few minuscules have two first-person pronouns, ἡμῶν ἡμῖν ('[suffered] for us [leaving] us [an example]'; 642 1243 2344), also seen in the *Textus Receptus*, while one reads ὑμῶν ἡμῖν ('[suffered] for you [leaving] us [an example]'; 2492): the limited attestation of both suggests that they reflect scribal confusion. The full attestation in Greek continuous-text manuscripts is given in *TuT Cath.* (TS29).[3]

3:8 ταπεινόφρονες (a humble mind) {A}

The Byzantine tradition is split between φιλόφρονες ('courteous'; 025 307[txt] etc.) and, in fewer manuscripts, ταπεινόφρονες ('a humble mind'; etc.; 𝔓[72] 𝔓[81vid] 01 02 03 etc.: see *TuT Cath.* TS30). Both external and internal evidence support the latter as the earlier reading: even though φιλόφρονες is less common in the New Testament, it suits the context better. Some witnesses have a conflation with both words, φιλόφρονες ταπεινόφρονες (020 1448[v.r.-vid] etc.), demonstrating how lists such as this increase over time.

3:15 τὸν Χριστόν (Christ) {B}

There is strong support for the editorial text with τὸν Χριστόν ('Christ'; 𝔓[72] 01 02 03 04 etc.), despite the unusual phrase 'the Lord Christ'. The majority reading τὸν θεόν ('God'; 025 5 81 307 436 etc.) stems either from assimilation to the more common phrase 'the Lord God' or a misreading of the *nomen sacrum* ΧΝ as ΘΝ. An incoherent branch of the attestation of Χριστόν in the CBGM suggests that this error occurred more than once.

3:16 καταλαλεῖσθε (you are maligned) {A}

The parallel at 1 Pet. 2:12 appears to have given rise to the two forms of text found in Byzantine tradition, καταλαλοῦσιν ὑμῶν ὡς κακοποιῶν ('[when] they malign you as an evildoer'; 01 02 04 025 etc.) and

---

[3] On this and the previous variant, see also Wachtel 1995: 246–249. Details of the CBGM are given in Wachtel 2008: 118–121.

καταλαλῶσιν ὑμῶν ὡς κακοποιῶν ('[when]ever they malign you as an evildoer'; 307 436 442 1243 etc.: see *TuT Cath.* TS32). Here, however, there is significant support for a different term, καταλαλεῖσθε ('you are maligned'; 𝔓⁷² 03 044 1175 etc.), which could not have been introduced through harmonisation or abbreviation, and has therefore been adopted as the editorial text. Indeed, the excellent coherence of the two majority readings suggest that they each stem from a single alteration. The one instance of καταλαλοῦσιν ('they malign'; 1448*) is a partial form of one of the variants. Languages which do not have a passive voice will need to use the active even when translating the editorial text.

3:18 περὶ ἁμαρτιῶν ἔπαθεν (suffered for sins) {B}

The most significant variant in this phrase is ἀπέθανεν ('died') in place of ἔπαθεν ('suffered'). As at 1 Pet. 2:21 (see above) and 4:1 (see below), this appears to be an editorial substitution to clarify that Christ actually died rather than suffered: although it is found in numerous manuscripts and goes back as far as Papyrus 72 and Codices Sinaiticus and Alexandrinus, it is not the majority reading. Variation between ὑπέρ ('because of') and περί ('concerning') is relatively common in the New Testament (cf. Gal. 1:4): while ὑπὲρ ἁμαρτιῶν ('because of sins') is preferred in the Pauline corpus (apart from Hebrews), περὶ [τῶν] ἁμαρτιῶν ('concerning sins') is more common in the Catholic Epistles. A number of the witnesses which read περὶ ἁμαρτιῶν here then include ὑπὲρ ὑμῶν ('on your behalf'); some have ὑπὲρ ἡμῶν ('on our behalf') or just ἡμῶν ('our [sins]'). The shortest reading, attested by the majority of manuscripts, also has early support in Codex Vaticanus and explains the development of the numerous other variants: περὶ ἁμαρτιῶν ἔπαθεν ('suffered for sins'; 03 025 642 etc.). Accordingly, this has been adopted as the editorial text. Despite the early attestation of περὶ ἁμαρτιῶν ὑπὲρ ὑμῶν ἀπέθανεν ('died for sins on your behalf'; 𝔓⁷² 02 [044] 1611 1735) and περὶ ἁμαρτιῶν ὑπὲρ ἡμῶν ἀπέθανεν ('died for sins on our behalf'; 01 04² 5 33^vid 436 etc.), the change of verb shows that these are secondary and also appears to have led to the expansion of the phrase (cf. Rom. 5:8, 2 Cor. 5:14).

3:18 ὑμᾶς (you) {C}

As noted above (e.g. 1 Pet. 2:21), itacism meant that the first- and second-person plural pronouns were pronounced identically. There is nothing in the present context to indicate whether Christ's suffering was for 'you' or for 'us', and the same variation is also found at 1 Pet. 3:21. External evidence, including the Byzantine tradition, is also split between ὑμᾶς ('you'; 𝔓⁷² 03 025 044 etc.) and ἡμᾶς ('us'; 01² 02 04 etc.), apart from the erroneous omission of the pronoun by the first hand of Codex Sinaiticus. Given the overwhelming preference in this letter for the second-person plural (ὑμεῖς appears at least forty times, ἡμεῖς just four times in the editorial text) and a tendency to make texts more inclusive, especially for liturgical reading, ὑμᾶς has been adopted here (as at 1 Pet. 2:21) with some hesitation.

4:1 παθόντος (suffered) {A}

Despite the replacement of παθεῖν with ἀποθανεῖν in 1 Pet. 2:21 and 3:18 (see above), only the first hand of Codex Sinaiticus has ἀποθανόντος ὑπὲρ ὑμῶν ('died on your behalf'; 01*). Other witnesses just read παθόντος ('suffered'; 𝔓⁷² 03 04 044 etc.) or παθόντος ὑπὲρ ἡμῶν ('suffered on our behalf'; 01² 02 025 5 33 etc.; see also *TuT Cath.* TS33). As noted at 1 Pet. 3:18, the longer text is likely to derive from assimilation to parallel passages, and the early evidence for the shortest reading justifies its adoption here.[4]

4:14 δόξης (glory) {B}

Again, there is good external evidence for the shortest reading here, δόξης ('glory'; 𝔓⁷² 03 044 642 1448 etc.). This is attested by the majority of minuscules and it is genealogically coherent, even though 'spirit of glory' is an unusual collocation. Numerous other witnesses have δόξης καὶ δυνάμεως ('[the spirit of] glory and power'; 02 025 5 33 81 etc.), while the first hand of Codex Sinaiticus reads δόξης καὶ τῆς δυνάμεως αὐτοῦ ('[the spirit of] his glory and power'; 01*). There is no obvious reason for the omission of the longer phrases (apart from eyeskip from καί to καί), while the combination elsewhere of δόξα and δύναμις (e.g. Matt. 24:30, Mark 13:26, Rev. 15:8 and

---

[4] See also the discussion at Wachtel 1995: 253–255.

19:1) could have led to the introduction of the latter here. The full attestation in Greek continuous-text manuscripts is given in *TuT Cath.* (TS35).[5]

4:14 ἐφ' ὑμᾶς ἀναπαύεται (is resting on you) {B}

At the end of this verse, the majority of Greek manuscripts include an additional observation: κατὰ μὲν αὐτοὺς βλασφημεῖται, κατὰ δὲ ὑμᾶς δοξάζεται ('on their part he is blasphemed, but on your part he is glorified'; 025 044 [1448] 1611 etc.). Although it is possible that this was omitted through homoeoteleuton between ἀναπαύεται and δοξάζεται, the strong attestation for the shorter reading ($\mathfrak{P}^{72}$ 01 02 03 5 etc.) suggests that it is original. The early core of the attestation is coherent, but the CBGM indicates that an abbreviation was introduced on multiple occasions; the absence of the first additional clause from GA 307 is due to eyeskip. One lectionary (not included in UBS6) has a further addition, reading κατὰ μὲν αὐτοὺς βλασφημεῖται καὶ ὀνειδιζόμενον φέρει, κατὰ δὲ ὑμᾶς δοξάζεται ('on their part he is blasphemed and bears that which has been scorned, but on your part he is glorified'; L921). This demonstrates how the text was supplemented over time with clarificatory or homiletic expansions: these may have been added to explain the unfamiliar designation 'spirit of glory' earlier in the verse (see previous unit).

4:16 μέρει (lit. part) {C}

There is very strong external evidence for the reading ὀνόματι ('[in this] name'; $\mathfrak{P}^{72}$ 01 02 03 044 etc.), including all the early translations. This refers back to the term χριστιανός ('Christian') earlier in the verse. Both the SBLGNT and THGNT adopt ὀνόματι, which was also read in UBS4. However, the ECM prefers the more difficult reading found in the majority of Greek manuscripts, μέρει (lit. '[in this] part' or 'in this respect'; 025 307 642 1448 etc.). Parallels for this are seen at 2 Cor. 3:10 and 9:3, although they hardly seem prominent enough to influence the wording here. The choice of ὀνόματι has been justified by the CBGM: the textual flow diagram for ὀνόματι shows several incoherencies indicating multiple emergence, in keeping with the

---

[5] See further Wachtel 1995: 257–259.

consideration that ὀνόματι was more likely to replace μέρει than vice versa.⁶

5:2 ἐπισκοποῦντες μὴ ἀναγκαστῶς ἀλλ᾽ ἑκουσίως κατὰ θεόν
(exercising the oversight, not under compulsion but willingly, as God would have you do it) {C}

The first participle, ἐπισκοποῦντες ('exercising oversight'), is missing from Codex Sinaiticus (first hand) and Codex Vaticanus as well as the Sahidic and Ethiopic. A few minuscules have the later form ἐπισκοπεύοντες ('to be a bishop'; 1175 1611: see further *TuT Cath.* TS36). After the verb ποιμάνατε ('tend'), this word may have been considered superfluous; in addition, as this charge is addressed to πρεσβυτέροι ('elders', 1 Pet. 5:1) it might have been felt inappropriate for them to act as ἐπίσκοποι ('bishops'). The word ἐπίσκοπος at 1 Pet. 2:25 is applied to Christ rather than Christian ministers. Some witnesses read ἀναγκαστικῶς ('compulsively'; 33 2344 etc.), which seems to be a synonym for ἀναγκαστῶς ('under compulsion'). The majority of Greek manuscripts, including Codex Vaticanus, lack κατὰ θεόν (lit. 'according to God'). It is unusual to find a shorter text in Byzantine tradition: the reason for the omission may have been the difficulty of understanding what this meant in context, yet the phrase is not uncommon in the New Testament (e.g. Rom. 8:27, 2 Cor. 7:9, 1 Pet. 4:6). When all these variants are taken into account, the choice of editorial text has relatively good and early attestation ($\mathfrak{P}^{72}$ 01² 02 025 044 etc.). The same reading is adopted in both the SBLGNT and THGNT.⁷

5:10 ὑμᾶς (you²) {A}

Alternation between pronouns due to itacism has already been observed at 1 Pet. 2:21 and 3:18 (see above). Here, the context of the preceding exhortation and the overwhelming manuscript attestation strongly support the second person, ὑμᾶς ('you'; $\mathfrak{P}^{72}$ 01 02 03 025 etc.). A few witnesses, however, have ἡμᾶς ('us'; 442 1735* 2492 etc.): al-

---

⁶ See the explanation in Wasserman and Gurry 2017: 71–74, as well as Mink 2004: 43–45, and Mink 2009: 205–224. Knight 2019 offers a detailed criticism of the CBGM here, preferring ὀνόματι.

⁷ This unit is also discussed in Wachtel 1995: 259–261.

though this is a simple sound change, its adoption in the *Textus Receptus* means that the first person is seen in a number of translations.

5:11 τὸ κράτος (the power) {B}

This verse has been influenced by the longer formulaic benediction at 1 Pet. 4:11, which includes ἡ δόξα καὶ τὸ κράτος ('the glory and the power') as found here in part of the Byzantine tradition (01 025 307 442 642 etc). The other most widely attested form is ἡ δόξα κράτος ('the glory, power'; [436] etc.: see *TuT Cath.* TS38), while a different group of minuscules reads τὸ κράτος καὶ ἡ δόξα ('the power and the glory'; 5 33 81 1175 1243 etc.). The fact that there is early evidence for just τὸ κράτος ('the power'; [𝔓⁷²] 02 03 044 lat^(vl-pt, vg)), which differs from the previous formula and explains the differing sequences in the other variants, means that it has been adopted as the editorial text.

5:14 Χριστῷ (Christ) {A}

The majority of witnesses include Ἰησοῦ ('Jesus'; 01 025 5 81 307 etc.): the ECM has a split guiding line, indicating that it is impossible to decide between Χριστῷ Ἰησοῦ ('Christ Jesus') and Χριστῷ ('Christ') by itself. The same variation is seen at 1 Pet. 5:10: these are the only two possible occasions of the sequence Χριστὸς Ἰησοῦς in this epistle (contrast Ἰησοῦς Χριστός at 1:1–7, 1:13, 2:5, 3:21, 4:11) and the expansion of such formulae in the textual tradition is to be expected. Here, there is a coherent core of early witnesses for Χριστῷ by itself, even though the overall attestation is not coherent, and the same phrase at 1 Pet. 3:16 offers further support for the shorter reading here and in 1 Pet. 5:10. The principal reason for the inclusion of this unit, however, is the final Amen. This, too, is attested by the majority of manuscripts (01 025 5 307 436 etc.), but its absence from a range of early and important witnesses (02 03 044 81 1175 etc.), including multiple translations, is hard to explain if it were not original. The entire final phrase is missing from Papyrus 72, presumably as an oversight.

The Second Letter of Peter

1:1 Συμεών (Simeon) {B}

Although the standard form of Peter's first name in the Gospels and Acts is Σίμων ('Simon'; 𝔓⁷² 03 044 5 81 etc.), there is extensive attestation here for Συμεών ('Simeon'; 01 02 025 33 307 etc.), and the Byzantine tradition is split. The latter form is otherwise only attested at Acts 15:14, and was therefore more likely to have been corrected towards the regular Greek spelling. The Hebraic form adds an element of verisimilitude, but it may be noted that the first name is absent from 1 Pet. 1:1. If translations adopt the principle of giving an individual the same name throughout in order to avoid confusion (cf. Gal. 2:9, 11) then this variation unit may be disregarded. Otherwise an explanatory note should be provided.

1:3 ἰδίᾳ δόξῃ καὶ ἀρετῇ (by his own glory and excellence) {B}

The majority of Greek manuscripts read διὰ δόξης καὶ ἀρετῆς ('through glory and excellence'; 𝔓⁷² 03 5 642 1175 etc.). The preposition διά after καλέσαντος ('called') is a common construction (cf. Gal. 1:15, 2 Thess. 2:14) and could easily have arisen from ἰδίᾳ through the omission of the initial letter (particularly given the other occurrences of διά in context), after which the dative would have been corrected to the genitive: the perfect genealogical coherence suggests that, if this scenario took place, it only happened once. The editorial text, ἰδίᾳ δόξῃ καὶ ἀρετῇ ('by his own glory and excellence'; 01 02 04 025 044 etc.), has strong external support, including most early translations. In addition, the adjective ἴδιος is used frequently in this epistle. Nonetheless, the genealogical coherence of this reading is not perfect.

1:10 σπουδάσατε βεβαίαν ... ποιεῖσθαι (be all the more eager to confirm) {A}

The longer form of this phrase, σπουδάσατε ἵνα διὰ τῶν καλῶν ἔργων βεβαίαν ... ποιῆσθε ('be eager through good works that you confirm'; 01 [02] 044 5 81 etc.), provides an explanation of how 'to confirm your call and election'. A similar expansion is found with a slightly different construction: σπουδάσατε διὰ τῶν καλῶν ἔργων βεβαίαν ... ποιεῖσθαι ('be eager through good works to confirm'; 442). The short reading is present in early witnesses as well as the majority of minuscules, σπουδάσατε βεβαίαν ... ποιεῖσθαι ('be eager to confirm'; 𝔓⁷² 03 04 025 etc.). There is no obvious reason for omission, and all other instances of σπουδάζω ('be eager') in the New Testament take an accusative and infinitive (including 2 Pet. 1:15 and 3:14). One witness has an abbreviated form, σπουδάσατε βεβαίαν εἰ ὑμῶν τὴν ἐκλογὴν ποιεῖσθε, ('be eager if you confirm your election'; 1243) which might have arisen in order to make sense of the form of the final verb: ποιεῖσθαι, ποιεῖσθε and ποιῆσθε were all pronounced identically in later Greek and so could have led to confusion in spelling.

1:17 ὁ υἱός μου ὁ ἀγαπητός μου οὗτός ἐστιν (this is my Son my Beloved) {B}

The majority of witnesses have this phrase in the form which occurs at Matt. 3:17 and 17:5, οὗτός ἐστιν ὁ υἱός μου ὁ ἀγαπητός ('this is my Son the Beloved' or 'this is my beloved Son'; 01 02 04¹ 044 etc.: see also *TuT Cath.* TS41). The strong influence exerted by these parallels—given that this is presented as a quotation—means that differing forms of text are hard to explain if this were original. Some witnesses read οὗτός ἐστιν ὁ υἱός μου ὁ ἀγαπητὸς οὗτός ἐστιν ('this is my Son, the Beloved this is'; [04*ᵛⁱᵈ] 025 1175 coˢᵃ⁻ᵐˢˢ,ᵇᵒ), which might be a conflation of the majority reading and that of the editorial text. However, ὁ υἱός μου ὁ ἀγαπητός μου οὗτός ἐστιν (lit. 'My Son, my Beloved, this is'; 𝔓⁷² 03 coˢᵃ⁻ᵐˢ) could have arisen through eyeskip between OYTOC and OYC (the *nomen sacrum* for ὁ υἱός) in that longer form. It is the presence of the second μου ('my') in this short text which suggests that this poorly-attested reading is the earliest on the grounds of transcriptional probability.[1] The THGNT prefers the majority reading, for which the external evidence is stronger.

1:21 ἀπὸ θεοῦ (from God) {B}

The majority of manuscripts read ἅγιοι θεοῦ ('holy [people] of God [spoke]'; 01 [02] 044 5 33 etc.). There is significant support for ἀπὸ θεοῦ ('[people spoke] from God'; 𝔓⁷² 03 025 442 1175 etc.). The latter might

---
[1] See Wachtel 1995: 272.

have been considered a harder reading, especially if it was construed as 'people from God'. Alternatively, in majuscule script ΑΠΟ could have been misread as ΑΓΙΟ(Ι) especially given that ἁγίου appears in the previous clause. There are a few examples of conflations reading 'holy [people] from God': ἀπὸ θεοῦ ἅγιοι (04), ἅγιοι ἀπὸ θεοῦ (81), demonstrating that both readings were ancient. The genealogical coherence is good for either shorter reading.[2]

2:4 σειραῖς (chains) {C}

A few important witnesses have σιροῖς ('pits'; 01 02 03 04 81 lat[vl-pt]), usually spelt as σειροῖς due to itacism. This is very similar to the majority reading σειραῖς ('chains'; 𝔓[72] 025 044 5 33 etc.). Given the relationship between 2 Peter and Jude, it is possible that this verse may reflect 'in eternal chains in deepest darkness' (δεσμοῖς ἀϊδίοις ὑπὸ ζόφον) at Jude 6. Either term could have been misread for the other, although 'pits of darkness' seems to make better sense than 'chains of darkness'. The majority reading, which has better genealogical coherence, has therefore been preferred here with some hesitation and is also seen in SBLGNT: the THGNT adopts the alternative in the form σειροῖς.

2:6 ἀσεβεῖν (lit. to be ungodly) {C}

The alternative readings involve different interpretations of μελλόντων ('to be about to'). The majority form, with the verb ἀσεβεῖν (01 02 04 044 etc.), takes it as referring to people: 'an example to those who were to be ungodly'. The noun ἀσεβέσιν (𝔓[72] 03 025 1175 1243 1852 sy eth) means that it must be understood impersonally, 'an example of what is coming to the ungodly'. A change could have been made in either direction to clarify the understanding, or the confusion of the majuscule forms ΑϹΕΒΕΙΝ and ΑϹΕΒΕϹΙΝ. While μέλλειν is usually followed by an infinitive, the genitive participle μελλόντων is difficult in this context, so ἀσεβεῖν may in fact be a harder reading than the dative ἀσεβέσιν. The latter is preferred by the SBLGNT, but unlike ἀσεβεῖν it is not genealogically coherent. Both the ECM and THGNT choose ἀσεβεῖν: in translating this, it may be more natural to render μελλόντων with a dative, such as '[an example] for those about to'.

---

[2] See also *TuT Cath.* (TS43) and Wachtel 1995: 273–275.

2:11 παρὰ κυρίῳ (lit. before the Lord) ◆

The second edition of the ECM has a split guiding line between the majority reading παρὰ κυρίῳ ('before the Lord'; 01 03 04 025 etc.) and the absence of the phrase (02 044 33 81 436 etc.), allowing that either may be original. The former is adopted in the THGNT, the latter in the SBLGNT. A third variant, παρὰ κυρίου ('from the Lord'; 𝔓⁷² 5 307 etc.), was preferred in UBS4, on the basis that it is a harder reading than παρὰ κυρίῳ because it presents God as the source of the 'slanderous judgement'.³ The parallel passage at Jude 9 does not include a reference to God: the shorter form could have been introduced through assimilation to this, or it could have been original and expanded in two different ways. Internal and external evidence thus point in different directions: although the attestation of παρὰ κυρίῳ is coherent, that of the shorter reading is not, indicating that it arose on multiple occasions.

2:13 ἀδικούμενοι (suffering) {B}

The internal rhythm of the editorial text, ἀδικούμενοι μισθὸν ἀδικίας (lit. 'being wronged the penalty for wrongdoing'; 𝔓⁷² 01* 03 025 044 etc.) matches the previous phrase, ἐν τῇ φθορᾷ ... φθαρήσονται ('in destruction ... they will be destroyed'), but it is unusual for ἀδικέω to be used with an accusative in the absence of a person as a direct object. This, or exegetical concerns that it was not appropriate for God to be the implicit agent of injustice or that the sinners are not in fact 'being wronged' for their wrongdoing, may have led to the substitution of ἀδικούμενοι with a similar participle, κομιούμενοι ('about to receive'; 01² 02 04 5 33 etc.; see *TuT Cath*. TS44). It is more difficult to explain the introduction of ἀδικούμενοι, which might perhaps have been an anticipation of ἀδικίας. In any case, the external evidence suggests that the easier majority reading is secondary.

2:13 ἀπάταις (pleasures) {B}

The visual similarity in majuscule script of ΑΠΑΤΑΙC and ΑΓΑΠΑΙC could easily have led to the substitution of one for the other. In the context of feasting (συνευωχούμενοι), the term ἀγάπαις ('love feasts'; 02 03 044 5 1243 1611 and several translations) is more likely to have been

---

³ Metzger 1994: 633.

introduced, hence the preference here for the majority reading ἀπάταις (lit. 'deceits'; 𝔓⁷² 01 04 025 etc.): the multiple emergence of ἀγάπαις in the CBGM is consistent with misreading on several occasions. There is also evidence for ἀγνοίαις ('ignorance'; 1739), which could have been a misreading of ἀγάπαις or possibly influence from 1 Pet. 1:14 or Eph. 4:18. Curiously, not only does the parallel at Jude 12 read ἀγάπαις (see below), but two of the manuscripts which have ἀγάπαις here read ἀπάταις there (02 1243).

2:15 Βοσόρ (Bosor) {A}

There are twelve instances of Βοσόρ ('Bosor') in the Septuagint, but always as the name of a place rather than a person (e.g. Deut. 4:43, 1 Sam. 30, Is. 63:1). All the references to Balaam describe him as the son of Beor (Βεώρ, Num. 22:5, 24:3, 24:15, 31:8; Deut. 23:4, Josh. 13:22, Mic. 6:5). The extremely strong attestation here of the unparalleled personal name Βοσόρ ('Bosor'; 𝔓⁷² 01² 02 04 025 etc.), also seen in Byzantine tradition, indicates that it is original (if probably erroneous), while Βεώρ ('Beor'; 03 lat^(vl-pt) sy^(ph) co^(sa)) is a correction.[4] The peculiar reading of the first hand of Codex Sinaiticus, Βεωρσορ ('Beoorsor'; 01*) is likely to reflect an attempt in its exemplar to correct Βοσόρ to Βεώρ by supplying the necessary letters, yet instead of being treated as substitutions they were incorporated as additions. As at 2 Pet. 1:1, if the principle of using a single name throughout is adopted, the customary proper noun would be supplied from the Old Testament.

2:18 ὄντως (lit. actually) {C}

There is significant support for ὀλίγως ('just'; 𝔓⁷² 01² 02 03 044 33 436), a word which is not found elsewhere in the Greek Bible (apart from Isaiah 10:7 in Aquila's version). The variant ὀλίγον ('a little'; 2344), the adverbial form normally used instead of ὀλίγως, is probably a development from this: the three early versions (lat sy co) reflect one of these two words. Despite the confidence of the previous committee for ὀλίγως (read in UBS4 and the SBLGNT), the textual flow shows a clear dependence on the majority reading ὄντως ('actually'; 01* 04 025 048 etc.), a perfectly coherent attestation in the CBGM, which is adopted

---

[4] Himes 2022 suggests that Bosor reflects a pun in Aramaic.

in the second edition of the ECM and the THGNT. This term is particularly prominent in 1 Timothy, but not otherwise found in the Catholic Epistles. It also seems harder in context, given the return to sin described in 2 Pet. 2:20. The change probably arose through the visual confusion of ΟΝΤΩΣ and ΟΛΙΓΩΣ. Translators should note that the ECM prefers a present participle as the following word (ἀποφεύγοντας, 'those who are [actually] escaping') in contrast to the aorist participle in the majority reading which also occurs in 2 Pet. 2:20 (ἀποφύγοντες, 'having escaped').

3:6 δι' ὅν (through which) {C}

The majority of witnesses here read a plural, δι' ὧν ('through which'; 𝔓⁷² 01 02 03 04 etc.). There are several options for an antecedent which matches this, although they are not straightforward. The closest on formal grounds is οὐρανοί ('heavens') in 2 Pet. 3:5 (compare the same noun in 3:7), which might also be taken in the form οὐρανοί … καὶ γῆ ('the heavens and the earth'); the two preceding instances of ὕδωρ ('water') could constitute a plural; a combination of ὕδωρ and λόγος ('word') is also possible. One of the challenges is the following reference to water (ὕδατι κατακλυσθείς, 'was deluged with water'), which risks being tautologous if 'water' is the previous subject.⁵ There is remarkably little support for δι' ὅν (lit. 'because of which'; 025 1175 lat^(vl-pt, vg-mss)), whose antecedent is the preceding phrase τῷ τοῦ θεοῦ λόγῳ ('the word of God'). Still, this makes better sense in context, and would then be reflected in the following verse by τῷ αὐτῷ λόγῳ ('by the same word', albeit not the majority reading). Because of vowel isochrony, the relative pronouns ὧν and ὅν would have sounded identical, yet the tendency would have been for this pronoun to be attracted to the immediately preceding singular even though that is only attested in ten manuscripts cited in the ECM: the CBGM indicates that, even if δι' ὅν is adopted as the initial text, it also arose independently on several occasions. In contrast, its emergence is more coherent if δι' ὧν is selected as the earliest form. This, along with its weak attestation, makes

---

⁵ I am grateful to Tommy Wasserman for the suggestion that 'the heavens and the earth' might relate to the text of Gen. 7:11 in the Septuagint, where different forms of water burst from these locations (αἱ πηγαὶ τῆς ἀβύσσου καὶ οἱ καταρράκται τοῦ οὐρανοῦ, 'the springs of the abyss and the torrents of the heaven').

δι' ὅν a very difficult choice despite its attractiveness: both THGNT and SBLGNT prefer the plural, as did UBS4.

3:9 εἰς ὑμᾶς (with you) {C}

As observed at 1 Pet. 2:21 and elsewhere, itacism meant that ὑμᾶς ('you') and ἡμᾶς ('us') came to be pronounced identically. The majority of minuscules have εἰς ἡμᾶς (lit. 'to us'; 307 442 642 2492 etc.) but the much earlier attestation for εἰς ὑμᾶς (lit. 'to you'; 𝔓[72] 03 04 025 048[vid] etc.) makes it preferable. Whichever of these two readings is adopted as the initial text, the second-person plural pronoun does not have perfect genealogical coherence—which would be consistent with multiple emergence through confusion of homophones. Surprisingly, however, εἰς ἡμᾶς has perfect coherence in either scenario. Another early strand of tradition has δι' ὑμᾶς ('because of you'; 01 02 044 etc., lat sy co[sa] eth). This preposition appears to improve the sense following μακροθυμεῖν ('be patient'), yet elsewhere in the New Testament this verb is followed by the preposition ἐπί ('upon'), which would have been a more expected replacement. What is more, there is also good overall genealogical coherence if δι' ὑμᾶς is taken as the initial text. As a result, although there is strong external evidence for εἰς ὑμᾶς, it is adopted with some hesitation.

3:10 οὐχ εὑρεθήσεται (lit. will not be found) {D}

This verse poses a textual conundrum which in the ECM is only resolved by adopting a reading which is not attested in any surviving Greek witness but implied by some manuscripts of the Philoxenian Syriac, the Sahidic version and, possibly, Coptic dialect V. Some important Greek manuscripts read εὑρεθήσεται ('will be found'; 01 03 025 1175 1448 1739[txt] 1852), yet this is in contradiction to the sense given by the previous καυσούμενα λυθήσεται ('will be dissolved with fire'). An early attempt to address this problem may be seen in Papyrus 72, which draws on the vocabulary of the preceding phrase to read εὑρεθήσεται λυόμενα ('will be found dissolved'; 𝔓[72]). The same approach—but based on the other term—underlies the majority reading κατακαήσεται ('will be burned up'; 02 048 33 81 etc.); some minuscules have the plural κατακαήσονται, taking γῆ as a separate subject even though this is not required grammatically. If κατακαήσεται were original, alternative readings would not have been necessary. Codex Ephraemi Rescriptus has ἀφανισθήσονται ('will vanish'; 04), a replacement which appears to be motivated by the sense of the phrase. Witnesses which lack the whole phrase (044 lat^vg) probably represent eyeskip from λυθήσεται to εὑρεθήσεται rather than an attempt to excise the problematic text. The endurance of εὑρεθήσεται suggests that it is at least part of the original text: there would be no reason for λυόμενα to be overlooked if it was initially present. Although there is nothing in context which would prompt the omission of οὐχ, the hypothesis of an early oversight of this key word restores the sense which many readers noticed was lacking here.[6] Nevertheless, both SBLGNT and THGNT prefer εὑρεθήσεται by itself, as the hardest reading to understand: it might be taken as a divine passive with the implication 'will be brought to judgment by God' or translated as 'will be disclosed' (NRSVue).[7] The full attestation in Greek continuous-text manuscripts is given in *TuT Cath.* (TS 49), while no fewer than sixteen conjectural emendations are listed in the *Amsterdam Database*.[8]

3:18 αἰῶνος (of eternity) {C}

The majority of Greek manuscripts include ἀμήν ('Amen'; 𝔓^72 01 02 04 025 etc.) here as at 1 Peter 5:14 (see above), but not at the end of James or the Johannine Epistles. It is unclear whether the few witnesses which lack Amen (03 1175 1243 1739*) represent an original shorter doxology, to which the addition of ἀμήν would have been natural, or an editorial deletion to match other epistles in these witnesses. Both the SBLGNT and THGNT choose to print ἀμήν, in keeping with the doxological formula (compare Jude 25 below).[9] A few expansions (including a triple Amen in GA 1848) are noted in *TuT Cath.* (TS52).

---

[6] *Amsterdam Database* cj11713 [Holwerda 1853]. See also the discussion at Mink 2004: 27. Another conjecture proposes that the the previous word be read as ἀργά, 'fruitless' (*Amsterdam Database* cj12787 [Stauffer 1945], cf. cj10389 [Bradshaw 1910]), but a positive verb retained here.

[7] For a full range of translation suggestions, see Bauckham 1983 *ad loc.* There is also a reference to this verse in BDAG s. v. εὑρίσκω 2 in support of the rendering 'judged'.

[8] Krans, Lietaert Peerbolte et al. 2016. The analysis of this variation unit in the CBGM is described at Wasserman and Gurry 2017: 74–78; see also Wachtel 1995: 285–287.

[9] In favour of its originality, see Wasserman 2023: 60–61.

The First Letter of John

1:4 ἡμεῖς (we) {B}

The majority of witnesses read ὑμῖν ('to you'; 02ᶜ 04 5 81 307 etc.), following the pattern of the indirect object for the two previous verbs. In contrast, an emphatic repetition of the subject ἡμεῖς ('we'; 01 02·ᵛⁱᵈ 03 025 044 33 latᵛˡ⁻ᵖᵗ coˢᵃ⁻ᵐˢˢ) is a harder reading, and its superior external attestation leads to its adoption here. As it indicates the writers of the letter, an exclusive pronoun should be used in languages where this is possible.

1:4 ἡμῶν (our) ♦

The confusion of the first-person and second-person plural pronouns due to the sound change known as itacism is frequently seen in this epistle. Here, the influence of the second person in the identical phrase in John 16:24 ('that your joy may be complete') is likely to have been strong, and it is surprising to find the Byzantine tradition split between ἡμῶν ('our'; 01 03 044 436 1175 etc.) and ὑμῶν ('your'; 02 04 025 5 33 etc.). If the first-person reading is interpreted as self-gratification, then ἡμῶν appears to be the harder reading: it is adopted by both SBLGNT and THGNT.[1] Nevertheless, the split guiding line in the ECM indicates that the editors felt unable to decide which form was original: the first person can be understood as inclusive, emphasising the desire for κοινωνία ('fellowship') expressed in the preceding verse and, with a few exceptions which are sufficiently explained by itacism, both attestations are coherent. (See also 2 John 12 below.)

2:14 ἔγραψα¹ (lit. I wrote) {A}

As the layout in the edition shows, this and the two previous verses present two sets of three co-ordinated addresses to the same groups of people. In the first group, each begins with the present-tense γράφω

---

[1] Metzger, however, characterises ἡμων as a reflection of the author's 'generous solicitude' (1994: 639).

('I am writing'), as is seen here at the beginning of the second group in the majority of minuscules (81 642 1175 1448 2492 etc.; see further *TuT Cath.* TS57). However, the latter two elements of the second group are uniformly attested as aorists, and the strong early support in the first of these addresses for the aorist ἔγραψα ('I wrote'; 𝔓⁷⁴ᵛⁱᵈ 01 02 03 025 etc.) indicates that all three addresses in this set were initially aorist and the variation is simply due to scribal inattention.² The coherence of both attestations suggests that the error was only made once. If ἔγραψα is considered to be an epistolary aorist, from the point of view of the recipient, then it too could be translated using the present tense. The change in tense, however, might be indicated in some way: for instance, by emphasising the consistency of the author in the present and in the past.

2:18   ὅτι¹ (that¹) {B}

The majority of Greek manuscripts include the definite article, reading ὅτι ὁ ('that the'; 01² 33 81 307 442 etc.). This leads to an appreciable difference in the understanding of the subject as 'the antichrist' rather than simply 'an antichrist' or the proper noun 'Antichrist'. However, the definite article stands in contrast to the plural ἀντίχριστοι ('antichrists') in the next phrase, and its absence from some important witnesses (01* 03 04 044 5 436 1739 Origen) suggests that it is secondary. There is a similar case at 2 John 7, although the evidence there is much weaker: in contrast, at 1 John 2:22 and 4:3, the inclusion of the article may be due to parallelism in context. A few manuscripts in the present verse read just ὁ ('the'; 02 1881), probably due to eyeskip within the longer reading, with the result that the phrase has to be treated as direct speech.

2:20   πάντες (all) {B}

The placing of the subject πάντες ('all'; 01 03 025 044 1852 sy co^sa) after the verb, in chiasmus with the initial ὑμεῖς ('you'), seems unexpected, especially as οἴδατε ('you know') has no direct object, unlike in the following verse. For this reason, πάντες could have been changed into the object πάντα ('[you know] all things'; 02 04 5 33 81 etc.; see *TuT Cath.* TS59), perhaps to be taken as 'all things necessary for salvation'. On the

---

² See also Wachtel 1995: 296–297.

other hand, in the previous verse πάντες also follows the verb to which it refers and this might have led to assimilation here: the CBGM suggests that πάντες was introduced more than once during transmission. Although the external evidence is divided, it suggests that πάντες is earlier.

2:23 ὁ ὁμολογῶν τὸν υἱὸν καὶ τὸν πατέρα ἔχει (everyone who confesses the Son has the Father also) {A}

Unusually, the majority of minuscules have a shorter text, lacking the whole of this phrase (81 642 1175 2492 etc.; see *TuT Cath.* TS60). Without this complement the observation appears to be incomplete, and there is excellent early evidence in favour of the longer text. Its omission must therefore have arisen through eyeskip between the two instances of τὸν πατέρα ἔχει (see also the next unit), possibly in a single manuscript which was important for the development of the Byzantine tradition.[3]

3:1 καὶ ἐσμέν (and that is what we are) {B}

The majority of minuscules lack this phrase, probably through eyeskip between κληθῶμεν and ἐσμέν: in majuscule script ΚΛΗΘΩΜΕΝ and ΚΑΙΕϹΜΕΝ are similar. Alternatively, it is possible that the phrase was deleted because it was considered an unnecessary parenthesis, or was even added by an editor concerned that 'being *called* children of God' was not the same as actually being so. However, the strong external evidence for καὶ ἐσμέν (lit. 'and we are'; 𝔓[74vid] 01 02 03 04 etc.) indicates that it is likely to be the earliest reading. The full attestation in Greek continuous-text manuscripts is given in *TuT Cath.* (TS63): Wachtel suggests that this is a relatively late omission in Byzantine tradition.[4]

3:5 ἁμαρτίας (sins) {B}

The external evidence is split between ἁμαρτίας ('sins'; 02 03 025 5 33 etc.) and the majority reading ἁμαρτίας ἡμῶν ('our sins'; 01 04 044 81 307 etc.). Although it is probable that the longer text was introduced through assimilation to verses such as 1 John 1:9, 2:2 and 4:2, it is also

---
[3] Wachtel 1995: 300.
[4] Wachtel 1995: 303.

possible that, mindful of the injunction at 1 John 2:2, an early editor deleted ἡμῶν so as not to limit the scope of salvation. The genealogical coherence of the shorter reading is perfect with only one exception, probably due to contamination or a scribal slip.

3:14   μὴ ἀγαπῶν (does not love) {A}

There is early support for the shortest text, μὴ ἀγαπῶν ('does not love'; 01 02 03 33 1243 etc.), including several ancient translations. This is a harder reading in that the participle has no object and therefore does not match the previous clause. The majority of manuscripts include the same noun as before as an object, reading μὴ ἀγαπῶν τὸν ἀδελφόν (lit. 'does not love the brother'; 04 044 5 81 307 etc.), while others also have a pronoun, μὴ ἀγαπῶν τὸν ἀδελφὸν αὐτοῦ ('does not love their brother'; 025 436 442 1448 1611 etc.: see further *TuT Cath.* TS64). There is a possibility that the object was deleted in order to make the statement broader in application (compare the previous unit), but the combination of the external evidence and more difficult reading leads to the choice of the editorial text (see also 1 John 4:19 below), which also provides the best overall genealogical coherence. In some languages, however, it may be necessary to supply an object for the verb.

4:3   μὴ ὁμολογεῖ (that does not confess) {A}

The editorial text μὴ ὁμολογεῖ ('that does not confess'; 01 02 03 044 etc.) is attested by early witnesses and the majority of manuscripts. A few minuscules have the subjunctive, μὴ ὁμολογῇ ('that is the sort that does not confess'; 442 1243 1881[c-vid]), but this is likely to be through itacism. The interest of this variant is in the intriguing reading *solvit* found in the Vulgate, which appears to stem from the Greek λύει ('that releases', 'that dissolves'), an odd verb to use of Christ. Its occurrence in multiple early Greek Christian writers is recorded in the margin of GA 1739. There is no obvious contextual reason for its emergence: it has been suggested that it was introduced as criticism of the Gnostic tendency to distinguish between the human Jesus and divine Christ, although such an implication is not immediately obvious given the absence of any mention of Christ here (see also the following unit).[5] The author's

---

[5] Metzger 1994: 645; see also the discussion in Ehrman 1988 and 2011: 147–158.

preference for identical structures and verbal repetition supports the majority reading.

4:3 τὸν Ἰησοῦν (Jesus) {A}

This variant illustrates how a short reading can grow over time. There is early support for τὸν Ἰησοῦν ('Jesus'; 02 03 1739 [1881] lat[vg] co[bo] etc.), while some witnesses have Ἰησοῦν Χριστόν ('Jesus Christ'; 1735 lat[vl-pt, vg-ms] co[sa, bo-mss] etc.) as seen in the corresponding clause of the previous verse. That verse also includes the statement that Jesus 'has come in the flesh' (ἐν σαρκὶ ἐληλυθότα). Some manuscripts feature this here, reading τὸν Ἰησοῦν ἐν σαρκὶ ἐληλυθότα ('Jesus has come in the flesh'; 044 33 81 436 1448 etc.)—and in doing so, provide support for τὸν Ἰησοῦν rather than Ἰησοῦν Χριστόν. Others match the previous statement exactly, Ἰησοῦν Χριστὸν ἐν σαρκὶ ἐληλυθότα ('Jesus Christ has come in the flesh'; 020 5 307 442 642 etc.), which is the Byzantine text. Evidence that this was circulating at an early stage is seen in the misreading in Codex Sinaiticus, Ἰησοῦν κύριον ἐν σαρκὶ ἐληλυθότα ('Jesus the Lord has come in the flesh'; 01), where the *nomen sacrum* ΚΝ (for κύριον) has been substituted for ΧΝ (Χριστόν). Other individual minuscules have different errors prompted by confusion between *nomina sacra* or the presence of the definite article. Although there is always a possibility that a shorter reading could have arisen from overlooking a *nomen sacrum*, and the genealogical coherence is not perfect, the primacy of the editorial text is supported by the variety of longer forms and its difference from the previous verse. The full attestation in Greek continuous-text manuscripts is given in two entries in *TuT Cath.* (TS66–67).[6]

4:19 ἀγαπῶμεν (we love) {A}

Several important witnesses attest the verb without a direct object, as ἀγαπῶμεν ('we love' or 'let us love'; 02 03 5 1243 1739 1852 1881 lat[vg]): compare the construction at 1 John 3:18. The main variant readings indicate that more than one editor supplied an object: ἀγαπῶμεν τὸν θεόν ('we love God'; 01 048 33 81 436 etc.) has earlier support and matches the following verse, while the majority reading ἀγαπῶμεν αὐτόν ('we love him'; 044 307 1175 2492 etc.) corresponds to the next clause. In

---

[6] See further Wachtel 1995: 305–307.

Sahidic, this unusual intransitive use of 'to love' has led to its replacement by the equivalent of γινώσκομεν ('we know [that he first loved us]'; co^sa). Once again, the strong support for the harder reading justifies its adoption. It may be noted that, although ἀγαπῶμεν is usually taken as subjunctive at 1 John 4:7 ('let us love'), the context here supports an indicative ('we love'). There are parallels for this at 1 John 4:14 and 16, which also begin with the emphatic ἡμεῖς ('we').[7]

4:20 οὐ δύναται ἀγαπᾶν (cannot love) ◆

The external evidence is divided between οὐ δύναται ἀγαπᾶν ('cannot love [God]'; 01 03 044 442 1243 etc.) and the majority reading πῶς δύναται ἀγαπᾶν; ('how can they love [God]?'; 02 048 5 [33] 81 etc.: see also *TuT Cath.* TS69). The latter is perhaps the harder reading, with the interrogative πῶς ('how') coming in the middle of the sentence after the object. On the other hand, a similar use of πῶς is seen at the end of a sentence at 1 John 3:17, which might have prompted its insertion here. With such evenly balanced internal and external evidence, the ECM has a split guiding line indicating that it is impossible to decide which of these two readings is earlier: both readings give the same result in the CBGM. The SBLGNT and THGNT adopt οὐ, and πῶς is often considered to be a later stylistic improvement: if it is not original, it must have been introduced at a very early point.[8]

5:6 αἵματος (blood[1]) {A}

A number of lectionaries and minuscules, under the influence of John 3:5, read πνεύματος ('[by water and] spirit') or πνεύματος ἁγίου ('[by water and] Holy Spirit'). Assimilation to that well-known verse is also seen in manuscripts with αἵματος καὶ πνεύματος ('[by water and] blood and spirit'; 01 02 33^vid 307 436 etc.) or πνεύματος καὶ αἵματος ('[by water and] spirit and blood'; 025 5 81 442 1243 etc.: see further *TuT Cath.* TS71). Although there is a possibility that one of the terms was omitted through eyeskip between the genitive endings or the connectives (ὕδατος καὶ αἵματος καὶ πνεύματος), the presence of two different sequences suggests that καὶ πνεύματος was a subsequent introduction,

---

[7] Thus Omanson 2006: 511.
[8] Wachtel 1995: 309.

perhaps anticipating its appearance later in the verse. External evidence also supports the adoption of the shorter text, with the majority of manuscripts as well as early witnesses reading αἵματος ('[by water and] blood'; 03 044 642 1175 1739* etc.).[9]

5:6 ὕδατι καὶ ἐν τῷ αἵματι (water and the blood) ◆

The ECM has a split guiding line between ὕδατι καὶ ἐν τῷ αἵματι ('[in the] water and in the blood'; 03 044 5 33 307 etc.) and the majority reading ὕδατι καὶ τῷ αἵματι ('[in the] water and the blood'; 01 436 442 636^txt 642 etc.), which only differ in whether or not they repeat the preposition ἐν ('in') from the beginning of the phrase. The former is adopted in the SBLGNT and the latter in the THGNT. Both readings are consistent with the text chosen in the previous variation unit, as are ὕδατι καὶ αἵματι ('[in the] water and blood'; 81 co^cv Cyril^pt) and αἵματι καὶ ἐν τῷ ὕδατι ('[in the] blood and in the water'; 025 1243 1739* [1881]). However, some of the witnesses which introduce spirit in that unit also have it here: ὕδατι καὶ ἐν τῷ πνεύματι ('[in the] water and in the spirit'; 02 1735) and αἵματι καὶ ἐν τῷ ὕδατι καὶ πνεύματι ('[in the] blood and in the water and spirit'; 1739^c). Although the evidence against the inclusion of πνεύματι is stronger here than in the previous unit, it is worth observing that its *nomen sacrum* abbreviation (ΠΝΑΤΙ) is similar to the other two terms (ΑΙΜΑΤΙ, ΥΔΑΤΙ), which may have led to copying errors.[10]

5:7–8 μαρτυροῦντες τὸ πνεῦμα καὶ τὸ ὕδωρ καὶ τὸ αἷμα (that testify; the Spirit and the water and the blood) {A}

The external evidence for the absence of the phrase known as the Johannine Comma (or *Comma Johanneum*) from Greek tradition is overwhelming: the shorter text adopted here is attested in all majuscules and the majority of minuscules (01 02 03 025 [044] 048^vid etc.). Out of 509 witnesses, *TuT Cath.* lists 500 in support of this form, with four others illegible or omissive (TS72). The earliest attestation of the additional text is in Latin: *testimonium dicunt in terra, spiritus aqua et*

---

[9] There is a detailed discussion in Wachtel 1995: 310–314; for a presentation of the CBGM for this unit, see Wasserman 2015c or Wasserman and Gurry 2017: 78–80.

[10] Ehrman 2011: 70–71 considers the possibility that the variants might represent assimilation to John 3:5.

sanguis et hi tres unum sunt in Christo Iesu. ⁸ *et tres sunt, qui testimonium dicunt in caelo, pater, verbum* [or *filius*] *et spiritus* ('that testify on earth, the spirit, the water, and the blood, and these three are one in Christ Jesus. ⁸ And there are three which testify in heaven, the Father, the Word [*or* the Son] and the Spirit.'). This is found in some Old Latin and Vulgate manuscripts, as well as the writer Priscillian, the *testimonia* collection known as the *Speculum* (*Liber de divinis scripturis*), and the *De trinitate* ascribed to Vigilius of Thapsus. The attestation suggests that this is a gloss introduced in the fourth century, like many other interpolations in the Latin text of the Catholic Epistles: it is not present in the earliest Latin quotation of these verses (*De rebaptismate*, composed around 256) or the major ancient Latin Christian authors.[11] Although the third-century writer Cyprian has the words *tres unum sunt* ('the three are one') alongside a reference to the Father, Son and Holy Spirit, the context does not support the identification of this as a reference to the Johannine Comma. The text of the Johannine Comma in Greek witnesses reflects a secondary Latin form with a different sequence, as found in the Clementine Vulgate: μαρτυροῦντες ἐν τῷ οὐρανῷ, ὁ πατὴρ ὁ λόγος καὶ τὸ ἅγιον πνεῦμα, καὶ οὗτοι οἱ τρεῖς ἕν εἰσιν. ⁸ καὶ τρεῖς εἰσιν οἱ μαρτυροῦντες ἐν τῇ γῇ, τὸ πνεῦμα καῖ τὸ ὕδωρ καὶ τὸ αἷμα ('that testify in heaven, the Father, the Word and the Holy Spirit, and these three are one. ⁸ And there are three which testify on earth, the spirit and the water and the blood'). This or a similar text is found in the margin of five Greek manuscripts as a variant reading (88 177 221 429 636) and in the main text of five others (61 629 918 2318 2473). In the sixteenth-century Codex Montfortianus (GA 61), which is believed to have been copied in order to persuade Erasmus to include the Johannine Comma in his edition, the absence of the Greek articles is an indication that this text was translated from Latin (cf. the bilingual 629, in which the following phrase is also lacking).[12] While the Comma is present in older translations based on one of Erasmus' later editions, it is generally omitted in modern versions. There are many detailed treatments of this variation unit.[13]

---

[11] See Houghton 2016: 178–180.

[12] See Wachtel 1995: 317; on the Greek text of GA 629, see also the comments of Wasserman 2006: 329–330. The variant in GA177 is not noted in *TuT Cath*.

[13] Among recent studies, see especially McDonald 2016 and Hernández 2020.

5:10 ἐν αὐτῷ (in their hearts) {C}

The Byzantine tradition is split between the reflexive pronoun ἐν ἑαυτῷ (lit. 'in himself'; 01 044 5 1243 1611 etc.) and the standard pronoun ἐν αὐτῷ (lit. 'in him'; 03² 81 307 436 442 etc.). Majuscule manuscripts which read EN AYTΩ without breathing marks (02 023* 025) could support either form (ἐν αὑτῷ or ἐν αὐτῷ). The genealogical coherence is the same for both readings. None of the other eighteen examples of this prepositional phrase in 1 John is reflexive, so internal evidence may be taken to support ἐν αὐτῷ. However, this reading is ambivalent, as it could be taken to refer to the believer or to the Son of God. Only the former interpretation is possible with the reflexive, which may have led to its introduction. In addition, there are instances of αὕτη as a reflexive pronoun in the verses on either side, which may have prompted assimilation. Notwithstanding this, both the SBLGNT (with αὐτῷ) and THGNT (with ἑαυτῷ, as in UBS4) prefer the reflexive. A similar variation is seen below at 1 John 5:18.

5:10 τῷ θεῷ (in God) {A}

There is strong external evidence, including the majority of manuscripts, for τῷ θεῷ ('in God'; 01 03 025 044 etc.). This is also the hardest reading, given that the complement of the same participle at the beginning of the verse is εἰς τὸν υἱὸν τοῦ θεοῦ ('in the Son of God'). Witnesses which read τῷ υἱῷ ('in the Son'; 02 5 81 436 642 etc.) and τῷ υἱῷ τοῦ θεοῦ ('in the Son of God'; co^(sa, bo-pt) eth^(mss)) represent assimilation to the preceding phrase, as the other reading could not have emerged from these through eyeskip.

5:18 τηρεῖ ἑαυτόν (lit. protects himself) {C}

This is the same type of variation as at 1 John 5:10 (see above). On this occasion, the majority of Greek manuscripts support the reflexive pronoun ἑαυτόν ('himself'; 01 02ᶜ 025 044 etc.), and there is much less evidence for αὐτόν (lit. 'him'; 03² 1852 lat), while AYTON in the first hand of Codices Alexandrinus and Vaticanus could be taken either way. The regular pronoun is the easier reading if the preceding subject, ὁ γεννηθεὶς ἐκ τοῦ θεοῦ ('the one born from God'), is understood as Christ, who would then protect the believer. However, this subject could also be taken to be the believer, as in the description at the beginning of the verse of Christians as 'those who are born of God', which makes more sense with the reflexive. This is the only instance of γεννηθείς in the Johannine Epistles, which favours distinguishing it from the author's use of γεγεννημένος for believers (normally in the phrase πᾶς ὁ γεγεννημένος ['everyone who is born'; 1 John 3:9, 5:4, 5:18, cf. 2:29, 4:7]). In addition, there is no other New Testament example of a reflexive with τηρεῖν ('keep'), although it does occur with φυλάσσειν ('guard') in 1 John 5:21. Given the sharp contrast between internal and external evidence, it is not easy to establish the earliest text. Whichever reading is chosen, the genealogical coherence is perfect for the reflexive but not for the other reading. On this occasion SBLGNT has αὐτόν (with UBS4), while THGNT prefers ἑαυτόν.[14]

5:21 εἰδώλων (idols) {A}

The majority of Greek manuscripts include a final ἀμήν ('Amen'; 025 81 307 1175 1852 etc.), as is customary at the end of letters, especially when they were read liturgically. However, without a preceding benediction or doxology it is unexpected, and there is strong support for its absence (01 02 03 044 etc. and most early translations: see further *TuT Cath.* TS75). It is worth observing that the situation is similar at 2 John 13 (see below), while at 3 John 15 there is hardly any attestation of a final Amen.

---

[14] On the broader context for this verse, see Ehrman 2011: 82–83 and, in contrast, Wasserman 2012: 337–339.

The Second Letter of John

8 ἀπολέσητε … ἀπολάβητε (you do not lose … may receive) {A}

The majority of Greek manuscripts have both these verbs in the first-person plural, ἀπολέσωμεν … ἀπολάβωμεν ('we may not lose … we may receive'; 025 1175 1448 etc.: see *TuT Cath*. TS78). This matches the preceding first-person plural verbs (e.g. 2 John 4, 5, 6), as well as the majority reading εἰργασάμεθα ('we have worked') in this verse (see the next variation unit). In such a context, the second-person plural seems more difficult, even though it follows the imperative βλέπετε ἑαυτούς ('be on your guard'); there is also very strong early attestation for ἀπολέσητε … ἀπολάβητε ('you may not lose … you may receive'; 01 02 03 044 etc.), including all early translations.

8 εἰργασάμεθα (we have worked for) {C}

There is early support for the second-person plural εἰργάσασθε ('you have worked for'; 01 02 044 048[vid] etc. and most ancient translations), matching the verbs on either side adopted in the editorial text (see the previous variation unit). The majority reading, the first-person εἰργασάμεθα ('we have worked for'; 03 025 1175 1448 2492 etc.), corresponds to Byzantine tradition in the previous unit, making the entire phrase consistent. However, Codex Vaticanus and three minuscules (181 1836 2492) have an unexpected switch from 'you do not lose' to 'what we have worked for'.[1] This is a harder reading which still makes sense in context, even though it could be a partial correction towards the majority reading: this variant is not genealogically coherent whichever form is taken as the initial text. While SBLGNT agrees with the ECM, THGNT prefers εἰργάσασθε. In translation, the first-person plural could be taken as inclusive or exclusive, depending on the extent to which the writer is considered to identify with the readers.

---

[1] See further Wachtel 1995: 331–335.

12 ἡμῶν (our) ◆

As in the occurrence of the same phrase at 1 John 1:4, both first-person and second-person pronouns are found, which would have sounded identical due to itacism. On this occasion, the majority of Greek manuscripts read ἡμῶν ('our'; 01 025 044 307 642 etc.) while there is significant support for ὑμῶν ('your'; 02 03 5 33 81 etc., lat co[bo] eth). Despite the strength of its attestation, the latter may be assimilation to the two second-person pronouns earlier in the verse. In contrast to 1 John 1:4, the CBGM indicates that the attestation here of ἡμῶν is coherent, but ὑμῶν is incoherent whichever is chosen as the initial text: there were multiple independent changes from ἡμῶν to ὑμῶν in transmission. Once again, the ECM has a split guiding line, allowing that either may be earlier: SBLGNT has ὑμῶν while THGNT reads ἡμῶν. The first-person singular in Sahidic, μου ('my [joy]'; co[sa]) is assimilation to the preceding singular verbs.

13 τῆς ἐκλεκτῆς (elect) {A}

The majority of Greek manuscripts have a final ἀμήν ('Amen'; 1175 1448 1611 1852 etc.), but in the original context this makes little sense and there is very strong support for its absence ($\mathfrak{P}^{74vid}$ 01 02 03 025 etc., lat[vl, vg] co). In some witnesses, a final benediction is added: ἡ χάρις μετὰ σοῦ ('grace be with you'; 442 lat[vg-ms]; see further *TuT Cath.* TS82). The unusual phrase 'the children of your elect sister' (cf. 2 John 1) has led to the replacement of ἐκλεκτῆς by the visually similar word ἐκκλησίας ('[the children of your sister] the church'; 307 lat[vg-ms]), but this is clearly an error: there is no other New Testament description of the church as sister.

The Third Letter of John

4 οὐκ ἔχω χαράν (I have no ... joy) {A}

There is strong support from early witnesses and the Byzantine tradition for οὐκ ἔχω χαράν ('I have no [greater] joy'; 01 02 025 044 048^vid etc.), although some manuscripts have the more natural word order χαρὰν οὐκ ἔχω (04 442 1739). Codex Vaticanus and the Latin Vulgate, however, read οὐκ ἔχω χάριν ('I have no [greater] grace'; 03² lat^vg), which also appears in the sequence χάριν οὐκ ἔχω (1243 2492). Despite the prevalence in the New Testament of χάρις ('grace'), the word χαρά ('joy') is more common in the Johannine Epistles and here reflects the verb ἐχάρην ('I was overjoyed') in the previous verse. It seems that χάριν is an error of inattention, perhaps prompted by the following word ἵνα: note also that the first hand of Codex Vaticanus mistakenly wrote the preceding word as ἔχων ('having') rather than ἔχω ('I have').

9 Ἔγραψά τι (I have written something) {B}

This is the only instance in the New Testament of ἔγραψα followed by the indefinite τι ('I wrote something'; 01* 02 048^vid 442 1739 co^bo-mss), but it has early attestation. Codex Vaticanus and the Coptic tradition support ἔγραψάς τι ('you wrote something'; 03 co), but the support for the second person is very slim and it is likely to be assimilation to the beginning of the previous section (3 John 5). Other important witnesses have ἔγραψα ἄν ('I would have written'; 01² 048 33 81 307 etc.), which suits the context: this reading might have been taken to explain why such a letter does not appear to be preserved.[1] At least one minuscule even has ἔγραψα ἄν τι ('I would have written something'; 1611*vid), combining the two readings. The Byzantine tradition, however, has no complement, reading just ἔγραψα ('I wrote'; 04 025 044 5 1175 etc.). This may be assimilation to Johannine usage elsewhere, or omission of τι by a form of haplography given the following homophone τῇ.

---

[1] Omanson 2006: 518 notes that some ancient and modern interpreters identified the letter implied by the editorial text as 2 John.

Conversely, it is possible but unlikely that τι could have arisen through dittography. The CBGM indicates that ἔγραψα ἄν is never genealogically coherent, and was introduced from the Byzantine text on more than one occasion. In contrast, the attestation of τι is coherent if it is adopted as the initial text: what is more, it is unusual, difficult to explain and well attested.

The Letter of Jude[1]

1 τοῖς ἐν θεῷ πατρὶ ἠγαπημένοις (to those … who are beloved in God the Father) {B}

There are two variants in this phrase. After τοῖς a few witnesses add ἔθνεσιν ('to the nations'; 307ᶜ 1243 1611 1739 2492 sy) in order to make the addressees explicit, but this is clearly secondary. The majority of manuscripts give the participle as ἡγιασμένοις ('to those … who have been made holy'; 025 307 642 1175 1448 etc.), while there is strong early support for ἠγαπημένοις ('to those … who are beloved'; 𝔓⁷² 01 02 03 044 etc.) including all ancient translations. The attestation of each participle is genealogically coherent. The similarity of the two terms has prompted the substitution: although ἠγαπημένοις might have been influenced by 1 Thess. 1:4, the external evidence suggests that the assimilated term is ἡγιασμένοις as seen at 1 Cor. 1:2. In addition, ἠγαπημένοις is a more difficult complement to the phrase ἐν θεῷ πατρί ('in God the Father'); the Revised English Bible translates this as 'who live in the love of God the Father'.

4 δεσπότην (master) {A}

There are three places in the New Testament where δεσπότης ('master') is used of God (Luke 2:29, Acts 4:24, Rev. 6:10), while at 2 Pet. 2:1 it probably refers to Christ; there is no other instance of the phrase δεσπότην καὶ κύριον ('Master and Lord'; 𝔓⁷² 𝔓⁷⁸ 01 02 03 04 etc.). The overlap in meaning of these two terms along with the possibility of reading them as two different referents because of the presence of καί ('and') seems to have led to the introduction of θεόν: the majority of manuscripts read δεσπότην θεὸν καὶ κύριον ('Master God and [the] Lord [Jesus Christ]'; 025 044 5 88 1175 etc.). It is possible that the *nomen sacrum* ΘΝ could have been overlooked, but the strong attestation of the shorter reading and the good sense it makes in context suggests that

---

[1] Because Wasserman 2006 offers an apparatus of all continuous-text Greek manuscripts of Jude, *Text und Textwert* is not cited here for this epistle: every variation unit may be compared with Wasserman's collation.

it is the earlier form. Wasserman concludes that the probable referent of δεσπότην here is Jesus Christ.[2]

5   ὑμᾶς ἅπαξ πάντα ὅτι Ἰησοῦς (you ... once and for all, that Jesus) {C}

This has been described as 'one of the textually most difficult passages ... in the whole NT'.[3] The reading adopted in the editorial text is only found in Codex Vaticanus (03), although other witnesses have it without ὑμᾶς ('you'), which is superfluous in context: ἅπαξ πάντα ὅτι Ἰησοῦς (02 33 81 2344 lat^vg eth), πάντα ὅτι Ἰησοῦς ἅπαξ ([88] 1739^txt etc.), πάντα ἅπαξ γὰρ Ἰησοῦς (1739^v. r.). The Greek name Ἰησοῦς can be translated as 'Jesus' or 'Joshua': while the reference to Egypt and subsequent destruction suits the latter, the following verse indicates that the subject is divine.[4] This was also the understanding of those responsible for the following variants: ὑμᾶς πάντα ὅτι ὁ κύριος ('you [know] entirely that the Lord'; 01 sy^h?), the majority reading ὑμᾶς ἅπαξ τοῦτο ὅτι ὁ κύριος ('you [know] this once that the Lord'; 1175 1448 etc.), ἅπαξ τοῦτο ὅτι ὁ κύριος ('this once, that the Lord'; 307 436 642), πάντα ὅτι ὁ κύριος ἅπαξ ('entirely that the Lord once'; [044] 1611 sy^h?), ἅπαξ πάντα ὅτι ὁ θεός ('once entirely that God'; 04²), ἅπαξ τοῦτο ὅτι ὁ θεός ('this once, that God'; 5), πάντα ὅτι ὁ θεὸς ἅπαξ ('entirely that God once'; 442 1243 2492 lat^vl-pt sy^ph) as well as ἅπαξ τοῦτο ὅτι κύριος Ἰησοῦς ('this once, that the Lord Jesus'; 1735). The adverbs ἅπαξ and πάντα clearly posed a problem of interpretation: are they to be taken with εἰδότας ('knowing') or σῶσας ('saving')? Semantically the concept 'completely' (πάντα) fits 'knowing' and 'once for all' (ἅπαξ) offers a better match for 'saving', yet they are rarely found in this order. In addition, ἅπαξ could alternatively be understood as 'once', 'a first time' in co-ordination with τὸ δεύτερον ('afterwards', 'a second time') later in the verse. As for the agent, there is the possibility of confusion between the *nomina sacra* abbreviations for Ἰησοῦς, κύριος and θεός (IC, KC,

---

[2] Wasserman 2006: 253; Wasserman 2015c explores this with reference to the CBGM.

[3] Wasserman 2006: 255.

[4] For the typological relationship of Jesus and Joshua, attested as early as the Epistle of Barnabas, see Wasserman 2006: 263.

ΘC).⁵ This may be the case in the extraordinary reading of Papyrus 72, ἅπαξ πάντα ὅτι θεὸς Χριστός ('once entirely that God Christ'; 𝔓⁷²); here, the *nomina sacra* ΘC XC might be an error for ΘΥ XC (θεοῦ Χριστός, 'God's Anointed One'), but equally this could be a deliberate editorial change.⁶ Another pertinent observation is that all six other mentions of Jesus in Jude are in the form Ἰησοῦς Χριστός. The full range of variants in Greek manuscripts is given in *TuT Cath.* (TS91). The external evidence supports the text adopted here (and in the SBLGNT) as the most difficult at each point of variation (the unnecessary inclusion of ὑμᾶς, the attestation of both adverbs before ὅτι, the reading Ἰησοῦς). The THGNT prints ἅπαξ πάντα ὅτι Ἰησοῦς (without the initial ὑμᾶς) and Wasserman prefers ὑμᾶς ἅπαξ πάντα ὅτι κύριος.⁷ It has been suggested that the writer's understanding that Jesus was present in Israel's history justifies using 'Jesus' in translation for clarity whichever noun is adopted.⁸

12 ἀγάπαις ὑμῶν (your love-feasts) {A}

Instead of ἀγάπαις ('love-feasts'; 𝔓⁷² 01 03 044 etc.), a few manuscripts read ἀπάταις ('deceits'; 02 04 88 1243 2492). The CBGM indicates that it was introduced multiple times during transmission, consistent with assimilation to 2 Pet. 2:13 (see above). Nevertheless, in that verse Codex Alexandrinus and GA 1243 read ἀγάπαις, so it is possible that it arose on some occasions through misreading instead.⁹ The third-person pronoun αὐτῶν ('their'; 02ᶜ latᵛᵍ syᵖʰ coˢᵃ⁻ᵐˢ) also matches 2 Pet. 2:13, and is a simpler reading which dissociates the unbelievers from the recipients of the letter. The external evidence for ἀγάπαις ὑμῶν ('your love-feasts'; 𝔓⁷² 01 03 044 and the majority of minuscules) is overwhelming. In translation, some explanation may need to be given of the technical

---

⁵ There is no variation unit in the CBGM for just the name alone: the attestation of κύριος appears to be coherent, while Ἰησοῦς has a strong core without being entirely coherent overall.

⁶ For an error, see Metzger 1994: 657; for a deliberate change, Ehrman 2011: 100.

⁷ Wasserman 2006: 148–149; 255–266 (reproduced in Wasserman 2009: 143–152); see further Osburn 1981b, Ross 1983: 71–72, Wachtel 1995: 349–357, Bartholomä 2008 and the discussion of this variant in the light of the CBGM in Wachtel 2008: 121–126.

⁸ King 2017: 21–23.

⁹ Wasserman 2006: 286–287 (reproduced in Wasserman 2009: 153–154) considers misreading more likely than deliberate harmonisation.

Christian usage of ἀγάπη for a communal meal, of which this is the only secure instance in the New Testament: in fact, two manuscripts not cited here in UBS6 read εὐωχίαις ὑμῶν ('your feasts'; 6 424²).[10]

15 πᾶσαν ψυχήν (lit. everyone) {C}

This passage is a quotation from 1 Enoch 1:9 which has been adjusted in this epistle: surviving witnesses indicate that the Greek text of the original source had two clauses, reading ἀπολέσει πάντας τοὺς ἀσεβεῖς καὶ ἐλέγξει πᾶσαν σάρκα ('he will destroy all the ungodly and convict all flesh').[11] The question is which of these terms was adopted in the single clause presented here. There is strong support for πάντας τοὺς ἀσεβεῖς ('all the ungodly'; 02 03 04 044 5 etc.), while the majority of minuscules have πάντας τοὺς ἀσεβεῖς αὐτῶν ('all the ungodly of them'; 88 1175 2492 etc.). Variants such as πάντας ἀσεβεῖς ('all ungodly people'; 1739 etc.) or τοὺς ἀσεβεῖς ('the ungodly'; 442 sy^(ph-mss)) seem to be omissive forms of these. Nevertheless, the Coptic translations and three surviving Greek manuscripts read πᾶσαν ψυχήν (lit. 'every soul'; 𝔓⁷² 01 1852 sy^(ph-mss) co^(sa, bo-mss)). This is close to the other element in this verse of Enoch, but not identical in that it reads πᾶσαν ψυχήν rather than πᾶσαν σάρκα ('all flesh'). Might this be the original reading, differing from the source text of the quotation, which was then partially corrected towards the original by substituting the other term? Or is it a partial correction by an editor who remembered that ἐλέγξει in Enoch was followed by πᾶσαν but who failed to supply the correct noun—perhaps under the influence of πᾶσαν ψυχήν in Rom. 2:9 (although the possibility of textual variation in Enoch should also be taken into account)? Each of these scenarios is possible, and the alteration was clearly made at an early stage. The SBLGNT, THGNT and Wasserman all prefer πάντας τοὺς ἀσεβεῖς as the earlier reading in Jude, which varies from the original source but fits well with the rest of the present verse as well as the reading ἀσεβεῖς in Jude 4. The ECM, however, reads πᾶσαν ψυχήν on the basis that it is closer to the original source and was then substituted with an easier reading. According to the CBGM, both πᾶσαν ψυχήν and the majority reading πάντας τοὺς ἀσεβεῖς αὐτῶν

---

[10] See Wasserman 2006: 169.
[11] See Wasserman 2006: 302.

provide overall genealogical coherence, but this is not the case for πάντας τοὺς ἀσεβεῖς.[12]

22 ἐλεᾶτε διακρινομένους (have mercy ... who are wavering) {C}

The Byzantine reading ἐλεεῖτε is an alternative spelling of ἐλεᾶτε ('have mercy') and the majority of minuscules also have a nominative plural participle, διακρινόμενοι ('have mercy when you are making decisions'; 025 307 642 1175 1448 etc.), matching the structure found in the following phrase. There is strong support for the accusative here, however, which must be understood in a negative way. The earliest witnesses are split between ἐλεᾶτε διακρινομένους ('have mercy on those who are doubting'; 01 03 04[2] 044 etc.) and ἐλέγχετε διακρινομένους ('convince/convict those who are wavering'; 02 04* 5 33 81 etc., lat[vl-pt, vg] co[bo]). While ἐλέγχετε could be a misreading of ἐλεᾶτε, under the influence of ἐλέγξαι ('convict') in Jude 15 or διακρινόμενος διελέγετο ('contended and disputed') in Jude 9, the reverse may be true, given that ἐλεᾶτε is read by many witnesses in the following verse (see below). Papyrus 72 and some versional witnesses omit this verb altogether and postpone διακρινομένους as part of a recasting of these two verses (see the comment on the next variation unit). The choice of ἐλεᾶτε διακρινομένους by the ECM, SBLGNT and Wasserman may be considered the more difficult reading if ἐλεᾶτε is repeated in the following verse, but THGNT prefers ἐλέγχετε διακρινομένους. The translation of διακρινομένους as 'doubters' is problematic, not least because it does not match Jude 9: a better option may be 'those who are under judgment' or even 'disputers'.[13]

23 οὓς δὲ σῴζετε ἐκ πυρὸς ἁρπάζοντες, οὓς δὲ ἐλεᾶτε ἐν φόβῳ (save others by snatching them out of the fire; and have mercy on still others with fear) {C}

The majority of variants present Jude 23 as dealing with a single group of people, identified by οὓς δέ ('others') in co-ordination with οὓς μέν ('some') in Jude 22. Papyrus 72 and some early translations give the text of the two verses as follows: οὓς μέν ἐκ πυρὸς ἁρπάσατε,

---

[12] There are discussions at Wasserman 2006: 301–304 and Wachtel 1995: 357–359; a worked explanation of the CBGM here is given in Mink 2011: 181–189.

[13] See respectively Wasserman 2006: 196, 327–328 and Prothro 2024: 368–369.

διακρινομένους δὲ ἐλεεῖτε ἐν φόβῳ ('Snatch some from the fire, but have mercy on those who are wavering in fear'; 𝔓[72] lat[vl-pt] sy[ph] co[sa]). Codex Vaticanus also applies the first element to the previous verse, reading σῴζετε ἐκ πυρὸς ἁρπάζοντες, οὓς δὲ ἐλεᾶτε ἐν φόβῳ ('save [those who are wavering] by snatching them out of the fire, have mercy on others in fear'; 03). The majority of minuscules have οὓς δὲ ἐν φόβῳ σῴζετε ἐκ πυρὸς ἁρπάζοντες ('save others in fear, snatching them out of the fire'; 025 1175 1448 2492 etc.). Variations on this may be seen in οὓς δὲ σῴζετε ἐκ πυρὸς ἁρπάζοντες ἐν φόβῳ ('save others, snatching then from the fire in fear'; 04 1243 1852 sy[h]) and οὓς δὲ σῴζετε ἐκ πυρὸς ἁρπάζοντες ('save others by snatching them from the fire'; 642). Two readings, however, identify three sets of people in this verse, in keeping with the preference for threefold grouping in this letter: οὓς δὲ σῴζετε ἐκ πυρὸς ἁρπάζοντες, οὓς δὲ ἐλεᾶτε ἐν φόβῳ ('save others by snatching them out of the fire, have mercy on others in fear'; 01 02 044 5 33 etc.) and οὓς δὲ ἐν φόβῳ σῴζετε ἐκ πυρὸς ἁρπάζοντες, οὓς δὲ ἐλεᾶτε ἐν φόβῳ ('save others in fear by snatching them out of the fire, have mercy on others in fear'; [88] 1611). This triple set extends the normal opposition of μέν ... δέ ('some ... others') and repeats the command to have mercy already seen in the first element in Jude 22, although it should be noted that some manuscripts replace this second ἐλεᾶτε with ἐλέγχετε ('convince/convict'; 88 307 442: compare the comment on the previous unit). Given that the strongest set of external evidence supports one of the more difficult forms, this has been adopted with some hesitation: the number of alternatives in the tradition demonstrate the problems posed by this variation unit (eighteen different readings with multiple subtypes are recorded in *TuT Cath.* TS94). Even so, this text is also preferred by SBLGNT, THGNT and Wasserman. It may be observed that Codex Vaticanus also supports the editorial text if the absence of οὓς δέ before σῴζετε was due to eyeskip following διακρινομένους.[14]

---

[14] For an extended discussion of these two verses and detailed engagement with previous scholarship, see Wasserman 2006: 320–331 and Prothro 2024 (who argues in favour of the reading of 𝔓[72]); the interpretation is considered by Robinson, Llewelyn and Wassell 2018.

25 μόνῳ (only) {A}

The reading μόνῳ σοφῷ ('to the only wise [God]'; 025 5 307 642 1175 etc.) in the majority of manuscripts looks like assimilation to the well-known doxology in Romans 16:27. Nevertheless, there remains the possibility that σοφῷ was omitted by eyeskip, even though there is strong external support for just μόνῳ ('to the only'; 𝔓⁷² 01 02 03 04 etc.), including all early translations. According to the CBGM, this has probably led to several incoherencies in an otherwise coherent attestation with a broad range of early witnesses. The majority reading is perfectly coherent but lacks early support. It may also be noted that the Byzantine tradition lacks the following phrase (διὰ Ἰησοῦ Χριστοῦ τοῦ κυρίου ἡμῶν, 'through Jesus Christ our Lord'), probably through eyeskip between the two instances of ἡμῶν ('our').

25 ἀμήν (Amen) {A}

Unlike the other Catholic Epistles, there is very good external evidence at the end of Jude for the final ἀμήν ('Amen'; 𝔓⁷² 01 02 03 04 025 etc.), which is in keeping with the context of the doxology. There are just seven minuscule manuscripts from which it is absent.[15] It has also been deleted by the corrector of GA 424, in order to conform the text to the manuscript used for comparison: this shows that an editor could remove a final Amen (compare 2 Pet. 3:18).

---

[15] Wasserman 2006: 338.

The Pauline Epistles

Overview

The principal surviving papyrus manuscript of the Pauline Epistles is the third-century Papyrus 46 ($\mathfrak{P}^{46}$). This is a collection of letters, including Hebrews, but it it is not extant beyond the end of 1 Thessalonians and it is not clear which other letters were present. There are almost forty other papyrus fragments from the third century onwards, only four of which contain more than one epistle. The most extensive other papyrus is the eighth-century Papyrus 61 ($\mathfrak{P}^{61}$), with portions of seven letters including Titus and Philemon. While Codex Sinaiticus (01) and Codex Alexandrinus (02) contain all fourteen Epistles, the original part of Codex Vaticanus (03) breaks off in the middle of Hebrews (lacking the four letters to individuals) and Codex Ephraemi Rescriptus (04) has multiple lacunae, one of which covers the whole of 2 Thessalonians. Codex Claromontanus (06) is a sixth-century manuscript of the whole Pauline corpus, the oldest representative of a Latin-Greek bilingual tradition which includes the ninth-century Codex Boernerianus (012).[1] The most important minuscule is the ninth-century GA 1739, whose colophon states that it was copied from a very ancient exemplar and agrees with the text of Origen's Pauline commentaries, especially in Romans.[2] Other significant minuscules are GA 6, 33, 81, 1175, 1506 and 1881, several of which have already been mentioned in the Overviews for Acts and the Catholic Epistles. The majority of later majuscules as well as the other minuscules constitute the Byzantine textual tradition.

Early translations provide valuable evidence for the Pauline Epistles, comprising the Old Latin (lat^{vl}) and Vulgate (lat^{vg}), the two Coptic versions of Sahidic (co^{sa}) and Bohairic (co^{bo}) and the Peshitta (sy^{p}) and Harklean Syriac (sy^{h}). In addition, the Latin tradition features numerous commentaries from the fourth and fifth centuries: Origen's commentary on Romans and the fifth-century Theodore of Mopsuestia are

---

[1] The Greek text of Codex Augiensis (010) appears to be a copy of Codex Boernerianus (Fisher 2024) and for that reason it has been removed from UBS6.

[2] For the text of this, see Parker 2008: 261–262.

largely preserved only in translation. Matching his version of the Gospel (see the Overview for Luke above), Marcion was responsible for a collection of Pauline writings in the second century consisting of ten letters (without Hebrews or the Pastoral Epistles): again, this is not known to be transmitted in any manuscripts and information is only provided by reports in early Christian writers. Even though there is evidence for different letter collections, it is not possible to reach back in the surviving manuscript tradition to a stage before Paul's epistles were first collected and circulated as a group. Nevertheless, comments from antiquity and other considerations point to the Pastoral Epistles (1 Timothy, 2 Timothy, Titus) and Hebrews as being of separate origin even though they are integrated into the Pauline corpus in the Greek manuscript tradition.

The earliest text of Paul is generally provided by the fourth-century majuscule tradition. The bilingual witnesses (06 012), sometimes joined by other manuscripts (including $\mathfrak{P}^{46}$ and 03), transmit a form which has been subject to an early editorial revision. This is sometimes described as a 'Western' form, because of its connection with Latin, although it is very different to the 'Western' readings in Acts.[3] As in other writings, the Byzantine tradition also bears the marks of revision, providing smoother readings and occasional expansions.

The position of the doxology in Romans, sometimes at the end of the epistle and sometimes at the end of Romans 14, is a variation which may shed some light on the formation of the corpus. Similarly, much has been made of the absence of the place name from some witnesses at Eph. 1:1. Other well-known places of variation include the subjunctive or indicative at Rom. 5:1, Paul's 'burning' or 'boasting' (1 Cor. 13:3), the location of 1 Cor. 14:34–35, 'simplicity' or 'holiness' at 2 Cor. 1:12, the description of Hagar and Sinai (Gal. 4:25), the sequence of Phil. 1:16–17, Christ identified with God at Col. 2:2, the injunction to be 'infants' or 'gentle' at 1 Thess. 2:7, the alternative 'without God' at Heb. 2:9, and whether Sarah is the subject of the sentence in Heb. 11:11. A number of variations involve names, such as Junia (Rom. 16:7), Prisca (1 Cor 16:19), Cephas (Gal. 1:18 etc.) and Nympha (Col. 4:15).

---

[3] See further Metzger 1994: 542 and Westcott & Hort 1896: 150, 256–260.

The text of Paul in UBS6 is unchanged from the previous edition, with the exception of the removal of a few sets of brackets. In keeping with the evidence of the oldest complete copies of the Greek New Testament, however, Hebrews has been moved from the end of the corpus to after 2 Thessalonians: here, it is the last of the letters addressed to churches, preceding the letters to individuals. Work on the *Editio Critica Maior* of Paul is ongoing, with some of the data (including manuscript transcriptions, synopses and the initial collations) being made available online.[4]

---

[4] See www.epistulae.org.

The Letter to the Romans

1:1 Χριστοῦ Ἰησοῦ (Christ Jesus) {C}

The vast majority of manuscripts read Ἰησοῦ Χριστοῦ ('Jesus Christ'; 𝔓²⁶ 01 02 012 etc.), whereas the reverse sequence is found only in just a few witnesses (𝔓¹⁰ 03 81 lat^(vl-pt, vg) etc.). Although Codex Claromontanus (06) now lacks the first page of Romans in Greek, both its Latin text and a copy made in the ninth century (Codex Sangermanensis, 0319) suggest that it had the majority reading. Elsewhere in Romans, there is an even distribution of both sequences of this name (yet there are no variants to 'Jesus Christ' at 1:4, 1:6, 1:7 and 1:8). In the introductory formula in other epistles there is a preference for 'Christ Jesus' (cf. 2 Cor. 1:1, Phil. 1:1, Col. 1:1, 1 Tim. 1:1, 2 Tim. 1:1, Phlm 1), which could well have prompted a change here and elsewhere (cf. 1 Cor. 1:1, Eph. 1:1, Titus 1:1). The weight of the external evidence for 'Jesus Christ' at this point is impressive, and it is the reading adopted in THGNT.[1] The sequence of these words is not significant for translation, yet it may be possible to reflect it: if Χριστοῦ is taken first, it could be interpreted as the title 'Messiah' rather than a proper noun, but such a usage would normally be expressed with a definite article.

1:29 πονηρίᾳ πλεονεξίᾳ κακίᾳ (evil, covetousness, malice) {C}

As is common in such lists, variations in sequence and additional terms are found in the textual tradition. One early order is κακίᾳ πονηρίᾳ πλεονεξίᾳ ('malice, evil, covetousness'; 04 33 81 1506 etc.), while Codex Sinaiticus and Codex Alexandrinus have πονηρίᾳ κακίᾳ πλεονεξίᾳ ('evil, malice, covetousness'; 01 02) and two bilinguals have κακίᾳ πορνείᾳ πλεονεξίᾳ ('malice, fornication, covetousness'; 06* 012): it is possible that ΠΟΡΝΕΙΑ arose from a misreading of ΠΟΝΗΡΙΑ. The majority of Greek manuscripts provide a conflated form, πορνείᾳ πονηρίᾳ πλεονεξίᾳ κακίᾳ ('fornication, evil, covetousness, malice'; [06²]

---

[1] On this sequence in Codex Vaticanus in the Pauline Epistles, see Jongkind 2019: 237–238.

[025] 0278 256 263 etc.). The sequence which appears best to explain the others is πονηρίᾳ πλεονεξίᾳ κακίᾳ ('evil, covetousness, malice'; 03 0172ᵛⁱᵈ 6 1739 1881 Chrysostom). Although its attestation is consistent with its being the initial reading, the other early variants make for some doubt.

1:31 ἀστόργους (heartless) {B}

Two terms are found here in the majority of Greek manuscripts, ἀστόργους ἀσπόνδους ('heartless, implacable'; 01² 04 06² 025 etc.). This appears to be assimilation to the list at 2 Tim. 3:3: while omission through eyeskip is a possibility, there is good external evidence in support of just ἀστόργους ('heartless'; 01* 02 03 06* 012 etc.).

2:5 ἀποκαλύψεως (lit. 'revelation') {B}

The shorter text, ἀποκαλύψεως ('revelation'; 01* 02 03 06* 012 81 1506 lat syᵖ co), results in a single idea, 'the revelation of God's righteous judgment'. However, the majority of Greek manuscripts read ἀποκαλύψεως καί ('revelation and'; 01² 06² 025 etc.), leading to a day with three elements, 'anger and revelation and God's righteous judgment'. In this alternative reading, the middle term might be interpreted as an eschatological 'revelation' without any specific content. However, because ἀποκάλυψις in the epistles is normally followed by a genitive complement (e.g. Rom. 8:19, 16:25) and there is strong early evidence for the shorter reading, it appears that the καί was duplicated in error at an early point.

2:16 Χριστοῦ Ἰησοῦ (Christ Jesus) {C}

The evidence for the sequence in the editorial text (01*ᵛⁱᵈ 03) is even more slim than at Rom. 1:1 (see above). This is certainly the more unusual reading: there are no other instances of διὰ Χριστοῦ Ἰησοῦ in the Pauline Epistles, while διὰ Ἰησοῦ Χριστοῦ appears four times in this letter (Rom. 1:8, 5:21, 7:25, 16:27). However, this could well be an early editorial change given the unique attestation of this sequence in Codex Vaticanus at Rom. 5:17. Both external evidence and Pauline usage point strongly towards Ἰησοῦ Χριστοῦ and this is again adopted in the THGNT. The reading Ἰησοῦ Χριστοῦ τοῦ κυρίου ἡμῶν ('Jesus Christ our Lord'; 06) is a typical reverential expansion.

2:17 εἰ δέ (But if) {A}

As ει and ι came to be pronounced identically in Greek through itacism, it would have been hard to distinguish aurally between εἰ δέ ('but if'; 01 02 03 06* 81 etc.) and ἴδε ('see'; 06² 33 365 1175 and the majority of minuscules). The strong external evidence in favour of εἰ δέ and Paul's extensive use of it in Romans (in contrast to the very limited appearance of the imperatives ἴδε and ἴδετε in the epistles) justifies taking this as the earliest form. Nevertheless, it makes for a very long sentence because the corresponding clause to this conditional one only appears in 2:21. The change to ἴδε (whether through sound change or simply overlooking the letter ε) results in a simpler text which can be more easily punctuated.

3:2 [γάρ] (for)

Although the explanatory γάρ is present in the majority of Greek manuscripts, its absence from a variety of important witnesses (03 06* 012 81 365 1506 2464* and some early translations) leads to doubt as to whether it was originally present. Alternatively, it may have been deleted in the light of the occurrence of γάρ at the beginning of the following phrase.

3:4 νικήσεις (you will prevail) {B}

The textual tradition is split between the future indicative νικήσεις ('you will prevail'; 01 02 06 018 81 etc.) and the aorist subjunctive νικήσῃς ('may you prevail'; 03 012 020 365 1175 etc.). The preceding ὅπως ἂν δικαιωθῇς ('so that you may be justified'), with which this verb is co-ordinated, expects another subjunctive—as seen in νικήσῃς in the original context of Psalm 51:4 [50:6 LXX]. The more difficult reading is therefore νικήσεις, an indicative whose continuing attestation despite the context suggests that it is the earlier form. However, the two words would have been pronounced identically in later Greek due to itacism and it remains possible that νικήσεις is simply a widespread error.

3:7 δέ (but if) {C}

The choice of connective influences the way in which the argument is constructed. The majority of Greek manuscripts read γάρ ('for'; 03 06 012 025 etc.), taking this verse in continuity with the previous assertions. However, there is a contrast here in that the previous rhetorical questions apply to an imagined situation, whereas the following one reflects Paul's reality. This suggests that the contrastive δέ ('but'; 01 02 81 256 263 etc.) has a stronger claim despite its relatively scarce attestation, hence its adoption as the editorial text here and in the SBLGNT. Still, it remains possible that an original εἰ γάρ, as preferred in the THGNT, could have been assimilated to the εἰ δέ of Rom. 3:5. See also the comments below on Rom. 4:15 and 1 Cor. 7:7.

3:22 εἰς πάντας (for all) {B}

The Latin Vulgate appears to support ἐπὶ πάντας ('onto all') rather than εἰς πάντας (lit. 'into all'; 𝔓⁴⁰ 01* 02 03 04 etc.). This could simply be a translational variant for an expression which appeared unusual in context. However, the majority of Greek manuscripts have a conflated form, εἰς πάντας καὶ ἐπὶ πάντας ('into all and onto all'; 01² 06 012 33 256 etc.). While it is possible that the shorter text arose through eyeskip between the two instances of πάντας, the external evidence and strong Pauline preference for εἰς πάντας rather than ἐπὶ πάντας (e.g. Rom. 5:18) suggest that it is likely to be the earlier form. The full attestation for this variation unit in Greek continuous-text manuscripts is provided in *TuT Romans* (TS2). The difference between εἰς and ἐπί in this verse is unlikely to be significant for translation.[2]

3:25 διὰ [τῆς] πίστεως (through faith)

The definite article τῆς is missing from important manuscripts (01 04* 06* 012 365 1506 1738 1881), casting doubt on whether it was originally present. The whole phrase is absent from a couple of witnesses (02 2127), either through oversight or to improve the logical flow: the preceding ἱλαστήριον, 'atonement', is more closely connected with αἷμα, 'blood'. The expression normally lacks an article when it is followed by a genitive complement (e.g. Rom. 3:22, Gal. 2:16, Phil. 3:9), whereas διὰ τῆς πίστεως tends to be used absolutely (e.g. Rom. 3:30 and 3:31, Gal. 3:14, but contrast 2 Cor. 5:7 and Eph. 3:12). This suggests that the longer form conforms better to Pauline usage, and the article may have been omitted through assimilation to Rom. 3:22. On the other hand, it could

---

[2] Thus Omanson 2006: 295.

have been added at a later point, perhaps with deliberate reference to that preceding instance. Whichever form is preferred, translation is unaffected.

3:28   γάρ (for) {B}

Most Greek witnesses have the connective οὖν ('and so', 'then'; 03 04 06² 025 etc.), but several early codices read γάρ ('for'; 01 02 06* 012 etc.). The latter corresponds to Pauline usage (Rom. 8:18, 2 Cor. 11:5), which could have led to assimilation here. Equally, οὖν may have been introduced as a repetition from the previous verse. As both instances of οὖν in the immediate context occur within a question (Rom. 3:27 and 3:31), this provides internal support for a different connective in the present statement. The choice of word affects the sequence of the argument: οὖν implies the result of the present deliberation, whereas γάρ indicates an existing position, which is consistent with Paul's use of ὁ λογιζόμεθα ('we hold'). It is not surprising that lectionaries have no connective here because this is the beginning of a liturgical lection.

3:30   εἴπερ (since) {A}

The majority of manuscripts read ἐπείπερ ('seeing that'; 01² 06*,² 012 025 etc.). Although the alternative form could have arisen from the omission of two letters, εἴπερ (lit. 'if indeed'; 01* 02 03 04 06¹ etc.) has strong early attestation. In addition, this shorter word is semantically more difficult, because it could be taken to imply doubt as to whether it is God who justifies. For these reasons, as well as Pauline usage (neither ἐπείπερ nor ἐπειδήπερ appears elsewhere in the epistles), εἴπερ has been adopted as the earliest form.

4:1   εὑρηκέναι Ἀβραὰμ τὸν προπάτορα ἡμῶν (was gained by Abraham our ancestor) {B}

The verb εὑρηκέναι (lit. 'has been found') varies in position: some manuscripts have it at the beginning of the phrase (01 02 04 06 012 etc.), while the majority of Greek manuscripts place it after ἡμῶν (025 33 1175 etc.). It is missing completely from a few witnesses (03 6 1739; cf. Rom. 3:12). While the differing locations might suggest that the verb was a later addition, the question seems to require a verb because Paul is not addressing Abraham directly. The later position is the more natural one, suggesting that the verb may have been moved and its absence is due to oversight in implementing the correction. Alternatively, if εὑρηκέναι originally stood next to ἐροῦμεν, the word might have been overlooked by an early copyist and later reintroduced. The unanimous choice of this verb when there is nothing obvious to prompt it in context and the better external evidence for the more difficult placing leads to its inclusion in the editorial text. In place of προπάτορα ('ancestor'; 01*, 2 02 03 04* etc.), the majority of Greek manuscripts read πατέρα ('father'; 01¹ 04³ 06 012 025 etc.). Although this is the only time that προπάτορα appears in the Pauline Epistles, its strong early attestation supports its adoption here: its replacement with a more common term would not be surprising (cf. Rom. 4:11, 4:12, 4:16). From the point of view of translation, the words are largely synonymous.

4:11 [καὶ] αὐτοῖς ([also] to them)

Even though καί ('also') is present in the majority of Greek manuscripts, it is missing from some important witnesses (01* 02 03 6 81 1506 1739 1881 2464). If καί is included, the result is to emphasise the inclusion of Abraham with his descendants, rather than set him apart as father. It may simply be that, following the verb λογισθῆναι ('reckoned'), καί was omitted through homoeoteleuton; alternatively, it might have been added here as an apparent improvement to the argument or on the basis of the other similar uses of καί in the context. The division of the external evidence makes a decision difficult.

4:11 [τὴν] δικαιοσύνην (righteousness)

The definite article is absent from certain manuscripts (01 04² 06* 6 365 1506 1739), and replaced by εἰς in others (02 1881). It is likely that these variant readings arose through assimilation to Rom. 4:5, 4:6, and 4:9; in context, there is no significant effect on translation.

4:15 δέ (but) {B}

The choice of connective affects the flow of the argument. There is good early support for a contrast to the previous phrase with δέ ('but'; 01* 02 03 04 81 etc.), while the majority of Greek manuscripts read γάρ ('for'; 01² 06 012 025 etc.). The latter word is found at the beginning of the verse, as well as the two previous sentences, suggesting that it was introduced here through assimilation.

4:19   κατενόησεν (he considered) {C}

Before this verb, the majority of Greek manuscripts include the negative οὐ ('not'; 06 012 025 etc.), stating that Abraham 'did not weaken in faith and did not consider his body'. While the logical consistency of this is clear, the sentence also makes good sense without a negative: 'he did not weaken in faith when he considered his body'. The shorter reading has good early attestation (01 02 03 04 etc., lat[vl-pt, vg] sy[p] co eth) and in addition might be considered a better match with the following verse.

4:19   [ἤδη] (already) {C}

This word is missing from some important witnesses (03 012 1739 1881 lat[vl-pt, vg] sy[p] cpa co[sa] eth etc.). It could be a later addition, to strengthen the observation, or have been overlooked because of its brevity. Paul's use of ἤδη before other instances of the perfect tense (e.g. 1 Cor. 4:8, 5:3; Phil. 3:12) might favour its originality (as in the THGNT), although the SBLGNT prefers the shorter reading.

5:1   ἔχομεν (we have) {D}

The textual tradition is evenly split in this famous variation unit between the indicative ἔχομεν ('we have'; 01[1] 03[2] 012 025 0220[vid] etc.) and the subjunctive ἔχωμεν ('let us have'; 01* 02 03* 04 06 etc.: the full attestation is provided in *TuT Romans* TS3). In later Greek pronunciation, the loss of vowel length (isochrony) made these words sound identical. The indicative was preferred in UBS4 (and SBLGNT) on internal grounds: Paul is making a statement about the result of righteousness through faith rather than urging his audience to make peace with God.[3] In addition, there is only one secure instance of ἔχωμεν elsewhere in the epistles (Rom. 15:4). Nevertheless, it may be noted that this verb is co-ordinated with the subjunctive καυχώμεθα ('let us boast') in the following verse, and there is a further subjunctive at the beginning of the the next sentence. A case can therefore also be made for ἔχωμεν, which

---

[3] Thus Metzger 1994: 452.

is adopted in the THGNT.[4] Other instances of the same type of variation can be seen at Rom. 6:1, 14:19 and 1 Cor. 15:49.

5:2 [τῇ πίστει] εἰς τὴν χάριν ταύτην ([by faith] to this grace) {C}

The words τῇ πίστει ('by faith'; 01*, 2 04 025 and the majority of minuscules) are missing from some early witnesses (03 06 012 0220 lat^{vl-pt} co^{sa} Origen^{lat-pt} Basil). Others read ἐν τῇ πίστει ('in faith'; 01¹ 02 1962 etc.), probably through duplicating the last two letters of the preceding word (ἐσχήκαμεν). The phrase could be a marginal gloss which was later incorporated into the text for clarification: conversely, it might have been deliberately removed because it was considered to be superfluous following ἐκ πίστεως ('by faith') in the previous clause or an interruption to the flow of προσαγωγήν … εἰς ('entry … into'). Internally, τῇ πίστει seems to be the more difficult reading and its appearance elsewhere indicates that it is stylistically plausible (e.g. Rom. 4:20, 11:20, 14:1). Consequently, it is retained in both the SBLGNT and THGNT. The full attestation in Greek continuous-text manuscripts is provided in *TuT Romans* (TS4).

5:6 ἔτι γάρ … ἔτι (for while … still) {C}

The confusing syntax and repetition in ἔτι γάρ … ἔτι ('for while … still'; 01 02 04^{vid} 06* 81 etc.) have good external support and are made simpler in a variety of alternative readings. The majority of Greek manuscripts lack the second ἔτι ('still'), which is likely to stem from a deletion of the unnecessary repetition. At the beginning of the verse, some witnesses read εἰς τί γάρ ('for why'; 06¹ 012 lat Irenaeus^{lat}), while others have εἴ γε ('if indeed'; 03 co^{sa, [bo]} [cpa]). These may be misreadings or attempts at clarification. Although εἴ γε has parallels in other epistles (e.g. Gal. 3:4, Eph. 3:2, Col. 1:23) and avoids the repetition of ἔτι, it introduces an aspect of doubt which seems contrary to Paul's argument. The editorial text seems to provide the best explanation for the origin of the other forms.

6:1 ἐπιμένωμεν (should we continue) {B}

The majority of Greek manuscripts are split between the present subjunctive ἐπιμένωμεν (lit. 'let us continue'; 02 03 04 06 012 etc.) and the

---

[4] See further Moir 1981 and Man 2016.

present indicative ἐπιμένομεν ('do we continue'; 01 025 1175 1881 2464 etc.), similar to Rom. 5:1 (see above). Two other forms are found: the future indicative ἐπιμενοῦμεν ('shall we continue') in the *Textus Receptus* and Latin tradition, perhaps under the influence of the form of the preceding ἐροῦμεν or the tense of the following ζήσομεν, and the aorist subjunctive ἐπιμείνωμεν ('let us continue' [as a single action]; 33 [365 1739]). A subjunctive offers the best match for the context of imagined speech following the previous question, which is swiftly contradicted by the following optative, and both internal and external evidence favour the present tense. The indicative probably developed through vowel isochrony (see Rom. 5:1, 14:19) or through attraction to ἐροῦμεν.

6:8   δέ (but) {A}

As with Romans 4:15, the connective has an effect on the structure of the argument. The external evidence in favour of δέ ('but'; 01 02 03 04 06 etc. and the majority of minuscules) is overwhelming. Notwithstanding the antiquity of the variant γάρ ('for'; 𝔓⁴⁶ 012 lat^(vl-pt) [sy^p]), it appears to be an assimilation to the previous or following sentence. Even if δέ is read, it could be translated as a transition rather than a contrast.[5]

6:11   [εἶναι] νεκρούς ([to be] dead)

There is some early support for the omission of εἶναι (𝔓^(46vid) 02 06* 012 33 Tertullian), which is unnecessary for the sense. Given Paul's use of a pleonastic εἶναι elsewhere (e.g. 1 Cor. 11:16, 2 Cor. 11:16), the infinitive may well be original here. Either way, it is likely to be required in translation.

6:11   ἐν Χριστῷ Ἰησοῦ (in Christ Jesus) {A}

A longer form, ἐν Χριστῷ Ἰησοῦ τῷ κυρίῳ ἡμῶν ('in Christ Jesus our Lord'; 𝔓^(94vid) 01 04 025 6 etc.) is found in the majority of Greek manuscripts. This seems to be a reverential expansion, perhaps under the influence of Rom. 5:21 or 6:23: its presence there makes it unlikely to have been deleted here if it were original. The full attestation in Greek continuous-text manuscripts is given in *TuT Romans* (TS6).

---

[5] See further Omanson 2006: 300.

6:12 ταῖς ἐπιθυμίαις αὐτοῦ (their desires) {B}

In place of this phrase, one early strand of text reads αὐτῇ ('[obey] it'; 𝔓⁴⁶ 06 012 etc.) referring back to ἁμαρτία ('sin'). The majority of Greek manuscripts conflate the two, with αὐτῇ ἐν ταῖς ἐπιθυμίαις αὐτοῦ ('[obey] it in its desires'; 04³ 025 [33] 1175 etc.), with the two pronouns referring first to 'sin' and then 'your body'. The strong external evidence for just ταῖς ἐπιθυμίαις αὐτοῦ ('its desires'; 𝔓⁹⁴ 01 02 03 04* etc.) justifies its adoption as the editorial text. The full attestation is provided in *TuT Romans* (TS7).

7:14 οἴδαμεν (we know) {A}

The extensive use of the first-person singular in this passage may lead readers to interpret the *scriptio continua* ΟΙΔΑΜΕΝ as two words, οἶδα μέν ('while I know'; 33). In early manuscripts, which have neither word divisions nor accents, it is often impossible to be certain of the intended reading (01 02 03* 04 06* 012 025). Nevertheless, the following ἐγὼ δέ ('but I'), with the emphatic first-person singular pronoun highlighting the contrast, indicates that the previous verb should be interpreted as plural, in keeping with Paul's practice elsewhere (e.g. Rom. 2:2, 3:19, 8:22, 8:26, 8:28 etc.): there are, in fact, no other instances of οἶδα μέν in the epistles (but note οἶδα γάρ at Rom. 7:18). This is confirmed by οἴδαμεν in the majority of Greek minuscules and its treatment in early translations.

7:18 οὔ (not²) {B}

The reading οὔ by itself ('not'; 01 02 03 04 etc.) is supported by the earliest manuscripts, and adopted as the editorial text. Its abruptness, however, has prompted later editors to supply a further verb, such as οὐχ εὑρίσκω ('I am not able'; 06 012 025 and the majority of minuscules) or οὐ γινώσκω ('I do not know'; 256 263 1573 2127). This may also be required in translation (e.g. the NRSV 'cannot'). The full attestation for this variation unit is provided in *TuT Romans* (TS8).

7:20 [ἐγὼ] τοῦτο ποιῶ (I do)

The first-person pronoun ἐγώ ('I') is already implicit in the verb, and is not present in various important witnesses (03 04 06 012 1506 2464 lat co^sa). This may be due to assimilation to the previous verse, or omission due to eyeskip following θέλω ('I want'). Alternatively, it may have been inserted by analogy with ἐγώ in the following phrase. A decision is difficult, but translation is unaffected.

7:25 χάρις δὲ τῷ θεῷ (but thanks be to God) {C}

This is an intriguing variation unit. Some witnesses supply a clear answer to the question of the previous verse, reading ἡ χάρις τοῦ θεοῦ ('the grace of God'; 06 lat[vl-pt, vg] Origen[lat-pt]) or ἡ χάρις κυρίου ('the grace of the Lord'; 012 lat[vl-pt]): the latter duplicates what is found in the following phrase and is therefore likely to be a misreading of the *nomen sacrum* in the former. The majority of Greek manuscripts, however, feature a statement which does not match the expected line of thought: εὐχαριστῶ τῷ θεῷ ('I thank God'; 01* 02 025 etc.). A similar break in flow is seen in χάρις δὲ τῷ θεῷ ('but thanks be to God'; 01[1] 33 81 256 etc.): witnesses with χάρις τῷ θεῷ ('thanks be to God'; 03 co[sa] Origen) may derive from this form with the omission of δέ through oversight, but the connective could have been added later to mark the disjunction. Despite its poor attestation here, χάρις τῷ θεῷ matches the other occurrences of this exclamation (Rom. 6:17, 2 Cor. 8:16; cf. 2 Cor. 2:14, 9:15), yet it may be the result of assimilation. The THGNT adopts εὐχαριστῶ τῷ θεῷ while the SBLGNT matches UBS6. Although the bilingual manuscripts offer a smoother reading, they appear to support χάρις as the earliest text. Some ancient writers quote the entire sentence as χάρις τῷ κυρίῳ ἡμῶν Ἰησοῦ Χριστοῦ ('thanks to our Lord Jesus Christ'; [Irenaeus[lat]] Origen[lat-pt]), which is probably a loose citation. In translation, it may be appropriate to indicate in some way that this exclamation is an answer to the preceding question.

8:1 Ἰησοῦ (Jesus) {A}

At the end of this verse, the majority of Greek manuscripts include a phrase also present in Rom. 8:4, μὴ κατὰ σάρκα περιπατοῦσιν ἀλλὰ κατὰ πνεῦμα ('who walk not according to the flesh but according to the Spirit'; 01[2] 06[2] 025 etc.). Some just read the first four words (02 06[1] 81 256 etc.): the full attestation is provided in *TuT Romans* (TS9). The longer form works better at 8:4, where both elements connect to the following verse. Such a long repetition is not characteristic of Pauline style and, given the early evidence for the absence of the phrase here (01* 03 06* 012 etc.), it is considered to be a subsequent addition.

8:2   σε (you) {B}

The majority of Greek manuscripts read με ('me'; 02 06 025 6 81 etc.), as might be expected given the emphasis on the first-person singular in the previous discussion. This makes the appearance of σε ('you'; 01 03 012 1506* 1739* lat$^{vl\text{-}pt}$ sy^p Tertullian^{pt}) the more unexpected reading. Although its attestation is limited, it is early, which supports its adoption as the editorial text. The first-person plural, ἡμᾶς ('us'; cpa co^{bo} eth etc.) is an adjustment in secondary sources which makes the application of the sentence broader and more inclusive.

8:11   διὰ τοῦ ἐνοικοῦντος αὐτοῦ πνεύματος (through his Spirit that dwells) {C}

The Pauline Epistles normally use the genitive in the phrase 'through the Spirit' (e.g. 1 Cor. 2:10, 12:8; Eph. 3:16; cf. Rom. 5:5), and a range of witnesses read διὰ τοῦ ἐνοικοῦντος αὐτοῦ πνεύματος ('through his Spirit that dwells'; 01 02 04 025^c etc.). The majority of Greek manuscripts have an accusative, διὰ τὸ ἐνοικοῦν αὐτοῦ πνεῦμα ('because of his Spirit that dwells'; 03 06 012 025* etc.). In context, the latter may be the stronger reading: not only is the construction less common and hence more likely to be adjusted to the genitive, but it also reflects the conditional clause at the beginning of the verse. The accusative is adopted by both the SBLGNT and the THGNT; the full attestation in Greek continuous-text manuscripts is provided in *TuT Romans* (TS11).

8:23   υἱοθεσίαν (adoption) {A}

In the majority of Greek manuscripts, υἱοθεσίαν ('adoption'; 01 02 03 04 etc.) is read in apposition to the following phrase, 'the redemption of our bodies'. The absence of this word from a few witnesses ($\mathfrak{P}^{46vid}$ 06 012 lat$^{vl\text{-}pt}$) represents an editorial smoothing of the text, possibly motivated by a perceived contradiction with the description at Rom. 8:15 of the 'spirit of adoption' (πνεῦμα υἱοθεσίας) which has already been received. Such intervention demonstrates that the so-called 'Western' witnesses have a secondary text. The full attestation for this variation unit is provided in *TuT Romans* (TS13).

8:26 ὑπερεντυγχάνει (intercedes) {A}

After this verb, the majority of Greek manuscripts include the prepositional phrase ὑπὲρ ἡμῶν ('on our behalf'; 01² 04 025 etc.). This is probably because the absolute form was felt to be incomplete: compare the complement at the end of the next verse. Nevertheless, there is very strong external evidence in support of the shorter reading (01* 02 03 06 012 etc.). In translation, it may be necessary to provide an indirect object to go with the verb.

8:28 συνεργεῖ (work together) {B}

A few important witnesses read συνεργεῖ ὁ θεός ('God works [all things] together'; 𝔓⁴⁶ 02 03 81 co^sa eth). The provision of a subject is normally a secondary clarification: without it, the sentence could be read with God as implied subject (based on the preceding phrase 'for those who love God'), the Spirit as subject (going back to the explicit subject in Rom. 8:26), or taking the neuter plural πάντα as subject ('all things work together'). In favour of the latter, absolute sense is the only other use of this verb in the epistles (1 Cor. 16:16). Nonetheless, it remains possible that the *nomen sacrum* for God (Ο ΘC) was overlooked at an early stage because of its similarity to the following word EIC.[6] If the editorial text is followed, translators may have to choose a subject from the three options above.

8:34 Χριστὸς [Ἰησοῦς] (Christ [Jesus])

The external evidence is split between manuscripts which include Ἰησοῦς ('Jesus'; 𝔓⁴⁶vid 01 02 04 012 6 33 81 365) and those which do not (03 06 0289 and the majority of minuscules). The sequence Χριστὸς Ἰησοῦς is often the locus of variation (cf. the comments above on Rom. 1:1, 2:16). Among numerous instances of Χριστός ('Christ') by itself in this epistle, it is commonly found as the subject of ἀποθνήσκειν ('to die'; e.g. Rom. 5:6, 5:8, 6:9, 14:9, 14:15; cf. 1 Cor. 8:11, 15:3; Gal. 2:24). External evidence is fairly evenly balanced and transcriptional probability is similar both for the addition of Ἰησοῦς out of habit and for the omission through oversight of one of the two *nomina sacra* (IC XC).

---

[6] For arguments in favour of the longer reading as original, see Rodgers 1995 and Ross 2003: 217–218.

However, the shorter reading in Byzantine tradition and Pauline usage both favour Χριστός alone as the earliest text, as seen in the SBLGNT and THGNT.

9:19 τί [οὖν] (why then)

The vast majority of Greek manuscripts do not read οὖν ('therefore', 'then') here, but it is present in some early witnesses ($\mathfrak{P}^{46}$ 03 06 012 lat^{vl}). Given that there are many instances of οὖν in context (including the word immediately preceding τί), it may have been deleted by an early editor. On the other hand, it could easily have been added by analogy with Rom. 9:14.

9:23 καὶ ἵνα (and what if he has done so in order to) {A}

The presence of the conjunction in καὶ ἵνα ('and ... in order to'; $\mathfrak{P}^{46vid}$ 01 02 06 012 etc.) is grammatically confusing, as there is no purpose clause in the earlier part of the sentence to which it is connected. Its absence from a few witnesses, which just read ἵνα ('so that'; 03 6 lat$^{vl\text{-}pt,\,vg}$ co$^{sa,\,bo\text{-}pt}$ Origen) is clearly an editorial improvement, and it is worth remarking on the secondary nature of the text of Codex Vaticanus here. If καί is retained in translation, some supplement may be needed to make good sense (as in the NRSVue's provision of 'what if he has done so').[7]

9:28 συντέμνων (decisively) {B}

After this participle, the majority of Greek manuscripts include the phrase ἐν δικαιοσύνῃ ὅτι λόγον συντετμημένον ('in righteousness because it is a shortened sentence'; 01² 06 012 025 etc.; only the first two words occur in 81). This text is present in the original context of this quotation at Isaiah 10:22–23 in the Septuagint, but is missing from early and important witnesses ($\mathfrak{P}^{46}$ 01* 02 03 etc.). Its omission could be explained as a copying error, skipping from συντέμνων to συντετμημένον, although one would expect the second rather than the first word to be retained in this scenario. In favour of the shorter reading, it may be noted that partial quotations from the Old Testament are often expanded in later tradition and in this instance the abbreviation

---

[7] On how the preceding verse affects the interpretation of the present phrase, see Moo 1996: 604–609.

provides a more focussed reference than the longer original. The strong external evidence also favours this as the earliest form. The full attestation is provided in *TuT Romans* (TS17).

9:32 ἔργων (works) {B}

The majority of Greek manuscripts qualify this word as ἔργων νόμου ('works of the Law'; 01² 06 025 etc.). Although this matches Pauline usage (e.g. Rom. 3:20, 3:28; Gal. 2:16, 3:2, 3:5 etc.), the external evidence for its absence is strong ($\mathfrak{P}^{46\text{vid}}$ 01* 02 03 012 etc.) and the shorter form is paralleled elsewhere in Romans (e.g. Rom. 4:2, 9:12, 11:6).

10:3 τὴν ἰδίαν [δικαιοσύνην] (their own [righteousness])

In the manuscripts with the shorter reading (02 03 06 025 81 365 1506 1739 1881), the preceding instance of δικαιοσύνην ('righteousness') also corresponds to ἰδίαν ('their own'). However, the majority of manuscripts—including some early witnesses—repeat the noun after this adjective ($\mathfrak{P}^{46}$ 01 012 etc.; the full attestation is provided in *TuT Romans* TS18). It is not clear whether this was a later addition or an editorial deletion of a word which already occurs twice in the sentence and thus seemed unnecessary. The repetition of the word δικαιοσύνην three times in one verse is seen at Rom. 9:30, showing that such pleonasm could be authorial. It is also possible that the noun was intended to clarify the different types of righteousness mentioned here (cf. Phil. 3:9). The SBLGNT prefers the shorter reading, but the THGNT follows the majority text. In translation, it may be necessary to repeat the noun regardless of the reading adopted.

10:15 [τὰ] ἀγαθά (good news)

There is very strong external evidence for the absence of the definite article (01² 02 03 04 06* 012 025 81 1506 1739 1881). However, as τά ('the') is also missing from the Septuagint text of Isaiah 52:7, its presence in the majority of Greek manuscripts may in fact be original. In either case, the translation is the same.

10:17 Χριστοῦ (of Christ) {A}

This is the only occurrence in the New Testament of ῥῆμα Χριστοῦ ('word of Christ'; 01* 03 04 06* etc.; cf. ὁ λόγος τοῦ Χριστοῦ at Col.

3:16). As such, it is unsurprising to see the alternative ῥῆμα θεοῦ ('word of God'; 01¹ 02 06¹ 025 and the majority of minuscules), which has parallels elsewhere (Luke 3:2; John 3:34, 8:47; Eph. 6:17; Heb. 11:3) as well as ῥῆμα κυρίου ('word of the Lord'; 𝔓⁴⁶, cf. 1 Pet. 1:25 quoting one of numerous instances in the Septuagint). The variation could have come about through assimilation or misreading of the *nomina sacra* (ΧΥ, ΚΥ and ΘΥ). Both internal and external evidence indicate that Χριστοῦ is likely to be the earliest reading. In translation, this could be interpreted as a genitive of origin ('the word from Christ') or an objective genitive ('the word about Christ').

10:20   εὑρέθην [ἐν] (found [among])

The preposition ἐν ('in') is missing from the majority of Greek manuscripts (01 02 04 06¹ 025 etc.) as well as the source of the quotation at Isaiah 65:1. It is difficult to know whether its appearance in a few important witnesses (𝔓⁴⁶ 03 06* 012 1506^vid) is a subsequent clarification or an original loose quotation. It may be significant that several of these witnesses (03 06* 1506^vid) also include a parallel ἐν before τοῖς in the next phrase.

11:6   χάρις² (grace²) {A}

At the end of this verse, the majority of Greek manuscripts include an additional phrase: εἰ δὲ ἐξ ἔργων, οὐκέτι ἐστὶν χάρις, ἐπεὶ τὸ ἔργον οὐκέτι ἐστὶν ἔργον ('but if it is by works, it is no longer on the basis of grace, since work is no longer work'; 01² 03 [with some variants] 6 33^vid 256 etc.); a shorter form due to eyeskip between the instances of χάρις is found in some witnesses, as reported in *TuT Romans* (TS20). There is no obvious reason which would prompt the omission of this phrase, and the strong external evidence for the shorter text (𝔓⁴⁶ 01* 02 04 06 etc.) suggests that it is the earliest form. The witness of Codex Vaticanus to the later text is notable (cf. Rom. 9:23). A similar addition of a parallel phrase in later tradition occurs at Rom. 14:6 (see below).

11:17   τῆς ῥίζης τῆς πιότητος (the rich root) {B}

The majority of Greek manuscripts read τῆς ῥίζης καὶ τῆς πιότητος ('the root and the richness'; 01² 02 06¹ 025 etc.), while one group of witnesses only have τῆς πιότητος ('the richness'; 𝔓⁴⁶ 06* 012 etc.). The reading τῆς ῥίζης τῆς πιότητος (lit. 'the root of the richness'; 01* 03 04 1175 1506 etc.) is the most difficult in terms of sense but it is attested by several important witnesses and provides a good explanation for the other, simpler readings. When translating this form, τῆς πιότητος could be a genitive of quality ('the rich root') or taken in apposition to τῆς ῥίζης ('the root, that is, the richness').

11:21 [μή πως] οὐδέ (neither) {C}

There is wide attestation for the concessive in μή πως οὐδέ ('perhaps neither'; 𝔓⁴⁶ 06 012 and the majority of minuscules). Nevertheless, just οὐδέ ('neither'; 01 02 03 04 025 etc.) is supported by strong external evidence. It seems that the extra text was added to mitigate the uncompromising condemnation of οὐδὲ σοῦ φείσεται ('he will not spare you'). Although μή πως does occur elsewhere in the epistles (e.g. 1 Cor. 8:9, Gal. 4:11), its use here is unique: on the other occasions it has the force of 'in case', introducing a remote possibility rather than reducing the force of an apodosis. In addition, it is not grammatically appropriate with the following future tense. The short reading is adopted in both the SBLGNT and THGNT.

11:25 [παρ'] ἑαυτοῖς (lit. [by] yourselves)

No preposition is required in context because the dative ἑαυτοῖς ('by yourselves'; 𝔓⁴⁶ 012 6 1506 1739) alone is sufficient for the sense. Some manuscripts have ἐν ἑαυτοῖς ('in yourselves'; 02 03), while the majority of Greek witnesses have παρὰ ἑαυτοῖς ('by yourselves'; 01 04 06 33 81 etc.). All of these constructions are paralleled elsewhere in the New Testament: ἐν ἑαυτοῖς is the most common, while the closest to the present context is φρόνιμοι παρ' ἑαυτοῖς ('wise by yourselves') at Rom. 12:16. It seems likely that both prepositions were introduced later, but the weak attestation of the shortest reading could be consistent with accidental omission.

11:31 [νῦν] (now) {C}

The second occurrence of νῦν ('now') in this verse is missing from the majority of Greek manuscripts (𝔓⁴⁶ 02 06¹ 012 etc.). Its inclusion in just a few witnesses (01 03 06*,³ 1506 co^(bo, fa-ms)), makes for a more difficult reading in the context both of the preceding νῦν and the sense of the purpose clause. It is possible that νῦν was added erroneously through misplaced parallelism with the preceding construction. At any rate, ὕστερον ('later'; 33 256 263 365 etc.) is clearly a secondary reading, as it conforms to the expected sequence of events.[8] If νῦν is adopted here, then its force is not to emphasise the immediacy of the action but rather the circumstances which have been established.[9]

12:14 [ὑμᾶς] (you)

Some important witnesses do not have ὑμᾶς ('you'; 𝔓[46] 03 6 1739 lat[vg]). The pronoun could have been added because διώκειν ('to persecute') was felt to require an object (perhaps through analogy with Matt. 5:44), or to differentiate its use here from that in the preceding verse. The absolute use of διώκειν at Phil. 3:12 offers a parallel for this shorter reading. On the other hand, ὑμᾶς could have been omitted through homoeoteleuton following διώκοντας, or deleted in order to enhance the parallelism with the latter half of the verse. The choice of reading may affect the interpretation: without an object, διώκειν could be understood as 'to practise [it]' (i.e. hospitality), as in the previous verse, but the rest of this sentence suggests that 'to persecute' is the intended meaning in context.[10] It may therefore be necessary in translation to provide an object for the verb.

14:4 ὁ κύριος (the Lord) {A}

The majority of Greek manuscripts read ὁ θεός ('God'; 06 012 048 0150 etc.), but there is strong early evidence for ὁ κύριος ('the Lord'; 𝔓[46] 01 02 03 04 025 [sy[p]] co). Although the variation could simply be due to the misreading of the *nomen sacrum* (ΘC for KC) or assimilation to ὁ θεός in a similar position in the previous verse, it is possible that ὁ κύριος was replaced by an editor to avoid confusion with τῷ ἰδίῳ κυρίῳ ('their own lord') earlier in the verse. Translators will need to distinguish between these two uses of κύριος, the first referring to a human master and the second to a divine one.

---

[8] Kaden 2011 offers a detailed study of this unit, preferring the shortest reading as original.
[9] See BDAG s. v. νῦν 2, 'as it is'.
[10] See further Omanson 2006: 315.

14:5 [γάρ] (lit. for) {C}

Most Greek manuscripts lack this connective ($\mathfrak{P}^{46}$ 01² 03 06 etc.), and there is no obvious causal connection with the previous sentence. However, γάρ ('for, indeed'; 01* 02 04² 025 0150 etc.) is sometimes used in the longer epistles to express continuation rather than cause (e.g. Rom. 1:18, 2:25; 1 Cor 11:18, 14:17; 2 Cor. 9:1).[11] The conjunction could therefore have been deleted by an early editor, perhaps through assimilation to the previous construction with ὃς μέν ('one person') in Rom. 14:2. There are several other instances of γάρ in neighbouring verses but none would obviously have prompted its insertion here. This balance of internal and external evidence makes a decision difficult.

14:6 κυρίῳ φρονεῖ (observe it for the Lord) {A}

After this clause, the majority of Greek manuscripts include a parallel phrase in the negative: καὶ ὁ μὴ φρονῶν τὴν ἡμέραν κυρίῳ οὐ φρονεῖ ('and those who do not observe the day, do not observe it for the Lord'; 04³ 025 33 81 365 etc.). This matches the structure of the following sentence. Although it could have been omitted by eyeskip from φρονεῖ to φρονεῖ, the strong early evidence in favour of the shorter reading (01 02 03 04²ᵛⁱᵈ 06 etc.) indicates that the extra text is a later expansion, like that at Rom. 11:6. The full attestation for this variation unit in Greek continuous-text manuscripts is provided in *TuT Romans* (TS27).

14:9 ἀπέθανεν καὶ ἔζησεν (died and lived again) {A}

There is good manuscript support for ἀπέθανεν καὶ ἔζησεν ('died and lived'; 01* 02 03 04 0150 etc.), which matches several places where Paul contrasts these two verbs (e.g. Rom. 6:2, 6:10; Gal. 2:19; Col. 2:20). Nevertheless, the aorist tense of ἔζησεν ('lived') is unusual in the New Testament outside Revelation (e.g. Rev. 2:8), and it is not surprising to find a few witnesses with the alternative ἀπέθανεν καὶ ἀνέστη ('died and rose again'; 012 lat^{vl-pt, vg-mss} Origen^{gr} Cyril^{pt}) which matches the credal statement at 1 Thess. 4:14. The majority of Greek manuscripts have a conflation of these readings, ἀπέθανεν καὶ ἀνέστη καὶ ἔζησεν ('died and rose again and lived'; 01² 06¹ 025 6 33 etc.), with an additional

---

[11] See further BDAG s.v. γάρ 2, where this instance is listed among several others from Romans with the meaning 'indeed'.

initial καί ('also') in many of these witnesses. Codex Claromontanus originally had the order ἔζησεν καὶ ἀπέθανεν καὶ ἀνέστη ('lived and died and rose again'; 06*), which is preferable as a theological sequence: placing the aorist ἔζησεν ('lived') after ἀνέστη ('rose') might call into question the duration of the resurrection.[12] At any rate, the attestation suggests that the conflated forms are secondary, and the most difficult reading is supported by the external evidence.

14:10 θεοῦ (of God) {B}

The majority of Greek manuscripts read Χριστοῦ ('of Christ'; 01² 04² 025 048 etc.). Given the references to 'Christ' and 'Lord' on either side, this would be a natural assimilation to the context. What is more, the phrase τὸ βῆμα τοῦ Χριστοῦ ('the judgement seat of Christ') also appears at 2 Cor. 5:10. In the light of this, the reading θεοῦ ('of God'; 01* 02 03 04* 06 etc.) is harder. It also has strong early attestation, leading to its adoption as the editorial text, although the possibility of confusion between the *nomina sacra* ΘΥ and ΧΥ cannot be ruled out. The full attestation for this variation unit in Greek continuous-text manuscripts is provided in *TuT Romans* (TS28).

14:12 [οὖν] (then)

Almost all instances of ἄρα at the beginning of a sentence in Romans are followed by οὖν: the exceptions are Rom. 10:17 and possibly here, where οὖν is missing from a range of important witnesses (03 06* 012 025* 6 1739 1881 lat). It is difficult to decide whether it was omitted due to an oversight, deleted in order to emphasise οὖν in the following verse, or added through assimilation to that or to the customary practice in this epistle (see also the comments below on Rom. 14:19).

14:12 [τῷ θεῷ] (lit. to God) {C}

Several important witnesses lack τῷ θεῷ ('to God'; 03 012 6 1739 1881 lat[vl-pt] Polycarp). Although this could be a clarificatory addition, specifying what is implicit in context and repeating the words at the end of the quotation in the previous verse, there are also occasions where some

---

[12] Omanson (2006: 317) observes that in this context ἔζησεν should be translated as 'he lived again'.

or all of these sources have a shorter text which appears to be secondary (e.g. Rom. 8:23, 9:23, 11:17, 13:9; cf. Rom. 4:19); note too their lack of οὖν in the previous variation unit. This suggests that the longer reading may be preferable, as chosen in the THGNT. Even if the shorter form is adopted with the SBLGNT, it might be helpful in translation to provide an indirect object for the phrase λόγον δώσει ('give an account'). In fact, it is worth noting that some of the witnesses to the shorter reading read λόγον ἀποδώσει ('render an account'; 03 06* 012): if an early editor felt that this alternative verb did not require a further complement, this could have led to the deletion of τῷ θεῷ.

14:19 διώκωμεν (let us pursue) {D}

There is much early evidence for the indicative διώκομεν ('we pursue'; 01 02 03 012 025 etc.), but the majority of Greek manuscripts have the subjunctive διώκωμεν ('let us pursue'; 04 06 33 81 256 etc.). As noted above (Rom. 5:1, 6:1), sound changes resulting in vowel isochrony made it very difficult to distinguish between these two forms. Elsewhere in Romans, ἄρα οὖν ('then') is always followed by an indicative (Rom. 7:3, 7:25, 8:12, 9:18, cf. 5:18, 9:16, 14:12).[13] Although there are a number of hortatory verbs in context (e.g. Rom. 14:13, 15, 16, 20, 22), which might favour the subjunctive, many of these are preceded by indicative statements (Rom. 14:12, 14, 17, 21) and the present verb could be indicative before the imperative κατάλυε ('destroy') in the following verse. While a decision is difficult, an alteration from subjunctive to indicative may be less likely than the opposite direction, especially in the context of liturgical reading of the epistle. Even so, both THGNT and SBLGNT also prefer διώκωμεν. A few lectionaries even have the imperative διώκετε ('pursue'), which is clearly secondary.

14:21 προσκόπτει (makes ... stumble) {C}

Most witnesses read προσκόπτει ἢ σκανδαλίζεται ἢ ἀσθενεῖ ('makes stumble or be upset or weakens'; 𝔓[46vid] 01[2] 03 06 012 etc.). It is possible that προσκόπτει alone ('makes to stumble'; 01* 02 04 048 81 etc.) derives from eyeskip to the end of ἀσθενεῖ. On the other hand, the two other verbs could have been introduced on the basis of similar passages

---

[13] Thus Metzger 1994: 469.

elsewhere (e.g. πρόσκομμα ἢ σκάνδαλον at Rom. 14:13; cf. 1 Cor. 8:13, 2 Cor. 11:29, 1 Pet. 2:8). The alternative λυπεῖται ('grieves'; 01*) is an assimilation to Rom. 14:15; this is also seen in λυπεῖται ἢ σκανδαλίζεται ἢ ἀσθενεῖ ('grieves or makes stumble or weakens'; 025). There are a few other instances of two verbs separated by ἤ in the Pauline Epistles (e.g. Rom. 1:21, 14:4; Gal. 3:15), but no groups of three, which underlines that the longer reading is unusual. Accordingly, it is preferred by both the SBLGNT and THGNT. The full attestation for this variation unit in Greek continuous-text manuscripts is provided in *TuT Romans* (TS30).

14:22 [ἣν] ἔχεις (that you have) {C}

The relative pronoun ἥν ('that'; 01 02 03 04 048 lat[vl-pt] Origen[lat]), although found in the four major majuscules, is surprisingly poorly attested in later tradition. The shorter reading, present in the majority of Greek manuscripts as well as early translations, requires punctuation after ἔχεις ('you have'). While this could simply be read as a statement, the use of σύ ('you') elsewhere in this epistle suggests that it should be treated as a question (Rom. 14:4, 14:10; cf. Rom. 2:3, 9:20). The lack of an interrogative particle, however, along with the absence of question marks in majuscule script, might have led an early editor to reinterpret the two clauses as a longer phrase and add the relative pronoun to make the grammar smoother. On the other hand, ἥν may have been accidentally omitted, perhaps because through itacism it sounded similar to the last syllable of the preceding word, πίστιν ('faith').

14:23 ἁμαρτία ἐστίν (is sin) {A}

The majority of Greek manuscripts have the final doxology, normally printed as Romans 16:25–27, at the end of chapter 14. As there are a few manuscripts which have the doxology in both places (02 025 0150 33 1506), it is advisable to treat the present instance as Romans 14:24–26.[14] The external evidence for the absence of these verses at this point is very strong ($\mathfrak{P}^{46}$ 01 03 04 06 [012] 048 etc., along with most

---

[14] This convention is found in Antoniades 1912, Robinson & Pierpont 2018 and the SBLGNT; see also Houghton et al. 2019: 151.

early translations and the *Textus Receptus*).¹⁵ In addition, placing the doxology here interrupts the treatment of the same topic in chapters 14 and 15. According to Origen, Marcion's text of Romans ended at this point: the explanation for the inclusion of the doxology at this point could be related to this shorter version of the epistle (compare the presence of both the shorter and longer additions to Mark in many Greek manuscripts).¹⁶ There is extensive literature on this structural variation, which also affects Rom. 15:33 and 16:25–27 (see below).¹⁷ The full attestation for this variation unit in Greek continuous-text manuscripts is provided in *TuT Romans* (TS31).

15:14 [τῆς] γνώσεως (knowledge)

The definite article τῆς ('the') is absent from the majority of Greek manuscripts (including 𝔓⁴⁶ 02 04 06 012), but present in some important witnesses (01 03 025 6 1506 1739 1881). The article could easily have been omitted through homoeoteleuton after πάσης or by analogy with the two preceding constructions involving 'being filled'. Its addition is more difficult to explain, although there is a loose parallel at 1 Cor. 13:2 where the article is present. In either case, translation is unaffected.

15:17 [τὴν] καύχησιν (reason to boast)

As at Rom. 15:14, most Greek manuscripts lack the definite article (01 02 025 etc.), but there is early and weighty support for τήν ('the'; 03 04 06 012 81 365 etc.). Other instances of καύχησις ('reason to boast') do not present a consistent practice (e.g. 2 Cor. 7:4, 14), yet the complements of ἔχω ('I have') in the Pauline Epistles often lack an article (e.g. 1 Cor. 7:25, 9:17, 13:1–3; Col. 2:1). Papyrus 46 has a different construction, ἣν ἔχω καύχησιν ('which reason to boast I have'; 𝔓⁴⁶), which appears to be secondary. Although the absence of τήν could be translated as an indefinite article ('I have a reason to boast'), the variation is of little importance for interpretation.

---

¹⁵ Codex Boernerianus leaves a blank space corresponding to the doxology at this point: this is in keeping with other places in this bilingual manuscript where text was present in the Latin manuscript consulted but missing from the Greek exemplar.

¹⁶ On Marcion, see further Schmid 1995: 289–294 and 335.

¹⁷ See especially Gamble 1977, along with Lampe 1985, Fitzmyer 1993: 55–67 and Metzger 1994: 470–473.

15:19 πνεύματος [θεοῦ] (of the Spirit) {C}

The majority of Greek manuscripts, including some ancient witnesses, read πνεύματος θεοῦ ('of the Spirit of God'; 𝔓⁴⁶ 01 06¹ 025 0150 etc.). This is a characteristic Pauline phrase (cf. Rom. 8:9, 8:14; 1 Cor. 7:40, 12:3; 2 Cor. 3:3; Phil. 3:3), but the alternative, πνεύματος ἁγίου ('of the Holy Spirit'; 02 06*,² 012 33 81 etc. and several translations) also occurs in the epistles, including Rom. 15:13 and 15:16. Codex Vaticanus has no complement at all, but just reads πνεύματος ('of the Spirit'; 03). This might be original (as in the SBLGNT), as it would explain the presence of two alternatives, yet it could also be one of the short omissions typical of this manuscript. The occurrence of the phrase ἐν δυνάμει πνεύματος ἁγίου ('in the power of the Holy Spirit') at Rom. 15:13 provides a strong reason for the assimilation of an original θεοῦ to ἁγίου in this verse, which, along with the external evidence, may tip the balance in favour of θεοῦ which is preferred in the THGNT.[18]

15:29 Χριστοῦ (of Christ) {A}

A longer form, τοῦ εὐαγγελίου τοῦ Χριστοῦ ('of the gospel of Christ'; 01² [0150] 33 256 365 etc.) is found in the majority of witnesses, yet there is very strong external evidence in favour of just Χριστοῦ ('of Christ'; 𝔓⁴⁶ 01* 02 03 04 06 etc.). There is no obvious mechanical reason to explain the omission of the longer text, so it seems that this is another expansion in later tradition, incorporating a typical Pauline phrase (cf. Rom. 11:6, 14:6, 15:19). One minuscule lacks any complement (263), presumably through an error. The full attestation for this variation unit is provided in *TuT Romans* (TS36).

15:30 [ἀδελφοί] (brothers and sisters)

All other instances of παρακαλῶ δὲ ὑμᾶς ('I appeal to you') in the Pauline Epistles are followed by the vocative ἀδελφοί (Rom. 16:17; 1 Cor. 1:10, 16:15; Heb. 13:22; cf. Rom. 12:1). Here, however, it is missing from two of the earliest witnesses (𝔓⁴⁶ 03). This may be an oversight, but there are examples of παρακαλῶ without a vocative (e.g. 1 Cor. 4:16, 2 Cor. 10:1, Eph. 4:1) which allow for the possibility that the

---

[18] Thus also Ross 1983: 68–69.

shorter reading could have been expanded through assimilation to the typical form.[19]

15:33 ἀμήν. (Amen) {A}

There are three earlier prayers in Romans which end with 'Amen' (Rom. 1:25, 9:5, 11:36), providing a parallel for the text of the majority of manuscripts. Nevertheless, 'Amen' is absent from a few important witnesses (𝔓46 02 012 1739 1881 lat^(vl-pt)). It is hard to explain why it would have been omitted, but several of these manuscripts in combination have already been noted as omissive (e.g. Rom. 12:14 and 14:12), suggesting that this is secondary. In the case of Papyrus 46, the word is not appropriate because the doxology of Rom. 16:25–27 (with final 'Amen') is added after this verse, before it continues with Rom. 16:1 (see further the comments on 14:23 and 16:25–27).[20] There is one commentary manuscript (1506) which does not contain Rom. 16:1–24, but leaves the rest of the page blank after 15:33 before resuming with 16:25 at the top of the following page. This may be due to a lacuna in its exemplar or a decision not to copy out the following long section of greetings which lacked commentary: it has no bearing on the original structure of the letter.

16:1 [καί] (lit. also)

The majority of Greek manuscripts do not include this connective (01* 02 04² 06 012 025 etc.). However, καί is present in some early witnesses (𝔓46 01² 03 04* 81 co^(bo)). There is no obvious reason for its addition or omission (apart from oversight), and the external evidence is inconclusive: corrections in each direction demonstrate that both readings were current.

16:5 Ἀσίας (Asia) {B}

Epaenetus is described in most Greek manuscripts as the first-fruits 'of Achaia' (Ἀχαΐας, 06¹ 025 33 1175 1881 etc.). This appears to be assimilation to 1 Cor. 16:15, where the household of Stephanas is given this title. There is very strong early evidence for Ἀσίας ('of Asia'; 𝔓46 𝔓118 01

---

[19] Aasgard 2004: 311–313 argues strongly in favour of the longer reading here.

[20] It may therefore be appropriate to number the verses with the doxology in Papyrus 46 as Rom. 15:34–36.

02 03 etc.). The two placenames are almost identical, and the fact that the only other location mentioned in this chapter is in Greece (Cenchreae in Rom. 16:1) might also have contributed to the introduction of the alternative reading. The full attestation for this variation unit is provided in *TuT Romans* (TS39).

16:6   εἰς ὑμᾶς (for you) {B}

In later Greek, the plural pronouns for 'you' and 'us' came to be pronounced in an identical way due to itacism. The majority of Greek manuscripts read the first person, εἰς ἡμᾶς ('for us'; 04² 33 1175 etc.), which is a less common construction in the epistles and may be the harder reading in context (cf. Gal. 4:11). The bilingual manuscripts read ἐν ὑμῖν ('in you'; 06 012), but there is very strong early support for εἰς ὑμᾶς ('for you'; 𝔓⁴⁶ 𝔓¹¹⁸ 01 02 03 etc.). The full attestation is reported in *TuT Romans* (TS40).

16:7   Ἰουνίαν (Junia) {A}

Five manuscripts read Ἰουλίαν ('Julia'; 𝔓⁴⁶ 6 606 1718 2685; see *TuT Romans* TS41) along with some early translations, but this is either a replacement by a more common form or an anticipation of Rom. 16:15. The other readings differ in their accentuation: Ἰουνιᾶν ('Junias') would be masculine, whereas Ἰουνίαν ('Junia') is feminine.[21] As the earlier manuscripts in majuscule script lack accents and the following adjectives are in the plural, it is not possible to determine whether they present a man or a woman. The majority of Greek manuscripts, however, along with older witnesses to which accents were added subsequently, have the feminine Ἰουνίαν ('Junia'; 03² 06² 0150 33 81 etc.). Early translations into Latin and Coptic also support the feminine, and no ancient attestation of the Latin name *Junias* (which is claimed to be a shortened form of *Junianus*) has been found.[22] There has been some controversy over the description of a woman as 'prominent among the apostles' (ἐπίσημοι ἐν τοῖς ἀποστόλοις), but the interpreta-

---

[21] The absence of accents in *Text und Textwert* means that the information provided there is of limited value.

[22] Metzger 1994: 475; for Coptic, see Plisch 1996.

tion of this phrase is a separate matter: the text is clear and the confidence of the committee covers the accentuation as well as the spelling.[23]

16:20 ἡ χάρις τοῦ κυρίου ἡμῶν Ἰησοῦ μεθ' ὑμῶν (**The grace of our Lord Jesus be with you**) {B}

Most witnesses read ἡ χάρις τοῦ κυρίου ἡμῶν Ἰησοῦ Χριστοῦ μεθ' ὑμῶν ('the grace of our Lord Jesus Christ be with you'; 02 04 025 0150 etc.). Just four manuscripts lack Χριστοῦ ('Christ'; om. 𝔓46 01 03 1881): this could be due to the accidental omission of one of the *nomina sacra* (ΙΥ ΧΥ), but such a shorter reading would have been very likely to be expanded to the full title. The importance of these documents elsewhere has led to the adoption of this as the editorial text. This phrase is very similar to Rom. 16:24 (see below). It is missing here from a few witnesses (06 012 lat[vl-pt]) which read it four verses later. This appears to be an early editorial deletion, which removes the repetition and incorporates the greetings of 16:21–23 into the rest of the letter.[24]

16:24 *omit verse* {A}

After verse 23, the majority of Greek manuscripts read ἡ χάρις τοῦ κυρίου ἡμῶν Ἰησοῦ Χριστοῦ μετὰ πάντων ὑμῶν ἀμήν ('The grace of our Lord Jesus Christ be with you all. Amen'; 06 [012] 6 1175 1881 etc.). Given that this is the final verse of the letter in most of these manuscripts (see the next unit), it is not surprising that a concluding grace should have been added (cf. 1 Cor. 16:23, 2 Cor. 13:13, Gal. 6:18, Phil. 4:23, 1 Thess. 5:28, 2 Thess. 3:18, Phlm 25) even though it is very similar to the text of Rom. 16:20 (see above). It is also worth noting that a few witnesses which do include Rom. 16:25–27 postpone this grace until after that doxology ([025] 33 256 263 365 etc.). The external evidence for the original absence of verse 24 is conclusive (𝔓46 𝔓61 01 02 03 04 etc., along with most Latin and Coptic witnesses).[25]

---

[23] Extensive discussion of this variant is seen in Fitzmyer 1993: 737ff., Cervin 1994, Burer and Wallace 2001 and Epp 2005. Most recently, and with attention to early Christian writers, see Hartmann 2020.

[24] For further considerations, see Gamble 1977: 129–132 and Fellows 2024: 14–15.

[25] The full attestation in Greek continuous-text manuscripts is provided in *TuT Romans* (TS45). See also Gamble 1977: 129–132 and Hurtado 1981.

16:25–27 *include in brackets* {C}

As noted at Rom. 14:23, the majority of Greek manuscripts have this doxology there (as Rom. 14:24–26) rather than here (6 1175 1881 etc.), while in the oldest witness ($\mathfrak{P}^{46}$) it occurs after Rom. 15:33. The external evidence for its presence at this point alone is considerable ($\mathfrak{P}^{61}$ 01 03 04 06 etc., lat[vl-pt, vg] sy[p] co eth Origen[lat]), along with the manuscripts which attest both 14:24–26 and 16:25–27 (02 025 0150 33 [1506]): the full attestation is provided in *TuT Romans* (TS46).[26] The omission or displacement of such a substantial section is unlikely to be accidental. Instead, it appears to relate to different forms of the letter in circulation. It has already been noted that, according to Origen, Marcion's text of Romans ended at 14:23. A version without the list of greetings—not that this is paralleled for any other epistle—would finish at 15:33. While it is plausible that a list of greetings formed part of the original letter (as in the case of the other epistles), questions have been raised as to whether the current text of Romans 16, with its two sets of greetings at 16:1–16 and 16:21–23, is actually part of the same letter.[27] In the face of this perplexity, which may reach to a period before the collection of the Pauline Epistles into a single corpus, and some doubt over the authenticity of these verses, the doxology is printed here in brackets. The SBLGNT omits these verses completely.

16:27 αἰῶνας (forever) {B}

Some early witnesses have the longer version of the benediction, common from liturgical usage, αἰῶνας τῶν αἰώνων ('for ever and ever'; $\mathfrak{P}^{61}$ 01 02 06 025 etc.). Elsewhere in Romans, the shorter form is unchallenged (Rom. 1:25, 9:5, 11:36; cf. 2 Cor. 11:31), but there are a couple of instances of the longer form in other epistles (Gal. 1:5, Phil. 4:20). Although it could be the result of assimilation to the earlier verses or accidental omission, the strong external evidence for αἰῶνας ('for ever'; $\mathfrak{P}^{46}$ 03 04 and the majority of minuscules; see *TuT Romans* TS47) leads to its adoption in the editorial text.

---

[26] On GA 1506, see the comment on Rom. 15:33 above.

[27] See further Gamble 1977, Elliott 1981a, Hurtado 1981, Fitzmyer 1993: 55–67 and 753, Metzger 1994: 470–473 and Collins 2002.

The First Letter to the Corinthians

1:1 Χριστοῦ Ἰησοῦ (Christ Jesus) {B}

The majority of Greek manuscripts have the word order Ἰησοῦ Χριστοῦ ('Jesus Christ'; 01 02 025 0150 etc.), but there is early attestation of Χριστοῦ Ἰησοῦ ('Christ Jesus'; 𝔓⁴⁶ 03 06 012 33 lat^{vl-pt, vg} co^{sa} eth Chrysostom Cyril). It may be noted that the majority of manuscripts read ἐν Χριστῷ Ἰησοῦ ('in Christ Jesus') a few words later, although that is followed by Ἰησοῦ Χριστοῦ at the end of 1 Cor. 1:2. As observed above at Rom. 1:1, 'Christ Jesus' is the preferred sequence in the introductory formula in multiple epistles: the external evidence for this is stronger here than in Romans. Once again, however, THGNT prefers the majority reading, with the implication that the alternative is an assimilation to Pauline practice elsewhere. While Χριστός could be interpreted as a title ('Messiah'), without an article is it best taken as a proper name.

1:13 μεμέρισται (has been divided) {A}

The reading μὴ μεμέρισται ('surely he has not been divided') is attested in a few witnesses (𝔓⁴⁶ᵛⁱᵈ 1962 2464* sy^p cpa co^{sa} eth). This is assimilation to the following phrase, which emphasises that this is a question expecting a negative answer. Without the addition, it is ambivalent as to whether this is a statement or a question. Despite the lack of punctuation in early Greek texts, it is preferable to consider this phrase as a rhetorical question and indicate it accordingly.

1:14 [τῷ θεῷ] (God) {C}

Some manuscripts read τῷ θεῷ μου ('to my God'; 02 33 81 lat^{vl-pt}), through assimilation to the same phrase at 1 Cor. 1:4 (cf. Rom. 1:8, Phil. 1:3, Phlm 4). Others lack the phrase altogether (01* 03 6 1739 co^{sa-mss, bo-pt}). It is possible that the latter was original and expanded on the model of the other Pauline instances of εὐχαριστῶ ('I give thanks'): the complement of τῷ θεῷ ('to God') is seen at 1 Cor. 14:18 and the shortest reading is the most difficult given that this verb usually has an object elsewhere: although there are exceptions (Rom. 16:4; 1 Cor.

10:30), neither of these occurs at the beginning of a sentence. There is strong external evidence here for the majority reading with τῷ θεῷ ('to God'; 01² 04 06 012 025 etc.) and ΤΩ ΘΩ could have been omitted through eyeskip after ΕΥΧΑΡΙΣΤΩ. Certain languages may, in any case, require the recipient to be specified after a verb of thanksgiving.

1:28 τὰ μὴ ὄντα (things that are not) {B}

Before this phrase, the majority of Greek manuscripts read καί ('and'; 01² 03 04³ 06² 025 etc.), which has the effect of including the 'things that are not' as another term in the list. The shorter reading, just τὰ μὴ ὄντα ('things that are not'; 𝔓⁴⁶ 01* 02 04* 06* etc.), has strong early attestation. It involves taking the phrase in apposition to 'what is low and despised in the world', contrasting them to the following τὰ ὄντα ('things that are'). It is therefore preferable on both internal and external grounds. It is possible to use the neuter to refer to people rather than objects when indicating a shared quality instead of a group of individuals: if this interpretation is followed, it would affect the whole of 1 Cor. 1:27–28.[1]

2:1 μυστήριον (lit. mystery) {C}

The majority of Greek manuscripts have μαρτύριον ('testimony'; 01² 03 06 012 025 etc.), which may be a reminiscence of the use of this word at 1 Cor. 1:6. In contrast, μυστήριον ('mystery'; 𝔓⁴⁶ᵛⁱᵈ 01* 02 04 lat^{vl-pt} sy^p co^{bo} Hippolytus) anticipates its occurrence in 1 Cor. 2:7. The latter word is more common in the Pauline Epistles, appearing with several similar verbs (cf. 1 Cor. 14:2, 15:51; Eph. 1:9, 3:3, 6:19; Col. 4:3). It is hard to decide whether this should be preferred on the basis of Pauline usage, or whether it was introduced through assimilation or misreading. The SBLGNT and THGNT both prefer μαρτύριον, which is perhaps the more difficult reading and has stronger attestation.[2] The full set of readings in Greek continuous-text manuscripts is provided in *TuT 1 Cor* (TS4).

---

[1] Omanson 2006: 328.
[2] See also Kloha 2006: 43–46.

2:4 πειθοῖ[ς] σοφίας [λόγοις] (with persuasive words of wisdom) {D}

Five different forms of this phrase are recorded in the apparatus, with additional subreadings: *TuT 1Cor* (TS5) lists no fewer than eighteen variants. The majority of Greek manuscripts have the longest reading, πειθοῖς ἀνθρωπίνης σοφίας λόγοις ('with persuasive words of human wisdom'; 01² 02 04 025 6 etc.). Also well attested is πειθοῖς σοφίας λόγοις ('with persuasive words of wisdom'; [01*] 03 06 0150 etc.). Shorter still is πειθοῖς σοφίας ('with persuasions of wisdom'; 𝔓⁴⁶ 012 Chrysostom^ms). However, the adjective πειθοῖς is only found here in Greek and has been explained as equivalent to πιθανός (present in GA 522).³ The other two variants have the standard form πειθοῖ, the dative of the noun πειθώ ('persuasion'): πειθοῖ ἀνθρωπίνης σοφίας λόγοις ('with persuasion by words of human wisdom'; 205 209 [2495] etc.) and πειθοῖ σοφίας λόγων ('with persuasion of words of wisdom'; [lat^vl-pt, vg-ms] sy^p Origen^gr-pt). While ἀνθρωπίνης ('human') is a later gloss, explaining the nature of 'wisdom' and anticipating the following verse, it is not clear whether πειθοῖς is original or a scribal error for πειθοῖ, duplicating the first letter of the following word (σοφίας). It is also worth noting that λόγοις breaks the parallelism with the second half of the the verse and is likely to have followed a change to πειθοῖς in order to provide a noun for this adjective: if λόγων were original, then it could have been altered to λόγοις after πειθοῖς was introduced. One explanation is to conjecture πειθοῖ σοφίας ('in the persuasion of wisdom') as the earliest form, as seen in the SBLGNT: this could have led to the variant in Papyrus 46 as well as πειθοῖ σοφίας λόγων before other, subsequent developments.⁴ Nevertheless, there remains the possibility that Paul himself coined the neologism πειθοῖς, perhaps writing πειθοῖς σοφίας which an editor later corrected to πειθοῖ after another had attempted to improve it by the addition of some form of λόγοι. Nowhere else does Paul use the noun πειθώ, although the word πιθανολογία ('use of probable arguments') which would have been ideal for the present context, is found at Col. 2:4. The THGNT adopts πειθοῖς σοφίας λόγοις, which is also the most common form in Origen's

---

³ See further the discussion of this verse in BDAG s. v. πειθός; the gloss with πιθανός is in Liddell-Scott-Jones.

⁴ *Amsterdam Database* cj10608 [Bentley 1628].

citations.[5] Whichever reading is chosen, the general sense of the phrase is clear for translation.

2:10   δέ (lit. but) {B}

The choice of connective at the beginning of the verse affects the structure of the argument. Even though δέ (01 02 04 06 012 and the majority of minuscules) often introduces a contrast ('but'), in the Pauline Epistles it can simply mark a transition (see Rom. 6:8 above). As the following observation is in keeping with the quotation in 1 Cor. 2:9, it seems that an early editor replaced δέ with γάρ ('for'; 𝔓[46] 03 6 256 263 etc.), which is also seen in the second half of this verse. The presence of a secondary text in Papyrus 46 and Codex Vaticanus is notable (compare Rom. 8:23 and 9:23 above).

2:15   [τὰ] πάντα (all things) {C}

Without the definite article, πάντα could be taken as masculine accusative singular ('every person') rather than neuter plural ('all things'). The article in τὰ πάντα ('all things'; 𝔓[46] 02 04 06* 025 etc.) fixes the reading as neuter plural. The absence of the article from the majority of Greek manuscripts (01[1] 03 06[2] 012 0150 etc.) corresponds to a slight preference in this epistle for the anarthrous use of πάντα (e.g. 1 Cor. 2:10), but it leaves the interpretation unclear: a singular would match ὑπ' οὐδενός ('by no-one') in the following clause. It is very difficult to decide which is original, although πάντας ('all people'; Irenaeus[lat]) is clearly secondary. The postpositive μέν is seen in most Greek manuscripts, but it is missing from early translations, ancient writers and a few important documents (𝔓[46] 02 04 06* 012). Its placement after the verb does not correspond to the following clause where the focal word for the contrast is αὐτός ('himself'), suggesting that it is not authorial.

2:16   Χριστοῦ (of Christ) {B}

As the phrase νοῦν κυρίου ('the mind of the Lord') has just appeared in the quotation from Isaiah 40:13, the repetition of it at the end of this

---

[5] I am grateful to Tommy Wasserman for calling my attention to Origen's citations, on the basis of which he strongly prefers the reading of the THGNT. For longer discussions, both of which favour ἐν πειθοῖ σοφίας, see Kloha 2006: 47–52 and Ebojo 2009.

verse (03 06* 012 lat^{vl-pt}) appears to be a simple error. This may have been exacerbated by the visual similarity between the two *nomina sacra* (ΧΥ and ΚΥ; compare 1 Cor. 4:17). Notwithstanding the potential of an error in the other direction, 'we have the mind of Christ' is a bold claim which is more likely to be original and is also very well attested.

3:3 ἔρις (quarrelling) {B}

The majority of Greek manuscripts include a third phrase in this list, reading ἔρις καὶ διχοστασίαι ('quarrelling and divisions'; 𝔓⁴⁶ 06 [012] 6 33 etc.). There is strong external evidence for ἔρις alone (𝔓¹¹ 01 02 03 04 etc.), which suggests that καὶ διχοστασίαι is a later addition, perhaps inspired by the occurrence of all three terms at Gal. 5:20. The full attestation is provided in *TuT 1 Cor* (TS6).

3:4 ἄνθρωποι (human) {B}

The support for ἄνθρωποι is impressive (𝔓⁴⁶ 01* 02 03 04 06 etc.). The alternative σαρκικοί ('fleshly'; 01² 025 and the majority of minuscules) may be considered a more negative term and therefore significant for Pauline anthropology. It is very likely that this has been carried over from its occurrence in the same phrase in the previous verse, whereas it is more difficult to explain ἄνθρωποι if it is not original. Again, full data for Greek continuous-text manuscripts is provided in *TuT 1 Cor* (TS7).

3:5 Ἀπολλῶς ... Παῦλος (Apollos ... Paul) {A}

A change in sequence, putting Paul first followed by Apollos, is found in the majority of Greek manuscripts (Παῦλος ... Ἀπολλῶς, 06¹ 6 256 263 etc.; see further *TuT 1 Cor* TS8). This clearly seems secondary: not only does it put Paul first, in the position of honour, but it also brings this verse into the same sequence as those on either side. The difference in order is the harder reading, with very strong early support (𝔓⁴⁶ᵛⁱᵈ 01 02 03 04 06*, ² etc.).

3:13 [αὐτὸ] δοκιμάσει (will test [it])

The pronoun αὐτό ('it') is supported by good external evidence (02 03 025 6 33 81 1175 1739 Origen). However, it is not required in context and is missing from the majority of Greek manuscripts (𝔓⁴⁶ 01 06 etc.).

The latter is the smoother reading, suggesting that αὐτό was originally present, but it is unusual to find a shorter text as the majority form (cf. 1 Cor. 4:17).[6]

4:6   γέγραπται (is written) {B}

The shorter reading with just γέγραπται ('it is written'; 𝔓⁴⁶ 01* 02 03 06* etc.) has strong attestation but it requires interpreting the complement of τό as a quotation in direct speech ('the saying "Nothing beyond what is written"'). The inclusion of φρονεῖν ('to think'; 01² 04ᵛⁱᵈ 06² 025 etc.) makes for a simpler construction, by creating an articular infinitive with τό ('not to think beyond what is written'). This appears to be a later addition: there is no obvious reason for φρονεῖν to have dropped out if it were original.[7] Some commentaries include an extensive discussion of whether this is a quotation and what its source might be: in certain translations, γέγραπται is taken as a reference to Jewish Scripture.[8]

4:14   νουθετῶ[ν] (to admonish)

The external evidence is split between the first-person indicative νουθετῶ ('I admonish'; 𝔓⁴⁶ 03 06 012 and the majority of minuscules) and the participle νουθετῶν ('admonishing'; 𝔓¹¹ᵛⁱᵈ 02 04 025 6 33 365 1175 1739). Each of these fits with the first half of the verse: the indicative matches γράφω ('I write'), while the participle stands in opposition to the initial οὐκ ἐντρέπων ('not to make you ashamed'). The latter is the more expected construction, suggesting that νουθετῶ is the harder reading. The indicative also finds some support in the same construction at 2 Cor. 2:17, in contrast to examples where the same main verb governs both clauses (1 Cor. 3:1, 2 Cor. 11:17, Eph. 5:15 etc.). This makes it very difficult to decide whether νουθετῶν is the author's original contrast or a stylistic improvement.

4:17   Χριστῷ [Ἰησοῦ] (Christ Jesus) {C}

The majority of Greek manuscripts only have Χριστῷ ('Christ'; 02 03 06² 025 etc.), but there is strong evidence for Χριστῷ Ἰησοῦ ('Christ Jesus';

---

[6] In favour of the absence of αὐτό, see Kloha 2006: 71–72.
[7] On the possibility that this verse incorporates a gloss, see Arzt-Grabner 2006 and Kloha 2006: 77–79.
[8] See Omanson 2006: 331–332 and the references there.

𝔓⁴⁶ 01 04 06¹ 6 etc.). The reading κυρίῳ Ἰησοῦ ('Lord Jesus'; 06* 012 etc.) derives from misreading the *nomen sacrum* ΧΩ as ΚΩ (cf. 1 Cor. 2:16 above), but supports the presence of Ἰησοῦ. The addition of the name following Χριστῷ, perhaps under the influence of 1 Cor. 4:15, would be an easy copying error: it is also striking that the majority of manuscripts have the shorter reading. Nevertheless, the support for Χριστῷ Ἰησοῦ is considerable, and it is possible that the second *nomen sacrum* could have been overlooked at an early point. The full attestation in Greek continuous-text manuscripts is provided in *TuT 1 Cor* (TS9).

5:4   τοῦ κυρίου [ἡμῶν] Ἰησοῦ ([our] Lord Jesus¹) {C}

Both this and the following unit involve the expansion of references to Jesus. In this verse, there is early evidence for three shorter readings: Ἰησοῦ ('Jesus'; 02), Ἰησοῦ Χριστοῦ ('Jesus Christ'; 01 lat^(vl-pt)) and ἡμῶν Ἰησοῦ ('our [Lord] Jesus'; 03 06* 1175 1739 lat^(vl-pt)). In contrast, the majority of manuscripts give the standard full title, ἡμῶν Ἰησοῦ Χριστοῦ ('our [Lord] Jesus Christ'; 𝔓⁴⁶ 06² 012 025 etc.). Although the shortest reading is paralleled at Col. 3:18, there seems to be no consistent practice across the epistles, which leads to frequent variation involving such titles (cf. 1 Cor. 6:11, 2 Thess. 3:6). While Χριστοῦ ('Christ') is likely to be an addition, it is more difficult to decide whether or not ἡμῶν ('our') was originally present: the slightly better external support may favour its inclusion.

5:5   κυρίου (of the Lord) {B}

In this verse, the shortest reading has substantial early support and, accordingly, κυρίου ('of the Lord'; 𝔓⁴⁶ 03 1739 Marcion^(acc. to Tertullian) Tertullian Origen^(gr-pt) etc.) has been adopted as the editorial text. The other variants, as in 1 Cor. 5:4, demonstrate the tendency to expand this title. Most Greek manuscripts read κυρίου Ἰησοῦ ('of the Lord Jesus'; 𝔓⁶¹ᵛⁱᵈ 01 6 81 1175 etc.), while a few witnesses read κυρίου Ἰησοῦ Χριστοῦ ('of the Lord Jesus Christ'; 06 lat^(vl-pt) Origen^(gr-pt)) and yet others have κυρίου ἡμῶν Ἰησοῦ Χριστοῦ ('of our Lord Jesus Christ'; 02 012 025 0150 etc.). The early attestation of the last of these and the possibility of influence from other references to 'the day of the Lord' (e.g. 1 Cor. 1:8, 2 Cor. 1:14, 2 Thess. 2:2) mean that some doubt remains about the initial reading.

6:7 [οὖν] (in fact)

Some important witnesses do not have οὖν ('therefore', 'then'; 𝔓⁴⁶ 01* 06* 6 33 1739 1881). It is possible that it was omitted by oversight after μέν, or that it was added to match 1 Cor. 6:4 (one of the few secure instances of μὲν οὖν in the Pauline Epistles).[9]

6:11 Ἰησοῦ Χριστοῦ (Jesus Christ) {C}

A variety of complements are found after 'in the name of the Lord' (cf. 1 Cor. 5:4 above). On this occasion, unusually, the majority of witnesses have a short reading, Ἰησοῦ ('Jesus'; 02 06² 0150 6 etc.). There is early evidence for Ἰησοῦ Χριστοῦ ('Jesus Christ'; 𝔓¹¹ᵛⁱᵈ 𝔓⁴⁶ 01 06* latᵛˡ⁻ᵖᵗ etc.) and also strong attestation for ἡμῶν Ἰησοῦ Χριστοῦ ('of our [Lord] Jesus Christ'; 03 04ᵛⁱᵈ 025 33 81 etc.). Witnesses with just ἡμῶν ('our [Lord]'; [coˢᵃ] Irenaeusˡᵃᵗ⁻ᵖᵗ) appear to be omissive. If ἡμῶν were originally present, it is surprising for it not to be seen in the Byzantine tradition: the latter could have arisen from Ἰησοῦ Χριστοῦ through oversight of the third of the *nomina sacra* abbreviations (ΚΥ ΙΥ ΧΥ) or assimilation to 1 Cor. 5:4. This explains the adoption of Ἰησοῦ Χριστοῦ as the editorial text, but the division of the manuscripts means that there is a considerable degree of doubt.

6:14 ἐξεγερεῖ (will raise) {B}

The tense of this verb is of theological importance: how does the resurrection of believers relate to that of Christ? All three possibilities are found in Papyrus 46, which has been corrected twice. The future-tense ἐξεγερεῖ is found in the majority of manuscripts ('he will raise'; 𝔓⁴⁶ᶜ¹ 01 04 06² 33 81 etc.). Some important manuscripts have the aorist, ἐξήγειρεν ('he raised'; 𝔓⁴⁶ᶜ² 03 6 1739 latᵛˡ⁻ᵖᵗ, ᵛᵍ⁻ᵐˢˢ), but this is probably the repetition of the verb from earlier in the verse: if the raising was in the past, this could be taken as referring to the time of Christian baptism. Finally comes the present tense, ἐξεγείρει ('he is raising'; 𝔓¹¹ 𝔓⁴⁶* 02 06* 025 etc.). The slim attestation suggests that this is a misreading of the future form rather than the earliest text, although the use of the present at 1 Cor. 15:15–16 may be noted.

---

[9] Zuntz 1953: 193 thinks that a subsequent addition is likely.

6:16 [ἤ] (lit. or)

The Byzantine tradition is divided here, with many manuscripts including the conjunction ἤ ('or'; 01 02 03 04 012 025 etc.) and numerous others which lack it ($\mathfrak{P}^{46}$ 06 etc.). This is the second of three occurrences of the phrase οὐκ οἴδατε ('do you not know?'): the first, at 1 Cor. 6:15, lacks the conjunction while the third, at 6:19, includes it. Paul's usage elsewhere is inconsistent (e.g. 1 Cor. 6:2, 6:3, 6:9), so both internal and external evidence are inconclusive.[10]

6:20 τῷ σώματι ὑμῶν (your body) {A}

There is excellent external support for the shortest reading, ὑμῶν ('your [body]'; $\mathfrak{P}^{46}$ 01 02 03 04* etc.), adopted as the editorial text. The majority of Greek manuscripts include two extra phrases: καὶ ἐν τῷ πνεύματι ὑμῶν, ἅτινά ἐστιν τοῦ θεοῦ ('and in your spirit, which are of God'; 04³ 06² 025 0150 etc.), while GA 2464 just has the first of these. The latter could have been omitted through eyeskip, but there is nothing in the Byzantine text to explain the editorial text as an accidental omission. Both phrases are irrelevant to the context, which concerns the body rather than the spirit (although there is a reference to spirit in 1 Cor. 6:17).[11] It may also be noted that ἐστιν with a genitive complement is rarely used to denote possession in the Pauline Epistles (cf. Rom. 8:9). All in all, the longer text is clearly an expansion made by a later editor in order to extend the scope of the command and render it more spiritual in application. The full attestation in Greek continuous-text manuscripts is provided in *TuT 1 Cor* (TS14).

7:5 τῇ προσευχῇ (to prayer) {A}

The attestation of the shorter reading, τῇ προσευχῇ ('to prayer'; $\mathfrak{P}^{11vid}$ $\mathfrak{P}^{46}$ 01* 02 03 etc.), is once again compelling. The majority of minuscules have τῇ νηστείᾳ καὶ τῇ προσευχῇ ('to fasting and prayer'; 01² 0150 256 365 etc.; see further *TuT 1 Cor* TS15). These terms often appear together in Christian practice (e.g. Acts 13:3, 14:23; cf. Matt. 17:21; Mark 9:29; Acts 10:30), but Paul never refers to fasting as a spiritual discipline (cf. 2 Cor. 6:5, 11:27), which confirms this as a secondary addition.[12]

---

[10] Zuntz 1953: 195 prefers the shorter reading.
[11] Thus Metzger 1994: 488.
[12] See also the discussion at Kloha 2006: 125–128.

7:7 θέλω δέ (I wish) {B}

The majority of manuscripts read γάρ ('for'; 01² 03 06¹ 025 etc.). The alternative, δέ ('but'; 𝔓⁴⁶ 01* 02 04 06* etc.) has strong external support. Although the numerous instances of δέ in context could have led to its introduction here, it is more likely that it was replaced with γάρ to emphasise that this verse complements rather than contrasts with the previous observation. Other examples of the alteration of an initial δέ are noted above in Rom. 3:7, 4:15 and 6:8, while the opposite scenario appears at Gal. 1:11 (see below).

7:14 ἀδελφῷ (brother) {A}

Most of the oldest Greek witnesses have ἀδελφῷ (𝔓⁴⁶ 01* 02 03 04 etc.), which literally means 'brother' but in context indicates 'a fellow Christian (to whom she is married)'; compare also the use of ὁ ἀδελφὸς ἢ ἡ ἀδελφή ('the brother or sister') in the following verse. The sense is made explicit in the majority of Greek manuscripts by the use of ἀνδρί ('husband'; 01² 06² 0150 6 81 etc.), with further clarification still in ἀνδρὶ τῷ πιστῷ ('husband who is a believer'; 629 lat^(vl-pt, vg) sy^p Irenaeus^lat Tertullian). Despite the early attestation of the latter, it seems that its repetition of the construction found at the beginning of the verse is a translational means of clarifying the sense. Similarly, modern translations may need to choose a word which indicates a believer rather than a blood relative in order to avoid the potential ambiguity which led to the textual variation. The full attestation in Greek continuous-text manuscripts is given in *TuT 1 Cor* (TS17).

7:15 ὑμᾶς (lit. you) {C}

The vast majority of witnesses read the first-person plural ἡμᾶς ('us'; 𝔓⁴⁶ 01² 03 06 012 etc.). Nevertheless, there is significant support for ὑμᾶς ('you'; 01* 02 04 0150 81 etc.). Sound changes in Greek meant that the two words were pronounced similarly. Other references to the divine call in the Pauline Epistles are found with pronouns in the first person (Rom. 9:24, 1 Thess. 4:7, 2 Thess 2:14) or the second person (Gal. 1:6, 5:8; 1 Thess. 2:12). The editorial text has adopted ὑμᾶς on the grounds that there is a tendency during transmission to extend the applicability of such observations by preferring a more inclusive pronoun, reflecting the hortatory use of these writings. On the other hand, the context of Paul's instructions to the Corinthians could easily have prompted the introduction of the second-person pronoun: both the SBLGNT and THGNT prefer ἡμᾶς.[13]

7:34 καὶ μεμέρισται. καὶ ἡ γυνὴ ἡ ἄγαμος καὶ ἡ παρθένος (and his interests are divided. And the unmarried woman and the virgin) {D}

There are two principal areas of variation in this phrase, involving the first three and last five words of the editorial text; the full Greek manuscript attestation for the latter is provided in *TuT 1Cor* (TS19).[14] The initial καί ('and') is missing from the majority of Greek manuscripts (06² 012 etc.) and the *Textus Receptus*: in this situation, the verb μεμέρισται ('is divided') could still be read in asyndeton with the male subject of the previous verse, but it could instead be applied to at least one of the following nouns, e.g. 'the wife is also divided' (see also the reading of 06* and 2464, which lacks καί after μεμέρισται). In fact, the sequence in the majority of manuscripts ἡ γυνὴ καὶ ἡ παρθένος ἡ ἄγαμος ('the wife and the virgin, the unmarried woman'; 06 012 0150 etc.) means that μεμέρισται could be taken impersonally with the next two nouns (as in the KJV): 'there is a difference also between a wife and a virgin'. One of the merits of this is that ἡ ἄγαμος ('the unmarried woman') becomes the subject of the following singular verb μεριμνᾷ ('she is anxious'), although it leaves two nominatives in apposition to μεμέρισται at the beginning of the verse. The same interpretation is inherent in some important manuscripts which read ἡ γυνὴ ἡ ἄγαμος καὶ ἡ παρθένος ἡ ἄγαμος ('the unmarried woman and the unmarried virgin'; 𝔓⁴⁶ 01 02 [6] 33 etc.): the double appearance of ἡ ἄγαμος seems to be pleonasm, making this a hard reading, but it could simply be a conflation of the other two readings. Papyrus 129 definitely has ἡ παρθένος ἡ ἄγαμος ('the unmarried virgin'), but it is not clear which of the other readings preceded it. Another difficult reading is ἡ γυνὴ ἡ ἄγαμος καὶ ἡ παρθένος ('the unmarried woman and the virgin'; 𝔓¹⁵ 03 025 256 263 etc.), which may have appeared tautologous. This has been adopted as the editorial text here and in both the SBLGNT and THGNT: it has

---

[13] The first person is also favoured in Kloha 2006: 142–143.

[14] In Latin tradition, the words corresponding to καὶ μεμέρισται *(et diuisus est)* occur at the end of 1 Cor. 7:33 rather than the beginning of 1 Cor. 7:34.

early attestation and provides an explanation of how the other forms developed as misreadings or simplifications. Still, it is possible that elements even of this form may be secondary.[15]

7:38 γαμίζων ... γαμίζων (marries ... from marriage) {B}

The majority of Greek manuscripts read ἐκγαμίζων for both these participles (025 2464 etc.), while there are a few witnesses which read γαμίζων ... ἐκγαμίζων (01² 365). There is strong support for γαμίζων twice ($\mathfrak{P}^{15vid}$ $\mathfrak{P}^{46}$ 01* 02 03 06 etc.). Although there do not appear to be any examples of ἐκγαμίζων ... γαμίζων, the first part of the sentence is often omitted through eyeskip from καλῶς ('well') at the end of the previous verse (see *TuT 1Cor* TS20). The structure of this verse indicates that it is the same agent for both participles, while the context on either side suggests that this is the unmarried man. A number of translations accordingly interpret γαμίζων as 'marry' rather than 'give in marriage', even though this contrasts with its use as a passive equivalent to γαμέω elsewhere in the New Testament (Matt. 22:30, 24:38; Mark 12:25; Luke 17:27, 20:35). Given this non-standard usage and its good external support, γαμίζων is most likely to have been replaced by ἐκγαμίζων, another relatively rare word, even though its sense of 'give in marriage' requires a new agent (parent rather than fiancé). Differing marriage practices in differing cultures are reflected in the vocabulary available in receptor languages and translators will have to choose the term which best corresponds to their understanding of Paul's argument in this passage.

8:3 τὸν θεόν ... ὑπ' αὐτοῦ (God ... by him) {B}

There are two variation units here. Papyrus 46 lacks both complements, reading εἰ δέ τις ἀγαπᾷ οὗτος ἔγνωσται ('anyone who loves is known'; $\mathfrak{P}^{46}$ Clement). This is somewhat telegraphic, and it is possible that the object and prepositional phrase were added later for clarification. In context, however, the text of Papyrus 46 seems to be the result of an editorial revision which removed all of the objects from the verbs in this sentence (it is also missing τι, 'something', in the previous verse) in

---

[15] See further the extensive discussion in Kloha 2006: 160–187, who concludes that the editorial text is the earliest form.

order to present a more general and memorable saying. It is striking to observe such evidence of stylistic alteration in the oldest surviving witness, corresponding to trends seen elsewhere in 'Western' readings. Some other important sources include τὸν θεόν but lack ὑπ' αὐτοῦ (01* 33 eth). This may be assimilation to the previous verse (where γνῶναι has no complement), partial influence from the text seen in Papyrus 46, or simply an oversight. There is also the possibility that the omission was influenced by 1 Cor. 13:12, where the passive has no complement. The external evidence is strongly in favour of the longer text τὸν θεόν ... ὑπ' αὐτοῦ ('[anyone who loves] God [is known] by him'; $\mathfrak{P}^{15\text{vid}}$ 01² 02 03 06 etc.); compare too the parallel at Gal. 4:9. Some languages may require complements in translation anyway.[16]

8:7 συνηθείᾳ (have become so accustomed) {A}

There is good external support for συνηθείᾳ (lit. 'in custom'; 01* 02 03 025 0150 etc.). The reading of the majority of Greek manuscripts, συνειδήσει ('in conscience'; 01² 06 012 256 etc.) is an assimilation to the same word later in the verse, which then becomes the topic of the following discussion. There is nothing in the context which would have led to the introduction of συνηθείᾳ, which is a rare word in the New Testament. The full attestation in Greek continuous-text manuscripts is provided in *TuT 1 Cor* (TS22).

9:13 [τὰ] ἐκ τοῦ ἱεροῦ (from the temple)

The definite article τά ('the') is not required for the sense of this clause, but its presence makes for a parallel with the second half of the sentence. Although its attestation is ancient (01 03 06* 012 6 81 1739), it is unusual to find the shorter reading in the majority of Greek manuscripts. The variation may affect translation: the presence of the article means that the object of the verb could refer to temple sacrifices, while its absence is less specific ('from the temple'). On the basis of this, it has been suggested that τά was deliberately removed by a reader to avoid indicating food offered to idols, even though this could still underlie the interpretation.[17] More significant may be the correspondence be-

---

[16] Both Kloha 2006: 199–203 and Letteney 2016 prefer the shorter text, largely on intrinsic grounds.

[17] Kloha 2006: 252–253.

tween the shorter reading here and the prepositional phrase at the end of the following verse. Assimilation in either direction is therefore possible, as well as omission through oversight, making it hard to decide on the original reading. The SBLGNT and THGNT both prefer the inclusion of τά.

9:15 οὐδεὶς κενώσει (no-one will deprive) {B}

The structure of the editorial text involves a break in this verse after ἤ ('than'), represented by the dash, as Paul interrupts himself using a rhetorical device called aposiopesis. There is limited but weighty support for οὐδεὶς κενώσει ('no-one will deprive'; $\mathfrak{P}^{46}$ 01* 03 06* 33 etc.). The reading of the majority of manuscripts, in contrast, does not involve this figure of speech but continues the original idea in a rather clumsy way: ἵνα τις κενώσῃ ('so that someone might deprive'; 01² 04 06¹ 025 etc.). However, through itacism, κενώσῃ and κενώσει became identical in sound, resulting in variation between these two forms regardless of the construction. For instance, τίς κενώσει ('who will deprive?', or 'someone will deprive'; 012 lat^(vl-pt)) could be an omissive itacistic form of the majority reading or a separate attempt to improve οὐδεὶς κενώσει. In some witnesses, μή ('not') is added between the two words to emphasise the negative sense of the phrase: οὐθεὶς μὴ κενώσει (lit. 'no-one will not deprive'; [02] 1175). In any case, the editorial text appears to provide the best explanation of the other forms.[18] The interrupted syntax could also be avoided if a full stop is placed after ἀποθανεῖν ('die') and the next word is accented as ἦ ('truly').[19] However, this is a classical usage which is not attested elsewhere in the Pauline Epistles.

9:20 μὴ ὢν αὐτὸς ὑπὸ νόμον (though I myself am not under the law) {B}

There is strong support for the presence of μὴ ὢν αὐτὸς ὑπὸ νόμον ('though I myself am not under the law'; 01 02 03 04 06* etc.), including most early translations. However, it is missing from the majority of Greek manuscripts (06² 1881 2464 etc.: see the full

---

[18] See also Kloha 2006: 255–258.
[19] Metzger 1994: 492.

attestation in *TuT 1Cor* TS30). While the content and context makes it conceivable that this was a marginal gloss subsequently incorporated into the text, the external evidence indicates that it is more likely that it was omitted through eyeskip between the two instances of ὑπὸ νόμον ('under the law'). The same type of explanation is also seen in the next verse but without any variation or the possibility of parablepsis.

9:22 ἀσθενής (weak) {B}

The majority of manuscripts read ὡς ἀσθενής ('as one who is weak'; 01² 04 06 012 025 etc.). This matches the pattern of the three previous units, when the qualifier ὡς indicates that Paul only matches his interlocutors in appearance. It would therefore be expected in this similar construction, and its absence is the harder reading. Although the shorter form is attested in a few key early witnesses ($\mathfrak{P}^{46}$ 01* 02 03 1739 lat$^{vl\text{-}pt, vg}$), it is not impossible that the short word was overlooked, perhaps because of the similarity of the following two letters (ΩC and AC). The absence of the qualifier would be of exegetical importance, indicating that Paul did present himself as weak (cf. 1Cor. 2:3, 4:10).

9:22 πάντως τινάς (by all means ... some) {A}

There is overwhelming external support for πάντως τινάς ('by all means [saving] some'; $\mathfrak{P}^{46}$ 01 02^{vid} 03 04 etc.), which limits Paul's success. The variant readings follow the pattern of the previous verses in having the same noun in both halves of the construction: τοὺς πάντας ('all people'; 33 Clement) and πάντας ('all'; 06 012 etc.). If the latter is a deliberate editorial change, it matches other 'Western' readings which enhance the status of the Apostle. In any case, there is a theological concern here regarding the scope of salvation.

10:2 ἐβαπτίσθησαν (were baptised) {D}

The majority of Greek manuscripts have the middle voice, ἐβαπτίσαντο ('they baptised themselves'; $\mathfrak{P}^{46c}$ 03 025 0150 etc.); the first hand of Papyrus 46 also has a middle but in the imperfect tense, ἐβαπτίζοντο ('they were baptising themselves'; $\mathfrak{P}^{46*}$). There is strong attestation for the aorist passive, ἐβαπτίσθησαν ('they were baptised'; 01 02 04 06 012 etc.). This also matches the exclusive use of the passive for this verb elsewhere in the epistles (Rom. 6:3; 1 Cor 1:13, 1:15, 12:13; Gal. 3:27; the present tense at 1 Cor. 15:29 is ambivalent). However, the middle is the harder reading, with no obvious reason for its introduction in context: in addition, this is the only reference to Jewish baptism in the Pauline Epistles, and the reflexive verb corresponds to the Jewish practice of converts administering baptism to themselves.[20] These considerations justify its adoption in the SBLGNT and THGNT. In translation, there are various ways of translating the middle voice (e.g. 'they baptised for their own benefit'), but the reflexive is probably the most appropriate here if this reading is followed.

10:9 Χριστόν (Christ) {B}

There is strong external support for Χριστόν ('Christ'; $\mathfrak{P}^{46}$ 06 012 and the majority of minuscules) even though this is the harder reading, as the Old Testament narrative does not mention Christ. On the other hand, Paul's identification of the rock as Christ in 1 Cor. 10:4 makes this consistent with the context. The alternatives θεόν ('God'; 02 81) and κύριον ('the Lord'; 01 03 04 025 0150 etc.) may either represent a deliberate alteration to the original context or a misreading of the *nomen sacrum* abbreviation (XN as KN or ΘN). The full attestation in Greek continuous-text manuscripts is provided in *TuT 1 Cor* (TS32).[21]

10:20 ἃ θύουσιν, δαιμονίοις καὶ οὐ θεῷ θύουσιν (what they sacrifice, they sacrifice to demons and not to God) {C}

The majority of witnesses include the subject, τὰ ἔθνη ('the gentiles'; $\mathfrak{P}^{46\text{vid}}$ 01 02 04 025 etc.). However, this appears ungrammatical after the plural verb θύουσιν ('they sacrifice') because the neuter plural noun normally takes a singular verb: Byzantine tradition does, in fact, read ἃ θύει τὰ ἔθνη δαιμονίοις θύει καὶ οὐ θεῷ ('what the gentiles sacrifice, they sacrifice to demons and not to God'; 6 1881 and most minuscules). On the other hand, there are several invariant cases of plural verbs fol-

---

[20] Thus Metzger 1994: 493. Kloha 2006: 276–277 suggests that the passive is likely to have been introduced through the influence of other Pauline passages.
[21] A fuller discussion in favour of Χριστόν is given in Osburn 1981a; Ehrman 2011: 104–106 prefers θεόν, but Wasserman 2012: 346–348 finds no pattern of theologically motivated change here.

lowing such nouns in the Pauline Epistles, especially τὰ ἔθνη as seen here (e.g. Rom. 2:14, 15:11, 15:12, 15:27).[22] There is very limited but early attestation for ἃ θύουσιν, δαιμονίοις καὶ οὐ θεῷ θύουσιν ('what they sacrifice, to demons and not to God they sacrifice'; 03 co[sa] Marcion? Eusebius). This has been adopted as the editorial text on the grounds that it explains the other readings: the reordering of the second verb into a more natural position immediately after δαιμονίοις ('to demons'; 06 012 lat[vl-pt] Marcion? Eusebius[ms]), the addition of τὰ ἔθνη in order to specify the subject (and to ensure that this was not interpreted as 'Israel according to the flesh' in 1 Cor. 10:18), and the later adjustment of the number of the verb to match the supplied noun. Nevertheless, the few witnesses to the shorter form of text are often related to secondary readings, including small omissions, which casts some doubt on their evidence here. It is therefore possible that the original text was the well-attested ungrammatical form ἃ θύουσιν τὰ ἔθνη δαιμονίοις καὶ οὐ θεῷ θύουσιν (as preferred in the THGNT), which was later corrected either by the omission of the subject or the alteration of the verb. In translation, a subject may be required in any case.[23]

10:28 συνείδησιν (conscience) {A}

At the end of this verse, the majority of Greek manuscripts include a quotation of Psalm 24:1 [23:1 LXX], τοῦ γὰρ κυρίου ἡ γῆ καὶ τὸ πλήρωμα αὐτῆς ('for the earth and its fullness are the Lord's'; 015[c] 6 263 etc.: see the full attestation in *TuT 1 Cor* TS37). This is a repetition of what follows the same phrase in 1 Cor. 10:25. Although there is a faint possibility that it was overlooked here because the first word of the next verse is also συνείδησιν, the strong external evidence for its absence (01 02 03 04* 06 etc.) indicates that the additional text is likely to have been introduced as a parallel to 1 Cor. 10:26. Papyrus 46 lacks the last five words of the shorter text of this verse as well as the quotation.

---

[22] See further Blass, Debrunner & Funk 1961: 73–74 (§133), which notes a range of examples across the New Testament. I am grateful to Tommy Wasserman for this reference.

[23] Kloha 2006: 301–305 suggests that καὶ οὐ θεῷ is a later interpolation, deriving from Deut. 32:17, but the external support for this is very weak.

11:15 [αὐτῇ] (to her)

There are three variants here: δέδοται αὐτῇ ('it is given to her'; 01 02 03 33 81 365 2464), αὐτῇ δέδοται ('to her it is given'; 04 015 025 1175 1739 1881) and simply δέδοται ('it is given'; 𝔓⁴⁶ 06 012 and the majority of minuscules). The varying position of the pronoun is typical of a later addition, and it is notable that the majority of manuscripts unusually have the shorter reading. Despite this, because an editor could have decided to delete the pronoun either to avoid repetition from the first part of the verse or to make the phrase more general in application (in keeping with similar 'Western' improvements, such as those in 1 Cor. 11:19–20), the pronoun has been included in brackets because of its strong external support.

11:19 [καί] (lit. also)

The majority of Greek manuscripts, including some early witnesses, do not have this word (01 02 04 06¹ 012 025 etc.), but there is good support for καί ('also'; 𝔓⁴⁶ 03 06* 6 33 1175 1739 1881 lat^vg co^(sa, bo-pt)). The presence of καί after ἵνα is relatively common in the Pauline Epistles (cf. 1 Cor. 4:8, 7:29, 14:19, 16:16) and it is not clear whether this is an early instance of assimilation to these other uses, or an original word which was overlooked.[24]

11:24 εἶπεν (said) {A}

After this verb, the majority of Greek manuscripts include λάβετε φάγετε ('take, eat'; 04³ 025 0150 etc.). This is a harmonisation to Matthew 26:26 or a liturgical form of the Eucharistic words of institution (see too the next unit). The external evidence for the absence of these words is very strong (𝔓⁴⁶ 01 02 03 04* 06 etc.), and there is nothing in context that would prompt their omission. The full attestation in Greek continuous-text manuscripts is provided in *TuT 1 Cor* (TS38) and this and the following unit are included in *ECM Parallel Pericopes*.[25]

---

[24] Kloha 2006: 335 suggests that καί here is an addition.
[25] An overview of the possible influence of liturgical texts is given in Kloha 2006: 339–347.

11:24 ὑμῶν (you) {A}

The phrase τὸ ὑπὲρ ὑμῶν ('that is for you'; 𝔓⁴⁶ 01* 02 03 04* etc.) may have been felt to be too telegraphic: at Luke 22:19, it is accompanied by the participle διδόμενον ('which is given for you', attested here in Latin, Coptic and Ethiopic). Here, however, the majority of Greek witnesses include the participle κλώμενον ('[which is] broken [for you]'; 01² 04³ 06¹ 012 025 etc.). This either derives from the previous verb ἔκλασεν ('he broke') or liturgical tradition (compare the previous unit and 1 Cor. 10:16). One manuscript has a synonym for this which is not found elsewhere in the Greek Bible: θρυπτόμενον ('[which is] broken in pieces [for you]'; 06*): for a similar variant in this manuscript, see 1 Cor. 15:51. The strong external evidence favours the shorter reading, which also explains the alternative forms.

11:29 πίνων (drink¹) {A}

After this word, the majority of Greek manuscripts have the adverb ἀναξίως ('unworthily'; 01² 04³ 06 012 025 etc.: see the full attestation in *TuT 1 Cor* TS39). This is a repetition from two verses earlier, apparently inserted to clarify that not all who consume will be subject to judgment (κρίμα) despite the concession about 'discerning the body' at the end of the sentence. There is good early support for the shorter reading (𝔓⁴⁶ 01* 02 03 04* 33 1739 lat^{vl-pt} co) and no obvious reason for its omission.

11:29 σῶμα (body) {A}

Again, the majority of Greek manuscripts have a longer form, reading σῶμα τοῦ κυρίου ('the body of the Lord'; 01² 04³ 06 012 etc.). This appears to be an assimilation to 1 Cor. 11:27, because there is no reason for its absence if it is original. The reading σῶμα ('the body'; 𝔓⁴⁶ 01* 02 03 04* 6 33 1739 1881* lat^{vl-pt, vg} co) is supported by the same witnesses as the editorial text of the previous unit, but it is ambiguous and therefore harder: the reference could be to 'the body of the Lord' or to the Church as 'the body' which shares in the communion.

11:32 [τοῦ] κυρίου (the Lord)

The definite article τοῦ ('the') is absent from the majority of manuscripts (𝔓⁴⁶ 02 06 012 025 etc.), but present in some important witnesses (01 03 04 33 1175). Although the inclusion of the article might be the expected Greek construction, the two parallels for this phrase in the Pauline Epistles both lack it (1 Cor. 7:25, 2 Thess. 2:13), suggesting that the shorter reading is original.[26] In either case, translation is unaffected.

12:10   ἄλλῳ [δέ] … ἄλλῳ [δέ] (to another² … to another³)

Manuscripts are agreed on the reading ἄλλῳ δέ in the first and fifth items in the list in this verse, but the conjunction δέ is missing from some important witnesses on the second and third occasions ($\mathfrak{P}^{46}$ 03 06 012 0201 6 1739 [1881] lat). If it were originally absent, it would have been a straightforward addition to harmonise to the other elements in the list: it is worth noting that most manuscripts which include it after the second and third instances of ἄλλῳ ('to another') also include it after the fourth item, ἑτέρῳ ('to someone else'). On the other hand, an early editor may have deleted the repeated conjunction in order to improve the style, the sort of adjustment which is seen in 'Western' readings elsewhere which lack δέ or replace it with another conjunction (cf. Rom. 4:15, 1 Cor. 2:10, Eph. 4:32). It seems that the slightly stronger external support for the lack of the fourth conjunction led to its exclusion from the editorial text, but the evidence was considered more evenly weighted on the second and third occasions. Despite the preference for conjunctions in Greek, there is no need for them to be included in translation (especially in such lists).

12:26   [ἕν] (one²)

The majority of witnesses have ἕν ('one') before both instances of μέλος ('member'). Nonetheless, it is missing on the second occasion from five important Greek manuscripts ($\mathfrak{P}^{46}$ 01* 02 03 1739), casting some doubt on whether it was originally present. If the number 'one' is not included in translation, an indefinite article will need to be supplied with broadly the same result.

13:3   καυχήσωμαι (I may boast) {D}

The reading traditionally identified as the Byzantine text is καυθήσωμαι ('I may be burnt'; 256 365 1573 1739ᶜ etc.) even though this is a non-

---

[26] See also the tables at Kloha 2006: 319–320.

standard grammatical form, namely a future subjunctive.[27] In fact, slightly more manuscripts read the future indicative καυθήσομαι ('I shall be burnt'; 04 06 012 6 81 etc.): according to *TuT 1Cor* (TS44), 274 manuscripts have καυθήσωμαι and 300 καυθήσομαι. The first-person singular aorist subjunctives καύσωμαι (middle) and καυθῶ (passive) are not found in the textual tradition. A few witnesses have the third-person aorist passive subjunctive καυθῇ ('it may be burnt'; 2127 [sy] [lat^(vg-mss)] Chrysostom^(pt)), taking τὸ σῶμα ('the body') as the subject, but this is a later alteration. There is early support for καυχήσωμαι ('I may boast'; 𝔓⁴⁶ 01 02 03 0150 etc.), along with a few instances of the future καυχήσομαι ('I will boast'; 048 1175*), yet Latin writers of the second and third century (Tertullian and Cyprian) knew the verse with the verb 'burn'. External evidence thus seems insufficient to determine the earliest form. In contrast to the frequency of the verb καυχάομαι ('I boast') in the Pauline Epistles, καίω ('I burn') only appears on one or two occasions (Rom. 1:27; cf. Heb. 12:18). This indicates that the direction of change to assimilate to Pauline usage would be towards καυχάομαι, yet after the verb παραδῶ ('hand over') the verb καίω might have been expected (compare 1Cor. 5:5). Two interpretative objections have been raised against καίω: first, if Paul's body were burnt, he would no longer exist to have love, as in the next phrase; second, the burning of Christians was a later development which did not take place at the time of Paul (but may have influenced later readers). On the other hand, the meaning of the phrase παραδῶ τὸ σῶμά μου ('hand over my body') is not entirely clear, especially in conjunction with 'boasting', and there were precedents in Hebrew Scripture for death by burning (e.g. Dan. 3:15). What is more, although classical Greek expects a subjunctive after ἵνα ('so that'), in the New Testament a future indicative is also acceptable (e.g. 1Cor. 9:15 [var.], 9:18; Gal. 2:4; Phil. 2:11 [var.]). In the light of these considerations, it is very difficult to determine the initial reading. Nevertheless, a preference has recently been expressed for καυθήσομαι, adopted in both the SBLGNT and THGNT.[28] The mechanics of the change may also favour this choice: the alteration

---

[27] On its 'impossibility' in Koine Greek, see Blass, Debrunner & Funk 1961: 15 (§28).

[28] It is also advocated in Elliott 1971 and Kloha 2006: 428–444; the latter rebuts the detailed arguments in favour of καυχήσωμαι in Petzer 1989. Further studies of this variation unit include Perera 2005 and Malone 2009.

from καυχήσωμαι to the grammatical form καυθήσομαι would require the change of two letters, but if the non-standard καυθήσωμαι was already in circulation due to the loss of vowel length (leading to the interchange of o/ω), then only one letter would be affected (θ to χ).

13:4 [ἡ ἀγάπη] (love³)

The first occurrence of ἡ ἀγάπη ('love') in this verse comes before two verbs in asyndeton. This is followed by another instance before a sequence of one or eight verbs in asyndeton, depending on whether or not the noun appears a third time. This further repetition is present in the majority of Greek manuscripts ($\mathfrak{P}^{46}$ 01 02 04 06 012 etc.) but absent from enough important witnesses (03 33 1175 2424 lat co^{sa}) to cast doubt on whether it is original. While there is no obvious reason to have added ἡ ἀγάπη yet again, the deletion of the third occurrence to make for an uninterrupted list of eight negative verbs is an obvious stylistic improvement; early translators may have done this independently. The full attestation in Greek continuous-text manuscripts is provided in *TuT 1 Cor* (TS45).

14:6 [ἐν] διδαχῇ ([in] teaching)

This is the fourth alternative in the list, and the three previous ones are all preceded by ἐν ('in'). The omission of the preposition is therefore the harder reading ($\mathfrak{P}^{46}$ 01* 06* 012 0243 1739 1881), but it may simply represent an early oversight. The meaning is unaffected, because the dative case of the noun can be taken with the previous preposition.

14:14 [γάρ] (for)

The conjunction γάρ ('for') is missing from some important witnesses ($\mathfrak{P}^{46}$ 03 012 0243 0289^{vid} 1739 1881) but is present in the majority of Greek manuscripts. The preceding instances of ἐάν ('if') have connectives (1 Cor. 14:8, 14:11), which might have led to its insertion. On the other hand, there are several other examples of ἐὰν γάρ in this epistle (1 Cor. 8:10, 9:16; cf. 4:15) and the conjunction could have been overlooked or deleted by an editor who felt that this sentence offers a new example which is not connected with the previous verse.[29]

---

[29] See also Zuntz 1953: 194.

14:16 [ἐν] πνεύματι ([in] the spirit)

There is relatively slim support for ἐν πνεύματι ('in Spirit'; 01² 03 06^supp 025 81 365 1175). The majority of Greek manuscripts read τῷ πνεύματι ('with the Spirit'; 018 020 044 1739 etc.), matching the previous verse. Given the difference from the previous verse and the fact that some important manuscripts simply read πνεύματι ('with [the] Spirit'; 𝔓⁴⁶ 01* 02 012 0243 33 etc.), there is some doubt as to whether ἐν was originally present. The alternatives are broadly equivalent in translation.

14:34 γυναῖκες (women) {B}

On the displacement of 1 Cor. 14:34–35 in some witnesses, see the entry on 1 Cor. 14:40 below. After γυναῖκες, the majority of Greek manuscripts include ὑμῶν ('your'; 06 012 lat^vl-pt, vg-ms). This may have been introduced in order to restrict the prohibition from 'women' in general to 'wives', in keeping with an interpretation of τοὺς ἰδίους ἄνδρας as 'their husbands' in the following verse. On the other hand, the pronoun could have been removed in order to produce a more general command, corresponding better to the church-wide context indicated by the previous phrase. The strong external evidence in favour of γυναῖκες alone (𝔓¹²³ 01 02 03 0243 etc.) leads to its adoption. It would still be possible to translate this as 'wives' without the qualifying pronoun (cf. Eph. 5:22–24, Col. 3:18).

14:38 ἀγνοεῖται (is not [to be] recognised) {B}

The majority of Greek manuscripts have the third-person imperative ἀγνοείτω ('may he not recognise' or 'let him be ignorant'; 𝔓⁴⁶ 01² 02ᶜ 03 06¹ etc.). This matches the structure of 1 Cor. 14:35 and 37. In contrast, the present-tense ἀγνοεῖται ('is not recognised'; 01* 02*vid 06* [012] 048 etc.) is the harder reading, as suggested by the direction of the corrections in the earliest majuscules. It is not impossible that this arose from a misreading of the final Ω as AI, but it is more likely that the pattern of the previous verses was extended to this one. The verb ἀγνοεῖται could be understood as a divine passive, with God as the implied agent (cf. James 1:12), or interpreted as the response of Paul or of the Church in general.

14:39 [μου] (my)

The use of the pronoun in ἀδελφοί μου ('my brothers'; 01 02 03* 06¹ 048 1175 2464) is frequent in the Epistles, especially after ὥστε (e.g. Rom. 7:4; 1Cor. 11:33, 15:58; Phil. 4:1). It is missing from the majority of manuscripts (𝔓⁴⁶ 03² 06* 012 etc.), perhaps through an oversight or through harmonisation to the previous instances of ἀδελφοί at 14:20 and 14:26. A shorter reading in Byzantine tradition, however, is often significant and assimilation of this to common usage is likely. In translation it may be idiomatic to include the pronoun whichever reading is followed.[30]

14:40 *include verses 34–35 here* {A}

A few witnesses have 1Cor. 14:34–35 after 14:40 (06 010 012 88* 915 lat^(vl, vg-ms); see further *TuT 1Cor* TS50). Although the displacement of text can indicate that it was a later gloss which was incorporated at different places, this does not appear to be the case here given the close relationship of the bilingual majuscule manuscripts and the observation that their text has elsewhere often been subject to deliberate alteration (e.g. Rom. 8:23 and 16:20, 1Cor. 9:22). It seems that the editor responsible for this change understood the final part of 1Cor. 14:33 as the conclusion to the previous section, from which 14:36 followed as a logical alternative. The intervening two verses were then relocated after 14:40, as an illustration of its injunction to act 'decently and in order'. Further support for this may have been provided by the preference for a clause introduced by ὡς ('as') to come after the main observation (as seen with καθώς in 14:34). Nevertheless, the use of ὡς at the beginning of a sentence is not unparalleled in the Pauline Epistles (e.g. 1Cor. 4:18, 10:15; Gal. 1:9, 6:10; Col. 2:6), and the latter part of 14:33 does not make particularly good sense when applied to the preceding description of God. The very strong external support for 14:34–35 following 14:33, plus the fact that no witnesses survive which lack these two verses, indicates that the differing order in the variant reading is a secondary attempt to improve both the abrupt shift from 14:35 to 14:36 and the way in which these two verses about women seem to interrupt the instructions about prophecy. It has also been suggested that these verses

---

[30] In favour of the longer reading, see Aasgard 2004: 315–317.

are a quotation from the letter of the Corinthians (which Paul then rejects in 14:37), but this is not widely accepted.[31]

15:10 [ἡ] (that is)

The definite article ἡ ('that is') is attested in the majority of Greek manuscripts but absent from some important witnesses (01* 03 06* 012 0243 0270* 6 1739). It is not required in context, and translation is unaffected: although this single letter may have been overlooked, it is also possible that it was added on the basis of the same construction in the first half of this verse.

15:14 ἄρα [καί] (then [both])

The external evidence is split between the absence of this instance of καί from the majority of Greek manuscripts ($\mathfrak{P}^{46}$ 01² 03 0243 etc.) and its presence in some important witnesses (01* 02 06 012 025 33 81). It could be that it was deleted by an editor to improve the style: as the adjective (κενή, 'in vain') is repeated in the following clause, the use of καί ... καί ('both ... and') is redundant. Alternatively, assimilation to ἄρα καί in 1 Cor. 15:18 is possible.

15:28 [καί] (also)

On this occasion, καί is present in the majority of witnesses (01 02 06² 025 etc.) and absent from a smaller group (03 06* 012 0243 33 1175 1739). It is likely that the latter represents an editorial deletion or oversight: a similar construction is seen at Col. 3:4, although that is unlikely to have influenced the wording of this verse.

15:28 [τὰ] πάντα (all)

The definite article τά ('the') is not required by the context, and is missing from some manuscripts (02 03 06* 0243 6 33 81 1739) but present in the majority. It may well have been added through assimilation to the two

---

[31] Thus Flanagan and Snyder 1981. Among the extensive literature on this variation unit, see Kloha 2006: 497–556 and Fellows 2024 as well as Ellis 1981, Allison 1988, Delobel 1994: 110–111 and Niccum 1997: the last of these shows that the marks in the margins of Codex Vaticanus (termed 'distigmai') which have been claimed to indicate early textual variants were added after the fourteenth century, a conclusion reinforced by recent analysis of the ink.

previous instances of τὰ πάντα in the present verse; compare too the same phrase in 1 Cor. 12:6 or Eph. 1:23. Still, it may have been overlooked and there is a parallel for its absence in a similar context at 1 Cor. 9:22.

15:31 [ἀδελφοί] (brothers and sisters) {C}

External evidence is split between witnesses which include ἀδελφοί (lit. 'brothers'; 01 02 03 025 0150 etc.) and those which lack it (𝔓⁴⁶ 06 012 0243 and the majority of minuscules). Even though this vocative was often added for liturgical lections, this is not an obvious place for it and its attestation is early. In contrast, its deletion would have improved the structure of the sentence by bringing the noun καύχησιν ('a boast') next to the relative pronoun ἥν ('that'). The tendency towards the omission of words in Papyrus 46 (cf. this word at Rom. 15:30, 2 Cor. 1:8) and the support for ἀδελφοί in early translations also favour its inclusion here.[32] The full attestation in Greek continuous-text manuscripts is provided in *TuT 1 Cor* (TS55).

15:49 φορέσομεν (we will bear) {B}

As noted, for example, at Romans 5:1, the sound change known as vowel isochrony led to the loss of a distinction between long and short vowels. The majority of Greek manuscripts have the aorist subjunctive φορέσωμεν ('let us bear'; 𝔓⁴⁶ 01 04 06 012 etc.). The future indicative φορέσομεν ('we shall bear'; 03 016 0150 6 1881 co^sa eth Cyril^pt) is much less well attested, although it is also found in the *Textus Receptus*. The liturgical reading of the Pauline Epistles may have prompted a tendency towards the subjunctive for exhortation. In context, however, this verb is descriptive as is shown by the use of the future tense in the following verses, so the indicative has been adopted as the editorial text.

15:51 οὐ κοιμηθησόμεθα, πάντες δὲ ἀλλαγησόμεθα (we will not all die, but we will all be changed) {B}

The variant readings in this unit convey the opposite sense to the editorial text, which is transmitted by the majority of Greek manuscripts (03 06² 025 048 0150 etc.: see the full attestation in *TuT 1 Cor* TS57). A change of word order is seen in κοιμηθησόμεθα, οὐ πάντες δὲ

---

[32] See too Aasgard 2004: 313–315; Kloha 2006: 316–317 considers it a later addition.

ἀλλαγησόμεθα (lit. 'we will fall asleep, but we will not all be changed'; 01 [02*] 04 0243* 33 etc.), while a conflated form of the two is οὐ κοιμηθησόμεθα, οὐ πάντες δὲ ἀλλαγησόμεθα ('we will not fall asleep, but we will not all be changed'; 𝔓46 02c). It is not clear whether the first or second variant is supported by Codex Boernerianus, which begins the sentence with πάντες μὲν οὖν κοιμηθησόμεθα ('And so while all of us will fall asleep'; 012): οὖν could be an error for οὐ or an independent expansion following μέν. Codex Claromontanus has ἀναστησόμεθα, οὐ πάντες δὲ ἀλλαγησόμεθα ('we will rise again, but we will not all be changed'; 06* lat^vl-pt, vg Marcion Tertullian), which has very early indirect support. Another single bilingual witness (not reported in UBS6) reads ἐνεργησώμεθα, πάντες δὲ ἀλλαγησόμεθα ('we will be made active, but we will be changed'; 628*). Although it has been claimed that the introduction of ἀναστησόμεθα was theologically motivated,[33] it is more likely that this is an anticipation of the same verb which occurs in the following verse in Codex Claromontanus and the Latin translation: a comparable example of a translational variant also attested in Greek by the first hand of this manuscript is seen at 1 Cor. 11:24. Most of the variants have ancient attestation, demonstrating early editorial intervention, yet only appear in a limited range of witnesses. The reading adopted as the editorial text has good support and explains the alternatives as adjustments made after Paul and his original addresses had died, in case their death was considered to invalidate his claim here.[34]

15:55   νῖκος; ποῦ σου, θάνατε, τὸ κέντρον; (victory? Where,
         O death, is your sting?) {B}

The variant readings reflect differences in the tradition of Hosea 13:14, with regard to the sequence of the nouns. The 'Western' reading has κέντρον; ποῦ σου, θάνατε, τὸ νῖκος; ('sting? Where, death, is your victory?'; 06* 012 lat^vl-pt etc.). The majority of Greek manuscripts also have this order, but with a change of addressee inspired by the text of the Septuagint: κέντρον; ποῦ σου, ᾅδη, τὸ νῖκος; ('sting? Where, Hades, is your victory?'; 01² 02c 025 6 etc.). The latter is also seen in νῖκος; ποῦ

---

[33] Metzger 1994: 502.

[34] This unit is considered in detail by Kloha 2006: 588–593, who prefers the reading of Papyrus 46: his argument against conflation, however, overlooks the correction in Codex Alexandrinus.

σου, ᾅδη, τὸ κέντρον; ('victory? Where, Hades, is your sting?'; 0121 0150 0243 33 etc.). Although ᾅδης ('Hades') appears in Luke, Acts and Revelation, it is not found elsewhere in the Pauline Epistles. There is early direct and indirect evidence in support of νῖκος; ποῦ σου, θάνατε, τὸ κέντρον; ('victory? Where, death, is your sting?'; 𝔓⁴⁶ 01* 03 04 088 etc.), which also provides an explanation for the subsequent developments. The full attestation in Greek continuous-text manuscripts is provided in *TuT 1 Cor* (TS58): through itacism, some manuscripts read νεῖκος (which means 'strife' or 'contention') in place of νῖκος ('victory').

16:19   Πρίσκα (Prisca) {A}

The majority of Greek manuscripts have the form Πρίσκιλλα ('Priscilla'; 04 06 012 81 365 etc.). This matches the three references to Priscilla and Aquila in Acts 18, but the Pauline Epistles appear to refer to a different couple, Prisca and Aquila (cf. Rom. 16:3, 2 Tim. 4:19).[35] A range of early and important witnesses support Πρίσκα here ('Prisca'; [𝔓⁴⁶] 01 03 025 0121 etc.), which is the harder reading given the presence of Priscilla in Acts.

16:24   Ἰησοῦ (Jesus) {B}

As at the end of most of the other Pauline Epistles, the majority of manuscripts include a final Amen (01 02 04 06 025 etc.), reflecting both the concluding benediction and the liturgical context in which they were read. Amen is lacking from a number of early witnesses (03 0121 0243 etc. and several translations), but there is no obvious reason for its omission if it were originally present. Codex Boernerianus should probably also be cited in favour of this shorter reading: the first hand wrote γενεθητω γενεθητω on a separate line before the colophon, yet while γενηθήτω ('let it come to pass'; 012) could be interpreted as a translation of the Hebrew Amen, the end of the biblical text is marked by punctuation and several *diplai* where there would have been space to include Amen if it were part of this epistle.[36]

---

[35] Fellows 2024: 20–34 suggests that the same couple is mentioned throughout and that the original sequence of the names in the present verse was Prisca and Aquila, as seen in GA 945 and most of the other references.

[36] On the double use of γένοιτο to indicate Amen at the end of a book, see Jerome's preface to his translation of the Hebrew Psalter.

The Second Letter to the Corinthians

1:10 τηλικούτου θανάτου (so deadly a peril) {B}

A few witnesses read the plural, τηλικούτων θανάτων ('such deadly perils', or literally 'such great deaths'; 𝔓⁴⁶ 1739^(v.r.) lat^(vl-pt, vg?) sy etc.). This might be under the influence of the plural 'sufferings' in 2 Cor. 1:6 or the two following verbs (see the next variation unit). However, an argument has been made for the plural as original: the hyperbole of risking more than one death could have been removed by an early editor and θανάτοι ('deaths') features in the list of tribulations at 2 Cor. 11:23. It is also possible that this phrase was assimilated to the singular θανάτου in the previous verse.[1] Nevertheless, in the context of the single event to which Paul refers in 2 Cor. 1:8–9 and the very strong external evidence for τηλικούτου θανάτου ('so great a death'; 01 02 03 04 06 etc.), the singular has been preferred. In translation, the word θάνατος here may be expanded as 'danger of death' (compare the Latin *periculis*).

1:10 καὶ ῥύσεται (and will continue to rescue) {B}

The majority of Greek manuscripts have the present tense, καὶ ῥύεται ('and is rescuing'; 06² 012 0121 0243 etc.). This gives the verse the expected sequence of past, present and future instances of ῥύεσθαι, yet it is likely to be an editorial correction based on the good external support for the future-tense καὶ ῥύσεται ('and will rescue'; 𝔓⁴⁶ 01 03 04 025 etc.). A few witnesses omit this phrase entirely (02 06* lat^(vl-pt) etc.), probably because it appeared to be redundant in context: this could offer further support for the future here, given that it also appears at the end of the verse.

1:10 [ὅτι] καὶ ἔτι (that ... again) {C}

There is good attestation for all three words, ὅτι καὶ ἔτι (lit. 'that also still'; 01 02 04 06² 025 and the majority of minuscules). In other manuscripts, only two appear: καὶ ἔτι ('and still'; 𝔓⁴⁶ 03 06* 0121 0243 1739 1881), καὶ ὅτι ('and that'; 012 lat^(vl-pt) [eth]) and ὅτι καί ('that also'; 06¹ 6

---

[1] Zuntz 1953: 104.

etc.). These alternatives can each be explained as the accidental omission of one of the three words (with reordering in one case). However, if καὶ ἔτι by itself were original, the apparent break in syntax may have led to the addition of ὅτι after the verb as a smoother reading. The external evidence confirms that this is a possibility.

1:12 ἁπλότητι (lit. simplicity) {B}

Numerous early witnesses support ἁγιότητι ('holiness'; 𝔓⁴⁶ 01* 02 03 04 etc.), while the majority of minuscules have ἁπλότητι ('simplicity'; 01² 06 012 etc.; see the full attestation in *TuT 2Cor* TS3) . The two words look very similar in majuscule script (ΑΠΛΟΤΗΤΙ and ΑΓΙΟΤΗΤΙ). Although there might have been an expectation for the phrase 'in holiness', the word ἁγιότης does not appear elsewhere in the Pauline Epistles. The construction indicates that the word should be synonymous with εἰλικρίνεια ('sincerity'; cf. 1 Cor. 5:8, Phil. 1:10), which favours ἁπλότητι. Still, it remains possible that this is an assimilation to the other uses of ἁπλότης in this epistle (2 Cor. 8:2, 9:11, 9:13, 11:3). See also the comment on 2 Cor. 11:3 below.

1:12 [καὶ] οὐκ ([and] not)

The majority of Greek manuscripts do not include the conjunction, but there remains extensive attestation of καί ('and'; 𝔓⁴⁶ 03 0121 0243 6 33 1175 1739 1881 2464 and some early translations). Internal evidence is also ambivalent: καί could have been added to connect this phrase with the previous elements to make a list, or deleted in order to improve the structure of the sentence. It may be advisable in translation to break this long sentence into smaller units.

1:14 τοῦ κυρίου [ἡμῶν] ([our] Lord) {C}

It might be expected that the pronoun ἡμῶν ('our'; 01 03 012 025 0121 etc.) would be a later addition into this common formula, yet the majority of Greek manuscripts unusually have the shorter reading (𝔓⁴⁶ᵛⁱᵈ 02 04 06 etc.; for parallels involving 'the day of the Lord', see 1 Cor. 1:8, 5:5; 2 Thess. 2:2). It is possible that ἡμῶν, an inclusive first-person plural in this context, was deleted by an editor to avoid inconsistency with the exclusive use of ἡμῶν earlier in the verse. On the other hand, there are several instances in the Pauline Epistles of the phrase τοῦ κυρίου Ἰησοῦ ('the

Lord Jesus') without a pronoun (e.g. 1 Cor. 16:23, 2 Cor. 11:31, Col. 3:17, 1 Thess. 4:2, 2 Thess. 1:7). Such conflicting considerations make a decision difficult, and in some languages a pronoun will be required anyway.

2:1 γάρ (so) {C}

The choice of connective determines how this decision is to be related to what has gone before. The majority of Greek manuscripts have δέ ('but'; 01 02 04 06[1] etc.), although in the Pauline Epistles this does not always convey a strong contrast (cf. the comments above on Rom. 6:8, 1 Cor. 7:7). A few important witnesses have γάρ (lit. 'for'; 𝔓⁴⁶ 03 0223 0243 etc.), which fits the context well as an explanation of why Paul chose not to come to Corinth. However, in some manuscripts the first four verses of this chapter all have γάρ in second position: the present connective could have been changed to δέ to avoid this, or through assimilation to δέ at the beginning of the section two verses earlier. The first hand of Codex Claromontanus, τε (06*), is simply an erroneous change of the preceding verb to a second-person plural (ἐκρίνατε, 'you decided') on the model of the previous word (ἑστήκατε), possibly as a misreading of δέ.

2:17 πολλοί (so many) {B}

Instead of Paul contrasting himself to 'the many' (πολλοί, 01 02 03 04 025 etc.), an alternative reads λοιποί ('the rest'; 𝔓⁴⁶ 06 012 020 etc.). The Byzantine tradition is split: *TuT 2Cor* (TS8) records 280 manuscripts with οἱ πολλοί and 315 with οἱ λοιποί, as well as two which conflate both terms. The similarity of the words in majuscule script (ΠΟΛΛΟΙ and ΛΟΙΠΟΙ) may have contributed to their interchange: λοιποί is perhaps the more expected term in a comparison (cf. 1 Cor. 9:5; Eph. 2:3 and the variant at Eph. 4:17; 1 Thess. 4:13, 5:6), which would explain its introduction here. The result, however, is a harsher saying with the implication that all other evangelists are blameworthy. The early attestation of λοιποί, largely restricted to 'Western' witnesses, also supports the adoption of πολλοί in the editorial text.

3:2 ταῖς καρδίαις ἡμῶν (our hearts) {A}

The sound change in Greek of itacism meant that η and υ were pronounced identically, leading to confusion between words such as ἡμῶν ('ours') and ὑμῶν ('yours'). Both first-person and second-person plural pronouns appear earlier in the verse, and either would make sense here: the Corinthians could be Paul's letter written on 'our hearts' or 'your hearts'.[2] However, there are few manuscripts in support of ταῖς καρδίαις ὑμῶν ('your hearts'; 01 33 1175 1881) and, in the light of Paul's reference to their being in 'our hearts' at 2 Cor. 7:3, the first-person plural attested by the majority of manuscripts has been adopted as the editorial text. The same variation appears at 2 Cor. 6:11; see also 2 Cor. 6:16 below.

4:5   διὰ Ἰησοῦν (for Jesus' sake) {B}

The theological interest of this variant is in the case taken by the preposition: are Paul and his companions slaves 'because of Jesus' (διά + accusative), or 'through Jesus' (διά + genitive)? The former appears to be the harder reading but is attested in the majority of Greek manuscripts, which have διὰ Ἰησοῦν (lit. 'because of Jesus'; 02*vid 03 06 012 015 etc.). There is also early support for διὰ Ἰησοῦ ('through Jesus'; 𝔓46 01* 02c 04 0243 etc.). The genitive could have been altered to the accusative under the influence of the accusative Ἰησοῦν earlier in the verse or in the same phrase at 2 Cor. 4:11, but consistency with the latter could also be taken to support the originality of the accusative here. The attestation of 'Christ' is too slim for it to merit consideration as the earliest text: διὰ Χριστοῦ ('through Christ'; 01¹ 2464) may represent the misreading of a *nomen sacrum* (ΧΥ for ΙΥ) or repetition of Χριστοῦ from the previous verse, while διὰ Ἰησοῦ Χριστοῦ ('through Jesus Christ'; latvl-pt cobo-ms Cyrilpt) is expansion prompted by the first half of the verse.

4:6   [Ἰησοῦ] Χριστοῦ (of [Jesus] Christ)

The majority of Greek manuscripts read the full form, Ἰησοῦ Χριστοῦ ('of Jesus Christ'; 𝔓46 01 04 015 025 etc.). The word order Χριστοῦ Ἰησοῦ ('of Christ Jesus'; 06 012 0243 1739* 1881 lat) seems to be an assimilation to Pauline usage elsewhere: it is worth noting that some of these manuscripts also have 'Christ Jesus' in the previous verse (0243 1739 1881), yet the only secure instance of this sequence in this epistle is at 2 Cor. 1:1. Even though a shorter reading is often compelling, there

---

[2] Larsen 2000: 346–347 argues that the context strongly supports the second person here.

is limited attestation for just Χριστοῦ ('of Christ'; 02 03 33 Tertullian), which could be explained as the oversight of one of the *nomina sacra* or an assimilation to the same phrase at 2 Cor. 2:10.

5:3   ἐκδυσάμενοι (lit. when we have taken it off) {C}

There is very strong external support for ἐνδυσάμενοι ('when we have put it on'; 𝔓⁴⁶ 01 03 04 06² and the majority of minuscules). In contrast, there is limited but early attestation of ἐκδυσάμενοι ('when we have taken it off'; 06*, c lat^(vl-pt) Marcion^(acc. to Tertullian) Tertullian), along with one manuscript in which this verb is misread as ἐκλυσάμενοι ('when we have loosened it'; 012). However, the claim that 'if when we have taken it off we will not be found naked' seems to be more logical (and hence potentially an editorial adjustment typical of 'Western' readings) than the apparent tautology of 'if when we have put it on we will not be found naked'. It may also be relevant that all the witnesses to ἐκδυσάμενοι read εἴπερ ('even if') rather than εἴ γε ('if indeed') at the beginning of the clause. The reference in the following verse to being 'further clothed' also suggests that the observation with ἐνδυσάμενοι is not as banal as it may initially appear, and it has accordingly been adopted in the SBLGNT and the THGNT.[3]

5:17   καινά (new) {A}

The shorter reading adopted in the editorial text, καινά ('new'; 𝔓⁴⁶ 01 03 04 06* etc.), has strong external support. Byzantine tradition is split between two forms, which is often indicative of a later alteration: καινὰ τὰ πάντα ('new all things'; 06² 025 0150 etc.) and τὰ πάντα καινά ('all things new'; 6 33 81 256 365 etc.: see the full attestation in *TuT 2 Cor* TS12). The addition of a subject serves as a clarification but is not required, as the verb γέγονεν ('has become') can be taken with the previous τὰ ἀρχαῖα ('the old'). Although the following τὰ δὲ πάντα might have prompted the omission of τὰ πάντα in this clause by eyeskip, the external evidence and alternative longer reading favour the shortest form as original. If τὰ πάντα is included, it could be taken as adverbial ('in all respects').

---

[3] The same conclusion is reached in the detailed study of Thrall 1981 and at Larsen 2000: 347.

6:16 ἡμεῖς γὰρ ναὸς θεοῦ ἐσμεν (for we are the temple of God) {B}

The sound change of itacism described above at 2 Cor. 3:2 has affected the pronoun here, with a corresponding adjustment of the verb. The majority of Greek manuscripts read ὑμεῖς γὰρ ναὸς θεοῦ ἐστε ('for you are the temple of God'; 𝔓⁴⁶ [01²] 04 06² etc.). This matches the references to the second-person plural in the previous verses, as well as the parallel at 1 Cor 3:16. Accordingly, the first-person plural is the harder reading and has been adopted on the basis of its good external support: ἡμεῖς γὰρ ναὸς θεοῦ ἐσμεν ('for we are the temple of God'; 03 06* 020 025 etc., lat^(vl-pt) cpa co eth Origen^(gr)). Further support for this reading is seen in the manuscripts which read ἡμεῖς γὰρ ναοὶ θεοῦ ἐσμεν ('for we are temples of God'; 01* 0243 1739 Clement), where the noun 'temple' has been changed to match the plural verb against Pauline usage (cf. 1 Cor. 3:16–17). An inclusive first-person plural should be used when possible in translation: the presence of the pronoun in Greek is emphatic.

7:8 βλέπω [γάρ] (for I see) {C}

If the verb alone is present, reading just βλέπω ('I see'; 𝔓⁴⁶ᶜ 𝔓¹¹⁷ 03 06* lat^(vl-pt) co^(sa)), this phrase could form the apodosis of the conditional clause with a new sentence starting at the following verse. This is a hard reading, as there is nothing to indicate that this phrase is the complement of εἰ καὶ μετεμελόμην ('even if I did regret it'). The other alternatives more clearly treat this as an aside, before beginning the apodosis with νῦν χαίρω ('now I rejoice'). The participle βλέπων ('seeing'; 𝔓⁴⁶* lat^(vg)), which makes this a subordinate clause explaining the preceding condition, is attractive but poorly attested. Another explanatory alternative, βλέπω γάρ ('for I see'; 01 04 06¹ 012 etc.) is found in the majority of manuscripts and fits the wider context well. It is difficult to decide whether this alternative is a later smoothing of the shorter form or whether the connective was omitted through oversight (or perhaps at some point after the insertion of δέ into the previous clause, as seen in 𝔓¹¹⁷ 03). It is also possible to interpret εἰ καὶ μετεμελόμην as part of the preceding sentence, and to begin a new sentence here.[4] Even though the SBLGNT adopts βλέπω alone, it puts the whole phrase in parentheses

---

[4] See Omanson 2006: 364.

to continue to mark it as an interruption within the conditional clause; the THGNT prefers the majority reading.

8:7 ἡμῶν ἐν ὑμῖν (our ... for you) {C}

Itacism leads to every possible combination of pronouns in the textual tradition (cf. 2 Cor. 3:2 and 6:16 above). The most widespread form is ὑμῶν ἐν ἡμῖν ('your [love] for us'; 01 04 06 012 025 and the majority of minuscules), followed by ἡμῶν ἐν ὑμῖν ('our [love] for you'; 𝔓⁴⁶ 03 0243 6 1175 etc.). Forms such as ὑμῶν ἐν ὑμῖν ('your [love] for you'; 2464) and ἡμῶν ἐν ἡμῖν ('our [love] for us'; 263) can be dismissed as clearly erroneous, while ὑμῶν εἰς ἡμᾶς ('your [love] into us'; 33) is very poorly attested. The context of the second-person plural suggests that the first-person ἡμῶν is the slightly harder reading, leading to its adoption as the editorial text here and in the SBLGNT, although the majority reading is preferred in the THGNT.[5]

8:19 [αὐτοῦ] (himself) {C}

The majority of Greek manuscripts read αὐτοῦ ('[the glory of the Lord] himself'; 01 06¹ 0150 etc.), while others have αὐτήν ('[the] same [glory of the Lord]'; 025 0243 263 1739 1881ᶜ) which is the form expected after the article τήν. Although the strong support for no qualifier at all (03 04 06* 012 etc. and most early translations) would normally be attractive because it is also the shortest text, the presence of any pronoun is unexpected and so the omission is a smoother reading: αὐτοῦ appears to offer the best explanation of the other variants.

9:4 ταύτῃ (this) {B}

At the end of this verse, the addition of τῆς καυχήσεως ('of boasting'; 01² 06² 025 0150 etc.) has the character of an explanatory addition to the noun ἡ ὑπόστασις whose meaning is not entirely clear ('endeavour' or perhaps 'confidence'; compare also 2 Cor. 11:17).[6] In contrast, there is excellent external support for the shorter reading (𝔓⁴⁶ 01* 03 04 06* etc.). The full attestation in Greek continuous-text manuscripts is provided in *TuT 2Cor* (TS14).

---

[5] Larsen 2000: 347–348 argues for the majority reading on internal grounds, noting too the difficulty of the preposition.

[6] BDAG s. v. ὑπόστασις 2 suggests 'undertaking' for this verse.

10:8 [τε] ('now')

This particle is present in the majority of Greek manuscripts (01 04 06 025 etc.) but lacking from numerous important witnesses ($\mathfrak{P}^{46}$ 03 012 015 0243 6 33 365 1175 1739 1881). There is no obvious reason for its addition apart, perhaps, from a possible assimilation to Rom. 14:8. This suggests that it was deleted by an early editor as superfluous before another postpositive (γάρ) even though there are other instances in the Pauline Epistles of τε without a corresponding καί (e.g. Rom. 1:20, 2:19, 7:7, 16:26 etc.)

10:12–13 οὐ συνιᾶσιν. ἡμεῖς δέ (they do not show good sense. We however) {B}

These four words are missing from some bilingual and Latin manuscripts (06* 012 lat$^{vl\text{-}pt}$), probably due to eyeskip in an ancestor between οὐ and οὐκ: subsequent users then emended the following verb accordingly (καυχησόμεθα ['we will boast'] is absent from 06* and replaced by the participle καυχώμενοι in 012). Other Latin sources support just ἡμεῖς δέ ('We however'; lat$^{vl\text{-}pt,\,vg}$), which may be a partial correction or translational variant. This is a striking example of how a single scribal error leads to a variety of further changes in a group of early witnesses. There is variation in the rest of Greek tradition between the verb forms συνιᾶσιν ($\mathfrak{P}^{46}$ 01^1 03 015^{vid} 0243 etc.) and συνίουσιν (06^2 025 0150 and the majority of minuscules), both third-person plural present active forms of συνίημι ('understand'): this is the only instance of this inflection of the verb in the Pauline Epistles, and the form in the older witnesses has been preferred. A few manuscripts have συνίσασιν ('know well', from σύνοιδα, e.g. 01*), which seems to be a replacement of συνιᾶσιν by a more common verb. The full attestation is provided in *TuT 2Cor* (TS16).

11:3 ἀπὸ τῆς ἁπλότητος καὶ τῆς ἁγνότητος (from a sincere and pure devotion) {B}

The reading has the appearance of a doublet, combining the two separate forms ἀπὸ τῆς ἁπλότητος (lit. 'from sincerity'; 01^2 06^{vid} 015 025 0121 0243 and the majority of minuscules) and ἀπὸ τῆς ἁγνότητος (lit. 'from purity'; only transmitted in some Latin writers). In this scenario, the latter would be a misreading of the former owing to their visual similarity (ΑΠΛΟΤΗΤΟΣ and ΑΓΝΟΤΗΤΟΣ) and the appearance of ἁγνήν ('pure') in the previous verse (cf. 2 Cor. 1:3, although there is a parallel for the word ἁγνότης at 2 Cor. 6:6). Their combination in a different sequence, ἀπὸ τῆς ἁγνότητος καὶ τῆς ἁπλότητος ('from a pure and sincere devotion'; 06*vid, 1 latvl-pt), would also make sense if they were conflated. However, it is very unusual that such a doublet is not found in Byzantine tradition, but present in some of the earliest and most important witnesses as ἀπὸ τῆς ἁπλότητος καὶ τῆς ἁγνότητος (lit. 'from sincerity and purity'; 𝔓46 𝔓124 01* 03 012 etc.). The full attestation is provided in *TuT 2 Cor* (TS18), which confirms the lack of any Greek continuous-text manuscript with ἀπὸ τῆς ἁγνότητος alone. Both this and the early evidence for the longer form suggest that it is original, with the latter element omitted through homoeoteleuton.[7] The alternative sequence in the first hand of Codex Claromontanus may be explained as the reintroduction of the missing term in the wrong place.

11:6   φανερώσαντες (we have made this evident) {B}

The majority of Greek manuscripts have a masculine plural aorist passive participle, φανερωθέντες ('they have been made evident'; 𝔓34 01² 06² 025 0278 etc.), referring back to the 'super-apostles' of the previous verse. The masculine singular, φανερωθείς ('he has/it is/I have been made evident'; 06* latvl-pt, vg) appears to be an improvement to this, relating it to Paul himself at the beginning of this verse. The most difficult reading is the aorist active participle φανερώσαντες ('having made evident'; 01* 03 012 33) because it has no object and is plural despite the preceding singular subject. This is not only attested by a few important witnesses but is also supported by manuscripts which include a reflexive pronoun in order to provide an object, φανερώσαντες ἑαυτούς ('having made ourselves/themselves evident'; 0121 0243 1739 1881). On the basis of this external evidence, the hardest reading has therefore been adopted as the editorial text although it is likely to be necessary in translation to add an object (e.g. 'this' in the NRSVue) to make grammatical sense. The entire clause from ἀλλ' to ὑμᾶς is missing from Papyrus 46, perhaps through a deliberate editorial decision to excise the problematic plural participle and continue with the first-person

---

[7] See also the discussion in Kurek-Chomycz 2007.

singular verb at the beginning of the next verse. The full attestation is provided in *TuT 2Cor* (TS19).

11:32 πιάσαι με (in order to seize me) {C}

The shorter reading adopted in the editorial text, πιάσαι με ('to seize me'; 03 06* lat^(vl-pt, vg) sy^p co^sa Eusebius) is not widely attested but makes tolerable sense with the infinitive taken as an expression of purpose after ἐφρούρει ('set a guard'). The inclusion of the participle θέλων ('wishing') makes for a smoother reading, but its insertion in different places suggests that it is secondary, appearing as both θέλων πιάσαι με ('wishing to seize me'; 012 [1739] etc.) and πιάσαι με θέλων (also 'wishing to seize me'; 01 06² 015 025 0121 and the majority of minuscules). On the other hand, the tendency for minor omissions in Codex Vaticanus, the potential influence of Latin on Codex Claromontanus (cf. 1Cor. 11:24, 15:51), and different ways of expressing purpose in early translations cast doubt on the shorter reading. A comparable construction in some modern languages may also involve an additional element.

12:1 καυχᾶσθαι δεῖ (it is necessary to boast) {B}

The concept of 'boasting' is often positive in the Pauline corpus, especially in this epistle (e.g. 2Cor. 1:12, 5:12, 7:4, 9:2 etc.), but in the previous chapter it is presented as negative (e.g. 2Cor. 11:12–13, 18, 21). In the light of this, the assertion καυχᾶσθαι δεῖ ('it is necessary to boast'; 𝔓⁴⁶ 03 06² 012 020 etc.), despite its wide attestation including numerous Byzantine witnesses, may have seemed to be too hard a reading. Alterations to this would explain two variant forms with the opposite sense, καυχᾶσθαι δή ('boasting indeed [is not beneficial]'; 018 0121 and the rest of Byzantine tradition, including the *Textus Receptus*) and καυχᾶσθαι δέ ('but boasting [is not beneficial]'; 01 06* co^bo eth), although they could have originated through itacism (the identical pronunciation of δεῖ and δή) or copying error. The addition at the beginning of the verse of εἰ ('if'; 01² 015 81 256 etc.) is an assimilation to the same phrase at 2Cor. 11:30.

12:6 [τι] (lit. something)

The manuscript tradition is split between those that include τι ('something'; 𝔓⁴⁶ 01² 06* 025 0243 0278 and the majority of minuscules) and those from which it is absent (01* 03 06² 012 015 6 33 81 1175 1739 lat^vg co). It could have been added to provide a direct object for the verb ἀκούει ('hears'), or deleted to improve the parallelism with the previous element (βλέπει με, 'sees me'). In translation, a direct object may anyway be required.

12:7   διό (therefore) {C}

The emphatic conjunction διό ('therefore') is missing from the majority of witnesses ($\mathfrak{P}^{46}$ 06 025 0150 etc. and several versions and ancient writers), but present in some important manuscripts (01 02 03 012 0243 etc.). Instead of beginning a new sentence with this word, Byzantine tradition (along with Latin and Sahidic) punctuates at the end of the previous verse, which makes διό superfluous. Accordingly, it seems that it was deleted in order to improve the reading of this verse as a single unit. Likewise, translations which follow the punctuation of the majority of manuscripts usually omit this conjunction; those which follow the editorial text have the challenge of interpreting the preceding words as part of the previous sentence, which may have led to this change.

12:9   δύναμις (power) {B}

The editorial text follows the shorter reading attested by the earliest witnesses ($\mathfrak{P}^{46vid}$ 01* 02* 03 06* 012 lat co^{sa, bo-pt} eth and ancient writers). The majority of Greek manuscripts have δύναμίς μου ('my power'; 01² 02^c 06¹ 025 0150 etc.). It is likely that this was introduced as a parallel to the previous noun phrase ('my grace'). Although it is possible that an original pronoun was deleted in order to broaden the application of the saying, the strong attestation of the shorter form suggests that it was initially absent. In some languages, the pronoun may be required by the grammar.

12:15   εἰ (if) {B}

The majority of witnesses read εἰ καί ('even if'; 01² 06¹ 025 0150 0243 etc.). The conjunction may have been added through assimilation to 2 Cor. 12:11 or the other instances of εἰ καί in this epistle (e.g. 2 Cor. 7:8). There is early support for εἰ by itself ('if'; $\mathfrak{P}^{46}$ 01* 02 03 012 33 81* co), which leads to its adoption as the editorial text. The absence of any word here in the first hand of Codex Claromontanus and some Latin witnesses appears to be an improvement to take account of the following participle (see the next variation unit, and compare 2 Cor. 10:12–13 above).

12:15 ἀγαπῶ[ν] (I love) {C}

Most Greek manuscripts have the participle ἀγαπῶν ('loving'; 𝔓⁴⁶ 01² 03 06 012 etc.), even though this is the more difficult reading grammatically because the following protasis of this conditional clause expects a finite verb. Some manuscripts have ἀγαπῶ ('I love'; 01* 02 0150 33 1573*), but the restricted attestation suggests that this is a correction. Translations which follow the participle may need to supply some form of the verb 'to be', as would Greek readers of this form of text: the removal of εἰ earlier in the verse (see the previous variation unit) provides another way of integrating the participle.

12:19 πάλαι (all along) {A}

The hardest reading, πάλαι (lit. 'long ago'; 01* 02 03 012 0243 etc.) has strong attestation, even though its meaning is unclear: is Paul referring to the time it has taken to read this letter aloud (bearing in mind that the next phrase is a repetition of 2 Cor. 2:17), or a longer period? It is also worth observing that this is the only occurrence of πάλαι in the Pauline corpus, apart from Hebrews 1:1. The text of Papyrus 46, οὐ πάλαι ('not long ago'; 𝔓⁴⁶), appears to be an editorial adjustment to make better sense, but supports the presence of πάλαι. The majority of witnesses read πάλιν ('again'; 01² 06 025 0150 0278 etc.: the full attestation is given in *TuT 2 Cor* TS25). This makes for a much smoother text in conformity with Pauline style (e.g. 2 Cor. 3:1, 5:12, 11:16), suggesting that it is likely to be secondary on both internal and external grounds. Translations which follow πάλαι may need to choose a rendering such as 'for a long time' or 'before now' in order to make sense in context. There is also the possibility of interpreting this sentence as a question, as seen in a number of English translations including the KJV and NRSVue (cf. 2 Cor. 3:1).

13:4 γάρ¹ (for¹) {B}

The majority of witnesses read γάρ εἰ ('for if'; 01² 02 06¹ etc.), but there is good external support for just γάρ ('for'; 𝔓⁴⁶ᵛⁱᵈ 01* 03 06* 012 etc.).

The introduction of εἰ seems to have been intended to mitigate the implication that Christ's crucifixion was 'from weakness' (ἐξ ἀσθενείας), yet it does not fit well with the introduction of the following clause by ἀλλά ('but'). There is therefore a possibility that an original εἰ could have been omitted through oversight, as a deliberate grammatical improvement, or by assimilation to the next sentence, although both internal and external considerations favour the shorter reading.

13:13 ὑμῶν (of you) {A}

As in the majority of the Pauline Epistles, most witnesses include a final liturgical Amen following this grace formula (01² 06 025 etc.). The strong external evidence for its absence ($\mathfrak{P}^{46}$ 01* 02 03 012 etc.) indicates that this is likely to be secondary.

The Letter to the Galatians

1:3 πατρὸς ἡμῶν καὶ κυρίου (our Father and the Lord) {C}

The majority of Greek manuscripts read πατρὸς καὶ κυρίου ἡμῶν ('the Father and our Lord'; 𝔓⁴⁶ 𝔓⁵¹ᵛⁱᵈ 03 06 etc.), while some important witnesses have πατρὸς ἡμῶν καὶ κυρίου ('our Father and the Lord'; 01 02 025 33 81 etc.). The latter sequence is predominant elsewhere in the Pauline Epistles (Rom. 1:7, 1 Cor. 1:3, 2 Cor. 1:2, Eph. 1:2, Phil. 1:2, Phlm 3), which is the reason for its adoption as the editorial text here: the common phrase 'our Lord Jesus Christ' would explain the transfer of the pronoun ἡμῶν to qualify κυρίου. On the other hand, it is possible that this greeting has been conformed to that of the other epistles: the majority reading is preferred by the SBLGNT, THGNT and several commentators.[1] A few manuscripts omit the pronoun altogether, reading πατρὸς καὶ κυρίου ('[from God] the Father and the Lord'; 0150 0278 etc.). This may be a reflection of textual instability at this point, perhaps arising from an adjustment between the two other readings which was only partially carried out, but it is not sufficiently well attested to have a claim to be the earliest form.

1:6 χάριτι [Χριστοῦ] (the grace [of Christ]) {C}

The tradition is split between χάριτι by itself ('grace'; 𝔓⁴⁶ᵛⁱᵈ 012 latᵛˡ⁻ᵖᵗ etc.), χάριτι Χριστοῦ ('the grace of Christ'; 𝔓⁵¹ 01 02 03 015ᵛⁱᵈ and the majority of minuscules), χάριτι Ἰησοῦ Χριστοῦ ('the grace of Jesus Christ'; 06 latᵛˡ⁻ᵖᵗ [coˢᵃ] syʰ ʷⁱᵗʰ *) and χάριτι θεοῦ ('the grace of God'; Origenˡᵃᵗ). On internal grounds alone, the shortest reading could have been expanded into the various forms which specify the source of this grace. However, its poor attestation suggests that it may have arisen through accidental omission of the *nomen sacrum* (XY). The external evidence is strongest for χάριτι Χριστοῦ, yet this would be the only instance of this phrase in the Pauline Epistles: elsewhere the preference is

---

[1] See Fee 1974: 454–455, Carlson 2015: 91–93 (who makes the point that this greeting may not have been standard in such an early epistle as Galatians) and Wasserman 2015b: 350–352.

for χάριτι θεοῦ (e.g. 1 Cor. 1:4 and 15:10, 2 Cor. 1:12), which seems to have influenced the reading in Origen. Hesitation between the internal and external evidence leads to the use of brackets in the editorial text. Nevertheless, the good support for the unusual reading χάριτι Χριστοῦ results in its adoption in both the SBLGNT and THGNT.[2] In this (and any of the other longer readings), the noun could be taken as the subject of καλέσαντος, leading to a translation such as 'from Christ, who called you by grace'.

1:8 εὐαγγελίζηται [ὑμῖν] (should proclaim [to you]) {C}

This unit comprises two variations: the absence or presence and placing of ὑμῖν ('to you') and the form of the verb, εὐαγγελίζηται (present subjunctive, 'should proclaim [continuously]'; $\mathfrak{P}^{51\text{vid}}$ 03 06 012 015 etc.), εὐαγγελίσηται (aorist subjunctive, 'should proclaim [once]'; 01 02 81 etc.) or εὐαγγελίζεται (present active, 'is proclaiming'; 018 025 0150 0278 etc.). The subjunctive is the expected mood after ἐάν ('if'): the present active appears to be a later development, perhaps as a result of the loss of vowel length (isochrony) in later Greek which has led to a split in the Byzantine tradition between εὐαγγελίζηται and εὐαγγελίζεται, although the latter may be an assimilation to the present tense in the following verse. The full attestation for the verb in Greek continuous-text manuscripts is provided in *TuT Galatians* (TS1). The stronger external support for the present subjunctive and its slightly less expected tense (in contrast to the following aorist) have led to its adoption here. The pronoun is lacking from a few early witnesses (01* 012 0150 etc.), while some have it before the verb and others afterwards. Such variation suggests that it may be a later addition, yet its absence could be due to confusion between the the different placings. Likewise, ὑμῖν could have been added to match the next phrase or removed by an editor to avoid repetition or to make the application of the saying broader. The THGNT prefers the dissimilar reading, ὑμῖν εὐαγγελίζηται ('should proclaim to you'; $\mathfrak{P}^{51\text{vid}}$ 03 015 etc.), which would have been likely to have been assimilated to the following clause. The SBLGNT adopts εὐαγγελίζηται ὑμῖν, as in UBS6 where the

---

[2] It is also supported by Carlson 2015: 145–149 and Wasserman 2015b: 352–353.

pronoun is in square brackets to indicate the difficulty of the decision.³ In some languages, a pronoun will be necessary regardless of the chosen reading.

1:11 γάρ (for) {C}

The majority of witnesses have the contrastive particle δέ ('but'; 𝔓⁴⁶ 01*, ² 02 06¹ 025 etc.). There is also early evidence for γάρ ('for'; 01¹ 03 06* 012 etc.), as well as one majuscule with οὖν ('and so'; 0278). Of these, δέ appears to be a smoother reading, breaking up the sequence of γάρ in the verses on either side and matching Pauline usage elsewhere (e.g. 1 Cor. 15:1, 2 Cor. 8:1). For this reason, γάρ has been chosen here and in the SBLGNT as a more difficult reading with early attestation: the THGNT prefers δέ, on the grounds that γάρ is more likely to have been introduced because of its predominance in context.⁴ If δέ is adopted, this has the effect of emphasising that this is the beginning of a new section. It is unsurprising that the connective is absent from lectionaries, where this is the first verse of a lection.

1:15 εὐδόκησεν ὁ θεός (lit. God ... was pleased) {B}

The noun ὁ θεός ('God') is not required grammatically, but serves to clarify the agent of the following participles. It is present in the majority of manuscripts (01 02 06 025 etc.), but lacking from some early witnesses which just have εὐδόκησεν ('he was pleased'; 𝔓⁴⁶ 03 012 0150 etc.). If the latter is original, it could reflect the Jewish practice of avoiding explicit mention of God. However, this is not regularly observed in the Pauline Epistles, and the limited attestation is consistent with accidental omission through eyeskip between the two instances of ὁ.⁵ Although the shorter form is preferred in the SBLGNT, the weak external support has led to the removal of the brackets around ὁ θεός in UBS5.

---

[3] Carlson 2015: 149–152 agrees with the THGNT; Wasserman 2015b: 353–354 prefers the reading in the SBLGNT.

[4] Thus also Zuntz 1953: 204 and Carlson 2015: 117–118. In contrast, the analysis of this verse in Silva 1990: 278 strongly supports γάρ as original, also favoured by Wasserman 2015b: 355–356.

[5] See further the discussions at Carlson 2015: 105–107 and Wasserman 2015b: 356–357.

Even if the shorter reading is adopted, translators may prefer to make the agent explicit.

1:18 Κηφᾶν (Cephas) {A}

There is no doubt that the Aramaic name 'Cephas' (which also means 'rock') is original, with Κηφᾶν supported by the earliest manuscripts (𝔓⁴⁶ 𝔓⁵¹ 01* 02 03 etc.). At a relatively early point, however, it was replaced by the Greek equivalent, Πέτρον ('Peter'; 01² 06 012 025 etc.), which became the Byzantine reading (see also Gal. 2:9, 2:11, 2:14 below). The full attestation for this variation unit in Greek continuous-text manuscripts is provided in *TuT Galatians* (TS2). Translations which follow the principle of using a single name for the same person throughout will have 'Peter' here anyway; if 'Cephas' is adopted then it may be appropriate to provide the more familiar name in a footnote.

2:5 οἷς οὐδέ ... εἴξαμεν τῇ ὑποταγῇ (we did not submit to them) {A}

External evidence overwhelmingly favours οἷς οὐδέ (lit. 'to whom neither'; 𝔓⁴⁶ 01 02 03 04 etc.) despite the grammatical inconsistency with the preceding verse. The reading οὐδέ alone ('not'; Marcion) makes for easier grammar, but is very poorly attested. Some sources reflect a text which lacks both words (06* lat^(vl-pt) etc.) or just reads οἷς ('to them'; 06^(1vid)), resulting in the opposite meaning. It has been suggested that this was a deliberate alteration to bring this statement into line with Paul's stated practice in 1 Cor. 9:20–23 and the circumcision of Timothy at Acts 16:3.[6] Nevertheless, it is also possible that this was simply due to a copying error. In any case, the difficulty of the most widespread reading leads to its adoption.

2:6 [ὁ] θεός (God)

The definite article is present in some early witnesses (𝔓⁴⁶ 01 02 0278 etc.) but missing from others (03 04 06 012 etc. as well as the majority of minuscules). Both SBLGNT and THGNT have the shorter form, but the article is preferred by others as the harder reading.[7] Translation is

---

[6] See Omanson 2006: 376.
[7] Carlson 2015:152–154, Wasserman 2015b: 357–358.

unaffected, although the absence of the article places more emphasis on the noun.

2:9; 2:11; 2:14   Κηφᾶς (Cephas) {A}

In each of these three verses, some manuscripts prefer the Greek form Πέτρος ('Peter'), but the early attestation of 'Cephas' is incontrovertible (cf. Gal. 1:18 above: the full attestation for 2:11 and 2:14 is given in *TuT Galatians* TS4–5). There is an inconsistency in Papyrus 46 (Πέτρος in 2:9 but Κηφᾷ in 2:14) which is indicative of later influence on its text. Conversely, Byzantine tradition usually has Πέτρος but reads Κηφᾶς in 2:9, which is an unexpected preservation of the earliest form. The different order of the three names in 'Western' witnesses in 2:9 is probably due to assimilation to the sequence in the gospels (e.g. Mark 5:47, 9:2, 14:33), although it also reflects the narrative in Gal. 1:18–19. The omission of Peter from Codex Alexandrinus (02) at 2:9 is likely to be eyeskip between the two instances of καί, compounded by the frequency of the name pair James and John (even though this James is not the apostle). As noted at Gal. 1:18, translations may choose to read 'Peter' throughout regardless of the form of the name adopted in Greek.

2:13   [καὶ] οἱ λοιποὶ Ιουδαῖοι (and the other Jews)

The repetition of καί, which would be translated as 'the other Jews also', is found in the majority of Greek witnesses. It is absent from a few important manuscripts ($\mathfrak{P}^{46}$ 03 6 630 1739 1881), but this may have been an editorial decision to simplify the sentence in the light of the following καί ('even Barnabas') or simply an oversight.[8]

2:16   [δέ] (yet)

The contrastive particle δέ ('but') is present in many majuscules, but missing from $\mathfrak{P}^{46}$ 02 and the majority of minuscules. It affects the relationship of this observation to the previous verse: as a connective might be expected, the absence of δέ is more difficult to explain and might therefore favour the shorter reading.[9]

---

[8] Carlson 2015: 108–109 prefers the longer reading.

[9] The detailed argument in Carlson 2015: 154–157, taking into account the exegetical implications, concludes with a slight preference for the inclusion of δέ.

2:20 τοῦ υἱοῦ τοῦ θεοῦ (the Son of God) {B}

The majority reading τοῦ υἱοῦ τοῦ θεοῦ ('[by faith] in the Son of God'; 01 02 04 06¹ 025 etc.) has been adopted in keeping with the immediate context and Pauline theology more generally. However, the alternative, τοῦ θεοῦ καὶ Χριστοῦ ('in God and Christ'; 𝔓⁴⁶ 03 06* 012 lat^(vl-pt)) is unexpected. This formulation does not appear elsewhere in Paul and there is no other instance in the Epistles of the genitive θεοῦ ('God') as the complement of πίστις ('faith'). Accordingly, the difficulty of this reading has led some to accept it as the earliest text.[10] On the other hand, it might be explained as arising through an error prompted by the juxtaposition of *nomina sacra*, perhaps involving the omission of τοῦ υἱοῦ through eyeskip and the subsequent addition of Χριστοῦ based on the previous verse.[11] Both the SBLGNT and THGNT agree with the editorial text here.

3:1 τίς ὑμᾶς ἐβάσκανεν (who has bewitched you) {A}

After ἐβάσκανεν ('bewitched'), most Greek manuscripts include a phrase also seen at Gal. 5:7, τῇ ἀληθείᾳ μὴ πείθεσθαι ('from obeying the truth'; 04 06² 025 0278 etc.). There is no obvious reason for its accidental omission or deliberate removal from the earliest majuscules and translations (01 02 03 06* 012 etc.). Rather, this is a secondary harmonisation between different parts of the same letter in order to clarify the sense. The full attestation for this variation unit in Greek continuous-text manuscripts is provided in *TuT Galatians* (TS8).

3:17 θεοῦ (by God) {B}

Most witnesses specify that the covenant was ratified 'by God in Christ', θεοῦ εἰς Χριστόν (06 012 016 0278 etc.). Although there is a slight possibility that the last two words were omitted by eyeskip between two *nomina sacra*, they are superfluous to the sense. Their absence from many important manuscripts which read only θεοῦ ('by God'; 𝔓⁴⁶ 01 02 03 04 etc.) suggests that they are a secondary gloss, per-

---

[10] Van Nes 2013; Carlson 2015: 96–101; Wasserman 2015b: 360–362. Carlson suggests that this reading might have been replaced in order to avoid any suggestion of the suffering of God (Patripassianism).

[11] On these two stages, see further Ehrman 2011: 101.

haps reflecting the end of the previous verse.[12] Compare also Gal. 4:7 below.

3:19 νόμος; τῶν παραβάσεων χάριν προσετέθη (law? It was added because of transgressions) {A}

The editorial text, νόμος; τῶν παραβάσεων χάριν προσετέθη ('law? It was added because of transgressions'; 01 02 03 04 06[1] etc.) is transmitted by the majority of Greek manuscripts and adopted on the basis of its strong attestation. The first hand of Codex Claromontanus erroneously wrote παραδόσεων ('traditions'; 06*) in place of παραβάσεων ('transgressions') as well as ἐτέθη ('it was instituted') for προσετέθη ('it was added'). Papyrus 46, however, has no response, instead reading νόμος τῶν πράξεων ('[Why then the] law of deeds?'; 𝔓[46]). The absence of a verb may be due to eyeskip from χάριν to ἄχρις, while πράξεων is a misreading which replaced παραβάσεων with a more common word. The same noun is seen in νόμος τῶν πράξεων; ἐτέθη ('[Why then the] law of deeds? It was instituted'; 012 lat^(vl-pt) Irenaeus^(lat)), which could also be read as a single question ('[Why then] was the law of deeds instituted?').[13] A case can be made for these poorly-attested alternatives reflecting a deliberate theological alteration by an editor in the 'Western' tradition.[14]

3:21 τῶν ἐπαγγελιῶν τοῦ θεοῦ (the promises of God) {B}

A few early witnesses read only τῶν ἐπαγγελιῶν ('the promises'; 𝔓[46] 03 lat^(vl-pt) [eth]), but there is extensive support for τῶν ἐπαγγελιῶν τοῦ θεοῦ ('the promises of God'; 01 02 04 06 [012] etc.). The latter could be a harmonisation (cf. Rom. 4:20, 2 Cor. 1:20), and there are other instances where Paul does not qualify ἐπαγγελία ('promise'; Rom. 9:4, Gal. 3:16–18). However, Codex Vaticanus is sometimes omissive and it is equally possible that an editor removed τοῦ θεοῦ in order to bring this verse into line with the preceding discussion. The external evidence is too slim to commend the

---

[12] See also the discussion in Carlson 2015: 191–192.

[13] The latter is supported by the punctuation in Codex Boernerianus (012), which has a large capital on the following ἄχρις.

[14] Carlson 2015: 192–193; see also Staples 2015, who notes Latin assimilation to Rom. 3:27 as a possible source for πράξεων.

shorter reading and the brackets in previous editions have been removed.[15]

3:28 εἷς ἐστε ἐν Χριστῷ (you are one in Christ) {B}

Most Greek manuscripts read εἷς ἐστε ἐν Χριστῷ ('you are one [person] in Christ'; 01² 03 04 06 etc.), but others have the neuter form of 'one', ἕν ἐστε ἐν Χριστῷ ('you are one [thing] in Christ'; 012 33 lat etc.). The latter may be a harmonisation to Paul's use elsewhere of the neuter phrase ἕν σῶμα ('one body'; cf. Rom. 12:5, 1 Cor. 10:17, 1 Cor. 12:12–13, Eph. 4:4). Three important witnesses have no numeral at all, reading ἐστε Χριστοῦ ('you are of Christ'; 𝔓⁴⁶ 01¹ 02). This appears to be assimilation to ὑμεῖς Χριστοῦ in the following phrase, perhaps compounded by the omission of εἷς after ὑμεῖς through haplography. The first hand reading of Codex Sinaiticus, ECTE EN XY, could be interpreted as ἐστε ἕν Χριστοῦ ('you are one [thing] of Christ'; 01*) or an error for ἐστε ἐν Χριστῷ ('you are in Christ'). The majority reading has been adopted as the editorial text: in some languages it may anyway not be possible to distinguish between the masculine and neuter forms of 'one'.

4:6 ἡμῶν (our) {A}

The majority of minuscules read ὑμῶν ('your'; 06² 0150 6 33 etc.), while most early manuscripts have ἡμῶν ('our'; 𝔓⁴⁶ 01 02 03 04 etc.). The two forms were frequently confused due to their similar pronunciation through itacism. The contrast between ἡμῶν and the second-person plural at the beginning of the verse makes it a more difficult reading: both internal and external evidence support the more inclusive observation as the earliest form.[16]

4:7 διὰ θεοῦ (through God) {B}

The oldest witnesses describe the heir as διὰ θεοῦ ('through God'; 𝔓⁴⁶ 01* 02 03 04* etc.). This is the only occurrence of this phrase in the New Testament. The majority of Greek manuscripts read θεοῦ διὰ Χριστοῦ ('of God through Christ'; 01² 04³ 06 0150 etc.), which appears to be a later expansion involving a more common complement (cf. Rom. 2:16;

---

[15] The longer reading is also preferred in Carlson 2015: 110–112 and Wasserman 2015b: 362–363.

[16] Thus also Carlson 2015: 222.

2 Cor. 3:4, 5:18; compare also Gal. 3:17 above).[17] Three other variants stem from misreading these forms: διὰ θεόν ('because of God'; 012 1881), διὰ Χριστοῦ ('through Christ'; 81 2464 etc.) and θεοῦ ('of God'; 1962), while there are two further expansions: διὰ Ἰησοῦ Χριστοῦ ('through Jesus Christ'; 1739ᶜ) and θεοῦ διὰ Ἰησοῦ Χριστοῦ ('of God through Jesus Christ'; 025 6 263 2127 sy eth). The variety of alternative readings is striking: a complete list is provided in *TuT Galatians* (TS12), one of which includes a harmonisation to Rom. 8:17. In translation, it may be appropriate to amplify the the preposition διά to reflect its indication of divine agency rather than simply mediation (e.g. 'by God's action'; cf. 1 Cor. 1:9, Gal. 1:1).

4:14 τὸν πειρασμὸν ὑμῶν (my condition put you to the test) {B}

The oldest manuscripts read τὸν πειρασμὸν ὑμῶν (lit. 'your testing'; 01* 02 03 04² 06* etc.). The article is repeated in some minuscules with τὸν πειρασμὸν ὑμῶν τόν ('your testing which is'; 6 1739 1881 Origen), offering a clarification. The plural pronoun is clearly the more difficult reading before the following σαρκί μου ('in my flesh'), although it can be understood as Paul's physical appearance being offputting to his audience (cf. 2 Cor. 12:7). Assimilation to the singular pronoun is seen in τὸν πειρασμὸν μου ('my testing'; $\mathfrak{P}^{46}$ lat$^{vl\text{-}pt}$) and the reading of the majority of of manuscripts, τὸν πειρασμόν μου τόν ('my testing which is'; 04*vid 06² 025 0150 etc.). Some witnesses have τὸν πειρασμὸν τόν ('the testing which is'; 01² 0278 81 etc.), which may reflect the removal of the difficult pronoun or the omission of μου by haplography. The full attestation for this variation unit is provided in *TuT Galatians* (TS13).[18]

4:25 τὸ δὲ Ἁγὰρ Σινᾶ (Now Hagar is Sinai) {D}

This phrase, explaining that Sinai is a mountain in Arabia, has long been suspected of being a gloss later incorporated into the text of the Epistle.[19] The variation partly reflects confusion as to how it is to be

---

[17] There is a brief discussion in Carlson 2015: 222–223.

[18] Carlson 2015: 223 suggests that the simple change to μου was made independently on more than one occasion.

[19] See Carlson 2014 and 2015: 163–169. Multiple similar conjectures are recorded in the *Amsterdam Database* (Krans, Lietaert Peerbolte et al. 2016). In particular,

connected with the previous verse. The editorial text is a difficult reading because the conjunction δέ does not correlate with the μέν of the previous verse and the contrast is unexpected. Nevertheless, there is early support for both τὸ δὲ Ἁγὰρ Σινᾶ ('but the "Hagar" is Sinai'; 02 03 06 0278 etc.) and τὸ δὲ Σινᾶ ('but Sinai'; 𝔓46 co^sa): as Ἁγάρ is feminine, the neuter pronoun can be understood as introducing a quotation of the previous verse or standing for τό ὄνομα ('the name'). This is also the case in the majority reading, τὸ γὰρ Ἁγὰρ Σινᾶ ('for the "Hagar" is Sinai'; 025 0150 6 33 81 etc.), the reading preferred in the THGNT. The smoothest reading is τὸ γὰρ Σινᾶ ('for Sinai'; 01 04 012 1739 etc.).[20] It has been been suggested that the replacement of δέ ('but') with the explanatory γάρ ('for') would have led to haplography with the following Ἁγάρ, but *TuT Galatians* (TS15) only records two instances of the omission of the conjunction.[21] An appealing conjecture is that the first word was originally a demonstrative, τόδε γὰρ Σινᾶ ('for this Sinai'), although this would usually be followed by a second article before Σινᾶ.[22] The alternative readings might then be explained as arising from the removal of δέ as an apparently superfluous double conjunction and/or the miswriting of γάρ as Ἁγάρ due to the context. However, as neither this nor the complete absence of the phrase is attested in any surviving manuscripts, the most difficult early reading has been adopted here and in the SBLGNT.

4:28   ὑμεῖς ... ἐστέ (you ... are) {B}

The majority of manuscripts have the first-person plural, ἡμεῖς ... ἐσμέν ('we ... are'; 01 02 04 06² etc.), but there is significant support for ὑμεῖς ... ἐστέ ('you ... are'; 𝔓46 03 06* 012 0278 etc.). The former can be explained as accommodation to the other occurrences of the first person in the passage (cf. Gal. 4:26, 4:31). Although an editor might have introduced the second-person plural in conjunction with

---

Carlson draws attention to the discrepancy between the conception of Arabia here and at Gal. 1:17.

[20] Although Tuckett 2015 prefers this as the earliest text, it is hard to account for the later introduction of δέ. See also Wasserman 2015b: 363–365, who opts for a split guiding line between τὸ δὲ Ἁγὰρ Σινᾶ and τὸ γὰρ Σινᾶ.

[21] For the suggestion, see Metzger 1994: 527.

[22] *Amsterdam Database* cj14734 [Pearce 1721].

the vocative ἀδελφοί, this contrasts with the construction in Gal. 4:31 and a difference between these two verses makes for a more difficult reading.[23]

5:1 τῇ ἐλευθερίᾳ ἡμᾶς Χριστὸς ἠλευθέρωσεν· στήκετε οὖν (For freedom Christ has set us free. Stand firm, therefore) {B}

This variation unit involves a number of small changes which may affect the division of the text: several editions start a new section after this verse rather than before it at the beginning of the chapter.[24] Most of the alternative readings can be construed as a continuation of the previous phrase, while the editorial text is quite abrupt: τῇ ἐλευθερίᾳ ἡμᾶς Χριστὸς ἠλευθέρωσεν· στήκετε οὖν (lit. 'For freedom us has Christ set free. Be standing firm, therefore'; $\mathfrak{P}^{135}$? 01* 02 03 [06*] etc.). Both the change of word order to Χριστὸς ἡμᾶς ($\mathfrak{P}^{135}$? 01² 04 015 0150 etc.) and the introduction of the relative pronoun ᾗ ('by which'; 06¹ [6] 263 etc.) appear to be attempts to soften this. The initial relative in Codex Boernerianus (ᾗ ἐλευθερίᾳ, 'for which freedom'; 012 lat etc.) may derive from the editorial text with the omission of the first letter, perhaps because a space was left for an enlarged capital.[25] The Byzantine reading, τῇ ἐλευθερίᾳ οὖν ᾗ Χριστὸς ἡμᾶς ἠλευθέρωσεν στήκετε ('Therefore be standing firm in the freedom by which Christ has set us free') is a further reworking which results in a greater disjunction from the preceding passage. There is also extensive attestation of τῇ ἐλευθερίᾳ Χριστὸς ἡμᾶς ἠλευθέρωσεν· στῆτε οὖν ('For freedom Christ has set us free. Therefore stand'; 015 0278 256 365 etc.), in which the aorist στῆτε may have been introduced through attraction to the tense of ἠλευθέρωσεν: the present-tense στήκετε ('stand firm') in the editorial text correlates with ἐνέχεσθε later in the verse and has overwhelming external support. The full attestation for this variation unit in Greek continuous-text manuscripts is provided in *TuT Galatians* (TS16).[26]

---

[23] This unit is also discussed at Carlson 2015: 125–126.

[24] e.g. UBS5, SBLGNT, THGNT.

[25] I am grateful to Amy Myshrall for this suggestion; Codex Boernerianus itself has a capital H here.

[26] Carlson traces the development of this verse over several stages (2015: 199–200, 216–217, 232 and 238).

5:19 πορνεία (sexual immorality) {A}

It is common for lists of virtues and vices to be supplemented with additional terms. This is the case here where μοιχεία ('adultery'; 01² 06 [0278] and the majority of minuscules) or the plural μοιχεῖαι (lit. 'adulteries'; 012 lat^(vl-pt) Irenaeus^(lat)) have been introduced before πορνεία under the influence of parallels elsewhere (Matt. 15:19 etc.). There is strong support for πορνεία by itself at the beginning of this list (01* 02 03 04 025 etc.) and the first word in a sequence is unlikely to be omitted through homoeoteleuton.

5:21 φθόνοι (envy) {C}

After φθόνοι (lit. 'envies'; 𝔓⁴⁶ 01 03 33 81 etc.), there is widespread attestation of φόνοι ('murders'; 02 04 06 012 and the majority of minuscules). The similarity of these words (ΦΘΟΝΟΙ ΦΟΝΟΙ) means that the latter could easily have been overlooked. On the other hand, there is early attestation of the shorter reading (including Sahidic and several ancient writers), and—as at Gal. 5:19 above—the longer reading can be explained as a harmonisation to other lists of sins (e.g. Rom. 1:29, Matt. 15:19 par.). It may be observed that 'murder' is unexpected in a list of vices, although not impossible. The SBLGNT prefers the shorter reading while the THGNT adopts both terms.[27]

5:24 Χριστοῦ [Ἰησοῦ] (Christ [Jesus]) {C}

Despite strong external support, the longer reading, Χριστοῦ Ἰησοῦ ('Christ Jesus'; 01² 02 03 04 025 etc.), is unusual in the Pauline Epistles: there are few parallels for these words preceded by a definite article (Eph. 3:1, 3:11; Phil. 3:8; Col. 2:6; two of which are also contested). The majority reading Χριστοῦ ('Christ'; 𝔓⁴⁶ 06 012 etc.) could have derived from the longer form through harmonisation to Pauline usage (cf. 1 Cor. 15:23) or the omission of the second *nomen sacrum* (ΙΥ) through eyeskip. Alternatively, it is possible that Χριστοῦ by itself was original and the expanded form is secondary: a shorter reading in Byzantine tradition is always worthy of consideration. While the THGNT has the longer text, the SBLGNT and other studies adopt the majority form.[28]

---

[27] See also the discussions at Carlson 2015: 129–131 and Wasserman 2015b: 366–367, who both prefer the shorter reading.

[28] Carlson 2015: 134–136; Wasserman 2015b: 368.

The first hand of Codex Sinaiticus, with κυρίου Χριστοῦ Ἰησοῦ ('Lord Christ Jesus'; 01*), includes a further honorific addition.

6:2 ἀναπληρώσετε (you will fulfil) {C}

The textual tradition is split between the future indicative, ἀναπληρώσετε ('you will fulfil'; 03 012 1962 lat co eth etc.) and the aorist imperative, ἀναπληρώσατε ('fulfil'; 01 02 04 06 025 etc. and the majority of minuscules). Papyrus 46 alone reads ἀποπληρώσετε ('you will complete'; 𝔓⁴⁶): this verb does not appear anywhere else in the Pauline Epistles and seems to be a misreading, although it too supports the future indicative. While the external evidence is stronger for the aorist, an imperative matches the form of the previous verb. The future indicative may therefore be considered the harder reading, despite its very limited attestation in Greek. It is also adopted in the SBLGNT and THGNT.[29] In translation, there may be comparatively little difference between these two forms.

6:13 περιτεμνόμενοι (the circumcised) {C}

The textual tradition is evenly split between the present participle, περιτεμνόμενοι ('those being circumcised'; 01 02 04 06 [012] etc.) and the perfect participle, περιτετμημένοι ('those who have been circumcised'; 𝔓⁴⁶ 03 020 6 365 etc.), both of which are found in Byzantine witnesses. The difference in tense is significant for the application of Paul's observation: does he refer to the keeping of the law by all those already circumcised, or only by this particular group? The present participle appears more appropriate for the immediate context and is also adopted in the SBLGNT, but the external evidence for the perfect (preferred by the THGNT) is also strong.[30]

6:15 οὔτε γάρ (for neither) {B}

The shorter form οὔτε γάρ ('for neither'; 𝔓⁴⁶ 03 33 1175 1739* etc.) makes for a rather brief statement. The majority reading, ἐν γὰρ Χριστῷ Ἰησοῦ οὔτε ('For in Christ Jesus neither'; 01 02 04 06 012 etc.), not only provides a context for the 'new creation' but brings this verse even

---

[29] Thus also Carlson 2015: 102–103.

[30] Carlson 2015: 116–117 and Wasserman 2015b: 368–369 both favour the present.

closer to Gal. 5:6. The longer text is therefore likely to be a later harmonisation (also evident in the replacement of ἐστιν ['is'] by ἰσχύει ['counts for'] later in the verse). The full attestation for this variation unit is provided in *TuT Galatians* (TS17).

6:17 Ἰησοῦ (of Jesus) {B}

The alternative readings illustrate the tendency to expand the name of Jesus: κυρίου Ἰησοῦ ('of the Lord Jesus'; 04³ 06² 1881 and the majority of minuscules); κυρίου μου Ἰησοῦ ('of my Lord Jesus'; 1739); κυρίου Ἰησοῦ Χριστοῦ ('of the Lord Jesus Christ'; 01 06¹); κυρίου ἡμῶν Ἰησοῦ Χριστοῦ ('of our Lord Jesus Christ'; 06* 012 lat^{vl-pt} [co^{sa-mss}]). The early attestation of Ἰησοῦ ('of Jesus'; 𝔓⁴⁶ 02 03 04* 33 etc.) as well as its brevity makes it likely to be the earliest form; the later manuscripts which have τοῦ Χριστοῦ ('of Christ'; 025 0278 81 365 etc.) probably represent a misreading of the *nomen sacrum* IY as XY, or an omissive form of one of the longer texts. This is the only place where Paul qualifies the noun 'stigmata'.

In contrast to the other Pauline epistles, there is almost unanimous support for the final 'Amen' in Galatians.[31] The only manuscript which appears to lack this is Codex Boernerianus (GA 012), which has a series of circular figures before a line of *diplai* (note too its unusual reading at 1 Cor. 16:24 above).

---

[31] See further Wasserman 2023: 60–61, who notes Güting's suggestion that this is not original.

The Letter to the Ephesians

1:1 [ἐν Ἐφέσῳ] (in Ephesus) {C}

The words 'in Ephesus' are missing from some early and important manuscripts (𝔓46 01* 03* 6 424c 1739 Marcion[acc. to Tertullian] Origen[vid]; see *TuT Ephesians* TS1), and Marcion knew this epistle as Laodiceans.[1] It has therefore been suggested that this work—which also has no concluding salutations, and addresses general topics—may originally have been a circular letter with no specific addressees. Nevertheless, even the six manuscripts which lack these words clearly identify it as Ephesians in the title. While the multiple attestation of the omission is remarkable, the presence of οὖσιν ('who are') suggests that a destination is likely to have been present, as the participle is otherwise superfluous. The trend in modern translations is to include 'in Ephesus' but with a note of the variant reading.

1:15 καὶ τὴν ἀγάπην τὴν εἰς πάντας τοὺς ἁγίους (and your love towards all the saints) {B}

Although the editorial text is attested in the majority of minuscules, the oldest witnesses lack τὴν ἀγάπην ('your love'), reading καὶ τὴν εἰς πάντας τοὺς ἁγίους ('and that towards all the saints'; 𝔓46 01* 02 03 025 etc.). In this case, the relative clause has to refer back to πίστιν, giving an unusual collocation ('your faith in the Lord Jesus and towards all the saints'). It is unusual to find πίστις with εἰς and a human object (the only other instance in the Pauline Epistles is Phlm 5, where the variation seems to reflect this; compare also Col. 1:4): it might be translated as 'faithfulness' or 'loyalty' to make better sense here.[2] It seems, however, that the omission of τὴν ἀγάπην is an early error caused by jumping between the two instances of τήν, while eyeskip on a smaller scale is responsible for the absence of τήν after ἀγάπην (06* 012). The displacement of ἀγάπην in minuscules reading καὶ τὴν εἰς

---

[1] See Schmid 1995: 111, 337.
[2] See Omanson 2006: 387.

πάντας τοὺς ἁγίους ἀγάπην ('and love towards all the saints'; 81 256 263 365 etc.) probably represents a later reintroduction of the noun to the early omissive form. The full attestation for this variation unit in Greek continuous-text manuscripts is provided in *TuT Ephesians* (TS2).

2:5 συνεζωοποίησεν τῷ Χριστῷ (made us alive together with Christ) {B}

The most widespread reading, τῷ Χριστῷ ('Christ'; 01 02 06 012 025 and the majority of minuscules), takes this noun as the indirect object of the verb συνεζωοποίησεν ('made alive with'). Other witnesses have a preposition, ἐν τῷ Χριστῷ ('in Christ'; 𝔓⁴⁶ 03 33 etc.) or σὺν τῷ Χριστῷ ('with Christ'; lat^{vl·pt} sy^{p, (h)} cpa [Origen^{lat}]). These are smoother forms, suggesting that they are secondary. However, either preposition could have been overlooked due to similarity with the final letters of the preceding verb. Although the appearance of the standard Pauline phrase ἐν Χριστῷ ('in Christ') three times in the following verses might support ἐν here, the harder but well-attested shorter reading offers the best explanation for the variants.

3:1 τοῦ Χριστοῦ [Ἰησοῦ] (for Christ [Jesus]) {C}

Most Greek manuscripts have τοῦ Χριστοῦ Ἰησοῦ (lit. 'of Christ Jesus' (𝔓⁴⁶ 01² 02 03 06¹ etc.; cf. Phlm 1 and 9). However, some early witnesses only read τοῦ Χριστοῦ ('of Christ'; 01* 06* 012 etc.): this could be an accidental omission of the second *nomen sacrum* abbreviation or the original reading which was later expanded (following Eph. 2:20). A few witnesses read Ἰησοῦ Χριστοῦ ('of Jesus Christ'; 6 1881 1962 etc.): this might be an error for the shorter form (reading ΤΟΥ as ΙΥ with a line above), a separate expansion or a reordering of the majority reading. Codex Ephraemi Rescriptus has τοῦ κυρίου Ἰησοῦ ('of the Lord Jesus'; 04), probably due to misreading the *nomen sacrum* ΧΥ as ΚΥ. An overly literal approach to the genitive, understanding Paul as 'the prisoner of Christ Jesus' rather than 'for Christ Jesus', or possibly a harmonisation to Eph. 4:1 could underlie the alternative ἐν Χριστῷ ('in Christ'; 365). The division in the external evidence leads to some doubt about the earliest form, but the SBLGNT and THGNT both agree with the majority reading.

3:9 φωτίσαι πάντας (to make everyone see) {B}

Some important manuscripts read only φωτίσαι ('to enlighten'; 01* 02 0150 6 1739 1881). The absence of a direct object means that the verb has to be understood as an absolute, e.g. 'to bring to light'. This is a difficult reading, but it may simply derive from an error of omission. There is very strong support for φωτίσαι πάντας ('to make everyone see'; $\mathfrak{P}^{46}$ 01² 03 04 06 and the majority of minuscules), which is also not entirely straightforward and it is possible to see how an editor could have thought that its deletion improved the grammatical construction. If an object were not originally present, later readers might have supplied differing words rather than the agreement seen for this term. The inclusion of πάντας could be of theological significance, broadening Paul's audience from gentiles alone in the previous clause to 'everyone' here.[3]

3:14 τὸν πατέρα (the Father) {A}

The majority of Greek manuscripts include the expansion τοῦ κυρίου ἡμῶν Ἰησοῦ Χριστοῦ ('of our Lord Jesus Christ'; 01² 06 012 0278 etc., cf. Eph. 1:3). This is a typical reverential addition, absent from the earliest witnesses ($\mathfrak{P}^{46}$ 01* 02 03 04 etc.). It should be noted that, if the longer text is read, the relative pronoun in the next verse could refer to Jesus rather than the Father; the latter offers the more appropriate etymological connection with πατρία, '(father)land', which seems to be the implication here.

3:19 πληρωθῆτε εἰς (you may be filled with) {B}

Early manuscripts join Byzantine tradition in reading πληρωθῆτε εἰς (lit. 'you may be filled into'; 01 02 04 06 etc.). One minuscule has πληροφορηθῆτε εἰς (lit. 'you may be fully assured into'; 81), a verb which is found elsewhere (e.g. Rom. 4:21, 14:5) but seems to be a misreading here. A few important witnesses read just πληρωθῇ ('it may be filled'; $\mathfrak{P}^{46}$ 03 0278 33 1175 co^sa). The subject of this would be the following τὸ πλήρωμα, but the idea that 'all the fullness may be filled' is tautological and is not paralleled in the other uses of this term in the Pauline Epistles.

---

[3] See further Omanson 2006: 390, and Best 1997: 319.

3:20 ὑπὲρ πάντα (more than all) {A}

The preposition ὑπέρ ('more than') is absent from Papyrus 46 and bilingual and Latin witnesses ($\mathfrak{P}^{46}$ 06 012 lat^{vl-pt, vg}). Given its otherwise unanimous attestation, this is either an oversight or a deletion by an editor seeking to rein in Paul's overabundant rhetoric, perhaps to avoid repetition with the following ὑπερεκπερισσοῦ ('abundantly by far').

4:6 ἐν πᾶσιν (in all) {A}

The majority of manuscripts read πᾶσιν ἡμῖν ('all of us'; 06 012 0278 etc.) at the end of the verse. The *Textus Receptus* has πᾶσιν ὑμῖν ('all of you'; 1739^c *TR*), which seems to be a secondary development from ἡμῖν due to itacism or the preceding second-person pronoun in Eph. 4:4. There is strong external evidence for just πᾶσιν ('in all'; $\mathfrak{P}^{46}$ 01 02 03 04 etc.) which also matches the three unqualified uses of πάντων ('all') earlier in the verse and fits the structure of this credal formula. Without the additional pronoun, πᾶσιν could be neuter ('all things') or masculine ('all people').

4:9 κατέβη (descended) {A}

Most Greek witnesses have an extra detail, κατέβη πρῶτον ('descended first'; 01² 03 04³ 025^{vid} 0150 etc.). This is missing from many early manuscripts ($\mathfrak{P}^{46}$ 01* 02 04* 06 etc.), and appears to have been added to clarify the sequence of events: there is no obvious reason for its omission if it were original.[4] The full attestation for this variation unit in Greek continuous-text manuscripts is provided in *TuT Ephesians* (TS8).

4:9 [μέρη] (parts) {C}

The presence or absence of the word μέρη ('parts') does not affect the sense, as its meaning is already covered by κατώτερα ('lower regions'). This is the only instance of each of these two words in the Pauline Epistles. Although μέρη looks like an expansion for clarification, its absence is restricted to a relatively small group of witnesses ($\mathfrak{P}^{46}$ 06* 012 lat^{vl-pt} co^{sa} eth and several ancient writers). This word may therefore be original and was removed by translators and at least one early editor on

---

[4] See further Ehrman 2011: 90.

the grounds that it was redundant. *TuT Ephesians* (TS8) also includes information about this variation unit.

4:17 τὰ ἔθνη (the gentiles) {B}

The variation in this unit affects the identification of the community to which this letter was written. The editorial text, supported by all the oldest witnesses, contrasts the addressees with τὰ ἔθνη ('the gentiles'; $\mathfrak{P}^{46}$ $\mathfrak{P}^{49vid}$ 01* 02 03 etc.), implying that it was sent to a Jewish community. The majority of Greek manuscripts, however, read τὰ λοιπὰ ἔθνη ('the rest of the gentiles'; 01^2 06^1 025 etc.), indicating that the addressees were also gentiles. The external evidence suggests that the addition is secondary. The full attestation is provided in *TuT Ephesians* (TS9).

4:19 ἀπηλγηκότες (lost all sensitivity) {A}

A small group of witnesses read ἀπηλπικότες ('lost all hope'; 06 [012] 025 lat sy^p eth Irenaeus^{lat}) rather than ἀπηλγηκότες ('lost all feeling'; $\mathfrak{P}^{46}$ 01 02 03 0150 etc.). The latter word is not otherwise found in the New Testament and it seems that, because it was an unusual term, it was replaced with a more common one. It is possible that this originally took the form of a gloss, as seen in Papyrus 99.[5] The similarity of the two words (ΑΠΗΛΠΙΚΟΤΕΣ and ΑΠΗΛΓΗΚΟΤΕΣ) means that this change may alternatively have been due to a misreading.

4:26 [τῷ] παροργισμῷ (anger)

The absence of the article from several early manuscripts ($\mathfrak{P}^{49}$ 01* 02 03 1739*) raises some doubt as to whether it is original, but translation is unaffected.

4:28 ταῖς [ἰδίαις] χερσὶν τὸ ἀγαθόν (good work with their own hands) {C}

There is good early support for ταῖς ἰδίαις χερσὶν τὸ ἀγαθόν (lit. 'with their own hands what is good'; 01* 02 06 012 0150 etc.), yet the oldest witnesses read only ταῖς χερσὶν τὸ ἀγαθόν (lit. 'with hands what is

---

[5] This manuscript appears to derive from a commentary and is no longer considered a direct witness to the New Testament: see Dickey 2019. I am grateful to Amy Myshrall for this suggestion.

good'; 𝔓⁴⁶ 𝔓⁴⁹ᵛⁱᵈ 01² 03 lat^(vl-pt, vg)). This casts doubt on whether ἰδίαις ('own') was originally present, although it makes little difference to the meaning. It is possible that it was added through assimilation to 1 Cor. 4:12, or accidentally omitted through eyeskip after ταῖς (see also 1 Thess. 4:11 below). In any case, one of these is likely to be the earliest text. The shorter reading may reflect the influence of Atticism (compare the deletion of ἰδίαις both here and at 1 Thess. 4:11 in Codex Sinaiticus), suggesting that the longer reading is preferable.[6] The re-ordering of the phrase as τὸ ἀγαθὸν ταῖς ἰδίαις χερσίν ('what is good with their own hands'; 018 1962 etc.) or τὸ ἀγαθὸν ταῖς χερσίν ('what is good with their hands'; 020 etc.) is a later simplification in order to place τὸ ἀγαθόν next to the verb to which it relates: the Byzantine tradition is split between these two readings. A number of manuscripts just read τὸ ἀγαθόν ('what is good'; 025 6 33 1739 1881 etc.), while there is also evidence for ταῖς χερσίν ('with their hands'; co^(sa-mss) Tertullian). Both make sense in context: they may have arisen through the partial implementation of corrections to change the word order to the later sequence. The full range of variants is given in *TuT Ephesians* (TS10).

4:29   τῆς χρείας (as there is need) {A}

A small group of witnesses reads πίστεως ('of faith'; 06* 012 lat^(vl) Tertullian etc.) rather than χρείας ('of what is needed'; 𝔓⁴⁶ 01 02 03 06² etc.). This is an obvious substitution of a more common term in place of an unexpected construction: an early editor may have found 'the building up of need' too ambiguous or hard to understand.

4:32   [δέ] (lit. but)

The majority of manuscripts (including 𝔓⁴⁹ 01 02) have the contrastive conjunction δέ at the beginning of the verse, which fits the context well. However, some of the earliest texts (𝔓⁴⁶ 03 0278 6 1739* 1881) have no conjunction, while a few read οὖν ('and so'; 06* 012 1175). The original form of text is therefore unclear: the SBLGNT prefers the shortest reading, but the THGNT includes δέ.

---

[6] I am grateful to Tommy Wasserman for this observation.

4:32 ὑμῖν (you) {B}

The reading ὑμῖν ('you'; 𝔓⁴⁶ 01 02 012 etc.), in which only the recipients of the letter are the beneficiaries of God's forgiveness in Christ, is present in several early witnesses as well as the *Textus Receptus*. The standard Byzantine reading is the first-person pronoun ἡμῖν ('us'; 𝔓⁴⁹ 03 06 0278 etc.), comprising the author along with the addressees. The immediate context of the second-person exhortation to imitate Christ and the parallel at Col. 3:13 have led to the adoption of ὑμῖν here and in the SBLGNT. On the other hand, ἡμῖν, preferred by the THGNT, might be considered the more difficult reading—unless an early editor adjusted the text to make sure that Paul was not left out. The confusion of these two words, due to the similar pronunciation of υ and η through itacism, is also seen in the next two variants.

5:2 ἠγάπησεν ἡμᾶς (loved us) {B}

In contrast to the previous variation unit, the editorial text here follows the majority of manuscripts in reading ἡμᾶς ('us'; 𝔓⁴⁶ 01²ᵃ 06 012 etc.) rather than ὑμᾶς ('you'; 01*,²ᵇ 02 03 025 etc.). The latter suits the context of imitating Christ, but the external support for the second-person plural is less strong here than in 4:32. The first-person plural in the next clause is very well attested, leading to the choice of ἡμᾶς in this verse too.

5:2 ὑπὲρ ἡμῶν (for us) {A}

The second-person ὑμῶν ('for you'; 03 0278ᶜ 1175 latᵛˡ⁻ᵖᵗ co eth) is very poorly attested. This suggests that the first person should be preferred throughout this verse (see the previous comment). There is strong early support for the majority reading ἡμῶν ('for us'; 𝔓⁴⁶ 𝔓⁴⁹ 01 02 06 etc.).

5:9 τοῦ φωτός (of the light) {B}

The majority of manuscripts read τοῦ πνεύματος ('[the fruit] of the spirit'; 𝔓⁴⁶ 06² 0150 263 etc.), matching the expression at Gal. 5:22. Although φωτός ('light') appears in the preceding clause and so could have been substituted for the *nomen sacrum* for 'spirit' (ΠΝΣ) through inattention, the predominance of the external evidence for φωτός ('[the fruit] of light'; 𝔓⁴⁹ 01 02 03 06* etc.) indicates that this unusual phrase is likely to be original and the alternative reading is a harmonisation. The full attestation in Greek continuous-text manuscripts is provided in *TuT Ephesians* (TS11).

5:14   ἐπιφαύσει σοι ὁ Χριστός (Christ will shine on you) {A}

The external support for the editorial text is overwhelming. The first hand of Codex Claromontanus, however, reads ἐπιψαύσεις τοῦ Χριστοῦ ('you will touch Christ'; 06* lat^vl-pt Origen^lat), a reading which was observed in manuscripts by Chrysostom. This surprising alternative is also seen in the Latin text of this manuscript and some other Latin sources. It appears to derive from a misreading of Ψ for Φ in the relatively rare verb and then incorporating the first letter of the next word, making it a second-person singular in keeping with the preceding imperatives. This was followed by the adjustment of the case of the following noun to match the verb. This mechanical explanation is more plausible than the attempt to explain this variant as a possible reference to an early Christian myth.[7]

5:15   Βλέπετε οὖν ἀκριβῶς πῶς περιπατεῖτε (be careful, then, how you live) {B}

The majority of Greek manuscripts have the word order πῶς ἀκριβῶς, which means that the adverb qualifies the second verb ('[Look] how carefully [you live]'; 01² 02 06 012 etc.). This corresponds to the expectation that βλέπετε would be closely followed by πῶς (cf. 1 Cor. 3:10, 8:9), but makes for poorer sense: ἀκριβῶς ('carefully') usually accompanies verbs of perception (cf. 1 Thess. 5:2). In addition, there is strong external evidence for ἀκριβῶς πῶς ('[Look] carefully how [you live]'; 𝔓⁴⁶ 01* 03 0150 0278 etc.). A few manuscripts with the later word order also add ἀδελφοί ('brothers'; 01² 02 2464 etc.), which seems to be a further secondary development corresponding to verses such as 1 Cor. 1:26 or Heb. 3:12. This is not widely attested in lectionary tradition, suggesting that it is not a liturgical addition.

---

[7] Metzger 1994: 540 suggests that it reflects a legend that Jesus was crucified on the place where Adam was buried and raised him from the dead by the touch of a drop of his blood.

5:19 [ἐν] ψαλμοῖς ([in] psalms)

Although most manuscripts have no preposition before ψαλμοῖς ('psalms'; 01 02 06 012 etc.) and none is required by the verb, the presence in some important witnesses of ἐν ('in'; 𝔓⁴⁶ 03 025 0278 6 33 1739 lat) raises the possibility that it might have been original. On the other hand, it may have been added to make a distinction from the preceding dative (ἑαυτοῖς, 'to yourselves'). The shorter reading is preferred in the SBLGNT and THGNT.

5:19 ᾠδαῖς πνευματικαῖς (spiritual songs) {A}

There is very strong external evidence, including all minuscules, for ᾠδαῖς πνευματικαῖς ('with spiritual songs'; 01 06 012 025 048^vid etc.). The absence of πνευματικαῖς ('spiritual') from Papyrus 46, Codex Vaticanus and some Old Latin witnesses is probably an omission due to the similarity of its *nomen sacrum* abbreviation (ΠΝΑΙC) to the preceding word (ΩΔΑΙC). The addition of ἐν χάριτι ('in grace'; 02) is assimilation to the parallel at Col. 3:16.

5:21 Χριστοῦ (for Christ) {B}

The object of the believers' reverence (φόβος, also 'fear') is, variously, Χριστοῦ ('Christ'; 𝔓⁴⁶ 01 02 03 020 etc.), Χριστοῦ Ἰησοῦ ('Christ Jesus'; 06 lat^vl-pt), Ἰησοῦ Χριστοῦ ('Jesus Christ'; 012), κυρίου ('the Lord'; 018 co^bo-ms), or θεοῦ ('God'; 6 81 1881 etc.). Byzantine tradition is split between the first and last of these. All these nouns would have been written as *nomina sacra*, with the possibility of confusion between the abbreviations. However, while examples are found in other epistles of φόβος θεοῦ ('the fear of God'; Rom. 3:18, 2 Cor. 7:1) and φόβος κυρίου ('the fear of the Lord'; 2 Cor. 5:11, cf. Col. 3:22), this is the only example of 'the fear of Christ'. This makes it the hardest reading, as well as the most likely source for the other variants: such internal considerations correspond to the external attestation.

5:22 γυναῖκες τοῖς ἰδίοις ἀνδράσιν (wives ... to your husbands) {C}

Only two manuscripts do not feature a verb here, instead relying on the participle ὑποτασσόμενοι ('being subject to') from the previous verse: γυναῖκες τοῖς ἰδίοις ἀνδράσιν ('wives [being subject] to your husbands'; 𝔓⁴⁶ 03 Clement^pt). Several forms of this verb are attested in different places. The imperative ὑποτάσσεσθε ('be subject to') appears after γυναῖκες (06 012 lat^(vl-pt)) or after ἀνδράσιν (0150 and the majority of minuscules), while the third-person plural passive imperative ὑποτασσέσθωσαν ('let them be subject to') is found after ἀνδράσιν in numerous important witnesses (01 02 016 025 0278 etc.; see further *TuT Ephesians* TS13). This leads to a conflict between the internal evidence favouring the shortest reading (adopted here and in the SBLGNT) and the external evidence which supports ὑποτασσέσθωσαν (preferred in the THGNT).[8] The variety in the form and placing of the verb are consistent with it being a later introduction, but it is possible that an early editor deleted ὑποτασσέσθωσαν as superfluous after its participle and ὑποτάσσεσθε was subsequently reintroduced on more than one occasion. If the shortest reading is adopted, it will be necessary to add a verb in translation: if γυναῖκες is taken as a vocative (cf. Eph. 5:25) then the second-person imperative is required.

5:25   γυναῖκας (wives) {A}

Even when the noun γυναῖκας ('women'; 01 02 03 048 etc.) appears by itself without a pronoun, the sense in context is clearly that husbands are commanded to love their own wives rather than women in general. In order to exclude the possibility of wilful misinterpretation, some witnesses have γυναῖκας ὑμῶν ('your [wives]'; 012 lat^(vl, vg-mss) sy), while the majority of manuscripts include the even more specific reflexive pronoun, γυναῖκας ἑαυτῶν ('your own wives'; 06 [025] 0278 etc., cf. Eph. 5:28). In most modern translations, a pronoun will be added even if the shortest text is followed.

5:28   [καὶ] οἱ ἄνδρες (husbands [too])

The majority of manuscripts lack καί ('also'), which is largely redundant given that the previous exhortation is also addressed to οἱ ἄνδρες ('husbands'; cf. Eph. 5:25). The presence in some important manuscripts of καί before οἱ (𝔓46 03 33 1175) or after ἄνδρες (02 06 012 025 etc.) means that it may be original in one of these places and was later removed, then reintroduced.

---

[8] The passive imperative is also adopted in Gurry 2021, which proposes that this verse marks the beginning of the household code. However, it may be noted that all of the following instructions are active imperatives.

5:30 τοῦ σώματος αὐτοῦ (of his body) {A}

The majority of witnesses include a reminiscence of Gen. 2:23 at the end of this verse, ἐκ τῆς σαρκὸς αὐτοῦ καὶ ἐκ τῶν ὀστέων αὐτοῦ ('of his flesh and of his bones'; 01² 06 012 025 etc.), anticipating the quotation of Gen. 2:24 in the following verse. While it is possible that the absence of this phrase is due to eyeskip between the instances of αὐτοῦ (as in the omission of ἐκ τῆς σαρκὸς αὐτοῦ, 'of his flesh', from 0150), the strong external evidence for the shortest reading ($\mathfrak{P}^{46}$ 01* 02 03 048 etc.) favours its originality. The addition serves to smoothe the transition into the following quotation, which otherwise begins rather abruptly. The full attestation for this variation unit is provided in *TuT Ephesians* (TS14).

5:31 [τὸν] πατέρα καὶ [τὴν] μητέρα (his father and mother)

The two definite articles, which in many languages would be translated as possessive pronouns, are absent from three majuscules (03 06* 012). This is more elegant, matching the anarthrous ἄνθρωπος, but the overwhelming support for the articles here and in the Septuagint of Gen. 2:24 (cf. Matt. 19:5, Mark 10:7) suggests that their omission is the work of an early editor.

6:1 [ἐν κυρίῳ] (in the Lord) {C}

The phrase ἐν κυρίῳ sits oddly: does it qualify τοῖς γονεῦσιν ὑμῶν ('your parents [in the Lord]') or ὑπακούετε ('obey [in the Lord]'), and what would this mean in either case? Such a modification to a command would normally be secondary, exonerating those whose parents were not 'in the Lord' or restricting obedience to matters deemed to be 'in the Lord'.[9] Although there is early support for the absence of these two words (03 06* 012 lat^{vl-pt} Cyril-Jerusalem^{vid}), the presence of ἐν κυρίῳ ('in the Lord'; $\mathfrak{P}^{46}$ 01 02 06¹ 025 and the majority of minuscules) may be deemed the harder reading. The attestation of the short form is consistent with removal by an early editor (compare Eph. 5:31 and 6:19). It is also relevant to note that ἐν κυρίῳ appears in the parallel at Col. 3:20, albeit at the end of the following phrase where its significance is far more straightforward. While it is not impossible that it could have

---

[9] The latter is the interpretation in Best 1997: 564.

been imported from there to the present verse, its displacement during the course of harmonisation makes this unlikely.

6:10   τοῦ λοιποῦ (finally) {B}

After these words, the majority of manuscripts include the vocative ἀδελφοί μου ('my brothers'; 01² 025 etc.) while a smaller group has just ἀδελφοί ('brothers'; 012 365 lat^vg). Some witnesses read ἀδελφοί before the following ἐν κυρίῳ ('brothers in the Lord'; 02 0278 2464). Both interjections are paralleled in the other epistles (2 Cor. 3:11, Phil. 3:1, Phil. 4:8, 1 Thess. 4:1, 2 Thess. 3:1), and their presence here appears to be due to harmonisation (compare Eph. 5:15): there is strong external evidence for the shortest text ($\mathfrak{P}^{46}$ 01* 03 06 016 etc.). The full attestation for this variation unit is provided in *TuT Ephesians* (TS15).

6:12   τοῦ σκότους τούτου (of this present darkness) {B}

The reading τοῦ σκότους τούτου ('of this darkness'; $\mathfrak{P}^{46}$ 01*, 2b 02 03 06* etc.) presents an unusual formulation: nowhere else in the New Testament is there a reference to 'the rulers of darkness' or the use of the demonstrative pronoun τούτου ('this') to qualify the noun σκότος ('darkness'). Most translators expand the phrase to explain its meaning and this is also seen in the majority of Greek manuscripts, which have τοῦ σκότους τοῦ αἰῶνος τούτου ('of the darkness of this present age'; 01²ᵃ 06² 025 81 etc.). The last three words are a standard Pauline phrase (cf. 1 Cor. 1:20, 2:6, 2:8; 2 Cor. 4:4), which results in a much easier reading. While it is possible that τοῦ αἰῶνος was omitted from the earliest text through eyeskip, the external evidence in favour of the shorter reading and its distinctiveness suggest strongly that it is original. The full attestation in Greek continuous-text manuscripts is provided in *TuT Ephesians* (TS16).

6:19   τοῦ εὐαγγελίου (of the gospel) {A}

Although there are references to 'the mystery of God' elsewhere in the epistles (1 Cor. 2:1, 4:1; Col. 2:2), and 'the mystery of Christ' at Eph. 3:4 and Col. 4:3, this is the only instance of 'the mystery of the gospel'. There is strong external evidence for the inclusion of τοῦ εὐαγγελίου ('of the gospel'; 01 02 06 016 025 and all minuscules) despite its absence from a small group of early witnesses (03 012 lat^vl-pt co^fa-ms Marcion^acc. to Tertullian).

It appears that it was deleted by an early editor as superfluous (cf. Eph. 5:31 and 6:1 above). However, 'gospel' makes good sense in conjunction with the two verbs of proclamation in the following verse rather than an unspecified 'mystery'. The full attestation for this variation unit is provided in *TuT Ephesians* (TS17).

6:20 ἐν αὐτῷ (lit. in it) {B}

The majority of Greek manuscripts have ἐν αὐτῷ ('in it'; 02 06 012 016 025 etc.), while a few important witnesses instead read αὐτό ('it'; 𝔓⁴⁶ 03 1739 1881 sy). Both these refer to 'the mystery of the gospel' (see previous variation unit). The prepositional phrase is a difficult reading with the verb παρρησιάσωμαι ('in it I may speak freely'), especially as it comes after the same construction in ἐν ἁλύσει ('in chains'). The postponement of ἐν αὐτῷ to after the verb (01 co) is an attempt to mitigate this, while αὐτό seems to be a replacement to give an easier reading ('I may speak it freely'). Even though αὐτό has the most ancient attestation, it is hard to see why this would have been changed to ἐν αὐτῷ except perhaps through the erroneous repetition of the preceding preposition.

6:24 ἀφθαρσίᾳ (undying) {A}

In keeping with the rest of the Pauline Epistles, Byzantine tradition includes a final 'Amen' (01² 06 025 0150 etc.). The strong external evidence for the editorial text (𝔓⁴⁶ 01* 02 03 012 etc.) indicates that 'Amen' was a later addition.

The Letter to the Philippians

1:11 καὶ ἔπαινον θεοῦ (and praise of God) {A}

The first hand of Codex Claromontanus wrote καὶ ἔπαινον Χριστοῦ ('and praise of Christ'; 06* 1962), perhaps under the influence of the previous phrases or as a misreading of the *nomen sacrum* (ΧΥ for ΘΥ). More intriguing is the reading of the other bilinguals, καὶ ἔπαινόν μοι ('and praise for me'; 012 lat$^{vl\text{-}pt}$). Nowhere else does Paul refer to praise for himself, and it would be tempting to dismiss this also as a misreading were it not for the text in Papyrus 46: θεοῦ καὶ ἔπαινον ἐμοί ('[for the glory] of God and praise for me'; 𝔓^{46} [lat$^{vl\text{-}pt}$]). Even though ἔπαινος ('praise') usually appears in the epistles with humans rather than God as its object, it is very unlikely that these poorly-attested variants represent the earliest form of text: this unit is included for its contribution to the characterisation of Paul in a part of the tradition.[1] The full set of readings in Greek continuous-text manuscripts is provided in *TuT Philippians* (TS3).

1:16–17 *Sequence of verses* {A}

The majority of Greek manuscripts reverse the order of these two verses, reading οἱ μὲν ἐξ ἐριθείας ... οἱ δὲ ἐξ ἀγάπης ... ('These out of selfish ambition ... the others out of love ...'; 06^1 etc.; see further *TuT Philippians* TS5). The motivation for this is to co-ordinate these verses with the sequence of Phil. 1:15, in which the negative reason appears first and the positive one second. There is overwhelming external evidence for the more difficult order of verses adopted here (𝔓^{46} 01 02 03 06* etc.), which offers a chiasmus in place of a straightforward correlation.

1:23 [γάρ] (for)

There is extensive early support for the connective γάρ ('for'; 𝔓^{46} 01^1 02 03 04 etc.) but it is absent from the majority of manuscripts (01* 06 012

---

[1] See, however, Nongbri 2009.

025 etc.). Although a shorter reading in Byzantine tradition is unusual, an editor may have decided to remove the interruption to the formulaic phrase πολλῷ μᾶλλον ('how much more') despite other parallels in the Epistles (Rom. 5:9, Phlm 16; see also Heb. 12:9 below). In either case, this phrase explains the previous clause and translations may supply a connective whichever Greek form is adopted.

1:24 [ἐν] (in)

The preposition ἐν ('in') is found in the majority of manuscripts, including early witnesses ($\mathfrak{P}^{46}$ 03 06 012 etc.). Its absence from other important sources (01 02 04 025 6 33 1739 Clement Origen etc.) casts some doubt on its originality, but translation is unaffected.

2:5 τοῦτο φρονεῖτε (let the same mind be) {B}

Most Greek manuscripts read τοῦτο γάρ (lit. 'for this'; $\mathfrak{P}^{46}$ 01^2 06 012 etc.), yet the connective is lacking from several early witnesses with just τοῦτο ('this'; 01* 02 03 04 etc.). As there is no obvious reason for its omission or deletion if γάρ was originally present, the shorter form has been adopted as the editorial text. The longer text may be due to assimilation to verses such as 1 Thess. 4:3 and 4:15. In translation, however, because this verse serves as a bridge between the previous exhortations and the description of Jesus, it may still be appropriate to add a connective.

3:3 θεοῦ (of God) {B}

There are six other references to 'the Spirit of God' in the Pauline Epistles (Rom. 8:9, 8:14, 15:19; 1 Cor. 7:40, 12:3; 2 Cor. 3:3), some of which are also places of textual variation. The phrase is clearly of theological importance, reflecting early Trinitarian developments, and the majority reading θεοῦ ('[in the spirit] of God'; 01* 02 03 04 06^2 etc.) has been adopted in the light of its early and widespread attestation. A number of witnesses, including the *Textus Receptus*, have the dative θεῷ ('[who worship] God in spirit'; 01^2 06* 025 256 365 etc.), while there is no qualifier at all in Papyrus 46. Both these alternatives can be explained as secondary: a copyist might have overlooked the second of the two *nomina sacra*, while the introduction of the dative is either assimilation to the preceding word or to provide the expected object for the verb λατρεύειν ('to worship'). Although πνεύματι by itself could be construed as the object, the worship of the Spirit would be unique in the Epistles: instead, this is normally treated as an instrumental dative ('in the Spirit' or 'by the Spirit'; cf. 'in Christ' in the next clause).[2]

3:7 [ἀλλ'] (Yet)

The majority of Greek manuscripts begin this verse with ἀλλά ('yet', 'but'; 01² 03 06 etc.). As it is not present in several important witnesses (𝔓⁴⁶ 𝔓⁶¹ᵛⁱᵈ 01* 02 012 0282 0289 33 81) and the text also makes sense without a conjunction, there is a possibility that it may not be original. Alternatively, the word may have been omitted through eyeskip, or deleted by an editor in the light of the initial ἀλλά in the next sentence.

3:13 οὐ (not) {B}

In place of the strongly attested οὐ ('not'; 𝔓⁴⁶ 03 06² 012 and the majority of minuscules), a number of manuscripts read οὔπω ('not yet'; 01 02 06* 025 etc.). This could be a simple error in the light of the sentiment of the previous verse (οὐχ ... ἤδη, 'not ... already'), or a deliberate alteration out of later reverence for Paul. The shorter reading favoured by external evidence has been preferred.

3:16 τῷ αὐτῷ στοιχεῖν (let us hold fast) {A}

Two additional elements are found in the majority of manuscripts. The presence of κανόνι ('rule') clarifies the pronoun αὐτῷ: 'let us keep to the same rule' (cf. Gal. 6:16). Such an expansion may be necessary in translation, as the reference of the preceding relative ὅ ('what') is not immediately apparent. The additional clause τὸ αὐτὸ φρονεῖν ('to think the same') offers a explanatory reformulation on the basis of the previous verse (cf. also Phil. 2:2). In the majority of minuscules, this comes second: τῷ αὐτῷ στοιχεῖν κανόνι, τὸ αὐτὸ φρονεῖν ('to keep to the same rule, to think the same'; 01² 025 1962 etc.). Other manuscripts have it first, as τὸ αὐτὸ φρονεῖν, τῷ αὐτῷ κανόνι στοιχεῖν ('to think the same, to keep to the same rule'; [06²] 81 256 263 365 etc.) or τὸ αὐτὸ φρονεῖν,

---

[2] Note that Papyrus 46 includes a preposition, ἐν πνεύματι ('in spirit'). For more on the translation of this phrase, see Fee 1995: 300 n. 62.

τῷ αὐτῷ συνστοιχεῖν ('to think the same, to keep with the same thing'; [06*] 012 lat^{vl-pt}). The shortest reading of all, τῷ αὐτῷ στοιχεῖν ('to keep to the same'; 𝔓^{16} 𝔓^{46} 01* 02 03 016^{vid} etc.) cannot be derived from any of these by simple eyeskip. The strong external attestation, the likelihood that such a concise form would be expanded and the variety of sequences involving the extra text indicate that it is the earliest form. The full attestation in Greek continuous-text manuscripts is provided in *TuT Philippians* (TS9).

4:13 με (me) {A}

While there is strong early evidence for με ('me'; 01* 02 03 06* 016 etc.; neither 𝔓^{16} nor 𝔓^{46} is extant here), most manuscripts read με Χριστῷ ('[in] Christ [who strengthens] me'; 01^2 06^2 [012] 025 etc.). In place of the whole phrase, a single minuscule reads ἐν τῷ δύνασθαι Χριστῷ ('in being strengthened for Christ'; 1573) which is a misreading of the majority form. There is no obvious reason for the omission of the *nomen sacrum*. Rather, Χριστῷ is a later addition which makes the agent of the participle explicit, perhaps through assimilation to 1 Tim. 1:12. In translation, it may be necessary to identify the subject even if the shorter reading is adopted.

4:19 πληρώσει (will fully satisfy) {B}

The future πληρώσει ('[God] will satisfy', 𝔓^{46} 01 02 03 06^2 etc.) is found in the majority of Greek manuscripts. There is fairly good support for the aorist optative πληρῶσαι ('may [God] satisfy'; 06* 012 6 33 81 etc.), including both the Latin and Ethiopic versions. Although such a wish might be expected at this point in the letter, the future is more direct: the early support for the majority reading and the nearest parallel in context (the future in Phil. 4:9) both favour πληρώσει here.

4:23 μετὰ τοῦ πνεύματος ὑμῶν (with your spirit) {B}

Most manuscripts read μετὰ πάντων ὑμῶν ('with all of you'; 01^2 2464 etc.), a formula which is found in several other epistles (e.g. Rom. 15:33, 1 Cor. 16:24, 2 Cor. 13:13, 2 Thess. 3:18, Titus 3:14). In contrast, μετὰ τοῦ πνεύματος ὑμῶν ('with your spirit'; 𝔓^{46} 01* 02 03 06 etc.) appears at Gal. 6:18 and Phlm 25. The adoption of this less common reading is supported by very strong external evidence, suggesting that the majority form is due to assimilation. The full attestation in Greek continuous-text manuscripts is provided in *TuT Philippians* (TS11).

4:23 τοῦ πνεύματος ὑμῶν (your spirit) {B}

A final Amen is widely attested (ἀμήν, 𝔓⁴⁶ 01 02 06 025 etc.), but it is missing from some important witnesses (03 012 6 263 etc.), including several early translations. Given the custom of concluding letters in this liturgical manner, the absence of Amen is best explained as the earliest form of text (cf. 1 Cor. 16:24, 2 Cor. 13:13, Eph. 6:24, Col. 4:18 etc.). However, it is preferred in the THGNT (cf. Gal. 6:18).

The Letter to the Colossians

1:2 πατρὸς ἡμῶν (our Father) {A}

The majority of manuscripts include the phrase καὶ κυρίου Ἰησοῦ Χριστοῦ ('and the Lord Jesus Christ'; 01 02 04 012 016 etc.). This appears to be an assimilation to the form of this greeting in other epistles (Rom. 1:7, 1 Cor. 1:3, 2 Cor. 1:2, Gal. 1:3, Eph. 1:2, Phil. 1:2, 2 Thess. 1:2, Phlm 3), perhaps influenced by the following verse. There is no obvious reason why it would be omitted if it were original and the shorter reading with just πατρὸς ἡμῶν ('our Father'; 03 06 33 81 1175 etc. and) has extensive support, including most early translations. A few manuscripts have an even longer expansion, καὶ Ἰησοῦ Χριστοῦ τοῦ κυρίου ἡμῶν ('and Jesus Christ our Lord'; 025 [0150] etc.), offering an alternative supplement to a short original reading which was felt to be incomplete.

1:3 θεῷ πατρί (God the Father) {C}

Most Greek manuscripts read θεῷ καὶ πατρί ('to the God and Father'; 01 02 04² 06¹ 016 etc.). References to 'the God of Jesus' may be of theological importance, and are paralleled elsewhere in the epistles (e.g. Rom. 15:6, 2 Cor. 1:3, 11:31; Eph. 1:3, 1:17; cf. 1 Pet. 1:3). The alternative, θεῷ πατρί ('to God, the Father'; $\mathfrak{P}^{61vid}$ 03 04* [06* 012] etc.), is a shorter reading which could have arisen through the simple omission of καί ('and') or assimilation to θεοῦ πατρός in the previous verse. On the other hand, the frequency of references to 'God and Father' in the epistles may have led to its introduction here through harmonisation. Both internal and external considerations are so balanced as to make a decision difficult. While the editorial text and SBLGNT prefer the shorter text, the THGNT adopts the majority reading. See also Col. 3:17 below.

1:7 ὑπὲρ ὑμῶν (lit. on your behalf) {B}

There is early support for ἡμῶν ('on our behalf'; $\mathfrak{P}^{46}$ 01* 02 03 06* 012 lat$^{vl\text{-}pt}$), but the Byzantine text has ὑμῶν ('on your behalf'; 01² 04 06¹ 025 etc.). In later Greek, both these pronouns came to be pronounced identically, leading to their frequent confusion. Both appear in the immediate context: this might favour ὑμῶν, giving a pattern of the first-person pronoun being followed by the second person twice in this sentence. Similarly, there is no other reference to someone as a διάκονος ('minister') on Paul's own behalf, but this term is used with the second person (Rom. 13:4, 2 Cor. 11:8, Phlm 13). Although this results in the choice of ὑμῶν here, the impressive external evidence for ἡμῶν has led to its adoption in the SBLGNT and THGNT.

1:12 τῷ πατρί (to the Father) {C}

The longest reading, τῷ θεῷ καὶ πατρί ('to the God and Father'; 04³ 0150 6 81ᶜ etc.), is found mostly in later manuscripts. Early witnesses are split between τῷ πατρί ('to the Father'; 𝔓⁶¹ 02 04* 06 etc. and the majority of minuscules), τῷ θεῷ πατρί ('to God the Father'; 01 [012] latᵛˡ⁻ᵖᵗ syᵖ etc.) and ἅμα τῷ πατρί ('at the same time to the Father'; 𝔓⁴⁶ 03). The last of these has been seen as a nonsense form, understanding ἅμα as 'together with' and making the Father a partner rather than the object of εὐχαριστοῦντες ('giving thanks').[1] The only other use of ἅμα in Colossians, however, is in a similar context following the participle προσευχόμενοι ('praying'; Col. 4:3), where it means 'at the same time'. This is also plausible in the present context and it has been suggested that this is the original text: a misinterpretation of ἅμα along the lines above might have led to its removal, giving the shortest reading which was then expanded in several ways.[2] Overall, the presence of τῷ πατρί in Papyrus 46 as well as Codex Vaticanus provides strong support for these words: it is likely that the longer readings are a harmonisation to Col. 1:3 (see above). It is less clear whether or not ἅμα should be included. Although these witnesses are early, the attestation is very restricted and there is a possibility that it is assimilation to Col. 4:3. The omission of the phrase from GA 1881 is due to eyeskip between the two instances of τῷ.

1:12 τῷ ἱκανώσαντι (who has enabled) {B}

Most Greek manuscripts read τῷ ἱκανώσαντι ('who has enabled'; 𝔓⁴⁶ 𝔓⁶¹ᵛⁱᵈ 01 02 04 06¹ etc.). The alternative, τῷ καλέσαντι ('who has called';

---

[1] Zuntz 1953: 40; Metzger 1994: 553.
[2] See Quarles 2021, which also proposes a reorganisation of the punctuation of this section.

06*, 2 012 33 1175 lat^vl-pt co^sa) appears to be an early substitution with a more common word. The antiquity of this simpler alternative is such that it is seen in two ancient translations and even in a conflation of both readings in Codex Vaticanus, τῷ καλέσαντι καὶ ἱκανώσαντι ('who has called and enabled'; 03).

1:12   ὑμᾶς (you) {B}

As noted at Col. 1:7 above, variations between the first- and second-person plural pronouns are common due to itacism. The majority of manuscripts have ἡμᾶς ('[who has enabled] us'; 02 04 06 012 025 etc.), in keeping with the first-person pronoun in the following verse and the first-person verb in Col. 1:14. The attestation of ὑμᾶς ('you'; 01 03 256 263 etc.) is more restricted, although it is still found in several important witnesses. Its implication that Paul does not here identify himself with those who have been enabled, along with the first-person context, makes this is the more unexpected reading and it has therefore been preferred in the editorial text.

1:20   [δι' αὐτοῦ] (through him) {C}

The repetition of δι' αὐτοῦ ('through him'; 𝔓^46 01 02 04 06^1 etc.) from the beginning of the verse occurs after τοῦ σταυροῦ αὐτοῦ ('of his cross') in the majority of manuscripts. This interjection is superfluous in context and not required for translation. It could have crept in as a marginal gloss, but the repetition and anaphora in the preceding verses suggest that it may be original. The absence of the phrase from a number of early witnesses (03 06* 012 016 etc. and most translations) could represent deliberate editorial excision, eyeskip between the two instances of αὐτοῦ, or the earliest form of text—which is hard to establish from the available evidence. The SBLGNT includes these words in brackets, while they are part of the editorial text in the THGNT.

1:22   ἀποκατήλλαξεν (he has reconciled) {C}

Most manuscripts read the aorist indicative ἀποκατήλλαξεν (or ἀπεκατήλλαξεν, both 'he has reconciled'; 01 02 04 06^2 etc). The implied subject is Christ, as in the rest of the paragraph. Two variants offer greater consistency with the second-person address in the previous verse. The participle ἀποκαταλλαγέντες ('having been reconciled'; 06*

012 lat^(vl-pt)) matches the participles in Col. 1:21.[3] Papyrus 46 and Codex Vaticanus have the second-person perfect passive ἀποκατηλλάγητε ('you have been reconciled'; [𝔓⁴⁶] 03). This could hint at the 'divine passive', with God as the unnamed agent (cf. James 1:12), and its early attestation has led to its adoption in the SBLGNT. However, both these variants could have been introduced through assimilation to forms in the parallel passage at Romans 5:10.[4] The majority reading, which also has early support, seems to be the hardest in context and has therefore been chosen for the editorial text, although ἀποκατηλλάγητε also poses problems for the syntax. It is difficult to construe the third-person singular perfect passive ἀποκατήλλακται ('it has been reconciled'; 33) with the rest of the sentence: this may be an error for the second-person plural form involving the common variation of AI in place of E.

2:2 τοῦ θεοῦ, Χριστοῦ (of God, Christ) {C}

As in Col. 1:12 and 1:22, Papyrus 46 and Codex Vaticanus share a distinctive reading, here τοῦ θεοῦ Χριστοῦ ('of God, Christ'; 𝔓⁴⁶ 03). The juxtaposition of the two nouns seems to have been problematic: without punctuation, the phrase could be translated as 'the mystery of the God Christ', which is a formulation of considerable theological significance. It is possible that Χριστοῦ ('Christ') was a gloss later incorporated into the text, but taking it as the earliest form provides an explanation for the variety of alternative readings: if τοῦ θεοῦ ('of God'; 06¹ 015 025 etc.) or τοῦ Χριστοῦ ('of Christ'; 81 [1739] lat^(vl-pt)) were original they would not require further explanation. As it is, these are likely to have arisen through deliberate or accidental omission of one of the *nomina sacra*. There are no fewer than six variants which expand the text following τοῦ θεοῦ. Most have relatively slight attestation: τοῦ θεοῦ ὅ ἐστιν Χριστός ('of God which is Christ'; 06* lat^(vl-pt)), τοῦ θεοῦ τοῦ ἐν Χριστῷ ('of God which is in Christ'; 33 [Clement]), τοῦ θεοῦ πατρὸς τοῦ Χριστοῦ ('of God the Father of Christ'; [01*] 02 04 [048] etc., which appears in the THGNT), τοῦ θεοῦ πατρὸς καὶ τοῦ Χριστοῦ ('of God the Father and of Christ'; 0208 0278 etc.), and τοῦ θεοῦ καὶ πατρὸς τοῦ Χριστοῦ ('of God and of the Father of Christ'; 01² 256 263 etc.). The

---

[3] For a theological interpretation of this variant, see Ehrman 2011: 113.
[4] See Araújo 2022.

majority of Greek manuscripts read τοῦ θεοῦ καὶ πατρὸς καὶ τοῦ Χριστοῦ ('of the God and Father and of Christ'; 06² etc.; see further *TuT Colossians* TS4), but the lack of early attestation tells against this as the initial form of text. Instead, the shortest and most difficult form has been adopted, as in the SBLGNT, with hesitation due to its slim attestation. The punctuation τοῦ θεοῦ, Χριστοῦ ('of God, Christ') is preferred, although it may well be necessary to expand the phrase in translation to indicate the way in which 'Christ' relates to the rest of the sentence (e.g. 'God's mystery, that is, Christ' in the NRSVue).

2:7 ἐν εὐχαριστίᾳ (in thanksgiving) {B}

After the participle περισσεύοντες ('abounding'), most Greek manuscripts read ἐν αὐτῇ ἐν εὐχαριστίᾳ ('in it, in thanksgiving'; 03 06² 015ᶜ 0278 etc.), with the feminine pronoun αὐτῇ referring to the previous τῇ πίστει ('in the faith'). A few witnesses have the masculine, ἐν αὐτῷ ('in him'; 01² 06* lat^(vl-pt) sy^hmg), repeating the reference to Jesus from the beginning of the verse. It is possible that one of these pronouns is original but was later omitted by eyeskip from ἐν to ἐν. However, the presence of two variants and good external evidence for ἐν εὐχαριστίᾳ by itself ('in thanksgiving'; 01* 02 04 015* 016^vid etc.) suggests that the longer readings are assimilation to the immediate context or a parallel: for instance, γρηγοροῦντες ἐν αὐτῇ ἐν εὐχαριστίᾳ ('keeping alert in it with thanksgiving') in Col. 4:2 may have inspired the majority reading here.

2:11 σώματος (body) {A}

After this word, the majority of manuscripts include τῶν ἁμαρτιῶν ('[the body] of the sins [of the flesh]'; 01² 06¹ [0278] etc.; see *TuT Colossians* TS5). This appears to be a simple addition for clarification, removing the possibility of interpreting the phrase as a complete rejection of the flesh. The shorter reading σώματος ('of the body'; 𝔓⁴⁶ 01* 02 03 04 06* etc.) is very strongly attested.

2:13 [ἐν] τοῖς παραπτώμασιν (in trespasses)

The Byzantine tradition is split between the presence of ἐν ('in'; 𝔓⁴⁶ 01¹ 02 04 06 012 025 048 etc.) and its absence (01* 03 0278 etc.). The preposition clarifies the function of the dative here and is likely to be required in translation, whether or not it was omitted or added in transmission.

2:13 συνεζωοποίησεν ὑμᾶς (made you alive) {C}

A large number of manuscripts, including the *Textus Receptus*, read just συνεζωοποίησεν ('made alive'; 01² 06 012 025 etc.), taking as its object the ὑμᾶς ('you') at the beginning of this verse. The repetition is superfluous, and the absence of a pronoun improves the flow. However, ὑμᾶς ('[made] you [alive]'; 01* 02 04 0150 etc.) is attested both in early witnesses and Byzantine tradition, while there is important evidence for ἡμᾶς ('[made] us [alive]'; 𝔓⁴⁶ 03 33 etc.). The latter is inconsistent with the initial ὑμᾶς yet matches the following ἡμῖν (see the next variation unit). A case can be made on internal criteria for any of these three readings as the earliest, but the redundancy of ὑμᾶς has led to its adoption in the editorial text.

2:13 ἡμῖν (us) {A}

The external support for ἡμῖν ('us'; 𝔓⁴⁶ 01* 02 03 04 etc.) is very strong: only a few manuscripts read ὑμῖν ('you'; 01² 018* 020 025 6), either under the influence of the preceding pronouns in this verse or through confusion due to through itacism (compare Col. 1:7). The variation is interesting for the insight it gives into whether the author chooses to identify with the recipients of the letter (cf. Col. 1:12 and 3:4), especially if a distinction is made between Jewish and gentile believers.

2:18 ἃ ἑόρακεν ἐμβατεύων (lit. dwelling on visions) {B}

The majority of manuscripts include a negative in this phrase, aligning it with the beginning of the sentence and the following εἰκῇ ('without cause'). The most common is ἃ μή ('which [he has] not [seen]'; 01² 04 06¹ 025 etc.; see *TuT Colossians* TS6), with the same meaning as ἃ οὐκ (012); one minuscule has just μή ('not'; 81) through the erroneous omission of the relative pronoun. There is strong external evidence for ἃ ἑόρακεν (lit. 'which he has seen'; 𝔓⁴⁶ 01* 02 03 06* etc.), a surprising reading in context which suggests that μή was added later to correspond to the negative sense expected in the rest of the verse. The exact sense of ἐμβατεύων, which only occurs here in the New Testament, is unclear although it may refer to initiation in ancient religion (cf. 'initiatory visions' in the NRSVue).⁵ It may be that a negative was supplied by an editor who interpreted this verb in a broader way, such as 'investigating' or 'searching into'.

3:4 ἡ ζωὴ ὑμῶν (your life) {B}

The majority of manuscripts have ἡμῶν ('our [life]'; 03 06¹ 015 0150 etc.). This is possibly the harder reading in a context full of second-person plural forms, including the phrase ἡ ζωὴ ὑμῶν ('your life') in the previous verse. Even so, external support is strong for ὑμῶν ('your'; 𝔓⁴⁶ 01 04 06* 012 etc.) here too, and the repetition is unexpected, leading to its adoption as the editorial text. As at Col. 1:12 and 2:13, the choice of pronoun reflects the extent to which the writer identifies with the audience.

3:6 ἐπὶ τοὺς υἱοὺς τῆς ἀπειθείας (on those who are disobedient) {C}

This phrase is absent from early witnesses in a variety of languages (𝔓⁴⁶ 03 06*ᵛⁱᵈ latᵛˡ⁻ᵖᵗ cpa coˢᵃ), resulting in the relative pronouns δι' ἅ ('on account of these') in Col. 3:6 and ἐν οἷς ('in these') in Col. 3:7 both referring back to the list of evils in Col. 3:5. In contrast, the presence of ἐπὶ τοὺς υἱοὺς τῆς ἀπειθείας (lit. 'on the sons of disobedience') makes the reference ambiguous for both ἐν οἷς and ἐν τούτοις ('in which'/'among them') in the following verse. While the shorter form could therefore have been an early editorial deletion for clarification, this phrase may have been added as a deliberate or subconscious harmonisation to Eph. 5:6. The arguments on both sides make a choice difficult regarding the earliest reading, but the SBLGNT and THGNT prefer the longer form. If this is adopted, translators must decide whether υἱούς is the antecedent of one or both of the two third-person pronouns in Col. 3:7.

3:13 κύριος (Lord) {C}

The majority of manuscripts read Χριστός ('Christ'; 01¹ 04 06¹ 025 0150 etc.), in keeping with the context and the following verses, and may thus be the result of assimilation. Two alternatives, both with very limited

---

⁵ For a collection of uses of this word in other ancient texts, see BDAG s.v. ἐμβατεύω.

attestation are θεός ('God'; 01* lat^{vg-mss}) and θεὸς ἐν Χριστῷ ('God in Christ'; 33), both of which seem to be assimilations to Eph. 4:32. The external evidence for κύριος ('Lord'; 𝔓^{46} 02 03 06* 012 etc.) has led to its choice as the editorial text, with some hesitation: the similarity between the two *nomina sacra* KC and XC means that one could easily be mistaken for the other.

3:14 τελειότητος (perfect harmony) {A}

There is no doubt here about the most ancient text, but the variant has been included as an alternative reading typical of 'Western' witnesses. In place of τελειότητος ('perfect harmony'; 𝔓^{46} 01 02 03 04 etc.), the Latin and bilingual traditions have ἑνότητος ('unity'; 06* 012 lat^{vl}). The latter noun might be expected after σύνδεσμος ('bond'; cf. Eph. 4:3); τελειότης only appears elsewhere in the New Testament at Heb. 6:1, but is a more theologically significant term.

3:16 ἐν [τῇ] χάριτι (gratitude)

The majority of manuscripts do not have the article, giving the standard form of the prepositional phrase ἐν χάριτι ('in gratitude'; e.g. Col. 4:6, Gal. 1:6, 2 Cor. 11:12). However, the external evidence for its inclusion here is strong (𝔓^{46} 01² 03 06* 012 6 1739), suggesting that it may be original. Either way, translation is unaffected.

3:16 τῷ θεῷ (to God) {A}

The editorial text is based on the very strong external evidence for τῷ θεῷ ('to God'; 𝔓^{46vid} 01 02 03 04* 06* etc.), including early translations. The reading τῷ κυρίῳ ('to the Lord'; 04² 06² 0150 and the majority of minuscules) is a straightforward assimilation to the parallel at Eph. 5:19, although confusion between *nomina sacra* may have contributed to this.

3:17 τῷ θεῷ πατρί (God the Father) {B}

The majority of manuscripts read θεῷ καὶ πατρί ('God and Father'; 06 012 0150 6 etc.). Both this and the shorter reading θεῷ πατρί ('God [the] Father'; 𝔓^{46vid} 01 02 03 04 etc.) are paralleled in other epistles, and a similar variation is found at Col. 1:3 and 1:12 (see above). Here, the stronger external evidence leads to greater confidence in the shorter form as the earliest text, but it remains possible that it may be an early editorial simplication of the longer phrase.

3:18 τοῖς ἀνδράσιν (husbands) {B}

There are two variants which qualify this noun, in order to provide greater precision as to whom should be obeyed (cf. Eph. 5:25 and Col. 3:19). Part of Byzantine tradition, including the *Textus Receptus*, reads τοῖς ἰδίοις ἀνδράσιν ('your own husbands'; 020 6 365 1175 1881 etc.), while some early witnesses have τοῖς ἀνδράσιν ὑμῶν ('your husbands'; 06* 012 lat^vl-pt sy^p, h with *). The former appears to be an assimilation to the parallel at Eph. 5:22, and the presence of two alternatives along with strong external support for the shortest reading, τοῖς ἀνδράσιν (lit. 'the men' or 'husbands'; 𝔓⁴⁶ 01 02 03 04 etc., as well as the rest of the Byzantine minuscules) means that this has been adopted as the editorial text. In some languages (especially when ἀνδράσιν is translated as 'husbands'), a personal pronoun will be required or advisable regardless of the Greek text.

3:19 τὰς γυναῖκας (wives) {A}

As in the identical phrase at Eph. 5:25 (see above), as well as the previous variation unit, two pronouns have been provided after this noun for clarification. One form reads τὰς γυναῖκας ἑαυτῶν ('your own wives'; 1175), while the other has τὰς γυναῖκας ὑμῶν ('your wives'; 04² 06* 012 lat^vl-pt, vg-mss sy). A correction to τὰς ἑαυτῶν γυναῖκας (also 'your own wives'; 01²) is seen in Codex Sinaiticus. The shortest reading of just τὰς γυναῖκας ('the women/wives'; 𝔓⁴⁶ 01* 02 03 04* etc.) is the most strongly attested and best explains the origin of the other variants.

3:22 κύριον (Lord) {A}

There is very strong external evidence in favour of κύριον ('Lord'; 01* 02 03 04 06* etc.), which is also the harder reading in the context of slavery due to its ambiguity. Although the majority of manuscripts read θεόν ('God'; 𝔓⁴⁶ 01² 06² etc.), this is likely to be secondary. It could be a misreading of the *nomen sacrum*, assimilation to a phrase such as Rom. 3:18 or 2 Cor. 7:1, or a deliberate alteration to dissociate this noun from κυρίοις ('masters') earlier in the verse. For 'the Lord' as the object of fear

3:24 τῷ κυρίῳ (the Lord[2]) {B}

The majority of Greek manuscripts include a connective in τῷ γὰρ κυρίῳ ('for [you serve] the Lord'; 06¹ 1175 etc.), making it clear that this observation is an explanation of what has come before. Without this, the phrase could be read as an imperative ('Serve the Lord!') or an indicative ('You serve the Lord.'). While it is possible that an original connective here was removed by an early editor to avoid repetition in the next clause, this could equally have been addressed by deleting the following instance of γάρ. The external evidence strongly supports the shorter reading, τῷ κυρίῳ ('the Lord'; 𝔓⁴⁶ 01 02 03 04 06* etc.), but there is no agreement in translations as to whether this is a command or a statement.

4:8 γνῶτε τὰ περὶ ἡμῶν (you may know how we are) {C}

There is early support for γνῶτε τὰ περὶ ἡμῶν ('you may know how we are'; 02 03 06* 012 025 etc.), which reflects what has already been stated in Col. 4:7. The majority reading γνῷ [or γνῶ] τὰ περὶ ὑμῶν ('he [or I] may know how you are'; 𝔓⁴⁶ 01² 04 06¹ 0150 etc.; see *TuT Colossians* TS10) contrasts both with the purpose expressed in the previous verse and the subsequent encouragement of the Colossians. Although this makes it a harder reading, it could have originated through two simple errors: the omission of ΤΕ through eyeskip before ΤΑ and variation between ἡμῶν and ὑμῶν due to itacism. The latter explains the almost nonsensical γνῶτε τὰ περὶ ὑμῶν ('you may know how you are'; 01*). On the other hand, the editorial text agrees verbatim with Eph. 6:22 and might therefore be the result of assimilation. Both the THGNT and a recent study prefer the majority reading, yet this is ambiguous because early manuscripts do not always include *iota*-subscripts: ΓΝΩ may be interpreted as a third-person subjunctive (γνῷ) through co-ordination with the following παρακαλέσῃ ('he may encourage'), but the THGNT adopts the first-person γνῶ ('I may know').[6]

---

[6] See Head 2014, who reads γνῷ in keeping with the role of Paul's letter carriers.

4:12 Χριστοῦ [Ἰησοῦ] (Christ [Jesus]) {C}

There is good external support for Χριστοῦ Ἰησοῦ ('Christ Jesus'; 01 02 03 04 016 etc.), as well as parallels in Paul's description of himself at Rom. 1:1 and Phil. 1:1. However, the majority of manuscripts read only Χριστοῦ ('Christ'; 𝔓⁴⁶ 06 012 0150 etc.) which corresponds to Eph. 6:6. It is difficult to decide whether the latter form arose through eyeskip of the second of the *nomina sacra* (ΧΥ ΙΥ) or was subsequently expanded in the light of other passages or general usage. It is unusual to find a shorter reading in Byzantine tradition: further support for this is offered by the existence of a further variant, Ἰησοῦ Χριστοῦ ('Jesus Christ'; 025 1962 cpa co^sa), but this could represent the reintroduction of Ἰησοῦ after it had been removed.

4:12 σταθῆτε (lit. you may be set) {B}

Most manuscripts have the aorist active subjunctive στῆτε ('you may stand'; 01² 02 04 06 012 etc.). This is a more common form of the verb than the aorist passive subjunctive σταθῆτε ('you may be set'; 01* 03 81 365 1739 1881), yet in practice there is little difference in meaning. It is unlikely that στῆτε would have been changed into the passive, but perhaps it was considered that the active voice implied more self-reliance than appropriate in the context of redemption. Even though σταθῆτε is limited to six Greek manuscripts, these are important witnesses which may preserve the earliest text. In any case, the poorly-attested and semantically-weak ἦτε ('you may be'; 016 2464 lat^vl-pt sy^hmg) appears to be a misreading of one of the other forms or assimilation to verses such as Phil. 1:10 or James 1:4.

4:13 ἔχει πολὺν πόνον (he has worked hard) {B}

Something about the phrase πολὺν πόνον (lit. 'much work'; 01 02 03 04 025 etc.), whose strong early attestation supports its adoption as the editorial text, has inspired numerous variants. Perhaps the collocation ἔχει πόνον ('he has work') was thought to be an unusual periphrasis: there is no other instance of it in the New Testament. It seems less probable that this observation was amended because of an implied criticism of the Colossians. The majority reading, ζῆλον πολύν ('much zeal'; cf. πολὺν ζῆλον in 06¹ 33) involves a term which is used in this sense at 2 Cor. 7:7. Two other variants replace πόνον with a synonym, πολὺν ἀγῶνα ('much struggle'; 6 1739 1881), possibly inspired by the context (cf. Col. 4:12; also Col. 2:1), and πολὺν κόπον ('much toil'; 06* 012, cf. 1 Thess. 2:9). Whatever the motivation for the alternative readings, some form of idiomatic translation can be offered for πολὺν πόνον.

4:15 Νύμφαν καὶ τὴν κατ' οἶκον αὐτῆς ἐκκλησίαν (Nympha and the church in her house) {C}

The majority of manuscripts accentuate the proper noun as the masculine Νυμφᾶν ('Nymphas'; 06² 0150 365 1175 1739* etc.) and, accordingly, read the masculine pronoun αὐτοῦ ('his') rather than αὐτῆς ('her') later in the verse. Accents are lacking from most majuscules, so the gender of the name has to be determined from the pronoun: those with αὐτοῦ ('his'; 06 012) correspond to the masculine, while αὐτῶν ('their'; 01 02 04 025 etc.) blurs the issue by combining this individual with the others in Laodicea. The editorial text, in which the accentuation and pronoun identify the person as female, is only attested in a few witnesses (03² 0278 6 1739ᶜ 1881 syʰ cpaᵐˢ coˢᵃ): the accentuation was added later in Codex Vaticanus and corrected in 1739, while in some manuscripts the feminine Νύμφαν ('Nympha'; 81 256 263 1573 etc.) is found with the plural pronoun. Given the expectation in later generations that a church leader would be male (cf. Rom. 16:7), the support for the female name and pronoun leads to its adoption in the editorial text, although the extensive support for αὐτῶν means that the plural (adopted in the THGNT) is also worthy of consideration alongside the name Nympha.

Col. 4:18 μεθ' ὑμῶν. (with you.) {A}

As in other epistles (e.g. Eph. 6:24, Phil. 4:23), the majority of manuscripts have 'Amen' at the end of the letter (ἀμήν, 01² 06 025 0150 0278 etc.). However, the strong external evidence for its absence (01* 02 03 04 012 048 etc.) indicates that this is a later development.

The First Letter to the Thessalonians

1:1 εἰρήνη (peace) {A}

At the end of this verse, the majority of manuscripts add ἀπὸ θεοῦ πατρὸς ἡμῶν καὶ κυρίου Ἰησοῦ Χριστοῦ ('from God our Father and the Lord Jesus Christ'; 01 02 016 025 etc.), while a significant number have just ἀπὸ θεοῦ πατρὸς καὶ κυρίου Ἰησοῦ Χριστοῦ ('from God the Father and the Lord Jesus Christ'; 06 0150 256 263 etc.). A longer salutation of this nature is found in nine of the other Pauline epistles, and it is likely that its presence here is secondary. There is no obvious reason for its omission from some important Greek witnesses (03 012 0278 1739 1881) and most early translations if it had originally been present (cf. 2 Thess. 1:1–2). The full attestation is provided in *TuT Thessalonians* (TS1).

1:2 μνείαν (mention) {B}

Most witnesses include the pronoun ὑμῶν ('of you'; 01² 04 06 012 025 etc.) after this noun. It is possible that it was overlooked, but its absence from several early manuscripts (01* 02 03 016 0278 etc.) suggests that the shorter reading is original. Five of the other six instances of μνεία ('mention') in the Pauline Epistles all have a genitive pronoun as object (e.g. 1 Thess. 3:6). The exception is Eph. 1:16, which offers an exact parallel with the present verse: the immediately preceding instance of ὑμῶν may have been intended to do double duty, but the repetition of the pronoun was inserted to provide a formal object. In translation, this is also likely to be necessary. Although the earlier ὑμῶν could be treated as the object, taking περὶ πάντων ('for all things') separately, the other examples as well as the majority text show that the natural place for the complement is after the noun μνεία.

1:4 [τοῦ] θεοῦ (God)

It makes no difference to the meaning or translation whether or not the definite article is present before 'God'. The external evidence in favour of its inclusion is weighty (01 02 04 025 etc.), but so too are the witnesses which exclude it (03 06 012 and the majority of minuscules). The parallel at 2 Thess. 2:13 might be taken to support its original absence.

1:5   [ἐν] ὑμῖν (among you)

The majority of manuscripts include this fifth instance in the verse of ἐν ('in'; 03 06 012 0278 etc.), but it is missing from some significant witnesses (01 02 04 025 048 33 81 1739 1881). There is a slight difference in meaning: ἐν emphasises Paul's presence ('among you'), whereas its absence would result in a broader reference ('to you'). The omission is probably secondary, due to haplography of the last two letters of the preceding word.

1:7   τύπον (example) {B}

Most Greek manuscripts have the plural, τύπους ('examples'; 01 02 04 06² 012 etc.), matching the plural of the preceding pronoun. The singular τύπον ('example'; 03 06*, c 6 33 81 1739 1881 lat$^{vl\text{-}pt}$ sy^h) is the harder reading, with multiple people constituting a single example. It is easy to imagine this being adjusted to the plural in context and its attestation is consistent with being the earliest text (compare Col. 4:12 and 4:15 above).

1:10   ἐκ [τῶν] νεκρῶν (from the dead)

The presence or absence of τῶν before νεκρῶν does not alter the meaning. The definite article is found in the majority of manuscripts (01 03 06 012 etc.), but the overwhelming preference for the phrase ἐκ νεκρῶν ('from the dead') throughout the Pauline Epistles suggests that witnesses with the shorter form ($\mathfrak{P}^{46vid}$ 02 04 018 etc.) transmit the original reading. This could easily have been expanded to match the previous phrase (ἐκ τῶν οὐρανῶν, lit. 'from the heavens').

2:7   νήπιοι (lit. 'infants') {C}

This is a well-known variation unit. The majority of Greek manuscripts (followed by the NRSVue), read ἤπιοι ('gentle'; 01^c 02 04² 06² 025 etc.). The alternative, νήπιοι ('infants'; $\mathfrak{P}^{65}$ 01* 03 04* 06* etc., with several early translations) could have arisen from the duplication of the final ν of the preceding word, just as haplography of an original double ν would result in the majority reading. The full attestation in Greek continuous-text manuscripts is provided in *TuT Thessalonians* (TS2). It is incorrect to claim that Paul only uses νήπιος of his converts (cf. 1 Cor. 13:11, Gal. 4:3, Eph. 4:14), but true that the only other occurrence of ἤπιος in the entire Greek Bible is at 2 Tim. 2:24.[1] However, the following image of the nurse features the only instance of τροφός in the New Testament, so patterns of usage are of limited help in determining the more likely reading. The word 'infant' might have prompted the parallel with the nurse and children, because Paul identifies himself with the nurse, yet νήπιοι could be considered the less appropriate correspondence with the preceding βάρει (lit. 'demanding'). While in other epistles the verb ἐγενήθημεν ('we became') refers to an object rather than a manner of behaviour (1 Cor. 4:9, 4:13; cf. Rom. 9:29, 1 Cor. 10:6, Eph. 3:7), this is not the case throughout 1 Thessalonians (1:5, 2:5, 2:10), which may offer further support for ἤπιοι. Editors who choose ἤπιοι, as in the SBLGNT and THGNT, normally finish a sentence after ἀπόστολοι ('apostles [of Christ]') rather than after ἐν μέσῳ ὑμῶν ('among you').[2]

2:12 καλοῦντος (who calls) {B}

A number of manuscripts and ancient translations have the aorist καλέσαντος ('who has called'; 01 02 2464 lat^(vl-pt, vg) sy co etc.), in contrast to the majority support for the present participle καλοῦντος ('calling'; 03 06 012 015 025 etc.).[3] The difference in aspect is of exegetical interest, as to whether the divine call is continuous or a single event. The external evidence seems too weak to justify the adoption of the aorist here: it may have arisen through assimilation to Gal. 1:6.

2:15 τοὺς προφήτας (the prophets) {B}

The majority of Greek manuscripts include an adjective, τοὺς ἰδίους προφήτας ('their own prophets'; 06¹ 0150 365 2464 etc.; see further *TuT Thessalonians* TS3). This appears to be an emphatic addition, probably under the influence of τῶν ἰδίων συμφυλετῶν ('your own compatriots')

---

[1] Thus Metzger 1994: 561–562.
[2] For more developed discussions of this variant, see Aland & Aland 1989: 284–285, Weima 2000, Sailors 2000 and Wasserman 2025, all of whom adopt νήπιοι.
[3] Despite the claim at Metzger 1994: 562 that the *Textus Receptus* reads καλέσαντος, the Oxford 1873 edition has καλοῦντος.

in the previous verse. There is no obvious reason for its absence had it originally been present, unless there was a very early instance of eyeskip between τούς and ἰδίους: the external support for τοὺς προφήτας ('the prophets'; 01 02 03 06* 012 etc.) is very strong indeed. In translation, it might be appropriate to indicate that the prophets were in a different time-period to Jesus, even though they are the object of the same verb.

2:16 ὀργή (wrath) {A}

A few witnesses read ὀργὴ τοῦ θεοῦ ('wrath of God'; 06 012 lat), a fuller expression which is seen in other epistles (e.g. Rom. 1:18, Eph. 5:6, Col. 3:6). There is compelling attestation for just ὀργή ('wrath'; 01 02 03 025 etc. and the majority of minuscules). The addition of τοῦ θεοῦ seems to be an independent clarification in the bilingual and Latin witnesses traditionally considered to be 'Western'. It may be exegetically helpful in modern translations to specify the source of this 'wrath' (as seen in the NRSV), even when the shorter reading is adopted.

3:2 καὶ συνεργὸν τοῦ θεοῦ (and God's co-worker) {C}

There is very limited attestation of καὶ συνεργὸν τοῦ θεοῦ (lit. 'and co-worker of God'; 06* 33 lat[vl-pt]). Codex Vaticanus just reads καὶ συνεργόν ('and co-worker'; 03), while other important manuscripts read καὶ διάκονον τοῦ θεοῦ ('and minister of God'; 01 02 025 0278 etc.). The majority of minuscules, however, have a combination of both terms: καὶ διάκονον τοῦ θεοῦ καὶ συνεργὸν ἡμῶν ('and minister of God and co-worker of ours'; 06[2] 0150 256 365 etc.). Such a conflation is typical of later tradition and is also seen in διάκονον καὶ συνεργὸν τοῦ θεοῦ ('minister and co-worker of God'; 012 lat[vl-pt]). The full attestation in Greek continuous-text manuscripts is provided in *TuT Thessalonians* (TS4). One of the shorter readings is most likely to be the earliest form. The external evidence is stronger for καὶ διάκονον τοῦ θεοῦ, which is preferred in the THGNT. In contrast, καὶ συνεργὸν τοῦ θεοῦ seems to be a harder reading, and is adopted in the SBLGNT: the differences in the majority text could suggest that the title 'co-worker of God' was perceived as problematic and adjusted through the deletion of τοῦ θεοῦ (lit. 'of God') or the replacement of συνεργόν with the more common διάκονον. Paul's description of himself as a 'co-worker of God' at 1 Cor.

3:9 shows that this title could be original. However, his other uses of συνεργός are normally qualified by a first-person pronoun, and the presence of ἡμῶν ('ours') in the Byzantine tradition appears to be assimilation to this practice. If a reading with συνεργόν is chosen, translators will need to decide on the significance of the following genitive: was Timothy God's partner (as in the NRSVue), or was he a co-worker with other disciples 'for God' (NRSV)?[4]

3:13 τῶν ἁγίων αὐτοῦ [ἀμήν]. (his saints. [Amen.]) {C}

Unusually, the addition of ἀμήν ('Amen') is not attested by the majority of Greek manuscripts, but by a handful of witnesses (01* 02 06* 81 lat^{vl-pt, vg} co^{bo}). It is easy to see how it could have been supplied later in the context of this formulaic statement. At the same time, there are other instances of Amen in the middle of an epistle which are clearly authorial (e.g. Gal. 1:5, Eph. 3:21). The brackets indicate doubt, although the stronger evidence is for the absence of Amen.

4:1 καθὼς καὶ περιπατεῖτε (as, in fact, you are doing) {A}

This entire phrase is missing from the majority of Greek manuscripts (06² 0150 1175 etc.), either through an oversight based on the previous clause (which also begins with καθώς) or an editorial deletion of this aside in order to improve the structure of the sentence. There is strong external evidence for the presence of καθὼς καὶ περιπατεῖτε (lit. 'as you also walk'; 01 02 03 06* 012 etc. and most early translations) and no obvious reason for it to have been inserted here. Some minuscules are not mentioned in the UBS6 apparatus here because they have a longer omission due to eyeskip (6 1573 1739 1881).

4:8 τὸν [καὶ] διδόντα (who [also] gives)

The word καί ('also') is absent from a sufficient number of important witnesses (02 03 06¹ 016 0278 33 365 1739* 2464) to cast doubt on whether it was originally included. On the other hand, it is difficult to find a plausible reason for its addition, whereas its absence makes for an easier reading.

---

[4] A fuller discussion of this variation unit is given at Metzger & Ehrman 2005: 337–339.

4:11 ταῖς [ἰδίαις] χερσίν (with your [own] hands) {C}

The adjective ἰδίαις ('own') is present in the majority of Greek manuscripts, but not in several early sources (01² 02 06* 012 0278 etc.). It could have been omitted through eyeskip after ταῖς, or deleted as unnecessary: it has been suggested that this adjective was a colloquial usage.[5] Equally, the presence of τὰ ἴδια ('your own affairs') earlier in the verse may have resulted in an addition here. The occurrence of ταῖς ἰδίαις χερσίν at 1 Cor. 4:12 and Eph. 4:28 (see above), with no textual variation in the former, offers significant parallels. While assimilation to either of these verses is a possibility, they could also support the longer reading at this point.[6] Even so, the shorter form is preferred in both the SBLGNT and THGNT.

4:13 κοιμωμένων (lit. who fall asleep) {B}

The majority of Greek manuscripts have the perfect passive participle, κεκοιμημένων ('who have fallen asleep'; 06 [012] 365 1881 etc.), rather than the present. The tense of the verb may affect the exegesis: does this situation relate only to those who have already died, or does it also apply to those who die subsequently? Both tenses are found elsewhere in the Pauline Epistles, along with the aorist (e.g. 1 Cor. 11:30, 15:19, 15:20). The two aorist passives (τοὺς κοιμηθέντας) in the following verses, each in conjunction with a future tense, may be taken to support the ongoing situation implied by the present participle: the external evidence also justifies the adoption of κοιμωμένων (lit. 'who fall asleep'; 01 02 03 0278 etc.).

5:3 ὅταν (when) {C}

There is early but limited attestation of just ὅταν ('when'; 01* 02 012 33 lat^vl-pt sy^p Tertullian Irenaeus^lat), and this shortest reading seems to offer the best explanation for the alternatives. Some important manuscripts read ὅταν δέ ('but when'; 01² 03 06 6 1739 etc.), while the majority of Greek witnesses read ὅταν γάρ ('for when'; 025 0278 81 365 etc.). The choice of connective plays a significant part in establishing the logical flow of the text: is the observation 'peace and security' a contrast to 'the

---

[5] Metzger 1994: 538, on Eph. 4:28. Contrast Omanson's suggestion in the present verse that it is a Hebrew idiom (2006: 427).

[6] Thus Wasserman 2025.

day of the Lord', or one of its signs? Either connective could have been introduced on the basis of the other instances of δέ and γάρ in context. The best argument for the omission of an original connective is the oversight of ΔΕ before the following ΛΕ, after which the alternative γάρ may have been supplied to fill the gap.

5:4   κλέπτης (a thief) {A}

There is very little evidence for the plural, κλέπτας ('thieves'; 02 03 co[bo-pt]). The overwhelming attestation of the singular κλέπτης ('a thief'; 01 06 012 025 etc. and the majority of minuscules) corresponds to the description of the 'day of the Lord' as a thief at 1 Thess. 5:2. Although this could have led to assimilation here, it is also the harder reading as it does not correspond exactly with the previous image. The plural κλέπτας was probably introduced under the influence of the preceding ὑμᾶς.

5:15   [καὶ] εἰς ἀλλήλους ([both] to one another)

The external evidence for the initial καί is evenly split, being present in the majority of Greek manuscripts ($\mathfrak{P}^{30}$ 03 etc.) and missing from some important witnesses (01* 02 06 012 6 33 1739 1881 2464). The closest parallel is at 1 Thess. 3:12, where there is no καί before the same five words: assimilation to this could have affected the present reading, but the earlier passage continues with καί used in the same sense ('both'), which might favour its inclusion here too.

5:25   [καὶ] περὶ ἡμῶν ([also] for us) {C}

As in 1 Thess. 5:15, the external evidence for καί ('and', 'also') is evenly split. On this occasion, it is lacking from the majority of manuscripts (01 02 06[1] 012 016[vid] etc.), but included in some early sources ($\mathfrak{P}^{30}$ 03 06* 0278 etc., with several ancient translations). In context, it serves no obvious purpose: the previous instance of προσεύχεσθε ('pray') in 1 Thess. 5:17 seems too distant to connect with this one. The shorter reading is better suited to the sequence of commands in context and is also supported by the parallel at 2 Thess. 3:1, but this might make it a secondary alteration. If it were original, then 'also' could have been added through assimilation to Col. 4:3.

5:27 τοῖς ἀδελφοῖς (to the brothers and sisters) {A}

The majority of Greek manuscripts read τοῖς ἁγίοις ἀδελφοῖς (lit. 'to the holy brothers'; 01² 02 025 0150 etc.). Apart from Heb. 3:1, the collocation 'holy brother' does not appear elsewhere in the New Testament: while ἁγίοις could have been omitted through homoeoarcton, the external evidence for its absence (01* 03 06 012 0278 lat^(vl-pt) co^(sa)) suggests that it was introduced later, perhaps through conflation with the Pauline phrase πᾶσιν τοῖς ἁγίοις ('to all the holy ones'; Eph. 3:18, Phil. 1:1; cf. Eph. 1:15, Phlm 5, Heb. 13:24). The presence of this word in the concluding formula at 1 Thess. 3:13 and the 'holy kiss' of the brothers in the previous verse may also have influenced its insertion. The full attestation for this variation unit is provided in *TuT Thessalonians* (TS5).

5:28 μεθ' ὑμῶν (with you) {A}

As with the other Epistles, the majority of Greek manuscripts conclude with a liturgical Amen (01 02 06¹ 025 etc.), particularly appropriate after the grace formula here. However, if this were original there is no good explanation for its omission from several early and important witnesses (03 06* 012 0278 6 33 1739* 1881 lat^(vl-pt, vg-ms) cpa co^(sa)).

The Second Letter to the Thessalonians[1]

1:2 πατρὸς ἡμῶν καὶ κυρίου (lit. our Father and the Lord) {C}

The word ἡμῶν ('our') is missing from some important manuscripts with just πατρὸς καὶ κυρίου ('the Father and the Lord'; 03 06 025 0111[vid] etc.). Almost all the Pauline Epistles (with the exception of the Pastorals) have ἀπὸ θεοῦ πατρὸς ἡμῶν ('from God our Father') in the initial greeting, although there is variation in the textual tradition at Galatians 1:3 as well as 1 Thess. 1:1 (see above). The shorter reading is therefore more unusual here, not least because ἡμῶν is present in the same context in the previous verse: while this suggests that the absence of this pronoun is original (as in the SBLGNT), it could have been omitted through an oversight. There is strong early support for the majority reading πατρὸς ἡμῶν καὶ κυρίου ('our Father and the Lord'; 01 02 012 016 etc.), but assimilation to the fuller forms seen elsewhere is the expected change and paralleled in other epistles. The different word order supported by some early translations, πατρὸς καὶ κυρίου ἡμῶν ('the Father and our Lord'; cpa co[sa-mss, bo-pt] eth), may provide further support for the shorter reading which was then harmonised to the form seen at Gal. 1:3.[2]

2:2 τοῦ κυρίου (of the Lord) {B}

Most Greek manuscripts have the unusual phrase ἡ ἡμέρα τοῦ Χριστοῦ ('the day of Christ'; 06[2] 1175 etc.).[3] The earliest witnesses read τοῦ κυρίου ('[the day] of the Lord'; 01 02 03 06* 012 etc.), which has led to its adoption as the editorial text. 'The day of the Lord' is the standard formulation in the Epistles (1 Cor. 1:8, 5:5; 2 Cor. 1:14; 1 Thess. 5:2) as well as the Septuagint, but there are parallels for 'the day of Christ' at Phil. 1:10 and 2:16 (cf. Phil. 1:6). The alternation is likely to be due to confusion between the two *nomina sacra* abbreviations (KY and XY).

---

[1] For a fuller textual commentary on 2 Thessalonians, see Edwards 2019: 99–160.

[2] Wasserman 2025 also prefers the shorter reading as original.

[3] Edwards 2019: 121 indicates, however, that the editorial text is found in numerous minuscules.

One minuscule reads τοῦ κυρίου Ἰησοῦ ('[the day] of the Lord Jesus'; 33).

2:3 ἀνομίας (lawless) {B}

Instead of ἀνομίας (lit. 'of lawlessness'; 01 03 0278 6 81 etc.), the majority of Greek manuscripts read ἁμαρτίας ('of sin'; 02 06 012 025 etc.). The latter word is far more common in the Epistles, suggesting that the former term is original and was substituted with a similar noun through inadvertence. The repetition of ἀνομίας in the resumption of the thought at 2 Thess. 2:7 (along with the explanatory γάρ) also favours its adoption here. The full attestation for this variation unit in Greek continuous-text manuscripts is provided in *TuT Thessalonians* (TS6).

2:4 καθίσαι (he takes his seat) {B}

The majority of Greek manuscripts read ὡς θεὸν καθίσαι (lit. 'to sit as God'; 06² 012ᶜ 0150 0278 etc.; see further *TuT Thessalonians* TS7). This appears to be a later clarification: while it is possible that the first two words were overlooked through eyeskip between the two *nomina sacra* (ΘΥ ... ΘΝ), their meaning overlaps with the following clause. There is strong external evidence for the shorter reading καθίσαι ('to sit'; 01 02 03 06* 025 etc.). The text of the bilingual Codex Boernerianus, ἵνα θεὸν καθίσαι ('in order to seat a god', or possibly 'in order to seat God'; [012*] latᵛˡ⁻ᵖᵗ), seems to be a retranslation of the majority reading mediated through Latin, as *ut* can represent both ὡς and ἵνα.

2:8 Ἰησοῦς (Jesus) {C}

The tradition is split between manuscripts which include Ἰησοῦς ('Jesus'; 01 02 06* 012 020ᶜ etc. with most early translations and ancient writers) and those which lack it (03 06² 020* and the majority of minuscules; see further *TuT Thessalonians* TS8). A shorter reading in Byzantine tradition is unusual and it has been suggested that references to the Septuagint in the Pauline Epistles tend to feature κύριος alone.[4] The shorter reading could easily have arisen through the oversight of one of the *nomina sacra* (ΚC ΙC), yet Ἰησοῦς may have been introduced as a gloss. While the phrase ὁ κύριος Ἰησοῦς without a final Χριστός

---

[4] Wasserman 2025, who notes this as a possible allusion to Isaiah 11:4.

but with a definite article is unusual, it is not unprecedented (e.g. 2 Cor. 11:31, Eph. 1:15, 1 Thess. 4:2, 2 Thess. 1:7). This, along with the external attestation, has led to the adoption of the longer reading with hesitation, although it is also preferred in the SBLGNT and THGNT.

2:13   ἀπαρχήν (first fruits) {B}

Most Greek manuscripts read ἀπ' ἀρχῆς ('from the beginning'; 01 06 0150 etc.). However, this phrase is not found elsewhere in the Pauline Epistles: instead, the preferred way of expressing 'from the beginning' is ἀπὸ τῶν αἰώνων (Col. 1:26) or πρὸ τῶν αἰώνων (1 Cor. 2:7). Ἀπαρχήν ('first fruits') occurs six times in Romans and 1 Corinthians: at Rom. 16:5 (and Rev. 14:4), ἀπ' ἀρχῆς appears as a variant in an early papyrus, indicating that the term ἀπαρχήν was problematic—in contrast to the regular attestation of ἀπ' ἀρχῆς in the Gospels and Catholic Epistles. The witnesses with ἀπαρχήν ('first fruits'; 03 012 025 0278 etc.) therefore appear to provide the earliest reading at this point.[5]

2:14   [καὶ] ἐκάλεσεν (he [also] called)

A few important Greek witnesses include καί ('also'; 01 012 025 0278 81 365 2464), presenting this as a supplement to the previous phrase. This intensifier is missing from the majority of manuscripts, including some early texts (02[vid] 03 06 33 1175 1739 1881 etc.) and not adopted in the SBLGNT or THGNT. Although a decision is difficult, there are parallels for the presence of καί before ἐκάλεσεν ('he called', Romans 8:30 and 9:24) and after εἰς ὅ ('for this purpose', Col. 1:29, 2 Thess. 1:11) which may have resulted in its introduction here.[6]

3:6   παρελάβοσαν (they received) {B}

The reading adopted in the editorial text, παρελάβοσαν ('they received'; 01* 02 0278 33 Basil[mss], cf. ἐλάβοσαν in 06*) is an alternative form of παρέλαβον ('they received'; 01[2] 06[1] 025 0150 and almost all minuscules). The same termination is attested frequently in the Septuagint. While the standard form would be an expected correction, the

---

[5] For extensive discussions of this variant, see King 2017: 30–32 and Edwards 2019: 136–139.

[6] In contrast, Fee 2009: 298 and Wasserman 2025 prefer the longer text, arguing that the insertion of καί is the harder reading.

third-person plural verb is still unusual in context and has to be understood as reflecting the implied plural of the antecedent in ἀπὸ παντὸς ἀδελφοῦ (lit. 'from every brother'). The grammatically correct singular verb παρέλαβεν ('he received'; 1962) is very poorly attested in surviving manuscripts but appears in the *Textus Receptus*. In contrast, the vocative ἀδελφοί ('brothers and sisters') and preceding second-person plural verbs are responsible for the variant παρελάβετε ('you received'; 03 012 2464 etc.). Despite being adopted by some modern translations, if this were original the alternative forms would be difficult to explain.

3:18   πάντων ὑμῶν (all of you) {B}

As in previous letters, the vast majority of Greek manuscripts include a final 'Amen' (01[2] 02 06 012 etc.). This is lacking from several early and important witnesses (01* 03 0278 6 33 1739 1881* 2464 lat[vl-pt, vg-mss] co[sa, bo-mss] Athanasius). As there is no obvious reason for its exclusion, the shorter form has been preferred in the editorial text.

The Letter to the Hebrews

1:3 τῆς δυνάμεως αὐτοῦ, καθαρισμόν (lit. of his power, purification) {B}

A few manuscripts have τῆς δυνάμεως, δι' ἑαυτοῦ καθαρισμόν ('of power, purification through himself'; [𝔓⁴⁶] 0243 6 1739 1881*), whereas there is extensive early support for τῆς δυνάμεως αὐτοῦ, καθαρισμόν ('of his power, purification'; 01 02 03 06¹ 015* etc.). The majority of witnesses have what appears to be a conflation of the two forms, τῆς δυνάμεως αὐτοῦ, δι' ἑαυτοῦ καθαρισμόν ('of his power, purification through himself'; 06*, ² 015ᶜ 0278 etc.). While it is not impossible that the shorter reading arose through homoeoteleuton, the external evidence suggests that it is earlier. The addition of διά ('through') along with the reflexive (AYTOY in majuscules could also be read as αὐτοῦ) may have been prompted by the middle voice in the following participle ποιησάμενος ('when he had made'). The full attestation for this variation unit in Greek continuous-text manuscripts is provided in *TuT Hebrews* (TS1).

1:8 τῆς βασιλείας σου (of your kingdom) {B}

The three oldest surviving Greek manuscripts read αὐτοῦ ('of his [kingdom]'; 𝔓⁴⁶ 01 03). Apart from two witnesses with no pronoun here (1573 cpaᵐˢ), all the other evidence is for σου ('of your [kingdom]'; 02 06 025 0150 etc.) which matches the original source of this quotation, Psalm 45:7 [44:7 LXX]. Although the reading which differs from this might be considered more compelling, it is difficult to construe αὐτοῦ in the light of the previous clause where all manuscripts have σου: this would involve either taking αὐτοῦ as a pronoun for ὁ θρόνος σου ('your throne') or reinterpreting ὁ θεός as a nominative rather than a vocative ('God is your throne …'). In any case the shift in person is very unexpected. For these reasons, it seems that αὐτοῦ is an error of inattention inspired by the numerous other instances of the phrase ἡ βασιλεία αὐτοῦ ('his kingdom'; e.g. Matt. 12:26, 13.41, 16:28 etc.). An alternative explanation could be that καί ('and') in this verse is an authorial conjunction intended to combine two separate citations (one with σου and the other with αὐτοῦ). However, as they are continuous in the context of the original Psalm, this is unlikely.

1:12   ὡς ἱμάτιον καί (and like clothing) {B}

The majority of witnesses read only καί ('and'; 06¹ 025 0150 0243 0278 etc.), and the other two words are also absent from the source of this quotation, Psalm 102:26 [101:27 LXX]. Nevertheless, early and important manuscripts have ὡς ἱμάτιον καί ('and like clothing'; 𝔓⁴⁶ 01 02 03 06* 1739 etc.), suggesting that this was an insertion by the author which was later removed in order to make the quotation match the Septuagint.¹ The full attestation in Greek continuous-text manuscripts is provided in *TuT Hebrews* (TS3). These words could be taken with the previous or the following verb; the punctuation in UBS6 adopts the latter, treating the similes as three clauses with identical structure.

2:7   ἐστεφάνωσας αὐτόν (you have crowned them) {B}

A large number of manuscripts, with most early translations and the *Textus Receptus*, include an additional phrase at the end of this verse: καὶ κατέστησας αὐτὸν ἐπὶ τὰ ἔργα τῶν χειρῶν σου ('and you have set them over the works of your hands'; 01 02 04 06* 025 etc.). This is present in the source, Psalm 8:6 (8:7 LXX), yet is missing from the majority of Greek manuscripts (𝔓⁴⁶ 03 06² 1175 etc.; see *TuT Hebrews* TS4). As at Heb. 1:12, it seems that a later editor has conformed the quotation to the Septuagint.

2:9   χάριτι θεοῦ (by the grace of God) {A}

The external evidence for the editorial text is overwhelming: almost all witnesses read χάριτι θεοῦ ('by the grace of God'; 𝔓⁴⁶ 01 02 03 04 06 etc.). Just two manuscripts read χωρὶς θεοῦ ('apart from God'; 0243 1739), a reading which was known to some early Christian writers (Origen, Jerome). This famous alternative may be a scribal error (ΧΩΡΙC for ΧΑΡΙΤΙ), or have originated as a marginal gloss noting that παντός ('everyone') two words later does not include God (cf. 1 Cor. 15:27): a

---

¹ On this practice in the textual tradition of Hebrews more generally, see Cadwallader 1992.

copyist might have mistaken such an annotation reading χωρὶς θεοῦ ('apart from God') as a correction and accordingly replaced the original text.[2]

3:6   ἐάν[περ] (if)

The majority of Greek manuscripts have the longer form, ἐάνπερ ('if only'; 𝔓⁴⁶ 01² 02 04 06² 0278 etc.). In the light of strong support for the shorter form, ἐάν ('if'; 𝔓¹³ 01¹ 03 06* 025 0243 33 1739 1881 lat), the intensifying suffix has been enclosed in brackets. It is worth noting that, in the parallel at Heb. 3:14, ἐάνπερ is uncontested, which may have led to its introduction here (see the next variation unit). The effect on translation is minimal.

3:6   κατάσχωμεν (we hold firm) {B}

Before the verb κατάσχωμεν ('we hold'), most Greek witnesses include the words μέχρι τέλους βεβαίαν ('firm to the end'; 01 02 04 06 025 etc.). They are absent from four early witnesses (𝔓¹³ 𝔓⁴⁶ 03 co^sa), yet there is nothing in context which would prompt their omission unless a whole line of an exemplar was overlooked. What is more, the feminine βεβαίαν is unexpected because this adjective should refer to the closer noun, τὸ καύχημα, which is neuter. It seems that the whole phrase has been introduced here through assimilation to μέχρι τέλους βεβαίαν κατάσχωμεν at Heb. 3:14, where the preceding noun is feminine. The full attestation in Greek continuous-text manuscripts is provided in *TuT Hebrews* TS5).

3:9   οὗ ἐπείρασαν … ἐν δοκιμασίᾳ (where they put … to the test) {C}

This long quotation from the Psalter differs from the Septuagint in a number of small ways. In this verse, corresponding to Psalm 95:9 [94:9 LXX], the majority of Greek manuscripts include με after ἐπείρασαν ('they tested me'; 01² 06² 025 0243 0278 etc.), even though this is not present in the source. Although there is strong evidence for the grammatically more difficult reading without a pronoun (𝔓¹³ 𝔓⁴⁶ 01* 02 03

---

[2] Among numerous discussions of this variant, see Parker 2008: 277–279 and—in support of χωρίς—Elliott 1972 and Ehrman 2011: 171–176.

04 06* 33 co^(sa)), its conformity to the Septuagint raises a question as to whether or not it is original. The situation is reversed in the next part of the phrase, where the majority reading ἐδοκίμασάν με ('they proved me'; 01² 06² 0278 etc.) is closer to the Septuagint, which just has ἐδοκίμασαν. The alternative, ἐν δοκιμασίᾳ ('in proving'; 𝔓¹³ 𝔓⁴⁶ 01* 02 03 etc.), differs from the Psalm text yet is attested by most of the same witnesses which agreed with the Septuagint in the first part of the phrase. For this reason, their text has been adopted with some hesitation. Much of the Latin tradition supports οὗ ἐπείρασάν με οἱ πατέρες ὑμῶν ἐδοκίμασαν ('where your fathers tempted me, they proved [and saw]'; lat^(vl-pt, vg)), which probably derives from overlooking the final pronoun in the majority text.

4:2   συγκεκερασμένους (united) {B}

The most widely attested form of this participle is συγκεκερασμένους, also spelt συγκεκραμένους (lit. 'mixed', 'blended with'; 𝔓¹³ᵛⁱᵈ 𝔓⁴⁶ 02 03 04 06 etc.), relating back to ἐκείνους ('them'). The application of this description to a group of people is unexpected, leading to two alternatives which relate it to other words in the sentence: the singular συγκεκερασμένος ('mixed'; 01 *TR* lat^(vl-pt) syᵖ co^(sa-mss) Cyril^(pt)) is to be taken with λόγος ('message'), while συγκεκραμένης (lat^(vg-mss) Chrysostom) agrees with ἀκοῆς (lit. 'of hearing'). As the majority reading is the most difficult, it has been adopted as the editorial text. There is an exegetical problem if ἐκείνους is taken to refer to 'all those who left Egypt' in Heb. 3:16, implying that none of them was faithful.³ However, if it is applied to the 'sinful and disobedient' of Heb. 3:17–18, it allows that 'those who listened' were an exception among the Israelites.

5:12   τίνα (lit. which) {D}

The earliest manuscripts have no accents (𝔓⁴⁶ 01 02 03* 04 06* 025), so provide no guide as to whether this word is an interrogative or an indefinite pronoun.⁴ Most Greek manuscripts have the interrogative τίνα (03² 06² 0150 0278 etc.), which should be taken with the following στοιχεῖα and translated 'which [are the basic elements]'. This also

---

³ See further Omanson 2006: 456.
⁴ This includes the minuscule GA 33, in which accents are sporadic.

represents the understanding of the term in all early translations. Accentuation marking this as an indefinite pronoun, τινά, is only seen in two witnesses in the apparatus (81 co^(sa-ms)): GA 81 punctuates after this word, indicating that it should be understood as '[to teach you again] some things, (namely) [what are the basic elements]'.[5] Attempts to translate it as 'someone' (accusative singular) involve a tortuous interpretation of the grammar: as an accusative, τινά cannot be the object of χρείαν ἔχετε, which takes a genitive, so it would have to be understood as part of an 'articular accusative-and-infinitive' phrase ('you have need of the-someone-teaching-you the elements') rather than the simpler articular infinitive. This interpretation may have been prompted by the active voice of διδάσκειν ('[you have need] of teaching you') rather than a passive ('[you have need] of you being taught'), but the former is not impossible even if it is less elegant. The accentuation τίνα has been adopted in this edition and the THGNT, on the grounds that the alternative is too hard a reading despite its adoption in UBS5 and SBLGNT and even going back to Westcott and Hort. The word is missing from three important minuscules (6 1738 1881), either through oversight or to improve the flow of the sentence.

5:12 [καὶ] οὐ ([and] not)

Although the majority of manuscripts read καί ('and'; 01² 02 03* 06 025 0278 etc.), this connective is absent from some important witnesses (𝔓⁴⁶ 01* 03² 04 33 81 81 1739 lat Origen Didymus). Both readings make sense in context, but the presence of καί offers a clearer construction by dividing the two complements and is therefore probably secondary: the shorter reading is preferred in the SBLGNT and THGNT.

6:3 ποιήσομεν (we will do) {B}

Greek manuscripts are split between the future indicative ποιήσομεν ('we will do'; 𝔓⁴⁶ 01 03 016 018 etc.) and the aorist subjunctive ποιήσωμεν ('let us do'; 02 04 06 025 0150 etc.). Vowel isochrony in later Greek would have made it very difficult to distinguish between the two, and there are numerous examples of similar variants (e.g. Rom. 5:1).

---

[5] The same accentuation and punctuation are seen in 044 (not included in the UBS6 apparatus).

While the Byzantine tradition is divided, the *Textus Receptus* has the future indicative, which also represents the understanding in the earliest translations. This is grammatically preferable and it is significant that all other conditional clauses in Hebrews are preceded by an indicative (e.g. Heb. 3:6, 3:14, 13:23). The subjunctive may have been assimilation to φερώμεθα ('let us go on') in the previous sentence.

6:18 [τὸν] θεόν (God)

External evidence is split between some important manuscripts which include the definite article τόν ('the'; 𝔓⁴⁶ 01* 02 04 025 0278 33 1739 1881) and the majority of witnesses which lack it (01² 03 06 81 365 etc.). The presence of the article is supported by the similar construction at Heb. 6:4, while its absence is matched by the close parallel at Heb. 10:4. Translation is unaffected.

7:4 [καί] (even)

This word is present in the longer reference to Gen. 14:20 at Heb. 7:2 but is missing here from some important Greek manuscripts (𝔓⁴⁶ 03 06* 6 1739 1881) as well as early versions. This suggests that καί may have been introduced in this verse through assimilation to the earlier quotation, where it functions as a connective ('and'). It is also possible, however, that it was removed from this second, shorter reference because in this context it has to be taken as a concessive ('even'), which an editor may not have felt was appropriate. On differences between quotations of the same text in this epistle, see the comment below on Heb. 7:21.

7:17 μαρτυρεῖται (it is attested of him) {B}

The majority of witnesses have an active verb, μαρτυρεῖ ('he/it attests'; 04 06² 1175 etc.). It is not clear whether the subject of this verb is the 'other priest' of the preceding verses (who might not be expected to address himself in the second person) or whether it is used impersonally of the scriptures. The use of the passive μαρτυρεῖται ('it/he is attested'; 𝔓⁴⁶ 01 02 03 06* etc.) avoids this change of subject and has been chosen as the earliest form based on its strong external support. It is surprising that what seems to be a more difficult reading is found in later tradition: it may have arisen through accidental omission of the letters ΤΑΙ (with similarities to the following ΓΑΡ), or it is possible that the passive construction preceding the direct quotation was felt to be too complicated.

7:21 εἰς τὸν αἰῶνα (forever) {B}

At the end of this quotation of Psalm 110:4 [109:4 LXX], most witnesses include the phrase κατὰ τὴν τάξιν Μελχισέδεκ ('according to the order of Melchizedek'; 01² 02 06 025 etc.), as is seen in the same quotation at Heb. 7:17. Here, however, the phrase is missing from some important witnesses which just have εἰς τὸν αἰῶνα ('for ever'; 𝔓⁴⁶ 03 04 0150 0278 etc.; see also *TuT Hebrews* TS11) while the first hand of Codex Sinaiticus lacks both phrases. It is not clear whether an original shorter quotation was later supplemented with the phrase from the earlier verse, or whether the extra text was omitted by eyeskip from the initial κατά to the same word at the beginning of the following verse. It may be observed that there are several instances of Septuagintal quotations being repeated in this epistle with slight textual differences or abbreviations (e.g. Heb. 7:2 and 7:4, 10:5–7 and 10:8–9, 8:10–12 and 10:16–17, all discussed in this commentary).[6]

7:22 [καί] (also)

This connective is missing from the vast majority of manuscripts and is only present in four Greek witnesses (01* 03 04* 33). Given that the tendency would be to omit a short word, its attestation in several early witnesses is striking. It is possible that 'also' was seen as superfluous in context and therefore deleted.

8:4 ὄντων τῶν προσφερόντων (since there are those who offer) {B}

The subject of the genitive absolute ὄντων τῶν προσφερόντων ('since there are those who offer'; 𝔓⁴⁶ 01 02 03 06* 025 etc.) has to be understood from the word ἱερεύς ('priest') which immediately precedes it. The majority of manuscripts make this explicit, by reading ὄντων τῶν ἱερέων τῶν προσφερόντων ('since there are priests who offer'; 06² 0278 1175 etc.). While it is possible that the plural noun was overlooked between the two instances of τῶν, the external evidence suggests that the

---

[6] See also Zuntz 1953: 163–164 and 171–175.

shorter reading was earlier. The full attestation in Greek continuous-text manuscripts is provided in *TuT Hebrews* (TS12).

8:8 αὐτούς (with them) {C}

The accusative αὐτούς ('them'; 01* 02 06* 016 etc.) has to be construed with the preceding participle ('finding fault with them'). The majority reading, the dative αὐτοῖς ('to them'; 𝔓⁴⁶ 01² 03 06² 0278 etc.) could be understood in the same way or with the following verb ('finding fault, he says to them'): μέμφομαι can take a dative or accusative of person, or be used as an absolute. This ambiguity could make αὐτοῖς the harder reading, although the idea of a fault in the first covenant has been already introduced in the previous verse so this is not in itself contentious. The adoption of the accusative in UBS4 (cf. the SBLGNT) was influenced by the correction to the dative in two majuscules, but this could simply be an adjustment to the Byzantine reading.[7] If the dative is adopted as in the THGNT, translators will have to choose how to interpret it.

8:11 πολίτην (each other) {A}

In this quotation of Jeremiah 31:34 [38:34 LXX], there is strong attestation of the Septuagintal word πολίτην (lit. 'fellow citizen'; 𝔓⁴⁶ 01 02 03 06 etc. and the majority of minuscules). In some witnesses, however, this is replaced by the simpler expression πλησίον ('neighbour'; 025 81 365 2464 lat^(vl-pt, vg) sy^(hmg) eth), which is also the form found in the *Textus Receptus*.

8:12 ἁμαρτιῶν αὐτῶν (their sins) {B}

This verse continues the quotation of Jeremiah 31:34 [38:34 LXX]. The reading ἁμαρτιῶν αὐτῶν ('their sins'; 𝔓⁴⁶ 01* 03 81 1739 1881 lat^(vl-pt, vg) sy^p co) matches the text of the Septuagint. However, the majority of Greek witnesses have a longer form which is also present at Heb. 10:17, ἁμαρτιῶν αὐτῶν καὶ τῶν ἀνομιῶν αὐτῶν ('their sins and their lawless deeds'; 01² 02 06 025 0285^vid etc.; for the full attestation see *TuT Hebrews* TS13). A few witnesses just read ἀνομιῶν αὐτῶν ('their lawless deeds'; 0278 33 Cyril), which is likely to be due to eyeskip. Although it is pos-

---

[7] Metzger 1994: 597; see further Wolmarans 1984, who argues in favour of taking the dative with λέγει.

sible that a jump from αὐτῶν to αὐτῶν was responsible for the other shorter reading, the external evidence suggests that the Septuagintal text was the original form which was then expanded on the model of Heb. 10:17.[8] See also the comment on Heb. 7:21 above.

9:1 [καί] (lit. even)

This conjunction is absent from some important witnesses ($\mathfrak{P}^{46}$ 03 6 1739 1881 syᵖ co). If it is included, as in most Greek manuscripts, it could be translated as 'also' or 'even', each with a slightly different nuance. Alternatively, it is possible that it was deleted by a later editor who read it as 'also' but considered that these attributes were missing from the second covenant; it may even simply have been overlooked following the preceding conjunction.

9:11 γενομένων (that have come) {B}

The majority of witnesses read μελλόντων ('[the good things] to come'; 01 02 06² 016ᵛⁱᵈ 025 etc.). There are only seven Greek continuous-text manuscripts with γενομένων ('that have come'; $\mathfrak{P}^{46}$ $\mathfrak{P}^{130}$ 03 06* 1611 1739 2005; see *TuT Hebrews* TS15). This is also supported by several early translations and is probably the harder reading: μελλόντων is likely to be an anticipation of the same phrase at Heb. 10:1. However, γενομένων could have been introduced under the influence of the preceding participle παραγενόμενος ('having come').

9:14 αἰωνίου (eternal) {A}

There is very strong attestation of the editorial text, which is the reading of the majority of manuscripts. The phrase 'eternal Spirit' (πνεύματος αἰωνίου, $\mathfrak{P}^{17\text{vid}}$ $\mathfrak{P}^{46}$ 01* 02 03 06² etc.) only occurs here in the New Testament and it is unsurprising to find that it was replaced with πνεύματος ἁγίου ('Holy Spirit'; 01² 06* 025 81 365 etc.).

9:14 ἡμῶν (our) {C}

Through itacism, ἡμῶν and ὑμῶν came to be pronounced identically and were often confused. Most Greek sources here read ὑμῶν ('your'; 01 06² 0150 0278 etc.), which fits the context just as well as ἡμῶν ('our';

---

[8] Thus also SBLGNT, THGNT and Zuntz 1953: 172.

02 06* 018 025 365 1739* and several early translations). The practice of the writer of Hebrews, however, appears to be to restrict the second person to imperatives and other direct forms of address, hence the preference for ἡμῶν here as an inclusive first person which identifies the author with the audience. This is also seen in the SBLGNT, while the THGNT prefers the second person on the grounds of its much stronger attestation (compare the division of witnesses in the previous variation unit too). Parallels are found for both phrases in another epistle (2 Cor. 1:12, 5:12). See also Heb. 13:21 below.

9:19   μόσχων [καὶ τῶν τράγων] (of calves and goats)

There is strong support for the shortest reading, μόσχων ('of calves'; 𝔓⁴⁶ 01² 0278 1739 1881 etc.), which would also explain the variety in the sequence of the alternatives. The majority of manuscripts have μόσχων καὶ τράγων ('of calves and goats'; 025 33 etc.), while others read μόσχων καὶ τῶν τράγων ('of calves and of the goats'; 01* 02 04 81 2464) or τράγων καὶ τῶν μόσχων ('of goats and the calves'; 06 365). The longer forms may have been inspired by τράγων καὶ μόσχων ('of goats and calves') a few verses earlier at Heb. 9:12. However, the shortest reading could have arisen from homoeoteleuton or as an editorial adjustment to bring this reference to Exod. 24:5 in line with the Septuagint, where only calves' blood is mentioned. It is therefore difficult to decide between this and μόσχων καὶ τῶν τράγων, which both have good early support. The full attestation in Greek continuous-text manuscripts is given in *TuT Hebrews* (TS16).

9:26   [τῆς] ἁμαρτίας (sin)

The definite article is lacking from the majority of witnesses (𝔓⁴⁶ 04 06 0278 etc.), but present in some early and important manuscripts (01 02 016 025 33 81 365). The other instance in Hebrews of ἀθέτησις ('removal', Heb. 7:18; see also Heb. 10:28) is not followed by the article, which may favour its absence here too. Either way, translation is unaffected.

10:9   τοῦ ποιῆσαι (to do) {B}

This quotation of Psalm 40:9 [39:9 LXX] follows a longer extract from the same psalm at Heb. 10:5–7. In the longer text, after the verb ποιῆσαι ('do'), a vocative address is included which also appears in the present verse in the majority of manuscripts, ὁ θεός ('O God'; 01² 0278^vid 81 365 1739 etc., see further *TuT Hebrews* TS17). Most early sources read the shorter text with just τοῦ ποιῆσαι ('to do'; 𝔓⁴⁶ 01* 02 04 06 etc.). This suggests that the original reading was expanded either on the basis of Heb. 10:7 or the text of the Septuagint. For other examples of inconsistency between quotations in this epistle, see the comment above on Heb. 7:21.

10:34   τοῖς δεσμίοις (those who were in prison) {B}

The external evidence for τοῖς δεσμίοις ('prisoners', lit. 'the chained'; 02 06* 015 0150 etc.) is strengthened by its appearance in most early translations. The alternative τοῖς δεσμοῖς ('the chains'; 𝔓⁴⁶ 256 Origen^mss) is attested as early as Papyrus 46. This continues to make sense in context if 'chains' is understood to mean 'prisoners' through metonymy. The reading of the majority of Greek manuscripts, τοῖς δεσμοῖς μου ('my chains'; 01 06² 025 263 etc.; see *TuT Hebrews* TS20) is clearly a secondary development. This is inspired by the same phrase which occurs four times in Phil. 1:7–17; the genitive pronoun μου does not appear in Hebrews outside quotations from the Septuagint and the first person does not suit the context. Some Old Latin manuscripts have a third-person pronoun equivalent to τοῖς δεσμοῖς αὐτῶν ('their chains'), referring back to the previous verse. Despite the difficulties of interpreting the readings with δεσμοῖς ('chains'), understanding these as stemming from the simple omission of an *iota* from δεσμίοις both accounts for this word here and matches its use at Heb. 13:3.

10:38   δίκαιός μου ἐκ πίστεως (my righteous one … by faith) {B}

The majority of Greek manuscripts read δίκαιος ἐκ πίστεως ('the righteous one [will live] by faith'; 𝔓¹³ 06² 015^c 016 025 etc.). This corresponds to the form of text quoted at Rom. 1:17 and Gal. 3:11, but differs from the Septuagint of Hab. 2:4. The reading δίκαιος ἐκ πίστεώς μου ('the righteous one [will live] by my faith'; 06* lat^vl-pt sy Eusebius^pt) matches the best Septuagint witnesses, while δίκαιός μου ἐκ πίστεως ('my righteous one [will live] by faith'; 𝔓⁴⁶ 01 02 015* 33 1739 lat^vl-pt, vg co^sa, bo-ms Clement) is found in some Septuagint manuscripts. On the basis of its deviation from the other instances of this quotation combined with strong early attestation, this has been adopted as the editorial text: the other readings appear to be corrections towards the forms attested elsewhere. Although in the New Testament context 'my righteous one' could be identified with Christ, in the original quotation this refers to God's people and it may be appropriate to make that clear in translation.

11:11 Σάρρα στεῖρα (Sarah ... was barren) {D}

The phrase δύναμιν εἰς καταβολὴν σπέρματος ἔλαβεν ('received power of procreation') is normally used in Greek with a male subject. Notwithstanding this, the text of the majority of manuscripts unambiguously presents Σάρρα ('Sarah'; 𝔓¹³ᵛⁱᵈ 01 02 06² 33 etc.) as the subject of the verb ἔλαβεν ('received'). The reading Σάρρα στεῖρα ('Sarah [herself] was barren'; 𝔓⁴⁶ 06*) could also be taken in this way, but it has been suggested that this is a form of absolute clause corresponding to a Hebrew circumstantial clause, acting as a concessive while Abraham, the subject of Heb. 11:8–10 and also the logical subject of ἡγήσατο ('he considered') in the following clause, is also taken as the subject of ἔλαβεν.[9] Minor variations which may have developed from this reading are seen in Σάρρα ἡ στεῖρα ('Sarah the barren woman'; 06¹ [150] 6 81 1739 etc.) and Σάρρα στεῖρα οὖσα ('Sarah being barren'; 025 256 263 365 etc.). Each of these may be taken as the subject of ἔλαβεν, though the form with the participle οὖσα could hint at an absolute clause. Nevertheless, the perplexities of interpretation remain, not least because Abraham is the subject of the other verbs in the immediate context as well as the masculine forms in Heb. 11:12. It has been suggested that the entire observation about Sarah was a marginal gloss, later incorporated into the text, or that the words CAPPA CTEIPA in majuscule script (along with the preceding AYTH) could be interpreted as a dative of accompaniment: the latter is adopted in the SBLGNT, which reads Σάρρᾳ ('with/through/in Sarah'; compare 'with Sarah's involvement' in the NRSVue).[10] The THGNT prefers Σάρρα in the nominative, matching the majority reading. On this analysis, στεῖρα is a gloss, perhaps inspired by its visual similarity to Σάρρα. Conversely, the text adopted in UBS6 implies that at some point στεῖρα was omitted through eyeskip

---

[9] Metzger 1994: 602.
[10] See further Metzger 1994: 602.

between the two visually similar words.[11] Translators will need to decide on the extent to which Greek usage is followed in δύναμιν … ἔλαβεν and establish the subject accordingly: a footnote may be helpful to explain the problems.

11:37 ἐπρίσθησαν (they were sawn in two) {C}

Most witnesses read ἐπρίσθησαν ἐπειράσθησαν ('they were sawn in two, they were tempted'; 𝔓[13vid] 02 06[1] 6 356 etc.). The latter term is unexpected in a list of deaths and torments. One possibility is that this is a conflation of two readings: ἐπρίσθησαν by itself ('they were sawn in two'; 𝔓[46] sy[p] [co[sa]] eth Origen[pt] Eusebius) and a misreading of this as the more common word ἐπειράσθησαν ('they were tempted'; lat[vg-mss] Clement), which were erroneously combined. This would also explain manuscripts with the word order ἐπειράσθησαν ἐπρίσθησαν ('they were tempted, they were sawn in two'; 01 025 048 [0150] 33 81). Alternatively, the similarity of these two terms could easily result in the omission of one by parablepsis: the very slim attestation of the single words favours this explanation.[12] A further suggestion is that ἐπειράσθησαν is an early corruption of another type of death, such as ἐπρήσθησαν ('they were burned').[13] This reading is found in a few manuscripts, apparently as an itacistic form of ἐπρίσθησαν (see further *TuT Hebrews* TS24). It may also be noted that the first hand of Codex Claromontanus wrote ἐπιράσθησαν ἐπιράσθησαν (lit. 'they were tempted, they were tempted'; 06*), demonstrating the potential for confusion. The better attested short reading ἐπρίσθησαν has been adopted here with considerable hesitation and also appears in the SBLGNT; the THGNT agrees with the majority.

12:9 [δέ] (lit. on the other hand)

A few important manuscripts include δέ ('on the other hand'; 𝔓[13] 𝔓[46] 01[2] 06* 1739 1881). This correlative to the initial μέν is expected by

---

[11] This longer text also appears to be the preferred text in Elliott 2017:84, although it seems that στεῖρα has been accidentally omitted in his conclusion. The longer text is also preferred by Black 1976: 83–89, who suggests that it is a Semitism.

[12] Thus Malik 2022.

[13] See further the list at Metzger 1994: 603–604 and the *Amsterdam Database* (Krans, Lietaert Peerbolte et al. 2016).

Greek grammar, as is seen in the same construction in the next verse. It could be that the rather unusual position of δέ within the phrase πολὺ μᾶλλον led to its removal (see also Phil. 1:23 above). Equally, δέ may originally have been absent when the author decided in the middle of the construction to switch to a rhetorical question, but was later added by an editor concerned for grammatical consistency. Either way, translation is unaffected.

12:18   ψηλαφωμένῳ (something that can be touched) {B}

Heb. 12:18–20 refers to Exod. 19–20 (cf. Deut. 4:11–12), where in Exod. 19:12 the Israelites are forbidden to touch the mountain. This is made explicit in the majority of Greek manuscripts, which read ψηλαφωμένῳ ὄρει ('a mountain that can be touched'; 06 025 0150 6 256 etc.); some minuscules have the sequence ὄρει ψηλαφωμένῳ (69 sy^h Chrysostom; see further *TuT Hebrews* TS27). However, there is early support for just ψηλαφωμένῳ ('something that can be touched'; 𝔓⁴⁶ 01 02 04 048 33 81 1175 lat sy^p co eth [Origen^(lat-pt)]) which, because it is also the least clear form, has led to its being adopted in the editorial text. In some languages, translators may need to include the noun 'mountain' from the original context regardless of the reading which is followed.

12:27   [τὴν] ... μετάθεσιν (the removal)

The definite article is missing from a few significant witnesses (𝔓⁴⁶ 06* 0243 1739). It is found in the majority of manuscripts immediately before μετάθεσιν ('the removal'; 06² 81 365 etc.), while others have it after δηλοῖ ('indicates'; 01*,[2] 02 04 0285 etc.). This sort of variation suggests that it may not originally have been present or could have been accidentally omitted and reintroduced in a different place. In the absence of τήν, an indefinite article may be used in translation ('a removal'). The full attestation in Greek continuous-text manuscripts is provided in *TuT Hebrews* (TS30).[14]

13:15   [οὖν] (then)

Most manuscripts include the connective οὖν ('then'; 01² 02 04 06¹ 0243 0285 etc.), yet it is absent from some early witnesses (𝔓⁴⁶ 01* 06* 025

---

[14] Note, however, that *Text und Textwert* is inaccurate for 020 and 323.

sy^p). It is possible that it was omitted through eyeskip following the last two letters of the preceding αὐτοῦ, or added into a phrase with the hortatory subjunctive as seen elsewhere in Hebrews (cf. Heb. 4:1, 4;11, 4:16). As this verse continues the exhortation of Heb. 13:13, there is minimal effect on translation.

13:21   παντὶ ἀγαθῷ (everything good) {B}

The evidence for παντὶ ἀγαθῷ ('everything good'; [𝔓⁴⁶] 01 06* lat co^bo) is limited but early. The majority of manuscripts read παντὶ ἔργῳ ἀγαθῷ ('every good deed'; 04 06² 025 0243 0285 etc.), making the phrase clearer through the addition of a noun. The shorter reading cannot be derived from the longer through homoeoteleuton, suggesting that the expansion is secondary. It may have been inspired by the same phrase in Col. 1:10 or 1 Tim. 5:10. A few manuscripts have παντὶ ἔργῳ καὶ λόγῳ ἀγαθῷ ('every deed and good word'; 02; see also the minuscules listed in *TuT Hebrews* TS32), apparently introduced through the influence of 2 Thess. 2:17 and demonstrating the possibilities for harmonisation between epistles.

13:21   ἐν ἡμῖν (among us) {B}

Byzantine tradition is split between ἡμῖν ('us'; 𝔓⁴⁶ 01 02 06 018 etc.) and ὑμῖν ('you'; 04 025 0150 6 etc.), with the latter appearing in the *Textus Receptus*. These two pronouns were frequently confused due to the sound change of itacism (cf. Heb. 9:14). With the second-person ὑμᾶς ('you') at the beginning of this verse and in Heb. 13:22, the first person may be considered the more unexpected reading. At the same time, the previous use of εὐαρέστως ('pleasingly') at Heb. 12:28 is in the context of several first-person plural verbs which could have influenced this phrase. This is the only occurrence of ἐν ('in', 'among') with a first- or second-person pronoun in Hebrews. The stronger early attestation of ἡμῖν leads to its adoption in the editorial text. In translation, it should be treated as an inclusive use of the first person because the author identifies with the recipients.

13:21   [τῶν αἰώνων] (lit. and ever)

The majority of witnesses have the longer phrase εἰς τοὺς αἰῶνας τῶν αἰώνων ('for ever and ever'; 01 02 04* 025 0243 0285 etc.). This is unanimously attested at 1 Tim. 1:17, 2 Tim. 4:18 and most of the occurrences in Revelation but does not otherwise appear in Hebrews. There are also examples elsewhere of the shorter form, εἰς τοὺς αἰῶνας ('for ever'; 𝔓⁴⁶ 04³ 06 6 365, cf. Rom. 1:25, 9:5, 11:36; 2 Cor. 11:31; Heb. 13:8). Although it is plausible that the shorter reading here was later expanded, it is also possible that the fuller form was abbreviated through eyeskip or by assimilation to Heb. 13:8 or the various instances of εἰς τὸν αἰῶνα ('for ever') in this epistle. The same variation is seen on numerous other occasions, including Rom. 16:27, Gal. 1:5, Phil. 4:20, 1 Pet. 4:11, 1 Pet. 5:11, Rev. 1:6.

13:25 πάντων ὑμῶν (all of you) {B}

As in the case of the other epistles in the Pauline Corpus, most manuscripts conclude the final benediction with ἀμήν ('Amen'; 01² 02 04 06 015 etc.). Its absence from several early witnesses (𝔓⁴⁶ 01* 016ᵛⁱᵈ 33 latᵛˡ⁻ᵖᵗ coˢᵃ) suggests that this is a later expansion, in keeping with the liturgical formula. A parallel for πάντων τῶν ἁγίων. ἀμήν ('all the saints. Amen'; 06*) is found in the newly-adopted text of Rev. 22:21 (see below). Here, however, it appears to be a repetition from the previous verse. The first hand of Papyrus 46 lacks ὑμῶν ('of you'), probably through eyeskip.

The First Letter to Timothy

1:4 ἐκζητήσεις (speculations) {B}

The majority of Greek manuscripts read ζητήσεις ('investigations'; 06 012 025 0285^vid etc.). The negative implication of ἐκζητήσεις ('speculations'; 01 02 0150 33 81 1175 1962) fits the context of the verse better despite its limited attestation. This specific term is only found here in the New Testament and would easily have been changed to the more common form, perhaps by overlooking EK following EC at the end of the previous word.

1:17 θεῷ (God) {B}

There is strong external evidence in support of the editorial text θεῷ ('to [the only] God'; 01* 02 06* 012 015* etc.). The parallel at Rom. 16:27 (or Rom. 14:26; cf. the majority reading at Jude 25) appears to have led to the introduction of the adjective in σοφῷ θεῷ ('to the [only] wise God'; 01² 06¹ 015^c 025 and most minuscules; see further *TuT Pastorals* TS1). While assimilation is the most likely explanation because it fits the pattern of attestation, there remains a possibility that σοφῷ was originally present but omitted by homoeoteleuton after μόνῳ.

2:7 ἀλήθειαν λέγω (I am telling the truth) {B}

After these words, most Greek manuscripts have ἐν Χριστῷ ('in Christ'; 01* 06² 015 33^vid 256 etc.). This is probably due to assimilation to Rom. 9:1. Although omission through homoeoteleuton is possible, albeit not seen in the parallel in Romans, the best explanation for the early attestation of the shorter reading with just λέγω ('I speak'; 01² 02 06* 012 025 etc.) is that it is the earliest form of text.

2:9 [καὶ] γυναῖκας (women [too])

The majority of Greek manuscripts actually read καὶ τὰς γυναῖκας ('the women too'; 06¹ etc.). The rest of the tradition is split between manuscripts which have καὶ γυναῖκας ('and women'; 01² 06* 012 6 365 1739) and those with just γυναῖκας ('women'; 01* 02 015 025 33 81 1175). The latter group is sufficiently weighty that it casts doubt as to whether καί was originally present: the shortest reading is adopted in the THGNT, while the SBLGNT retains καί. The other instance of ὡσαύτως ('likewise') at the beginning of a sentence in this epistle is followed by καί, which may be an indication of authorial preference (cf. 1 Tim. 3:8 and 3:11). The full attestation for this variation unit in Greek continuous-text manuscripts is provided in *TuT Pastorals* (TS2).[1]

3:16   ὅς (he) {A}

In the editorial text, the relative pronoun ὅς ('who'; 01* 02* 04* 012 etc.) refers to Jesus, who is not named in context. This provides the best explanation for the two alternative readings. The neuter ὅ ('which'; 06* [061] lat) is an adjustment to make the relative agree with the preceding word μυστήριον ('mystery'). The majority reading, θεός ('God'; 01³ 02ᶜ 04² 06² 025 etc.) is either an editorial attempt to supply a subject (which does not entirely suit all the following attributes) or a misreading of OC as the *nomen sacrum* ΘC. The relative pronoun appears to be the beginning of a quotation of an early Christian hymn or creed, in which its antecedent would have been clear.[2]

4:10   ἀγωνιζόμεθα (lit. we struggle) {B}

The majority of Greek manuscripts read ὀνειδιζόμεθα ('we suffer reproach'; 01² 06 025 0150 etc.), which is adopted in the SBLGNT and NRSVue. However, several important witnesses have ἀγωνιζόμεθα ('we struggle'; 01* 02 04 012 018 33 1175). It is possible that the latter arose through assimilation to Col. 1:29 (κοπιῶ ἀγωνιζόμενος, 'I toil and struggle'), although the parallel is not particularly close. A more likely scenario is that an original ἀγωνιζόμεθα was changed to the similar form ὀνειδιζόμεθα under the influence either of Psalm 119:42 [118:42 LXX], where ὀνειδίζειν also precedes the phrase ὅτι ἤλπισα ἐπί ('because I have my hope set on'), or the occurrences of ὀνειδίζειν before θεὸν ζῶντα ('the living God') in Isaiah 37:4 and 37:17. Co-ordinated

---

[1] For a longer discussion of this and the verses on either side, see Zamfir & Verheyden 2008.

[2] Ehrman 2011: 91–92 observes that early creeds usually begin with relative pronouns. For arguments against this as a theologically-motivated change, see Wasserman 2012: 344–345.

verbs with a similar semantic field are a stylistic feature of this epistle (e.g. παράγγελλε ... καὶ δίδασκε, 'insist on and teach' in the following verse), which offers further support for the choice of κοπιῶμεν καὶ ἀγωνιζόμεθα ('we toil and struggle') as the editorial text both here and in the THGNT.

4:12 ἐν πίστει (in faith) {A}

Before this word, an extra item is present in the majority of Greek manuscripts, ἐν πνεύματι, ἐν πίστει ('in spirit, in faith'; 025 365 etc.). The strong support for just ἐν πίστει ('in faith'; 01 02 04 06 012 etc.) indicates that it is the earliest reading. It is possible that the addition was inspired by verses such as Col. 1:8 or 1 Cor. 4:21 or it was a misreading or accidental duplication of some or all of the following term, which was then reinterpreted as the *nomen sacrum* ΠΝΙ (πνεύματι). The full attestation for this variation unit in Greek continuous-text manuscripts is provided in *TuT Pastorals* (TS5).

5:16 πιστή (believing woman) {B}

A significant number of early witnesses support πιστή alone ('believing woman'; 01 02 04 012 025 etc.). The best-attested alternative, πιστὸς ἢ πιστή ('believing man or believing woman'; 06 0150 and the majority of minuscules) appears to be a later insertion in order to increase the applicability of this instruction. There is also a possibility that the first part of this longer phrase was omitted through eyeskip. The alternatives πιστός ('believing man'; lat[vl-pt] eth) and πιστάς ('believing women'; lat[vl-pt]) are misreadings which are restricted to early translations.[3]

6:5 εὐσέβειαν (godliness) {A}

At the end of the verse, the majority of Greek manuscripts include an additional phrase: ἀφίστασο ἀπὸ τῶν τοιούτων ('withdraw from such people'; 06[2] 025 061 0150 etc.). There is no obvious biblical parallel for this, apart perhaps from the 'Western' reading at Acts 5:39 (see above): instead it appears to be a gloss, attested as early as Irenaeus and Cyprian. Not only is there strong support for the shorter form (01 02 06* 012 048 etc.), and no obvious factors which would prompt an omission, but the

---

[3] *TuT Pastorals* (TS7) indicates that just one minuscule reads πιστός (1780*).

repetition of πορισμός ('gain') and εὐσέβεια ('godliness') in the next verse has more effect if it follows their occurrence here without interruption. The full attestation in Greek continuous-text manuscripts is provided in *TuT Pastorals* (TS8).

6:7   ὅτι (so that) {A}

The use of ὅτι by itself results in a causal relationship with the previous phrase, even though they are not necessarily logically connected. The flow of the argument is simplified by the alternatives ἀληθὲς ὅτι ('it is true that'; 06* lat[vl-pt, vg-mss] sy[hmg]) or δῆλον ὅτι ('it is clear that'; 01² 06¹ 025 [0150] and most minuscules), as well as the absence of any connective from some secondary sources (co[bo] Chrysostom[mss] Cyril). The best explanation for all these variants, which also has early attestation, is the simple conjunction ὅτι ('so that'; 01* 02 012 048 etc.).[4]

6:13   [σοι] (you) {C}

Some important witnesses do not have σοι ('you'; 01* 012 6 33 1739 lat[vl-pt] co[sa-mss]), but the majority of manuscripts include it in anticipation of σε in the following verse and it is adopted in both the SBLGNT and THGNT. In many languages, the verb παραγγέλλω ('I charge' or 'I insist') would require an explicit object regardless of whether or not it was present in Greek.

6:17   ἐπὶ θεῷ (on God) {B}

Most Greek manuscripts read ἐν τῷ θεῷ τῷ ζῶντι ('in the living God'; 06² 1573 1962 etc.), which may have arisen through a reminiscence of 1 Tim. 3:15 or 4:10; earlier witnesses strongly favour a shorter text. All the occurrences of ἠλπικέναι ('to set one's hopes') in this epistle are followed by ἐπί ('on'; see 1 Tim. 4:10, 5:5, and earlier in the present verse), and this preposition has very strong manuscript support here (01 02 06* 012 016 etc.): ἐν appears to be a misreading, possibly under the influence of the phrases on either side. The inclusion of the article before θεῷ is less clear. It is only absent from a few witnesses (01 06* 012 Origen[gr]) and could have fallen out through eyeskip or assimilation to

---

[4] Marshall 1999: 646–648 presents nine ways in which ὅτι here may be understood and translated; see also BDAG s.v. ὅτι 5.c, which refers to this verse as an example of ὅτι meaning 'so that' rather than 'because'.

ἐπὶ θεῷ at 1 Tim. 4:10. Still, it is preferred here to ἐπὶ τῷ θεῷ ('on God'; 02 016 025 0150 etc.) and there is no difference between the two in translation. The full attestation for this variation unit in Greek continuous-text manuscripts is provided in *TuT Pastorals* (TS9).

6:19   τῆς ὄντως ζωῆς (that really is life) {A}

The relatively rare word ὄντως ('really') occurs three other times in this epistle (1 Tim. 5:3, 5:5 and 5:16), and is well supported here by external evidence (01 02 06* 012 0150 etc.). It was probably replaced by αἰωνίου ('eternal'; 06² 025 and the majority of minuscules), a much more common complement to the noun ζωῆς ('life'), under the influence of 1 Tim. 6:12. At least one minuscule has a conflated reading, αἰωνίου ὄντως ζωῆς ('that really is eternal life'; 1175).

6:21   ἡ χάρις μεθ' ὑμῶν. (Grace be with you) {B}

The plural pronoun for 'you' (ὑμῶν) is surprising in a letter addressed to one person, especially given the vocative singular in the previous verse. However, as the plural is supported by strong external evidence (01*, ² 02 012 025 0150 33 81; compare also 2 Tim. 4:22), it has been adopted as the more difficult reading. The majority of Greek manuscripts read the singular μετὰ σοῦ ('with you'; 06 048^vid 6 256 etc.), and the whole phrase is missing from some secondary witnesses (co^sa Chrysostom).

6:21   ὑμῶν. (with you) {A}

As in other epistles, most manuscripts include a final liturgical Amen (01² 06 025 0150 etc.). Its absence from the earliest witnesses (01* 02 06* 012 048^vid etc.) indicates that this is secondary.

The Second Letter to Timothy

1:11   καὶ διδάσκαλος (and a teacher) {B}

The majority of Greek manuscripts read καὶ διδάσκαλος ἐθνῶν ('and a teacher of the nations/gentiles'; 01² [04] 06 012 [025] etc.). This seems to be an assimilation to 1 Tim. 2:7, where there are no variants to this longer phrase. Nevertheless, there is only slim attestation for καὶ διδάσκαλος alone ('and a teacher'; 01* 02 016 1175 cpa^ms). The reading καὶ διάκονος ('and a minister'; 33) is the erroneous substitution of a similar word which might also be expected in context: this indirectly supports the text without ἐθνῶν. The full attestation for this variation unit in Greek continuous-text manuscripts is provided in *TuT Pastorals* (TS10).

2:14   θεοῦ (lit. God) {C}

Most witnesses read κυρίου ('Lord'; 02 06 025 048 etc.), which is the most common complement of ἐνώπιον ('in the sight of') in the Septuagint. There is no other instance of this in the Pastoral Epistles, however, where the regular construction is ἐνώπιον τοῦ θεοῦ ('in the sight of God'; e.g. 1 Tim. 2:3, 5:4, 5:21, 6:13; 2 Tim. 4:1) and there is early support for this here (01 04 012 016 etc.). Either reading could have arisen from the other, through assimilation or through confusion between the *nomina sacra*: the alternative Χριστοῦ ('Christ'; 429) is probably a misreading of ΚΥ as ΧΥ. It is on the basis of usage that θεοῦ ('God') has been adopted as the editorial text.

2:18   [τὴν] ἀνάστασιν ([the] resurrection)

The definite article τήν is missing from a few important witnesses (01 012 048 33). This could be of theological significance, as it affects the interpretation of 'resurrection'. It is not clear whether τήν was originally present and then deleted (perhaps to remove the possibility of this being understood as Jesus' resurrection), or whether it was added to ensure that the statement was understood to be more specific than simply 'a resurrection', referring instead to the resurrection of faithful Christians.[1]

3:14 τίνων (whom) {B}

There is strong external evidence in favour of the plural τίνων ('whom'; 01 02 04* 012 025 etc.), yet the majority of manuscripts have the singular τίνος ('whom'; 04³ 06 0150 etc.). The latter appears to be a substitution in order to make this a reference to Paul, in keeping with the focus on the first person in the preceding verses. The reference to Timothy's childhood in the next clause offers internal support for the plural, suggesting that the author did not intend Timothy's teacher to be a self-reference (cf. 2 Tim. 1:5).

3:15 [τὰ] ἱερὰ γράμματα ([the] sacred writings)

Some witnesses do not have the definite article τά ('the'; 01 04² 06* 012 33 1175 co Clement). It is likely that this was added later for clarity, to ensure that the reference was to the Jewish Scriptures rather than 'sacred writings' more generally. Still, it may have been omitted at an early point through an oversight.

4:1 καὶ τὴν ἐπιφάνειαν αὐτοῦ (and in view of his appearing) {B}

The majority of Greek manuscripts read κατὰ τὴν ἐπιφάνειαν αὐτοῦ ('according to his appearing', i.e. 'at the time when he appears'; 01² 06¹ 025 0150 etc). This makes for a simpler construction than καὶ τὴν ἐπιφάνειαν αὐτοῦ ('and his appearing'; 01* 02 04 06* 012 etc.), whose attestation also supports its adoption as the oldest form. In translation, it may be necessary to expand the conjunction (e.g. 'in view of' in the NRSVue).

4:10 Γαλατίαν (Galatia) {C}

Γαλατίαν ('Galatia'; 02 06 012 025 etc.) is the destination named in the majority of manuscripts, but some significant witnesses have Γαλλίαν ('Gaul'; 01 04 81 lat^vg co^sa, bo-pt Eusebius). This is probably a misreading, as seen in another variant, Γαλιλαίαν ('Galilee'; lat^vg-ms [co^bo-mss]).

---

[1] On the interpretation of this phrase, see Marshall 1999: 751–754; Elliott 1975: 148 prefers the longer reading based on the context.

However, even the reading Γαλατίαν can be translated as 'Galatia' or 'Gaul', according to early Christian usage.[2] It is therefore possible that Γαλλίαν was substituted in order to remove this ambiguity or, conversely, that an original, unique occurrence of Γαλλία in the New Testament was replaced by the more common biblical place name 'Galatia' with its customary reference to Asia Minor. This geographical location would fit better with the place names on either side, also making it the easiest option. The choice of reading is of significance for mapping the geography of Paul's networks.

4:22   κύριος (Lord) {B}

Most manuscripts include the name Ἰησοῦς Χριστός ('Jesus Christ'; 01² 04 06 025 0150 etc.), while a few sources support Ἰησοῦς ('Jesus'; 02 lat^(vl-pt, vg)). Both appear to be expansions of the shortest attested form, κύριος ('the Lord'; 01* 012 33 1739 1881 lat^(vl-pt) co^(sa)). This appellation is unusual in the Pauline corpus (compare Gal. 6:18, Phil. 4:23, Phlm 25): its attestation is fairly slim but consistent with its being the earliest text. It is also worth noting that there is no other instance of κύριος Ἰησοῦς or κύριος Ἰησοῦς Χριστός in the Pastoral Epistles.[3]

4:22   ἡ χάρις μεθ' ὑμῶν. (Grace be with you) {A}

Unlike 1 Tim. 6:21, the plural is found here throughout Greek tradition. In keeping with the pattern already established, the majority of manuscripts include a liturgical Amen but its absence from key witnesses (01* 02 04 012 etc.) is likely to represent the earliest form of text.

---

[2] Metzger 1994: 581.
[3] Elliott 1975: 148.

The Letter to Titus

1:4 χάρις καὶ εἰρήνη (grace and peace) {A}

The majority of Greek manuscripts have the threefold greeting χάρις ἔλεος εἰρήνη ('grace, mercy, peace'; 02 04² 0150 etc.). This appears to be assimilation to 1 Tim. 1:2 and 2 Tim 1:2 (cf. 2 John 3). The form adopted as the editorial text differs from this and the standard pattern χάρις ὑμῖν καὶ εἰρήνη ('grace to you and peace') in other epistles, yet it has strong early attestation (01 04* 06 012 025 088 etc.). The full evidence for this variation unit in Greek continuous-text manuscripts is provided in *TuT Pastorals* (TS15).

1:10 πολλοὶ [καὶ] ἀνυπότακτοι (many rebellious people)

The conjunction καί ('and') is present in the majority of witnesses (06 012 016 etc.), resulting in the rhetorical device known as hendiadys (the use of two words to express one concept).[1] The external evidence for its absence is strong too (01 02 04 025 088 81 365). It is unclear whether καί is original and was later removed by someone who did not understand the construction, or whether it was added by analogy with the following phrase. In either case, the translation is the same in languages where such a construction is not idiomatic (although in the NRSVue it seems that this word underlies 'also').

2:7 ἀφθορίαν (integrity) {B}

This is the only instance in the Greek Bible of the word ἀφθορίαν ('integrity'; 01* 02 04 06* 018 etc.), but it has the support of important witnesses. In addition, it provides a plausible origin for the two other readings, ἀφθονίαν ('freedom from envy'; 𝔓³² 012 1881) and ἀδιαφθορίαν ('sincerity'; 01² 06¹ and the majority of minuscules; see further *TuT Pastorals* TS16). While it is possible that one of these forms was misread to result in the other two (ἀδιαφθορίαν is also unique in

---

[1] Elliott 1975: 148 observes that it is a Semitism as well as a classical Greek construction.

the New Testament), the external evidence leads to the adoption of ἀφθορίαν as the editorial text.

2:7   σεμνότητα (gravity) {B}

The inclusion at the end of this verse of ἀφθαρσίαν ('incorruption'; 06² etc.) has been claimed to be a harmonisation to 2 Tim. 1:10, but the context there is very different.[2] Given that the attestation of ἀφθαρσίαν is largely restricted to manuscripts which read ἀδιαφθορίαν two words earlier ('sincerity'; see the previous variation unit), a better explanation might be that this stems from a marginal note with the variant reading ἀφθορίαν ('integrity') which, misread as the more common word ἀφθαρσίαν, was then incorporated out of sequence.[3] The extensive early support for the shorter reading of just σεμνότητα ('gravity'; $\mathfrak{P}^{32\text{vid}}$ 01 02 04 06* etc.), including the Latin and Coptic translations, is a strong indication that it is the most ancient form.

3:1   ἀρχαῖς (rulers) {A}

Although the majority of Greek manuscripts include the conjunction καί between ἀρχαῖς and ἐξουσίαις ('rulers and authorities'; 06¹ 025 0278 etc.), this appears to be assimilation to other instances of this word pair such as Eph. 1:21 and Col. 2:10 (even though in those contexts the reference is to heavenly rather than earthly powers). The absence of καί is attested by multiple early witnesses (01 02 04 06* 012 etc.) and the whole sentence is a model of asyndeton: in some languages, it may be more natural to supply connectives.

3:15   ὑμῶν (of you) {A}

As in other epistles, most manuscripts include a final 'Amen', but its absence from key sources (01* 02 04 06* 048 etc.) suggests that it is a subsequent addition.

---

[2] See the apparatus to NA28 *ad loc.*

[3] Although ἀφθορία is translated in the previous unit as 'integrity', like ἀφθαρσία it could also mean 'incorruption': see BDAG s.v. ἀφθορία.

The Letter to Philemon

2 τῇ ἀδελφῇ (our sister) {A}

The reading of the majority of Greek manuscripts, τῇ ἀγαπητῇ ('the beloved'; 06² 0150 etc.) seems to have arisen through assimilation to τῷ ἀγαπητῷ (lit. 'the beloved') in the previous verse. The external evidence in favour of τῇ ἀδελφῇ ('sister'; 01 02 06* 012 016 etc.) is very strong indeed. A few witnesses have τῇ ἀδελφῇ τῇ ἀγαπητῇ ('our beloved sister'; 629 lat[vl-pt, vg-mss] sy[h with *]). Although this appears to be a conflation of both readings, it has been proposed as the original form because it would explain both shorter readings and it matches the combination of these terms on six occasions elsewhere in the Pauline Epistles.[1] However, the influence of its Latin version on the Greek text of the bilingual manuscript GA 629 means that it is very unlikely to preserve the earliest text (see above at Acts 20:4, 1 John 5:7–8 etc.). The full attestation for this variation unit in Greek continuous-text manuscripts is provided in *TuT Pastorals* (TS18).

6 ἐν ἡμῖν (that we share) {B}

Sound changes in Greek meant that ἐν ἡμῖν (lit. 'in us'; 02 04 06 048[vid] etc.) came to be pronounced the same as ἐν ὑμῖν ('in you'; 𝔓⁶¹ 01 012 025 0278 etc.). The former appears in most Greek minuscules, while the latter is found in the *Textus Receptus*. The choice of pronouns has implications for Paul's rhetorical strategy: ἐν ἡμῖν is less common than ἐν ὑμῖν in the other epistles but it suits the context here, especially if the first-person plural is read inclusively. As ἐν ὑμῖν would be the only occurrence of the second-person plural in this letter outside the initial and final greetings, this could lead to its preference as the harder reading or offer stylistic support for ἐν ἡμῖν. Either phrase is slightly cumbersome, and the omission of these words (629 lat[vg-mss] [eth]) results in a smoother text.[2]

---

[1] Elliott 2017: 83.

[2] For more on the interpretation and translation of this difficult verse, see the literature mentioned in Omanson 2006: 450. For Latin influence on GA 629, see the previous entry.

11 [καὶ] σοί ([both] to you)

Although only a few witnesses include καί ('both'; 01*, 2 012 33 lat^vg sy^p), their textual importance makes it uncertain whether or not it was originally present. It could have been omitted before σοί by eyeskip, although one might rather expect a jump from καί to καί. However, a shorter reading in the majority of manuscripts is unusual and this has been preferred in both the SBLGNT and THGNT.

12 ὃν ἀνέπεμψά σοι, αὐτόν, τοῦτ' ἔστιν τὰ ἐμὰ σπλάγχνα
(I am sending him, that is, my own heart, back to you) {B}

Several variants are found which simplify the structure and sense of this rather convoluted verse. The majority of Greek manuscripts read σὺ δὲ αὐτόν ('but you, him') in place of σοι αὐτόν ('him to you') and include προσλαβοῦ ('welcome') from Phlm 17 after σπλάγχνα ('heart'): their full text can be translated as 'may you welcome the one whom I sent back, that is, my own heart.' (01² [06²] 025 0150 etc.). The similarity in later pronunciation of σύ and σοι due to itacism may well have contributed to the first difference. Some witnesses have προσλαβοῦ but retain σοι αὐτόν ('him to you'; 04*), one has σὺ δὲ αὐτόν but without the additional verb ('but you, him'; 012), and in another, προσλαβοῦ comes after αὐτόν rather than at the end of the verse (048). The editorial text is only attested by three manuscripts (01* 02 33), but this shorter, more telegraphic form offers the best explanation for the variety in the textual tradition and is also adopted in the SBLGNT and THGNT.[3]

25 τοῦ πνεύματος ὑμῶν (your spirit) {B}

The grace formula is addressed to the people named at the beginning of the letter (cf. Phlm 3). One Vulgate witness, however, supports the second-person singular, σοῦ ('your'; lat^vg-ms; compare 1 Tim. 6:21 above), through harmonisation to the rest of the text. It is worth noting that the third-century Papyrus 87 matches several other epistles in reading μεθ' ὑμῶν ('with you'; cf. 1 Cor. 16:23, Col. 4:18, 1 Thess. 5:28, 1 Tim. 6:21, 2 Tim. 4:22) rather than μετὰ τοῦ πνεύματος ὑμῶν ('with

---

[3] *TuT Pastorals* (TS20) erroneously also cites GA 1996 and 1999 in support of the editorial text, when in fact they both read σὺ δὲ αὐτὸν προσλαβοῦ.

your spirit'). The focus of this variation unit, however, is the final Amen. As at the end of most of the Pauline Letters, the external support for its absence ($\mathfrak{P}^{87\text{vid}}$ 02 06* 048^{vid} etc.) suggests that ἀμήν is a later addition: it is unlikely to have been deleted if it were originally present. Even so, the THGNT adopts 'Amen' in keeping with the early attestation of this liturgical formula.

The Revelation to John

Overview

There are seven papyri of Revelation. The earliest is Papyrus 98 ($\mathfrak{P}^{98}$), a fragment of Revelation 1 possibly from the second or third century; Papyrus 47 ($\mathfrak{P}^{47}$) is the most substantial, containing most of Rev. 9–16; Papyrus 115 ($\mathfrak{P}^{115}$), also from the third century, has portions of twelve chapters. Revelation is present in Codex Sinaiticus (01), Codex Alexandrinus (02) and Codex Ephraemi Rescriptus (04), although the last of these is very lacunose. This book is not extant in the original portion of Codex Vaticanus (03): a Byzantine form of text was later supplied in minuscule script (GA 1957). There are few other majuscules with Revelation: the most complete are GA 025 and 046, both from the ninth or tenth century, but the latter is a Byzantine witness. The most important of the other fragments is the fourth-century GA 0207, a single page of Rev. 9. The most significant minuscules for the earliest text are GA 254, 1006, 1611, 1637, 1854, 2019, 2050, 2053, 2080, 2329, 2344 and 2846. In many manuscripts, this book is transmitted separately from the rest of the New Testament and accompanied by a commentary. The best attested early translation of Revelation is the Old Latin (lat^{vl}), revised in the Vulgate (lat^{vg}). There is very limited Coptic evidence, with just one Sahidic manuscript (co^{sa}) alongside the Bohairic (co^{bo}). Revelation is excluded from the Peshitta, so the oldest Syriac versions are the Philoxenian (sy^{ph}), produced in the year 508, and the seventh-century Harklean Syriac (sy^{h}).

The oldest form of text is often that found in Codex Alexandrinus and Codex Ephraemi Rescriptus, joined by Papyrus 115. However, these and Papyrus 47 and Codex Sinaiticus feature a number of singular readings which are not original and recent work has shown that GA 025, 1611 and 2846 are of considerable importance. Byzantine tradition is often split between manuscripts with the commentary of Andreas of Caesarea (Byz^A, constituted by the agreement of GA 2081 with 2814 or 2495) and the Koine tradition (Byz^K, constituted by the agreement of GA 82 with 1849 or 2138), both of which underwent later development. Only when these both agree is the siglum *Byz* used. Other lines of tradition are the text found in the sixth-century commentary of Oecumenius, best represented by GA 2053, and that adopted by the sixteenth-century Complutensian Polyglot.

The Greek of Revelation often departs from standard usage, leading to a variety of textual problems. These include 'freeing' or 'washing' in Rev. 1:5, whether Antipas is a name (Rev. 2:13), the gnomic saying in Rev. 13:10, 'linen' or 'stone' in Rev. 15:6, 'wine' or 'anger' in Rev. 18:3, and 'washing garments' or 'doing commandments' in Rev. 22:14. The textual problem involving the number of the beast (Rev. 13:10) is particularly noteworthy. It is also worth observing that the *Textus Receptus* reproduces the sixteenth-century edition of Erasmus, a text based on a single manuscript supplemented by several passages translated from Latin, leading to readings with no independent parallel in Greek manuscripts. Most earlier translations into modern languages stem from this unsatisfactory text.

The text and apparatus of UBS6 reflect the *Editio Critica Maior* of Revelation (*ECM Revelation*). This has been preceded by numerous studies, including the publication of a separate volume of *Text und Textwert* examining the relationship of the different types of text.[1] In keeping with other ECM volumes, there are no brackets in the editorial text, although readings where the editors were unable to come to a decision are indicated by a split guiding line in the ECM and a diamond (♦) in the UBS apparatus. The ECM apparatus does not indicate the two Byzantine groups, nor a single Byzantine reading when they both agree. Other features of *ECM Revelation* include the presentation of most numbers as Greek numerals rather than written out as words and a revised system of punctuation, neither of which has been adopted in the hand editions.

1:4 ἀπὸ ὁ ὤν (from him who is) {A}

After ἀπό, the majority of Greek manuscripts include θεοῦ ('from God [who is]'; 82 [91] 250 1006 1611 etc.). The absence of this noun is grammatically difficult, with no genitive following the preposition, but all the oldest witnesses support just ἀπό ('from [him who is]'; $\mathfrak{P}^{18}$ 01 02 04

---

[1] Lembke et al. 2017.

025 etc. and most early translations). The *Textus Receptus* reads ἀπὸ τοῦ ('from him'), an unusual construction which may be a back translation from the expanded form in the Latin Vulgate. Although it is possible that an original *nomen sacrum* (ΘΥ) was overlooked, its presence does not remove the following inconsistency: it appears that the formulaic threefold title of God was treated as indeclinable even when θεοῦ was included. For this reason, the strong external evidence in favour of the hard but possible shorter reading leads to its adoption. As in the NRSVue, translators may prefer to follow standard usage in the target language rather than try to reproduce the unusual Greek. The full evidence in continuous-text Greek manuscripts for this variation unit is given in *TuT Rev.* (TS1).

1:5 λύσαντι ἡμᾶς (freed us) ◆

Both Byzantine traditions have λούσαντι ἡμᾶς ('washed us'; 025 1006 [1854 2053] etc.). There is early attestation of λύσαντι ἡμᾶς ('freed us'; 𝔓¹⁸ 01² 02 04 etc.), with some manuscripts reading just λύσαντι ('freed'; 01* 1611 2344^(vid)). The words λύσαντι and λούσαντι look similar and there is alternation between ο and ου elsewhere in this book (see Rev. 3:18 below). It has been suggested that λύσαντι was changed to λούσαντι due to a literal understanding of the following clause ἐν τῷ αἵματι αὐτοῦ ('in his blood') instead of its idiomatic use of ἐν to indicate a price.[2] However, the ECM editors could not decide between this and the Byzantine reading as the initial text (see the *ECM Revelation* Textual Commentary): by convention, the reading of the previous edition is maintained in UBS6.

1:8 Ὦ (Omega) {A}

After 'Alpha and Omega', a large number of Greek manuscripts include ἀρχὴ καὶ τέλος ('the beginning and the end'; 01* 254 1854 [2019] 2050 etc.; see further *TuT Rev.* TS3). This appears to be an assimilation to Rev. 21:6, where the words are firmly attested: there is no obvious explanation for their absence here from most early witnesses and Byzantine tradition (01¹ 02 04 025 etc.). Translations may need to explain the significance of these Greek letters if the shorter reading is followed.

---

[2] Metzger 1994: 662.

1:9   ἐν Ἰησοῦ (in Jesus) {B}

The Koine tradition reads ἐν Χριστῷ Ἰησοῦ ('in Christ Jesus'; [01ᶜ] 82 91 1006 1637 etc.), while the Andreas tradition has Ἰησοῦ Χριστῷ ('in Jesus Christ'; 254 1854 2329 etc.). Most early witnesses support ἐν Ἰησοῦ ('in Jesus'; 01* 04 025 1611 etc.), although Codex Alexandrinus has ἐν Χριστῷ ('in Christ'; 02). Expansion of one of the shorter forms seems the most likely explanation, with external and internal evidence favouring ἐν Ἰησοῦ: the term Χριστός alone is rarely used in Revelation. There remains a possibility that one of the two *nomina sacra* (ΙΥ and ΧΥ) was omitted through eyeskip, but there is no occurrence of 'Jesus Christ' or 'Christ Jesus' in the editorial text of this book after the initial greeting in Rev. 1:5.

2:13   καὶ ἐν ταῖς ἡμέραις (even in the days) ◆

The reading καὶ ἐν ταῖς ἡμέραις ('even in the days'; 02 04 2053 2080 2344 latᵛᵍ) has early attestation but is difficult on two levels: it is not clear where the main verb is for a new clause beginning with καί ('and') and the construction normally expects some form of qualifier (see also the next variation unit). The majority of witnesses are split between the Andreas text, ἐν ταῖς ἡμέραις ἐν αἷς ('in the days in which'; 01 025 254 1611 etc.) and the Koine form ἐν ταῖς ἡμέραις αἷς ('in the days which'; 1006 etc.). Both of these could be attempts to remedy the difficulties of the shorter reading. The same is true of καὶ ἐν ταῖς ἡμέραις μου ('even in my days'; 2329 2846), καὶ ἐν ταῖς ἡμέραις ἐν αἷς ('even in the days in which'; 1854 *TR*) and καὶ ἐν ταῖς ἡμέραις μου ἐν αἷς ('even in my days in which'; 2050); further variants are reported in *TuT Rev.* (TS18–19). The SBLGNT and THGNT follow the hardest reading, as in previous UBS editions, but the ECM has a split guiding line between the two oldest attested forms, καὶ ἐν ταῖς ἡμέραις and ἐν ταῖς ἡμέραις ἐν αἷς. If the shorter reading is followed, some expansion is likely to be needed in translation. See also the following unit and the overview of readings in the *ECM Revelation* Textual Commentary.

2:13   ἀντίπας (Antipas) ◆

Part of the difficulty of the previous variation unit lies in this word which comes immediately afterwards. It could be a name, 'Antipas' in the form Ἀντίπας (1611 1637 1849 etc.) or perhaps Ἀντιπᾶς (lat)—the latter accentuation is not attested in any Greek manuscript in *ECM Revelation* but is preferred in several printed editions. A few minuscules, including GA 254, have an overline above the word indicating that it was considered to be a proper noun. This form seems to provide a nominative matching the following phrase ('my witness') rather than the expected genitive qualifier in the form Ἀντιπᾶ ('of Antipas'): it has been conjectured that this was the original reading but became ΑΝΤΙΠΑΣ through partial dittography of the following Ο.[3] There is also a slight possibility that Ἀντίπας is an indeclinable name in the genitive, followed by a nominative in apposition (cf. the comment on Rev. 1:4 above), but it may be noted that none of the early Greek commentaries treats this word as a genitive noun. On the other hand, ἀντίπας could be taken as an itacistic form of the nominative participle ἀντείπας ('having answered'): this is the most common accentuation in Greek tradition, but would involve parsing the next words ('my witness') as a vocative, which is very convoluted. A significant number of other witnesses, however, give the word as ἀντεῖπας ('you answered'; 82 1006 2050 2846^vid sy^h-mss co) a second-person singular verb. It is not possible to decide between these forms using the CBGM: ἀντίπας is widely attested but incoherent, while ἀντεῖπας has a consistent attestation but is found in few witnesses with a close relation to the initial text. Accordingly, they have been placed in a split guiding line.[4] Neither Codex Sinaiticus nor Codex Alexandrinus have accentuation which might help to resolve the question. The difficulty in deciding on the reading poses challenges for translation. Despite previous practice, a proper noun may no longer be considered the best option and some form of the verb 'to answer' may be preferred, along with a note explaining the ambiguity.

4:11 ἦσαν καί (they existed and) {A}

The unexpected chronology of the sequence ἦσαν καὶ ἐκτίσθησαν ('they existed and were created'; 01 1006 1611 etc.), which has the strongest external evidence, seems to have led to numerous attempts to improve it. The most widespread is replacing ἦσαν with the present-tense εἰσίν

---

[3] *Amsterdam Database* cj10678 [Ewald 1828].

[4] The *ECM Revelation* Textual Commentary raises the possibility of a triple split, to indicate that ἀντίπας could be a name or a participle.

('they are'; 025 254 1637 1854 etc.). One witness has ἐγένοντο καί ('they came to pass and'; 2329), Codex Alexandrinus lacks καὶ ἐκτίσθησαν but offers support for ἦσαν ('they existed'; 02) and a few sources omit ἦσαν καί (2019 lat[vl-pt]). A striking reading is οὐκ ἦσαν ('they did not exist'; 2080 and other manuscripts in the ECM). This could be a deliberate emendation to restore the expected sequence of divine creation *ex nihilo*, or a copying error through dittography of the last two letters of the preceding σου: the suggestion that it is the earliest reading, and that the first two letters of οὐκ were overlooked by haplography after σου, does not account for the whole word or the widespread attestation of the harder reading.[5] Exegetically, the two verbs of the editorial text may be harmonised by taking them as referring to the same event: God's will that all things exist brought them into being.

5:9 τῷ θεῷ ἡμᾶς (lit. us for God) {C}

Codex Alexandrinus and some early translations have a short reading, τῷ θεῷ ('for God'; 02 sy co[sa-mss] eth). This was adopted in UBS5 and is also preferred by the SBLGNT: it offers an explanation for the varying position of ἡμᾶς ('us') in τῷ θεῷ ἡμᾶς ('for God us'; 01 025 1006 1611 and the majority of minuscules) and ἡμᾶς τῷ θεῷ ('us for God'; 254 2019 2050 2344 etc.). On the other hand, if ἡμᾶς were originally present but fell out accidentally, it could have been reintroduced as a direct object for ἠγόρασας ('you ransomed') in a different position. The ECM and THGNT select τῷ θεῷ ἡμᾶς as the initial reading, which also presents interpretative difficulties: the object 'us' does not match 'them' (αὐτούς) in the latter part of this sentence.[6] The shorter reading in Codex Alexandrinus could thus be a deliberate omission, like the removal of τῷ θεῷ resulting simply in ἡμᾶς (lat[vg-ms]; see also see *TuT Rev.* TS37). If the shorter reading is followed, translators will need to supply an appropriate object.

5:10 βασιλείαν (kingdom) ◆

The textual tradition is split between βασιλείαν ('kingdom'; 01 02[vid] 1611*[vid] 1637 1854 etc.) and βασιλεῖς ('kings'; 254 1006 1611[c] 2019 2053

---

[5] The suggestion is made in Ross 1983: 72, followed by Elliott 2014: 74–75.
[6] The longer reading is also preferred in Malik 2017.

etc.). The latter is the majority reading, which is easier in context: it corresponds to the preceding plural αὐτούς ('them') and the following ἱερεῖς ('priests'), although two of the manuscripts which read βασιλείαν here continue with ἱερατείαν ('priesthood'; 01 2344). In addition, it may be noted that elsewhere in Revelation βασιλεῖς is always negative, usually qualified by τῆς γῆς ('kings of the earth'), whereas βασιλεία is positive. Despite the arguments in favour of βασιλείαν, there is a possibility that it was introduced through assimilation to the close parallel at Rev. 1:6. This, along with the general pattern of external evidence observed in the ECM and the early coherent attestation of βασιλεῖς according to the CBGM, has led the editors to place these readings in a split guiding line, indicating that it is impossible to decide which is the earliest form.

5:10 βασιλεύσουσιν (they will reign) {C}

Many Greek manuscripts and the early translations read βασιλεύσουσιν ('they will rule'; 01 025 82 1006 etc.), but there is also support for βασιλεύουσιν ('they are ruling'; 02 254 1611 1849 etc. and the Byzantine Koine tradition). The latter appears to be the more difficult reading, given the future tense of this verb elsewhere in the book (Rev. 11:15, 20:6, 22:5), but it may be a simple error of the omission of C before O (which also occurs in Codex Alexandrinus at Rev. 20:6).[7] While the THGNT also has the future, the SBLGNT prefers the present. The *Textus Receptus* reads ἡμᾶς … βασιλεύσομεν ('us … we will rule'). This harmonises with the variant ἡμᾶς ('us') in the previous verse, but has no independent support in Greek manuscripts: as it is found in the Clementine Vulgate, it is likely to derive from the Latin version used by Erasmus to supply gaps in his Greek source.[8]

5:11 φωνήν (voice) ◆

Both the Byzantine tradition and the early versions are split between simply φωνήν ('a voice'; 02 025 1611* 2053 etc., with the Andreas text) and ὡς φωνήν ('like a voice'; 01 254 1006 1611ᶜ etc. and the Koine text).

---

[7] Thus Metzger 1994: 667.

[8] The nine minuscule manuscripts listed in support of the first-person plural in *TuT Rev.* (TS39) have all been identified as copies of printed editions (Lembke et al. 2017: 89*); compare also Rev. 6:1 below.

The exegetical significance of the variation is clear: is it actually the voice of angels, or something 'like a voice'? There is no obvious reason for the accidental omission of ὡς but in context the shorter reading seems easier because the following speech is indeed in a loud voice (φωνῇ μεγάλῃ). Several other units in Revelation feature the same variation (e.g. Rev. 14:3 and 19:11; see below). With the external evidence so evenly divided, it is not clear whether an editor sought to add or remove the qualifier; the incoherent attestation in the CBGM indicates that the change was made on several occasions. Accordingly, the ECM editors left the decision open about the earliest reading, placing the two alternatives in a split guiding line. The SBLGNT and THGNT prefer the absence of ὡς here.

6:1-2 ἔρχου. καὶ εἶδον ("Come!" I looked) {B}

The same variation is found on four occasions in this passage, all with similar attestation. A few witnesses have three verbs, ἔρχου καὶ ἴδε. καὶ εἶδον ("Come and see!" And I saw'; 01 2344 lat[vl-pt, vg-mss]; see also thirty-two minuscules in *TuT Rev.* TS42), but most have only two. The Byzantine Koine text reads ἔρχου καὶ ἴδε ('Come and see!'; 2329 lat[vl-pt]), while the Andreas tradition is joined by early manuscripts in ἔρχου. καὶ εἶδον ('"Come!" And I saw'; 02 04 025 1006 1611 etc.). A powerful argument in favour of the latter reading, as the repetition throughout the passage indicates, is that the command is addressed not to the narrator but to each set of horse and rider.[9] The Koine reading could be a misreading of εἶδον, perhaps through assimilation to the same phrase in John 1:46 and 11:34. Even so, it is not impossible that a longer form was abbreviated through eyeskip, especially as the phrase continues with καὶ ἰδού ('and lo!'): this is probably the case in manuscripts which have ἔρχου alone ('Come!'; 254 1854). The reading of the *Textus Receptus*, ἔρχου καὶ βλέπε. καὶ εἶδον ('"Come and look!" And I saw'), seems to be a retranslation by Erasmus based on a Latin Vulgate tradition but introducing a synonym: it is only attested by manuscripts which are copies of printed editions (compare Rev. 5:10 and 6:3-4).

---

[9] Elliott 2014: 76 supports the longest reading in this and the following four units, proposing that the first ἔρχου (but not the others) is addressed to the narrator even though this breaks the sequence.

6:3-4 ἔρχου. καί ("Come!" And) {A}

TuT Rev. (TS43) shows that twenty-five minuscules have ἔρχου καὶ ἴδε. καί ('"Come and see!" And'; 2344 lat^(vl, vg-mss)). This appears to be assimilation to the majority reading at the end of Rev. 6:1 (see above) or looseness in translation. Codex Sinaiticus and seventeen minuscules read ἔρχου καὶ ἴδε. καὶ εἶδον καὶ ἰδού ('"Come and see!" And I saw, and lo!'; 01), matching the longer reading in Rev. 6:1-2 and Rev. 6:5, yet if this form were original more support for readings involving just one of the references to seeing (εἶδον or ἰδού) would be expected here. As it is, there is only one minuscule in the entire tradition with ἔρχου. καὶ ἰδού ('"Come!" And lo'; 254). The shortest reading, ἔρχου. καί ('"Come!" And'; 02 04 025 1006 1611 etc.) has very strong external support, including both Byzantine traditions and most early translations. As at Rev. 6:1-2, the *Textus Receptus* and copies of printed editions have ἔρχου καὶ βλέπε. καί ('"Come and look!" And'), again matching a Latin Vulgate variant.

6:5 ἔρχου. καὶ εἶδον ("Come!" I looked) {B}

As at Rev. 6:1-2 (see above), Koine witnesses read ἔρχου καὶ ἴδε ('come and see'; 2329 2344 etc.) rather than ἔρχου. καὶ εἶδον ('"Come!" And I saw'; 02 04 025 etc.). Codex Sinaiticus, again, has all three terms (see Rev. 6:1-2, 3-4, 7-8), but the external evidence and context (as described in Rev. 6:1-2 above) support the editorial text. Once more the *Textus Receptus* and derivative manuscripts have ἔρχου καὶ βλέπε. καὶ εἶδον ('"Come and look!" And I saw').

6:7-8 ἔρχου. καὶ εἶδον ("Come!" I looked) {B}

On this fourth occasion, the attestation is almost identical to the previous unit. Koine tradition has ἔρχου καὶ ἴδε ('come and see'; 254 *Byz*^K lat^vl, cf. 2344) while the earliest Greek witnesses read ἔρχου καὶ εἶδον ('"Come!" And I saw'; 𝔓^24vid 02 025 etc.). Codex Sinaiticus has all three terms and the *Textus Receptus* tradition has a synonym, ἔρχου καὶ βλέπε. καὶ εἶδον ('"Come and look!" And I saw'). There are, however, a few differences: some manuscripts have ἔρχου. εἶδον ('"Come!" I saw'; 04 2053) and others just ἔρχου ('Come!'; 1854 2329). The ECM here prefers the orthography ἴδον rather than εἶδον on the basis of its attestation in older witnesses, but the meaning is unchanged.

6:17 αὐτοῦ (lit. his) {C}

The ECM adopts the reading of the majority of Greek manuscripts, the singular pronoun αὐτοῦ ('[the day of] his [wrath]'; 02 025 1006 1637 2846 etc.: see *TuT Rev.* TS50). This corresponds to the singular in 'the wrath of the Lamb' in the previous clause. The plural αὐτῶν ('[the day of] their [wrath]'; 01 04 254 1611 1854 etc.) relates both to the Lamb and 'the one seated on the throne'. Depending on where the direct speech ends, it is possible to take the plural as referring to other subjects in the previous two verses but this is unlikely. The change could have been made in either direction: the plural may have been introduced to match the two figures, or changed to the singular through assimilation to the immediately preceding singular. The CBGM indicates that the attestation of αὐτῶν is incoherent and so it was probably added on multiple occasions: αὐτοῦ is completely coherent and has therefore been selected as the initial text. Both the SBLGNT and THGNT prefer αὐτῶν, the reading of UBS5.

11:1 ῥάβδῳ (staff) {A}

The majority of manuscripts read ἐδόθη μοι κάλαμος ὅμοιος ῥάβδῳ λέγων (lit. 'there was given to me a measuring rod like a staff, saying'; $\mathfrak{P}^{47}$ 01* 02 025 254 etc.), which makes it appear that the rod itself was speaking. A smoother reading is presented by the addition after ῥάβδῳ of the phrase καὶ εἱστήκει ὁ ἄγγελος ('and the angel stood [saying]'; 1637 1854 2329 etc.); the verb form ἑστήκει ('was standing'; 01²) is a later development. The longer text is not widely attested and there is no obvious reason for it to have been omitted if it were original. In translation, it may be appropriate to treat λέγων as a passive ('and I was told', NRSVue) or to supply an alternative subject ('and someone said', NASB).

12:18 ἐστάθη (lit. it stood) ◆

Most manuscripts have a first-person verb, which entails treating this verse as the beginning of a new paragraph, ἐστάθην ('I stood'; 025 1006 1611 1637 etc.). This provides logical consistency with the departure of the dragon, as narrated in the previous verse, and the narrator's following vision of a beast rising from the sea. There is very strong external evidence for a third-person verb, ἐστάθη ('it stood'; $\mathfrak{P}^{47}$ 01 02 04 1854 etc.), whose subject must be the dragon. The ongoing presence of the dragon in Rev. 13:2 indicates that this reading, while more difficult, still makes sense in context. Although the omission of a final *nu*, especially if written as a supralinear stroke, is a simple scribal mistake, the attestation suggests that the third-person verb was changed to match the first person of the next verse. The ECM leaves the decision open, allowing that either form may have been original: the SBLGNT and THGNT prefer the third person. Some translations do not number this verse as 12:18 but treat it as the first clause of 13:1.

13:1 ὄνομα (lit. name) {C}

The plural ὀνόματα ('names [of blasphemy]'; 02 254 1611 1637 etc.), present in Koine tradition, is consistent with the rest of the verse and also matches the multiplicity of the heads on which this is found. However, the singular ὄνομα ('[a blasphemous] name'; $\mathfrak{P}^{47}$ 01 04 025 etc. and the Andreas text) has early and widespread support too and appears to be the harder reading because it leaves open the question of what this name is. Either form could be assimilation to passages elsewhere (e.g. the singular name of the beast at Rev. 13:17 and the phrase ὀνόματα βλασφημίας ['names of blasphemy'] at Rev. 17:3) or could have arisen through a copying error which still made grammatical sense in context (the same variation is seen at Rev. 17:13). While the SBLGNT has the plural, the ECM and THGNT opt for the singular.[10] The full evidence for this variation unit in continuous-text Greek manuscripts is given in *TuT Rev.* (TS51).

13:6 τοὺς ἐν τῷ οὐρανῷ σκηνοῦντας (those who dwell in heaven) {A}

Before this phrase, some manuscripts read καί ('and' or 'even'; 01² 025 254 2019 etc.), treating the dwelling and dwellers as two separate items. The only extant papyrus simply reads ἐν τῷ οὐρανῷ ('in the heaven'; $\mathfrak{P}^{47}$), as a description of the dwelling. Both of these are smoother readings than the Koine form τοὺς ἐν τῷ οὐρανῷ σκηνοῦντας ('those who dwell in heaven'; 01* 02 04 025 [1006] etc.), which is grammatically awkward: it has to be taken as a gloss or explanation of the preceding noun σκηνή ('dwelling'). Even so, this qualification makes sense,

---

[10] The singular is also preferred in Elliott 2014: 87.

deriving from an understanding that blasphemy is properly directed at people rather than a place. Both internal and external evidence justify its adoption in the editorial text. Translations following this text will need to expand the sentence to identify it as a gloss, as is seen in the NRSVue ('that is').

13:10   εἰς αἰχμαλωσίαν ὑπάγει (into captivity you go) {B}

This saying, with its gnomic quality, has caused many problems in transmission and is also hard to translate. Most early witnesses read just εἰς αἰχμαλωσίαν ὑπάγει ('[if someone] goes into captivity'; 𝔓⁴⁷? 01 04 025 254 etc.), which seems to give an unbalanced conditional clause consisting of a protasis without an apodosis. This is also supported by manuscripts with εἰς αἰχμαλωσίαν ἀπάγει ('goes off into captivity'; 𝔓⁴⁷? 1854). Codex Alexandrinus has εἰς αἰχμαλωσίαν, εἰς αἰχμαλωσίαν ὑπάγει ('[if someone] into captivity, into captivity one goes'; 02 lat^vg): adopted in the SBLGNT and UBS5, this provides a partial protasis, but still lacks a verb.[11] The other readings offer a smoother text by supplying a verb in the first clause: αἰχμαλωτίζει, εἰς αἰχμαλωσίαν ὑπάγει ('[if someone] takes captive, into captivity one goes'; 2019); εἰς αἰχμαλωσίαν ἀπάγει, εἰς αἰχμαλωσίαν ὑπάγει ('[if someone] goes off into captivity, into captivity one goes'; lat^{vl, vg-mss} sy^{h with *-ms} Irenaeus^{lat}); αἰχμάλωτός ἐστιν, αἰχμάλωτος θήσεται ('[if someone] is a captive, one will be made a captive'; 2344); ἔχει αἰχμαλωσίαν, ὑπάγει ('[if someone] has captivity, one goes [away]'; 𝔓⁴⁷? 1637 and Byzantine tradition); εἰς αἰχμαλωσίαν συνάγει, εἰς αἰχμαλωσίαν ὑπάγει ('[if someone] gathers into captivity, into captivity one goes'; *TR*). Although the shorter readings could be haplography from a longer form, they are supported by the strongest external evidence: the Byzantine reading with ἔχει appears to be a misreading of εἰς or a slight adjustment, while ὑπάγει is the best attested verb form. Both the ECM and THGNT read εἰς αἰχμαλωσίαν ὑπάγει, treating the form in Codex Alexandrinus as accidental dittography.[12]

---

[11] Elliott 2014: 78–79 also prefers this reading and draws attention to Delobel's analysis of the rhetorical context, suggesting that the verse should not be interpreted as retribution but as the impossibility of resisting God (cf. the parallels at Jer. 15:2 and 43:11 [50:11 LXX]).

[12] There is an extensive discussion of this unit in the *ECM Revelation* Textual Commentary.

Nevertheless, the lack of balance with the following conditional clause in the editorial text, as well as the variants described in the next unit, pose a problem for translation and it may be necessary to expand the saying in order to make sense.

13:10 ἀποκτενεῖ δεῖ αὐτόν (if you kill ... you must) {B}

The challenges of the first part of this clause, described in the previous variation unit, continue in the second. Codex Alexandrinus has a unique short form, lacking a finite verb in both parts of the conditional clause: ἀποκτανθῆναι αὐτόν (lit. '[if someone with a sword] to be killed, him [with a sword to be killed]'; 02). The Byzantine Koine tradition reads δεῖ αὐτὸν ἀποκτανθῆναι ('[if someone is with a sword,] it is necessary for him to be killed'), lacking a second reference to being killed with a sword probably through eyeskip between two instances of ἀποκτανθῆναι. Andreas tradition and the earliest manuscripts read ἀποκτενεῖ δεῖ αὐτόν ('[if someone with a sword] will kill, he must [be killed with a sword]'; 𝔓⁴⁷ᵛⁱᵈ 04 025 254 etc.), which is very similar to the present-tense ἀποκτείνει δεῖ αὐτόν ('[if someone with a sword] kills, he must [be killed with a sword]'; 01 1006 1854 2846). The SBLGNT and UBS5 again choose the hard reading of Codex Alexandrinus, which could account for the other forms in circulation, but the ECM and THGNT opt for the longer text with the future tense on the basis of its external attestation. It has been suggested that the difficulty of the Greek here reflects a Hebrew construction, yet this does not fit the context in Codex Alexandrinus where, as the final sentence of this verse indicates, the subject of the saying is 'the saints' themselves.[13] *TuT Rev.* (TS58) lists no fewer than twenty-two variants in this unit; the *ECM Revelation* Textual Commentary also includes notes on the interpretation of the whole verse.

13:18 ἑξακόσιοι ἑξήκοντα ἕξ (six hundred and sixty-six) {C}

The number of the beast is a well known text-critical problem. The ECM adopts the numeral 666, written as ΧΞϹ in majuscules (𝔓⁴⁷) or χξϛ' in the majority of minuscules (1637 2019 2329 etc.), corresponding to ἑξακόσιοι ἑξήκοντα ἕξ ('six hundred and sixty-six'; 01 02 025 254

---

[13] Metzger 1994: 675.

1006 etc.). The masculine ἑξακόσιοι is unexpected, but has been adopted from Codex Alexandrinus (02); other witnesses have the regular neuter ἑξακόσια for 'six hundred'.[14] There is early evidence for an alternative number. The second-century writer Irenaeus of Lyons observes that some manuscripts read six hundred and sixteen, a reading preserved in full in Codex Ephraemi Rescriptus (ἑξακόσιαι δέκα ἕξ; 04) and also supported by the numeral in Papyrus 115 (ΧΙϚ, '616'; 𝔓[115]). It is possible that the middle numeral could have been misread, but the difference is more likely to be deliberate. The call for the reader to calculate the number indicates that this is an instance of *gematria*, when the numerical values of the letters add up to the total number. The referent is unclear: while the emperor Nero has been associated with both numerals (via a Hebrew transliteration of the Latin form *Nero Caesar* or the Greek Νέρων Καῖσαρ), another possibility is the emperor Caligula. Known as *Gaius Caesar*, Caligula was hated in Jewish circles for his attempt to set up a statue of himself in the Temple in Jerusalem and Γάιος Καῖσαρ adds up to 616. Other readings are also attested, which may reflect alternative forms of *gematria* or possible misreading of numerals: one important manuscript reads ἑξακόσια ἑξήκοντα πέντε ('six hundred and sixty-five'; 2344), perhaps through misinterpreting a final Ϛ as Ε, while the Old Latin Book of Armagh has 646 (DCXLVI, which could reflect a mistake of XL for LX).[15] Despite the continued preference for the reading 666, it remains unclear whether this was indeed the earliest form.[16] The full evidence for this variation unit in continuous-text Greek manuscripts is given in *TuT Rev.* (TS66), and other readings are transmitted in versional evidence.[17]

14:3   ὡς ᾠδήν (lit. like a song) ◆

Although Andreas tradition and some early manuscripts read ὡς ('like'; 02 04 254 1006 2846 etc.), this qualifier is lacking from the others

---

[14] Note also the feminine ἑξακόσιαι in the variant in Codex Ephraemi Rescriptus (04), which offers further evidence against the neuter form.

[15] The only possible evidence for 646 in Greek is GA 110, in which the numeral is mostly illegible.

[16] Elliott considers that it could be 'a secondary improvement' (2014: 92).

[17] See the collation at Hoskier 1929: 2.364–365; more detailed discussions of this variant may be found at Birdsall 2002 and Parker 2008: 242–244, while Allen 2020: 126–148 presents a full account of interpretations attested in Greek manuscripts.

including the Koine text ($\mathfrak{P}^{47}$ 01 025 1611 1637 etc.). In context, the longer reading is harder to interpret: what is the significance of something 'like' a new song? The shorter reading could therefore be a deletion to simplify the text, or assimilation to the same phrase without ὡς in Rev. 5:9. On the other hand, it is possible that ὡς was introduced erroneously on the basis of its appearance three times in the previous verse in a similar context. The frequent use of ὡς in Revelation and the difficulty of interpretation lead many to accept it as original here (including SBLGNT and THGNT), but the ECM has a split guiding line allowing that either could be the earliest form.[18] Full evidence for continuous-text Greek manuscripts is given in *TuT Rev.* (TS68). Other variations with ὡς are found at Rev. 5:11 and 19:12.

14:5   ἄμωμοί εἰσιν (they are blameless) ◆

There is good external support for both ἄμωμοί εἰσιν ('they are blameless'; 02 04 025 1854 2053 lat) and ἄμωμοι γάρ εἰσιν ('for they are blameless'; $\mathfrak{P}^{47}$ 01 1611 1637 etc.). Other readings are poorly attested: a different form of the adjective is seen in ἀμώμητοι γάρ εἰσιν ('for they are blameless'; 1006), GA 2019 lacks the phrase altogether, and the *Textus Receptus* appears to incorporate a phrase from the Clementine Vulgate in ἄμωμοι γάρ εἰσιν ἐνώπιον τοῦ θρόνου τοῦ θεοῦ ('for they are blameless in the sight of the throne of God'). The presence of the connective improves the flow of the sentence, explaining the application of the previous reference to the Jewish Scriptures (cf. Ps. 32:2, Is. 53:9, Zeph. 3:13). For that reason, γάρ appears secondary and could have been added as a parallel to παρθένοι γάρ εἰσιν ('for they are virgins') in the previous verse. Nevertheless, the ECM has a split guiding line indicating that the editors were unable to decide between the two main forms of text. The full evidence for this variation unit in continuous-text Greek manuscripts is given in *TuT Rev.* (TS70).

14:18   κραυγῇ (cry) {B}

Early manuscripts and Byzantine tradition have κραυγῇ ('cry'; $\mathfrak{P}^{47}$ 04 025 254 etc.). The adoption of this as the editorial text is a change from previous editions which read φωνῇ ('voice'; 01 02 1006 2053 etc.). In

---

[18] Elliott 2014: 79–80 also prefers ὡς.

context, κραυγῇ is the harder reading: it is a relatively rare word which only appears once elsewhere in this writing (Rev. 21:4), where its meaning is negative (cf. Eph. 4:31). There are over twenty instances of φωνή in Revelation, which also matches the preceding verb (ἐφώνησεν, 'he called'), so the likely direction of change is towards this form. The reassessment of external evidence in the ECM is complemented by the CBGM, which indicates that φωνῇ was introduced on multiple occasions.

15:3   ἐθνῶν (of the nations) {C}

The words of this hymn are a patchwork of verses from the Jewish Scriptures, with no obvious source for this particular phrase. The majority of Greek manuscripts read ἐθνῶν ('[king] of the nations'; 01²ᵃ 02 025 254 1637 etc.), while some of the oldest witnesses have αἰώνων ('[king] of the ages'; 𝔓⁴⁷ 01*, ²ᵇ 04 1006 1611 2846 lat^vg sy co^sa). The latter word does not otherwise occur in Revelation outside the formula 'for ever and ever' and may have been introduced under the influence of 1 Tim. 1:17 (cf. Tobit 13:7, 13:11 LXX). Further support for ἐθνῶν in context is offered by the reference to πάντα τὰ ἔθνη ('all the nations') in the following verse. Even so, it is not clear whether the parallels for αἰώνων are strong enough to have led to assimilation, and the possibility that this is an authorial inconsistency cannot be discounted: the SBLGNT prefers αἰώνων while the THGNT has ἐθνῶν. The reading of the *Textus Receptus*, ἁγίων ('[king] of the saints') is an unusual collocation, also attested in some early Latin writers. It can be explained as a misreading of the Latin *sclorum*, the abbrevation for *saeculorum* ('of the ages', αἰώνων), as *scorum*, the abbreviation for *sanctorum* ('of the saints', ἁγίων). Alternatively, haplography and the pronunciation of γ as a glide in later Greek could have led to the transformation of αἰώνων into ἁγίων, but this seems less likely.

15:6   λίνον (linen) {C}

Important witnesses support λίθον ('stone'; 02 04 254^c 2053 2080 lat^vg sy^hmg). This appears to provide a parallel to the Septuagint of Ezek. 28:13, where the same noun (in the form πᾶν λίθον, 'every stone') is the object of the same verb ('clothed in'). However, the absence of πᾶν here and the adjective καθαρόν ('pure') qualifying 'stone' make the sense very difficult. The noun λίθον is not otherwise found in Revelation before 18:12, where it is described as τιμίου ('precious'), i.e. a jewel. The reading of the majority of Greek manuscripts, λίνον ('linen'; 025 1006 1611 1637 etc.), may be a correction of λίθον or an original form which was misread at an early stage. The variant λινοῦν ('a garment made of linen'; 𝔓⁴⁷ 254* 2019 lat^{vg-ms}) could be an improvement to λίνον, but in either case the singular is a hard reading given the plural ζώνας ('sashes') at the end of the sentence, and the change could have gone in the opposite direction. The simplest reading is that of Codex Sinaiticus, which gives the whole phrase as ἐνδεδυμένοι καθαροὺς λινοῦς λαμπρούς ('clothed in pure bright garments of linen'; 01 lat^{vl-pt}). The presence of so many early variants indicates a problem with the reading, which could support the apparently nonsensical λίθον as original: the ECM editors considered a split guiding line here (see the *ECM Revelation* Textual Commentary). The final decision, with some support from the CBGM, was to prefer the majority reading, also adopted in the SBLGNT and THGNT.[19]

16:17 ναοῦ (temple) {A}

The word ναοῦ ('temple'; 𝔓⁴⁷ 01 02 1006 1611 etc.) matches the source of the voice in Rev. 16:1 and is supported by the oldest manuscripts and most early translations. The majority of manuscripts lack the relevant clause in that verse, and here are split between the Andreas tradition with οὐρανοῦ ('heaven'; 254 1854 2019 etc.) and the Koine text reading ναοῦ τοῦ οὐρανοῦ ('the temple of the heaven'; 1637 etc.). The former is a replacement with the expected noun (cf. Rev. 10:4, 11:12, 14:13 etc.), perhaps influenced by the form of the *nomen sacrum* (ΝΑΟΥ to ΟΥΝΟΥ), while the latter is a conflation of the two readings. Compare also the Byzantine preference for οὐρανοῦ in Rev. 21:3 below.

16:18 ἄνθρωποι ἐγένοντο (people were) {B}

Almost all witnesses support the plural, ἄνθρωποι ἐγένοντο ('humans were'; 01 1006 1611 [1637] etc.). Just three manuscripts have a singular, ἄνθρωπος ἐγένετο ('humanity was'; 02 254) or ἐγένετο ἄνθρωπος (also 'humanity was'; 2080), while Papyrus 47 is ambiguous with the un-

---

[19] Elliott 2014: 96 favours λίνον too, as do Westcott and Hort (*ad loc.*).

grammatical ἄνθρωποι ἐγένετο (lit. 'humans was'; 𝔓⁴⁷). There is no obvious parallel to this phrase elsewhere in Revelation. One possibility for the change is a misreading of the final letter, as lunate *sigma* (C) and *iota* (I) can be similar (compare Rev. 21:3 below); singular and plural forms of γενέσθαι ('become') both appear earlier in the verse. In contrast to UBS5, the plural has been adopted on the basis of the external evidence and matches the SBLGNT and THGNT. The variation in the sequence of the verb and noun reflects the parallels in this and the following verse.

18:2 ἀκαθάρτου καὶ μεμισημένου (foul and hateful) {C}

The textual tradition includes up to three different phrases in this verse beginning with καὶ φυλακή ('and a haunt'). The first, with παντὸς πνεύματος ἀκαθάρτου ('of every unclean spirit') is lacking from a few witnesses (04 1854 1611). More manuscripts do not have the second, which refers to παντὸς ὀρνέου ('of every bird'), including the Andreas tradition (02 025 etc.). The third, reading καὶ φυλακὴ παντὸς θηρίου ἀκαθάρτου ('and a haunt of every unclean beast'; 02 254 1611 2329) is only attested by a few manuscripts, some of which lack one of the other elements. Although it is present in the SBLGNT, this third phrase is not adopted in the ECM or THGNT.[20] There are various other variations in this series, which are only to be expected given the large number of words shared between them and the likelihood of eyeskip.[21] Parallels with Isaiah 13:21 and 34:11 are very loose; the combination of bird and beast is more likely to be a commonplace.

18:3 τοῦ οἴνου τοῦ θυμοῦ τῆς πορνείας (the wine of the wrath of her fornication) {C}

The reading here may depend in part on the verb, which is discussed in the next variation unit. Some important witnesses simply read τοῦ θυμοῦ τῆς πορνείας ('from the wrath of her fornication'; 02 [04] 1611 2053 2846 lat^vg). The presence of οἴνου ('wine') may be an expansion, in conjunction with a form of 'to drink' as the following verb, making the object more explicit. This is seen in the the Koine text, τοῦ οἴνου

---

[20] The reading of the SBLGNT is also preferred by Elliott 2014: 96.
[21] Full details are given in *ECM Revelation*; see also Metzger 1994: 682–683.

τοῦ θυμοῦ τῆς πορνείας ('the wine of the wrath of her fornication'; 01 1006 2080 2329 etc.), possibly an assimilation to the same phrase in Rev. 14:8; the alternative sequence τοῦ θυμοῦ τοῦ οἴνου τῆς πορνείας ('the wrath of the wine of her fornication'; 025 254 1637 2019 and Andreas tradition) also appears. Less well attested is τοῦ οἴνου τῆς πορνείας ('the wine of her fornication'; 1854), which may be assimilation to Rev. 17:2. While the longer forms could be due to conflation or independent expansion, οἴνου may have been omitted through eyeskip given the visual similarity of ΟΙΝΟΥ and ΘΥΜΟΥ. It is therefore difficult to decide between τοῦ θυμοῦ τῆς πορνείας and τοῦ οἴνου τοῦ θυμοῦ τῆς πορνείας: if the shorter reading is adopted, the metaphor may still need to be expanded in translation. It should also be noted that θυμός can be rendered as 'wrath' or 'passion': if the first of these is chosen, it may be appropriate to add a divine subject ('God's wrath at …'). All readings in continuous-text Greek manuscripts are provided in *TuT Rev.* (TS89).

18:3 πεπτώκασιν (have fallen) {D}

Witnesses are divided between some form of the verb 'to drink' and the very similar verb 'to fall'. The former comprise the singular πέπωκεν ('he/she has drunk'; 025 254 1637 2053* and Andreas tradition), two forms of the third-person plural (πέπωκαν or πεπώκασιν, 'they have drunk'; 1006^c 2080 2329 lat^{vg}), and a transitive singular πεπότικεν ('she has made to drink'; 2019). The latter similarly involve a third-person plural πέπτωκαν or πεπτώκασιν ('they have fallen'; 01 02 04 1006* etc., including the Koine text) and a singular πέπτωκεν εἰς ('she has fallen into [all nations]'; 1854 2053^c 2062 and the *Textus Receptus*). The full attestation in Greek continuous-text manuscripts is given in *TuT Rev.* (TS90). The reading 'to drink' would explain the presence or introduction of οἴνου ('wine') in the previous variation unit and match the parallel at Rev. 14:8, which is probably responsible for the variant πεπότικεν here. In contrast, while 'to fall' makes sense (e.g. 'all nations have fallen out [or 'because'] of the wrath of her fornication' in Codex Alexandrinus) and matches the opening words of this speech in Rev. 18:2, it seems a less appropriate—but therefore harder—reading in the context of the sensual pleasures later in the verse. The replacement of πέπωκαν ('they have drunk') by the more common verb πέπτωκαν ('they have fallen') is seen in Rev. 14:8, where the object οἶνον ('wine') is secure: the same change could have been inspired here by the presence of ἔπεσεν in the previous verse. However, despite adopting τοῦ οἴνου in the previous unit, the ECM prefers πεπτώκασιν here while the SBLGNT and THGNT choose πέπτωκαν, all resulting in a mixed metaphor. The complexity of the textual tradition and the inconsistency between the two parts of this phrase make for considerable doubt regarding the earliest form of text: the ECM considers them as a single unit, leading to a large number of variants, but notes that readings with 'to drink' are less coherently attested, suggesting that these may be secondary (see the *ECM Revelation* Textual Commentary).

19:12   φλόξ (flame) {B}

The qualification ὡς φλόξ ('like flame'; 02 1006 1854 2080 etc.) has very early support in indirect witnesses, appearing in all ancient translations and writers such as Irenaeus and Origen. The majority of manuscripts have the shorter reading φλόξ ('flame'; 01 025 254 1611 etc.). This contrasts with the same phrase at Rev. 1:14, where the angel is described in similes: in the present verse there are no other qualifiers in the portrayal of the horse's rider, and the literal depiction of his eyes as fire suits the dramatic context. Although ὡς was included in brackets in UBS5, it is very likely that this is a harmonisation to the earlier instance. The CBGM indicates that its attestation is incoherent, suggesting that it was added on multiple occasions. A similar variation is seen in the parallel at Dan. 7:9, where the Septuagint has ὡς but Theodotion lacks it (compare the preference for Theodotion's text of Daniel at Rev. 1:7, 10:6, 13:7 and 20:11).

20:5   αὕτη (this) {C}

Many witnesses, including the Andreas tradition, have a parenthetical phrase at the beginning of this verse, such as καὶ οἱ λοιποὶ τῶν νεκρῶν οὐκ ἔζησαν ἄχρι τελεσθῇ τὰ χίλια ἔτη ('And the rest of the dead did not come to life until the thousand years were ended'; [02] 254 1006 [1611] 1637 etc.). This is absent from Codex Sinaiticus and the Koine text (01 2053 etc.). It would be very easy for the longer text to have been omitted through eyeskip from the preceding χίλια ἔτη ('a thousand years') and the phrase is included in the previous hand editions as well as the SBLGNT and THGNT. Nevertheless, the variety of forms in which it is found and its clarificatory content, as well as the smoother reading which results from its absence, led the ECM editors to consider it as a later gloss formed of text from the two preceding verses (see the long discussion in the *ECM Revelation* Textual Commentary). It may be noted that all Greek manuscripts here and at Rev. 20:3 read ἄχρι ('until'): the appearance of ἕως ('until') in the *Textus Receptus* is a synonym consistent with a retranslation from the Latin by Erasmus (cf. Rev. 1:4, 6:1, 21:6 etc.).

20:9 ἀπὸ τοῦ θεοῦ ἐκ τοῦ οὐρανοῦ (lit. from God out of heaven) {C}

The phrases ἐκ τοῦ οὐρανοῦ ('out of heaven'; 02 lat^(vl-pt, vg-ms) eth?) or ἀπὸ τοῦ οὐρανοῦ ('from heaven'; 2080 eth?) appear to reflect a Septuagintal expression prominent in the Elijah narrative (2 Kings 1:10, 12, 14). There is also very slim external evidence for ἀπὸ τοῦ θεοῦ ('from God'; 1854). Most witnesses have a combination of these readings, such as ἀπὸ τοῦ θεοῦ ἐκ τοῦ οὐρανοῦ ('from God out of heaven'; 01² 025 1006 1611 2050 etc.), ἐκ τοῦ οὐρανοῦ ἀπὸ τοῦ θεοῦ ('out of heaven from God'; 1637 2329 *Byz*^K etc.), or even ἐκ τοῦ θεοῦ ἀπὸ τοῦ οὐρανοῦ ('out of God from heaven'; 254 [*Byz*^A]). The variety in the longer readings suggests that they arose as conflations of the two shorter forms or through assimilation to Rev. 21:2 and 21:10 (where there is also variation in the sequence). On the other hand, ἐκ τοῦ οὐρανοῦ by itself might have been an early harmonisation to the Septuagint, while the omission of either clause could be explained through eyeskip between instances of τοῦ or the *nomina sacra*. The ECM prefers ἀπὸ τοῦ θεοῦ ἐκ τοῦ οὐρανοῦ due to its strong attestation in witnesses related to the initial text, even though both the SBLGNT and THGNT have ἐκ τοῦ οὐρανοῦ by itself. It may be noted that the previous reference to fire coming out of heaven at Rev. 13.13 is the work of one of the beasts, so the addition of 'from God' may have been felt to be a necessary clarification despite disrupting the parallel with Elijah.

21:3 θρόνου (throne) ◆

The majority of Greek manuscripts read οὐρανοῦ ('heaven', 025 254 1006 1611 etc.), which matches other passages elsewhere in this book (e.g. Rev. 14:13, 18:4). The oldest witnesses, however, have θρόνου ('throne'; 01 02 lat^(vl·pt,vg) sy), which corresponds to the reading at Rev. 19:5. Assimilation could thus have worked in either direction, especially given the similarity between ΘΡΟΝΟΥ and the *nomen sacrum* ΟΥΝΟΥ (compare Rev. 16:17 above). While the parallels for οὐρανοῦ elsewhere and its appearance in the preceding verse suggest that θρόνου is the harder reading, the ECM has a split guiding line allowing that either could be the initial text. One minuscule lacks the phrase entirely (2050).

21:3 λαοί (peoples) ◆

There is strong external evidence for the plural λαοί ('peoples'; 01 02 2050 2053 etc. and the Andreas tradition), which is the harder reading: other references to the 'people of God' are in the singular, as seen in the Koine reading λαός ('people'; 025 254 1006 1611 etc.; cf. Rev. 18:4 and, for example, Jer. 31:33 [38:33 LXX], Ezek. 37:27, Zech. 8:8). If the plural is adopted, it has a theological implication in suggesting that many 'peoples' have now replaced one 'people of God'. Still, λαοί could be an early adjustment prompted by the plural verb and the preceding αὐτοί. There is also the possibility for misreading either term as the other due to the similarity between *iota* and lunate *sigma* (I and C: compare Rev. 16:18 above). For these reasons, the ECM has a split guiding line, allowing that either λαός or λαοί may be the initial text. The full evidence for this variation unit in continuous-text Greek manuscripts is given in *TuT Rev.* (TS107).

21:3 μετ᾽ αὐτῶν ἔσται αὐτῶν θεός (with them and be their God) ◆

Most Greek manuscripts have a shorter text, with Koine witnesses reading μετ᾽ αὐτῶν ἔσται (lit. '[God himself] with them will be') and ἔσται μετ᾽ αὐτῶν ('will be with them'; 01 254 1637 etc.) in Andreas tradition. The inclusion of αὐτῶν ('their') and θεός ('God') appears superfluous, as both words appear in the first part of the verse. The longer readings take a variety of forms, which is often an indication that they are secondary: the *Textus Receptus* has ἔσται μετ᾽ αὐτῶν θεὸς αὐτῶν ('will be with them, their God'; 025 etc.). some minuscules read μετ᾽ αὐτῶν ἔσται θεός ('will be with them, God'; 1006 1611), while others cluster around μετ᾽ αὐτῶν ἔσται αὐτῶν θεός ('with them will be their God'; 02^(vid) [1854] [2050] [2053] etc.). It is possible that the last of these is an expansion in keeping with the broader reference to Ezek. 37:27 (compare also Jer. 32:28 and Lev. 26:12; cf. 2 Cor. 6:16), but it has several difficulties: the unemphatic placing of the possessive pronoun before the noun is only otherwise found in this book at Rev. 18:5, while the additional text requires either the repetition of the verb ('God will be with them and *will be* their God') or a composite subject ('God-himself-with-them will be their God').[22] The ECM has a split guiding line between αὐτῶν θεός and its absence, reflecting the external attestation and internal problems. If μετ᾽ αὐτῶν ἔσται αὐτῶν θεός is the earliest text, as adopted in the THGNT, the other longer forms can be understood as attempts to simplify the structure before the problematic phrase was eventually omitted. The SBLGNT prefers μετ᾽ αὐτῶν ἔσται, treating the other forms as incoherent expansions. No fewer than eighteen different readings are listed in *TuT Rev.* (TS108).

21:6   γέγονα ἐγώ (I have become) {C}

Early witnesses and Byzantine tradition have γέγονα ἐγώ ('I have become'; 01* 025 1611 [1637] etc.), although the pronoun is lacking from the Koine text, γέγονα ('I have become'; 1637 2081* 2814 etc.). Two majuscules attest a third-person plural form of the verb: a correction in Codex Sinaiticus reads γέγοναν ἐγώ ('They have come to pass. I, [the Alpha]'; 01[2] co[bo]), while Codex Alexandrinus and a range of other evidence support γέγοναν ἐγώ εἰμι ('They have come to pass. I am [the Alpha]'; 02 254 1006 2053 etc.; some of these have γέγονασιν, the standard form of the perfect tense). The singular in the *Textus Receptus*, γέγονε ἐγώ εἰμι ('It has come to pass. I am [the Alpha]') is a back-translation from the Latin Vulgate by Erasmus with no prior attestation in any Greek manuscripts (cf. Rev. 5:10, 14:5 above). The inclusion of εἰμί ('I am') appears to be a harmonisation to Rev. 1:8 (cf. 1:17). It is superfluous with the first-person γέγονα ('I have become'). There is no other instance in Revelation of the plural γέγοναν ('they have come to pass'): the closest is the singular γέγονεν ('it has come to pass') at Rev. 16:17. With some hesitation, the ECM has adopted the reading with the strongest external attestation, introducing the first person in the place of the third-person plural in UBS5; because the latter is clearly the

---

[22] On the translation of this verse and its textual history, see Shepherd 2023.

harder reading, it is preferred in the SBLGNT (which matches the correction in Codex Sinaiticus) and the THGNT (which agrees with Codex Alexandrinus). An extensive discussion is provided in the *ECM Revelation* Textual Commentary.

21:27   ὁ ποιῶν (anyone who practises) ◆

The reading ὁ ποιῶν ('the one who does'; [01*] 1854 2080 2344 etc.) is the predominant Koine form. The definite article specifies a new, human subject in contrast to the preceding noun, but is lacking from manuscripts which have simply ποιῶν ('practising'; 01² 02 1006 2050 2329 2846). Byzantine witnesses in the Andreas tradition have the neuter participle, ποιοῦν ('practising'; 025 254 1611 1637 etc.), which treats πᾶν κοινόν ('nothing unclean') as the subject throughout. The hardest reading is ποιῶν alone, whose grammatical connection to the rest of the sentence is unclear. Despite its restricted attestation, this is adopted in both the SBLGNT and THGNT and would explain the origin of both other forms. In contrast, the ECM has a split guiding line between ὁ ποιῶν and ποιοῦν, yet none of the readings is completely coherent. The full evidence for this variation unit in continuous-text Greek manuscripts is given in *TuT Rev.* (TS123).

22:12   ἔσται (lit. will be) {B}

There is early evidence for the present tense, ἐστίν ('is'; 01 02 [Origen]), but the majority of manuscripts have the future, ἔσται ('will be'; [254] 1006 [1611] 1637 etc.). A few indirect witnesses (lat^vg Clement Cyril) lack any verb: although this is the smoothest reading, it is not sufficiently well attested to be original. The present tense is consistent in form with ἔρχομαι ('I am coming') at the beginning of the verse, while the future corresponds to the sense: a change could therefore have been introduced in either direction. Similar constructions with ἔρχομαι in Revelation might favour the future (cf. Rev. 2:5 and 2:16), but there is no clear parallel. There is a potential theological difference between the two forms, as to whether the judgment relates to current or future deeds. The ECM editors chose ἔσται on the basis of its wide attestation, claiming that the early majuscules reflect a stylistic revision (see *ECM Revelation* Textual Commentary). This contrasts with the present tense in UBS5, SBLGNT and THGNT.

22:14 πλύνοντες τὰς στολὰς αὐτῶν (who wash their robes) {B}

The oldest witnesses, including several early translations, support πλύνοντες τὰς στολὰς αὐτῶν ('who wash their robes'; 01 02 1006 [2050] 2053 etc.). It is possible that this is a harmonisation to the same phrase in Rev. 7:14. The reading in the majority of witnesses, ποιοῦντες τὰς ἐντολὰς αὐτοῦ ('who do his commandments'; 254 1611 1637 1854 etc.), is a more banal phrase which fits the context better. The visual similarity of the two phrases is obvious: yet another variant which appears to be due to a misreading is πλατύνοντες τὰς στολὰς αὐτῶν ('opening wide their robes'; Pseudo-Athanasius, not cited in UBS6). While the majority reading appears to be easier, the verb associated with 'commandments' throughout the New Testament (and at Rev. 12:17 and 14:12) is τηρέω ('keep', which may be reflected in Latin and Syriac manuscripts listed under φυλάσσοντες, 'guarding') rather than ποιέω ('do'). Accordingly, some commentators prefer this form, noting the use of ποιεῖν τὰς ἐντολάς at 1 John 5:2 and observing that the people referred to here are still on earth at the coming of the Lamb, unlike those in Rev. 7 who are in heaven.[23] Even so, the ECM, SBLGNT and THGNT all adopt πλύνοντες τὰς στολὰς αὐτῶν. In translation, it may be helpful to indicate that 'washing robes' is a metaphor for spiritual cleansing, perhaps with an implication of baptism or martyrdom.

22:21 κυρίου Ἰησοῦ (of the Lord Jesus) ◆

Support for the shortest form, κυρίου Ἰησοῦ ('of the Lord Jesus'; 01 02 1611 2053 lat[vg-mss] eth) is consistent with this being the earliest text, given the tendency of such formulae to expand during transmission: the majority of manuscripts have κυρίου Ἰησοῦ Χριστοῦ ('of the Lord Jesus Christ'; 254 1006 1637 1854 etc.), while other witnesses support κυρίου ἡμῶν Ἰησοῦ Χριστοῦ ('of our Lord Jesus Christ'; *Textus Receptus* lat[vl-pt, vg] sy[ph] [co[sa]]). While it is possible that the second *nomen sacrum* was overlooked at an early point in the tradition or that this phrase was harmonised to the preceding verse, the shortest reading is most likely to be original. Nevertheless, the ECM has a split guiding line between κυρίου Ἰησοῦ and κυρίου Ἰησοῦ Χριστοῦ, given the better coherence of the majority text and the antiquity of the uniform Byzantine reading.

---

[23] Elliott 2014: 99; see also Ross 2003: 220–221 and Goranson 1997.

Due to eyeskip from Ἰησοῦ to Ἰησοῦ, GA 2329 and the Bohairic version omit the first part of this verse (see the next variation unit).

22:21   μετὰ πάντων τῶν ἁγίων. ἀμήν (with all the saints. Amen) {C}

There is limited manuscript support for a number of shorter readings. The briefest text of all is μετὰ πάντων ('with all'; 02 lat[vl-pt, vg]) and there is also early attestation of μετὰ τῶν ἁγίων. ἀμήν ('with the saints, Amen'; 01). One manuscript has μετὰ πάντων ἡμῶν. ἀμήν ('with all of us, Amen'; 2050), while the minuscule which omits the first part of the verse (see above) reads μετὰ τῶν ἁγίων σου. ἀμήν ('[Come Lord Jesus Christ] with your saints, Amen'; 2329). The Byzantine tradition has μετὰ πάντων τῶν ἁγίων. ἀμήν ('with all the saints, Amen'; 254 [1006] 1611 1637 1854 etc.), while the Andreas witnesses lack the final Amen. As in the previous variation unit, it is plausible that a short form was expanded: even though μετὰ πάντων might be an assimilation to a Pauline doxology (cf. 2 Cor. 13:13, 2 Thess. 3:18), it is adopted by the SBLGNT and UBS5. Because ἅγιοι ('saints') is a common term in Revelation and there is no other instance of a grace formula with μετὰ τῶν ἁγίων ('with the saints'), this too is a strong contender for the earliest form.[24] The THGNT prefers the text of Codex Sinaiticus while the ECM adopts the majority reading (see further the *ECM Revelation* Textual Commentary). The *Textus Receptus* has μετὰ πάντων ὑμῶν. ἀμήν ('with all of you, Amen'). Although this could be an itacistic version of the text of GA 2050, its correspondence to the wording of the Clementine Vulgate suggests that, once again, this is a back translation by Erasmus from Latin.

---

[24] Note the variant at Heb. 13:25 above, which does not seem to be related to this.

Glossary

agraphon A passage which originally circulated independently of the biblical canon.

anarthrous Lacking an article (i.e. without 'the' or 'a').

Andreas tradition A group of Byzantine manuscripts in the book of Revelation whose biblical text is accompanied by the commentary of Andreas of Caesarea.

apodosis The second part of a conditional clause (i.e. the result; see also *protasis*).

aposiopesis Breaking off in the middle of a sentence.

apparatus A separate presentation of information relating to a text. In UBS6, this usually refers to the list of variant readings at the foot of the page.

assimilation Making two elements resemble each other. This may involve different passages (see *harmonisation*), or individual letters or sounds.

asyndeton The absence of connectives, usually in a list of multiple items.

Atticism The adjustment of Koine Greek to the higher literary register known as Attic Greek.

bilingual In two languages.

block mixture Portions of a manuscript with different textual affiliations.

catena A commentary consisting of extracts from early Christian writers. These are often accompanied by the biblical text of the book in question, either in a central panel framed by the commentary or in alternating portions of text and commentary.

CBGM Coherence-Based Genealogical Method. A digital method of combining individual textual decisions in order to assist editors in establishing the history of a work's transmission through the groupings of witnesses which attest different readings (see also *coherence*).

chiasmus A mirror-image sequence (e.g. ABCCBA), named after the Greek letter *chi* (χ).

citation A quotation of the New Testament in a work by an early Christian author.

codex A manuscript formed of folded pages joined at the spine, written on both sides, matching the format of a modern book rather than a scroll.

coherence When the attestation of a reading is explained by the extant groups of witnesses (see also *CBGM* above).

collocation The positioning of two or more words next to each other.

conflation A longer reading created by combining two shorter forms.

conjecture A reading reconstructed by a scholar which is not attested in surviving witnesses.

continuous text The text of a complete biblical book presented in sequence (rather than selected or rearranged extracts).

contrastive A word which indicates that the following phrase is a contrast to the previous one.

coronis A decoration to mark the end of a work.

deictic Pointing to a specific agent or object.

demonstrative An indication of a particular item or group (e.g. 'this' or 'that').

diamond reading A reading marked in the *ECM* as a *split guiding line*, where the editors could not decide between different reconstructions of the *initial text*.

direct tradition Witnesses which transmit a work in its original language (see also *primary evidence*).

dittography Writing the same thing twice (compare *haplography*).

divine passive Constructing a sentence in the passive voice in order to avoid naming God as the agent.

doxology Portion of a prayer offering praise to God.

eclecticism The process of choosing readings from different sources.

ECM *Editio Critica Maior*: the major, twenty-first-century edition of the Greek New Testament based on an assessment of all surviving evidence.

euphony Something which sounds well when read aloud.

exemplar The source manuscript from which a copy was made.

external evidence Historical information about witnesses, such as date or place of production (contrast *internal evidence*).

eyeskip The omission of text while copying, usually due to jumping from one sequence of letters to the same sequence later in the text.

family A group of related manuscripts whose distinctive ancestor can be reconstructed.

first-hand Written by the copyist of the manuscript.

GA Gregory-Aland: the standard system for identifying Greek New Testament manuscripts using numbers (sometimes with a prefixed letter).

genitive absolute A phrase in the genitive case with no grammatical connection to the main clause describing its circumstances.

gospel harmony A single gospel combining elements from the four canonical gospels, usually so as to eliminate repetition and contradiction.

haplography Writing something once which appears twice in the original (compare *dittography*).

harmonisation Removing differences in order to make one passage more closely resemble another (see also *assimilation*).

harmony: see *gospel harmony*

hendiadys The use of two co-ordinated words to express a single concept.

homoeoarcton Omitting text by jumping between two words which start with the same sequence of letters (see also *eyeskip*).

homoeoteleuton Omitting text by jumping between two words which end with the same sequence of letters (see also *eyeskip*).

homophone A word which sounds the same as another but is spelt differently.

inchoative A verb form which indicates an action is beginning to happen.

indirect tradition Witnesses which transmit the text of a work in the form of quotations or a translation into another language (see also *secondary evidence*).

initial text The wording which underlies all surviving forms of text.

intensification Heightening the narrative by increasing the number of a noun or adding an adjective or adverb.

internal evidence Considerations relating to a text's style, grammar or other form of consistency.

interpolation An insertion of text from another source (see also *Western non-interpolation*).

intransitive A verb without a direct object.

isochrony Loss of distinction in vowel length due to changes in pronunciation (i.e. confusion of *omicron* and *omega*, or *epsilon* and *eta*).

itacism Changes in Greek pronunciation which resulted in the vowels η, ι, υ, ει and οι all being pronounced as 'ee'.

Koine The common form of Greek, in which the New Testament was written. In Revelation, this is a large group of Byzantine manuscripts which contrast with the textual tradition of Andreas of Caesarea.

lacuna A gap where text is missing due to the loss of the physical material on which it had been written.

lectionary A manuscript containing biblical passages to be read during Christian worship.

lemma The portion of biblical text which is the subject of a passage of commentary.

LXX: see *Septuagint*

majority text A reading transmitted by more than half the surviving Greek New Testament manuscripts, and thus predominant in minuscule tradition (see also *Textus Receptus*).

majuscule Greek script consisting only of capital letter forms, with each usually written separately. In common use until around the tenth century. (See also *uncial*.)

mechanical errors Mistakes introduced during the process of copying, without the awareness of the scribe.

metonymy Identifying something by one of its attributes.

minuscule Greek script consisting of capital and smaller letters, in which the characters are often joined within a word. The most common style of handwriting in New Testament manuscripts, first attested in the eighth century.

nomen sacrum A two- or three-letter abbreviation for a key Christian term (God, Lord, Jesus, Christ, Spirit, Father, Son etc.). The plural is *nomina sacra* (lit. 'sacred nouns').

NTVMR New Testament Virtual Manuscript Room. Online portal with manuscript images, textual databases and other resources.

palimpsest A re-used manuscript in which the original layer of text has been erased in order to permit another text to be copied on the same page.

parablepsis The Greek term for 'eyeskip' (see above).

patristic Relating to early Christian writers after the time of the New Testament ('Church Fathers').

pleonasm Excessive and unnecessary use of the same word.

postpositive A word which can never stand first in a sentence.

primary evidence Manuscripts of a text in its original language (see also *direct tradition*).

protasis The first part of a conditional clause (i.e. the element beginning with 'if'; see also *apodosis*).

qualifier A word which modifies the scope of another, usually an adjective or adverb.

recension A thorough editorial revision of an entire work, often involving extensive textual changes.

scriptio continua Text written without spaces between words.

secondary evidence Witnesses to a text in the form of quotations in another writing or translations (see also *indirect tradition*).

Septuagint The Greek translation of the Old Testament.

siglum An identifier for a witness as used in an apparatus (e.g. a *Gregory-Aland* number).

singular reading A textual form only attested in one witness.

split guiding line A variation unit in the *ECM* where two or more variants are presented as equally likely to be the initial text (see also *diamond reading*).

stemma A family tree diagram indicating the relationship of witnesses (or their text).

supralinear Above the line of writing.

synonym A word which means the same as another word.

synoptic Treatment of the same material in different writings, used here of overlaps between Matthew, Mark and Luke (the Synoptic Gospels).

tautologous Saying the same thing twice.

text-type A grouping of witnesses based on distinctive textual features, sometimes connected with a *recension*. Used in a much broader sense than *family*.

Textus Receptus 'Received Text': although deriving from an edition of the Greek New Testament published in 1633 by the Elzevir brothers, this is used to describe early printed editions of the Greek New Testament which often (but not always) match the *Majority Text*.

TuT *Text und Textwert:* a book series listing the readings of all Greek continuous-text manuscripts in a set of variation units across the New Testament.

uncial A form of *majuscule* script (see above), used especially of a type of Latin handwriting.

version In New Testament scholarship, another word for an early translation from Greek.

vowel isochrony: see *isochrony*

Western non-interpolation A verse or portion of a verse which is missing from so-called 'Western' witnesses to the gospels. Given the tendency of this tradition to expand the text, these shorter readings have occasioned much debate.

witness A source which transmits the text of a work, whether an original-language manuscript, a translation, or a quotation in another work.

Bibliography

Abbreviations used only in the bibliography

ABC	Anchor Bible Commentary
ANTF	Arbeiten zur neutestamentlichen Textforschung
BETL	Bibliotheca Ephemeridum Theologicarum Lovaniensium
BT	*The Bible Translator*
BTS	Biblical Tools and Studies
BZNW	Beihefte zur Zeitschrift für die neutestamentliche Wissenschaft
CBQ	*Catholic Biblical Quarterly*
ConBNT	Coniectanea Biblica New Testament Series
CUP	Cambridge University Press
ETL	*Ephemerides Theologicae Lovanienses*
FilNeot	*Filología Neotestamentaria*
HTR	*Harvard Theological Review*
ICC	International Critical Commentary
JBL	*Journal of Biblical Literature*
JSNT	*Journal for the Study of the New Testament*
LNTS	Library of New Testament Studies
NICNT	New International Commentary on the New Testament
NIGTC	New International Greek Testament Commentary
NovT	*Novum Testamentum*
NovTSup	Supplements to *Novum Testamentum*
ns	New Series
NTS	*New Testament Studies*
NTTSD	New Testament Tools, Studies and Documents
os	Old Series
OUP	Oxford University Press
SBL	Society of Biblical Literature
SBLRBS	Society of Biblical Literature Resources for Biblical Study
SBLTCS	Society of Biblical Literature Text-Critical Studies
SD	Studies and Documents

SNTSMS   Studiorum Novi Testamenti Societas monograph series
TC   *TC: A Journal of Biblical Textual Criticism*
T&S   Texts and Studies
WUNT   Wissenschaftliche Untersuchungen zum Neuen Testament
ZNW   *Zeitschrift für die neutestamentliche Wissenschaft*

Aasgard, Reidar (2004). 'Brothers in Brackets? A Plea for Rethinking the Use of [ ] in NA/UBS.' *JSNT* 26.3: 301–321.
Achtemeier, Paul J. (1996). *1 Peter: A Commentary on First Peter*. Hermeneia; Minneapolis, MN: Augsburg Fortress.
Aland, Barbara, Kurt Aland†, Gerd Mink, Holger Strutwolf and Klaus Wachtel, ed. (2013). *Novum Testamentum Graecum Editio Critica Maior. IV. Die Katholischen Briefe/Catholic Epistles*. Second edition. ECM IV; Stuttgart: Deutsche Bibelgesellschaft.
Aland, Barbara, and Klaus Wachtel (2005). *Text und Textwert V. Das Johannesevangelium. 1. Teststellenkollation der Kapitel 1–10*. 2 vols. ANTF 35–36; Berlin & New York; De Gruyter.
Aland, Kurt (1968). 'Eine Untersuchung zu Joh. 1.3–4: Über die Bedeutung eines Punktes.' *ZNW* 59: 174–209.
Aland, Kurt (1969). 'Bemerkungen zum Schluss des Markusevangeliums.' In *Neotestamentica et Semitica*, ed. E. Earle Ellis and Max Wilcox. Edinburgh: T&T Clark, 157–180.
Aland, Kurt (1994). *Kurzgefasste Liste der Griechischen Handschriften des Neuen Testaments*. Second edition. ANTF 1; Berlin & New York; De Gruyter.
Aland, Kurt with Annette Benduhn-Mertz and Gerd Mink (1987). *Text und Textwert I. Die Katholischen Briefe*. 3 vols. ANTF 9–11; Berlin & New York; De Gruyter.
Aland, Kurt with Annette Benduhn-Mertz, Gerd Mink and Horst Bachmann (1991). *Text und Textwert II. Die Paulinischen Briefe*. 4 vols. ANTF 16–19; Berlin & New York; De Gruyter.
Aland, Kurt with Annette Benduhn-Mertz, Gerd Mink, Klaus Witte and Horst Bachmann (1993). *Text und Textwert III. Die Apostelgeschichte*. 4 vols. ANTF 20–21; Berlin & New York; De Gruyter.
Aland, Kurt & Barbara Aland (1989). *The Text of the New Testament. An Introduction to the Critical Editions and to the Theory and Practice*

of Modern Textual Criticism. Second edition. English translation by Erroll F. Rhodes. Grand Rapids, MI: Eerdmans.

Aland, Kurt & Barbara Aland, with Klaus Wachtel and Klaus Witte (1998). *Text und Textwert IV. Die synoptischen Evangelien. 1. Das Markusevangelium*. 2 vols. ANTF 26–27; Berlin & New York; De Gruyter.

Aland, Kurt, Barbara Aland, Klaus Wachtel with Klaus Witte (1999). *Text und Textwert IV. Die synoptischen Evangelien. 2. Das Matthäusevangelium, 3. Das Lukasevangelium*. 4 vols. ANTF 28–31; Berlin & New York; De Gruyter.

Allen, Garrick V., ed. (2019). *The Future of New Testament Textual Scholarship*. WUNT 417; Tübingen: Mohr Siebeck.

Allen, Garrick V. (2020). *Manuscripts of the Book of Revelation. New Philology, Paratexts, Reception*. Oxford: OUP.

Allison, Robert W. (1988). '"Let Women Be Silent in the Churches (1 Cor. 14.33b–36)": What Did Paul Really Say and What Did It Mean?' *JSNT* 32: 27–60.

Amsterdam Database see Krans, Lietaert Peerbolte et al.

Antoniades, Vasileios (1912). Ἡ Καινὴ Διαθήκη ἐγκρίσει τῆς Μεγάλης τοῦ Χριστοῦ Ἐκκλησίας. Revised edition; Constantinople: Ecumenical Patriarchate.

Araújo, Diego dy Carlos (2022). 'The Passive ἀποκατηλλάγητε in P46 and B03 Colossians 1:22a: An Original Grammatical Anomaly or Another Case of Scribal Assimilation?' *Tyndale Bulletin* 73: 23–44.

Arzt-Grabner, Peter (2006). '1 Cor. 4:6 – a Scribal Gloss?' *Biblische Notizen* 130: 59–78.

Ascough, Richard S. (1998). 'Civic Pride at Philippi. The Text-Critical Problem of Acts 16.12.' *NTS* 44.1: 93–103.

Baarda, Tjitze (1969). 'Gadarenes, Gerasenes, Gergesenes and the "Diatessaron" Tradition.' In *Neotestamentica et Semitica* ed. E. Earle Ellis and Max Wilcox. Edinburgh: T&T Clark, 181–197.

Barrett, C.K. (1994–98). *A Critical and Exegetical Commentary on the Acts of the Apostles*. ICC; Edinburgh: T&T Clark.

Bartholomä, Philipp (2008). 'Did Jesus Save the People out of Egypt? A Re-examination of a Textual Problem in Jude 5.' *NovT* 50.2: 143–158.

Bauckham, Richard (1983). *2 Peter and Jude*. Word Biblical Commentary 50; Nashville: Thomas Nelson.

Bauer, Walter, Frederick W. Danker, William F. Arndt, Wilbur Gingrich (2001). *A Greek-English Lexicon of the New Testament and Other Early Christian Literature.* Third Edition (BDAG). Chicago: University of Chicago Press.

Becker, Ulrich (1963). *Jesus und die Ehebrecherin. Untersuchungen zur Text und Überlieferung von Joh. 7,53–8,11.* BZNW 28; Berlin: Alfred Töpelmann.

Best, Ernest (1997). *Ephesians.* Sheffield New Testament Guides. Sheffield: Sheffield Academic.

Billings, Bradly S. (2006). *Do this In Remembrance of Me. The Disputed Words in the Lukan Institution Narrative. Luke 22:19b–20. An Historico-Exegetical, Theological and Sociological Analysis.* LNTS 314; London: T&T Clark.

Birdsall, J.N. (1960). 'John X. 29.' *JTS* ns 11.2: 342–344.

Birdsall, J.N. (2002). 'Irenaeus and the Number of the Beast: Revelation 13, 18.' In *New Testament Textual Criticism and Exegesis: Festschrift J.Delobel,* ed. A. Denaux. BETL 161; Leuven: Peeters, 349–359.

Black, David Alan (1985). 'The Text of John 3:13.' *Grace Theological Journal* 6.1: 49–66.

Black, David Alan (1988a). 'The Text of Mark 6.20.' *NTS* 34.1: 141–145.

Black, David Alan (1988b). 'Jesus On Anger: the Text of Matthew 5:22a Revisited.' *NovT* 30.1: 1–8.

Black, David Alan, ed. (2008). *Perspectives on the Ending of Mark.* Nashville, TN: Broadman & Holman.

Black, Matthew (1967). *An Aramaic Approach to the Gospels and Acts.* Third edition. Oxford: Clarendon.

Black, Matthew (1981). 'The Holy Spirit in the Western Text of Acts.' In Epp & Fee 1981: 159–170.

Blass, Friedrich, Albert Debrunner & Robert W. Funk (1961). *A Greek Grammar of the New Testament and Other Early Christian Literature.* Cambridge: CUP.

Blumell, Lincoln H. (2014). 'Luke 22:43–44: An Anti-Docetic Interpolation or an Apologetic Omission?' *TC* 19: 1–35.

Brown, Raymond E. (1966). *The Gospel According to John (I–XII).* ABC 29; New York: Doubleday.

Brown, Raymond E. (1970). *The Gospel According to John (XIII–XXI).* ABC 29A; New York: Doubleday.

Bryan, Steven M. (2021). 'Scribal Tendencies and Name Forms: "Mary" In the New Testament.' *TC* 26: 155–186.

Burer, Michael H. & Daniel B. Wallace (2001). 'Was Junia Really an Apostle? A Re-examination of Rom 16.7.' *NTS* 47: 76–91.

Burkholder, Benjamin J. (2012). 'Considering the Possibility of a Theological Corruption in Joh 1,18 in Light of its Early Reception.' *ZNW* 103.1: 64–83.

Cadbury, Henry J. (1939). 'The Meaning of John 20:23, Matthew 16:19, and Matthew 18:18.' *JBL* 58.3: 251–254.

Cadwallader, Alan (1992). 'The Correction of the Text of Hebrews towards the LXX.' *NovT* 34.3: 257–292.

Caragounis, Chrys C. (2007). 'What Did Jesus Mean by τὴν ἀρχήν in John 8:25?' *NovT* 49.2: 129–147.

Carlson, Stephen C. (2014). '"For Sinai is a Mountain in Arabia." A Note on the Text of Galatians 4,25.' *ZNW* 105.1: 80–101.

Carlson, Stephen C. (2015). *The Text of Galatians and Its History*. WUNT II.385; Tübingen: Mohr Siebeck.

Cervin, Richard S. (1994). 'A Note Regarding the Name "Junia(s)" in Romans 16.7.' *NTS* 40.3: 464–470.

Ceulemans, Reinhart (2007). 'The Name of the Pool in Joh 5,2. A Text-Critical Note Concerning 3Q15.' *ZNW* 99.1: 112–115.

Clarke, Kent D. (2002). 'Textual Certainty in the United Bible Societies' *Greek New Testament*.' *NovT* 44.2: 105–133.

Clivaz, Claire (2010). *L'ange et la sueur de sang. Lc. 22,43–44*. BTS 7. Leuven: Peeters.

Clivaz, Claire, Mina Monier & Dan Batovici, ed. (2022). 'The Transmission of Mark's Endings in Different Traditions and Languages.' *Comparative Oriental Manuscript Studies Bulletin* 8.2: 297–745.

Cole, Zachary (2017). 'P^{45} and the Problem of the 'Seventy(-two)': A Case for the Longer Reading in Luke 10.1 and 17.' *NTS* 63: 203–221.

Collins, Raymond F. (2002). 'The Case of a Wandering Doxology: Rom 16,25-27.' In *New Testament Textual Criticism and Exegesis: Festschrift J. Delobel*, ed. A. Denaux. Leuven: Peeters, 293–303.

Crawford, Sidnie White & Tommy Wasserman, ed. (2025). *The Oxford Handbook of Textual Criticism of the Bible*. Oxford: OUP.

Crisp, Simon (2021). 'Eugene Nida and the UBS Greek New Testament.' In *Βιβλικές Μεταφράσεις: Ιστορία και Πράξη*, ed. Costas G. Tsiknakes and Maria Sik. Athens: Greek Bible Society, 89–105.

Crouzel, Henri (1972). 'Le texte patristique de Matthieu V.32 et XIX.9.' NTS 19.1: 98–119.

Croy, N. Clayton (2022). '"That They Also Might Be [One] in Us": Establishing and Interpreting the Text of John 17:21.' NovT 64.2: 229–248.

de Jonge, Henk Jan (2013). 'The Chronology of the Ascension Stories in Luke and Acts.' NTS 59: 151–171.

Delobel, Joël (1994). 'Textual Criticism and Exegesis: Siamese Twins?' In *New Testament Textual Criticism, Exegesis, and Early Church History: A Discussion of Methods*, ed. Barbara Aland and Joël Delobel. Kampen: Kok Pharos, 98–117.

Dickey, Eleanor (2019). 'A Re-Examination of New Testament Papyrus P99 (Vetus Latina AN glo Paul).' NTS 65.1: 103–121.

Ebojo, Edgar Battad (2009). 'How Persuasive is "Persuasive Words of Human Wisdom"? The Shortest Reading in 1 Corinthians 2.4.' BT 60.1: 10–21.

Editio Critica Maior (ECM), see editions listed under Aland, Strutwolf and Karrer.

Edwards, Grant G. (2019). 'The Text and Transmission of 2 Thessalonians.' Unpublished PhD thesis, University of Birmingham.

Ehrman, Bart D. (1988a). '1 Joh 4:3 and the Orthodox Corruption of Scripture.' ZNW 79: 221–243; reprinted in Ehrman 2006: 221–246.

Ehrman, Bart D. (1988b). 'Jesus and the Adulteress.' NTS 34.1: 24–44.

Ehrman, Bart D. (1989). 'A Problem of Textual Circularity: The Alands on the Classification of New Testament Manuscripts.' Biblica 70.3: 377–388.

Ehrman, Bart D. (1991a). 'The Text of Mark in the Hands of the Orthodox.' In *Biblical Hermeneutics in Historical Perspective: Essays in Honor of Karlfried Froehlich*, ed. Mark S. Burrows and Paul Rorem. Grand Rapids MI: Eerdmans, 19–31; reprinted in Ehrman 2006: 142–155.

Ehrman, Bart D. (1991b). 'The Cup, the Bread, and the Salvific Effect of Jesus' Death in Luke-Acts.' *Society of Biblical Literature Seminar*

Papers. Atlanta, GA: Scholars Press, 576–591; reprinted in Ehrman 2006: 156–177.

Ehrman, Bart D. (2003). 'A Leper in the Hands of an Angry Jesus.' In *New Testament Greek and Exegesis: Essays in Honor of Gerald F. Hawthorne,* ed. Amy M. Donaldson and Timothy B. Sailors. Grand Rapids: Eerdmans, 77–98; reprinted in Ehrman 2006: 120–141.

Ehrman, Bart D. (2006). *Studies in the Textual Criticism of the New Testament.* NTTSD 33. Leiden & Boston: Brill.

Ehrman, Bart D. (2011). *The Orthodox Corruption of Scripture.* Updated edition. Oxford: OUP.

Ehrman, Bart D. & Mark A. Plunkett (1983). 'The Angel and the Agony: The Textual Problem of Luke 22:43.' *CBQ* 45.3: 401–416; reprinted in Ehrman 2006: 178–195.

Ehrman, Bart D. & Michael W. Holmes, ed. (2013). *The Text of the New Testament in Contemporary Research. Ess ays on the Status Quaestionis.* Second edition. NTTSD 42; Leiden: Brill.

Elliott, J.K. (1971). 'In Favour of καυθήσομαι at I Corinthians 13:3.' *ZNW* 62: 287–288; reprinted in Elliott 2010: 221–223.

Elliott, J.K. (1972). 'When Jesus was Apart from God: An Examination of Hebrews 2:9.' *Expository Times* 83.11: 339–341; reprinted in Elliott 2010: 226–234.

Elliott, J.K. (1975). 'The United Bible Societies' Textual Commentary Evaluated.' *NovT* 17.2: 130–150.

Elliott, J.K. (1979). 'Μαθητής with a Possessive in the New Testament.' *Theologische Zeitschrift* 35: 300–304; reprinted in Elliott 1992: 139–145.

Elliott, J.K. (1981a). 'The Language and Style of the Concluding Doxology to the Epistle to the Romans,' *ZNW* 72: 124–130; reprinted in Elliott 2010: 315–324.

Elliott, J.K. (1981b). 'An Eclectic Textual Commentary on the Greek Text of Mark's Gospel.' In Epp & Fee 1981: 47–60; reprinted in Elliott 1992: 159–170.

Elliott, J.K. (1988). 'The Text of Acts in the Light of Two Recent Studies.' *NTS* 34: 250–258; reprinted in Elliott 2010: 275–286.

Elliott, J.K. (1992). *Essays and Studies in New Testament Textual Criticism.* Estudios de Filología Neotestamentaria 3; Cordoba: El Almendro.

Elliott, J.K. (2000). 'Mark 1.1–3 – A Later Addition to the Gospel?' *NTS* 46.4: 584–588; reprinted in Elliott 2010: 235–242 .

Elliott, J.K. (2002). 'The Parable of the Two Sons: Text and Exegesis' In *New Testament Textual Criticism and Exegesis. Festschrift J. Delobel*, ed. A. Denaux. Leuven: University Press and Peeters, 67–78; reprinted in Elliott 2010: 359–372.

Elliott, J.K., ed. (2004). *The Collected Biblical Writings of T. C. Skeat*. NovTSup 113; Leiden & Boston: Brill.

Elliott, J.K. (2010). *New Testament Textual Criticism: The Application of Thoroughgoing Principles*. NovTSup 137; Leiden & Boston: Brill.

Elliott, J.K. (2014). 'A Short Textual Commentary on the Book of Revelation and the "New" Nestle.' *NovT* 56.1: 68–100.

Elliott, J.K. (2017). 'Majority Text or Not: Which Criteria Should be Adopted When Assessing Textual Variation in the New Testament?' In *Getting into the Text. New Testament Essays in Honor of David Alan Black*, ed. Daniel L. Akin & Thomas W. Hudgins. Eugene, OR: Pickwick, 77–89.

Ellis, E. Earle (1981). 'The Silenced Wives of Corinth. 1 Cor. 14:34–5.' In Epp & Fee 1981: 213–220.

Epp, Eldon J. (1966) *The Theological Tendency of Codex Bezae Cantabrigiensis in Acts*. SNTSMS 3; Cambridge: CUP.

Epp, Eldon J. (1981). 'The Ascension in the Textual Tradition of Luke–Acts.' In Epp & Fee 1981: 131–145.

Epp, Eldon J. (1999). 'The Multivalence of the Term "Original Text" in New Testament Textual Criticism.' *HTR* 92.3: 245–281.

Epp, Eldon J. (2005). *Junia. The First Woman Apostle*. Minneapolis, MN: Fortress.

Epp, Eldon J. (2015). 'Critical Editions and the Development of Text-Critical Methods: Part 2: From Lachmann (1831) to the Present.' In *The New Cambridge History of the Bible Vol. 3*, ed. John Riches. Cambridge: CUP, 13–48.

Epp, Eldon J. & Gordon D. Fee, ed. (1981). *New Testament Textual Criticism. Its Significance for Exegesis. Essays in Honour of Bruce M. Metzger*. Oxford: Clarendon.

Eubank, Nathan (2010). 'A Disconcerting Prayer: On the Originality of Luke 23:34a.' *JBL* 129.3: 521–536.

Fee, Gordon D. (1974). 'Review of Bruce M. Metzger, *A Textual Commentary on the Greek New Testament.*' *Biblica* 55.3: 452–455.

Fee, Gordon D. (1981). '"One Thing is Needful?" Luke 10:42.' In Epp & Fee 1981: 61–75.

Fee, Gordon D. (1982). 'On the Inauthenticity of John 5:3b–4.' *Evangelical Quarterly* 54.4: 207–218.

Fee, Gordon D. (1995). *Paul's Letter to the Philippians.* NICNT. Grand Rapids MI: Eerdmans.

Fee, Gordon D. (2009). *The First and Second Letters to the Thessalonians.* NICNT. Grand Rapids MI: Eerdmans.

Fellows, Richard G. (2023). 'Early Textual Variants That Downplay the Roles of Women in the Bethany Account.' *TC* 28: 67–82.

Fellows, Richard G. (2024). 'The Interpolation of 1 Cor. 14.34–35 and the Reversal of the Name Order of Prisca and Aquila at 1 Cor. 16.19.' *JSNT* 47.2: 179–217.

Fennema, D.A. (1985). 'John 1.18: "God the Only Son".' *NTS* 31: 124–135.

Ferda, Tucker S. (2019). 'Flesh from Heaven: The Text of John 6:52 and its Intertext.' *NTS* 65.3: 371–387.

Fisher, Alec (2024). 'Codex Augiensis is a Copy of the Greek Text of Codex Boernerianus.' *NTS* 70.2: 187–203.

Fitzmyer, Joseph A. (1993). *Romans.* ABC 31; New York: Doubleday.

Fitzmyer, Joseph A. (2008). *The Acts of the Apostles.* ABC 33; New York: Doubleday.

Flanagan, Neal M. & Edwina Hunter Snyder (1981). 'Did Paul Put Down Women in 1 Cor 14:34–36?' *Biblical Theology Bulletin* 11.1: 10–12.

Förster, Hans (2017). 'Possible Similarities in the Linguistic Structure of John 8.25b and John 8.45a.' *BT* 68.2: 164–178.

Foster, Paul (2001). 'A Tale of Two Sons: But Which One Did the Far, Far Better Thing? A Study of Matt. 21.28–32.' *NTS* 47: 26–37.

Gäbel, Georg (2021). 'Evidence, Evaluation, and Edition: The Evaluation and Presentation of the Secondary Traditions and Approaches to Critical Editing – The Example of Acts 1:2.' In *Ancient Texts, Papyri, and Manuscripts. Studies in Honor of James R. Royse*, ed. Alan Taylor Farnes, Scott D. Mackie & David Runia. NTTSD 64; Leiden: Brill, 77–106.

Gamble Jr., Harry (1977). *The Textual History of the Letter to the Romans.* SD 42; Grand Rapids, MI: Eerdmans.

Glover, Daniel B. (2020). 'The Promises Fulfilled for Whose Children? The Problem of the Text of Acts 13:33 in Contemporary Debate.' *JBL* 139.4: 789–807.

Goler, Sarah et al. (2019). 'Dating Ancient Egyptian Papyri through Raman Spectroscopy: Concept and Application to the Fragments of the Gospel of Jesus' Wife and the Gospel of John.' *JSNT* 42.1: 98–133.

Goodacre, Mark (2002). *The Case Against Q. Studies in Markan Priority and the Synoptic Problem.* Harrisburg, PA: Trinity Press International.

Goranson, Stephen (1997). 'The Text of Revelation 22.14.' *NTS* 43: 154–157.

Gurry, Peter J. (2021). 'The Text of Eph. 5.22 and the Start of the Ephesian Household Code.' *NTS* 67.4: 560–581.

Gurtner, Daniel M., Juan Hernández Jr. & Paul Foster, ed. (2015). *Studies on the Text of the New Testament and Early Christianity. Essays in Honor of Michael W. Holmes.* NTTSD 50; Leiden & Boston: Brill.

Haelewyck, Jean-Claude (2013). 'The Healing of a Leper. Mark 1,40–45: A Textual Commentary.' *ETL* 89.1: 15–36.

Hartmann, Andrea (2020). 'Junia – A Woman Lost in Translation: The Name ΙΟΥΝΙΑΝ in Romans 16:7 and its History of Interpretation.' *Open Theology* 6: 646–660.

Head, Peter M. (1991). 'A Text-Critical Study of Mark 1.1, "The Beginning of the Gospel of Jesus Christ".' *NTS* 37.4: 621–629.

Head, Peter M. (1993). 'Christology and Textual Transmission: Reverential Alterations in the Synoptic Gospels.' *NovT* 35.2: 105–128.

Heater Jr., Homer (1986). 'A Textual Note on Luke 3.33.' *JSNT* 9.28: 25–29.

Hendriks, Wim M. A. (2005). 'Brevior Lectio Praeferenda est Verbosiori.' *Revue Biblique* 112.4: 567–595.

Hengel, Martin (1969). 'Mc 7 3 πυγμῇ. Die Geschichte einer exegetischen Aporie und der Versuch ihrer Lösung.' *ZNW* 60.3: 182–198.

Hernández Jr., Juan (2020). 'The *Comma Johanneum*: A Relic in the Textual Tradition.' *Early Christianity* 11: 60–70.

Hill, Charles E. & Michael J. Kruger, ed. (2012). *The Early Text of the New Testament.* Oxford: OUP.

Himes, Paul A. (2022). '*Lectio difficilior potior* and an Aramaic Pun—Βεώρ vs. Βοσόρ in 2 Peter 2:15 as a Test Case for How a Classic Rule Might Be Refined.' *TC* 27: 69–83.

Hirunuma, Toshio (1981). 'Matthew 16:2b–3.' In Epp & Fee 1981: 35–45.

Hixson, Elijah & Peter J. Gurry, ed. (2019). *Myths and Mistakes in New Testament Textual Criticism*. Downers Grove, IL: IVP Academic.

Holmes, Michael W. (1986). 'The Text of Matthew 5.11.' *NTS* 32: 283–286.

Holmes, Michael W. (1990). 'The Text of the Matthean Divorce Passages: A Comment on the Appeal to Harmonization in Textual Decisions.' *JBL* 109.4: 651–664.

Holmes, Michael W., ed. (2010). *The Greek New Testament: SBL Edition*. Atlanta, GA: SBL.

Hoskier, Herman C. (1929). *Concerning the Text of the Apocalypse*. 2 vols. London: Quaritch.

Houghton, H. A. G. (2016). *The Latin New Testament. A Guide to its Early History, Texts, and Manuscripts*. Oxford: OUP.

Houghton, H. A. G. (2018). 'The Text of the Gospel and Letters of John.' In *The Oxford Handbook of Johannine Studies*, ed. J. M. Lieu & M. C. de Boer. Oxford: OUP, 5–22.

Houghton, H. A. G., & D. C. Parker, ed. (2008). *Textual Variation: Theological and Social Tendencies?* T&S 3.6; Piscataway, NJ: Gorgias.

Houghton, H. A. G., D. C. Parker, Peter Robinson & Klaus Wachtel (2020). 'The *Editio Critica Maior* of the Greek New Testament: Twenty Years of Digital Collaboration.' *Early Christianity* 11.1: 97–117.

Houghton, H. A. G., C. M. Kreinecker, R. F. MacLachlan & C. J. Smith (2019). *The Principal Pauline Epistles: A Collation of Old Latin Witnesses*. NTTSD 59; Leiden & Boston: Brill.

Hüffmeier, Annette (2015). 'The CBGM Applied to Variants from Acts.' *TC* 20: 1–12.

Hurtado, Larry W. (1981). 'The Doxology at the End of Romans.' In Epp & Fee 1981: 185–199.

Hutton, Jeremy M. (2008). '"Bethany beyond the Jordan" in Text, Tradition, and Historical Geography.' *Biblica* 89.3: 305–328.

Hyytiäinen, Pasi (2019). 'Evolving Gamaliel Tradition in Codex Bezae Cantabrigiensis, Acts 5:38–39: A Novel Application of Coherence-Based Genealogical Method (CBGM).' *TC* 24: 1–22.

IGNTP (1984/1987). *The New Testament in Greek. The Gospel according to St. Luke. Edited by the American and British Committees of the International Greek New Testament Project.* Two vols. Oxford: Clarendon.

Johnson, Nathan C. (2017). 'Anger Issues: Mark 1.41 in Ephrem the Syrian, the Old Latin Gospels and Codex Bezae.' *NTS* 63.2: 183–202.

Jongkind, Dirk (2008). 'Singular Readings in Sinaiticus: The Possible, the Impossible, and the Nature of Copying.' In Houghton & Parker 2008: 35–54.

Jongkind, Dirk (2019). 'Redactional Elements in the Text of Codex B.' In Allen 2019: 231–246.

Jongkind, Dirk (2022). 'The Various Scribal Habits Behind Substitutions.' In *Ancient Texts, Papyri and Manuscripts. Studies in Honor of James R. Royse*, ed. Alan Taylor Farnes, Scott D. Mackie & David T. Runia. NTTSD 64; Leiden: Brill, 141–159.

Jongkind, Dirk & Peter J. Williams et al., ed. (2017). *The Greek New Testament Produced at Tyndale House Cambridge.* Wheaton, IL: Crossway.

Kaden, David A. (2011). 'The Methodological Dilemma of Evaluating the Variation Unit in Romans 11:31. A Text Critical Study and a Suggestion about First Century Social History and Scribal Habits.' *NovT* 53.2: 165–182.

Kannaday, Wayne C. (2006). '"Are Your *Intentions* Honorable?": Apologetic Interests and the Scribal Revision of Jesus in the Canonical Gospels.' *TC* 11: 1–30.

Karrer, Martin, Darius Müller, Marcus Sigismund, Holger Strutwolf, Annette Hüffmeier, Gregory S. Paulson et al., ed. (2024). *Novum Testamentum Graecum Editio Critica Maior. VI. Die Offenbarung/ Revelation.* ECM VI; Stuttgart: Deutsche Bibelgesellschaft.

Keith, Chris (2009). 'The Initial Location of the Pericope Adulterae in Fourfold Tradition.' *NovT* 51.3: 209–231.

Kilpatrick, George D. (1968). '"Kurios" in the Gospels.' In *L'Évangile hier et aujourd'hui. Mélanges offerts au Professeur Franz-J. Leenhardt.* Geneva: Labor et Fides, 65–70.

Kilpatrick, George D. (1969). 'Some Problems in New Testament Text and Language.' In *Neotestamentica et Semitica. Studies in Honour of Matthew Black*, ed. E. Earle Ellis & Max Wilcox. Edinburgh: T&T Clark, 198–208.

King, Daniel (2017). 'The Textual History of the New Testament and the Bible Translator.' *BT* 68.1: 20–37.

Kloha, Jeffrey J. (2006). 'A Textual Commentary on Paul's First Epistle to the Corinthians.' Unpublished PhD thesis, University of Leeds.

Kloha, Jeffrey J. (2014). 'Elizabeth's Magnificat (Luke 1:46).' In *Texts and Traditions. Essays in Honour of J. Keith Elliott*, ed. J.J. Kloha & P. Doble. NTTSD 47; Leiden & Boston: Brill, 200–219.

Klostermann, A. (1883). *Probleme im Aposteltexte*. Gotha: Perthes.

Knight, Jarrett W. (2019). 'Reading Between the Lines: 1 Peter 4:16, MS 424, and Some Methodological Blind Spots in the CBGM.' *JBL* 138.4: 899–921.

Knust, Jennifer & Tommy Wasserman (2018). *To Cast the First Stone. The Transmission of a Gospel Story*. Princeton, NJ: Princeton UP.

Krans, Jan, Bert Jan Lietaert Peerbolte et al., ed. (2016). *The Amsterdam Database of New Testament Conjectural Emendation* (https://ntvmr.uni-muenster.de/nt-conjectures/). Release 32 (July 2024).

Kurek-Chomycz, Dominika A. (2007). 'Sincerity and Chastity for Christ. A Textual Problem in 2 Cor. 11:3 Reconsidered.' *NovT* 49.1: 54–84.

Lampe, Peter (1985). 'Zur Textgeschichte des Römerbriefes,' *NovT* 27.3: 273–277.

Landon, Charles (1996). *A Text-Critical Study of the Epistle of Jude*. Sheffield: Sheffield Academic Press.

Lanier, Gregory R. (2016). 'A Case for the Assimilation of Matthew 21:44 to the Lukan "Crushing Stone" (20:18), with Special Reference to $\mathfrak{P}^{104}$.' *TC* 21: 1–21.

Larsen, Iver (2000). 'Variant Readings in 2 Corinthians.' *BT* 51.3: 342–348.

Lembke, Markus, Darius Müller and Ulrich B. Schmid, with Martin Karrer (2017). *Text und Textwert VI. Die Apokalypse*. ANTF 49; Berlin & New York; De Gruyter.

Letteney, Mark (2016). 'Toward a New Scribal Tendency: Reciprocal Corruptions and the Text of 1 Corinthians 8:2–3.' *JBL* 135.2: 391–404.

Malik, Peter (2017). '"And You Purchased [Whom?]": Reconsidering the Text of Rev 5,9.' *ZNW* 108.2: 306–312.

Malik, Peter (2022). 'Rid Us (Not) of the Temptation: A Note on the Text of Hebrews 11.37.' *JSNT* 44.4: 580–589.

Malone, Andrew S. (2009). 'Burn or Boast? Keeping the 1 Corinthians 13,3 Debate in Balance.' *Biblica* 90.3: 400–406.

Man, Loretta H. Y. (2016). 'The Textual Significance of Corrected Readings in the Evaluation of the External Evidence: Romans 5,1 as a Test Case.' *ZNW* 107.1: 70–93.

Marshall, I. Howard, with Philip H. Towner (1999). *The Pastoral Epistles*. ICC. Edinburgh: T&T Clark.

Martin, Michael Wade (2005). 'Defending the "Western Non-Interpolations": The Case for an Anti-Separationist *Tendenz* in the Longer Alexandrian Readings.' *JBL* 124.2: 269–294.

Martyn, J. Louis (1997). *Galatians*. ABC 33A. New York: Doubleday.

McCollum, Joey (2024). 'The Intrinsic Probability of τοῖς ἰδίοις ἀνδράσιν ὑποτασσέσθωσαν in Eph. 5.22.' *JSNT* 46.4: 556–578.

McDonald, Grantley (2016). *Biblical Criticism in Early Modern Europe: Erasmus, the Johannine Comma and Trinitarian Debate*. Cambridge: CUP.

McReynolds, Paul R. (1981). 'John 1:18 in Textual Variation and Translation.' In Epp & Fee 1981: 105–118.

Mees, Michael (1981). 'Realer oder irrealer Kondizionalsatz in Joh 8:39?' In Epp & Fee 1981: 119–130.

Metzger, Bruce M. (1972). 'The Text of Matthew 1.16.' In *Studies in New Testament and Early Christian Literature*, ed. David E. Aune. NovTSup 33; Leiden: Brill, 16–24.

Metzger, Bruce M. (1994). *A Textual Commentary on the Greek New Testament*. Second Edition. Stuttgart: Deutsche Bibelgesellschaft.

Metzger, Bruce M. & Bart D. Ehrman (2005). *The Text of the New Testament, its Transmission, Corruption, and Restoration*. Fourth edition. Oxford & New York: OUP.

Miller, J. I. (1986). 'Was Tischendorf Really Wrong? Mark 8:26b Revisited.' *NovT* 28.2: 97–103.

Min, Kyoung Shik (2005). *Die früheste Überlieferung des Matthäusevangeliums (bis zum 3./4. Jh.)*. ANTF 34; Berlin & New York: De Gruyter.

Mink, Gerd (2004). 'Problems of a highly contaminated tradition: the New Testament. Stemmata of variants as a source of a genealogy for witnesses.' In *Studies in Stemmatology II*, ed. P. van Reenen, A. den Hollander & M. van Mulken. Amsterdam: Benjamins, 13–85.

Mink, Gerd (2009). *The Coherence-Based Genealogical Method (CBGM) - Introductory Presentation.* Release 1.0. http://egora.uni-muenster.de/intf/service/downloads_en.shtml.

Mink, Gerd (2011). 'Contamination, Coherence, and Coincidence in Textual Transmission.' In Wachtel & Holmes 2011: 141–216.

Moir, Ian A. (1981). 'Orthography and Theology: The Omicron–Omega Interchange in Romans 5:1 and Elsewhere.' In Epp & Fee 1981: 179–183.

Moo, Douglas J. (1996). *The Epistle to the Romans.* NICNT; Grand Rapids: Eerdmans.

Moses, Robert E. (2011). 'Jesus Barabbas, a Nominal Messiah? Text and History in Matthew 27.16–17.' *NTS* 58.1: 43–56.

Moss, Candida (2024). *God's Ghostwriters: Enslaved Christians and the Making of the Bible.* London: William Collins.

Muddiman, John (1972). 'A Note on Reading Luke xxiv. 12.' *ETL* 48: 542–548.

Müller, Klaus W. (1986). 'ΑΠΕΧΕΙ (Mk 14 41) — absurda lectio?' *ZNW* 77.1: 83–100.

NA29. See Strutwolf et al. 2026.

Nässelqvist, Dan (2018). 'The Question of Punctuation in John 1:3–4: Arguments from Ancient Colometry.' *JBL* 137.1: 175–191.

Niccum, Curt (1997). 'The Voice of the Manuscripts on the Silence of Women: The External Evidence for 1 Cor 14.34–5.' *NTS* 43: 242–255.

Nolland, John (1996). 'A Text-Critical Discussion of Matthew 1:16.' *CBQ* 58.4: 665–673.

Nongbri, Brent (2009). 'Two Neglected Textual Variants in Philippians.' *JBL* 128.4: 803–808.

Nongbri, Brent (2018). *God's Library. The Archaeology of the Earliest Christian Manuscripts.* New Haven: Yale University Press.

North, J. Lionel (2005). 'Praying for a Good Spirit: Text, Context and Meaning of Luke 11.13.' *JSNT* 28.2: 167–188.

Omanson, Roger L. (2006). *A Textual Guide to the Greek New Testament.* Stuttgart: Deutsche Bibelgesellschaft.

O'Loughlin, Thomas (2018). 'One or Two Cups? The Text of Luke 22:17–20 Again.' In *Liturgy and the Living Text of the New Testament*, ed. H. A. G. Houghton. T&S 3.16; Piscataway, NJ: Gorgias, 51–69.

O'Neill, J.C. (1994). 'John 13:10 Again.' *Revue Biblique* 101.1: 67–74.

Osburn, Carroll D. (1981a). 'The Text of 1 Corinthians 10:9.' In Epp & Fee 1981: 201–212.

Osburn, Carroll D. (1981b). 'The Text of Jude 5.' *Biblica* 62.1: 107–115.

Parker, D.C. (1997). *The Living Text of the Gospels*. Cambridge: CUP.

Parker, D.C. (2008). *An Introduction to the New Testament Manuscripts and Their Texts*. Cambridge: CUP.

Parsons, Mikeal C. (1988). 'The Text of Acts 1:2 Reconsidered.' *CBQ* 50.1: 58–71.

Perera, C. (2005). 'Burn or Boast? A Text Critical Analysis of 1 Cor 13:3.' *FilNeot* 18: 111–128.

Petzer, J.H. (1989). 'Contextual Evidence in Favour of καυχήσωμαι in 1 Corinthians 13.3.' *NTS* 35.2: 229–253.

Plisch, Uwe Karsten (1996). 'Die Apostelin Junia: Das exegetische Problem in Röm 16,7 im Licht von Nestle-Aland[27] und der sahidischen Überlieferung,' *NTS* 42: 477–478.

Porter, Calvin L. (1967). 'John ix. 38, 39a: A Liturgical Addition to the Text.' *NTS* 13.4: 387–394.

Prothro, James B. (2024). 'Triads, Groups, and the Text of Jude 22–23. Internal Evidence and the Shortest Reading.' *NovT* 66.4: 364–381.

Pryor, John W. (1997). 'John the Baptist and Jesus: Tradition and Text in John 3.25.' *JSNT* 19.66: 15–26.

Quarles, Charles L. (2020). 'Matthew 16.2b–3: New Considerations for a Difficult Textual Question.' *NTS* 66.2: 228–248.

Quarles, Charles L. (2021). 'Colossians 1.12a: A Case for the Reading of the Earliest Witnesses.' *BT* 72.3: 380–392.

Quek, Tze-Ming (2009). 'A Text-Critical Study of John 1.34.' *NTS* 55: 22–34.

Rico, Christophe (2006). 'Jn 8,25: Les aléas d'une transmission textuelle.' *Revue Biblique* 113.3: 398–435.

Robinson, Alexandra, Stephen Llewelyn & Blake Wassell (2018). 'Showing Mercy to the Ungodly and the Inversion of Invective in Jude.' *NTS* 64.2: 194–212.

Robinson, Maurice A. & William G. Pierpont, ed. (2018). *The New Testament in the Original Greek. Byzantine Textform*. Nuremberg: VTR Publications.

Rodgers, Peter R. (1995). 'The Text of Romans 8:28.' *JTS* ns 46.2: 547–550.

Ropes, James H. (1926). *The Text of Acts.* = *The Beginnings of Christianity; Part I, The Acts of the Apostles, vol. 3*, ed. F.J. Foakes Jackson and Kirsopp Lake. London: Macmillan.

Ross, J.M. (1983). 'Some Unnoticed Points in the Text of the New Testament.' *NovT* 25.1: 59–72.

Ross, J.M. (1992). 'The Extra Words in Acts 18:21.' *NovT* 34.3: 247–249.

Ross, J.M. (2003). 'Further Unnoticed Points in the Text of the New Testament.' *NovT* 45.3: 209–221.

Roth, Dieter T. (2015). *The Text of Marcion's Gospel.* NTTSD 49; Leiden & Boston: Brill.

Royse, James R. (1983). 'The Treatment of Scribal Leaps in Metzger's *Textual Commentary*.' *NTS* 29.4: 539–551.

Sailors, Timothy B. (2000). 'Wedding Textual and Rhetorical Criticism to Understand the Text of 1 Thessalonians 2.7.' *JSNT* 23.80: 81–98.

SBLGNT, see Holmes 2010.

Schmid, Ulrich (1995). *Marcion und Sein Apostolos. Rekonstruktion und historische Einordnung der Marcionitischen Paulusbriefausgabe.* ANTF 25; Berlin & New York: De Gruyter.

Schmid, Ulrich (2008). 'Scribes and Variants – Sociology and Typology.' In Houghton & Parker 2008: 1–23.

Schmid, Ulrich (2011). 'Conceptualizing "Scribal" Performances: Reader's Notes.' In Wachtel & Holmes, 2011: 49–64.

Schrader, Elizabeth (2016). 'Was Martha of Bethany Added to the Fourth Gospel in the Second Century?' *HTR* 110.3: 360–392.

Shepherd, Thomas R. (2023). 'The Textual History and Translation of Revelation 21.3b.' *BT* 74.1: 110–125.

Skeat, T.C. (1988). 'The "Second-First" Sabbath (Luke 6:1): the Final Solution.' *NovT* 30.2: 103–106; reprinted in Elliott 2004: 254–257.

Skeat, T.C. (1990). 'A Note on πυγμῇ in Mark 7:3.' *JTS* 41: 525–527; reprinted in Elliott 2004: 250–251.

Silva, Moisés (2001). *Interpreting Galatians: Explorations in Exegetical Method.* Second edition. Grand Rapids, MI: Baker Academic.

Silva, Moisés (1990). 'Text and Language in the Pauline Corpus with special reference to the use of conjunctions in Galatians.' *Neotestamentica* 24.2: 273–282.

Smit Sibinga, J. (1981). 'Matthew 14:22-33—Text and Composition.' In Epp & Fee 1981: 15–34.

Snodgrass, Klyne (1972). 'Western Non-Interpolations.' *JBL* 91.3: 369–379.

Staples, Jason (2015). 'Altered Because of Transgressions? The "Law of Deeds" In Gal 3,19a.' *ZNW* 106.1: 126–135.

Strange, James F. (1992). 'Beth-Zatha.' In *The Anchor Bible Dictionary*, ed. David Noel Freedman. 6 vols. New York: Doubleday, vol. 1: 700–701.

Strange, W. A. (1992a). *The Problem of the Text of Acts*. SNTSMS 71; Cambridge: CUP.

Strange, W. A. (1992b). 'The Text of Acts 19.1.' *NTS* 38.2: 145–148.

Strutwolf, Holger (2011). 'Original Text and Textual History.' In Wachtel & Holmes 2011: 23–41.

Strutwolf, Holger (2014). 'Urtext oder frühe Korruption? Einige Beispiele aus der Apostelgeschichte.' In In *Texts and Traditions. Essays in Honour of J. Keith Elliott*, ed. J. J. Kloha & P. Doble. NTTSD 47; Leiden & Boston: Brill, 255–280.

Strutwolf, Holger (2021). 'Remarks on the Patristic Evidence.' In Strutwolf et al., ECM I.2, Teil 2.3 *Studien*, 76–104.

Strutwolf, Holger, Georg Gäbel, Annette Hüffmeier, Gerd Mink & Klaus Wachtel, ed. (2017). *Novum Testamentum Graecum Editio Critica Maior. III. Die Apostelgeschichte/The Acts of the Apostles*. ECM III; Stuttgart: Deutsche Bibelgesellschaft.

Strutwolf, Holger, Georg Gäbel, Annette Hüffmeier, Marie-Luise Lakmann, Gregory S. Paulson & Klaus Wachtel, ed. (2021). *Novum Testamentum Graecum Editio Critica Maior. I. The Synoptic Gospels. 2. Das Markusevangelium/The Gospel according to Mark*. ECM I.2; Stuttgart: Deutsche Bibelgesellschaft.

Strutwolf, Holger, & Klaus Wachtel, ed. (2011). *Novum Testamentum Graecum Editio Critica Maior. The Synoptic Gospels. Parallelperikopen/Parallel Pericopes*. ECM I *Sonderband*; Stuttgart: Deutsche Bibelgesellschaft.

Strutwolf, Holger, Hugh Houghton, Christos Karakolis, David Parker, Stephen Pisano, David Trobisch & Klaus Wachtel, ed. (2025). *The United Bible Societies' Greek New Testament*. Sixth edition. Stuttgart: Deutsche Bibelgesellschaft.

Strutwolf, Holger, Hugh Houghton, Christos Karakolis, David Parker, Stephen Pisano, David Trobisch & Klaus Wachtel, ed. (2026).

Nestle-Aland Novum Testamentum Graece. Twenty-ninth edition. Stuttgart: Deutsche Bibelgesellschaft.

Text und Textwert (TuT), see under Aland and Lembke.

THGNT, see Jongkind & Williams 2017.

Thiselton, Anthony C. (2000). *The First Epistle to the Corinthians: A Commentary on the Greek Text*. NIGTC; Grand Rapids, MI: Eerdmans.

Thomas, John Christopher (1997). 'A Note on the Text of John 13:10.' *NovT* 29.1: 46–52.

Thrall, Margaret E. (1981). '"Putting on" or "Stripping off" in 2 Corinthians 5:3.' In Epp & Fee 1981: 221–237.

Trobisch, David (2013). *A User's Guide to the Nestle-Aland 28 Greek New Testament*. SBLTCS 9; Atlanta, GA: SBL.

Tuckett, Christopher M. (2015). 'The Text of Galatians 4:25a.' In Gurtner, Hernández & Foster 2015: 372–388.

Turner, C.H. (1926). 'A Textual Commentary on Mark 1.' *JTS* os 28: 145–158.

UBS6. See Strutwolf et al. 2025.

Vaganay, Léon (1940). 'Marc VI, 45. Essai de critique textuelle.' *Revue Biblique* 49.1: 5–32.

Van Nes, Jermo (2013). 'Faith(fulness) of the Son of God"? Galatians 2:20b Reconsidered.' *NovT* 55.2: 127–139.

Victor, Ulrich (2009). 'Textkritischer Kommentar zu ausgewählten Stellen des Matthäusevangeliums.' *FilNeot* 22: 55–90.

Wachtel, Klaus (1995). *Der Byzantinische Text der Katholischen Briefe*. ANTF 24; Berlin & New York: Walter De Gruyter.

Wachtel, Klaus (2008). 'Towards a Redefinition of External Criteria: The Role of Coherence in Assessing the Origin of Variants' In Houghton & Parker 2008: 109–127.

Wachtel, Klaus (2012). 'The Coherence-Based Genealogical Method: A New Way to Reconstruct the Text of the Greek New Testament.' In *Editing the Bible. Assessing the Task Past and Present*, ed. John S. Kloppenborg & Judith H. Newman. SBLRBS 69; Atlanta, GA: SBL, 123–138.

Wachtel, Klaus (2019). 'The Development of the Coherence Based Genealogical Method (CBGM), its Place in Textual Scholarship, and Digital Editing.' In Allen 2019: 433–444.

Wachtel, Klaus (2020). 'Die kohärenzbasierte Methode und ihre Ergebnisse.' *Biblische Notizen* 184: 43–72.

Wachtel, Klaus, and Michael W. Holmes, ed. (2011). *The Textual History of the Greek New Testament: Changing Views in Contemporary Research*. SBLTCS 8; Atlanta, GA: SBL.

Wallace, Daniel B. (1989). 'The *Majority Text*: A New Collating Base?' *NTS* 35.4: 609–618.

Wallace, Daniel B. (2015). 'The Son's Ignorance in Matthew 24:36: An Exercise in Textual and Redaction Criticism.' In Gurtner, Hernández & Foster 2015: 178–205.

Wasserman, Tommy (2006). *The Epistle of Jude: Its Text and Transmission*. ConBNT 43; Stockholm: Almqvist and Wiksell.

Wasserman, Tommy (2009). 'Proposal for a New Rating System in Greek New Testament Editions.' *BT* 60.3: 140–157.

Wasserman, Tommy (2011). 'The "Son of God" was in the Beginning. Mark 1:1.' *JTS* ns 62.1: 20–50.

Wasserman, Tommy (2012). 'Misquoting Manuscripts? The Orthodox Corruption of Scripture Revisited.' In *The Making of Christianity: Conflicts, Contacts, and Constructions: Essays in Honor of Bengt Holmberg*, ed. M. Zetterholm & S. Byrskog. ConBNT 47; Eisenbrauns, 325–350.

Wasserman, Tommy (2015a). 'Historical and Philological Correlations and the CBGM as Applied to Mark 1:1.' *TC* 20: 1–11.

Wasserman, Tommy (2015b). 'A Short Textual Commentary on Galatians.' In Gurtner, Hernández & Foster 2015: 345–371.

Wasserman, Tommy (2015c). 'The Coherence Based Genealogical Method as a Tool for Explaining Textual Changes in the Greek New Testament.' *NovT* 57.2: 206–218.

Wasserman, Tommy (2017). 'A Short Textual Commentary on the Lucan Travel Narrative. Luke 9:51–19:46.' In *Getting Into the Text: New Testament Essays in Honor of David Alan Black*, ed. Daniel L. Akin & Thomas W. Hudgins. Eugene, OR: Pickwick, 90–115.

Wasserman, Tommy (2018). 'Bringing Sisters Back Together: Another Look at Luke 10:41–42.' *JBL* 137.2: 439–461.

Wasserman, Tommy (2020). 'Scribal Alterations to the "Canonical" Gospels in Second- and Third-Century Manuscripts.' In *The Reception of Jesus in the First Three Centuries: Volume Two: From Thomas to Tertullian*, ed. Jens Schröter & Christine Jacobi. London: T&T Clark, 305–327.

Wasserman, Tommy (2023). 'Liturgical Influences on the Text of the New Testament.' In *Why We Sing: Music, Word, and Liturgy in Early Christianity*, ed. Carl Johan Berglund, Barbara Crostini & James A. Kelhoffer. Leiden: Brill, 49–79.

Wasserman, Tommy (2025). 'A Short Textual Commentary on 1–2 Thessalonians'. *Forthcoming*. Berlin & New York: De Gruyter.

Wasserman, Tommy & Peter Gurry (2017). *A New Approach to Textual Criticism. An Introduction to the Coherence-Based Genealogical Method*. SBLRBS 80; Atlanta, GA: SBL; Stuttgart: Deutsche Bibelgesellschaft.

Wasserman, Tommy & Peter Gurry (2019). 'Textual Criticism and the Editio Critica Maior of James.' In *Reading the Epistle of James: A Resource for Students. Edited by Eric F. Mason and Darian R. Lockett.* SBLRBS 94; Atlanta, GA: SBL, 209–229.

Weima, Jeffrey A. D. (2000). '"But We Became Infants Among You": The Case for ΝΗΠΙΟΙ in 1 Thess 2.7.' *NTS* 46.4: 547–564.

Wenham, John W. (1979). 'How Many Cock-Crowings? The Problem of Harmonistic Text-Variants.' *NTS* 25.4: 523–525.

Wernberg-Møller, P. (1956). 'A Semitic Idiom in Matt. v.22.' *NTS* 3.1: 71–73.

Westcott, B. F., & F. J. A. Hort (1896). *The New Testament in the Original Greek. II. Introduction and Appendix*. Second edition. London: Macmillan.

Wettlaufer, Ryan D. (2007). 'A Second Glance at Matthew 27.24.' *NTS* 53.3: 344–358.

Wikgren, Allen P. (1981). 'The Problem in Acts 16:12.' In Epp & Fee 1981: 171–184.

Williams, P. J. (2011). 'Not the Prologue of John.' *JSNT* 33.4: 375–386.

Williams, P. J. (2012). 'An Examination of Ehrman's Case for ὀργισθείς in Mark 1:41.' *NovT* 54.1: 1–12.

Wolmarans, Johannes L. P. (1984). 'The Text and Translation of Hebrews 8.8.' *ZNW* 75.1: 139–145.

Wyant, Jennifer (2019). 'Giving Martha Back Her House: Analyzing the Textual Variant in Luke 10:38b.' *TC* 24: 1–11.

Zamfir, Korinna & Joseph Verheyden (2008). 'Text-Critical and Intertextual Remarks on 1 Tim 2:8-10.' *NovT* 50.4: 376–406.

Zuntz, Gunther (1953). *The Text of the Epistles: A Disquisition on the Corpus Paulinum*. London: OUP.

Zwiep, Arie W. (1996). 'The Text of the Ascension Narratives. Luke 24:50-3; Acts 1:1-2, 9-11.' *NTS* 42: 219–244.